A Theory of the Literary Text
by Antonio García-Berrio

Research in Text Theory
Untersuchungen zur Texttheorie

Editor
János S. Petöfi, *Macerata*

Advisory Board
Irena Bellert, *Montreal*
Antonio García-Berrio, *Madrid*
Maria-Elisabeth Conte, *Pavia*
Teun A. van Dijk, *Amsterdam*
Wolfgang U. Dressler, *Wien*
Nils Erik Enkvist, *Åbo*
Robert E. Longacre, *Dallas*
Roland Posner, *Berlin*
Hannes Rieser, *Bielefeld*
Dieter Viehweger †, *Berlin*

Volume 17

Walter de Gruyter · Berlin · New York
1992

A Theory of the Literary Text

By
Antonio García-Berrio

Walter de Gruyter · Berlin · New York
1992

Translated from Spanish into English by Kenneth A. Horn.

First published in the original language with the title *Teoria de la literatura* by Ediciones Catedra, S.A., Madrid, in 1989.

∞ Printed on acid-free paper which falls within the guidelines of the ANSI to ensure permanence and durability.

Library of Congress Cataloging-in-Publication Data

```
García Berrio, Antonio.
   [Teoria de la literatura. English]
   A theory of the literary text / by Antonio García-Berrio ;
[translated from Spanish into English by Kenneth A. Horn].
      p.    cm. — (Research in text theory = Untersuchun-
gen zur Texttheorie. ISSN 0179-4167 ; v. 17)
   Translation of: Teoria de la literatura.
   Includes bibliographical references and indexes.
   ISBN 3-11-012809-8 (Germany ; acid-free paper). —
ISBN 0-89925-803-4 (USA ; acid-free paper)
   1. Literature—Philosophy.  I. Title.  II. Series.
PN45.G31513   1992
801—dc20                                          91-44794
                                                       CIP
```

Die Deutsche Bibliothek — Cataloging-in-Publication Data

```
García-Berrio, Antonio:
A theory of the literary text / by Antonio García-Berrio.
[Transl. from Span. into Engl. by Kenneth A. Horn]. — Berlin ;
New York : de Gruyter, 1992
   (Research in text theory ; Vol. 17)
   Einheitssacht.: Teoria de la literatura <engl.>
   Literaturverz. S. 497—530
   ISBN 3-11-012809-8
NE: GT
```

ISBN 3 11 012809 8
ISSN 0179-4167

© Copyright 1992 by Walter de Gruyter & Co., D-1000 Berlin 30
All rights reserved, including those of translation into foreign languages. No part of this book may be reproduced or transmitted in any form or by any means, electronic or mechanical, including photocopy, recording, or any information storage and retrieval system, without permission in writing from the publisher.
Printed in Germany
Typesetting and printing: Arthur Collignon GmbH, Berlin
Binding: Lüderitz & Bauer, Berlin

Preface

At the present time, the current importance and need for a theory of the literary text is best justified when we keep in mind the extreme complexity of artistic texts of a verbal nature, often overly automatized by their use. I published this book in its first Spanish version of 1989 with the uncomfortable suspicion that it might represent, given the circumstances then predominating in international scientific circles, an excessively polemical counterpoint, against my own estimation and intentions. In setting out to construct and shape a book of literary criticism in terms of a theory of the artistic text, I was not unaware of the general situation prevailing in the critical environment, which currently tends to advise against both the will to theoretical systematization, opposed to fragmentarism, and the possible constructive understanding of the literary message as an entity of special poetic communication, considering such a position somewhat unusual and out of place. Still, to be aware of the dissemination and predominance in current criticism of relativist, antithetical, fragmentary, or even absolutely skeptical attitudes towards the conditions and possibilities of meaning, does not in any way imply the acceptance of these tendencies in all of their most radical conclusions. Presently, a theory of the literary text can assume these anxieties as productive subjects of debate while nevertheless assimilatively relativizing the most apocalyptic and deconstructive proposals about literature, in terms of its own awareness and security as a constructed theory.

In the few years that have passed from the completion of the Spanish version to the publication of this English translation, importance scientific developments have appeared which have contributed towards reaffirming my confidence in the suitability and opportuneness of having formulated my conception of the critical activity in terms of a theory of the literary text. This current translation therefore also represents a revision of the earlier book in order to take into account the evidence of this modified scientific awareness. Beyond the well-known polemic, representative but external, concerning the "case" of de Man and American deconstruction, the revisions are a matter of internal readjustments arising at the heart of the German school of reception, and of authoritative, symptomatic and nuanced evolutions, such as the illuminating critical development of Bloom, the recently disseminated, timely and precise discrepancy Eco has emphasized between his own work and Derrida's, the sense of balance Gombrich has urged towards the relativism of the spiritual sciences as the culmination of his artistic experience, and so forth. At the same time, the current edition insists on and restructures — alternatively amplifying and reducing certain considerations — a flexible model of the literary text, while nevertheless respecting the basic constitutive divisions of the 1989 version: the examination of literariness in terms of literary expressiveness, of artistic conventionality as the traditional "context" internal to literary culture, and, finally, of poeticity as an aesthetic value translating the artistic imagination's activity. All of which presupposes the effort to critically modernize and readjust the complementary triple division regarding the nature of the artistic event which has invariably continued to be set forth since its origins in classical Greek culture and which is represented in the work of Aristotle, Longinus, and Gorgias, and even in the compartmentalized periodization of the gradual formation in the West of a theoretical ideal concerning literature: the Renaissance rhetoric of the literary text, the Romantic aesthetics of the artistic imagination, and the fragmented modern awareness of poetic drift.

A theoretical effort of this nature is difficult to realize at the present time if one is unable to rely on a suitable scientific environment and much personal encouragement to facilitate it. I have had the good fortune to lack neither. To the assistance and understanding I have received in the course of pursuing this undertaking from the administration of the Universidad Complutense de Madrid and my colleagues and collaborators there, I must add the frequent opportunity to compare and contrast my thought with that of others provided by my visits and courses at important universities both here in Europe — especially that of Bologna — and in the United States — especially Harvard. Finally, I should like to express my gratitude to those who have been most directly linked to the genesis and realization of this English translation, including Claudio Guillén, Paolo Valesio, and, especially, János S. Petöfi. Many thanks to Mr. Paul Quinn for his important assistance in reviewing and making revisions to this translation, realized with energetic enthusiasm by Kenneth Horn, to whom I especially wish to express my gratitude.

Madrid, September 1991   Antonio García-Berrio

Contents

Preface V

Introduction

Between Literary Theory and a General Poetics 3

- 0.1. A Methodological Assessment of Modern Literary Theory. The Starting Point: A Conflictive Present 3
- 0.2. Poetics as a Classical Science and as a Contemporary Discipline: Traditional Contents 6
- 0.3. Romantic Literary Theory: Fantasy and Imagination in the Artistic Construction of Sentimental Intimacy 13
- 0.4. The Contents of Modern Semiological and Linguistic Poetics ... 20
- 0.5. The Crisis of Structuralist Poetics: Towards the Construction of a General Poetics 33

First Part

1. Literary Expressiveness 39
   - 1.1. Literariness: The Linguistic Structure of the Literary Option ... 39
   - 1.1.1. Towards the Linguistic Characterization of Literature 39
   - 1.1.2. Poetic Specificity vs. Linguistic Generality: Phono-Acoustical and Grammatical Levels 44
   - 1.1.3. Semantic Structures of Literariness 49
   - 1.1.4. Literariness and the Pragmatic Point of View: The Systematic Practice of Communicative Exception 55
   - 1.2. Literariness and the Text 63
   - 1.2.1. The Text as the Level of Decision for the Linguistic Specificity of Literature 63
   - 1.2.2. Text Grammar's Contribution to the Explanation of Literariness 71

1.2.3.	The Textual Typology of Classical Lyrical Poetry and the Characterization of Literariness	78
1.2.4.	Literariness and Poeticity: The Insufficiency of the Linguistic Definition	85
1.3.	Artistic Modes and the Aesthetic Law of Expressiveness ...	94
1.3.1.	Literary Expressiveness: Its Verbal and Fantastic Constituents	94
1.3.2.	The Aesthetic Norms of Literary Expressiveness	97
1.3.3.	Classical Modes of Literary Expressiveness: Mechanisms of Expressiveness and Levels of Style	103
1.3.4.	On General Rhetoric as a Science of Artistic Expressiveness	112
1.3.5.	The Integration of Rhetoric and Linguistic Poetics: The Thematic Macrostructure of Expressiveness	123

Second Part

2. Artistic Conventionality and Ambiguity		145
2.1.	The Pragmatic Relativity of Meaning	145
2.1.1.	Objections to Meaningful Textual Construction: Conventionality and Arbitrariness	145
2.1.2.	The Poststructuralist Crisis of Literary Meaning	152
2.1.3.	The Relativization of Meaning in the Aesthetics of Reception: A Criticism of the Fundamental Concepts	170
2.1.4.	The Formalist Mechanism of "Reader Implication": Textual "Gaps" and the Work of the Imagination	179
2.1.5.	The Modern Itinerary of Meaning: Umberto Eco	190
2.2.	The Deconstructive Lodging of Poetic Experience	210
2.2.1.	Deconstruction in Literary Criticism: The Intensified Undermining of Meaning	210
2.2.2.	From Deconstruction as an Aporia of Meaning to the Poetic Space of Original Experience	220
2.2.3.	The Poetic Concept of "Writing" in Jacques Derrida	231
2.2.4.	The Experience of the Poetic as Space and the Limits of Meaning. The Paradoxical Inscription of Writing	240
2.2.5.	Otherness as a Reference Forming Experience's Essential Emplacement	253
2.3.	The Aesthetic Capacity of Cultural Conventionality	262

2.3.1. The Aesthetic Structure of Traditional Conventionality: The Historical Relativity of Artistic Meaning and the Non-Arbitrary Foundations of Cultural Conventionality 262
2.3.2. Literary Tradition as a Typologizable Conventional Context 272
2.3.3. Traditional Conventionality as a Poetic Principle of Cultural Recognition 285
2.3.4. Artistic Ambiguity as a Poetic Property 294
2.3.5. Cervantes' Irony as an Instrument of Poetic Ambiguity 300

Third Part

3. Poetic Universality 311
   3.1. Fictionality: Imaginary Forms of Fantastic Activity 311
   3.1.1. Introduction. The Imaginary Structure of the Material Text: From the Immanence of the Material Text to the Poetics of the Imagination 311
   3.1.2. The Structure of Fictionality: The First Traditional Feature of a Poetics of Fantasy 317
   3.1.3. The Rules of Verisimilitude in Realist Fictionality 329
   3.1.4. The Realist Control of Fantasy: The Law of Semantic Maxima in Fictional Production 337
   3.1.5. Literary Fantasy's Conceptual Forms: The Cultural Imagination 342
   3.2. Poeticity: The Imaginary Structure of Symbols in the Temporal Domains 355
   3.2.1. On the Imaginary Structure of Poetic Value: Traces in the Text's Material-Verbal Scheme of Temporal and Spatial Orientations, Anthropological Symbols, and Patterns of the Imagination 355
   3.2.2. The Anthropological Roots of Temporal Regimes' Symbolic Semantics 369
   3.2.3. The Structure of the Poetic Imagination: The Spatial Pattern of the Imagination's Anthropological Orientation 388
   3.2.4. Versions of the Personal Articulation of the Spatial Myth and the Universality of the Imaginary Orientation 417
   3.2.5. Imaginary Poeticity in Narrative Prose Texts: Cervantes' Spatial Myth 436

3.3. Universality as a Property of Poetic Value 446
   3.3.1. Textual and Anthropological Foundations of Poetic Universality: On the Frustration of the Arts' Diversity 446
   3.3.2. The Generic Deployment of Universal Artistic Structures .. 455
   3.3.3. The "Natural" Limitation of Historical Literary Genres 468
   3.3.4. The Universal Structure of the Artistic Text: From Diversity to Singularity 480
   3.3.5. The Imaginary Foundations of the Universality of Artistic Systems: Painting and Poetry 489

Bibliography 497
Index of Contents 531
Index of Names 537

Introduction

0. Between Literary Theory and a General Poetics

0.1. A Methodological Assessment of Modern Literary Theory. The Starting Point: A Conflictive Present

At every step of its progression through the ages, the history of scientific thought seems invariably to be in the throes of a crisis. In science, the stabilization of any momentary achievement, the dogmatic prolongation of a fixed idea, commonly conceals a fallacy, a simplification, or even indicates a momentary exhaustion of creativity. In the specific case of ideas concerning literature and, more generally, in that of aesthetic judgments on the nature of artistic phenomena, this general feature of the scientific system is more acutely felt. The speculation dedicated to aesthetic, artistic, poetic and literary phenomena surely lends itself to a wide and discordant dispersion of opinions, many of them the result of attitudes which are more of a sentimental nature than rigorously rational or rationalizable.

These characteristics, common to the aesthetic and literary sciences of every age, are even more powerfully felt today. Some contemporary ideas are absolutely opposed to fundamental traditional conceptions of literariness, going so far as to question verbal art's very basis for existence. Thus, a widespread and prestigious contemporary trend in the United States, namely *deconstructionism*, has been known to negate meaning in verbal texts and, consequently, in poetic and literary texts as well (M. Ferraris, 1984; W. Martin, 1984). That is, it denies the validity of attributing a universal and objective meaning to the texts under analysis.

It seems to me that one of the most important elements contributing to the current crisis in literary theory is the undeniable disproportion that exists between the advances achieved by modern formalist criticism in the understanding of the literary text's material-verbal structure, and the far inferior level of knowledge and experience concerning other conceptual, imaginary and aesthetic dimensions of the artistic text, missing links which are in the end decisive for properly attributing properties of literariness and poeticity. Nevertheless, this disproportion should not, in my opinion, detract from the merit of the efforts of those who have so energetically contributed to its creation. For this very reason, when the time comes for passing judgment, we value Doležel's moderate balance (1979 a, pp. 521—530) more than van Dijk's pessimistic impatience (1979, pp. 571—577). In the twentieth century the various schools and modes of critical formalism — from the original Russian phenomenon to recent structural and semiological neoformalisms, not to mention European and American stylistics — have contributed a very rich set of analytical categories and strategies to literary science, so that the crisis of disproportion I am referring to, resulting from the overexertions of the formalist schools, should ultimately be judged as a *crisis of superproduction* (A. García-Berrio, 1977 a).

A second factor contributing to criticism's current problems lies in the recent tendency towards overvaluing the *receiver's* activity in the communicative process. The original call to arms in this area, issued by a group of Anglo-Saxon critics among whom T. S. Eliot's efforts stand out, had in its time the reasonable aim of calling attention to an important and systematic omission on the part of literary historiography. What is most problematic about these and similar efforts has always been, to my mind, the inevitably radical factionalization of their original hypotheses. Hence, with the initially reasonable goal of correcting an excess or omission, they rush headlong towards formulating the opposite exaggeration. The critical assignment of the receiver to his proper place in the constitution of textual meaning is in itself very correct, original and necessary. Such notable figures of poststructuralism as R. Barthes (1970a, 1975) and U. Eco (1979) have popularized this concept in all its brilliant paradoxes, and the German school of reception, including W. Iser (1972, 1976) and H. R. Jauss (1967, 1977), has definitively braced it in its possible theoretical development. But I believe the enthusiastic excesses committed in defence of reception, together with a certain laxness in controlling its extreme shifts towards utopian aporia have drastically contributed to the erosion of the critical credit these theories initially merited, to the point where it is now necessary to adopt certain reservations and precautions in order to avoid being carried away by the excesses of one of receptive theory's numerous deformed and extremist versions.

In summary, criticism currently has some of the paths it must follow well mapped out for it. With regard especially to the structural analysis of texts' linguistic material, the present crisis can be seen as one of disinterest and a lack of conscientiousness, manifested in the current practice of insistently delving ever more deeply into relatively secondary and specialized minutiae while disregarding other more fundamental constituents of literary phenomena still requiring attention. Moreover, the healthy opening towards the receptive axis runs the risk of devaluating its credit and authority as criticism when it becomes violently isolated from the textual meaning lodged in the creative relationship between author and text. The temptation to allow an infinite multiplication of readings without promoting or even recognizing the existence of any controls and limits in the interests of correctness and accuracy has led in practice to the tedious abandonment of critical reading, engendering in its place a form of critical writing which aspires to literariness itself, yielding efforts which can never match the interest of true artistic originals.

Furthermore, literary criticism still has decisive questions to address in its examination of the structure of literary phenomena. As I have indicated, the poetics of reception has to its merit the fact that it has completed the configuration of the author/text/receiver relationship, thus fully cataloging and describing the areas wherein the literary work's meaning is produced. The texts' channels of communication permit the identification of this global area of general and aesthetic meaning. Finally, communication in terms of aesthetic meaning between author and reader is possible due to the existence of imaginary impulses of a homogeneous nature traversing the text's material scheme, ranging over the entire area in which literary and artistic communication occur (A. García-Berrio, 1985, 1987). Hence, the psychological component of imaginary activity in the artistic text is an area requiring exploration, a field still open to literary investigation.

Psychological participation and communication in artistic processes yields an understanding framed in terms of mythical sequences, involving the manipulation and combination of anthropologico-fantastic symbols and archetypes which reveal themselves to be universalizable instruments of man's imaginary representation of the world. At the same time, symbols are semantic entities lodged in spatial rhythms. In the poem, painting or building, they create an understanding between transmitter and receiver based on the essential coordinates of anthropologico-spatial orientation. In my own experience, the most urgent tasks for the *development* of our conscious knowledge of the artistic text include articulating the known inventories of symbols and patterns of fantastico-imaginary spatialization contained in the structure of the textual scheme and establishing the proper correlations between textual indexes and their corresponding fantastic representations.

As prospects for critical attention, these suggestions for exploration and development, in proposing the permanent collation of the immanent textual scheme with its psychological and anthropological imaginary extensions, outline a mechanism of *projection*. Future developments in literary textual analysis ought to avail themselves of this mechanism in order to formulate a more ambitious and satisfactory aesthetic of literary forms. But all of these projective leaps in the general structure of literary knowledge, which I believe are currently required to achieve progress, also constitute tasks that have been largely unformed and unformulated to date. They are, therefore, going to be costly to implement, albeit inevitable in spite of their difficulty. Moreover, the demanding and problematic task of filling these gaps, in my opinion, also helps explain the vacillations and uncertainties characterizing the current critical crisis.

In short, it appears literary aesthetics and poetry fulfill their function by corroborating the existence and operation of *aesthetic universals* which exist beyond any chance form of conventionalism, beyond any purely social consensus. The aesthetic effect essentially results from the operation of a system of universal convergences within the sphere of artistic communication framing the text. To discover and explain the textual contents and mechanisms for the production and reception of meaning — immanent in the text's material scheme, yet transcending its confines — is the current challenge facing criticism.

0.2. *Poetics as a Classical Science and as a Contemporary Discipline: Traditional Contents*

Poetics, literary theory's first historical product — and presently its chief alternative — is an ancient science, originating in classical antiquity after the division and specialization of scientific disciplines. It develops in Greece as part of a set of materials on the formation of discourse, encompassed within the disciplines of Grammar, Rhetoric and Dialectics. Rhetoric was the classical science of expression, concerning itself with the practical, logical, and communicative aspects of discourse. Dialectics was a science diluted at a very early date, corresponding to the intellectual constitution of discourse's contents, which in turn were structured and expressed by rhetoric. Poetics deals with the study of a special mode of verbal discourse, namely, artistic discourse (J. J. Murphy, ed., 1983).

In his *Poetics*, the treatise which founded the discipline of poetics and first set forth its outlines and contents, Aristotle noted that "the art of imitating with words does not yet have a name" (47 b, 22). That is, "poetics", the word Aristotle uses from the very opening of his text, was not a technical term for the Greeks, as it is for us. "Poetics", like "poetry" and "poet", derives from the Greek root *poiein*, meaning "to make". In other words, Aristotle addresses the poet's labors in terms of an exemplary activity of manufacture or construction. Hence, this term, so general and inexpressive at first glance, is actually a very precise and ambitious characterization of the poet's work and, in general, of poetry's significance (D. Romero de Solís, 1981).

We must not forget that Aristotle is first and foremost a philosopher. In all of his work he seeks to formulate his own position on the fundamental question facing Greek philosophy: the problem of knowledge. In the *Physics*, the *Metaphysics*, and the *Organon*, he describes man's only possible mode of experience as a mixture of sentient and rational knowledge, active and passive. That is, Aristotle believes it is possible for man, through knowledge, to connect with his own *identity*, his consciousness of self, and with the general reality of the world, with *otherness* as the consciousness of the other and what is outside the self. Hence, Aristotle's position is absolute and optimistic, in contrast with the skepticism of philosophical and sophistical relativism, which asserts man's inability to acquire an exact conception of reality (S. H. Butcher, 1955; C. F. Else, 1957).

Given this context, poetics, for Aristotle, is a faculty complementary to philosophical knowledge. Poetry implies the possibility of man's ability to duplicate reality, creating via *imitation* or *mimesis* a fictional world he himself structures and governs. The principle of truth, which regulates man's experience of events in reality and in historical discourse, enormously restricts his possibilities for ethical and imaginative foresight. Through poetic invention, governed by the conventions of *verisimilitude*, man definitively expands and enriches his experience, situating characters and events in all possible hypothetical positions, however extreme, beyond the limited articulations of his experienced reality (E. Lledó, 1961). This explains Aristotle's assertion that history, narrating only what has occurred, is less universal and philosophical than poetry, which narrates what might have happened, in terms of the necessary and verisimilar (51 a, 37—38).

As can be seen, in the classical conception of the world, poetics was viewed as a science dedicated to regulating a fundamental facet of human experience. Poetry's mimetic fiction multiplies the possibilities for experiencing, experimenting and enhancing consciousness by constructing true yet hypothetical *models*, which is, after all, what the terms "imitation" and "mimesis" refer to. With these models, reproducing the fantastic feeling of reality, man empowers his imaginary experience. The characters, events and settings he creates in fiction satisfy his imagination's need for sentimental expansion or test his ethical or passionate experience in hypothetical situations of extreme conflict, without true risk (the principle underlying Aristotle's notion of *catharsis*).

The classical world, therefore, exalted poetry and the science which studied it as among the most serious and powerful operations by which man forms and situates his experience of the world and of his own existence (R. R. Bolgar, 1971). This high esteem for the poetic corresponds with the *mythic* structure of classical thought, an understanding of myth as the exemplary — and therefore poetic — symbolic narration (W. Jaeger, 1934; E. R. Dodds, 1957, pp. 80—82).

It goes without saying that in historical stages in which positivist, intellectualist or technological conceptions predominate, the value of poetic experience is relegated to those individuals and minorities especially sensitive to this form of affirming knowledge and feelings (G. Weise, 1969). Along general lines, it can be said that the "modern world", with which the majority of the patterns of our present historical circumstances are linked, embraces technological positivism. For this reason, poetic humanism survives socially as an attitude restricted to the few in number and, consequently, we find ourselves obliged to explain and justify the wide and profound meaning poetics possesses in a mythical conception of experience.

The much more limited scientific sense the term "poetics" has acquired in recent years must be distinguished from the classical discipline of the same name. Structuralist literary thought divulged this renewed conception of poetics via well-known authors like Jakobson and the Russian or Czech formalists, or through the French neoformalism of Barthes and his disciples. In this manner, it came to be popularized in numerous books, articles and even journal titles. But, compared to its classical namesake, structuralist poetics refers more concretely to a theory of literary language, or rather to a part of descriptive linguistics which studies the artistic use of language (T. Todorov, 1968; R. Pajano, 1972; R. Jakobson, 1977; J. Culler, 1978; J. M. Pozuelo Yvancos, 1988).

A book which today makes use of the word "poetics" should begin by acknowledging its two different meanings: a traditional one, which understands poetics in its most ample and decisive form, and the modern linguistic sense, restricted in its orientation to the study of the verbal constituents of the literary text. We should not forget, though, that it has been the enthusiastic and scientific cultivation of the linguistic and semiological orientations of modern poetics which have fundamentally reactivated the present dissemination of the old classical discipline, a discipline which had been progressively corrupted, stripped down to a purely theoretical and didactic dimension by the end of the last century.

In order to resolve this ambiguity and attenuate the serious doctrinal confusion it produces, the generic, traditional designation used for poetics should be adjectivized. By denominating the more reduced and monographic speciality of structuralist literary criticism as *linguistic poetics*, or semiological poetics, as others have suggested, it is possible to refer precisely to the scientific content of the modern theoretical literary discipline, without severing its connections with the general disciplinary branch of poetics, and without depriving structuralist poetics, in its absolutely broadest scope, of the wider and more universal contents included in the domain of poetics in its traditional sense. Certain noted structuralist "poetologists" have in fact used and disseminated this same restrictive adjectivization in referring to modern poetics.

Classical and classicist literary theory defines its contents in terms of the documents of Plato, Aristotle and Horace, preserved and extended in a large number of medieval texts (E. Faral, 1928; H. Caplan, 1934—1936; J. J. Murphy, 1974, 1985), before culminating with the Renaissance's further consideration and amplification of the tradition, beginning with Dante's *De vulgari eloquentia* (1957 edition) and Boccaccio's *De genealogia deorum* (1951 edition). With good reason, Baxter Hathaway (1962), an excellent historian of Renaissance literary theory, designated the sixteenth century as "the age of criticism" (G. Saitta, 1949—1951; P. O. Kristeller, 1956; R. Scrivano, 1959; G. Weise, 1961, 1978; E. Garin 1952, 1965). I myself have designated the century from 1550 to 1650 as the period of "modern literary theory's formation" (A. García-Berrio, 1977—1980).

Classical European theory of the seventeenth century caps this long process of the accumulation of ideas and materials (J. E. Spingarn, 1908; Ch. S. Baldwin, 1939; V. Hall, 1945; A. Buck, *et al.*, 1972; B. Weinberg, 1961, 1970—1973), generally through the exegesis and commentary of fundamental canonical texts. This process is articulated in four traditional currents. From Plato's *Ion, Phaedrus,* and *Republic*, and from the series of commentaries generated by these dialogues, an initial, very sketchy theory is formulated concerning the literary genres and the discursive modes of verbal imitation. Above all, these sources give rise to basic beliefs about the poet's psychological disposition, the nature of the creative process, and the myth of *inspiration*, together with ideals regarding poetry's morality and social utility (J. W. Atkins, 1934; A. Reyes, 1941; G. M. Grube, 1968, pp. 46—65).

Horace's *Epistola ad Pisones*, the basic text for the historical pattern of ideals in the Horatian topical current, popularized and perpetuated the concepts of Alexandrian poetics in the classical world, thanks particularly to the driving force and synthetic capacity of the great Latin poet's versified formulas. Horace's *Ars* contains many stylistic suggestions relating to *inventio* — the thematic content of the work — and to its *dispositio* or structure, both governed by the principle of aesthetic proportionality known as *decorum* (C. O. Brink, 1963—1982; G. Stégen, 1960; C. Becker, 1963; E. Pasoli, 1964).

Above all, Horace's *Ars Poetica* systematizes and disseminates the general principles of literary aesthetics (G. Williams, 1968). In Horace's definition of poetry's essence in terms of *causes*, the *efficient cause* regulates notions regarding the nature of artifice and the creative process, according to the topical polarity between *art* (or rules) and *genius* (or inspiration). The *final cause* of poetry is expressed by means of the opposition between *entertaining* and *teaching*, between which extremes ideas are formulated concerning the aims of literature in terms of its didactic or pleasure-giving service to society and the individual. Finally, the *material cause*, corresponding to the literary work's *content*, is opposed, in terms of its role in the work's composition, to the formal artistic verbal structure, or *form* (A. García-Berrio, 1977—1980).

As can be seen, the Horatian systematization of the three primary dualities sets forth a complete scheme, forming the very backbone of the literary and artistic aesthetics of classicist literary theory. Classical taste will oscillate between the two poles formed by these three dualities. The *rules-didacticism-content* axis represents a conservative system of the artistic ideal, which allies itself with the understanding of literature as complementary to philosophical thought. Literature and art's submission to the pattern of social organization in Greek tragedy, in Augustan literature and in Medieval Christian art relied on this ideological option of the classical poetic ideal (A. García-Berrio, 1981, 1988, pp. 18—19).

By way of contrast with this conservative ideal, art will always contain the ferment of recreative, playful liberty which obeys a poetics based on *inspiration*, *delight*, and *formal artifice*. The absolutist tendency of official conservative poetics has always regularly attempted to impose itself on those symptoms of revitalizing liberalism which are to be found in the aesthetic ideology of any great artist — whether Horace or Cervantes — beyond the conscious content of ideas in his official poetic program. Certain figures, like Pindar, Ovid and Ariosto, demonstrate more radically in their work the presence of this poetic ideal. And whole ages or schools, like Mannerism, can be explained as the gradual displacement of a didactic, content-oriented poetics by this second, recreative-formalist ideal, increasingly fashionable within the mass of aesthetic ideas and options constituting the poetics of the *Renaissance Age* (A. García-Berrio, 1977–1980, II, pp. 247 ff.).

The Aristotelian tradition, based on the fundamental ideas of Aristotle's *Poetics*, was a late development. Technically, its influence in antiquity is hardly recognizable, as a result of its being filtered and diffused in the aesthetic thought of the moral philosophical schools, among the Sophists, and in the extensive tradition of the Alexandrian grammarians and rhetoricians. In Western Europe, this current does not really become active until its dissemination in the sixteenth century through the humanists' Latin and Italian translations and paraphrases, especially Francesco Robortello's influential commentary. As a result, in spite of Aristotle's prestige throughout the Middle Ages as a philosopher and rhetorician, his poetic ideas have to be considered as a relatively small and late component of classicist poetics (M. T. Herrick, 1946; B. Weinberg, 1961).

The most evident Aristotelian contribution to classical poetics can be located especially in the distorted specialization of the entire subject of the purpose and object of art to the narrow ideal of *catharsis* or the purging of the passions, together with the universal acceptance of the principle conceiving *poiesis* in terms of *mimesis*. In fact, this is a question of the illustration and strengthening of the didactic poetic ideal, blended with the rhetorical principle of *movere*. As we will soon see, Aristotle's conception of art's purpose was actually far more complex than his initial humanist commentators allowed for, with room for an intellectual mode of specifically artistic pleasure; but, as always happens, the *pattern* of reception of Aristotle's ideas by his commentators differs from the objective content of the original ideas as he first proposed them (A. García-Berrio, 1975, p. 95; 1988, pp. 106–114).

Aristotle's *Poetics* also decisively influenced the characteristic classical conception of the text's *structure*, of its macrostructural *dispositio*. Without exaggeration we can today conceive of the *Poetics* as a rigorously structural treatise on the construction of the tragic text. In the fragment dealing with the definition of tragedy, not only is the determination of the mechanism of the passions and their cathartic purging considered fundamental, as in fact it has been down to the present, but so too is the enumeration and description of the content of the *qualitative parts* which compose the tragic text: plot, character, diction, thought, spectacle and song. Through a process of analogical extension, Aristotle's conception of tragedy's quantitative and qualitative constituents and its argumentative structure or plot gave rise to classicist poetics' fundamental notions of the artistic text's structure (A. García-Berrio, 1975, p. 111; 1988, pp. 119–131.

The fourth of the traditional components of classical literary theory is rhetoric. As is known, rhetoric was the classical disciplinary setting which framed poetics. Originally, its specific concern was the construction of verbal discourse based on the practical objectives of *movere* and *adherence*, utilizing, above all, the de-automatizing mechanisms of verbal *expressiveness* (A. García-Berrio, 1983, 1984). As a science of communicative discourse, its true content referred to the theory and description of the civil and legal argumentation of *rhetores* — lawyers, politicians and those involved in public life. Nevertheless, in treating this system of argumentation and expressiveness in terms of a brilliantly embellished verbal language, it touched on facets of concern to the poetics of artistic discourse (Ch. S. Baldwin, 1939; G. A. Kennedy, 1963).

From the beginning, this situation was also complicated by the lack of interest among the classical treatises of poetics in questions specifically related to *elocutio*. That is, neither Aristotle's *Poetics* nor Horace's *Ars poetica* include a treatment of poetic elocution equivalent to what modern literary theory and poetics generally understand as a theory of literary language. As concerns *elocutio*, Aristotle sketches what is basically a grammatical discussion and Horace provides beautiful images of lexical dynamics (A. García-Berrio, 1976, pp. 181–201), but no more. In fact, in his *Poetics*, Aristotle designates questions of language as material for the rhetoricians.

Thus, classical rhetoric initially, if inadequately, displaced poetics as a science of literary eloquence. From this position, rhetoric gradually began to develop theories of poetic *dispositio* and even many elements of the theory of *inventio*. Hence, in practice, classical poetics abandoned to rhetoric all reflection dealing with the specific nature of artistic language, which in our own time has become the object of what has been called linguistic poetics. Stripped of these concerns, classical literary theory focused its attention on *dispositio* in order to address problems of the textual macrostructure, together with general questions of aesthetic causality, and stylistic issues of *decorum* (H. Lausberg, 1966–1968).

Disassociated from the aesthetic orientations of classical poetics, broadened by the speculative transcendentalism of Romantic theory and favoring a more pragmatic, textual and elocutive specialization of rhetoric, poetics in our century, from its beginnings in Russian formalism and stylistics, has concentrated exclusively on the immanent and textual aspects of literary works (L. Ritter Santini and E. Raimondi, eds., 1978; A. Leoni and M. A. Pigliasco, eds., 1979). That is, with regard to the literary work, linguistic poetics has assumed as its own field of attention those structural aspects of the artistic text's verbal material which had previously been exclusively attended to by rhetoric, thus creating the paradox, which I pointed out at the beginning of this chapter, in which the term "poetics" simultaneously refers to two naturally complementary views: the traditional philosophico-aesthetic one, fruit of the Romantic perfection of classical poetics, and a modern linguistico-rhetorical sense.

The process I have just sketched shows how rhetoric's shadow came to be cast over an area normally belonging to poetics: the theory of literary language, and in particular speculation as to the nature of poeticity and the verbal devices which produce the poetic effect. My presentation of these facts attempts to conform to their historical nature, as produced in the classical sciences of discourse. Hence, as opposed to the complete vacuum existing in the Aristotelian and Horatian poetic treatises, all of the classical theory of literary embellishment appears systematized in Athenian and Alexandrian rhetorical works, and in the Roman treatises of Cicero and Quintilian. The most specifically stylistic and artistic considerations of literary and poetic language are to be found in treatises normally considered rhetorical — Theophrastus, Hermogenes or Demetrius on style (G. M. A. Grube, 1968, pp. 111) — and, above all, in the aesthetic speculation on the sublime nature of discourse in pseudo-Longinus. Known as *Progymnasmata*, rhetorical manuals on the practice and exercise of eloquence, among which Theon's stands out, functioned in classical education on the basis of literary hypotheses and examples (G. A. Kennedy, 1963).

What is therefore produced in antiquity is the progressive indistinction and synthesis of the two great disciplines dedicated to discourse, poetics and rhetoric, and not simply a rhetoricalization resulting in the impoverishment of poetics (A. Battistini and E. Raimondi, 1984, pp. 5—13). Little by little, the initially rhetorical considerations concerning artistic eloquence are incorporated during medieval times into works entitled *Poetics* (Ch. S. Baldwin, 1928; E. Faral, 1928; J. J. Murphy, 1974, 1985), the most famous of which are those of Geoffrey of Vinsauf or John of Garland. In Dante, for example, we already find rhetoric's analytico-discursive schemes completely assimilated to the service of an artistic and poetic preoccupation with discourse and literary style (P. V. Megaldo, 1978). Along the same lines, already at the beginning of the Renaissance (R. A. Lanhan, 1976; W. J. Kennedy 1978; T. O. Sloan and R. B. Waddington, eds., 1974; J. J. Murphy, ed., 1983), a more specialized rhetoric conscious of its exclusive role as a theory of non-poetic elocution (A. García-Berrio, 1977—1980; W. S. Howell, 1961; G. Mazzacurati, 1961) begins to suffer from the well-known process of decline that would carry through to its absolute depletion and discredit by the end of the nineteenth century. On the other hand, poetics, now more complete as a speculative-philosophical and stylistico-rhetorical whole, does not follow the same path towards exhaustion, but rather flourishes in the work of the likes of Boileau, Muratoni and Luzán in the eighteenth century (R. Bray, 1957), or Hegel and Dilthey in the nineteenth (A. García-Berrio and M. T. Hernández, 1988, pp. 24—32; T. Albaladejo, 1989, pp. 23—40).

In this process of influences and contamination, rhetoric, beginning in the eighteenth century, grew to be more eroded and corrupted than poetics (A. García-Berrio, 1983). An increasingly more literary rhetoric, both in its examples and its models (E. Raimondi, 1983), began to lose its initial identity as a linguistic science of communicative discourse, a role in which it would be supplanted by general and speculative grammar and later, in our own century, by linguistics. Meanwhile, rhetoric's unsurpassable foundations as a science of rationally argued expressive discourse tended to invalidate and restrict it from addressing the progressive development of literary and poetic styles, the latter being much more autonomous with regard to their imaginary and sentimental sources, as well as in many of their subconscious registers.

Throughout the history of their collaboration as complementary disciplines of discourse, rhetoric, the science of verbal *expressiveness*, and poetics, the science of expressive-imaginary *poeticity*, have labored under an ever-changing, differing understanding of the nature of standard language and of literary and poetic discourse. The rhetoricalization of classical poetics was made possible by the confusion reigning in Greco-Latin culture over the nature of artistic language. Literature, and especially poetry, was considered in terms of an adorned, *embellished discourse*, without significant interest being paid to the specific constitution of its autonomous, transrational and fantastic sources (E. Norden, 1898; K. Borinski, 1914). This common, overly generic appraisal nevertheless seems generally valid and definitive, beyond the unique partial or momentary cases of sublime self-awareness we may be able to attribute to certain exceptional classical artists (A. Michel, 1982).

On the other hand, the modern consolidation of the autonomous ideal of literary art and, above all, of the most pure forms of poetry, initiated during the Renaissance (F. Tateo, 1960; E. Garin, 1952) and consecrated by Romanticism, introduced an unshakable belief in the insufficiency of the *embellished style* as a means of justifying the aesthetic specificity of literature (G. Mazzacurati, 1961; M. Fumaroli, 1980). Rhetoric as a science of communicative verbal expressiveness pursued a stylistic use of language the pragmatic, rational and persuasive results of which differed essentially from the aesthetic effects produced in the artistic — literary and poetic — use of language (E. Raimondi, 1983).

The radicalization of literature as a sentimentally and imaginatively autonomous experience began during the *Romantic revolution* (G. Gusdorf, 1976; G. Carnero, 1983) and deepened by the textual experimentation of modern art's *vanguards* (R. Poggioli, 1962; B. Goriély, 1967) has, among its many consequences, brought about the present definitive separation between rhetoric as an adequate linguistic science of communicative verbal experience and poetics as the science of a specific artistic mode of verbal discourse. The latter today offers itself, more than ever, as an emphatically alternative *aesthetic experience* to the rationalist discourse of reflective and philosophical knowledge (M. Raymond, 1947; M. Nadeau, 1945—1948).

0.3. Romantic Literary Theory: Fantasy and Imagination in the Artistic Construction of Sentimental Intimacy

Up to this point I have been speaking of traditional poetics as a single whole, set against the twentieth century's linguistic poetics. Nevertheless, the great shift produced in European poetic tastes and ideals beginning in the eighteenth century obliges us to identify the profound differences which need to be taken into account in any discussion of that moment's poetic tradition. Basically, the principal change consists in the displacement of the center of interest from the classicist reflection on questions related to the artistic text and its structure towards those which deal with the organization of the psychological, fantastico-imaginary and sentimental processes involved in the creation and reception of works of art (S. Timpanaro, 1965; A. Battistini and E. Raimondi, 1984, pp. 85–86; A. García-Berrio and M. T. Hernández, 1988, p. 43).

The Hegelian symbol, also prevalent among other thinkers of the period, serves as an example expressing the distinctiveness of Romantic art in terms of a shift of vision from the perfect surfaces and solid, impenetrable corporeal masses of classical statues to the visceral, intimate commotion of human emotional conflict. Romantic literary theory represents above all the anthropological radicalization of aesthetics, the search for the causes of poeticity in the emotive roots of man's "cosmovision" (W. J. Bate, 1946).

In one sense, Kants's *Critique of Judgment* represents the definitive crystallization of the double current of antithetical ecclecticism, subjectivist and proportionalist, external and textual, which runs through the history of aesthetics since antiquity (O. Walzel, 1952). As is well known, Kant affirms, as the foundation of the aprioristic universalization of aesthetic judgment, the agreement between the structural characteristics of the aesthetic object and the theoretical conditions of the subject's sensibility. The classicist tradition of artistic theory, especially that of poetics, provided him with the structural principles of objective consciousness. And in the reasonable appeal to the intimate foundation of subjective sensibility, Kant echoed the passionate feelings of his own age (T. E. Uehling, 1971; T. Cohen and P. Guyer, eds., 1982).

In spite of this, nobody would, of course, consider Kant as one given over to the sentimental passions of Romanticism. Moreover, the subjective radicalization of aesthetic judgment constituted a current with numerous known antecedents, like the objective tradition itself. Kant's insight consists, once more, in the natural ease of his balanced intuition. That he would succeed in properly intuiting the Romantic demands for an intimate psychological space, a sphere where the textual propositions of artistic objects bear fruit or are frustrated as effects of emotion and fantasy and as constructions of the imagination, is certainly an unexpected synthesis for him to achieve in view of his own intellectual habits.

The Romantic inversion even reaches the emotional forms discussed in Aristotle's *Poetics*, the triumphal essence of censured classical taste. The poetic delight of *mimesis*, which Aristotle had identified, was made concrete under the form of man's intellectual pleasure in *re-cognition*. Even the passionate mobilization of cathartic commiseration and terror had as its goal the extirpation of "those passions", the purge of passions at the service of the well-balanced ideal of a citizenry without vehement emotions. Obviously, we are at the opposite pole from the passionate imagination recognized and favored by Romantic literary theory (M. H. Abrams, 1953).

It is customary to cite, as the first traditional impulse for this change, Longinus' treatise *On the Sublime*, which only achieved wide dissemination in Europe at the beginning of the eighteenth century with Boileau's academic commentary and Bouhours' enthusiastic annotations (C. A. Litman, 1971; T. E. Wood, 1972). It should be noted that this new document, incorporating itself into the European aesthetic fashions of the 1700s, was also a basic element of classical poetics. *On the Sublime* symbolizes the rhetorical appeal to the explanation of paradox and of poetic aporia: the enthusiastic consecration of a language which consumes its useful coherence in order to appeal poetically beyond the conventional meanings inevitably adhering to language's *presence* in texts. The sublime explosion of poetic meaning comes more from the silent and negative than from any substantial, solid plenitude.

But not even the influence of *On the Sublime* exhaustively explains the radical alternative meaning of Romantic subjectivist sentimentalism, compared to the descriptive structural nature of classicist poetics. After all, Longinus' work is a rhetorically-oriented treatise, which explores the properties inherent in language more than the psychological, emotional and imaginary constitution of poetic sentiment. At the most, he is able to locate the dazzling sensation produced by verbal sublimity. The Romantic exploration of the poetic imagination's intimate sentimental nature begins only with the radical discovery of a new image of man (C. M. Bowra, 1961).

If I find it interesting to highlight both the differences and the complementarity that exist between the classicist and Romantic components of traditional literary theory, it is not because I have surrendered to some form of historical stupefaction nurtured by monumentalist nostalgia. The duality of the complementary constituents structuring traditional poetics faithfully illustrates, in my judgment, the "burning questions" of current literary theory (J. Veltruský, 1977).

The structural and textual interests of the various currents of modern formal poetics correspond approximately to the fundamental content of classicist poetics and rhetoric. In reacting against their immediate past, that is, traditional literary theory as it existed in the first decades of this century, the various formalisms set out to surpass the aesthetic idealism of Romantic theory, branded as transcendental intimism and sentimentalism (G. Morpurgo Tagliabue, 1960). Scarcely noticed by the young and inexperienced formalists, their immanent location of textual mechanisms at the center of their own interests helped to restore the interest of classical poetics and rhetoric in the text as a verbal construction. In this respect the European cultivators of stylistics, like Spitzer, Hatzfeld and the two Spanish Alonsos, had sufficient time and composure at their disposal, both of which the formalists lacked, to explicitly establish and confirm the continuity of their interests with these traditions, which would explain the widely circulated definition of rhetoric as "the stylistics of the ancients" (D. Alonso, 1952; A. Alonso, 1955).

Evidently, as I have been indicating in this chapter, linguistic poetics has not restricted itself to the passive and limited retrieval of the experience of the classical sciences of poetics and rhetoric relating to discourse. The conscious remodeling of the artistic text's structural mechanisms, thanks especially to the tutelage and stimulus of the formal revolution in linguistics, has profitably transformed and modernized classical poetic's metalinguistic reflections on the literary text. The breadth of this systematic completion, together with the rigor and metatheoretical explicitness of its descriptions, represents formalist poetics' current option for constituting a sector of general poetics — which I, for one, view as entirely appropriate and reasonable (A. García-Berrio and M. T. Hernández, 1988, pp. 67—71).

For their part, the emphasis on sentimental irrationality and imaginary symbolism characterizing the essential core of the Romantic alternative in poetics, both constitute excellent models for the integrative amplification, in due course, of the anthropological and imaginary sector in the theory of the text and of the artistic system produced by this general poetics.

Romantic aesthetics is, as is known, notably characterized by its passion for that which cannot be made concrete (L. R. Furst, 1979). The fixation and assimilation of a certainty is itself sufficient evidence proving it to be fraudulent and, hence, discardable. The Romantic tendency towards locating the poetic absolute in a radically unstable area, alien to the coherence of word or meaning, corresponds exactly to the predifferentially lodged type — of the "différance" in Derrida's own terms (1967 [1978, p. 92]; 1967a [1976, p. 260]). The myth of the unattainable primogenial evident in Vico or Herder's idea of pure lyric as pure language (I. Berlin, 1976; A. Battistini and E. Raimondi, 1984, pp. 138—144; A. García-Berrio and M. T. Hernández, 1988, pp. 36—39) or the concept of unaffected art which runs throughout Romantic poetics from Schiller and Goethe to Schlegel and Coleridge in one form or another (R. Wellek, 1955, II), all correspond to this Romantic intuition concerning the proper location of the poetic absolute. What Derrida proposes in our time as the location of deconstructive aporia, Blanchot had formulated positively as the translinguistic space of the experience of otherness. At the same time, for the Romantics, it was the ground where a vehement desire of the imagination and the sentiments lay positively rooted.

For general poetics, Blanchot's existentialist experience, with his poetics of paradoxical negativity, as well as the current skeptical resurgence of Derridean deconstruction — both sharing the common remote and general antecedent of Heidegger's aesthetic radicalization of "poetry as truth" and the more immediate precedent of Emmanuel Levinas' ethics of the *other* — only hint at a sense of direction. Both, although with different intentions, point to the immanent, sentimental and imaginary conception of *poeticity*, already and inevitably designed as a transcendent experience. I have written "only", but I could also add "nothing less than", because freeing reference in the transcendental space of *poeticity* implies a whole program for literary theory, familiar to Romanticism or to the psychoanalytical and mythopoetic sectors of modern criticism, but unknown until now to formal and structuralist poetics.

The faculty called upon by Romantic theory to explore poetry's journey towards the absolute was the *imagination*. In the case of the modern aesthetics of despair, be it in the form of Blanchot's existentialist aesthetics or the deconstructive aesthetics of Derrida — a positive aesthetics after all and in spite of himself — the hermeneutical power of imagination is invalidated in view of the differential variation of the depth in which the direct experience of *the other* is lodged. The general poetics which we may currently aspire to establish gathers in all of its validity the Romantic incitement towards the imaginary and towards the maximalization of the imagination's capacities. Existentialism's silent suspension of judgment on this point and deconstruction's skeptical nihilism, neither of which should affect general poetics with their negative perspectives of analysis, also cannot help very much, except, as I said before, in providing a general prospective direction. A general poetics can rediscover and complete the founding stimuli of the Romantic concepts of imagination in view of the contribution of the present school of the poetics of the imagination which, with Bachelard and Durand, has already constructed a *symbolic semantics* of mythic representations and which is on its way towards constructing, as I myself have set forth, an *imaginary syntax* of the fantastic designs and schemes of anthropological orientation (A. García-Berrio, 1985, 1987; A. García-Berrio and M. T. Hernández, 1988, pp. 100—107).

Fantasy — "Phantasie" — and *Imagination* — "Einbildungskraft" — are the two progressive constituents of the Romantic theory of the poetic imagination. Presently they are almost always used as synonymous terms. Romantic theory regularly needed to distinguish between them, but their respective conceptions changed from one author to another. For A. G. Schlegel, *fantasy* represented reason's highest and most absolute capacity, and that most independent from any conscious, controllable support. In the later terms of Freudian psychoanalysis, it corresponds to the suddenly discovered images provoked by subconscious impulses. Imagination, on the other hand, represented, in Schlegel's opinion, the elaborative level of combinatory associationism, a capacity linked to the sentimental fantastic iridescence corresponding to the verbal stimuli of *expressiveness* and to the control of *fictionality*. On the contrary, Coleridge attributed the powers and capacities of what Schlegel understood as the imagination ("Einbildungskraft") to fantasy ("fancy") and vice versa (R. Wellek, 1955, II, Chs. I and VI; A. García-Berrio and M. T. Hernández, 1988, pp. 52—53). At the present crossroad, the imaginary section of a general poetics must adhere to the global Romantic concept of the imagination, but also control the manner in which all of the concept's reclassifications and differences operate, especially in all that relates to the difference between imagination and fantasy.

The origin and cause for the hierarchical division of imaginary activity into two levels and modes in Romantic literary theory lies, in my judgment, in the need to distinguish between the least concrete forms of imaginary experience, understood until then as "ineffable", and the fantastic context at work in the connotative sentimental periphery of classical expressiveness (F. Schlegel, 1956 edition, pp. 130 and 185). Considerable activity and effort in Baroque art centered precisely on this latter context (R. Wellek, 1946; G. Getto, 1951; O. Macrí, 1962; F. Lázaro Carreter, 1966; A. García-Berrio, 1968).

However, the differential pathetic condition of the Romantic understanding of the imaginary is always in evidence. The Baroque's fantastic activity is permeated by its classical inheritance (E. Raimondi, 1961, p. 196), textually reorganized throughout the Renaissance, of which the Baroque represents only the final episode, the natural end result of the tensions inherent in the age's materials (A. García-Berrio, 1977—1980, II, pp. 247—355; W. Sypher, 1956; J. A. Maravall, 1975). The connotative sentimental periphery of the regular and controlled verbal rhetorical expressiveness and nomic productivity of *conceptismo*'s metaphoric combinations aspires to constitute the Baroque imagination as a new instrument for the hitherto unknown exploration of the natural correspondences in the rational poetic of wit (*ingenio*) (J. Rousset, 1945; E. Raimondi, 1961; F. Lázaro Carreter, 1966; A. García-Berrio, 1968; M. T. Hernández, 1986). The Romantic imagination, also firmly rooted in the literary tradition of nomic fantasy, aggressively projects itself towards the sublime inklings of the poetic imagination, governed by unstable, volatile and subconscious impulses. Unlike the Baroque, Romanticism does not seek a renovation of its conception of the world, but rather abandons itself to the delight of the tormenting sweetness of a sentimental shipwreck. Ezio Raimondi, a keen observer of these two areas of the historical imagination, has successfully indicated the "milestones" of the Romantic sentimental dream (E. Raimondi, 1974, 1985).

The reasons for the continued validity of the dichotomy which today we lay claim to from the perspective of the imagination's role in a general poetics are approximately the same as those recognized by the Romantics. As will become clearer as my scheme is developed and set forth in this book, the Romantic distinction is both useful and legitimate, establishing a first set of *nomic* forms, controllable by the conscious imagination — which I prefer, in order to resolve the terminological vacillation plaguing the Romantics, to conventionalize as products of *fantastic operations* — in contrast to a second set of deeper manifestations, subconscious drives, which do not proceed immediately from the stimulation predictable from an experience or examination of the form of textual *expressiveness*. Insofar as they are effects produced by imaginary and sentimental activity, both forms of the imagination — the fantastic and that properly imaginary — correspond in my scheme to the sphere of *poeticity* as an unpredictable *value*, which is to be distinguished from the pragmatic and conventionalizable reaches of the choice or *option* of *literariness* in its strictest sense.

Nevertheless, the *fantastic* nature of expressiveness' connotative results, together with the referential work of *fictional* construction in the mimetic illusion, indicate a first level, more accessible and concrete, of the *poetic effect*. On the other hand, the most unpredictable, accidental forms of *poeticity*, those that cannot be the fruit of cultural convention because they are of an unknown and unforeseeable nature, symbolize the more radical anthropological limits of the imagination, constituting the fortuitous essence of the poetic as a *value of aesthetic experience*.

In the corresponding chapters of this book I will specify the respective contents of both structures of the poetic imagination. Here I will limit myself to proposing the idea that the unexpected imaginary mass which makes its way to the forms of the text guided by "impulses" and revelations, never clearly conscious or predictable, is an affirmation of man's encounter with his own anthropological structures. Man constitutes and orders in time and space his *diurnal* vision and his *postural* relationship with cosmological otherness, at the same time as he makes visible the shadowy spaces in this relationship and in the microcosm of his own identity in terms of symbolic and impossible representations, faint exhalations in the imagination, under the effect of death's crude reflection, of *nocturnal* and *digestive* depths, alien to the measurement of time and irreducible to any structure of spatial support (G. Durand, 1960; A. García-Berrio, 1985). Skeptical annulment, the projection of the mystical and Romantic reverie, or the concept of "listening" recently distinguished by Paolo Valesio (1986), are all constituted by these means. In the gap between the imagination of the diurnal coordinates of time and space and their loss in the shipwreck of the nocturnal imagination, the creative abundance of *eros* maintains the cyclical and regenerative symbols of its triumph over time and the removal of spatial limits in the poetic representation of paternity and copulative ecstasy.

I have already indicated that it is characteristic of Romantic poetics and, in general, of its literary aesthetics, to examine in depth the psychological conditions and effects of the artistic illusion. In this sense, it seems to me that Hegel specifies very accurately the principle constituting literary and poetic operations: man in search of a procedure to express and represent his own conceptual and imaginary configuration of reality as a dialectical structure of identity-otherness. By erecting his typology of literary texts on the precise principle of the essential and communicative constitution of literary activity, Hegel founds, develops and consolidates a *universalist* model for poetic literary reflection.

Presently, the opposite trend predominates among the cultivators of literary studies. Considering artistic effects in terms of universal categories is as foreign to the *relativist* fashion of the radical aesthetics of reception and reading as it is to the *skeptical* beliefs of deconstruction. Obviously, a general poetics must assume convictions of a *universalist* type, corresponding to examples such as Hegel's dialectical theory of genre, A. Jolles' development of "simple", elemental forms (1930), or the proto-imaginary and anthropological constructions of N. Frye (1957). It is an entirely plausible task, as I trust I am illustrating in this book; one which attempts to adjust itself precisely to the nature of literary phenomena. In other words, it is plausible only on the condition that it fulfills its commitment to adequately consider and actualize the cultural tradition of literary theory, without simplifying or deforming it.

0.4. The Contents of Modern Semiological and Linguistic Poetics

As I have already indicated, a modern poetics aware of its disciplinary status began to take shape in Europe during the second decade of this century. Its concrete content was the analysis of the textual structure of literary works. Precisely through this analytical immanentism concentrated in formal structures of the artistic text, the new poetics tried to remedy the inattention paid to the textual physiognomy of literary works already customary in philosophically-rooted Romantic poetics, which concentrated on the major meaningful structures of the literary system. At the same time, the incipient poetics of the Russian formalists called attention to the unsatisfactory petrification of rhetorical analysis, already almost entirely reduced to the automatic identification of tropes and figures in the text, beginning with the conventionally accepted inventories in the rhetorical manuals of the time (V. Erlich, 1955; A. García-Berrio, 1973; J. Striedter, 1989).

Modern poetics' physiognomy and interest are also characterized by its willingness to adapt and give the corresponding analytical response to the profound changes appearing in artistic practice beginning with Romanticism and accelerating with the futurist and symbolist vanguards. The concept of the poetic word's *transrationality* and *deautomatization* as it was circulated by the Russian formalists translates the unsalvageable disproportion of the old rhetorical conception of poetry as the mere adornment of rational communication into new terms in order to justify the most sought-after effects of the new poetry (Y. Tynjanov, 1924).

Some of the new formalist poetics' essential peculiarities are explained in terms of its attempt to rectify the insufficiencies of traditional thetorical analysis. Particularly in this century, poetics has been characterized by its extension to the criticism of narrative structures (M. Bal, 1977). Since its first appearance, the novel became a suspicious genre in the debates of traditional rhetoric. The absence, since Aristotle, of precedents in the classical treatment of the genre was a frequently mobilized argument in the Renaissance disputes over the place and value of Italian *romanzi*. Of course, the development and consolidation in Europe of the novelistic text's form and reputation from Cervantes to its great nineteenth century creators led critics to discard the primitive arguments over the "authorized" genres. Nevertheless, there remained a very significant lack of methods to deal with the specific structure of narrative texts.

Moreover, we must keep in mind the fact that the prestylistic, rhetorical hermeneutic focused exclusively on elocutionary phenomena, restricting even this investigation to the text's most superficial structures. Rhetorical analysis confined itself to highly limited and concrete features or stylemes, the reach and extension of which tended to coincide with that of the word, as in the study of adjectivization, or with phrases not extending beyond the sentence or verse in the case of poems. Stylistics later inherited these restrictions almost unaltered (C. Bally, 1921; P. Guiraud, 1955; B. Terracini, 1966; M. Riffaterre, 1971; N. E. Enkvist, 1973). As a result, under these premises, novelists' styles could only be considered in terms of the *stylemes* of artistic prose. Hence, the fundamental textual aspects of *dispositio* or the textual macrostructure of narration remained absolutely unknown (J. S. Petöfi and A. García-Berrio, 1979). In fact, these more extended structures, first approached by Tynjanov, Tomashevsky and Shklovsky, were only brought into a revolutionary and renovating focus by Vladimir Propp's functional analyses at the end of this century's third decade (A. García-Berrio, 1973, pp. 214—284; T. Albaladejo Mayordomo, 1986, pp. 95—112).

In summary, modern poetics in its formalist period has constructed a complete theory of literary and poetic language, highly adequate in its current form. All of the features of the different levels of literary language, from the phonological to the grammatical, in morphology as in syntax, were the object of a rigorous revision in the hope of defining the differential principle constituting *literariness*. From a renewed linguistic and stylistic perspective, that investigation reviewed the old poetic, grammatical and rhetorical concepts of vocalic coloring, alliteration, enjambement, line and stanza, adjectivization, the stylistic value of essential and active nouns, deixis, the stylistic connectors, the specificity of the poetic lexicon, etc. (T. Albaladejo Mayordomo, 1984, pp. 141—207; J. C. Coquet, 1972; J. Culler, 1975; W. U. Dressler, 1978; N. E. Enkvist, 1973; N. E. Enkvist, J. Spencer and M. Gregory, 1971; R. Fowler, ed., 1966; D. C. Freeman, ed., 1970; J. Ihwe, 1972; R. Jakobson, 1960; R. Kloepfer, 1975; J. Lotman, 1970; J. M. Pozuelo Yvancos, 1983, 1988; R. Scholes, 1976; T. A. Sebeok, ed., 1960; C. Segre, 1985).

A more detailed study of the poetological reactivation and modification of the traditional arsenal of poetic, rhetorical and critical concepts is undertaken elsewhere in this book. For this synthesis, it will suffice to mention them, noting that modern poetics has produced a reasonably definitive and sufficient description of the *verbal material* of literary and poetic texts from the linguistic revision and critical readaptation of these concepts. In terms of its real explanatory utility and its accomodation to literary and poetic phenomena, this new poetological rearrangement and readjustment has revitalized traditional rhetorical analysis. The muffled, microstructural study of rhetorical *elocutio* can consider itself to have been definitively secured with all critical accuracy by modern poetics, although this level of rhetorical revitalization of the elocutionary component is just the beginning of a balanced inventory of its achievements. It is especially worth calling attention to modern poetics' articulation of previously partial analyses of linguistic features, phenomena and levels into a new vision of the textual whole (E. Gülich and W. Raible, 1977; J. S. Petöfi, 1975). That is, modern poetics definitively established the organic principle of the *text's general structure as a level of decision*, even before the phenomena was generally accepted in linguistic theory (A. García-Berrio, 1979, pp. 145—152.). In the artistic text's unique structure, individual literary phenomena of *intensification*, like hyperbaton, or of *anti-tendency*, like rhyme, attain their definite *qualitative differential* status as material features of literary specificity. At the textual level they acquire the aesthetic potential which differentiates them essentially from modes of the standard logical-communicative norm (A. García-Berrio, 1987).

A distinct limitation of the extension in our century of the immanentist poetic to the textual level has been the practical identification of the nature of the literary text with that of the narrative text. The novel, modern literature's major protagonist, has also monopolized the field as the object of criticism. Of course, there existed, as I have previously indicated, a necessary and even urgent reason for this state of affairs, arising from the absence of a critical tradition dedicated to the novel in traditional poetics and rhetoric (W. Booth; 1961; C. Bremond, 1973; G. Prince, 1973, 1982; T. Todorov, 1969; J. Kristeva, 1974; L. Doležel, 1976; R. Barthes, 1977a; G. Genette, 1980). Still, the novel's monopolization of critical effort is already clearly disproportionate and has had inestimable deforming consequences. Often, the "poetologists" have inadvertently generalized with regard to the nature of the artistic text and its meaningful and aesthetic properties solely on the basis of their experience of the narrative text in general and the novel in particular.

The Russian formalists began the study of literary texts by attending to their least known and most ignored aspect at the time the school was constituted at the beginning of the twentieth century: the text's material-linguistic structure (A. García-Berrio, 1973, pp. 99 ff.; I. Ambrogio, 1968, pp. 13 ff.). In fact, the formalist school of criticism was, to a large degree, a poetic branch of structural linguistics organized under the Saussurean impulse and specializing in the literary and poetic characteristics of artistic discourse as a deviation or specific "gesture" of standard language, the latter considered specifically in terms of its use in fulfilling practical logical-communicative functions.

The general assessment of formalist contributions has already been adequately presented in a large number of studies. Among them, Erlich's history (1955) and Todorov's anthology (1965) must be counted as those that have lead in the dissemination of the movement's methods and achievements in the West. In my own book, *Significado actual del formalismo ruso* (1973), I attempted to show and document the expansion of the Russian group's initial efforts and enthusiasms into a complete international formalist methodology. At that time, the critical phenomena's participants did not have a clear awareness of their situation. But structuralist neoformalist criticism reached such a complete theoretical development towards the end of the seventies that we may say that the formal analysis of classical and modern literary texts is now completely established as a methodological achievement (A. García-Berrio, 1977; J. Culler, 1975; F. Lentricchia, 1980).

Many of these studies customarily do not emphasize formalism's immediate and remote precedents; still, I believe these to be very illustrative and worth explanation. Russian formalism, like literary stylistics, is unforgettably linked to the trends since the end of the last century called "formalist" in aesthetic theory in general and, more concretely, in the aesthetics of the figurative arts. This tendency alternated with others we could consider "subjectivist" and which dominated German aesthetics during the second half of the nineteenth century. Comparing formalist literary criticism to this more general framework permits us to see the reasons for its existence, namely, its necessity within the general currents of the parcelization of the Kantian subjective-objective synthesis, as formulated in *The Critique of Judgment* (I. Ambrogio, 1968, pp. 39 ff.; E. M. Thompson, 1971, pp. 12 ff.).

Artistic aesthetics and criticism since Kant have developed alternatively and separately the study of the *subjective* nature of aesthetic perceptions and emotions and that of the structural characteristics of artistic *objects*. I believe only very rarely throughout this century can we point to conscious and systematic initiatives to combine and integrate, in an organically solid way, this double dimension constituting artistic phenomena and their meaning. The more common procedure has been the polarization of these interests and efforts into one or another camp of experience. In this light, I repeat that the explicit description of the structure of literary discourse seems to be far closer to completing the description of the parcel granted to it than can be said of the psychological tendencies of subjective studies. Even conceding that the objects of this second task are more diffuse, complex and difficult to handle does not alter the fact that, as the objective basis for critical judgment, the inventory of scientific effort dedicated to them has until now been far poorer and more reduced in scope than that of the formal study of the literary text (A. García-Berrio and M. T. Hernández, 1988, p. 39).

Moreover, I believe that the explanation of the formalists' success in satisfying their critical objectives must take a second factor into account: critical formalisms' reconstruction of the analytical tradition of rhetoric. Evidently, the Russian formalists did not have at their disposal a fully developed or even minimally useful analytico-rhetorical method. Even they themselves declared that the reason for the primary urgency of their effort lay in the degeneration and absence of critical devices needed for examining the formal dimension of artistic texts. Traditionally, the rhetorical categories of eloquence had served as the only criteria used in the increasingly impoverished analysis of texts' poetic configuration. Hence, the Russian formalists' efforts to repair these deficiencies clearly led to the revival of rhetorical analysis.

The type of objective analysis initiated and practiced by the formalists on the verbal materials composing the literary work's textual scheme has not been simply a reiteration of rhetorical concepts and categories. Clearly, the new formalist analyses have occupied, by way of perfecting it, the "objective" space of rhetoric's classical patterns, as it existed before rhetoric's neoclassical degradation and annihilation. Formalism's categorical support has invariably come from the extraordinary boom of post-Saussurean linguistic structuralism. For more than fifty years, this has been, in its various branches and orientations, the inspiration behind the image of the verbal text and of the operations which constitute it which literary criticism has made use of (R. Fowler, 1986; R. Selden, 1985; T. Albaladejo Mayordomo, 1986 b; A. Jefferson and D. Robey, eds., 1986, pp. 46—72; J. Y. Tadié, 1987, pp. 185—209).

Precisely because of this habit of cooperating with linguistics, the formalists' work has sometimes imperiled, with good reason, their stature as literary critics, since they appear, both in their methods and interests, to be undertaking linguistic investigations. The neoformalist model, which is often improperly called poetics and must be readjusted to its linguistic dimension by means of the more exact and reasonable denomination of semiological or linguistic poetics, illustrates their limitations in this regard (A. García-Berrio, 1973). Basically, linguistic poetics and literary criticism coincide in the objects of their investigation — texts of verbal art — but they differ in their respective metalinguistic exigencies — more similar in the case of criticism to the language which is the object of the texts it analyzes — as in their very scientific stature and their purposes: linguistic poetics has fundamentally linguistic interests, which may serve the critic as background information, while he, in turn, concentrates his efforts more appropriately on the tasks of mediating between the text and its readers and on the interpretation of literary meanings (A. García-Berrio, 1981 a).

The extensive work of different formalist methodologies, which has resulted in the creation of poetic linguistics as a discipline of synthesis, has consisted in explaining textual literary characteristics, especially poetic features, as initiatives and mechanisms of *intentional stylistic deviation* (J. Mukařovský, 1964; S. Levin, 1965; N. Gueunier, 1969; M. Riffaterre, 1971; S. Chatman, 1973). The first step in the detection and measurement of this intentional deviation of stylemes has been signaled in many different ways, perhaps the most explicit and brilliant of which was that presented many years ago in Shklovsky's formula of "art as procedure" or as "artifice"

(V. Shklovsky, 1925). Thus, the principle of literary language's *anti-economy* is considered as specifically artistic and poetic, in opposition to the economy which governs the standard language's communicative system. In my opinion, the broader and more general ideal of anti-economy is a more efficient way of referring to many concrete features, more commonly appealed to in terms like "redundancy" (R. Jakobson, 1973, pp. 234—279), "plurisignification" or "polysemy" (R. Barthes, 1953; J. Kristeva, 1969, p. 142). The advantage of using the term anti-economy to refer to the dominant tendency of the literary "norm" to diverge from particular logical-communicative norms, is that it seems to distinguish a distinctive feature of poetic language without having to dialectically lodge the concept in an alternative entirely autonomous and independent from the general linguistic standard.

A thorough examination of each of the different features traditionally considered indexes of literariness and poeticity reveals, in my judgment, their inability as individual elements to affirm the autonomy and specificity of a poetic language as such. In view of this situation, it seems necessary to propose the broadest and most inclusive solution possible. Being unable to locate the differential standard in any of the individual linguistic features regularly invoked in formalist and poetological analyses and methods, I have elsewhere proposed the *textual level* as the place where all of these singular linguistico-poetic features converge, transforming the limitations of their structural and communicative-artistic singularity in their joint and aggregate articulation (A. García-Berrio, 1979, pp. 145 ff.). For example, the greatest burden and responsibility for lexical selection in literary texts originates in and is justified by the detectable tendencies toward isotopy that traverse and dynamize the kinds of texts that are literary — and to an even greater extent those that are poetic — in which identical conditions of extension, either prearranged or carefully considered by the text's transmitter, serve to heighten the proportional responsibility of each element belonging to the set.

All the same, not even the textual solution adequately satisfies the demand for qualitative specificity attributable to *literariness* and, even less so, to *poeticity*. Considering the text as a level or degree of reference broadens considerably, in my judgment, the differential experience of poetological formalism. Nevertheless, in order for the textual solution of the problems of literariness or of poeticity to be adequate, the scope of the formalists' notion of the text needs to be broadened, extending it to a more multi-faceted and complex level. In short, their conception of the text must go beyond seeking to understand only its material-verbal scheme, which is the narrow and exclusive way in which both they and the stylistic critics have always conceived of the problem, at least until the onset of structuralist neoformalism.

Still, I do believe that the methodology of literary analysis has gained great experience and solidity from the formalists' proposals, ranging from the most unformed and least articulate formulations to the most clearly functional and textual models. To objectively analyze a text at the linguistic level presupposes being able to neatly and securely fix the most concrete domain of its artistic difference and uniqueness. And this can be done today exceedingly well, with relatively customary ease and consistency, as any philologist with a basic professional formation knows. Literary criticism's experience in examining the specific physiognomy and structural workings of the text of the classical or modern poem is no longer a secret to anyone. The same applies to the information concerning the narrative structures which organize the novel's text and, perhaps in a less explicit way, although still in a not overly unpredictable manner, to the texts of theatrical works. In order to properly judge the achievement this degree of familiarity attests to we need only contrast the present situation with the almost total ignorance of the novel's structure in the second decade of this century, when formalist methodologies first began to be formulated.

Of course, if we aim at explaining to our complete satisfaction the complex aesthetic meaning of literary and poetic texts, it is not enough to be able to determine precisely the linguistic foundations of texts, but there is no doubt that this is an essential starting point for beginning to do so. Strictly speaking, the text is, as we already know today, a communicative entity which does not deplete its own capacities for communication, meaning or form at the most immanent surface level of its verbal, material complexity. Operative at this surface level is what I prefer calling the textual *scheme* or material textual scheme (A. García-Berrio, 1985, p. 257). Acting on the textual scheme are components of a different conceptual, emotional and, especially, imaginary order, the independent nature of which naturally transcends the text's linguistic materiality. Yet these immaterial and non-immanent components of the text could not exist independently from its linguistic scheme. In the section of this book dedicated to the poetics of the imagination, I will reflect more thoroughly on these anthropological and poetic characteristics. For now, let it suffice us to say that they are the complementary constituents in which the verbal physiognomy of the textual scheme is produced and projected. Thus, integrated in its various components, the concept of the artistic text can be set forth, in my judgment, in terms of an entity which distinctively justifies any and all attributions of *literariness* and *poeticity*.

A decisive concept of great reliability and transcendence concerning the structures of artistic texts follows from all of this: the objectifiable reality of their aesthetic characteristics. Or, what amounts to the same thing, the rejection of opinions which explain the origin of judgments and evaluations of literary texts' artistic uniqueness based on the *pragmatic relativism* (J. M. Ellis, 1974; S. Fish, 1980) of consensual and ever-changing values and attributions (T. A. van Dijk, 1976; M. Corti, 1976; M. L. Pratt, 1977; S. J. Schmidt, 1980). This pragmatic proposal for defining and explaining the literariness, poeticity and aestheticity of artistic works has had a profound effect on the present methodological crises; we will evaluate this here in the book's second part, which deals with the notion of conventionality and the critical methods

0.4. The Contents of Modern Semiological and Linguistic Poetics

of "reception" and "reading" (W. D. Stempel, 1979; D. Coste, 1980; M. Steihmetz, 1981; R. C. Holub, 1984). Beyond its reasonable contributions, that is, creating the image of the receiver as an important controller of the meaning of certain messages originating in the textual propositions of the author or artist, the radicalization of the receiver's role which attempts to dispel the objectifiable reliability of aesthetic meaning appears to me to be an abusive segmentation of the literary entity.

The formal analysis of a literary and poetic text, beyond being absolutely feasible and relatively easy and accessible, guarantees the possibility of verifying in artistic texts the existence of certain structural constants which characterize aesthetic intentionality. *Don Quijote* or *Las Meninas* are not what they are in the fulfillment of the free play of some consensual fad. There is something in those great works of art, in the most immanent and material structures of their composition, which places them safely beyond any whimsical and irresponsible forms of consensually and culturally ascribed value. The formalist methodology already offers us a secure basis, in the breadth and depth of its experience of conceptual categories and analytical strategies for making those "constants" evident in the text, the necessary effects and results of which testify to the fact that artistic texts acquire a characteristic sense precisely because they participate in a system of aesthetic universals, within the context of which their special features are substantially explained.

In the evolution of formalist methods two principle paths need to be distinguished depending on the class of texts being analyzed, each with its own markedly characteristic evolution. In its first period, the work of Russian formalism established, above all, the structural characteristics of the new Russian poetry (A. García-Berrio, 1973, pp. 101—198). In a certain sense, as we have already explained, the school thus made its entrance as a continuation of the traditional rhetorical analysis of poetic texts. Studies of prose, which we are not lacking in this initial period of the school's evolution, basically coincide in their orientation with poetic analyses, given that the works of Gogol, Tolstoy and even Lenin were examined as "artistic prose" (B. Eikhenbaum, 1922). That is, studying the fundamental expressive-syntagmatic features exhibiting an artifice deviating from the norm was of more concern than investigating works' general textual constitutions.

A preoccupation with the structure of the narrative text in its broad and macrodispositive dimension was, as is known, the late and important contribution of one of the formalist group's followers, the famous Vladimir Propp (1928). The studies of Tynjanov and of Shklovsky on the structure of *Don Quijote* or *Tristram Shandy* are also numbered among the school's relatively mature contributions. Still, in spite of their intention of examining these works' general structure, they are in fact not exhaustive investigations, centering on characteristic features, symptomatically generalizable. As for the theories of "motivation" formulated especially by Tomashevsky (B. Tomashevsky, 1965, pp. 263—307), they attend to isolated syntagmatico-semantic areas of the text, without really putting into practice the desire to achieve a global description of the textual entity's structural constitution, an objective which would later characterize the formalist study of narrative texts.

Thus, in my view, the Russian group inaugurated a kind of critical uneasiness towards narration and the poetic text which, directly or indirectly, would manage to influence all subsequent critical activity. As regards the poem, perhaps the most suggestive and adequate formalist concept was that of *zaum*. *Zaum* is a general term covering a diversity of poetic mechanisms and properties (A. García-Berrio, 1973, pp. 161 ff.). The *zaum* effect is usually translated as *transrationalism*, referring to the property of poetic meaning capable of evoking certain kinds of sentimental association, differing from the objective communicative neutrality of the practical, non-poetic use of language.

The formalists' principle of transrationality has since been transferred in two important ways to an explanation of what is potentially specific to the poem and foreign to language's general communicative use. In the first place, the "non-neutrality" of the poetic signifier appears to be a decisive component — although in this case not the only component — reflecting the *connotative* capacities of literary and, above all, of poetic language (M. N. Gary-Prieur, 1971, pp. 104—106; M. Arrivé, 1972, pp. 19 ff.; J. M. Adam, 1976, pp. 17— 20, 85—88), in contrast to the *denotative* role characterizing language's logico-symbolic use (J. Molino, 1971, pp. 9—10; C. Kerbrat-Orecchioni, 1977; V. M. de Aguiar e Silva, 1967 [1984, p. 81]). On the other hand, Yuri Lotman — indirectly responsible for the present continuation of formalistically-rooted Soviet semiology — has subjected the poem's meaningful form to a meticulous analytical frame by virtue of which the relevance of the signifier is autonomously configured (Y. Lotman, 1970). Lotman's well-known definition of poetry as a *secondary modeling system* alludes to this double insertion of the poetic signifier, which is not only associated with its automatic and habitual meaning at the level of its everyday sense, but also, by way of that first meaningful association, with a second specific and poetic sense arising in a different plane of evocative-sentimental meaning (W. Rewar, 1976; A. Shukman, 1977, 1978). Each one of these two planes of meaning in Lotman can be shifted to its corresponding connotative-denotative terms. Louis Hjelmslev, in effect, described the behavior of semiotic systems as a non-neutral activity of the signifier (J. Trabant, 1970) in terms of a "connotative semiotics".

The Russian formalists' characterization of *zaum* in terms of the concrete poetic mechanisms which produce it does not differ from some of the ancient practices of classical rhetoric. Thus, for example, the stylistic effect of so-called "vocalic coloring" corresponds rigorously to the ancient prejudices concerning the "virtues of the letters" as asiduously practiced by the rhetorical *exercitatio* of elocution (A. García-Berrio, 1975, p. 199). The same occurs with the isotopic awareness of the correspondences and contrasts between rhythmic

0.4. The Contents of Modern Semiological and Linguistic Poetics

accentuation, vocalic coloring and the reinforcement of meaningful elements in the poem's text. Precisely because rhythmic-acoustical resources are basic in the traditional inventory of poetry's formal mechanisms, they would once again be extensively exploited by European stylistics in the fifties and sixties. Amado and Dámaso Alonso, and especially the latter, have used the sentimental parameters of meaning associated with poems' acoustical material to generate some of the most profound reflections these materials have yielded in the long history of their critical exploitation (D. Alonso, 1952; A. Alonso, 1955).

Every mechanism for the communicative and aesthetico-sentimental demonstration of form participates through *zaum* in the fundamental exercise of *de-automatization* specific to poetic language, insofar as this language is a result of artistic "procedures" (V. Shklovsky, 1925; T. Todorov, ed., 1965, pp. 76—97). Nevertheless, the principle of de-automatization is broader and more universal than that of *zaum*, which is consequently one of the former notion's individual facets. Not only mechanisms for the artistic distancing of the signifier, but all those resources which possess and exhibit differential stylistico-poetic intentionality contribute to de-automatization. Enjambement, for example, is the archetypal case, studied by O. Brik, of the *conflict between two syntaxes*: a logical syntax, with its sense of unity located in the phrase, and a metrical syntax, with its unity located in the line of verse. Together, these two syntaxes illustrate the basic way de-automatization reinforces the structurally asymmetrical impulse (O. Brik, 1965, pp. 143—153).

Moreover, the principle of poetic de-automatization is not only represented by the unexpected and asymmetrical. Stylistics has superceded formalism in the revelation of the intentionally de-familiarizing effect of reiteratively *serial structures* (F. Lázaro Carreter, 1980, pp. 7—27), the *symmetrical effects* of parallel reiteration. Dámaso Alonso has exploited this ancient principle of rhetorical disposition (D. Alonso, 1952, pp. 117—222) with a consistency and discernment unsurpassed in modern stylistics. Constructive parallelism and serialized reiteration (S. R. Levin, 1962, p. 22), which indicate similarities or demarcate divergences one wishes to positively demonstrate, are examples of the artistic construction elevated by R. Jakobson to a primary principle characterizing the constitution of artistic language (R. Jakobson, 1970).

The analyses of European stylistics and North American New Criticism have insisted basically on these principles of parallelism and contrast in the construction of literary texts and, above all, the heavily weighted importance of the poem's textual space. Dámaso Alonso described his critical itinerary as a "stylistics of exterior form", that is, of the analytical progression from sound to meaning, relying on the "coupled" solidarities between differently ordered elements, but in complementary relations (D. Alonso, 1952, pp. 32—33). The same route would have to be followed in establishing the path of connections and couplings constituting a "stylistics of interior form" — as a progression from meaning to sound —, a methodological inversion predicted by Dámaso himself and one which I have attempted to carry out in the construction of my typological system of lyrical texts (A. García-Berrio, 1982, pp. 261–263). The advantage which permitted me to realize the old aspiration envisaged by Alonso has been that of being able to conveniently make use of methods and analytical categories offered to current criticism by the formalist hermeneutical experimentation of linguistic poetics and of general and literary semiology — and, especially, having been able to count on the instruction provided by textually based formal grammars (J. S. Petöfi and A. García-Berrio, 1979).

The concept of *convergence* or *coupling* (S. R. Levin, 1962) has been the most important single contribution to our understanding of the poem's structure, fusing the analytical experience of formalist methods. The ancient rhetorico-poetic principle of the "decorous" coupling of the artistic utterance's conceptual and formal constituents (*res — verba*) is thus extended in the analyses of modern structural poetology, from the simplest and most conventional critical exercises, like that of Jakobson and Lévi-Strauss in their famous analysis of Baudelaire's poem *Les chats* (1962, pp. 401–419), to the more rigorous and profound journey Greimas' school launched through complex isotopic nets (A. J. Greimas, 1972; see especially the contribution by F. Rastier, 1972, pp. 80–105). In the principle of convergence — of textual planes, structural levels of language, the units constituting the text's range, etc. — (M. Arrivé, 1973, pp. 53–63; J. M. Klinkenberg, 1973) the poem finds its stability in being permanently threatened (K. Shapiro, 1976). Convergence is a dynamic construction, a kinetic mechanism that invariably represents the image of wholeness resulting from the interdependent instability of each one of its units and constitutive parts.

Compared to the usual formalist and neostructuralist criticism, stylistic analysis of the poem was persistently richer in *grammatical-semantic* elements, as illustrated by studies on the epithet and its modes (G. Sobejano, 1970) or on the stylistic consequences of a predominance of active verbal symbols or essentially stable, substantival symbols. It also knew how to measure the effects of stylistic intentionality deduced from the characteristic abundance, presence or absence of grammatical elements, such as the article (A. Alonso, 1961, pp. 125–160), all in the natural practice of language and in its intentionally artistic use. Finally, it made a powerful effort towards the systematic constitution of a stylistics of the units of content, with abundant stylistic studies of themes: solitude, fame, the other world, etc.

The Russian formalists' earliest initiatives in the study of narrative texts opened the second of the great paths towards establishing critical methodologies I will study in this chapter. I have indicated already how the praiseworthy advances of this school before V. Propp rarely ever move beyond the general stylistic ideal of examining features of syntagmatic fragmentation. In both proto-formalism and stylistics the artistic characteristics of extensive narrative texts are usually examined under the same isolationist and fragmentary microtextual premises used in the analysis of individual aspects of the poem in terms of lyrical stylemes. Of greatest interest in early formalist analyses were the phenomena of *skaz*, a complex index alluding to a broad set of "procedures constituting the unique artifice" characterizing narration in the novel (B. Eikhenbaum, 1969, pp. 169 ff.; V. Vinogradov, 1969, p. 203): point of view, models of narrative omniscience or of objectivist neutrality, epic mechanisms of enunciation, archetypal manipulation of characters in the attempt to create effects supporting and encouraging interest and sympathy, etc. (A. García-Berrio, 1973, pp. 249 ff.).

In this context, V. Propp's importance is immeasurable. It is he who begins the macrotextual study of narration as a process of specific significance. It has been repeated so often that it is now common knowledge that the great shift of perspective Propp contributed to macrotextual formalism is the functional study of narrative, breaking with a more or less pure tradition of semantic structural studies. From my point of view, the outstanding feature of the study of narrative structure in terms of functions, assembled into units based upon the principle of conflict as a "transgression of the interdict or prohibition", consists in its assumption of the option of the *universal* or general construction of the tale, in contrast to the traditional critical habit of emphasizing and describing the particular. For Propp, the interest of a character lies in pointing to the principle and the dialectical functional option it represents in the *logic* of the narrative, rather than in itemizing its fictionality (V. Propp, 1928).

Propp's starting point, tending towards the construction of a general order of the story's *universalist logic*, represents the most characteristic feature of the neoformalist study of narrative texts, and its most controversial peculiarity as well. In effect, narratology's enormous merit rests, in my judgment, on its discovery and description of one of the fundamental artistic and anthropological activities of the human enterprise: that which mythically reproduces in the tale the processes of activity constituting real events. In so doing, it has also complementarily illustrated the process in terms of a solid economy of logical constants (C. Bremond, 1973). As in other communicative products, the tale appears subjected to a strict general logic of highly controlled movements and types, from which only end-products may diverge, and subsequent transformations to deep structures of highly convergent systematicity. This effort at describing our knowledge of the universals of artistic-anthropological behavior is, in my opinion, both fascinating and essential for the correct understanding of art's deepest meaning.

Still, there is no doubt that the exclusive radicalization of a narratological logic can greatly detract from many other aspects of the aesthetic range of narrative texts (E. Muir, 1928). Artistic stories — including authored novels and stories and not only the popular tales with a collective author and schematic functional structure which inspired Propp's studies and folklorist typologies — capture the very best aesthetic meaning in the verbal psychological portrait of some unique, unrepeatable characters: Fabrizio del Dongo, Julien Sorel, Ana Ozores, and Anna Karenina, for example (E. M. Forster, 1927). The efficiency of the realistic representation of archetypes and individual characters, the interesting curiosity of fictional creatures as the autobiographical transcription or likeness of the author's own rich personal experiences, or the interest of the novel's own verbal-aesthetic texture, of its "voice" as proclaimed by Bakhtin, and in the "polyphonic" representation of a complex social world (M. Bakhtin, 1929), all point towards the individuality of each novel, the uncommunicated singularity of its own utterance as a unique product, as an inexhaustible universe for exegesis and critical reading (M. Baquero Goyanes, 1970, pp. 125, 167).

Up until now in this century, criticism of the novel has developed between these two poles: the functional universalization of a logic of narrative structuralization and the semantic construction of a singular universe of referential experiences. Formalist and neoformalist critical activity (T. Todorov, 1967; C. Bremond, 1973; J. Kristeva, 1970; etc.) has contributed almost exclusively to the development of the former aspect. The explicit description of the story's logic, with a validity and applicability universalizable to the various processes of narrative utterance, constitutes an achievement the importance of which, it seems to me, ought not to be ignored or relativized in spite of the disorder it may indirectly have contributed towards unleashing.

The objection that is usually leveled against structural narratology is that it is evidently a deforming textual exercise; specifically, that traditional narratological analysis in its most characteristic manifestations does not take into account narrative *discourse* as much as narrative *story*, that is, the structural summary or skeleton of the novel (L. Doležel, 1976a, pp. 5—14). I believe this is explained well, at the same time as it better confirms the seriousness of the limitation being criticized, from the perspective of the Aristotelian enumeration of tragedy's "qualitative parts". Structuralist narratology attended only to the summary of the argumentation, to the "fable" or "mythos", practically ignoring the other parts: diction, thought and spectacle, and even ignoring characters, conceived strictly in terms of semantics and fictional personality. Characters were of interest to narratology only in the opposite sense, that is, in their relational-syntactic aspect, as mere functional *capacities*, semantically empty forms existing to support and advance the action.

It is not that there haven't been initiatives in narratology attempting to close the gap between narrative discourse and story. Years ago, W. O. Hendricks (1973) took some merit-worthy steps in this direction. Nevertheless, it seems to me that this concrete trajectory is always difficult, and would surely require hundreds of *ad hoc* analyses to achieve a satisfactory overview or at least to illustrate the most certain regularities of this process of osmosis. Finally, the effort would surely not be efficient and economical.

If narratology exaggerates the reductive and schematic approach to the text, analyzing the textual summary it has previously established rather than the work in all of its complexity, there is nevertheless no doubt that this undeniable *simplification* of literary reality is not necessarily equivalent to its *deformation*. Rather, these operations, stylizing and essentially purifying the material, lead to the only possible way of discovering the *logic of possible narratives* spoken of by C. Bremond (1966), a task involving the profound deduction of the anthropological foundations underlying and originating the narrative constitution of myths. Foundations, moreover, which become evident through narratological analyses, revealing the art of narration as one of the most deeply rooted human exercises and presenting its forms and peculiarities as fundamental structures of the mechanisms of individual expression and the processes of social communication. In this sense, I believe that Greimas and Fillmore's collection of semiotico-actantial categories has perhaps contributed the richest and most rigorously well-founded and structured material from which it is presently possible to carry out analytical exercises on narrative texts (A. J. Greimas, 1966, 1970, 1972).

In short, the future methodical and systematic study of the novel as a genre of discourse, and not only of novels as single units of experience, should significantly modify the semiotico-narratological exclusivity of analysis. Today, it is more important to root stories in the universes of argumentative social-aesthetic discourse (A. García-Berrio, 1983, pp. 134—139; M. Bakhtin, 1929; F. Jameson, 1981), and of anthropological-imaginary discourse (G. Durand, 1960), both of which approaches differ noticeably from the previous interest in the logical features of discourse, properly belonging to its structural constitution as a text. Nevertheless, we should not forget that, if today we can perceive the legitimacy of these other interests, it is because the plots of knowledge linked to the structural constitution of the novel's text prove to be already overly familiar to us. Narratology, like the formal theory of the poem, is not yet a field closed to the continuing search for curious data (W. Mitchell, ed., 1981; E. Gülich and U. M. Quasthoff, eds., 1986). Still, in comparison to other aspects of analytical interest concerning literary objects, it appears already to be solidly and sufficiently consolidated (G. Prince, 1982). And this situation sanctions, in a settling of accounts, its merit and importance, at the same as it justifies the possibility of considering the question relatively closed.

0.5. *The Crisis of Structuralist Poetics: Towards the Construction of a General Poetics*

Ten or fifteen years ago, structuralist linguistic poetics suffered a general crisis, the meaning and extent of which has given rise to very different analyses and explorations, which we will examine in greater detail elsewhere in this book (J. Culler, 1975). Judging it all from our present juncture of reflection — that is, between a partially modern poetics and traditional philosophic poetics —, it seems clear that the past crisis of linguistic poetics was the result of a *maladjusted superproduction* which does not, from my point of view, imply only negative features and values.

The positive balance of results of modern linguistic poetics translated, as has been indicated, into the almost definitive establishment of a theory and description of the literary work at the level of the constitution of its *textual scheme* as a differentiated structure of *verbal materials*. The crisis could have come from, among other positive factors, an awareness satisfied by the results achieved at this level. For example, as I said before, the structural analysis of the novel has gone from an absolute void of categories, critical methods and analytical strategies to a general normalization of results such that a correct narratological analysis can presently be the object of an exercise for college students at the introductory level (F. Jameson, 1972).

Nevertheless, the methodological focus in formalist poetics' study of the textual material has become, by virtue of its very perseverance and excellent results, hypertrophic and unbalanced regarding other levels of the text's constitution, as well as towards other interests of the literary, cultural and artistic system. In the former respect, what is urgently needed is a balanced reflection concerning the psychological, anthropological-imaginary and sentimental constituents of textual meaning, one which takes full advantage of the already well-formulated conception of the text's material scheme (A. García-Berrio, 1985). An understanding of the imagination's work in symbols and schemes of representation is fundamental, as we shall see, in the constitution of the literary and poetic text as a whole (M. Bodkin, 1934; G. Durand, 1981).

With regard to the necessary expansion of the poetological enrichment of our understanding of the text to other constituents of the literary, artistic, cultural and social series, the personal evolution of many representatives of neoformalist poetics shows an impatient shift in their ever-mobile interests, characterizing what has been called the poststructuralist trend in poetics. From my point of view, this evolution explains the shift in interests of such well-known structuralist poetologists as T. van Dijk or S. J. Schmidt towards the socio-cultural content of the textual frame. Also, an important internal corrective factor was provided by the reasonable initial claim by the founders of the German school of reception, Iser and Jauss (D. Fokkema and E. Ibsch, 1986; M. Steihmetz, 1981, pp. 193—209; R. C. Holub, 1984), following the cultural precedent of Gadamer (1960), towards the relativist appraisal of the reader's role in the constitution of general and, particularly, aesthetic meaning (A. Jefferson and D. Robey, eds., 1986, pp. 121—144). Simultaneously, the more drastic corrective effect of Derrida's *deconstructive* skepticism towards the value of meaning made its influence felt (J. Culler, 1982; C. Norris, 1982; V. B. Leitch, 1983; A. García-Berrio and M. T. Hernández, 1988, pp. 86—89).

The *poststructuralist* evolution of two outstanding protagonists of modern poetics, Roland Barthes and Umberto Eco, is paradigmatic of the intersecting influence of the pragmatic relativisms of reception aesthetics and deconstructive aporia (J. Culler, 1975; F. Lentricchia, 1980). As we will see in greater detail in the second part of this book, the radicalization of the concepts of the *open text* and *plurisignification*, negative in terms of the valorization of objective meaning, has cast aside the stable poetological confirmation of a *preferential* structure, a structure capable of guaranteeing and controlling the required degree of meaning's polysemy. In its place poststructuralism has favored Eco's algorithm (1971, 1978, 1979), — not developed in the theory of the implied reader — of the "reader in the *fabula*", and Roland Barthes' axiomatic myth of an infinite number of readings of an absent structure, which he himself was never able to substantiate (1970 a).

In my judgment, reception aesthetics has contributed very positively to the restoration of the generalist dimension of philosophical poetics, although excesses may again result from the absolute radicalization of its premises (S. Fish, 1970, 1980; D. Coste, 1980). In the more positive vein, Hans R. Jauss has recovered an awareness of the primitive complementary scheme of artistic theory, divided into a *poietic* axis, beginning with creation and ending in the text, and an *aisthetic* axis, perceptive and receptive in nature, beginning with the textual utterance and ending with the meaning which the reader acquires and constructs from this same utterance (H. R. Jauss, 1977). Criticism and literary history in particular should become aware of the position of responsibility pertaining to the historical tradition of reception and its contemporary physiognomy in constituting the meaning of each individual act and each historical and social moment of reading. In order to take these elements into account, observations within the aesthetic range of the text's cultural "series" are obviously necessary, being of a still complementary nature to analysis linked exclusively to the text's formal structure, as investigated by structuralist linguistic poetics (R. Selden, 1985, pp. 72—105).

For the purposes of expanding linguistic poetics towards the creation of a general poetics, in its traditional aesthetic sense, solid and very original proposals of a broad, general design, like those of Mikhail Bakhtin, Lucien Goldmann and Frederic Jameson, can be modernized and put into practice. In my opinion, these in particular are very productive models precisely because their criticism of formalism is not motivated by a desire to exclude or forget its positive achievements, but rather to recognize the utility and positive rigor of formal poetic's conception of the artistic text's physiognomy. Such programs of amplification are designed, in different ways, according to the requirements for a *projection* of linguistic poetics, which I have on various occasions cited as a precondition for profitable extensions of this kind.

The Bakhtinian program, deserving more attention in this respect, overcomes the deficiencies of formalist poetics by elevating the analysis of the *compositional* forms constituting the text's syntactic and semantic artifice, as the Russian formalists emphasized in their practice of textual hermeneutics, to the level of *architectonic* forms characteristic of the general aesthetic and poetic system underlying the very nature of art (M. Bakhtin, 1975, pp. 34—35). In applying these conceptions we would, for example, transcend the indications of *comicalness* in the structure of Molière's *Le Misanthrope*, in order to generate general categories useful in the diagnosis of *the comic* as a universal of literary representation. Clearly, we are dealing with a project involving the reinsertion of the data of a rigorously developed linguistic poetics, without any preliminary exclusions, into the context of a general poetics with aesthetico-philosophical ambitions.

As far as the general sociological application of the discoveries of immanent textual analysis, Lucien Goldmann's "genetic structuralism" (1955, Ch. I), offers interesting and very creative possibilities in line with the transfer and generalization of data and categories required by the shift from a modern formal poetics to a general poetics or theory of literature (A. García-Berrio, 1985 a).

Poetics, or general poetics, as we have just envisaged it in its broadest dimension, essentially coincides in content with a well-founded theory of literature. The present moment is thus decisive for the possible elaboration of such a general poetics. As we have previously mentioned, the broad traditional branch of classical poetics, stirred up and amalgamated in all the complexity of its constituents by the classicist poetics of Humanism, definitively gains considerable density and universality with the philosophical re-elaboration of literary theory as an aesthetic discipline in Kant, Hegel and Schlegel. To which may be added the important enrichment contributed by poetics in its more restricted modern linguistic sense which, as an immanentist theory of the artistic text, has readjusted and revitalized the important traditional materials of literary rhetoric as a science of expressiveness.

First Part

1. Literary Expressiveness

1.1. Literariness: The Linguistic Structure of the Literary Option

1.1.1. Towards the Linguistic Characterization of Literature

It has not been very long since one of the most solid traditional principles on which the artistic condition of literary and poetic texts was founded collapsed or at least fell into a state of turmoil and debate. The traditional conviction of classical rhetoric and poetics confided the artistic efficacy of literary resources to the expressiveness of stylistic features, exceptional schemes of language and procedures for the metaphoric and figurative use of meaning (A. A. Hill, 1976, pp. 116—117). Briefly stated, the roots of literary aestheticity were understood to reside in the *verbal artifices* constituting the linguistic structure of literary and poetic texts (T. A. van Dijk, 1979, pp. 571—577). Against this traditional conception, a linguistic trend of relativism arose, banding together with the new *pragmatic perspective*, which conceived of linguistic phenomena as communicative events. This trend came to deny the possibility of objectively defining the artistic specificity of those texts traditionally considered literary and/or poetic (M. Corti, 1976; T. A. van Dijk, 1977; M. L. Pratt, 1977; S. J. Schmidt, 1980, etc.).

Their strongest argument lies in the fact that all of the linguistic features considered especially artistic are also represented in the most habitual communicative uses of language (J. Ellis, 1974, pp. 24 ff.; C. Di Girolamo, 1978). Even for those features most particularly understood as artistic, such as the metamorphic ornamentation of poetry, rhythm and metrical-strophic divisions, equivalents could easily be found in the principles and tendencies regulating the linguistic standard. From this point of view, artistic language and the aesthetic properties generally known as *literariness* and *poeticity* would be interpreted as phenomena of *social conventionalism*, as a series of cultural compromises with no objective basis for any claim to artistic specificity (E. Miner, 1976, 1976a; S. Fish, 1980). Moreover, notice the convergence of the results this *pragmatic hypothesis* yields, which, in spite of their importance, have not as such achieved further critical notoriety, with the basic assumptions of the widely circulated relativisms known as the *poetics of reception and reading*. In effect, even though these poetics prefer to concentrate on the relativization of the text's meaning in view of the plural response of its receivers, implied in their shifted emphasis could be the principle which skews the closure of all judgments concerning the literary work, including its aesthetic and artistic values, towards the act of reading (R. C. Holub, 1984).

For my part, I have already set forth in this book my intention of defending the absolute values of aesthetic meaning as properties inherent in the artistic text, which, I will argue, simultaneously establishes and consecrates *aesthetic and artistic universals*. In this chapter, my position will entail the recovery of the traditional arguments of rhetoric and poetic theory, together with the various currents of formalist, linguistic and stylistic analysis developed in our own century up to the present moment. Undoubtedly, the objections, often well-reasoned, which these principles raise in this day and age, will force me into a defensive position which the critics and theorists of other ages did not know and would not have anticipated. In this regard, the most powerful apologetic instrument is to be found, in my judgment, in the present maturity of the linguistic understanding of the text's nature and constitutive structure, as well as that of the psychological and anthropological contributions to the comprehension of textual meaning, all of which are especially pertinent to artistic texts.

I should make clear from the beginning that my disagreement with relativism and with the conventionalist pragmatic-receptivist positions is not complete, nor lacking the necessary nuance of discerning and acknowledging the positive contributions which underlie the most radical aspects of their ideas. The role played by readers' cultural consensus in the configuration of aesthetic values should be recognized as real and has often been ignored in the past (H. R. Jauss, 1967, 1977). Recording this role and giving it its due has both corrected this past neglect and contributed an important perspective towards the understanding of textual meaning. The trouble lies in the radicalization of this concept, which serves to reinforce the argument that cultural history proceeds more by a mechanism of bumps and jolts guided by a logic of reaction than through synthesis. Hence, from one error, the old absolute understanding of meaning as residing entirely in the space linking author and text, we proceed to another, consciously yet involuntarily, thereby shifting to the opposite extreme (W. Iser, 1976). A much healthier and more accurate synthesis would involve reconciling the double axis constituting textual meaning, projecting the proposal constructed by the author onto the reader's interpretative response.

As far as the artistic mechanisms of language are concerned, there no doubt exists a conventionalized tradition of verbal *stylemes* (A. Marchese, 1978, pp. 263–264) specifically recognized as *literary* specializations of the general linguistic *norm* (J. A. Martínez, 1975). The most elementary and immediate experience proves this set of stylistic features, "deflected" (J. Mukařovský, 1964; S. Levin, 1965; N. Gueunier, 1969; R. Chapman, 1973, p. 40) with regard to the communicative standard, do not constitute a systematically autonomous and special language. Clearly, for example, we recognize the Italian of even the very learned Leopardi as being Italian. In any case, the first problem posed is the designation of this standard level of language as the starting point or degree zero from which deviation is then measured (J. Cohen, 1966; F. Rodríguez Adrados, 1974, II, p. 618). Still, that same immediately direct and elementary experience persuades us to recognize in the great, inspired and inspiring poem and in the passionate pages of the great novel a manner of employing language contributing to produce a perceptible aesthetic effect. The undifferentiated identity of the poetic probably cannot be attributed to this set of linguistic peculiarities or deviations (N. Ruwet, 1972); personally, I believe poeticity is more of an *effect* and a product-value. Nevertheless, it appears clear the *cause* of the aesthetic emotions and of the interchange of fantastic contents, established by the communication of the readers with the author through the immanent verbal text and particularized by resources and devices of language, resides in that immediate textual scheme (N. Enkvist, 1978, pp. 176—182). Certainly, the effect of poeticity transcends the literariness of the text, but literariness must be this effect's necessary and direct cause.

Thus, *literariness*, as a set of linguistic-aesthetic properties and characteristics of a text (M. Margghescou, 1974), presupposes a recognizable social reality and, as such, can be considered in terms of a conventionalized cultural tradition. It is evident that this conventional tradition, understood and inventoried according to its most general and basic features, can be adapted by the artist as a verbal performance in the production of a text. The adaption of said features for textual production is a choice, an *option*, immediately translating an artistic intention. We recognize the resulting object, the intentionally artistic verbal text, as a special object which we, in turn, conventionally call "literary". Hence, literariness is an artistic property of the text derived from a verbal *option* (D. Delas and J. Filliolet, 1973). Still, literariness, chosen in these terms, does not guarantee a positive aesthetic result. Having passed a beginning course on poetry, the student who decides to write his first sonnet will surely concoct a verbal product in which we recognize the stylizations typical of literature, but which will probably not move us as poetry when considered in terms of its aesthetic value. In short, if *literariness* is a conventionalizable cultural *choice* or option, poeticity is an unpredictable aesthetic *value*.

But if the cultural conventionality of literature is a reality so self-evident on the historical plane that proclaiming it as a discovery would seem almost ridiculous, the radical affirmation of literature's conventionality, which extends the total lack of any non-conventional elements to its very origins and to the level of constitutive necessity, implies that we are certainly in the presence of a crucial opinion (C. Di Girolamo, 1978). In this way, the most common and rash affirmation of the pragmatic cultural relativism of literature either unjustifiably — since reasons are not cited by its proponents — assumes the validity of the principle of radical conventionalization or else subscribes only to the innocent recognition of a relative, historical conventionalism, an apologetics for which, as Aguiar e Silva has indicated (1967 [1984, pp. 19—42]), is unnecessary. It could also be the case that through the failure to distinguish between these two very different degrees of conventionalism, the radical conception is considered automatically proven by the obvious veracity of the historically-based argument. And I should add that this third hypothesis is not entirely speculative, but is at the very basis of the majority of the exaggerated lapses and abusive generalizations which the plural theory of reading incurs in its relativizations of the meaning of artistic texts (J. Ellis, 1974; E. Miner, 1976, 1976 a).

The immanently textual plane of the literary work cannot by itself justify or guarantee, in the linguistic materiality of the stylemes and verbal artifices, the phenomena and aesthetic effect of poeticity (R. Harweg, 1973, pp. 86—87). The reason for this lies in the fact that poeticity is a result with sentimental, imaginary roots linked to the complete textual globality of the literary work. It involves not only the immanently material-verbal structure of the text, but also pragmatic-communicative projections in the double instance of emission and reception which, moreover, within their "transcendental" properties, constitute cultural, historical and anthropological solidarities. The artistic text is really that polyhedral and, clearly, the complexity of the aesthetic phenomena of poetry stems from this very multiplicity. As far as possible, this book is dedicated to discerning and clarifying this complexity.

Nevertheless, poeticity as an aesthetic phenomenon and general value must be fulfilled in all instances, and, naturally, in the decisive component of the immanent material scheme of the text. In this way, the verbal structures of literariness in the work of art turn out to be radically *selective*. Far from being capricious and changeable conventions, they correspond to linguistic mechanisms of the greatest rigor, by reason of their psychological link to the connotative-sentimental and imaginary structures of the general aesthetic effect. It is not a question of making literature about literature; on the contrary, in this book, I attempt to make explicit, insofar as possible, the verbal, psychological, imaginary and cultural mechanisms determining the complex aesthetic phenomenon of poeticity. Concerning the present problem of literary language and its contribution to the general poetic effect, I will for now limit myself to paraphrasing a conventional plastic convention, which I've made use of in another book (A. García-Berrio, 1985, p. 59): poeticity cannot be just "a matter of words", but — although a phenomena of far greater complexity — it nevertheless begins with words.

In spite of all of this, recent poetic bibliography has been invaded by an absolutely negative trend in the treatment of the subjects of literariness and poeticity (J. M. Pozuelo Yvancos, 1988, pp. 74—75). Traditional concepts of stylistics and structuralist poetics referring to poetic and literary expression have found themselves affected recently by a wave of skepticism (C. Di Girolamo, 1978). Traditional objections against these trends, such as the impossibility of substituting any element of the poetic utterance, are answered, with reason, by pointing out that the same argument could be advanced concerning the communicative and pragmatic efficacy of a good joke or a successful advertising slogan. Evidently, it can be taken as well established that the generalized "ingenuous" argument we have just referred to — and which, in reality, originated with Aristotle's *Poetics* and applied more to poetic textual *dispositio* — must be banished. Irreplaceability is not a poetic property, but a general linguistic feature related to the *communicative success* of any speech act, literary or otherwise (F. Lázaro Carreter, 1976; M. Riffaterre, 1979).

Still, I wish to make clear that, as powerful and well-argued as the reasons of those partial to erasing the notion of a poetic literary specificity from the relevant discourses may have been, the resistance of the assiduous reader of literature has permanently rebelled against such activity, based upon the evidence provided by acts of poetic reading felt as a special expression. Moreover, I'm convinced this is not, as might be argued, a question of subconscious cultural prejudices. There exist specific reasons in the strictly linguistic domain to support this proclamation of poetic or literary discourse as an obviously singular, special and distinct realization, compared to the usual communicative act of language (J. Kristeva, 1969, pp. 258—259; S. R. Levin, 1971, p. 181).

To begin with, it is worth asking how the defenders of the pragmatic hypothesis believe this conventional accord is reached; because, with all due respect, in practice they run the risk of resurrecting the dilemma of the chicken and the egg. The cultural-pragmatic accord on the literariness or poeticity of a message must necessarily be constituted on the basis of some set of traits — linguistic features, undoubtedly, in addition to others — grasped intuitively and conventionalized as specific by virtue of a generally accepted agreement as to their specificity. If not, then where does the cultural-pragmatic convention originate?

Recently, there has been much insistence on the differential force of non-linguistic elements in the constitution of literary convention. We will, for now, set aside the possibility of discussing such a consideration under the renewed perspective of textual pragmatics and linguistic semiology. But, leaving aside as interchangeable and general, which they clearly are, such evidence as the volume bound in a book, margins, the division into parts and chapters, etc., it is evident that it is not possible to turn to purely conventional reasons apart from artistic writing for establishing the foundations of a pragmatics of literariness or of poeticity. The previously enumerated features adapt as easily to the textual-pragmatic properties of a novel as they do to a treatise of history or economics.

Nor is it sufficient to argue the deceptive value of the "fame" of the text or its author or of the work's "title". Obviously, if I am wrong about the fictional or poetic nature of a chemistry book, either because it has been misrepresented to me as such or because someone has written on the cover a false title or label — novel, poetry, etc. — I can react and, in fact, people do generally react by discounting the possibility of said book being literary. Recall the range and importance of the topical discussion in classical poetics regarding the status of versified treatises such as Lucretius' works of philosophy or natural science and Lucan's history, *Pharsalia*. Versification alone did not guarantee poeticity, even assuming as true the author's intention of conferring on them a literary nature by versifying them (A. García-Berrio, 1975, pp. 72−81; 1988, pp. 71−73).

Verse and fiction, or verisimilar imitation, are explicit literary tags. It would be difficult to deny their stature as objective differential features of literary discourse. Without ignoring the intrinsically linguistic-systematic status of poetic rhythm (V. Zirmunsky, 1966; R. Fowler, 1970, pp. 347−365; P. M. Bertinetto, 1973; J. Domínguez Caparrós, 1981), or the possible non-literary linguistic-expressive manifestation of fiction (S. J. Schmidt, 1976, pp. 162 ff.), it is clear that the possibility of belonging to both non-literary and literary linguistic systems does not invalidate the fact that it is in the literary or poetic subsystem where both rhythm and fictionality have gained true acceptance and recognition.

1.1.2. Poetic Specificity vs. Linguistic Generality: Phono-Acoustical and Grammatical Levels

The analysis of the importance of the linguistic-expressive component in the constitution of poetic meaning involves surveying and examining the principal characteristics identified and stabilized by linguistic poetics throughout its gestation in our century, from its very origins in Russian formalism and European structuralism. In each case, we will pay close attention to the reasons favoring the literary specificity of the phenomenon being explored and, in contrast, those which serve to link it with the general system of language.

I will undertake this survey following the semiotic order of planes or levels, from least to greatest linguistic complexity (R. Ingarden, 1931; E. H. Falk, 1981, pp. 23 ff.; M. Pagnini, 1970; C. Segre, 1985, pp. 53−57), as I have done in previous works (A. García-Berrio, 1973; 1977, pp. 227−260; 1979), to which I refer those interested in consulting in greater detail the doctrinal questions relative to the different features cited. In this chapter I will attend to these questions only insofar as they refer to the central theme concerning us here. Such a systematization is already familiar to both traditional rhetoric and modern linguistic poetics; its detailed repetition and synthesis would only serve to make this summary irritating (J. Ihwe, 1972; R. Kloepfer, 1975; J. A. Martínez, 1975; J. Culler, 1975; R. Scholes, 1976; J. M. Pozuelo Yvancos, 1983; T. Albaladejo Mayordomo, 1984).

On the phono-phonological level of rhythm and verse, traditional literary characteristics already present us with two of the marks of literary and poetic specificity most unanimously sanctioned by the historical tradition (R. Ingarden, 1931 [1973, pp. 42−61]). In his *Poetics*, Aristotle poses the problem of verse as the constitutive feature of poetry. Although he discards

1.1. Literariness: The Linguistic Structure of the Literary Option 45

it as a decisive principle affecting imitation or verisimilar fiction (47 b, 13—27), he does not restrict the view of its fundamental specificity, as it was traditionally received and understood. Thus, the very fact that Aristotle submitted it for debate gives us some idea of its importance for the classical consciousness of literariness or poeticity (A. García-Berrio, 1988, pp. 81—87).

If verse as such is discarded by Aristotle as being a determining and essential property, the same is not true of rhythm (48 b, 21), the generic element of artistic language (S. Chatman, 1965). Poetic rhythm, especially in its classical form, incorporates a series of physiological and psychological properties which justify its implantation in the inventory of poetry's resources, apart from its linguistic meaning (A. García-Berrio, 1975, pp. 72—80).

Evidently, standard communicative language also tends to exhibit rhythm in its sequences, albeit to a less systematic and intensive degree than in artistic prose and poetry, but nothing leads us to believe that the ultimately aesthetic reason for this tendency is detached from prose and poetry in a clear and conscious way (I. Paraíso, 1976). Historical explanations of poetic rhythm link it to origins quite far removed from any expressive proclivity standard language might possess. In literature, poetic rhythm appears associated with musical recitation, through song or the accompaniment of musical instruments, or even associated to phenomena of mnemonic retention.

Historically, then, we can count on sufficient evidence to justify the specificity of the phenomenon of literary poetic rhythm, independent from similar tendencies observable in standard language. It is a matter of the simultaneous trajectory followed in both literary and standard language by phenomena with a common cause but which, naturally, precedes both. Moreover, the feature of rhythm demonstrates a degree of poetic specialization so specifically marked (S. Chatman, 1965, pp. 30—76) in comparison to the equivalent rhythmical tendencies of standard communicative language, that the explanation of the former as a simple deduction from the latter strikes me as unreasonable.

Also, keep in mind that to the central fact of rhythm (V. Zirmunsky, 1966) it is customary and necessary to add an entire set of marginal tendencies, which are either antilinguistic — in the sense of the common economical uses of the communicative "standard" — or are autonomous and independent from the general phenomena of language. Consider, for example, acoustic phenomena like the signaling of nonrational-communicative, sentimental products, by means of *vocalic coloring*, autonomous rhythmic accentuation, etc. These are clearly phenomena of an anti-linguistic competence which, through verse and enjambement, create a rhythmical syntax (O. Brik, 1965, pp. 143—153), distorting the logico-communicative syntax regularized in the general system of language. The rhythmical language of verse, compared to the common tendencies of language, cultivates abnormal phono-phonological features such as alliteration (P. Valesio, 1967), phonic anaphoras, rhyme, etc. (A. García-Berrio, 1973, pp. 124—160).

These same *anti-tendencies* of poetic rhythm with regard to the habits of the logico-communicative standard are equivalent to the written anti-linguistic features supposedly specific to literature, which are put into play in the cultural-historic shift from sung-heard to written-read poetry (P. Valesio, 1967).

Acoustic rhythm, co-naturally pleasurable to man, in Aristotle's phrase (*Poetics*, 48 b, 20—23), perhaps because, as the treatise-writers of the Renaissance proclaimed, it responds to the consonance of heartbeat, the pulses of circulation and respiratory periods, gives way to the rhythm of reading, a visual rhythm. Free verse, the devices offered by the organization of the poem and the blank spaces on the page and many other graphic-written artifices generated in modern poetry are the ocular-rhythmical equivalents of classical acoustic melody, only in a new age presided over by the imposed dissemination and multiplication of written communication (J. Derrida, 1967). Both of these equivalent manifestations, the acoustic and the visual, reflect the identical, definitive triumph of the abnormal literary expedients relative to standard communicative uses of language, as is convincingly set forth in the collection of theoretical contributions assembled by R. Cremante and M. Pazzaglia (1972) in their comprehensive anthology.

Leaving aside the general fact of rhythm, which is simply the implantation of a musical order in the sphere of verbal discourse, has made it possible, correctly, to discuss whether many other concrete features of the phono-phonological poetic series correlate more or less directly with the situation as it exists at this level in standard language (V. Zirmunsky, 1966, p. 88). In this respect, characteristic and illustrative evidence has been cited regarding basic national meters and their close connection to the tonal rhythms belonging to the corresponding languages — for example, the octosyllabic meter of the Spanish *romance* (T. Navarro Tomás, 1966, p. 8) and the interdependence of syllabic quantity in Latin and Greek rhythmic feet. Analogously, anti-use is a paradoxical use, an exception in proportion to the rules, and thus dependent on them. This can be seen as an operative notion in the case of some of the poetic phono-phonological features already indicated characteristically exhibiting themselves in competition with the uses of the system.

In any case, if it is true that we are forced into maintaining a great deal of prudence in speaking of exclusively poetic features relative to the features of the general system of language at the phono-acoustical level, it is equally true that the differences are noteworthy. If not the *causes* of specificity, at least its *symptoms*, at the level of differentiation which we seek, can be established from these differences. Such phenomena are not, if one prefers, exclusive features, but are signs of a positive solidification, made evident and intentional with respect to their ideal and tolerable proportion in standard communication.

When we ask ourselves, in conclusion, about the organizational framework of the phono-phonological characteristics of poetic language, we find ourselves, already at this level, in the domain of the utterance. In effect, notes of adaption and reinsistence in the phono-phonological features of poetic language are produced from the overall grasp of the text. This works like the restrictive frame creating the dimension and *domain* in which alliterations, parallelisms and phonic antitheses, rhymes, etc., have their effect and become evident (I. Fonagy, 1965).

The textual organization of acoustical rhythm also turns out to be decisive in the production of general rhythmical-imaginary effects. Aristotle's notion of rhythm as one of the two "physical" causes of poetry is, in my judgment, a valid explanatory principle, given its proper weight only with great difficulty, perhaps because of its very straightforwardness and simplicity (A. García-Berrio, 1987). As will be explained in the corresponding chapter of this book, Aristotle's understanding of the purely acoustico-verbal rhythms of the poem, insofar as they represent a correspondence with more general anthropological tendencies, transcends the concrete phenomenon of these same oral rhythms in order to suggest their translation into fantastic impulses of spatial orientation. By means of this rhythmical organization of the impulse, the text of the poem proposes and activates subconscious designs, patterns in which man lodges his most radical means for the imaginary construction of the universe (A. García-Berrio, 1985, 1987).

Nevertheless, in these general poetic rhythms — decisive, it seems to me, in adjusting the production of the poetic effect as a transcendental modulation of verbal communication — the role of the purely acoustical components is important, yet partial. In the construction of the poem's rhythmic spatial-imaginary design, the physical acoustical elements of poetic rhythm do not transcend the value of the subconscious suggestions communicated by symbols themselves, like the ascensional suggestion of the tree, the dynamic suggestion of wind, etc. Nor are they more efficient in their value for fantastic orientation than the spatial deixes of the text's demonstratives, or the semantic suggestion of impulse and action communicated by names and verbs, as demonstrated in my own analysis of Jorge Guillén's poems (A. García-Berrio, 1985, pp. 261—263).

Something analogous to all of this is also apparent when it comes to considering the distinctive features of literary and poetic language at the morphosyntactic level (R. Ingarden, 1931 [1973, pp. 62—94]). Historically-speaking the most characteristic feature of poetry at this level is the syntactical distortion in the order of its elements. Poetic hyperbaton is not, of course, a feature specific to poetry, compared to standard expression, but it evidently functions as an *accepted risk* in the economy of verbal-poetic communication. It is not a kind of linguistic *de-automatization* unknown to the general usage of languages, but, as at the phono-phonological level, here too we find ourselves in the presence of an anomaly of very significant proportions. In languages with the most marked syntactic order and in the most extravagantly divergent poetic realizations, violent hyperbaton reaches a level of complete infraction of the linguistic norm, dictated by an opposing rule of communicative economy.

The example of hyperbaton, with its power of defamiliarization, is even more markedly anti-systematic when considered as a general symptom of the conflict between rhythmical or poetic syntax and logico-communicative syntax (O. Brik, 1965, pp. 143—144). Enjambement represents the extreme case of a voluntary distortion of the normative, of aggression against the syntactico-tonal system of standard language. Obviously, there again, the textual *frame* is the limit in which the set of distortions of the morphological order is implanted, supporting and restricting them.

On the lexical-semantic level the arguments supporting poetic deviation are even stronger (L. Doležel, 1966, 1966, pp. 257—266). This is not the case as far as the traditional and most cited argument of lexical selection, whether poetic or literary, is concerned (T. Todorov, 1978, pp. 45—46). Classical literary discourse affirmed what is perhaps its most basic self-awareness in this lexical expedient. In the same way as the heroic pantheon of classical literature conventionally restricted to a very drastic extent the total inventory of literary characters, conflicts and themes, vocabulary, corresponding to the requirements of *decorum*, also found itself affected by restrictions and by a high degree of control, both of which worked towards imposing a conventionalized inventory and a process of selection.

However, one should keep in mind the fact that classical poetics did not by any means consider poetic or literary discourse as an abnormal, non linguistic discourse. All to the contrary, the lexical selection which determines the limits of artistic vocabulary, conventionalizing and fixing the inventory of "literary" terms available for each theme together with its colloquial or communicative lexical representation, consciously acts within the framework of the general convention, hierarchical but unitary in nature, of the "language's treasure-house" (A. A. Hill, 1976, p. 115).

The classical poet's task of lexical selection cannot take place with his back turned on his fundamental sense of discourse as it is standardized in available inventories. The guiding concept in the artistic ideology of the classical world is of a global, mythical and metaphysical nature, insofar as art is conceived of as a sublime metamorphosis of common material linguistic components. The artistic construction within the "limitation" of common linguistic materials, still forming part of the linguistic standard although lodged in its most noble quarters, is where the secret of poeticity and the motor of the literary situation is located for the classical creator, not in any belief in the autonomous nature of such materials (A. García-Berrio, 1977—1980, I, pp. 150—155).

But if the classical awareness of the non-specificity of the lexicon signals the exclusion of any conception of an autonomous literary language, the strongly rooted hierarchical and differential conception of poetry's words presupposes a limited but definite counterweight to this non-specificity. Once again, we see the same situation repeating itself. Examining each of the linguistic features most manifestly characterizing the poetic, it turns out that the explicit boundary between the specifically literary and poetic and the concise, general and systematic dimension of the linguistic standard cannot be located or affirmed with regard to lexical considerations. But it is also evident that, in terms of *density*, each of the previously mentioned resources strongly singularizes different kinds of discourse, those which we perceive and denominate as literary being artistically marked.

The density alluded to is at the very least contrary to the economy of practical communication. In the particular case of the lexicon, the hierarchical selection and marginalization within the set of materials of the linguistic system presents an increasingly convincing picture of the literary domain of language as a space so justly differentiated that it can be considered autonomous by reason of the density and reiteration of certain features. All of the features analyzed up to this point — like those we will soon discuss in the semantic domain of poetic language — would, in my opinion, overcome any objection to the linguistic distinctiveness of poetic expression, if the scruple distinguishing between distinctiveness and autonomy were not raised. The former requires only that a *quantitative* condition be met, whereas the latter requires a specifically essential difference be demonstrated.

At the very least, it could be argued that the requirement that complete autonomy be demonstrated represents a maximalist's way of closing his eyes to certain overwhelming evidence. But, in addition, all of the facts summarized so far gain solidarity and significance, performing not only a quantitative change, but also a differentially qualitative one, when the reality of literary or poetic discourse is addressed from a textual perspective. That is, when they are considered at the level of the text, in a very broad conception of the text viewed as a linguistic *scheme*, a *domain* of meaningful constructions and a *sphere* of imaginary specifications.

1.1.3. Semantic Structures of Literariness

The gradual increase in the number of possibly distinctive features relative to standard communicative language is visible in the semantic aspect of poetic language. In the great range of literary language's peculiarities — and, in this case, especially of poetic language — references to artistic semantics, habitual in linguistic poetics since Russian formalism (J. Striedter, 1989), are articulated with regard to the concept of multiple meanings. The poetic word is defined in the text's interior by its semantic plurifunctionality and its aesthetic polysemy, with the result that these features have become an essential point raised in the current theory of reading (J. Kristeva, 1969, p. 142). From this point of view, the literary text is presented as a reality pierced by changeable isotopies (A. J. Greimas, 1972, p. 18), open (U. Eco, 1968, pp. 66–67) to a variable play of readings (W. Iser, 1976), which promise or threaten, according to one's point of view, the eternal consistency of aesthetic meaning.

If said characteristic were to be formally consolidated in terms of its most radical formulation, we would find ourselves before the verified thesis of the essential difference between the two languages and their systems, the poetic and that belonging to standard communication. The univocal intention of the latter, dictated by its tendency towards communicative economy, would exclude the plural and equivocal condition of poetic semantics, informed by an ideal of anti-economic experimentation, pursued at the expense of fixed meaning. In this case we find ourselves, in my opinion, with another one of the marks differentiating standard and poetic language, based on criteria of conscious intensification and quantitative density, and not with a truly essential difference organized in terms of binary oppositions of presence/absence or existence/non-existence.

At the most, the foundation offered by the verbal artistic text's structure for the plurality of readings of innumerable readers ought to be located in the connotative periphery of the work, where the "effects of evocation" which Bally speaks of (1951, pp. 204—205) are produced, in the compounding of what could be designated as the text's linguistic features lodged in the textual microstructure, in combination with the essential breadth of the textual semantic organization, which deliberately increases in the case of the literary or poetic artistic text. Thus, *connotation*, the famous concept put into circulation by L. Hjelmslev and later generalized in logical-linguistic explanations of poetry (S. Johansen, 1949; J. Trabant, 1970; A. J. Greimas, 1970, pp. 93 ff.; syntheses in V. M. de Aguiar e Silva, 1967 [1984, pp. 81 ff.], in J. Molino, 1971, pp. 9—10, and in the books of K. Kerbrat-Orecchioni, 1977, and B. Garza Cuarón, 1978), is evoked as one of the most intuitive, but also unstable categories in the semantic definition of artistic language.

Still, the literary work, any work, has been conceived in an act of organizing meaning, with the firm intention on the part of its author of endowing it with a substantive personality, of isolating it from all that it is not. For this reason it always appears before us as what it is, with an essentially identical message. There is no possible reading of *Don Quijote* which makes it the summary of the contents of the *Divine Comedy*, or vice versa. Limiting interpretive extensions to the cases, always deliberate and conscious, of works conceived in modern literature as programatically pluri-structural or open, the affirmative and balanced situation of classical works derives from the fact that the text of the artistic message corresponds to a structural plan.

People will probably think that I am exaggerating when I use this type of extreme argument. After all, though, perhaps my distortions are proportional to the kind of relativist exaggerations which deny the artistic text's objective meaning, relegating it to variables of individual receptive appreciation. I will not here repeat my defense of the opportunity represented by the theory of reading and the utility and convenience of the receptive parameter in establishing the definitive and complete meaning of the artistic text. It will suffice to say without reservations that the receiver's role is undeniable in the construction of meaning (M. Pagnini, 1970). But nobody has until now really counted, since it would be impossible to do so, the combinatory infinitude of receptive clues offered by the textual base of the artistic utterance. By the same token, to dismiss or forget the causal or intentional relationship of author and text, such as is practiced consciously or by simple forgetfulness in the most dramatic arguments of the relativism of reception and reading, is to deny another more radical and active fact.

Moreover, the relativism of reader theory and the more extreme deconstructive developments favors a capricious understanding of the "legality" of language, as Paolo Fabbri says. Our understanding by means of language is incomplete and we know it, but it is incomplete in terms of a demand for absolute objectivity, while being sufficient and satisfactory in the terms necessary for communication. The author's communicative intention enunciated by the text is discovered in normally satisfactory terms by the average reader, whose culture and linguistic ability are up to the level of the utterance (J. Rousse, 1972; W. Krysinsky, 1977). After all, it is true that the text is by nature *porous*; but, as speakers, we are familiar with the loose objective permeability of language. For this reason, we develop many other strategies of comprehension complementary to — yet outside of — language's strict objective code.

To cite the porosity of language as an obstacle for the acceptance of the objectivity of the utterance's meaning amounts to negating the principle of intuition and complementary approximation, which peripherally accompanies man's every cognitive and communicative activity. In brief, to deny the legitimacy of these resources and capacities corresponds to a requirement of complete induction, a physical universe without secrets, the theoretical hypothesis *ab ovo* or a completely existential experience without limits of space and time. This ultimate "legality" is not, we know, what it is all about (M. Ferraris, 1984). Human knowledge progresses by means of the relative legality of the sufficient and the novel, of the progressive and partial satisfaction of our curiosity. So, too, with regard to poetry and art, as with any form of knowledge whatsoever.

Faced with the skeptical relativization of the meaning contributed in the author-text relation, the aesthetics of reading confers an illusory measure of confidence on the true powers of the receptive situation (D. Coste, 1980, p. 4; Steihmetz, 1981; R. C. Holub, 1984), which has problems of its own. The "porosity" of meaning in the sphere of creation corresponds to forms of elasticity, no less fickle, in reading. Faced with texts, truly complex in their creative axis, like *Don Quijote* or the *Divine Comedy*, we can take it for granted that even the most attentive reading, known or possible, will never have exactly restored the complex circumstances of their artistic production. The relationship between the author and the text he produces is always affected by the breadth of his conceptual idea and his linguistic expression. Likewise, the exact link between the text and its readings will inevitably be marked by the same inconsistent adjustments of conceptualization and expression on the receiver's part. Moreover, in addition to these limitations, one would have to add other circumstantial restrictions inherent to the situation. For example, the *estrangement* between the text and its reader, who by nature does not know the entire integrated universe of the transmitter as reflected in the construction of his utterance (J. Fetterley, 1978; F. Martínez Bonati, 1981).

As we were saying, the specifically literary or poetic phenomenon of multiple meanings raises the level of unitary cohesion between standard and poetic language to its maximal degree of tension. This is perhaps due to the fact that here, more than in any other feature, the directive trends are radically opposed. In fact, they are polarized. Standard language in its logical communicative modes *tends* towards monosemy, while poetry *tends* towards polysemy. It is not a matter, as in other cases we have discussed, of the proportional fulfillment of one and the same tendency, with different degrees of quantitative or qualitative magnitude, with one and only one meaningful origin and end. On the contrary, we are dealing here with a phenomenon of *anti-tendency*. Two opposing forces, which do not differ more only because each one appears ballasted by the weight of its opposing tendency. The multiple meanings of poetic language are limited by the communicative requirements inherent in poetry's words in their non-aesthetic function and in the structural habits of the artistic transmitter's textual plan. Absolute plurisignification is thus presented as poetry's ideal desideratum, as its formula of maximal capacity. On the other hand, communicative-standard language seeks univocality, the absence of equivocal references, as the most efficient and complete realization of the speech act.

Images, within the semantic domain of literary language and, especially in this case, of poetry, throw some clarifying light on the subject with which we are presently concerned. Classical consideration of poetry generally centered the greatest responsibility for the poetic effect in tropes and images, coining the popular notion of poetry as a "language with images". Thus, under this simple additive principle — a quantitative extension of standard communicative language of the "bottleneck" type — poetic language was conceived of and realized as an accumulation of tropes, especially metaphors, stretched to its possible limits within the poetic message's margins of communicative elasticity.

The classical concept of the accumulation of images, functioning on the basis of the general formula equating poetic language with a more ornate standard language, has been powerfully restricted in the case of modern art. The instances of polysemy, like the playful polyvalency of the poetic message which we spoke of before, have largely supplanted the conception of poetry oriented purely by notions of image and adornment (R. Barthes, 1953). Nevertheless, although perhaps displaced from its primary role in the intentional order, the image continues to be the most notable linguistic mechanism in the current conception of poetry and, of course, the element offering the most solid basis for differentiating — within the series of linguistic processes — features specific to poetic language in contrast to standard language.

By definition, images presuppose a procedure of *illumination* shared by the artist and his receiver. The support of the essential idiomatic terms creates results which, although we cannot denominate them as absolutely autonomous, can be conceptualized with every reason as independent or outside the physiognomy of this support. Consider, for example catachresis as the ideal metaphoric type supporting the image (K. W. A. Shibles, 1971). The surprise and brilliance of the image is sustained in a no man's land, in the sphere of lexical emptiness equidistant between the semantic representations placed in an unfamiliar contrast by the image, with greater returns the more the zone of semantic non-tangency of the evoked lexical supports is dilated (Group µ, 1970; A. Henry, 1971; M. A. Le Guern, 1973; special issue of *Poetics Today*, 1983). This process for the production of meaning, in which an excision operates between the *semantics represented* by the lexicon and the *semantic evoked* in the communication, indicates a clear way of differentiating between the uses of communicative and standard language.

In the history of the debates on poetry's linguistic specificity — which, in one form or another, includes the greater part of the linguistic-poetic speculation of our century since the Russian formalists (R. Scholes, 1976) — the parties on either side of the issue have introduced obvious excesses regarding the precise position for the location of differential limits. Neither those who have taken the position of affirming poetry's "original independence" nor those who have tried to reduce it to a superficial stylistic mode of standard language have adequately taken the time to agree on and state precisely at what level their discussions should begin. There has not even been any attempt to take stock of the concrete features constituting such a differential level. In examining many of the phenomena analyzed here, I have consistently signaled — discarting it as insufficient — the guiding principle of quantitative intensification. There is no doubt that if, in the most rigorously demanding method, said principle is unsatisfactory, its capacity to clarify the peculiarities of the poetic linguistic order is nevertheless very illustrative and surprisingly convincing when all the evidence discussed here is added and combined together at the textual level (M. Margghescou, 1974).

Yet, even renouncing as superficial the principle of quantitative intensification, the practice among some critics of seeking to obligate everyone to argue substantiveness at such a unique, basic and radical level of autonomy so as to approach the non-human is obviously fallacious. Still other critics either have nothing to do with or repudiate the need to penetrate and explain the origin of discrepancies at this maximal level, or — although such critics are in the minority — naively fall into the trap their adversaries have set for them, attempting to probe the linguistic evidence for a level of difference beyond what is reasonable and necessary between the linguistic standard and literary poetic communication (M. Riffaterre, 1979). In my opinion, the similarities between both languages are not so great so as to permit us to ignore the level at which differences are produced. Nor are the differences so substantial and deep so as to make it necessary to situate them in radical domains in order to justify both activities, the standard communicative and the literary or poetic, as phenomena entirely distinct in spite of their common linguistic, cultural and even anthropological roots (J. Mukařovský, 1964, p. 28).

Evidently, there is no reason for disregarding an awareness of the general linguistic norm in order to justify poetic production as an autonomous reality. Thus, for example, the essential comprehension of the poetic image as a reality produced and understood by means of *normative habits*, linguistic as well as cultural and semiological, is not incompatible with the literary specificity of the pragmatic rules governing the communication of images, as we have indicated before.

On the concrete level of this discussion, I believe it is pertinent to repeat the radical difference that I have been reiterating here between *literariness as an option* and *poeticity as a value*. In my judgment, the primary difference that has set the two critical currents against one another on the question of the specificity or autonomy of artistic language can be attributed to the shared lack of sharp and clear definitions establishing the characteristics and differences existing between the literary and poetic, in the sense, for example, in which Croce opposed poetry as the expression of truth to literature as a testimony of civilization. Since Russian formalism, literariness and poeticity have not been systematically distinguished. Still, it is a question of far more than two progressive degrees of complexity in the artificially "deflected" use of language. It is clear that, via the analytical control of linguistically distinctive characteristics, one cannot reach a reasonable explanation of a notion like poeticity, traditionally coupled, and quite rightly so, with axiological-artistic convictions. The poetic is an aesthetic value rooted in the universe of emotions constructed by fantasy: hence, it belongs to the ethics of the imagination. For the gifted creator, the poetic is completed only in the text, with a unique dynamic which accellerates and broadens insurmountable limits and areas of suggestion. For his part, the reader extracts the poetic from the text's verbal formulas, but, like the creator, interiorizes the verbal stimuli in the ultimately unfathomable regions of his feelings and imagination.

Literature is *opted for* from among certain conventional procedures — or, better still, let us denominate them "known procedures" in order to put an end to the use of an unnecessarily equivocal term — of the language's stylization: from modes of fictional or realist reference to the reality denoted by language, and from linguistic structures conventionalized in their artistic topicality. Thus, the artist bets on sure and known "procedures", from which aesthetic and imaginary effects may or may not flow. Thus, literariness is an entry-level option, while poeticity is a terminal value. The exploitation of certain linguistic mechanisms makes the option adopted recognizable as literary, but does not in itself guarantee poetic value, which is not assured by the adoption and use of any particular mode of the linguistic game.

In this way, the insurmountable dichotomy constructed by the two, until now, opposing notions of artistic language can be resolved or, better yet, diluted. The recognizable and calculated optative nature of its paradigms of linguistic constitution locates artistic language within the scope of pragmatic cultural explanation, while the uncertain nature of its imaginary effects, depending on unforeseeable powers of subconscious repercussion, places poetic emotion at levels unattainable by the certain, automatic effect of any consciously anticipated and articulated linguistic options.

1.1.4. *Literariness and the Pragmatic Point of View: The Systematic Practice of Communicative Exception*

The conscious incorporation of the pragmatic point of view into general linguistic analysis and, above all, its recently thriving success, necessarily motivated a similar modification in the domain of linguistic poetics. Some of the pragmatic arguments against the specificity of literary and poetic language (especially M. Corti, 1976, and M. L. Pratt, 1977), in spite of their radically negative appearance, show themselves relatively open to admitting the specificity of artistic language, although only as a question justifiable exclusively from the pragmatic perspective. Others are more radical in their stances (J. Ellis, 1974; C. Di Girolamo, 1978).

Normally in such works the insufficiency of distinctively literary and poetic features on other levels — phono-phonological, morphosyntactic and semantic — is extended in order to insist that only with the conscious assumption of the literary "act of expression", constituted as such, that is to say, as a specifically coined cultural convention, can one locate the differential linguistic root between communicative language and artistic language. Relying, reasonably or abusively, on the rich critical and linguistic proposals of Mikhail Bakhtin, these critics come to insist on the practice of the "literary act" as a culturally and historically conventionalized event.

For the advocates of this position, not only are violations of the basic linguistic system acceptable, but, contradictorily, this set of conventionalized exceptions is privileged as an essentially poetic sign. This being the case, then, in the opinion of such authors, poetic signs are quantitatively intensified yet normal features of the general system of language.

Until this point in my examination of the linguistic features that tend to be offered as distinctive and specific to literary language, the least definitive of the cases discussed, for example, that of phono-phonological features, are those where the invocation of the pragmatic perspective proves most fruitful. That is, pragmatics yields the most when specificity is more a question of quantitative intensification than a genuinely original feature of artistic language, unsupported by the general scheme of the language or by its communicative economy. As far as other cases are concerned, like that of images, the invocation of literary pragmatic conventionalism fulfills other purposes. Basically, it suggests answers to those who seek to explain how certain abnormal signs, non-existent as such in the general system of language, are nevertheless usually acceptable in the literary or poetic system.

As far as the debate on the examination of the pragmatic distinctiveness of literariness, it seems necessary to me that we take note of the initial propensity towards centering a feature that includes a very broad range of events entirely on conventions of fictionality and verisimilitude. Of course, these conventions do not exhaustively explain the full scope of literariness. This, I believe, is the logical consequence of the boom in literary studies dedicated to the novel, so characteristic of twentieth century literary criticism. But it seems unnecessary to warn critics of the fact that narrative fiction — be it in stories, novels or theater — is just one more of the many aspects included in the cultural pragmatic convention of literariness. Even realist fictionality amounts to a relatively small segment of the total domain of objects affected by the convention of poeticity.

Undoubtedly, an important starting point for the pragmatic approach to literariness was offered in the set of studies collected and edited by T. A. van Dijk in *Pragmatics of Language and Literature* (1976). Van Dijk's efforts, as evidenced both in his own contribution to this volume as well as in the paper he presented in 1977 to the First International Congress of Literary Investigation of Puerto Rico (E. Forastieri, ed., 1980, pp. 3—16), were very directly motivated by the criticism Roland Posner levied against the suggestive book van Dijk had published in 1972, *Some Aspects of Text-grammars* (R. Posner, 1976).

According to Posner, the inadequacy of van Dijk's work concerning the search for a poetic language with the exclusion of communicative attributions was evident from the very beginning, an accusation Posner extended to the most distinguished figures associated with structural poetics: Bierwisch, Doležel, Levin, Zolkowski, etc. (R. Posner, 1976, pp. 1—10).

I believe the central idea of van Dijk's pragmatic characterization of the literary event and object owes a great deal to Posner's attack: namely, its privileged condition established by the preconceptions and biases of traditional conventionalism, its nature as a linguistic entity. The effect of Posner's vigorous shake-up was also evident in the healthy pragmatic reaction which immediately followed his criticisms, extending even to Lotman who, without abdicating the traditional explanation of poeticity set forth in his earlier books "as a function of the internal organization of the text" (Y. Lotman, 1970), now sought to establish its complementary pragmatic element "in terms of the communicative function" of the poetic act (Y. Lotman, 1976).

The affirmation of an identically pragmatic focus was also noticeable in the United States. A speech by the famous critic and linguist Samuel Levin

1.1. Literariness: The Linguistic Structure of the Literary Option

at a conference in 1973, retouched and published in 1976 in van Dijk's volume on literary pragmatics, was noticeably instigatory in its effects. Basing himself on Richard Ohmann's well-known literary pragmatic ideas, Levin, between 1971 and 1973, intensified the value and importance of the communicative characteristics of the poetic "speech act" as the best way of defining the act of literary communication (S. R. Levin, 1976, pp. 141—160). The pragmatico-communicative characteristic of "poetic faith", or verisimilar credibility, as an *entendu* between author and listener/reader, is the general principle which, until now, has sustained all of the efforts towards formulating a pragmatic explanation of literary characteristics.

All of the linguists asked by van Dijk to contribute to his 1976 collection of pragmatic texts agreed on this point. Schmidt (1976, pp. 161—178) establishes his reflections on the nature of fiction along more predominantly philosophical than empirico-literary lines. Kuroda assimilates the fictional, insofar as the "story" is concerned, to *poiein* (1976, pp. 107—140), contrasting it with the non-narrative fictional experience, which he identifies with *legein*. Levin perhaps exceeds everyone else in the keenness and accuracy of his treatment of the pragmatic properties of verisimilar fiction, not just limited to narrative-fictional features. But Levin is far from having explained, first, how the degree of pragmatic fictionality of a poem by Ezra Pound, for example, can be assimilated to that of a novel, at least without establishing so many distinctions so as to make such a notion, in the best of cases, not very profitable and of very doubtful explanatory value. Moreover, one can find fault with his claim that verisimilar fiction is the only perlocutionary principle to confer specificity on the poetic message, not to mention the case of literary communication. I believe, resorting once again to traditional poetics and rhetoric, that at least one series of the poetic message's perlocutionary effects — *docere, delectare, movere* — has not been put to adequate use by this pragmatic-poetic reaction, not to mention the value of characteristics of an illocutionary type and the perlocutionary results involved in the mysterious, unfathomable notion of sublimity.

Having established the value of the literary features of verisimilar fictionality in terms of its positive pragmatic importance for defining the linguistic specificity of one type of literary message it governs, questions of the pragmatic statute of poetic specificity still remain pending as regards other literary and especially lyrical messages, not characterized, as I said before, by the feature of fiction. Moreover, even in the cases we admit as fictional, the presence of other features of literariness and poeticity, possibly also within the scope of pragmatic considerations, is evident.

From my point of view, the usual pragmatic perspective of the literary act as an act of expression yields features clearly different from those contributing to standard communication, different to the extent of serving to powerfully distinguish the former discourse from the latter. Beginning with the pragmatic mode of the literary act itself, the normalcy of the receiver's customary *absence* and of the *distance* or *mediated nature* of his response is immediately apparent compared to the scheme of things in standard communicative language (F. Lázaro Carreter, 1976 a). Literature is the consecration of an inexistent dialogue, except in certain rare cases which choose to thematize the violation of this general principle (J. Domínguez Caparrós, 1981, pp. 113—116). Reading is nothing more than a metaphor of response. And the proof of this lies in the very fact that, by definition, the modes of reading-response are multiple, depending on different allocations of ability and interest (Y. Lotman, 1970). Clearly, the literary transmitter anticipates (U. Eco, 1979; M. Pagnini, 1980) a wide range of responses which — like it or not — unquestionably yields a variety of performative modes in the literary message (C. Segre, 1985, pp. 19—21), as well as preventing operations of self-reflection, correction and response by which communicative messages are normally completed and produced in standard language (H. Weinrich, 1971 a; M. Charles, 1977).

As concerns the literary "speech act" from the transmitter's perspective, this process' pragmatic distinctiveness is marked by the fact of the transmitter's constant awareness of being and moving in the domain of an *exceptional "plus"* (B. Romberg, 1962; F. K. Stanzel, 1955, 1964; W. Krysinsky, 1977). The artistic creator elicits the receiver's surprise within the margins set by a certain tolerance for deviation in the general system of the language. To a large extent, the transmitter-creator's *poetic competence* results from his keen awareness of the poetic message's differential nature and of the final limits possibly open to this message with respect to the standard's communicative viability (V. M. de Aguiar e Silva, 1980). This competence is thus established and realized as a conscious practice of communicative *exception* to standard language (A. García-Berrio, 1985, p. 49).

In the receiver's case, literary or poetic competence also plays a role. Here, competence is realized in terms of the perception of the message with an awareness of its status as exceptional communication. However, the differences are very noticeable between this *secondary literary or poetic competence* and the functioning of the general competence of language's communicative standard. In effect, general linguistic competence is seen as the capacity to determine a message's grammaticality and appropriate formation, both by the transmitter and by the receiver. Which amounts to saying that every speaker can normally create any message he would be able to understand.

However, poetic competence differs essentially in its pragmatic functioning. The receiver, even a sensitive and well-read speaker, although he may perfectly understand the contents of the poetic message, is rarely in the position to formulate an explicit linguistic response in the same poetic terms. In other words: there are excellent readers of poetry that have in fact never written a poem; and there are many who, having attempted it, achieve nothing more than a mechanical reproduction of what they've read, without "inspiration". Or, worse still, they end up composing a positively inferior poem.

The preceding evidence abundantly demonstrates (M. Bierwisch, 1970) the differential condition of poetry's linguistic nature, and to a lesser degree, of literature, as *practices of exception*. To the extent that exception is created, it is invented on each occasion, especially in the outstanding cases of the most respected poetry, the richest in linguistic surprises for the receiver. It does not exist as an automatically activated standard system. The myths of "inspiration" and of "poiesis" refer to the blind production of the poetic message; that is, an unconscious process unguided by the usual standardized practices of general linguistic production (D. Romero de Solís, 1981, p. 101).

This argument, reduced to its minimal claims, even denying the myth of inspiration any role, is not without substance. It is evident that, expressed in terms of degrees of competence, the poetic "act of expression" powerfully differs from standard language. To begin with, one might think the language's general communicative competence recognizes cases similar to that of poetry. We know there are people perfectly capable of understanding linguistic utterances, yet lacking the same capacity to produce or transmit other texts of the same nature. In addition, the complexity of, for example, a philosophical utterance is similar to the poetic, in that we can come to understand the *Discourse on Method* or the *Critique of Pure Reason*, but, obviously, those who do understand such discourses do not generally have the capacity to create other similar, totally new and original discourses.

Nevertheless, everyday experience tells us that what is exceptional in the first case — i. e., those with the capacity to understand linguistic utterances, but not to create them — is general in the case of poetry. In the second example, the problem is not so much an expressive impotence, that is, a problem of competence, as a question of the capacity of conceiving the thoughts and reasoning of a philosophical discourse. Clearly, the case of poetry is different. When we think of a beautiful poem, like the one beginning "Gather ye rosebuds while ye may" by Robert Herrick, we find ourselves confronted with a topical thought — the *carpe diem*. None of the poem's parts achieves any degree of novelty in the domain of intellectual enrichment. Nevertheless, we feel the poem to be a positive development (A. García-Berrio, 1978). Hence, although we can predict the general syntactico-semantic structure of a literary topic, the majority of a language's speakers are not in any condition to be able to recreate it in a beautiful, surprising way, until the great creator arrives on the scene to erect it as a *practice of exception*.

The explanation for this *partial mechanism* of poetic-literary competence is perhaps best achieved by attentively considering the process and limits of the receiver's linguistic comprehension. Evidently, in the *reception* of a poetic or literary linguistic message, an operation of detachment takes place which confirms our previous hypothesis about the process of transmission as a practice of linguistic exception. The receiver is aware of the fact that, upon understanding a poetic message, a great part of that comprehension has been distilled outside of the normal activities of his general linguistic-communicative competence (S. R. Levin, 1962; B. Herrstein-Smith, 1980). Customarily, modern poetics has appealed to the concept of transrationality or metarationality to designate — if not explain — this pragmatic peculiarity of poetry. It seems clear that that which from a poetic message is convertible by the receiver of the same to a rational scale is normally identified with that which from that same message can be translated into the terms of communicative-linguistic normality.

The clarification of the concrete laws governing the practice of exception is urgently required, important and, without doubt, very difficult. Hence, the very obvious merit of Yuri Lotman's proposal in this regard, although he only intended to establish an explanation for determined aspects of a much broader problem. In applying and adapting the semiological notion of a "secondary modeling system" to literary and poetic acts as artistic practices, Lotman has succeeded in precisely indicating, at the very least, where the problem is really located (Y. Lotman, 1970, Ch. I).

After Lotman's clarification, it is clear that the practice of poetic exception is carried out by virtue of the exceptional nature of the *second meaning* which linguistic signifiers acquire when symbolized as poetic signifiers. The old intuition about the *non-neutrality* compared to standard communication of the poetic signifier — manipulated, for example, in poetry's complete destabilization of communicative synonyms — makes sense in view of Lotman's linguistic discourse. A complete textual theory at all levels of the signifier is thus articulated.

Nevertheless, the problem persists beyond Lotman's explanation, to the extent that the discussion of the systematic autonomy of artistic language is reasonably raised. In effect, it is true that even intuitively we are convinced that literary language has a meaningful implicitness, translated into the degree of density and intensity of signification. And it is evident that this phenomena becomes meaningful through the terms of transrational communication, being more or less fully explained for poetry thanks to the semiological theory of secondary modeling. But it is also undeniable that the very fact we talk about and claim the existence of a language of poetry communicates another no less accurate intuition: the *systematic nature* — and thus a combination of theoretically limited principles and resources — of literary and poetic linguistic practice.

It is in the wisdom of this hunch where we believe the foundations of the recently emphasized distinction between poetic language and the language of standard communication are to be found. The same sense of literature or poetry as a cultural agreement, manifested in terms of the *understanding* between the parties involved in the communication at the pragmatic level reinforces this idea of systematicity. Rather than being seen as a code open to verbal experimentation, literary and poetic language is conceived, especially in the classical tradition, as an artistic system of rules. The existence of this inventory of rules codified in poetics and, especially, in rhetoric, encourages the belief that the linguistic practice of poetry or literature is nothing more than the extension of the practices of the general linguistic-communicative system.

This perspective conceeds, at the most, that the aforementioned amplification results from the specialization of certain domains rarely frequented in general communicative practice, precisely as a function of their relative efficiency and economy.

It is necessary to examine in greater depth poetry's linguistic characteristics in the sense of its *systematicity as a practice of exception*. It is not a matter of giving in to the temptation of affirming or denying its condition of integration or autonomy with regard to standard language. In this sense, I believe long dormant traditional rhetoric has done much to shed some light on the traditional debate, now modernized, perhaps more than all of the vigilant, active poetics of our century. This perhaps may explain the nostalgia of so many for a general literary rhetoric which for the moment is to found, in the sense of an effort at integration, only at very tentative levels (Group μ, 1970; A. García-Berrio, 1983, 1984). This systematization must retrace the paths of classical rhetoric, but with the awareness that it carries out the task of demonstrating a system of constituted exceptions, since another of the contaminations and confusions engendered by a habitual prejudice results in not perceiving the exceptions to a system forming, in their own right, a systematic set. But along with the logic of rules of a system, the systematicity of artistic exceptions can be established and, at least in its broad outlines, effectively constituted as a system of transgressions.

The problem which immediately arises is the lack of differentiation between the concepts of *transgression* and *exception*. The first presupposes a more immediate presence of the transgressed base system. It is understood that the set of transgressions can be organized resorting to the same lines and tendencies governing the basic system of rules. The same direction is thus maintained, inverting its sense. Exception — not transgression — requires the identification of the base system, admitting the possibility of multiple systems acting to produce the set of exceptions. The previous rule of contrast with transgression is of no use here. Exception implies great autonomy with respect to its basic paradigm: not only does the direction of its lines have to be altered, but often the exception's lines of direction will not coincide with any of the directions signaled by the system creating the rule. In my judgment, a first task for creating the necessary inventory of rules for a general poetics in our times lies in determining specifically poetic norms as norms of exception or rules of transgression of the standard system of the language.

I have myself undertaken this project, developing a poetics in terms of the systematic practice of linguistic exception in an extensive chapter on Jorge Guillén's poetic language, part of my general study of *Cántico* (1985, pp. 49—134). Note that in order to realize it, just as I had previously thought, it was not necessary to resort to any new inventory of exceptional linguistic stylemes. On the contrary, the best known and most reliable terms and concepts of traditional rhetoric and literary stylistics, like anaphora, deixis, emphatic exclamation, rhetorical question, enjambement, vocalic coloring, etc., are sufficient, provided one does not lose sight of the systematic interaction and symptomatic, selective exploitation of the chosen resources, which are gradually specialized in the physiognomy of an individual aesthetic style.

In this sense, the exceptional systematicity of an artistic voice is always defined by the distinctive physiognomy of its options. Not only are a concrete number of commitments to stylistic resources selected, but the omissions by abstention also turn out to be analogously systematic. In this way, the symptomatic code of an individual style is configured. The constitution of a singular artistic style, in its positive and negative dependence — through its commitments and omissions — on the traditional inventory of expressive resources, is easily situated within the tradition of rhetorical practices, which the metalinguistic advances of modern investigation help clarify. For example, the generative notion of "subcategorization", anomalous in this case, permits a more effective illustration of some of the specific personal characteristics of Guillen's style in *Cantico* than would have been possible with the traditional metaphorical concept (A. García-Berrio, 1985, pp. 119—134).

The systematic paradigm of an author's individual artistic style will logically show a first stage characterized by extension and selection with respect to the framework of expressive resources at his disposition, which constitute the artistic rhetoric of a determined age. Thus, we can speak of the *exorhetorical* stage of stylistic constitution as a practice of exception. On the other hand, once the author stabilizes the expressive system in the conventionally customary terms of consolidating his personal poetic "voice", an interesting process of purification begins. This process, as systematic as the exorhetorical stage, involves the purification of the author's own expressive powers, in terms of the *endorhetorical* perpetuation of his style as a general value of constants.

If the concept of *exception* partakes, in the sense of the standard norm, of the limit of *transgression*, as we have already indicated, another perhaps more immediate and necessary form establishes the boundary which, in my study of *Cantico*, I set in terms of *violation*, a term already managed in a distinctively positive way by J. Mukařovský (1964). Nevertheless, in my own analysis, violation is found at the apex of agrammaticality and meaninglessness (A. García-Berrio, 1985, pp.52—54). Violation is not poetic, precisely because it destroys the rigorous requirements for meaningfulness, highest of all in poetry. In the analysis of a successful poetic style it is possible to see that the licenses of linguistic exceptionality always result in the production of meaning, insofar as they are capable of submitting the paradigms of grammaticality to their most extreme flexible tensions, without breaking their constitutive principles (G. Leech, 1970, pp. 121—122).

Between the expressively irrelevant pure verbal exercise of transgression and the annihilation of meaning resulting from linguistic violation, the systematic order of the stylistic exceptions constituting the individual artistic-expressive mode enriches the language's possibilities of symbolic signification. It extends them to unexpected regions, illuminating new and unexplored areas. In the systematic practice of linguistic exception, the text's material skeleton finds a vehicle for dynamic imaginary communication, through which the artistic work fosters the participation of meaningful subjects and subconscious drives.

In conclusion, under the pragmatic perspective we have invoked in this section, the linguistic peculiarities of poetry and literature take shape in contrast to the norms of standard language (M. Pagnini, 1980; C. Segre, 1985, pp. 11–35). Especially in the domain of the receiver of the "literary speech act", the reality of the awareness with which the specific nature of the literary system as a secondary modeling system of acts results in distinctive characteristics of artistic language that are not, in any case, attributable to the standard, is undeniable. But perhaps the most surprising and definitive result is the fact of the *systematicity* of the double mechanism of transgressions and exceptions to the norm of standard language by which the set of features of literary language can be organized. Perhaps, as I've already said, this very systematicity has served until now to camouflage the autonomous conception of poetic exception, to the extent that exception and transgression have been incorrectly and abusively assimilated to asystematism. It is not — far from it — by way of tracking the supposed organic nature of the set of features of poetic language that one is able to affirm their autonomy from standard language. The most rigorous path surely consists in rejecting unproven allegations that all of the features of artistic language *proceed* from the standard — and not simply that they are represented therein, which is another matter. Because I am convinced of the necessary and essential *systematicity* of artistic language, at any level of autonomy one wishes to think of it (A. García-Berrio and M. T. Hernández, 1988a), I think this characteristic does not offer a sufficient basis for differentiating it from the linguistic standard, also proven to be systematic. The interesting question requiring an explanation here lies in the autonomous nature of the concrete content of linguistic features, rules and elements constituting each of the two systematic complexes of language.

1.2. Literariness and the Text

1.2.1. The Text as the Level of Decision for the Linguistic Specificity of Literature

What the invocation of the pragmatic level in the search for an extraformalist definition of literariness and of extraformalist and extralinguistic poetics meant to a certain tradition of theoretical-literary containment, the possible encounter of instances at the textual level has meant for the tradition of linguistic poetics. The substitution, now definitively justified, of the sentence by the text as the broadest level for making the linguistic plan explicit (A. García-Berrio, 1979a), has an important advantage for our present purposes. Many of the features partially intuited as properly literary and poetic reveal their most radical specificity when contemplated in the light of their reinforcement and intensified functioning in the general domain of the text.

The literary or poetic text establishes, effectively, certain more precise and even conventional fixed limits for the creator of literary or poetic types of expression, which are unknown in the elaboration of the standard communicative text. From the very start, the author of a sonnet works under the pressure of a closed textual space. He accepts a pre-set dimension for his discourse, which artistically specializes each of his operations and decisions regarding thematic invention, structural arrangement and elocution at every level (F. Lázaro Carreter, 1976, pp. 315—332; M. Riffaterre, 1971). Without knowing such stringent limits, the constructor of a theatrical piece or a novel is similarly aware of the existence of relatively conventional boundaries, experienced, adapted and patterned for the communicative-aesthetic efficacy of said discourses. Hence, the resulting interdependence among all of the singular components of the literary and, especially, poetic text is so much more permanent and solid than that determining the reciprocal selections of the standard communicative speech act.

Frequently, this fact has been raised only as a sort of consequence associated with virtuosity, freely assumed by the artistic creator, but at bottom entirely pointless. This attitude is not only historically present among the ranks of poetry's "enemies", but, through the ages, is to be found even among the most passionate partisans and cultivators of classical art, an activity conceived basically as "artifice", rhetorical flourish or embellishing effort. In this respect, the translation of the formalist technicality *priem* as "procedure", seems to me more appropriate in English for reflecting the distinctive nature of literary art than the previously used translation of the term as "artifice" (A. García-Berrio, 1973, pp. 91—93).

The artistry of the manufactured literary "procedure" is determined by the exigency of multiplying the capacity for the creation of standard language's meaning. I have already shown in my discussion of Lotman's contributions how literature and especially poetry presuppose a greater capacity for meaning than standard communicative practice, through fairly vague formulas like "transcendental enrichment", sentimental expressivity, etc. The literary text reinforces the coherence among its components in an equilibrium of tensions that, without exception, traverse the entire body of a great artistic work, powerfully highlighting each of its elements while, at the same time, reinforcing the cement which joins it all together. Thus, the textual components blur their own substantive boundaries to the benefit of their reference to the text's general multiplicity.

Nevertheless, let's not forget that, in the current conception of the linguistic domain's compartmentalization, the nature of the pragmatic *level* and the terms of reference of the textual *domain* mutually imply one another's existence. The text is, above all, a concrete entity of discourse, which as a result determines the corresponding perspective or point of view. It is measurable within absolutely precise limits, and includes as constituents the totality of concrete linguistic entities making up other levels. In this sense, the "act of expression" originating the text as a pragmatic component is the energy which produces a linguistic result: the text which covers and envelops it. From a concrete utterance it is possible to reconstruct the structure of the expressive act in all of its steps; but if said act is made known to us only in its structural scheme, we still do not have a text. That pragmatic template must be filled with concrete linguistic contents — phono-phonological, morphosyntactic, lexical-semantic, etc. — that is, with the set composed of all of the component elements of the text.

Also keep in mind that in the present comprehension of the text I am referring to, together with the concrete material linguistic understanding of the same, areas which are not strictly material-textual are also recognized as parts, considered as components as far as the *context* is concerned. That is, any text as a linguistic entity cannot be reduced to the merely expressable discursive dimension, or that which is subsidiarily writable or printable. Because if the text were reduced to such a state, without extending to the domains of *premises*, of referential incorporation, etc., it would become progressively more and more opaque, ambiguous and uncommunicative (C. Segre, 1985, pp. 36—37).

Hence, if we conceive the *contextual* above the *co-textual* (T. A. van Dijk, 1972, p. 39), as a pragmatic reality outside the text, we thereby reduce the text to an unviable condition. The text as a level of consideration of the language and as a concrete entity possessing unity assumes, organizes and relates the pragmatic perspective with its other linguistic integrals. In the concrete case of the literary text, its power to definitively organize the set of features of literary or poetic expressiveness is unquestionable. We will now proceed to re-examine, from the textual perspective, the system of fundamental features of literary and poetic specificity, which we have previously alluded to. We will see that each of the features we discussed before, even those appearing least definitive, gain unusual strength and support from their reconsideration from the literary textual point of view as essential linguistic mechanisms of literary specificity, unable to be approached and explained by the considerations of standard language.

As a whole, the phono-phonological literary and poetic features perhaps seem to be the least likely to be affected by the perspective offered by their textual insertion. The limited range of their presence in the terminal chain of the text's lineal manifestation encourages this sense of their restricted condition, their short-term influence: one thinks of their intersyntactic expansion in microtextual terms. Nevertheless, the old presupposition of rhetorical hermeneutics, brought up to date by Jakobson and, in greater detail, by the analyses of Greimas and Rastier (F. Rastier, 1972, pp. 80—106), have obliged us to consider phono-phonological events of rhyme, accentuation, vocalic coloring, alliteration, etc., as strongly solidified elements in the thematic *isotopy* of the text's contents. The text is the great unit determining the broad scope and outlines of said networks. Its boundaries, its own structure, wisely establish zones of concentration and emptiness, of tension and recovery.

Phonic isotopies, closely linked to the textual dimension of the poetic and literary work, create a pattern in which we can already perceive the text's pressure in determining the organization of the artistic utterance in certain delimited and immanent terms unknown in standard communicative discourse. Poetry in every age, the prosodic organization of the text, of oratorical pieces and, in general, even the accentual distribution of phonic coloring, etc., are not generated and distributed non-hierarchically and casually, but within a perfectly calculated *tonal concert*, and executed in the text.

Without doubt, among the set of analogous phenomena at the morphosyntactic level, the literary and poetic morphological feature of greatest importance is also the most directly derived from the articulation of the textual perspective. That which I've frequently denominated the morpheme's *textual dynamization* in the domain of poetic expression, represents the correspondence on this plane of the general phenomena of textual isotopy, which I am considering here as a basic differential feature of the literary text (A. J. Greimas, 1966; F. Rastier, 1982, pp. 80—105; C. Segre, 1985, pp. 40—42). Each element of the text — on this level, each morpheme, plereme or moneme — receives in the case of the poetic message a burden of "textual responsibility", which translates in the sphere of poetic cenesthesis into a balanced situational value (M. Arrivé, 1973, pp. 53—56). In the most concrete domains of the lexicon and of semantics, textual dependence appears under very well-defined features of suitability and under characteristics of the lexical selection's special motivation. Similarly, the contextual semantic dependency is normally translated by the blurring of its automatically meaningful outlines in the general semantic system, in the case of the meaning of the poem's lexical piece.

The current of textual dynamization bears much of the responsibility for the effect, so notable in literary messages (B. Gray, 1975), of the *defamiliarization* or *de-automatization* of each morpheme as an isolated textual piece. The production of distance in the artistic text, automatically returning the text's lexical pieces or syntagmatically unitary constructions to a pristine and original state of meaning, is achieved by way of the powerful co-textual cohesion realized within the artistic utterance. The pressure exerted by a context densely solidified in the cooperative convergence of the artistic effect of the literary and poetic message paradoxically makes evident the manifestation of each singular piece's isolation and, simultaneously and compatibly, also produces the permanent and unforgettable manifestation of the text's unitary whole (A. García-Berrio, 1973, pp. 142—160).

Intimately related to these phenomena of the morphematic level are the two most obvious features of literary expression on the lexical level: the *selection* and the suitability or *decorum* of terms. Both are strongly linked with the processes of dynamization and interdependency of pieces within the textual whole.

As far as *selection* is concerned, it would not appear necessary to insist at great length on the differential importance that has been atttributed to it since the very origins of verbal artistic expression for the purposes of distinguishing said expression from the standard communicative uses of language. Lexical selection was the only consciously apparent linguistic principle classical art proclaimed as forming the basis of its autonomous efficiency compared to normal communicative expression. Logically, this process of selection acted according to the principle of the substitutability of forms within the textual utterance. It was produced by the simultaneous action of a double system of meaningful equivalencies and hierarchical-stylistic differences among said interchangeable pieces. The final element regulating this hierarchy was, again, the *text*, operating, in this case in the totality of dimensions and virtualities of its contextual and co-textual integrals.

In the first place, the hierarchical principle was founded on the most intuitive or capricious elements of the material or acoustical order. The euphony and beauty of the material components of a word or syntagm created an order of preferences, recognizable even today. Naturally, the consideration of the textual environment in which the pieces set in said hierarchy were located was a decisive factor in the decision governing the suitability of their placement in the utterance.

Euphonic considerations, though still meriting attention, were nevertheless a minimal ingredient in the general decision of the *suitability* of a piece within a text. The sanctions regarding the *decorum* of a unit of artistic discourse, based on the application of the system of hierarchies previously mentioned, involved many considerations. Together with superstitious biases with regard to the material components of the lexical piece — euphony, sentimental ictus, etc. — there were many arguments concerning suitability which here, as a reinforcement to our hypothesis, we will group into *contextually motivated causes* and *cotextually motivated causes*. By these means, the importance of the textual parameter in the consideration of the linguistic reponsibilities in defining the expressive substantiveness of literary language is well represented.

The textual reasons defining *decorum* were patterned in classes under the influence of the metaphor of social structure (A. García-Berrio, 1975, pp. 100 ff.). Transmitter, receiver and message formed a triangle of selective interdependencies which determined all of the literary text's components, especially from the lexicon onwards. At least, this was how it was explicitly set forth. Schematically, the system of pluri-dimensional relationships constituted by these elements can be set forth in the following diagram:

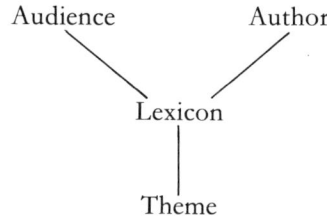

Obviously, this graph is only true for the "exegematic" mode of expression (A. García-Berrio, 1975 pp. 81 ff.), in which the subject of the enunciation and the subject of the utterance are identical. For the cases where this identity does not exist, that is, when characters appear, displacing the author as the subject of the utterance and appropriating the fiction to a voice suitable to their own nature, the previous triangular graph representing *decorum* was extended to a square scheme. In this hypothesis, the addition of the characters' diction as an interdependent factor of the decorous production is reflected in the following schematization:

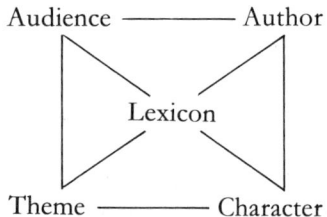

Any of the trajectories passing through the lexicon is possible. Those situated on the diagonal of the graph place the lexicon at the center of the author-theme or character-audience dialectic. The axes formed by the vertical or horizontal columns recognize lexical determination by means of the audience-author, audience-theme, character-theme, author-character dialectics and, of course, those represented by the inversion of each of these pairs.

As is well known, classical theory played on the combinations created by all of these elements in order to justify the formal stylistic features of its linguistic utterance, concretely evoked in order to legitimize decisions of lexical selection and combination. The type of audience imposed on the author, for reasons of decency or propriety, a certain theme viewed as most suitable. This in turn invoked the corresponding characters. For each, verisimilitude demanded a given type of language. Sometimes, though, the causes for legitimization were inverted, beginning first with those of linguistic decorum as determined by the kind of audience (A. García-Berrio, 1977, pp. 155 ff).

I believe all of this argumentation regarding the classical principle of *decorum* is equally applicable to modern literary expression. The social contextual parameters that provided the classical system with its reason for being

1.2. Literariness and the Text

may have changed, but the substitution of this social order by others — cultural, counter-cultural, postmodern, etc. — should not in any case be confused with its complete elimination. The consideration of such principles, in the final analysis, determines the necessarily transitive nature of artistic enunciation in the sense of *transmission-reception*, as well as defining the efficacy of the message in the sense of *representation*.

The acts of lexical determination in the literary text motivated by *co-textual causes* are centered in even more definitively textual zones. Lexical pieces are definitely components determined by the text's linguistic utterance. This fact, apparently ignored by the classical, hypertrophic conception of the lexicon, is explicitly recognized, contrary to that of the traditional order, in the modern experience of literature. But the objective fact, beyond extreme appraisals, is that the powerful influence of the lexicon is just one more element among the formal components, interacting with the rest, which make up any linguistic utterance. If the influence of all of these constituents is fundamental for the communicative efficacy of the standard language's messages, it is even more decisive for the messages of literary language, where it is necessary to add to the normal communicative effect those of, among others, aesthetic and imaginative efficiency and performance.

The co-textual conventionalisms of the genre-text, reflecting the contextual exigencies we have already examined, create a selective lexical structure, in which each piece is inserted according to how it best fits together with all of the other components of the text. In classical artistic writing, co-textual dissonance was the governing principle preventing the frustration of the artistic, literary or poetic utterance (A. García-Berrio, 1988). The same applies, in my judgment, to the case of the *intentionally* anti-classical textual constructions of modern art. These, even those based on lexical irregularities, are simply following a proportionally analogous principle of negation (A. García-Berrio and M. T. Hernández, 1988a).

Awareness of the textual plane of analysis contributes a powerful reinforcement to the definition of the linguistic specificity of literary expression, reflected almost entirely analogously on the semantic level. The previously presented evidence of the doubly antithetical dynamic which the global text introduces with regard to lexical textual units — namely, isolating and making them visible by means of processes of defamiliarization and, simultaneously, integrating them solidly into the constructions's totality through mechanisms of textual dynamization and perspective — are reproduced when considering the meanings of these same lexical pieces integrated in the global semantic representation of the text.

The meaningful result of this general tendency of the poetic text is manifested in the reinforcement of the poetic word's *polysemy* as compared to the usually monosemic values of the word in communicative-standard discourse. The same process takes place with regard to its logical correlate, the *polysemy* of the total, ideal artistic text as opposed to the univocal nature of the communicative-standard utterance.

The polysemic foundations of poetic discourse result from the calculated density of the network of intertextual and co-textual relations of each element of the message, a density unknown in the normal communicative text. The essential characteristic responsible for the pattern of poetic texts is the *pluriaxiality* of the co-textual lines of reference (M. Arrivé, 1973, pp. 53—56; J. M. Klinkenberg, 1973). Cataphoric and anaphoric intratextual deixes create a network of meanings that traverse the literary text in all directions, even occasionally fostering delay or backtracking in the reading of this type of utterance. Of course, this condition is not fulfilled in the communicative text of primarily progressive-terminal interests, where the textual-communicative dynamic does not usually recognize any possibility other than the linear progression of the message (J. S. Petöfi, 1973).

Compared to the co-textual causes of the poetic word's polysemy, the influence of contextual reasons is even greater. Thanks to special freedoms created by its intratextual location, the poetic voice acquires very dense possibilities of referential combination. This set of referential allocations, richer and far more varied than that of the standard in logico-rational and conceptual meaning, nevertheless finds its true dimension in the resonance of sentimental, transmental or irrational connotation. The combination of a certain order of referential ambiguity in poetry, produced by the superposition of a dense network of co-textual connections, makes possible the richness of the concrete allocations of meaningful value, their *polyvalency*, in the domain of the context.

Supporting the complex and dense world of contextual and co-textual relationships among its components, the textual composition offers itself as the culmination of the polyvalent condition demonstrated by the verbal work of art. From this there results a much more powerfully evocative and meaningful utterance than that which characterizes communicative discourse.

As a privileged textual element in the case of literary discourse, the *image* finds in its role at the textual level many of the characteristic features which it is usually identified with. In spite of its immediate appearance as an autonomous, endo-significative element of unexpected brilliance, the image's textual function is undeniable.

Jean Burgos' studies on the associationism of images within the utterance (J. Burgos, 1982) reinforce and amplify the ancient arguments regarding the decisive value of the text's material scheme as a constitutive setting for aesthetic meaning. The various kinds of data of isotopic correlation — phonological, grammatical or lexico-semantic — are much more decisive in the polysemic construction of the meaning of the verbal artistic text when considered in the light of metaphoric associationism. The structural aesthetico-imaginary network, which the artistic text depends on substantially for its fantastic effects, is the result, in the first place, of the constellation of meaning associated with the lexico-semantic constituents of the text, always tending toward monosemy by the recollection of their practical communicative use.

But this network is above all else the result of the inventory of images which constitute the most important source of meaning in artistic works.

The meaningful results of the text's set of images do not immediately stem from the sum of the potential valencies of each of those images, isolated in their respective inventories. They selectively and automatically restrict the plural potential of their individual valencies when they are associated in the utterance. The operations of meaningful image selection by virtue of the images' functional dynamic in the text are not physiognomically different from the equivalent phenomena on the level of lexico-semantic meaning. They do vary though, and very noticeably, in their influence in establishing the more open yield of meaning. In effect, the referential substance of the image is much more diffuse than that involved in the lexico-semantic relationships between words. The profile of meanings images offer is also by nature more fluid than in the case of words. Overall, the possibilities for the plural articulation of metaphoric and imaginary associationism in the artistic text decisively enrich its symbolic plurivalency.

When the exegetes of radical polysemy have stated their case, they have habitually counted on a type of textual constitution founded on lexical or syntagmatico-semantic units (R. Barthes, 1970, p. 12; W. Iser, 1976), without paying sufficient attention to the decisive ingredient of fluid images and their unstable associative structure. In this sense, Burgos' severe criticism of the blindness of a poetics with a vocation towards a radical polysemic openness, nevertheless restricted exclusively to the possibilities for freedom in verbal combinations, seems very reasonable to me (J. Burgos, 1982, pp. 26—27).

In short, the text as a perspective and final limit of discourse is, in the end, the area where the concrete differential peculiarities between literary language and standard communicative language are coined and defined.

1.2.2. *Text Grammar's Contribution to the Explanation of Literariness*

In view of what has previously been said, it is clear that the disciplines that have occupied themselves with defining the text's linguistic laws and in describing its structure and functional rules are in a position to make important contributions towards clarifying the notions of poeticity and literariness. This is especially evident when the text is valued, according to our proposal, as the decisive linguistic level for demonstrating the specificity of literary language, defined in contrast to standard logico-communicative language (G. Wienold, 1978a; N. E. Enkvist, 1978).

This is not the appropriate place to introduce any kind of general synthesis of the accomplishments and the development of the textual disciplines, notably of so-called textual linguistics (J. S. Petöfi, 1975; J. S. Petöfi and A. García-Berrio, 1979). This I will take for granted is well-known to my readers (W. U. Dressler, ed., 1978). I would, however, like to indicate the need to integrate, towards the ends which currently concern us, the results of all of the linguistic disciplines that have examined the text from a secular tradition.

Thus, in the first place, it is urgently necessary to incorporate the contributions of classical rhetoric to a science of the text. The proposals in this vein (T. A. van Dijk, 1972, p. 24) have so far amounted merely to programs of good intentions. Among all of the rhetorical parts, *inventio*'s domain can contribute to the explanation, in very substantial terms, both of the text's extensional semantics and of the process of selecting and articulating the discourse's topic, its subdivivision and its links to other topics in the course of textual development. The discussions of *dispositio* in classical rhetorical treatises, especially in the medieval manuals of concionatoria (H. Caplan, 1934—1936; Th. M. Charland, 1936) and in the *artes dictaminis* (Rockinger, 1863—1864), could shed incalculable light on the subject, enabling the complete description of the macrostructure as a set of macrotransformations. Finally, the rhetorical rules of *elocutio* — the least macrotextual element of rhetoric — could contribute indirectly to the enrichment of our knowledge of the text, to the extent that it is definitively organized in the segments of the microcomponent (J. Kopperschmidt, 1976; J. Plett, ed., 1977; P. Valesio, 1980, 1986; A. García-Berrio, 1983, 1984; T. Albaladejo Mayordomo, 1989).

As urgent and potentially enriching as this incorporation is the comparison of the traditional contents of rhetoric with the modern thought of general linguistics, poetic linguistics and literary criticism. The Russian formalists' attention to the traditional domains of rhetoric was centered, on the one hand, on the demonstration of the literary specificity of artistic verbal discourse and especially on textual phenomena and types — lyric poems and brief texts of artistic prose — already well described by rhetorical hermeneutics as mechanisms of the expressiveness of language in general. On the other hand, the formalists' most immediately and clearly textual attention was focused on the expressive literary genres traditionally ignored by rhetorical hermeneutics, such as those of narrative prose: story, short novel and novel. The textual scheme of the story — including features of structure, motives, perspectives, point of view, *skaz*, etc. — was the basis for the formalist definition of *procedure* through which literariness was perfectly profiled (A. García-Berrio, 1973).

The continuity of the formalist legacy in modern experience is evident, universally recognized and, to a certain extent, exploited. Still, the late date at which Russian formalism was incorporated into European neoformalist criticism has helped shape important peculiarities of this coupling. At times, these distortions have served to mask elements well developed in formalist thought (J. Striedter, 1989).

Other critical currents, especially European stylistics (B. Terracini, 1966; N. E. Enkvist, 1973) and North American New Criticism (J. C. Ransom, 1941), also made important contributions in the structural investigation of the text. Spitzer's hermeneutical "philological circle" (1974, pp. 37—41) coincided basically with the schemes of distribution of homologous organizational features along the axis of textual simultaneities looked for from the

Prague Circle to Jakobson, with the demonstration of textual isotopies in French structuralism (A. J. Greimas, 1973), and with the establishment of thematic networks and referential diagrams in text grammars (J. S. Petöfi, 1975).

On the other hand, the general awareness of the notion of literary language as a dialect or deflected language coined by European stylistics (J. M. Pozuelo Yvancos, 1988, pp. 20—24), in spite of its concrete irregularities, represents the obligatory basis from which to begin the confrontation of the singularities of literary and poetic texts. Bennison Gray demonstrates this all very well when, in dividing all of the literary poetological models into those oriented towards the phenomena of *deviation* and those oriented towards defamiliarization — a scheme Pozuelo Yvancos follows (B. Gray, 1975; J. M. Pozuelo Yvancos, 1988) — each literary or poetic styleme, or special "gesture" (J. Mukařovský, 1964) of the artistic work, continues to be what calls the attention of textual observation and reflection, which then considers and values each of them within the artistic text's universe.

Within this current of continuous and contiguous effort, the most indisputable outlines of which I have been tracing here, the most urgent path for contact, practical and fruitful, is that which can be established between the rich tradition of critico-textual reflections on the literary text offered by the so-called literary criticism of French structuralism and the considerations derived from the powerful theoretical effort of the text grammars developed recently within the Germanic cultural domain (T. Albaladejo Mayordomo, 1984).

As in the formalist tradition, European structuralism has augmented the kind of reflections dedicated to the domain of *textual dispositio* thanks to its multiplication of studies on the narrative genre, no doubt a reaction against its own deeply rooted national tradition of "explication de textes", generally aimed at brief and artificially fragmentary or episodic lyric structures (A. J. Greimas, 1966, 1973, 1976). The correlation between this tendency and the norms generalized in the text grammars is above dispute; moreover, the fruits of this contrast appear inevitable and easily predictable, although no serious comparison has been attempted to date (C. Chabrol, ed., 1973).

It is certainly true that the text grammars' predominant interest in the facts of textual *dispositio* — at least in their first urgent developments — was governed by different causes than those which characterized French structuralism. Text grammars' interest resulted from the methodological need to overcome the basic limitations evident in sentence-based grammars, generative or otherwise, by evolving descriptions and explanations of the text's linguistic and communicative reality (P. Hartmann, 1978, pp. 93—105). This explains the preferential attention paid to the macrotextual component, compared to the sparing consideration of the microtext's data, already partially addressed by sentence-based grammars and stylistic criticism, in spite of the immense limitation in both efforts stemming from the lack of a functional-textual perspective. Still, without a doubt, this coincidence, in the case of two unquestionably productive scientific methodologies, offers a very fruitful basis for collaboration (T. Albaladejo Mayordomo, 1989, pp. 115−116).

At present, the text grammars' investigation has not advanced very much in the determination of literary and poetic specificity (N. E. Enkvist, 1978, pp. 174−190). No doubt, even French critical structuralism, although not having indicated the investigation of poeticity as one of its fundamental intentions, has contributed more in this area, especially in programatically fixing and demonstrating the statute of narrative *procedure*, which for this genre of texts is linked to its ultimate literary condition (C. Chabrol, ed., 1973, R. Barthes, *et al.*, 1966). But it is no less certain that, in terms of advances in the real understanding of the text as a linguistic event and especially the formalization of its structures, the text grammars developed in Germany have profitably formulated the critical intuitions of the French school (J. S. Petöfi and A. García-Berrio, 1979; W. Dressler, ed., 1978).

It does not seem necessary for me to exhaustively list all of the possible approaches of the French and German critics working in this area, in line with my previous discussion of the rhetorical tradition, Russian formalism and the trends of North American and European stylistics, all of which form the fundamental baggage of French neoformalist structuralism. I will limit myself to describing some of the most important and obvious points of contrast and mutual enrichment.

In the first place, we must indicate the transcendence achieved by A. J. Greimas' initiatives in providing a very broad basis for the comprehension of the text on its various levels — especially because he has afforded us the basic instruments for contemplating isomorphism — through the predicative logical model and its actantial inventories (A. J. Greimas, 1966, 1973). For their part, the text grammars have generalized and radicalized, to an overall congruence unknown in French criticism, even that most directly influenced by Greimas, this system of predicative formalization (E. Gülich and W. Raible, 1977). Nevertheless, it seems that with Greimas and his school the trend towards the linguistico-theoretical enrichment of French structuralism ends insofar as the highly formalized text grammars are concerned.

Recalling the most outstanding lines of argument traced by Janos S. Petöfi (J. S. Petöfi and A. García-Berrio, 1979), one of the last of these models, and projecting them onto the traditional achievements of French textual criticism, we may contemplate the literary and poetic text far more clearly. In the first place, we acquire a sharper picture of its general condition as text, thanks to the very detailed explicitness of Petöfi's system of conceptualization and formalization (J. S. Petöfi and H. Rieser, eds., 1973). In the second place, precisely to the extent that said generally explicit clarity and detail mark out with greater accuracy the specific domains of the literary trait (J. S. Petöfi, 1973, pp. 205−275; 1975, 1987), the text's special literary or poetic rules are illuminated. Above all, Petöfi's contribution is important because these characteristics, in the traditional prejudiced conception of their ineffability, were portrayed as mechanisms of *ambiguity*. The clarification and formalization of the text proposed by the textually-based formal grammars, Petöfi's work among them, constitute the most useful system, in many cases, for stripping away the notions of ambiguity which have encumbered the critical interpretation of artistic features (T. Albaladejo Mayordomo, 1979, p. 272).

Even at first sight we can see the importance for the clarification of the critical-literary process contributed by the basic, general distinction of *rules of formation and rules of transformation* on the textual plane, a classification adapted from generative grammar. The literary distinction between *historical res* and *fabula* — each with its own specific *ordo naturalis* and *poeticus* and each with its own measure of coherence, namely, that of truth and verisimilitude — makes up this category of classical poetics with its equivalencies in Russian formalism and narratology (A. García-Berrio, 1979 a, pp. 33—35; W. O. Hendricks, 1973), and very plausibly connects with the conception of the genesis and definitive verbal structure of the work as an aggregate of the two sets of different rules (T. Albaladejo Mayordomo, 1989, p. 115).

The composition of the poetic *fabula* (plot), is clearly established at the level of optative textual transformations. The artist's decisions about the text he creates are not exercised solely — as a certain reductionist rhetoric might suggest — in the domain of phrasal optative transformations. The artist obviously has options available to him for the structuring of his text (U. Eco, 1979). In their origin, many of these possibilities would be offered to him by a code of aesthetic behavior, individual or transindividual-cultural, with the result that these decisions determine the *artistic* nature of the linguistic text. Recall how the set of motivations Tomashevsky (1965, pp. 270 ff.) considered artistic basically coincide with this kind of optative transformation (which we can also term artistic) in the domain of the macrotextual structure of literary discourse. In another sense, the majority of the stylemes examined by stylistic hermeneutics would be, comparably, cases of optative artistic transformations of a more microtextual nature.

We can perhaps shed some light on the problem in another way, namely, through a broad duality, to some extent approaching the previously stated method, but more genuinely linguistico-textual in its formulation. I am referring here to Petöfi's excision (1973) in the *textual basis* between a *semantic representation of the text* (Text Se Re) and a *block of information* (Text Ω). In my judgment, this set of components more directly represents the structure of the traditional rhetorical system, according to the following possibilities of distribution:

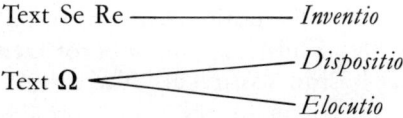

This much is certain, at least if we understand the rhetorical divisions as operative thresholds for the text's realization. Notwithstanding this clarification, the problem of the proper distinctions could once again arise in the form of the obligatory dependencies between *inventio-dispositio* and *inventio-elocutio*. For example, in certain lexical operations arranged by the block of information, but determined from the semantic textual representation, and even between the structurally obligatory nature of certain character's "roles", theoretically the domain of *dispositio*, which are, however, selected in thematic terms — such as parricide or adultery — corresponding to the domain of *inventio*.

We see, then, that what literary theory has been dragging along since its origins is an error of schematization, consisting in the confusion of the terms *operation* and *theoretical structural component*. The categories of text production in traditional rhetoric, along with the organization of semantic and syntactic elements in the first models of formal grammars, have been conceived exclusively as structural components and never as true operations. From this followed the secular isolationist-successive conception of thought and language. The scars this theoretical prejudice has left on linguistic and literary theory are still patently obvious (A. García-Berrio, 1979 b, pp. 35—37).

However, I do not believe the diffusion of this linguistic simplification is attributable only to the discipline of rhetoric. What has in fact happened is that rhetoric itself has been impoverished and simplified by the philosophical conception of language. In this way, the horizontalism of the schematization of the three structural components has been made possible, positively disregarding the creative categories offered by rhetoric itself, which as a result crystalize in the principle of *decorum*. Decorum dynamizes the horizontal isolation in a parallel manner, activating a vertical axis. It indicates the dependencies and decisions created by *inventio* through theme in the domain of *dispositio*, in its textual semantic, syntactic and pragmatic forms, together with its influence in decisions of *elocutio*. That is to say, it proclaims the instability of textual boundaries between semantics, syntax, lexicon and phonology, when one wishes to consider them, in practice, as successive and closed spaces in the text's production (A. García-Berrio, 1977, pp. 155—162).

In summary, a productive approach for pinpointing the literary or poetic specificity of the artistic text may be achieved from the adequate combination of a set of rhetorical, linguistico-sentential (both generative and structural) and linguistico-textual categories. All of which is feasible because we can count on text linguistic's more definitive image of the literary and poetic object as, above all, a *textual* object.

In these terms, literary reality is presented to us as the product of a *double system of options*, cultural and linguistic. By means of the first, accomplished at the level of *inventio*, the thematic specification of literariness is produced, of determining value at least in classical art. The concrete mechanism of this type of specification can be, in its own turn, prolonged by means of a collection of optative transformations, culturally known as artistic, operating from the *historical res* according to easily conjectured rules of elimination, addition and combination. The obligatory condition of the successive textual transformations — semantic, syntactic and syntactico-semantic — when dealing with transformations also common to linguistic discourse in general, can precipitate again the equivocal image of the literary and poetic text as a discourse of rigorously linguistic dependencies, obscuring the distinctiveness of the same compared to the system of standard language. Nevertheless, we should not forget that, at its root, in terms of the theme within the level of *inventio*, the action of a selective system of optative artistic transformations has already been produced (J. S. Petöfi and A. García-Berrio, 1979).

The second system of options, acting as a set of optative textual transformations, is introduced at different decisive moments in the text's structure. These transformations, where the artistic choice or option is operative, *select* concrete types in the textual nodes of optative transformation. The problem here is to avoid returning to posing the question of the exclusively linguistic or non-linguistic condition of these literary and poetic transformations with respect to the inventories of standard language. What interests us is the explicit reduction of the zone of optative artistic transformations, as sets of semantic representations of the text and as blocks of information of the text, establishing in this way a double space, in which the linguistic singularity of the material scheme of the literary and poetic text becomes evident.

Recalling the basic error previously indicated concerning the comprehension and representation of the text in the parcelled rhetorical consideration of the three domains — *inventio*, *dispositio*, and *elocutio* —, I think it necessary to emphasize here the attention to the forms of textual creation as a process of synthesis. The hypothesis of French structuralism, expecially the narratological models of Greimas, Todorov, and Kristeva (A. J. Greimas, 1973; T. Todorov, 1969), broke with the analytical perspective of the text imposed by the hermeneutical tradition of rhetoric and stylistics.

The consideration of the text predominantly in terms of being a *product of synthesis*, implanted from these perspectives, apart from its novelty, presupposes a restitution of *reality* to the linguistic description of human discourse as a result, not only of reception analysis, but also of its complementary and previous stage of production and synthesis. This tendency is seen equally in the previously mentioned examples from French narratology, in the generative-textual model of van Dijk (1976), and as an explicit and conscious basis in the algorithm of textual synthesis, present from the very basic exposition of its model in Petöfi (1973).

Strongly influenced in this by predominantly creative habits, imposed since North American and Russian generativism, the neoformalist cultivators of European narratology and generative-based textual linguistics have shifted their attention and priorities to the generative domains of the text, those closest to the development of the narrative nucleus as a topic of discourse, and in general, to the macrotextual sector. Along this route, the critical activity of some narratologists has come to justify itself, with their predominant attention turned to *discourse* as opposed to *story* or, better still, to the problems of the synthesis of the two (W. O. Hendricks, 1973).

Beyond its possible excesses, the linguistic opportunity present in the synthetic tendency appears unquestionable to me. At least within literary criticism, it is invaluable for selecting features of literariness and poeticity. In this way, the identification and explanation of the mechanisms of literary poetic *creation* is made possible, this being an area generally mystified in the critical tradition, which alluded only vaguely to it, ascribing all kinds of responsibility to it for the final aesthetic reality of the artistic work, but not studying it in the multiplicity of its components or of the linguistic and non-linguistic operations it included. The definitive proposal of a functional-actantial formulation of the topic of discourse, made by Greimas and extended under Todorov's grammatical metaphor (A. J. Greimas, 1966; T. Todorov, 1969), Julia Kristeva's succinct description of the geno-text's medullary zones (1969, p. 280) or van Dijk's description of the process transforming the textual topic to a linear manifestation through a macro-microtextual continuum (1972, pp. 92 ff.), are only a few of the explanatory models that originate from the same principle of critico-linguistic *methodological inversion*, in which attention is shifted from an invariably analytical perspective to a synthetico-productive one.

The consequence of this tendency is decisive in the definition of the literariness and poeticity of poetic texts. Minutely examined in its processes, clarified as a complex set of causes, and explicitly and coherently formalized, the vague traditional notion of the process of artistic creation, literary or poetic, has shed many of the veils which made it appear as a creative act of uncertain and imprecise intentions. Under the new synthetic methodological vision, literary creation is described as a conveniently organized linguistic process, in which it is possible already to establish the boundaries between the impulses of sentimental, aesthetic and connotative motivation and the normal linguistic processes of standard expression. Also, at this point, the collaboration between the different methodological tendencies which we have been placing in contact suggests the necessity of establishing an effort of synthetic conciliation. In such a synthesis, the linguistic-textual methodologies lend the clarity of their formalizing capacities to the properly analytical-literary habits of description.

1.2.3. The Textual Typology of Classical Lyrical Poetry and the Characterization of Literariness

The most noteworthy and decisive element among the literary context's components, in addition to being the most influential in the historical-literary evolution of classical art, is the context properly created by the literary *tradition* itself. My own understanding of this context is explicitly represented in *typological schemes*. In this sense, I have been examining a highly topicalized genre of texts, the amorous sonnets of the European Renaissance, on the basis of their integration in corresponding typologies (A. García-Berrio, 1984 c). Considering the metrical identity of the text, the sonnet, is given by definition, the textual varieties appear organized according to a double syntactic and semantic typological scheme (A. García-Berrio, 1978, 1978 a, 1979 c, 1979 d, 1980, 1980 a, 1980 b, 1981 b, 1983 a, 1983 b, 1983 c, 1985 a, 1985 b).

In its semantico-thematic macrotextual aspect, the general typology of the sonnet includes all of its typological-thematic varieties, such as amorous, moral, commemorative, funerary, etc. (A. García-Berrio, 1984 b). Each of these varieties is configured as a collection of sets which fulfill the syntactico-semantic requirements of a common definition, or *initial formula*, from which typological variants begin to unfold. For example, in the case of the amorous sonnet, the modes are determined by the nature of the predication, beginning before this with regard to the premises of the textual behavior of the actant-object, *lady*, towards the subject (correspondence/noncorrespondence), which give rise to the differentiation between *song* and *suffering* (negative predication without actant-object).

Each one of these types, at a new level, is further subdivided following the specification of object actants and confidant. In turn, each of these branches, resulting in a new level, appear divided in two by the modality — real or not — of the predication. Finally, at another still lower level, properly semantico-thematic branchings are established, both central and marginal. Thus, the typology of contents is conceived as a progressive disposition, in which the initial formula at the first level is branched out until it reaches a terminal state, a goal, where each of the different sonnets appears censused, except for the theoretical cases of complete plagiarisms or versions which entirely coincide. From the combination of the thematic definition of each sonnet-text, obtained in accordance with the previous categories, and its structural-dispositive definition, we have the characteristic macrotextual typology of the sonnet. Beginning with this characteristic macrotextual typology, we are then able to establish analytical microtextual extensions, of the kind found in traditional stylistic analyses.

Having sketched out the organization and basic workings of the typology I have developed, I will outline the items pertinent to our present concern: that is, the degree to which the typological-linguistic characterization contributes to illustrate the literary and poetic specificity of artistic texts, compared to other products considered normal in standard language (see also Section 2.3.2).

As I have indicated elsewhere in this book, the pragmatic initiative in which the text's literariness consists of its degree of conventional adherence to a set of characteristics vaguely denominated as "cultural" has recently been making itself felt. This pragmatic effort does not attempt to make a positive contribution to the definition of literariness, as much as it seeks to negate the concept entirely. I have already argued the fallacy hidden behind the label of "consensually cultural characteristics". The intention here is to strip these distinctive features of their nature as linguistic facts, since, even when all of the truly differential features are reduced to those derived only from the pragmatic perspective, as a singular kind of expressive act — which also seems unacceptable —, this pragmatic approach will not have demonstrated the non-linguistic nature of specificity. On the contrary, it will have shown specificity's linguistic nature.

What the typologies clarify about this problem is the precise and explicit terms of the "cultural accord". If, like every social agreement, the consensus on the artistic nature of the literary text was originally arbitrary, it is undeniably justified from a historical point of view. The basis of the linguistic cultural decision regarding literariness is what is explicitly manifested in the typological scheme. Within these bounds, everything culturally and linguistically conventionalized as literature is included; whatever is not admitted remains outside the limits of the scheme. Thus, in the case of our example, sonnets considered in the Europe of the Romance countries as amorous lyrical poetry during the sixteenth and seventeenth centuries are those which meet the conditions of the initial formula and its subsequent developments as hierarchicalized in the typological scheme. In this sense, a linguistic discourse that does not correspond to precise isosyllabic and tonal schemes, grouped in relatively fixed combinations, is not versified poetry. It is not lyrical poetry if its mode of exposition is not "exegematic". Any discursive combination, poetic or otherwise, is not a sonnet if it does not have a set number of lines (fourteen), each with eleven syllables, grouped into two quartets and two triplets. It is not amorous, if the subject of the enunciation is not the agent of the utterance *to love* and even, within this last feature, if a large number of other conditions are not met, such as that the poet loves one single lady, that he does not explicitly consider any type of carnal love but rather a platonic devotion, etc.

It is clear that the typology does not explain, nor does it pretend to, the historical, social, psychological or other causes for the constitution of these conventions (A. García-Berrio, 1985a, 1985b), but rather only describes the framework and the concrete content of the referred-to accord. In this sense, the typology syntactically, semantically and pragmatically establishes the framework for a text's literary condition.

This typological description and resolution of literariness is exercised in a double sense: in that of the text as a genre and also in that of the individual text. In the first case, the directive nature of the description is established in terms of the systems's *completeness* or *restriction* and, hence, of the *value* of the same. In the second case, the determining characteristic consists in the degree of *originality* or degree of *topicality*, and also is resolved in the resulting *value*.

1.2. Literariness and the Text

Considering the typological set as a closed system or as a linguistico-cultural text, its exhaustive nature is measured in terms of its selection from reality. Syntactically, the received habits and the prestige of traditional models insured that the text could be organized only as a very limited combination of argumentative structures from among all of those linguistically possible. Following Helmslev's model, the genre-text in its structural-syntactic aspects constitutes a concrete and demarcated *form* within the total expressive-syntactic *substance*, which includes all of the real and possible textual-literary structures.

In its semantico-thematic concreteness, the limited condition of the text-genre "courtly-amorous sonnet" is always constructed as a conventional restriction of reality or, to put it in another way, as a thematic "possible world", in a dialectic excluding all the other possible worlds, the real world included among them. For example, the characteristics of amorous univocality, platonic love, the generally non-explicit nature of the lady's correspondence, the limitation and conventionalization of the real and metaphoric class of confidants, etc., that we have indicated in the text-genre of the amorous sonnet, evidently involve a pattern drastically restricting the normal and real possibilities of love, which would also include infidelity, the lady being in love and not the gentleman, possible confidants of a different nature, the physical consummation of the amorous relationship, etc.

The result of contrasting the world textualized in the text-genre with other thematic organizations of the same (T. Albaladejo Mayordomo, 1986), as, for example, those which may be considered as real, dreamt, historical-contemporary, historical-present, etc., determines the genre-text's *value*. According to this value, it is possible to discuss, taking the historical perspective of our present example as a starting point, what it is which seeks to establish the degree of sexual inhibition exhibited in the text-genre of the amorous sonnet and its possible social causes, such as the role of the patron-client relationship between the troubador and the lady's gentleman and husband in the historical genesis of this kind of poetry, etc. (A. García-Berrio, 1985a). In this sense, it seems to me it is useful to elaborate truly meaningful — if not exhaustive — typologies before proceeding to risky theoretical generalizations, like those which stylistics has sometimes constructed on the formal plane and, on the thematic plane, those proposed by sociological or psychological criticism. These theories often, in terms of the value of the textual basis they operate on, have not first established its effective and symptomatic adequacy, with the result that they sometimes make abusive generalizations based on an insignificant feature of the text-genre.

Historically, the scientific-literary disciplines have, in practice, restricted themselves almost entirely to identifying artistic value with degree of *originality* or *topicality*. At least at first sight, one would think that this has been done from the perspective of the general and current system of values. However, art, and especially literary art, offers one notable exception here. In the first place, for that classical art most immediately influenced by Greco-Latin characteristics, the situation needs to be seen as entirely the reverse of the currently prevailing one (F. Lázaro Carreter, 1981, pp. 193—224). Only with the generalization of the social and aesthetic conception which we may call "modern" does the consciousness of positively evaluating absolute originality emerge, even exaggerated in recent times to the pretension of the permanent and revolutionary renovation of each and every artist. In antiquity, it is well known that the opposite consciousness prevailed; that is, true merit was compatible with the imposed *retractatio*, which came to consist in the exhaustive artistic re-elaboration of relatively fixed and well known themes and models (A. García-Berrio, 1981; H. Bloom, 1973, 1975, 1978).

In any case, we have until now spoken of originality or *retractatio* in very relative terms. Originality, of course, has always been a necessary prerequisite of value. Hence, it seems that the modern concept of novelty needs to be substituted, in the case of classical art, with the more general notion of the effect of *marvelous surprise*, the enrichment of intellectual, sentimental and aesthetic experience in the transmitter-receiver interchange. On this point, the typological illustration becomes decisive for making this intuition more explicit. In general terms, we could explain this intuition by saying that the inventory of semantic and pragmatic macrotextual features, censused in the typology, constitutes the *frame* of originality, in the double sense of the word frame understood as limit and *capacitas*. That is to say, in terms of *capacity*, the typology represents all of the features of the typologized subsystem as an inventory of frequency and as a surface plan of the distribution of solutions. On the basis of which, it is possible for us, at every moment and with each concrete example, to functionally define the feature quantitatively and qualitatively, measuring it against the set or subset it forms a part of. Two matters are involved in the notion that the typology constitutes a limit defining originality. The most obvious is that, thanks to the typology, conceived of as a result, we know the system's delimitative-performative capacity is explained in terms of a principle of exclusion.

At the same time, the typology is also a limit in the sense of its dynamic nature. The historical-evolutionary consideration of the phenomena the typology exercises its control over permits us to maintain as a parameter, at every moment, the element of novelty introduced to and assumed by the system, within a coherent definition of its very essence.

Thus, thanks to this theoretical-typological control of reality's data, the diachronic perspective of the literary system can be defined in terms very similar to the diachronic version of other systematic inventories of complex sets, like that of phonology. The *degree of originality* is thus also measured in this way with regard to whether the innovation presupposes a change of system, by affecting the postulates of the set of formulas constituting said typologized system, as in the case of the previously discussed examples. If the innovation does not presuppose a change of system, an adequate ranking or gradation would have to be established, which as a rule would be accomodated to the hierarchical sanction, indicated according to the degree of proximity of the relevant feature to the initial formula. Thus, innovation as an attempted exception to the consolidated rule could affect, to a greater or lesser degree, the system's structure without altering the initial formula. As examples of a descending hierarchy of such innovations relating to our semantic typology of the amorous sonnet we might find the following (A. García-Berrio, 1978 a): the modification of a predicate, of an actant, of a thematic feature centrally positioned within its text, or of a variant within a feature (an unusual metaphor with a metaphoric type, like Phaethon within the mythological type), also considered in terms of its central or marginal position, etc.

The consideration of the hierarchy I have just established and of the problem of originality as a whole obliges us to pursue this question in light of the textual constitution of discourse, which underlies the establishment of typologies. In our case, the conception of the text, which is that commonly held within the currently used textual grammars, corresponds to a macro and microcomponential complex, functioning in both domains upon the pragmatic, thematico-semantic and formal-syntactic planes.

Textual typology, as it has been set forth here, exclusively considers the domain of the macrocomponent. Microcomponential decisions cannot be typologized, or at least not with results differing from those offered by the syntactic and semantic typologies common in the sentential grammars of different languages, an area outside our sphere of investigation. Nevertheless, it is obvious that the textual value of the microcomponent cannot be discounted in any sense. I am not unaware of its final performative function with respect to the text at the general grammatical level, nor do I minimize its decisive nature, as we shall see, in the concrete problem of the artistic text's literariness or poeticity.

The macrotextual typology itself demonstrates that, in most cases, decisions of poetic originality and value preferentially depend on microcomponential features, at least in the domain of the classical lyric. The great artistic-expressive revolutions, putting new syntactico-semantic and pragmatic macrocomponential textual structures into circulation, are very rare and, culturally, are not assigned decisive values of poeticity. For example, we know that not even Dante and Petrarch are the inventors, in a strict sense, of the metrical and grammatical macrostructures constituting the lyric in the Romance languages, which they nevertheless powerfully propelled. Their predecessors, who invented macroforms like the "ballad" and the "sonnet", appear silenced or relatively minimized in the domain of literary history. And if we say this about the formal plane of rhythmical syntax, we could perhaps claim no less in the more independent and mobile plane of thematico-semantic structures. Generally, we speak of the tradition of the Petrarchist lyric, but a merely superficial analysis would suffice to show that in its rhythmic and pragmatic syntactico-semantic macrostructures, this lyrical type is a label suitable to refer to poetic success, but inaccurate, in the strictest terms, for denoting invention.

All of these phenomena are being explained in an approximately identical manner by the historians of literature, both by those applying mechanical socio-historical schemes, and those seeking explanations internal to the literary series itself, generally called "formalists". The former affirm the power of "conditions" as a way of disparaging the individualist exaplanatory power of "genius" in the development of literary production. The latter, especially through the examination of sources — and, recently, not only thematic sources, but especially thematico-formal ones — conceive literary evolution in terms of changes-in the systems of forms (A. García-Berrio, 1973, pp. 288—312). They therefore are able to exhume the topical infrastructure of every historical product, describing the basis for any novelty regularized as a topical transformation. As we have pointed out, both ways of understanding cultural tradition and creation, antithetical on the surface, confirm the principle on which my typological work is founded: the double condition, topical and recurrent in history, of cultural products, requiring us to act with prudence in formulating decisions about originality, novelty and value in cultural history (A. García-Berrio, 1979 b).

In terms of textual composition and typological understanding, the culturally novel feature is revealed by its historical survival in macrotextual typological systems. For example, the literary series of "courtly love", in its Petrarchist conventionalized expression, prolonged its validity in Europe for centuries. The textual-typological definition of such a socio-historical attestation is the stability and perseverance, unaltered at all levels, of a macrostructural poematic type. Precisely the participation of such an immutable macrostructure determined for contemporaries the *literariness* of textual predicates seeking to incorporate themselves to it. Literariness, in terms of the classical conception of art, was thus defined by *adherence* to a precise topical inventory, the powerful restrictions of which are emphasized in our typologies. Inversely, for the modern artistic consciousness, the *anxiety* of artistic merit is established by the degree of each text's *exclusion*, preferably in terms of its macrotext, with respect to the space conventionalized by typologies of preceding macrotextual solutions (H. Bloom, 1973).

What is happening is that the modern conception of art — at least at the level of aspirations — imposes a non-existent association on classical consciousness between literariness and poeticity, understood as synonyms of value, on the one hand, and macrotextual originality, on the other. The characterization of a text's literariness did not figure in the classical mind as a value in and of itself. The respect for the topical convention constituted a prerequisite condition, a simple mode of adherence, a code perfectly defined in terms of macrostructures. Originality, which in each case only required the definition of its *exclusion* in microtextual terms (A. García-Berrio, 1977,

I, pp. 146—149), was not synonymous with value in the classical axiology. All of this leads me to believe, on the basis of the evidence provided by the typologies, that the effectiveness of the ideal of *retractatio* in post-classical artistic textual creation has been very prolonged, perhaps to the same extent that within modern art itself the inversion of said effort at adherence, which constituted the base of *retractatio*, has been unable to emerge in open systems of violation, truly independent of the classical textual counter-model.

1.2.4. Literariness and Poeticity: The Insufficiency of the Linguistic Distinction

In the preceding paragraphs the great differences revealed in the literariness-poeticity pair have made themselves felt in light of the examination of the artistic text's linguistic features. This fact no doubt imposes a new perspective on the development of this chapter, which until now has implicitly presented as an undifferentiated set the aggregate formed by literariness and poeticity in order to compare it, in its artistic intentions and results, to the standard and objective use of language, or of more practical and rational verbal communication. Nevertheless, it is now time to discuss in a more detailed way the differences existing between the two terms of the set, *literariness* and *poeticity*, habitually considered as constituting the artistic use of language.

The problem, however, is further exacerbated by the fact that recent critical tradition has regularly neglected the distinction itself and the fitting and discriminating use of the terms *literariness* and *poeticity*. For the majority of recent critics, in contrast to what may have been the case in the past for the cultivators of idealism such as Croce (1907, Ch. XVII), literariness and poeticity are designations, if not perfectly synonymous in the conscious domain of culture, then at least synonymous in practice and usage (J. Mukařovský, 1964; J. Kristeva, 1969, p. 247; M. J. Lefebve, 1971, pp. 26—27; G. Leech, 1970; S. R. Levin, 1971, p. 189. See the summary in V. M. de Aguiar e Silva, 1967 [1984, pp. 150—151]). Literariness, even more than poeticity, has come to be the unique, marked term in the opposition to a usage of language not conventionalizably artistic. Every other distinction has been considered inoperative, resulting in a dangerous predicament in which there is a total lack of categories.

Not many years ago, Paul de Man detected, in very rough terms, the need to make the appropriate distinctions within this problematic state of confusion, precisely to the extent that it is necessary to clearly differentiate in deconstructive criticism between the literary, grammatical and exoreferential factors of language that are insufficient or falsified within deconstructive ideology, and those more strictly poetic, rhetorical or sacredly endoreferential elements in the great Yale critic's unique conception of the matter: "Literariness, however, is often misunderstood in a way that has provoked much of the confusion which dominates today's polemics. It is frequently assumed, for instance, that literariness is another word for, or another mode of, aesthetic response. The use, in conjunction with literariness, of such terms as style and stylistics, form or even 'poetry' (as in 'the poetry of grammar'), all of which carry strong aesthetic connotations, help to foster this confusion, even among those who first put the term in circulation" (P. de Man, 1986, p. 9). The exaggerated assimilation of literariness and poeticity denounced by de Man corresponds precisely to the distinction I am proposing between literariness as a feasible pragmatic option (affected by deconstructive analytics in the terms in which it is conceived by de Man) and poeticity as an aesthetic value, the powers of imaginary, sentimental and aesthetic allusiveness of which escape predictable logical circuits, thereby rendering it undeconstructible.

Nevertheless, in de Man's own usage, one may observe many instances in which this distinction is neglected, abandoned through the failure to consistently make use of it, as in the following symptomatic example: "And this is the point at which literariness, the use of language that foregrounds the rhetorical over the grammatical and the logical function, intervenes as a decisive but unsettling element which, in a variety of modes and aspects, disrupts the inner balance of the model and, consequently, its outward extension to the nonverbal world as well" (1986, p. 14). In this case, the concepts of grammatical optionality and aesthetic unforeseeableness appear clearly distinguished by way of the implication that the predictability of the former is deconstructible while the destabilization characteristic of the latter is undeconstructible; however, "literariness" is applied in its customarily imprecise sense to designate what ought to be attributed to the poetically absolute, beyond the reach of deconstructive differentiation in de Man's particular understanding of the notion.

The causes behind this diacritical neglect derive, to a large extent, from the propaedeutic and immanentist nature of the majority of the basic questions poetic linguistics has recently posed for itself, under the weight of its rigorous epistemological requirements of scientific explicitness, in contrast to the more transcendent and intuitive usage of past critical practice. This situation explains, for example, the complete absence of this type of questioning within the scientific current of what is called "pragmatics". In other cases, it is simply a further consequence of the general lack of focus the critical disciplines are suffering from as far as the nature of their objects of study is concerned. The interest in narrative texts, praised in recent poetics for reasons of objective necessity and the convenience of its modes (A. García-Berrio, 1977; 1978a, p. 22), has been especially responsible for the displacement of the questions dealing directly with poeticity to a secondary level of consideration. In any case, displacement of the *ad hoc* notion of fictionality as the structure encompassing literariness is symptomatically observed (S. J. Schmidt, 1976, 1980, 1984; C. Segre, 1985, pp. 214–233, Ch. II).

Nevertheless, considering the literary event in its broadest scope, it is beyond doubt that the notion of *poeticity* is necessary and cannot be assimilated to that of *literariness*. Clearly, Manzoni's *The Betrothed* or Tolstoy's *War and*

Peace are literary objects, seldom referred to as strictly poetic, while Baudelaire's *Flowers of Evil* or Lorca's *Poet in New York* are poetic books incarnated within a much broader and more varied set of literary products. This is a popular and conventional distinction, posing little risk, which criticism ought not to divorce itself from, in spite of the fact it involves a basic fallacy, which must be pointed out from the start. The positive and excessive stress of Croce's adherence (1969) to Vico's protolinguistic hypotheses (P. Verene, 1981) does not deprive his restricted sense of the poetic within the creative linguistic universe of either its importance or its utility.

Hence, *literariness* and *poeticity* are never synonymous terms, nor are they alternating qualifiers applicable to one and the same feature of language. In principle, both are different characteristics of certain artistic texts, opposed to the norm of standard communicative language by means of a set of features incompatible with said norm. These characteristics are commonly defined by the *aesthetic function* (S. J. Schmidt, 1972), which can prudently be established without greater abuse from the strictly linguistic perspective by virtue of the exceptions it supports and encourages compared to the fundamental principle of standard language, which consists in the *verbal economy of communication*, in the predominantly *representative-conceptual condition* and the *practice* (L. Bloomfield, 1933) of the same, and in its predominantly *denotative* mode.

But *literariness* and *poeticity*, in turn, are notions representing very different degrees of the same linguistic tendency opposing them to standard language. In order to establish the distinction between them it is not enough to cite observations like the well-known ones of Jakobson (1960, pp. 350–379), Levin (1962), and Lotman (1970), which I have already repeatedly referred to, all based on the signifier's non-neutrality. Actually, such characteristics dispense with the problem of distinguishing between literature and poetry by referring more to the linguistic block which includes both and to its general differentiation from the communicative-verbal standard. It is no coincidence Jakobson began speaking, in 1921, of the *aesthetic function*. Its evolution afterwards to the more widely disseminated and polemical denomination of *poetic function* (A. M. Pelletier, 1977; V. M. de Aguiar e Silva, 1967 [1984, pp. 57–74]; E. Flahault, 1978, pp. 31 ff.) was attributed to the good fortune and expansion, in many cases abusive and improper, of the term poetics used in referring to linguistic poetics. But, to the extent that it involves a doctrinally irresponsible evolution (F. Lázaro Carreter, 1975), it was not motivated by the intention of differentiating between poeticity and literariness within the general aesthetic function (J. A. Martínez García, 1975, pp. 131–140; M. A. Garrido Gallardo, 1978). More adequately, Lotman has returned to Jakobson's initial incisiveness by speaking of the characteristics of the *artistic text*; in his most fundamental book, he predominantly refers to verbal poetic usage, but also frequently to literary usage (D. W. Fokkema, 1976; W. Rewar, 1976; A. Shukman, 1977, 1978).

If the lack of terminological distinction between literariness and poeticity is so widespread or, what amounts to the same thing, the irresponsible permutability of the two terms is so general, it should not surprise us to find a relative frugality — not to mention absence — of recent attempts in literary science tending towards establishing criteria for distinguishing between the two terms. Still, explaining the difference is very convenient for achieving a better and more complete understanding in the critical disciplines, although the task is predictably going to be complicated. Keep in mind that the purely linguistic distinction between verbal texts in representative function and texts in artistic or aesthetic function, which has already been depleted in innumerable exercises, is still a long way from constituting a category of truth deferred to without reservations, in spite of my own belief in its reality. The distinction suffers from the same general mistrust, as a result of its drastic schematism, common to all of Jakobson's theories concerning the functions (M. Shapiro, 1976, p. 82). Consequently, the internal distinction between texts with artistic functions, literary and poetic, has not been explored in very much depth and is almost unknown critically.

The difference between the text's material scheme and poetry's fantastic effect, which I have already repeatedly linked as a principle for distinguishing literariness from poeticity, does not imply that the former is absolutely neutral and indifferent with regard to the latter. If, as a way of countering certain kinds of philological, formalist and aesthetic analyses, it is possible to say that poeticity does not consist of a "mere question of words", it is also possible, on the other hand, to assert that it begins with words. Literary analysis of poetry should above all trace those registers associated with effects of poeticity. Nevertheless, those verbal structures that are poetically effective in a given text are extremely uncertain; they turn out to be poetic in one context and not in another. The best proof against those of the opinion that the aesthetic and poetic effect is to be located in formulas of pure cultural consensus is this changing and uncertain condition from one text to another of the poetic capacity of verbal structures. The poetic suggestion of verbal constructions with effects privileged in a particular author, take Cervantes as an example, is never again present in the work of those who reiterate them.

On the contrary, the poeticity emanating from a verbal formula in the stylistic context of a given author certainly is totally amortized with that single expressive achievement. Undoubtedly, the elegant efficacy of the topical rhetorical questions in Manrique's *Coplas* is so strictly identified in Spanish with the concrete context of that work that its capacity for pathos, personalized in Manrique, becomes opaque and not viable for any other subsequent author. Hence, we see that, in practice, the pragmatic cultural hypotheses of poeticity as a generic convention must be substituted by a principle of the general success of the individual and non-repeatable text as an expressive structure.

The enormous constitutive complexity of the text is by definition unconventionalizable. The poetic work is unforeseeable and cannot be repeated. The verbal structure it achieves, once it has revealed its aesthetico-communicative structure in the unique act of its original formulation, becomes — at this point, certainly — culturally stereotyped as a literary scheme at the disposition of subsequent cultural options. Stylistic Cervantism or Quevedism, for example, are historico-literary phenomena, by their very nature impeded from attaining, in the style of their imitators, the surprise of poetic value.

A great distance exists between the concrete, unrepeatable poetic text and the literary paradigm, conventionalizable and open to individual poetic achievement, guaranteeing the unpredictable liberty of the aesthetic act. We can say in these cases that what we denominate as the conventionalizably literary, open to the poetic, is concretized in structural paradigms as vast as classical Asianism or Renaissance Ciceronianism, within the breadth of which the achievements of Boccaccio's *periodare* or Cervantes' *cursus* can easily fit. Only conventional structures as broad as these, frameworks that remote from the poetic achievement in the singular text, are acceptable within the genre of literary conventions that safeguard and guarantee the unpredictable unrepeatbility of the expressive literary achievement, capable of successfully establishing the imaginary poetic construction.

The aesthetic effect of poeticity takes shape through a privileged verbal structure, which by definition cannot be reduced to any prior conventional foresight. Beyond the innocuous verbal appearances of the poetic effect's limitedly directive expression, it is in the infinitely varied textual articulation of such syntagmatic formulas — "e il naufragar mi è dolce in questo mare", for example — where the aesthetic manifestation of what is poetic is elevated above the material web of the words themselves.

Until now, I have been referring too generally to the aesthetic effect which provides the foundations for the value of the "poetic". Still, the kinds of aesthetic experiences existing in poetry are very complex and respond to many different types of emotion, stemming from its immediate and unique origin, the mediation of the text's material verbal structure. In principle, we can speak of a possible genre of poetic effects more explicitly linked to the denotative function of the literary utterance. This reflects what we feel in regard to, for example, Greco-Latin classical poetry and the modern poets electing a more direct and non-symbolic kind of *expressiveness*. Surely this is the source of the best poetic values of Miguel de Unamuno's narratives or Robert Frost's poetry.

The *poetics of expressiveness*, which I will study extensively in the next chapter, is undoubtedly that which most immediately counts on the artful or artistic effect of language itself, insofar as it is an autonomous instrument of the nominalist exploration of reality's mysteries. Under the values of expressiveness, poetry exploits the surprises deriving from the free play of an autonomous verbal discourse, in great measure foreign to intellectual discourse's investigation of reality. The *conceptista* art of the Baroque, a cipher of the procedure, was only an exaggeratedly simplified stylization of that eternal spring of poeticity, founded on the language's powers of expressiveness without being foreign to its denotative logic (F. Lázaro Carreter, 1966; A. García-Berrio, 1968).

The free play of poetic expressiveness presents us with the "unexpected brainchild of wit", products almost exclusively lodged in the logical-denotative activity of language, their aesthetic value deriving from the effect of surprise associated with their conceptual novelty. I do not conceive this kind of aesthetic emotion as something entirely alien to the poetic work — that is, the constructive work of the imagination and of subconscious drives —, but there is no doubt that the poetic effects of linguistic *expressiveness* have to do with the specific constructions of *fantasy*, different and inferior in degree to other poetic devices which I will discuss shortly. In any case, the emotional-aesthetic values of poetic expressiveness are absolutely relative to the game of *topicality* in artistic discourses. Features of expectation and exceptional novelty are located in the topical nature of styles, which assimilate and temper the normal experience and define the unique and new feature, isolating it as exemplary and manifesting it historically.

Fiction in the novel (T. Albaladejo Mayordomo, 1986), the form of literary discourse which is currently the closest to the operations of mimetic verisimilitude through which Aristotle conceived of the poetic effect of tragic narration, offers one of the most distinctive and widespread sources of poeticity. In modern literature, the novel surely represents the most generalized and prestigous type of poetic discourse and, of course, the form our century's literary criticism has given preference to. *Fictionality* is one of the surest sources of poeticity, the generator of aesthetic emotions of value, linked to verbal utterances. Fictional aesthetics is naturally founded on conventional structures of literariness — the so-called narrative structures. Nevertheless, as with any other case of poetic value, the simple and automatic use of literary narrative structure does not guarantee nor necessarily accompany the kind of aesthetico-fantastic effects demonstrating fiction's poetic value in the great constructions of Tolstoy, Dostoyevsky or Balzac.

Fictionality includes the collaboration between fantasy and a very particular and fixed type of discursive structure. In his study of realism, Tomás Albaladejo has faithfully established a theory of fiction and the realist illusion framed by the components of a truly semiotic doctrine. Thus, he distinguishes a semantics of artistic realism in terms of the degree of the language's tolerance for the conventional contents of fictionality, and announces the formulation of a syntax and a pragmatics of realism (T. Albaladejo Mayordomo, 1991). The linguistic mechanisms of the narrative text translate and control the shift from the terms of objective reality to those of fictional universes, conventionally hierarchicalized in a general structure of possible worlds (C. Segre, 1985, p. 123, Chs. 3, 10; T. Albaladejo Mayordomo, 1986). Fictionality thus shares the same general structure as the imaginary operations, contributing other poetic products of different kinds.

The imaginary base of fictionality has more to do with the capacity of fantasy than it does with that of imagination itself, as it is today commonly understood — following here the sense in which Coleridge conceived and disseminated the notions of imagination and fancy (here, fantasy), the very opposite conception from the understanding of the terms prevailing among the German theoreticians. Fictional fantasy is contiguous to the logical and rational analysis of reality. It must keep close at hand the facts of referential experience in order to create a set of representations and forms which, while elaborations of the imagination, are also simultaneously verisimilar — that is, capable of being framed among the phenomena of sensible and referential experience. Fantastic fictionality thus utilizes the conscious and rational control of experience. It operates differently from the anthropologically symbolic work of the imagination, which creates the absolute forms of poeticity and forms its artistic results according to subconscious drives, indirectly expressing an irrational conception and orientation of the world as an experience of otherness.

The most immediate difference, in my judgment, between the imaginary type of poetico-narrative fictionality and the non-fictional activity of the imagination, consists in the equivalence between the characters or *ethical symbols* (M. Bakhtin, 1975, [1978, pp. 50—54]) of the novel's fiction and the *anthropological* symbols (G. Durand, 1960) of lyrical construction. This last kind of poeticity translates a cosmovision to the textual discourse (N. Frye, 1957), one not directly conceptual like that of expressive poeticity, nor ethical or personified as in that of fictionality. Symbolic poeticity represents, through cosmological intermediaries — like the tree, the cup, the technology of weapons and the cyclical seasonal system of agrarian cultures — man's systemic interpretation of his cosmic orientation. The symbols of day and night, with the copulative dismissal of time in amorous ecstasy and procreation, are part of the poetic system of representation, the underlying mythical structures enveloped by individual poetics.

To the extent that we perceive this genre of lyrical poeticity of anthropological symbols as something purer than the referential condition of fantastic fictionality, the corresponding archetypes come closer to being very abstract conceptual images. In them, the pillars of conscious knowledge and understanding are diluted in the unreachable zone of sensations and subconscious drives. This is the domain, for example, of dew as a regenerative, fertile element in Wallace Steven's poetry or of the lit torch as a commitment to an essential faith in the nocturnal depths of nothingness in Saint John of the Cross' artistic expression. In short, what we are referring to is the privileged space of symbolic representation as an obsessive metaphor (Ch. Mauron, 1962), in which the symbol ambiguously alludes to a diffuse conglomerate of subconscious contents, scarcely open to differentiation.

In that symbolic universe of poetry, surrealism has given the definitive version of a situation of literary experience that, since Mallarmé, Baudelaire and Lautréamont, has formed the foundation for modern poetry (E. Wilson, 1931; M. Raymond, 1947), in which man's orientation in the universe is poetry's fundamental issue (M. Nadeau, 1945—1948; M. Raymond, 1947). The artistic world preceding that of imaginary symbols, conceptualized and ethical, of sensations and of more concrete and conscious aesthetic emotions, is revealed in its rational and fantastic structure from this new imaginary and poetic perspective, deeper and more universal, located at the limits of the subconscious impulse, almost a poetic epiphenomenon. Compared to the ultimately and necessarily rational adjustment of fantastic constructions, the poetic imagination sinks its roots in the anthropological justification pure symbols assume. By means of these symbols, man proposes to embark on the exploration of the *space* around the self, an area which is sometimes familiar, immediate and accessible to his postural activity of illuminated, sensitive and diurnal recognition. But also, and at the same time, it is an area which includes the foreboding of nocturnal space, of uncertain dimensions, chaotically reflected in the mysterious nocturnal *digestive* experience. Altogether, the nocturnal represents a perplexing wait in which the frustration of the representations of temporal duration even presupposes the translation of a more profound, damaging and vital failure: the destruction of the dimensional calculation of space, crushed by the immeasurable dimension in which the infinitely dilated and the infinitely contracted are confused in an anguish of useless and inhuman eternity (G. Durand, 1960; A. García-Berrio, 1985, 1987).

The radical anthropological experience of space is translated by poetry (M. Blanchot, 1955) under a privileged form of symbolic capacity, in which the effort towards anthropological orientation surpasses the space of the semantics of symbols, frequently in order to construct within the meaningful space of the poem genuinely fantastic schemes of spatial orientation. In this way an imaginary organization of otherness is constituted as a sense of emotion and extension, a constructive condition by which it can be denominated, in contrast to the semantics of fantastic symbols, a syntax of the imagination. In effect, the whole of the textual body, the semantic substance of the symbols under the dynamic animation of acoustico-temporal rhythms lodged in the text, delineates consistent outlines of movement measuring off privileged dimensions of space or probing from premonitions of stationary equilibrium the encompassing space as a welcome sphere or as a bare, menacing field. The majority of poets designated as "pure", such as Paul Valéry, Jorge Guillén or Wallace Stevens, are pure from the perspective which translates into their poetic systems of representation the predominance of these distinctive syntactico-imaginary schemes of spatial orientation over the semantic corporality of symbolic systems (A. García-Berrio, 1985).

The three generic modes of poeticity I have just set forth (the denotative-expressive, fictional-narrative and imaginary-symbolic) impose the prerequisite of a suitable and efficient textual material scheme. If we conceive of poeticity, as I have done, as an effect of imaginary-fantastic mobilization, depending on the literary-verbal stimuli implied in the text's material scheme, the participation of the artistic text's literary structures is clearly involved in this phenomena. It being, nevertheless, well understood that not just any verbal initiative with artistic intentions will in and of itself assure the production of the poetic effect, nor is a prior inventory available of rhetorical-expressive structures and resources with guaranteed poetic effects.

This same unpredictable and asystematic condition of the verbal structures capable of generating the informed poetic effect is a feature which can, in turn, encourage yet another mode of pragmatic objections insisting on poetry's social conventionality. The pragmatic critic may perhaps think that what I have been denominating poetic value is founded upon a conventional effect, purely capricious and unjustified, given the fortuitous condition of the imaginary and verbal association which produces it. Nevertheless, the situation is analogous to that previously set forth distinguishing between the unforeseeable and unrepeatable concrete textual *occurrence* producing the poetic effect, and the broad paradigmatic linguistico-structural *frame* which assures the predictions of poeticity and is able to explain them. Analogously, here the structural-linguistic frame in which the effects of poeticity are located, offers in its own structure and constitution a rigorous design of patterns of linguistic behavior, associated with certain regularity with the imaginary effects of poeticity.

To determine and describe the terms of this correlation between the text's literary structures and the various imaginary effects of poeticity could be the great task of a contemporary literary theory. This would already, at the very outset, count on the many advances of linguistic poetics and the various current methods of stylistic and formal criticism, developed against the background, incalculable but in need of recovery, of inventories of categories and of the analytico-descriptive strategies of traditional rhetoric. It also seems to me that psychologists and psychoanalysts, anthropologists, historians and analysts of culture today can offer materials which are more than just fascinating, but adequately disposed and able to be assimilated by philologists and literary critics for their reasonable use. I, at least, conceive the most profitable efforts of literary theory and of critical analyses, present and future, in terms of this mediation.

Finally, one must keep in mind that we are not dealing with an extreme or eccentric proposal, neither reductive nor anti-traditional. In my opinion, the text remains the ideal focus for the literary analysis of poeticity. In effect, what has changed are the perspectives for understanding the text, which enlarge and deepen its conception and physiognomy in terms I judge to be suitable and realistic. Poeticity seeks its explanation, as a result, in the aesthetic space of the text's imaginary behavior, brought together through its prolongation in the immanent verbal scheme's communicative space, in which the global poetic text achieves the density of its immediate corporality, its literary formulation.

1.3. Artistic Modes and the Aesthetic Law of Expressiveness

1.3.1. Literary Expressiveness: Its Verbal and Fantastic Constituents

The measure of aesthetic value close to the linguistic registers of the literary text's verbal scheme is what I have been denominating as *expressiveness*. This, together with the fictional illusion and the symbolic-imaginary construct, form one of the manifestations of poeticity as the connotative result of literary utterances. Expressiveness as a property and poetic effect of literary language is very directly linked to the potential for conceptual and sentimental resonance of our cultural experience deposited as language. In contrast to what occurs with the imaginary effects of poeticity, which are symbolic and anthropologically oriented, poetic expressiveness does not privilege the recovery of subconscious drives; on the contrary, its own space is marked by the unexpected illumination of the conscious and habitual and it is valued on the merits of the singularity of its evocative expressive mechanism. Poetic expressiveness exists in the domain of the de-automatization of conceptual values. The Russian formalists were the first to outline this source of poetic value, although they may have exaggerated in exploiting it as the primary source of poetic expressiveness.

Poetic expressiveness is also neatly differentiated from the fantastic poeticity proper to fiction. Fictional construction fundamentally acts by means of a system of shifting between "worlds" or fictional universes different from the data produced by linguistic denotation (T. Albaladejo Mayordomo, 1986). The poetic values of expressiveness are commonly accomodated in the positive universe of reality, where they are lodged by the coupling of man and language. The poetic value of expressiveness originates in the infinite possibilities inscribed in linguistic combinations. Its measure is the rhetorically sustained pitch, the expressive mechanism which, making the artifice evident, dislodges the softened, habitual contact of man with reality consecrated in the logic of communicative language.

Expressiveness adds an emotional edge to the logical neutrality of the linguistic expression. Undoubtedly, the opposition between poetic expressiveness and communicative expression can be illustrated in part by way of the traditional opposition between connotation and denotation (B. Garza Cuarón, 1978). The basis for expressiveness lies in the domain of the purely connotative, where the action of the rhetorical mechanism of linguistic de-automatization deposits its best sentimental effects. Literature's rhetorical expressiveness creates the most distinctive effects of affective connotation, but since the sentimental effects of connotation are also inseparable from the denotative use of language, the connotative poeticity belonging to rhetorical defamiliarization certainly partakes of expressive results which are more difficult to define. Nevertheless, rhetorical expressiveness became the most representative option and, in many cases, perhaps the only option for classical poetry. Before the literary revolution of poetic symbols, which, as is well

1.3. Artistic Modes and the Aesthetic Law of Expressiveness   95

known, was an extraordinarily modern development (G. H. Gusdorf, 1976), poetry achieved that degree of illumination which is inseparable from it and necessary to it almost exclusively from impulses of expressiveness. One of the channels of that great current of poetic expressiveness runs between Horace and Fray Luis de León, for example.

To oppose the rhetoric of poetic expressiveness to fiction's fantastic operations and to the imaginary mechanism of symbolic construction does not, however, mean stripping it totally of its imaginary element. With regard to poetic and fictional expressiveness, the imagination acts according to the differences I have set forth previously. Still, in another of the ways in which fantasy operates, the imaginative sheath enveloping verbal mechanisms exists as a well-known fact demonstrated, for example, in a linguistic phenomenon as thoroughgoing and representative as that of presupposition. Furthermore, rhetorical-expressive devices — and not only those known as "images" — commonly appeal to the propulsive tool of fantasy's sheath: ironic inversions, interrogative emphases, the proportional effects of "climaxes", the proportional calculation of the length and weight of phrases and sentences, etc. Throughout all of this, fantasy's imaginative cement inserts itself to consolidate the overly bare suggestion of plain words.

This participation in the processes of fantasy, which literary expressiveness places above the strict immanence of the direct and literary meanings of rhetorical stylemes, powerfully serves to make possible the homologation of the different classes of aesthetic phenomena which we consider poetic. Through it all, the basic ingredient of the textual scheme is glued to a kind of imaginative coating carrying the aesthetic emotion of poeticity. The nature and density of this imaginative supplement is extremely varied, as this book attempts to illustrate, but the imaginative sheath's presence in every case ratifies it as a basic constituent of the poetic *effect* and result, developing from its origins in the immanent verbal structures constituting its textual *cause* or raison d'être.

In denominating this expressive mode of the poetic as *rhetoric*, it is not my intention to identify it strictly with the traditional inventory of images, figures and schemes of expression conserved under the classical identification of rhetorical science. It seems to me that one way to conceive of classical rhetoric today would be as a *science of verbal expressiveness,* as I have myself repeatedly denominated it (A. García-Berrio, 1983, 1984). In this sense, rhetoric is open to whatever new attempts at linguistic combination are necessary to represent less than immediately evident modes of reality, or even to confront radically new explorations in that same objective space. As a result, without exaggeration, I believe I understand the kind of literary rhetoric I'm calling for: an authentic *general rhetoric*, capable of accounting for all of the special features characterizing linguistic expressiveness already collected or still lacking in the classical inventories of schemes and figures.

The predictably rhetorical structures — that is, those properties of enduring expressiveness conventionalized by their having typically appeared in inventories — immediately form part of the arsenal of literary structures arrived at through consensus, as I have already set forth in the previous chapter. Analogously, the same holds true for other, new constructions of discourse, encouraged by the expressive experimentation of modern literature. The doubly expressive intentionality of one or another present them as schemes of literariness, proposals of aesthetic intentionality. It will be the degree of their aesthetic effect, sentimental and fantastic, which will enable them to either constitute themselves as principles of poeticity, or be definitively frustrated in the effort.

The class of poetic effect which is understood as fundamentally expressive is produced in the formulas of stylized language and leaps into contact with the kind of experiences which are neither immediate nor habitual, the kind of experiences which are impenetrable and recondite. They are a genre of truths that reveal themselves as original by their unheard of twisting of the language that expresses them, in the rare virtue of metaphoric parallelism discovering its cosmological reach. A rhetoric of the manifest, a rhetoric of the vacuum inhabited by suggestion, a rhetoric of silence (G. Mendonça Telhes, 1979; P. Valesio, 1986). Language in polemical friction with the flint of reality, yielding the dazzling, inspiring image. And a stimulating, suggestive reality, rendered in a linguistic formula — experience creating the pure, essential word. That rhetorical universe of expressive literariness, opening a path for itself, perhaps towards the more generalized kind of poetic illuminations, can be critically studied with the traditional rhetoric we have at hand and expanded and made more flexible in a *neorhetoric*, in the terms recently proposed (H. Plett, 1971, 1977; J. Kopperschmidt, 1976; L. Heilmann, 1978; P. Valesio, 1980), or in a general literary rhetoric, as I prefer to call it (A. García-Berrio, 1983, 1984).

The anomalous and exceptional behavior of literary language, that is, its deviation from the communicative standard for aesthetic-connotative motives, relies among its foreseeable schemes on numerous canonic devices of traditional rhetoric. Born, as is known, with a purpose different from that of constituting or explaining the poeticity of verbal artistic messages, classical rhetoric came to serve as a poetics of eloquence due to the original lack of an *elocutio* in the tradition of poetic treatises (A. García-Berrio and M. T. Hernández, 1988, pp. 21—22).

Moreover, with an expressive concept of poeticity like that predominating in classical literature and art, it is not unusual that this stylistic rhetoric, progressively centered on the features of eloquence, schemes and figures, decisively occupied a place above the verbal literary mechanisms of a still imprecise literary science.

In the dense rhetorical inventories dealing with the expressive-intentional deviations of linguistic behavior, we find typified the greater part of the features constitutive of literariness established by classical literature. In their concrete textual articulation, under certain individual circumstances and in fortuitous combinations, some of those literary schemes of verbal stylization achieved a degree of expressive accomodation with the objective reality of their contents, transfiguring them into moments of highly expressive poeticity. The processes of this transfiguring course are already familiar to us, as set forth in the preceding chapter. But, as I have said before, the inventories of the schemes of classical rhetoric's literariness do not exhaust the possibilities for the aesthetic stylization of language. Furthermore, considering the subsequent performance of the discipline, rhetoric presently is not yet in a position to provide explanations and answers to the profound evolution of the procedures of expressiveness established by modern literature, beginning especially with Romanticism.

1.3.2. The Aesthetic Norms of Literary Expressiveness

The most immediately evident and explicit signs of literariness are mostly of a linguistic nature, and those that are not entirely so, like fictionality, still possess correspondingly formal lines in the semantic and pragmatic verbal structure of texts. Traditionally, the set formed by these verbal features and signs has been searched for some objective evidence of texts' aesthetic or poetic value. Undoubtedly, the verbal conditions of the text can communicate, when fortunate, certain effects of an intellectual and sentimental nature, comprising a first stage of poetic distinctiveness as a value. It is on this first aesthetico-expressive level of the poetic effect where I endeavor to locate the linguistic principles of expressiveness.

I understand literary expressiveness as a property in itself of certain successful verbal texts. In my opinion, it is a primordial and simple form of aesthetic value, achieved under certain not entirely foreseen structures of linguistic usage. As such, it must be distinguished from the verbal forms that support the imaginary and sentimental constructions of texts with poetic value. Poeticity is necessarily generated in an accurate structure of language, in a text of singular expressive success, a verbal scheme associated with, expressing and provoking the general imaginary effect we recognize as poetic. Literary expressiveness, in turn, has particularly intellectual consequences; it is a property of verbal wit or ingenuity, the imaginary features of which are easily and immediately recognizable in the linguistic structures which have produced it. The unforeseeable nature of the effects of expressiveness frees them from the automatism of the conventional, which is the inevitable consequence attached to the features of literariness. Expressiveness rests on regular grammatical — and especially rhetorical, typologized and normal — mechanisms, but the combining and compounding of constants which generates expressiveness achieves unforeseeably adventitious forms. Expressiveness sets itself apart from literariness by the absence of conventional and automatic features; in this manner, it constitutes the simplest rhetorico-verbal expression or form of aesthetic value.

1. Literary Expressiveness

By itself, expressiveness formed the conscious continuum of artistic discourse in classical literature. I mean deliberately conscious, since the poetic value of the majority of the sublime cases of Greco-Latin and classicist art has to be attributed to forms, whether voluntary or involuntary, of the imaginary construction. Nevertheless, at least in the terrain of explicit and normative theoretical awareness, classical poetics was formulated as an art of ornamental-rhetorical expressiveness (A. García-Berrio, 1984).

Reading the *Epistola ad Pisones*, perhaps the most characteristic text of classical normativity in literature, we are today surprised and find it incomprehensible that an artist of Horace's high poetic stature, with all of his skill and success, can defend the technical normalcy of *ars*, providing such convincing proof of its pedagogical tenacity. From within the perspective of the text's role as a piece of propaganda in the Augustan dictatorship's political campaign of cultural improvement, Horace appears convinced of the possibility of educating the refined youth of Roman society at the time, like Pison's own sons, to be above-average poets, according to his proposal. The guidelines and advice Horace sets forth in his *Ars Poetica* do not in any case move beyond the expressive-verbal wariness and ingeniousness of what we are here denominating expressiveness (A. García-Berrio, 1977, I, pp. 212–225).

Horace's sincerity as to his pedagogical confidence in poetry is and will always be an enigma, hard to pin down and judge. But what is certain is that his theoretical proposals came to be embodied in and represent the general spirit of classicist poetics and aesthetics. The Ciceronian ideal of stylistic elegance is founded, naturally, on nothing more than exquisite forms of rhetorical expressiveness. And the very abdication by poetics of the task of constructing a theory of artistic and poetic language independent from rhetoric's efforts represents the conscious surrender to the ornamental and intellectual forms of rhetorical expressiveness of any aspiration or prospect of formulating a theory of artistic language possessing poetic, imaginary or sentimental foresight superior to or different from those of rhetorical intellectual persuasion.

Pseudo-Longinus himself, in spite of surely being the purest exponent we know in Greco-Latin rhetoric of the poetic aspiration towards the sublime, does not escape the expressive-verbal emphasis characteristic of the classical aesthetic ideal. In his treatise *On the Sublime*, the emancipation of poetic value from the rhetorical structure of expressiveness reaches its peak. Yet, still, the separation is not so complete so as to permit one to consider the possibility that the imagination generating the poetic effect is entirely autonomous. The process of disassociating the two categories will not be entirely completed until, at the earliest, the European Enlightenment and Romanticism, in the thought of such figures as Herder, Friedrich Schlegel or Coleridge (A. García-Berrio and M. T. Hernández, 1988, pp. 32–53).

In indicating Romanticism as the line of systematic and total rupture with the classicist ideal of poetic expressiveness, we run the risk of raising objections on behalf of the Baroque's claim to this position. The significant range of a poetics of expressiveness is evident as far as the most pure and representative Baroque art, as an art of excess, is concerned. In effect, certain interpretations of this art are characterized by an understanding of it as a phenomenon of the overflowing irrational imagination. Perhaps this impression is justified in plastic, architectural or musical expressions, or even in other historical features of an age which embraces a fairly extensive period of time and in which many different social historico-political manifestations are included (A. García-Berrio, 1990).

The broad reach of a poetics of expressiveness is clear in the Baroque, in its purest and most representative literature, considered as an art of excess. This is in fact the case within the double stylistic line — euphuist and conceptist — in which the antithetical tendencies balanced in classical style are exaggerated and not maintained in harmonious suspension. The art of euphuistic verbalism is a basic exercise in expressiveness, which dwells on the splendor of the neologism, the extravagant voice or the forced metaphor, practicing with rhetorical means aimed at impressing the reader, at dazzling him, at compelling him to suspend the conceptual analysis of their artifice, wit and ingenuity in the name of the marvelous effect of surprise (M. T. Hernández, 1986).

The European art of witty conceits (*conceptismo*) does not diverge from fustian expressivism except in its verbal economy and the serene dose of its forms' austerity — in the Attic tradition and under Tacitus' influence. Nevertheless, as has been indicated so often, its understanding of the metaphor as conceit (*concepto*) is analogous. The conceit, a central mechanism of Baroque art, equal in depth to the superficial differences of the verbal expressiveness of *ornatus*, is the basic operation of witty imagination (*ingenio*), conceived as an intellectual faculty by all of the European theoreticians of Baroque conceptualism, from Gracián to Pellegrini and Tesauro (A. García-Berrio, 1968).

The Baroque understanding of metaphor as "the art of wit" may even be paradigmatic for recognizing the behavior and limits of an art of expressiveness. The already well-described activity of the Baroque conceit (*concepto*) lodges the phenomenon of expressiveness in the sphere of formal creativity, approximating the pun to the invocation of its semantic representations. For Gracián, as well as for Tesauro, the intellectual art of the conceit modifies the rules of verbal associationism in the metaphor in order to renovate the image and representation of the world. We are dealing here with a non-sylogistic innovation, although one that is just as intellectual, as the fruit of the *mind's wit (agudeza de ingenio)* (E. Raimondi, 1961, pp. 1–33; E. Hidalgo Serna, 1983; M. T. Hernández, 1986).

The separation between what on the one hand I denominate the phenomenon of *verbal expressiveness*, and which I appraise as the first classical manifestation of conventional aestheticity, and what, on the other hand, I consider as artistic procedures of poetic value, is based on the constitution of the literary signifier as a fortuitous mechanism. Here expression is presented turned inward, towards itself, and towards the play of effects of rational combinations, rather than as a scheme of the text eliciting and conducting the imagination's unconscious symbols and drives.

Literary expressiveness is achieved by means of a varied set of verbal procedures the general effect of which can be summed up in terms of the de-automatization of language (J. M. Pozuelo Yvancos, 1988a, pp. 19—68). Within a conventionalized form of rhetorical narration, that which describes the character, his name, country, description, career, etc., Cervantes, for example, achieves a successful effect of expressiveness at the beginning of the *Quijote*, stating that the *hidalgo* lives "In a certain place in La Mancha, the name of which I do not wish to recall."

Expressiveness is produced by every sort of mechanism, from the purely acoustically meaningful, like alliterations and other rhythmico-onomatopoeic forms — "and murmuring of innumerable bees in immemorial elms" — to the broadest of textual constructions, such as the highlighted ironic effect of the respective discourses produced in the confrontation of the three characters' points of view in the preface to Goethe's *Faust*. Grammatical features also contribute to the effects of distancing and surprise in discourse, like the hyperbaton of E. E. Cummings' "All in green went my love riding", or verbal equivocations and other lexical-semantic games, as in Thomas Hood's famous pun, "They went and told the sexton and the sexton tolled the bell" (A. García-Berrio, 1973, pp. 101 ff.).

The inventories of resources of discursive artifice accumulated in the tradition of rhetorical science constitute an exhaustive and vast treasure trove. In this sense, consulting any of the manuals and lists of tropes and figures yields numerous illustrations of the phenomenon of expressiveness. In the case of, for example, the rhetorical treatises of Baroque *conceptismo*, like Gracián's *Agudeza y arte de ingenio* or Tesauro's *Il canocchiale aristotelico*, one is in the presence of catalogued paradigmatic modes of a manifold resource, the conceit, which established an entire art of expressiveness. They include everything from allegories and compound conceits to the thoughtful appraisal of enigmas and emblems, forms of "catachresis" or metaphoric violence, ambiguities, word play and other manifestations of nominal wit, even to actual examples of quick-wittedness like that twisting of bad fortune in the case of the fallen general who, after a ridiculous grin, proclaims the "teneo te Africam," cited by Gracián, or the example of the officer who transforms the explosion of his own powder keg into a sign of hope and a "lamp of victory".

Literary expressiveness is linked to the verbal resources of the artistic text and its effects are tightly bound to the immediate intellectual repercussion of these resources. Hence, it is a phenomenon well differentiated from imaginary products, which are channeled by the text's formal structures, but whose origin is located in subconscious drives and in symbolic forms of the elementary dominants — postural, digestive and copulative — which organize the phenomena of consciousness, distributing them among the respective regimes of the imagination: diurnal, nocturnal and erotic (G. Durand, 1960).

Nevertheless, expressiveness shares an element of unforeseeability with the artistic text's poetic products. Hence, due to the fact that they are not conventionalizable, expressive surprise and illumination are hierarchicalized as *values* of variable intensity. And, as I will later discuss, the condition of value necessary in terms of automatic convention is a constitutive frame in my understanding of poeticity.

Insofar as it is dependent on the nature and linguistic constitution of texts, the verbal principle of expressiveness must be explained in its unconventional poetic character according to the properties and structure characteristic of language. The material component of every artistic text — verbal, visual or musical — is at the same time the source of weighty limitations and the cause of its driven poetic condition (A. García-Berrio, 1985, pp. 257 ff.).

The experience which has dominated the activity of the purest creators, like Mallarmé and Juan Ramón Jiménez, is well known: the ideal of the blank page is the symbol of perfect poetry. In our time, Maurice Blanchot has been the philosopher of art that has most agonizingly represented the paradoxical limitation of the materials in artistic products, in order to express the spiritual and imaginary objects in the genre of aesthetic, sentimental and existential intuitions entrusted to poetic language (M. Blanchot, 1969, p. 43). Michelangelo's mythical wounding of the marble of his Moses to secure its cry of life is the exemplary case of the artistic imagination's battle against the limiting bulk of its materials.

The verbal constitution of literary texts or the plastic ingredients of visual texts live contaminated by their everyday communicative limitations. "The sweet lament of two shepherds", in Garcilaso, in order to achieve its extensive poetic vibration, has previously transfigured the realistic representation of the shepherd's work and transformed the concepts of sweetness and lament. Consider the poetry of Velázquez's roguish philosophers. In the same way, he achieves the poetic with his clowns and court personalities, in the mysterious, ungraspable distance of the difference between their representation and the insignificant vulgarity of their realism (A. García-Berrio and M. T. Hernández, 1988a, pp. 230−231).

The mechanisms of that artistic transfiguration of materials have more frequently been diffused than approached and concretized by critical and technical descriptions. The aestheticity of the forms of expressiveness has often been relegated, in terms of its explanation, to the inconcrete chain of the ineffable. Still, at the very least, a literary theory must give some indication of the origin of the aesthetic consistency of its materials.

The historicity of language's forms, on the one hand, demarcates their concrete aesthetic limitation, their inevitable association with utilitarian, communicative and apoetic representations and contexts, while, simultaneously, that very same historicity has been endowing forms with the full weight of their poetic, sentimental and imaginary complexity. The accurate reproduction of the contextual structure, in the plenitude or void of other forms, capable of achieving the work or expression transfigured at the level of poetic manifestation, creates the situation in which the poetic expressiveness of language sheds the vulgar contaminations of use and makes its entry into the sentimental space of aesthetic efficiency (L. Doležel, 1986, p. 28).

Transcendental historicity, the poetic tradition of language, provides entities and expressive combinations with the energy which, properly searched for and located, produces the phenomena of poetic expressiveness as sentimental resonances. Every poetic voice stores and treasures the historical precedents of all of the previous strains of its artistic use. In this way, expressive discourse exploits the vast universe of *intertextuality*.

The intertextual condition of aesthetic resonance tends to be invoked frequently since Julia Kristeva's *Semeyotiké* (1969, pp. 255—257; A. Popovich, 1979, pp. 521—544; C. Segre, 1985, pp. 85—90, Ch. 2.29), above all in order to explain the simultaneous encounters and contaminations of communicative and literary forms (J. Stierle, 1977, pp. 425—426). Undoubtedly, this is more useful for pondering the sociable condition of texts and their textual components than for evoking the explanation of their capacities for aesthetic resonance. But the poetic vibration of expressive utterances sinks its roots above all in the history of words and languages. In their role as traditional forms of the historical expressive community current voices awaken the memory of the past occasions of their artistic glory. Language — familiar and strange, friend and foe, core, key and limit, rich and lacking — discovers in the complicated depths of its artistic history the poetic reason for its expressiveness (B. Terracini, 1976, pp. 198—199).

Until this point I have only considered the emotional results of expressiveness. Still, present among its effects are the connotative poetic factors of imaginary activity. The forms of verbal ingeniousness which I have alluded to previously as characteristics of expressiveness, for example those of baroque metaphorism, include the production of images, as well as the complex networks of association between them. Nevertheless, these products of the imagination are of a *nomic* nature, that is, regulated by operational norms and rules which distinguish them from properly free and involuntary poetic features. The images emerging from expressiveness logically have their imaginary stamp, but the traces of their dependent ties to the textual scheme's expressive signs are evident, as is the automatism of cause end effect regulating their associated genesis and development in the conscious imaginary production of the text.

If we return to the Romantic distinction between fantasy and imagination, in the precise senses I fixed for these terms before, we can attribute the imaginary quality of the phenomena of expressiveness to the elaboration and production of fantasy. The other more spontaneous forms remain excepted from this process, undiscovered in their conscious origins, and with less obvious automatic links than those of fantastic expressiveness, in terms of the perceptible stimuli of the verbal text's material scheme.

For all of the reasons examined up to this point — the relative unpredictability of their exceptional linguistic behavior, their broad sentimental and cultural historical resonances and, especially, the fantastic constitution of their connotative periphery — the expressiveness of artistic works should be considered among the constitutive factors of poetic value (J. P. Weber, 1960). In fact, there are many works, especially novels and manifestations of mimetic narration, such as epics, romances, etc., which establish the ostensible and conscious foundations of their aesthetic pretensions exclusively in these verbal sentimental and fantastic values of literary expressiveness. And, above all, many receivers of literary works do not seek or demand from them any more fundamentally poetic guarantees in return for their adherence and their interest.

Nevertheless, the unfathomable depth of great artistic creations — the mythical universe of the Homeric epics and of Euripides' tragedies, the *Divine Comedy* or *Paradise Lost*, Shakespearean tragedy or Cervantes' *Don Quijote* — imply the existence of other forms of imaginary reverberation, surpassing the nomic automatism of fantastic associations in the connotative sentimental periphery of expressiveness. I try to approach these pure poetic forms of imaginary activity in the third part of this book. For now, it will suffice to note the differences between the forms belonging to expressive fantasy and all of these other symbolic consolidations of the subconscious imagination, lodging poetic expression in the essential coordinates of space and time, of anthropological orientation and symbolization. The foundations of absolute poeticity are to be found at this other level of the imaginary structure.

1.3.3. *Classical Modes of Literary Expressiveness: Mechanisms of Expressiveness and Levels of Style*

The verbal and fantastic registers on which expressiveness is founded are very numerous, as I have just indicated. Therefore, the possible specimens of phenomena of artistic expressiveness are almost infinite. There is hardly a brilliant literary page that does not abound in successful strokes of expressive vigor, since, as has been indicated, the expressive is the inevitable support through which every dazzling construction of fantasy or feeling passes in literary messages. To establish a typological inventory of the forms of expressiveness which assembles and surpasses those already in existence in the historical tradition is surely an important and necessary task. But because of its specific complexity and its predictable extensiveness, it would certainly be a job removed from the general construction of a theory of the literary text, which is the subject I have proposed to outline and develop in this book.

The existing repertories of expressiveness are to be found particularly in the manuals and treatises of rhetoric, in the abundant exemplification of figures and schemes extracted from the quarries of classical and modern eloquence. I have already referred to one of the most extreme and visible manifestations of this type of inventory with Baroque rhetoric's classifications of conceptual ingenuity in works as well-known as those of Gracián and Tesauro (A. García-Berrio, 1968). In them, however, the modes of expressiveness represent fairly monographically one type of restricted example: those items derived from comparison and from conceptist "ponderatio" in conceits, under the proportional schemes of simile and metaphor (J. A. Mazzeo, 1933). Given this situation, and with the warning that I am not here going to provide an exhaustive system of literary expressiveness' classes, I will limit myself to offering some illustrative examples of the phenomenon.

In the first place, I will insist on the most obvious and self-evident mode fundamentally nourishing the literature of the Baroque: ingenious allusiveness. In the play on words, exploiting the spontaneous semantic associations of homophony and homonymy, language reveals itself as an inexhaustible mine, by virtue of its own evocative-associative dynamics, for the extraction and production of images of powerful imaginative plasticity. Word play particularly exploits the fantastic effect of surprise produced by an unusual association between concepts and very different facets of reality, which nevertheless have a common feature, although perhaps only that derived from the purely nominal construction.

Some examples from Quevedo's work will serve to illustrate the workings of this rhetorical-fantastic kind of expressiveness, as in the very animated flood of metaphoric associations inspired by the anomalous size of a nose in "To a Man With A Great Nose": "Érase un hombre a una nariz pegado, / érase una nariz superlativa, / érase una alquitara medio viva, / érase un peje espada mal barbado; // era un reloj de sol mal encarado, / érase un elefante boca arriba, / érase una nariz sayón y escriba, / un Ovidio Nasón mal narigado. // Érase el espolón de una galera, / érase una pirámide de Egito, / las doce tribus de narices era; // érase un naricísimo infinito, / frisón archinariz, nariz tan fiera, / que en la cara de Anás fuera delito". ["There was a man appended to a nose, / there was a hyperbolic nosiness, / there was a live alembic in repose, / there was a swordfish snooted to excess, // there was a sundial poorly aimed, but stout, / there was an elephant tipped upside down, / a scribe and executioner of snout, / Ovidius Nasus nosed to sad renown. // There was a galley ram long as a tree, / there was a pyramid from Egypt brought, / twelve tribes of noses snorting overtime; / there was an infinite nasality, / nosisimus, so fiercely overshot, / that stuck on Annas' face 'twould be a crime"] [Francisco de Quevedo, *Songs of Death and Love and in Between*, trans. and ed. by David M. Gitlitz (Lawrence, Kansas: Coronado Press, 1980), p. 257]. The effect of expressiveness Quevedo seeks is achieved from the very first line, in the manipulation of the inchoative values of the narrative formula of the singular case, linked to the anaphorical expression "érase" ("there was"). At the same time, the image produces its effect of noticeable surprise, inverting the normal anatomical relationship between the nasal appendage and the rest of the body: "Érase un hombre a una nariz pegado" ["There was a man appended to a nose"]. The verbal focalization of the expressive effect isolates the nose through the absolute evidence of the superlative "Érase una nariz superlativa" ["there was a hyperbolic nosiness"], in order to round out the effect of an absolutely predominant exaggeration in variants like the "muchísimo nariz" ["nosisimus"; literally, "lots of nose"] in the final tercet. Meanwhile, hyperbole has been testing the unexpected expressive effects of the joke based on the evocation of increasingly prominent forms — alembic, "swordfish snooted to excess," "a sundial poorly aimed," elephant, galley ram, "pyramid from Egypt brought" — building up to a "climax" full of great allusive intensity in the terms of Quevedo's satiric universe: the collective proliferation of the image of the "twelve tribes of noses snorting overtime".

The animated scenes of witty associations illustrating Quevedo's best pages are constructed on the basis of the varied range of forms possible in this mode of nominal expressive wit. Consider, for example, the spiralled succession of ingenious developments constituting the obsessive plot of his most celebrated satiric and burlesque pieces.

Customarily, Quevedo exploits in an asystematic and spontaneous manner the sudden, instantaneous associations of the chance pun a particular word affords him in order to sprinkle his prose with a great variety of surprising images. But, on occasion, Quevedo's fertile talent for associative expressiveness centers on one particular image, illustrating the whole absurd range of its possible caricatural associations which surpass the normal capacities of evocation by way of contiguousness, similarity and contrast, as in the obsessive spirals of expressiveness in the sonnet we have just discussed. Elsewhere, the effect of the allusive ponderation of one sole feature serves to exploit a general expressive register of the language's rhetorical system, as in the famous case of the sarcasm of the letter from Pablo's uncle in *El Buscón (The Swindler)*, informing him of his father's fate. An "indecorous" rhetorical-verbal skewing is evident in this scene, especially in the disproportionate use of a middle or elevated level of language by "low" characters. The same resource, as Cervantes uses it, creates the absurd and burlesque expressiveness of the delinquents and prostitutes in Monipodio's patio and, to a different degree, in the improperly urban formulas of a colloquial middle style adopted by Rincón and Cortado in their adult, courtly greetings. Not to mention the extreme satirical effect of the absurdities involving vulgarisms, ambiguities, popular etymologies and other anomalies constituting the characteristically burlesque expression of absolute social and ethical inversions in this same novel.

The cooperation of the fantastic faculty is obvious in these forms of discursive expressiveness. The accumulation of images in the description of Dr. Goat in *The Swindler*, one of the most successful products of Quevedo's satiric art, demonstrates the degree and manner in which the strictly verbal mechanisms of expressiveness are developed and correspond with fantasy's elaboration of images: "El era un clérigo cerbatana, largo sólo en el talle, una cabeza pequeña, pelo bermejo. No hay más que decir para quien sabe el refrán que dice, ni gato ni perro de aquella color. Los ojos, avecindados en el cogote, que parecía que miraba por cuévanos; tan hundidos y escuros, que era buen sitio el suyo para tiendas de mercaderes; la nariz entre Roma y Francia, porque se le había comido de unas búas de resfriado, que aun no fueron de vicio, porque cuestan dinero; las barbas, descoloridas de miedo de la boca vecina, que de pura hambre, parecía que amenazaba a comérselas; ..." ["He was a peashooter priest, generous only in height, with a small head and red hair (for those who know the proverb, I need say no more); his eyes resided at the back of his head, as though he looked out from the depths of a pannier, so sunken and dark, they were a good spot for a trader's store; his nose, between Rome and France, because it had been eaten up by the pustules of a cold (not signs of a vice, which costs money to indulge); his beard was as white as a sheet from the fear of the neighboring mouth which, from sheer hunger, was threatening to eat it; I don't know how many of his teeth were missing, but I think they had been exiled for being idlers and vagrants; his gullet was as long as an ostrich's, with an Adam's apple so pronounced it looked as though it were off to find food, forced by necessity; ..."] [translated from: Francisco de Quevedo, *El Buscón*, ed. Domingo Ynduráin (Madrid: Cátedra, 1983), pp. 99—100].

The tense *ellipsis* of the simile's grammatical indicators — of the kind: *as long as* a peashooter — metaphorizing the noun in "He was a peashooter priest", imposes the first pressure in the fantastic displacement towards the prosopography's transformation of characters into objects. This process is accelerated in the description by the unbroken succession of expressive forms, each requiring analogous imaginative effort. Immediately, *ambiguity* comes into play — "generous only in height" — establishing, among other things, the conflictive semantic contamination in the moral universe between the should-be (charitable generosity as a virtue required of a priest) and the frightful reality of the physical being: the caricatural height of the image of the avaricious guardian.

The cascading accumulation of descriptive signs and elements calculatedly forces the plural mobilization of fantasy's visual capacities. We are not dealing here with the normal evocative activity implied in the visual-imaginary reconstruction of any given realistic literary portrayal; the effect of expressionist tension in this description is achieved by means of the multiple levels which intervene. Thus, even from the most neutral touches, like the syntagm "a small head", which immediately follows the description of Dr. Goat's height and generosity, we expect some burlesque effect of deformed stylization, by virtue of the strong caricaturist stamp marking the description's first components. An expectation which is immediately confirmed in the next

1.3. Artistic Modes and the Aesthetic Law of Expressiveness 107

feature to be described. The reference to "red hair" permits Quevedo to introduce the association with a widely-known anti-Semitic joke which appears habitually and frequently in his work. A suggestion expressively reinforced by the elliptical predicative void, with the reference to an anti-Semitic proverb which itself is absent from the text "(for those who know the proverb, I need say no more)".

In these first steps of the description, Quevedo has relied especially on verbal forms for achieving expressive efficiency, forms in which the accelerated progression of the imaginary-expressive rhythm of the portrait, secured through the negative resources of ellipsis and absence, immediately flows into a stratum of the text with an extraordinary density of verbal stimuli. To begin with, the successful effect of "the eyes resided at the back of his head", is created by the autonomous animation of a pair of eyes fantastically transformed by means of the verb's semantic valency ("*avecindados*") into willfully and mobile citizens in the microcosm of this physiognomy. And, on this expressive base, syntactical expansions succeed one another, insisting on the imaginary growth of the frightful vision. First, there is the reinforcing expansion provided by the adjectival phrase: "as though he looked out from the depths of a pannier". Then, immediately, the formula, very common in Quevedo's style, developing the previous phrase with the consecutive correlation "so sunken and dark, they were a good spot for a trader's store", a verbal and imaginary formula involving the cooperation of a whole latent system of extensional semantic factors. Anyone familiar with Quevedo's fantastic and conceptual universe is sensitive to the nuances of his disdain and loathing for the merchant's world of self-interest and calculation, expressively accused of avarice and represented in images provoked by the gloomy darkness of their store, resembling caves (an association also evoked by the Spanish word for pannier, "cuévanos"). A subject closely linked to the author who so mocked and reproached merchants in the unforgettable scenes of his *La hora de todos* (*Everyone's Hour*).

This collaboration between the explicit verbal explanation and the *implications* of fantasy's images, in the service of the general effect of expressiveness, is extended along similar lines — although never identical in the Quevedesque architectural variety of each of the text's units — in the subsequent syntactical blocks. This is the case, for example, in the set of four descriptive entries which follow that of the eyes. First, the nose, immediately and ironically reinforced by the playful "between Rome and France", which at the same time implies the unexpressed association with beliefs concerning the nature of "pustules" as symptoms of the "French disease". And, following that of the nose, the descriptions of his beard, his teeth and his throat are linked in an unbridled crescendo of jokes governed by the obsessive fear of hunger.

The result of this sustained exercise of expressionist cooperation between language's verbal forms and the anomalous tensions produced by fantasy's imaginary associations is the synthesis of a vigorous, densely expressive image in which the portrait is transformed into a still-life (M. Baquero Goyanes, 1963). In this transfiguration, live nature is increasingly "objectified" towards the ironic stratum of a "dead nature". By means of its powerful capacity for suggesting and convoking abnormal fantastic images, the verbal expressiveness of Quevedo's linguistic formulas introduces us to a carnavalesque universe of representations entirely foreign to the language's usual, normal powers of extension.

In this general assault on the imagination, posed by so many simultaneous partial suggestions, the expressive forms produce their miraculous total transfiguration; to the point that, in the end, we find the final geometric and acoustic abstractions, through which the creature portrayed here ends up transformed into the cipher of a compass and the macabre serenade of a leper's rattle, to be perfectly meaningful: "Looked at from the waist down, he looked like a fork or a compass, with two long, skinny legs. He walked very slowly; if something went wrong, his bones sounded like lepers' rattles".

The rhetorical-fantastic expressiveness corresponding to all of these conceptual and absurd effects represents, as I was saying before, one of the most obvious and self-evident forms of the phenomenon. But the artistic principle of verbal expressiveness cannot be reduced, of course, to these most immediate and visible forms of satire and mockery, linked to the effects of the verbal joke and the "humble" style. On the contrary, every stylistic effect in the intentional, expressionist and artistic use of language originates in the linguistic support which provides it with an intentionally structured verbal formula, in such a way, that it permits and facilitates the type of fantastic and sentimental suggestions to which the verbal features of expressiveness stream or are translated.

In this way, the expressiveness of the ironic use of verbal forms in the *conceptista* model does not present itself as an exclusive characteristic, linked to a personal style or a given age, since it appears in moments and authors as distant from one another as in the origins of the epic and those of the Greek lyric - recall, for example, the images about the power of the lyre over Zeus' eagle in Pindar's first *Pythian Ode* — or in recent prose and theater, as in the *greguerías* of Ramón Gómez de la Serna or in Nabokov's narratives. By the same token, it is also not a mode exclusive to a certain stylistic level or thematic tone. The symptomatic fact of the contempt for Quevedo's ingenious verbal jokes may be offered as evidence of this non-exclusivity, considered by Gracián to represent easy and debased modes of the witty use of conceits. As the first theoretician and anthologizer of *conceptismo*, Gracián selected his inventory from among the best examples of keen expressiveness and anthologized them in his *Agudeza y arte de ingenio*, in which an ample classification appears of the legitimate expressions of this mode of expressiveness, extending from the classical Romans — Martial, Quintilian, Cicero, etc. — to his own contemporaries, and from very extensive and elaborate textual forms of compound wit to brief witticisms, phrases and even the quick-witted gestures of famous characters.

In this sense, we may consider Cervantes as a clear example and superior expression of all of the genres of expressiveness' registers. But we will invoke him here particularly for the purposes of pondering the active, intentional stylistic framework that underlies the classical modes of expressiveness, under a double register, pronounced in the sublime and pathetic styles, but not in the middle style of *urbanitas*.

As Mikhail Bakhtin has indirectly indicated in regard to Cervantes' novelesque art, the poetics of verbal expressiveness constitutes the great key to his capacities for creating fantastic worlds, initiating the conditions which in Dostoyevsky form the foundations for the origin of the modern "polyphonic" novel. Personally, I believe Cervantes' poetic complexity cannot be reduced to a basic set of resources incorporating narrative "voices" to the "polyphonic" phenomena of the "aesthetic" representation of a social chronotope (M. Bakhtin, 1929, 1975, pp. 133, 134, 221–225). Still, there is no doubt that Cervantes' extraordinary capacity for idiomatic expressiveness is one of his most outstanding resources.

Traditional criticism of Cervantes has also highlighted this same principle of linguistic expressiveness as one of Cervantes' fundamental capacities in the construction of his world of images in the novel. Recall, to cite just one aspect, the habitual emphasis placed on Sancho Panza's popular speech as serving to profile his carnavalesque personality (M. Bakhtin, 1955, p. 26). This is patently clear in the almost constant and dense features of discourse as, for example, with the dense multiplication of proverbs and colloquial digressions, the intentionally expressive excesses of which Don Quijote himself criticizes. What is indicated in the case of Sancho Panza's speech is a type of expressiveness manifested in counterpoint. But the literary phenomenon of expressiveness is much more universal and generic in Cervantes' art. The first implantation in Cervantes' prose of the imaginary-poetic seduction of colloquial persuasion in the delicious urbanity of a middle style, common to all of the characters and appropriately balanced moments that form the foundations of Cervantes' novelesque history, provides another example of this literary phenomenon of expressiveness. As used by Cervantes, the expressiveness of the middle style can be seen beginning with Alonso Quijano himself, in his moments of sanity, or in the delicious conversation of his neighbors: the priest, the barber, the Bachelor Sansón Carrasco, etc.

The poetic underpinnings of expressiveness in the mid-level discourse of Cervantes equates the majority of his non-parodic characters under a common kind of suggestive formula, which the expressive *cursus* of the narrative voice reserves for itself. More than the social polysemy of voices characteristic of the modern novel's realistic individualization, the universe of Cervantes' characters exists and is forged in the archetypal community of the ideal classic idyll. In this basic identity of conventional discourse, Cervantes' expressiveness exercises its immense powers, suggesting the concepts, feelings and emotions corresponding to the exalted expressiveness of moments of emotional tension in impassioned discourse. The latter is signaled by expressive forms at least as self-evident and differential as those of the middle style, such as the colorful examples of the colloquialism and vulgarism of Sancho's popular "voices" and the slang of Monipodio's "brotherhood".

Recall, for example, the unsurpassable opening of *El amante liberal*: "Oh lamentables ruinas de la desdichada Nicosia, ¡apenas enjutas de la sangre de vuestros valerosos y mal afortunados defensores! Si como carecéis de sentido, le tuviérades ahora, en esta soledad donde estamos, pudiéramos lamentar juntos nuestras desgracias, y quizás el haber hallado compañía en ellas aliviara nuestro tormento; esta esperanza os puede haber quedado, ¡mal derribados torreones!, que otra vez, aunque no para tan justa defensa como en la que os derribaron, os podéis ver levantados; mas yo desdichado, ¿qué bien podré esperar en la miserable estrecheza en que me hallo, aunque vuelva al estado en que estaba antes deste en que me veo? Tal es mi desdicha, que en la libertad fui sin ventura, y en el cautiverio, ni la tengo ni la espero" (M. de Cervantes, *El amante liberal*, M. Baquero Goyanes, ed., I, p. 175) ["Oh the lamentable ruins of unfortunate Nicosia! The blood of your valiant and most unfortunate defenders is yet scarcely dry. Though now you are senseless, if you had any feeling at all in this loneliness we inhabit, we could lament our misfortunes together, and perhaps having found company in them would ease our torment; this hope may have been left you — most fallen towers! —, that once more, though not in so just a defence in which they fell, you may see them raised; but I, unfortunate one, what good can I hope for in the miserable straights in which I find myself, though I were to return to the state of mind I was in before I found myself like this? Such is my misfortune, that in freedom I was without happiness and in captivity, I neither have it nor expect it"].

The rhetorical emphasis of the initial apostrophe finds itself plaintively diluted, particularly in the semantic waning of the adjectivization, redoubled in view of the expressive resonance of the two notions themselves, one natural and the other historical, which come into play in the invocation: "Oh the lamentable ruins of unfortunate Nicosia!" All of the natural weight of the exclamative impulse appears compressed and regulated by countless factors of very careful exclamative effect: the solemn and well-tempered prose rhythm, delighting in the elegant parallel reiterations, the careful selection of the least explosive terms — "lamentable" or "dry" — unfolding slowly, even, in phrases of explicitly sustained length: "your valiant and *badly fortunate* defenders" (not "unfortunate," for example). And together with these and other verbal factors of the expressive regulation of rhetorical vehemence, true to the figure of apostrophe, the powerful aesthetic effect of the fragment's expressiveness is, simultaneously, controlled by the decisive role of other discursive elements of an implicit nature.

1.3. Artistic Modes and the Aesthetic Law of Expressiveness 111

To begin with, the system of *premises* the author has immediately and in an automatic way brought into play in the readers' evocative associations, contributes powerfully to the sentimental result dominating the captive lovers' discourse of complaint. The first of these is the distancing structurally adopted by the rhetorical convention underlying the apostrophe: the conscious personification of an inanimate referent, Nicosia's ruins. A premise which makes ready and signals the opening note of the argumentative-syntactic game of implicitly unreal conditions: "though now you are senseless", etc. The awareness of the impossibility of dialogue with the inanimate ruins, which is the next piece in the expressive process of the emphatic rhetorical argumentation in this novelesque deployment of the topic of the complaining lover, archetypal in Petrarchist poetry, contributes to the sentimental structure of the discourse. A spoken, impossible dialogue with an inanimate confidant that, if here represented by a ruined city, was a river by antonomasia in Petrarchist poetry (A. García-Berrio, 1979 c, pp. 45—448; 1980 b, pp. 70—73).

The extension of the argumentative construction in this conventional rhetorical dialogue, regulated and, at the same time, maintained by the discursive play of the literary premises of the cultural system, launches the spirit of verbal expressiveness in the renewed and progressive game of conjecture: those ruins — the "*¡mal derribados* torreones!" — in remote expressive correspondence with the adjectival phrase of the "*mal afortunados* defensores" — can be reconstructed, but not the wounded lover's hope. A forlorn and plaintive argument, foreign to any vehement urgency, which finds the room at every moment to take pleasure in the circumlocutions of evocative orientation with the *restriction* of the concessive clause: "*que* otra vez, aunque no para tan justa defensa como *la en que* os derribaron, os podéis ver levantados." The game of rhetorical questions about the impossibility of escaping his destiny, knowingly prepares the expressive *tempo* of the final synthesis, also internally vigorous in its emotional emphasis, by means of the heightening of the consecutive play between protasis and apodosis and the climax deriving from the pessimistic parallelism of the two seasons of his destiny: "Such is my misfortune, that in freedom I was without happiness and in captivity, I neither have it nor expect it".

As tends to occur habitually in the model of Cervantes' narration, a scheme of doubly ironic expressive distancing is implanted which was imitated and continued by many others, especially Galdós. This ironic distance is achieved when the narrative voice immediately introduces the metalinguistic emphasis which, at the same time, makes evident and de-automatizes the artifice of the resources of expressiveness. If there is any doubt about this, consider how, immediately after the above-cited fragment, the personal voice of the narrator establishes a reasonable contrast with the lover's voice which nevertheless contributes more towards reinforcing rather than restricting the narrative expressiveness in the system of conventions regulating the rhetorical scheme of apostrophe: "Estas razones decía un cautivo cristiano, mirando desde un recuesto las murallas derribadas de la ya perdida Nicosia, y así hablaba con ellas, y hacía comparación de sus miserias y las suyas, como si ellas fueran capaces de entenderle". ["These words were spoken by a Christian captive looking at the fallen walls of the already lost Nicosia from a hill, speaking to them in this manner and comparing his miseries with theirs, *as if* they were able to understand him".]

But the metalinguistic contrast with the artifices of emphatic expressiveness in the high style of the pathetic "voice", is not only realized in the preceding example through the direct denunciation of the artificiality of the mechanism of the premise within the argumentative process of the plaintive dialogue with the confidant in the apostrophe. The same change of expressive register, produced with the middle style of the narrator's normal voice, particularly contributes to yield this calculated stylistic effect. In order to achieve this, Cervantes makes use of the narrator's *reductive paraphrase* in contrast to the apostrophe's emphatic use in the *amplificatio*. Note the strict precision of the reference, without any of the rhetorical adornments strewn throughout the preceding emotional deliberations delivered in the pathetic style: "y así hablaba con ellas y hacía comparación de sus miserias y las suyas." Closing, in turn, with the pithy style of narrative onmiscience, which sanctions the new synthetic closure of the *conclusion* with the same absence of emphatic marks corresponding to the middle style: "propia condición de afligidos" ["condition proper to afflicted persons"] — notice here the well-known essential-universalist effect produced by the absence of the article (A. Alonso, 1961, pp. 155—160) — "que, *llevados de sus imaginaciones*" ["who, carried away by their imaginations"] — Cervantes here explicitly calls attention to the fantastic mechanism: "hacen y dicen cosas ajenas de toda razón y buen discurso" ["do and say things beyond all reason and proper speach"].

1.3.4. On General Rhetoric as a Science of Artistic Expressiveness

In the course of the past twenty years, two kinds of scholars, with very different backgrounds and interests, have approached rhetoric. On the one hand, there are those investigating the classical tradition, like Lausberg (1960; J. Martin, 1974), motivated by a desire to exhume rhetorical science in all of its various aspects and dimensions. It is necessary that we recognize these investigators lack, even in the best cases, such as that of Lausberg himself, the capacity or, perhaps, the will to integrate that science, recovered perfectly in the majority of its utterances and appropriately articulated in its classifications, within the schemes of the modern disciplines of discourse. On the face of it, this seems inexcusable and scarcely well-conceived, since modern linguistics, genetically so closely linked to rhetoric in the great variety of its methodological approaches to the phenomenon of language, offers an exemplary — if not perfect — balance to rhetorics' own efforts within the development of the so-called human sciences.

1.3. Artistic Modes and the Aesthetic Law of Expressiveness 113

Since I have singled out Lausberg's work, it is only fair, in order to explain and excuse in his case the defect of pursuing or permitting the disciplinary divorce I have alluded to, to indicate in the first place that, given the enormous volume of his investigation, it may well have created distortions to have established throughout the book a permanent system of parallels between the materials of classical rhetoric and those of contemporary linguistics. Moreover, in the fifties, when Lausberg elaborated his great synthesis, the value of modern linguistics perhaps did not make the effort at interdisciplinary integration as essential as it is now. But this fact, which, in all justice, Lausberg himself can in no way be censured for, as though it were his own defect, has nevertheless been translated into a bad example for many of his followers.

The second sector of recent approaches to rhetoric encompasses those who, coming from different modern disciplines dedicated to the study of discourse — including linguistics, poetics and semiology and, in many respects, logic — have caught a glimpse of the possibility of finding in the categories and analytico-interpretative paradigms of rhetoric some productive assistance for expanding or even resolving certain crises in their own respective disciplines. In many of these cases, true in very different fields (P. Kuentz, 1971, pp. 112—114; Group μ, 1977; J. Kopperschmidt, 1977), the concept of rhetoric was little more than a flexible framework in which some vaguely pragmatic intuitions could comfortably be lodged. Rhetoric, as they had recently discovered it, would be a kind of universal mechanism of persuasion, with not overly well-defined rules, or, at most, a weak, stunted and inadequate system of strategies for dialogue or argumentation, barely measuring up to anything more than the common sense of the neorhetoricians themselves. Obviously, rhetoric as a plurisecular science has far more to contribute and offers far more in the way of real backing to researchers than this caricature would suggest (J. M. Pozuelo Yvancos, 1988a, pp. 181 ff.; F. Chico Rico, 1988, pp. 49—63).

From these criticisms of the current situation, it is already possible to predict the general lines in which I would set forth a collaboration between rhetoric and the modern disciplines of discourse, with the goal in mind of constructing a general rhetoric particularly suitable for scientifically appraising the resources of literary expressiveness. In the first place, we are dealing with a collaboration possible and most fruitful only on the condition that it be an authentic *integration*, in the terms that will be set forth below. Secondly, it is absolutely necessary that the somewhat empty denomination of rhetoric or neorhetoric be endowed with its genuine stock of principles, categories and hermeneutical strategies for the analysis of literary discourse. This task is justified on its own terms, if only in consideration of the enormous doctrinal deposits made by a tradition of thought unceasingly active for over twenty centuries, to which some of the most brilliant minds of the West have contributed. In this sense, we should indicate that none of the syntheses of rhetoric — neither the most ambitious modern examples nor those that survive from antiquity — can be considered a sufficient and definitively balanced view of the general tradition of the discipline. The history of rhetoric, like that of poetics, is so rich, and the documents that constitute it are so numerous and, in spite of appearances, varied, that the current project of scientifically laying the foundations for a re-implantation of rhetoric at the center of the disciplines of discourse presupposes a preceding stage dedicated to the adequate *recovery of historic thought*. Only in this manner will the current initiative not find itself frustrated and defeated, once again, by irresponsible adventures in poetics and semiology.

Precisely in the context of this progress of integration which I am setting forth and defining here, the project of a general rhetoric would acquire its full meaning. Certainly the greatest merit of Dubois and his collaborators is the respect and prudence with which they attempted to organize the French classical doctrine on the tropes of Fontanier and Du Marsais from the perspective of a set of elemental categories, along the lines of categorical taxonomies and systemic genetics, already familiar in structuralist explanation. Of course, as Group μ participants recognize, their rhetoric is a long way from being a general rhetoric. Although possessing the will for integration, it is clear that, from the start, the project of an *elocutio* has almost entirely lacked the integration of the doctrines of *dispositio, inventio* and *actio*, all of which together made classical rhetoric the most scientific instrument for the analysis, interpretation and practice of discourse.

An authentic general rhetoric, like that Habermas glimpsed since its hermeneutical re-insertion (1971, p. 123), or that which Kopperschmidt has energetically been calling for (1977, p. 216), cannot disregard its complex relationship with the science of dialectics (H. G. Gadamer, 1967, pp. 113—130). In principle, the examination in depth of *inventio* constitutes one of the most urgent debts which current rhetorical-scientific speculations owe the powerful technique of elaboration of the products of human discourse which, in its origins, rhetoric was. But, having declared these priorities, it also does not seem realistic to me to think that the possibility exists today to efficiently navigate the remote and uncertain waters which made up the difficult boundary between rhetoric and dialectics in Greek cultural ideology. In any case, I believe the prudent demarcation of these spheres by linguists and poetologists, which left the speculation corresponding to dialectics in the care of logicians and philosophers of science (C. Perelman and L. Olbrechts-Tyteca, 1958; L. Gianformaggio, 1981, pp. 110—188), cannot be branded as a capricious disciplinary division of labor. Moreover, it is a fact that whatever breadth it may have possessed at its foundation, rhetoric left Greece already largely converted into an art of verbal persuasion (G. A. Kennedy, 1963; A. García-Berrio, 1977—1980; J. J. Murphy, 1983).

General rhetoric's tasks should not exclude any of those belonging to each of its traditional sectors. It is well-known that the recently disseminated work of neorhetoricism in practice has been reduced to the development of a literary rhetoric (W. C. Booth, 1965). Lausberg himself did not see any problem in placing his own work under that specific designation and the members of Group μ even came to identify the poetic and rhetorical functions as absolute synonyms (Group μ, 1970, p. 81; R. Lachmann, 1977, p. 181). Nor is the situation at all altered by the oratorical-persuasive nature characterizing the studies of eloquence in American neorhetoricisms, perhaps the broadest and oldest tradition among those which come together to form this neorhetorical rebirth (I. A. Richards, 1936; E. Black, 1965).

But a literary rhetoric, which in itself can become a truly interesting, powerfully complex system, still does not exhaustively recover the original value and commitment of rhetoric as a science or art of persuasion. Moreover, it cannot be considered a general rhetoric. This discipline, while ideal for the present moment, must generalize its capacities in order to be applied to the great extension of the verbal text, to any text with communicative-actuational intentionality. Literary or poetic texts will thus be attended to within the sphere of that general rhetoric in terms of their generic condition as articulated and "uttered" texts. Furthermore no fortuitous circumstance should be permitted to invert this image of the facts: although, historically, the chronicles of the discipline and its recent reactivation illustrate very clearly that this did take place in the past. A small part of rhetoric's materials, dealing with the figures, has been specialized in error since French classicism as literary rhetoric (P. Fontanier, 1968 edition), resulting in the incorrect generalization that a general rhetoric is largely or solely a literary rhetoric. Dubois and his collaborators have intelligently recognized this traditional excess as a case of Gallocentrism (Group μ, 1977, pp. 13–14).

Rhetoric, then, or general rhetoric, is unmistakenly identified with linguistics as far as its most complex common object, the text, is concerned (A. García-Berrio, 1979). In this sense, moreover, and thanks to the convergence of interest in certain current linguistic developments for the general construction or semantic genesis of the utterance, I do not believe it exaggerated to insist on the possible correlation between this ambitious general rhetoric, integrated in linguistics, and a properly developed *textual linguistics* (J. S. Petöfi and A. García-Berrio, 1979; A. García-Berrio, 1979 a).

As regards its interest, also justified and even fundamental, in special types of verbal utterances of a lyrical and poetic nature, rhetoric can, if so desired, specialize and allocate this particular field to literary rhetoric. This kind of specialized rhetorical investigation would be the most important and effective instrument for the study of literary expressiveness.

Take, for instance, one of the most characteristic examples of expressiveness. Compared to recent contributions, none of the taxonomies and lists of categories established by non-rhetorical stylistics can offer us today a more complete system for analyzing those authentically *intentional stylemes of expressiveness*, namely, the *figures of speech*. In addition, as far as this question is concerned, the *integration* of present linguistic thought — a prerequisite for a general rhetoric — with expressive schemes or figures of speech is already a relatively firm reality. This is the case, both as concerns concrete aspects — like metonymy and metaphor (M. Black, 1962; Group μ, 1970, p. 108; A. Henry, 1971; M. Hester, 1967; M. Le Guern, 1973; P. Ricoeur, 1975; H. Kubczak, 1977; S. Sacks, ed., 1980) — and also the development of a general system of the figures of speech, which Genette opportunely called attention to (1968), immediately awakening Todorov's fleeting interest (1967), itself preceded by Leech's more mature reflections (1966) themselves and followed by Plett's more complex efforts in this area (1977). Finally, the development of a global system led to Group μ's (1970) meritworthy proposal for a rhetoric of the figures of speech, the major weakness of which may be, not the careful way in which the treatment of the figures was integrated, but the inaccurate title selected for the work, referring as it does to a general rhetoric (Group μ, 1977, p. 19).

Certainly, being able to consider a doctrinal element as important as that of the figures of speech as being relatively firmly and satisfactorily established is no small accomplishment from the perspective of the formulation of a literary rhetoric, within the course of the development of a general rhetoric. In this chapter, I will consider this systematization of the figures as an accomplished fact, as providing us with a ready and available set of theoretical and analytical instruments. But I do not believe the program I am delineating in these pages should stop there. On the contrary, as I will set forth more fully at the end of the chapter, the rigorous investigation of the materials of textual construction deposited in the historical quarries of rhetorical *dispositio*, and especially the revitalization of the activity of *movere* or persuasion through an *argumentation of the transmitter's values*, are decisive for the revitalization from the rhetorical perspective of an exegesis of literary expressiveness that now finds itself listing heavily to port under the weight of a crisis of conflicting interests.

Among the causes for the attention being paid to rhetoric by diverse sectors of literary investigation, aside from those of a general social nature commonly alluded to (H. Plett, 1977; B. Luking, 1977, pp. 49—50), I should point out the situation of methodological crises currently affecting literary studies. Many critics are coming to view literary rhetoric as offering a hopeful, redemptive perspective (R. Lachmann, 1977, pp. 169—170). In fact, the arsenal of textual categories and hermeneutical strategies which rhetoric has at its disposal can contribute to revitalizing the linguistic and poetological disciplines dedicated to the artistic text, especially as regards its mechanisms of verbal expressiveness. The different modes or levels of collaboration I am referring to can be catalogued according to the following scale of expectations:

a) *Simple and direct reimplantation of rhetoric*. In reality, this consists of replacing the different analytical algorithms and inventories of categories developed throughout this century by modern semiological poetics of a formal cast,

from Russian formalism to structural neoformalisms (E. Black, 1965; G. Ueding, 1976).
b) *Completion and perfection.* In this understanding of the matter, rhetoric presents itself as a rich mine of materials destined to fill the empty *slots* in formalist textual analysis (Group μ, 1977).
c) *Interdisciplinary integration.* This perspective presupposes an intimate collaboration between rhetoric and linguistic poetics. It would tend to definitively reorganize studies of the literary text, restoring the old doctrinal branch of classical rhetoric, integrated with the accurate contributions of current poetics and linguistics. This, clearly, is the option I consider as the most viable path for a general rhetoric.

Next, I will examine in greater detail the distinctive advantages and disadvantages each of the three options presents, always in view of the generalized crisis of critical methods I have established as the starting point and framework for this collaboration. It should be kept in mind that the objective of this methodological recovery lies particularly in the acquisition of the classical science's rich casuistry for identifying and typifying discourse's artistic effects of expressiveness. The reimplantation of rhetoric, as a means purely and simply of recovering its past hermeneutical textual laws, is the option most attractive to that current of opinion traditionally most reticent towards the recent successes of linguistic poetics. Attempts in this direction are not lacking. Though today they tend more or less to be concealed, they still exist, especially among the most conservative sectors of the European sciences dedicated to the study of Romance languages and literatures, classical philology and the "explication de textes". To the thousands of systematic rhetorical treatises written throughout Europe between the fifteenth and nineteenth centuries, which by themselves already could offer an organized base available for immediate use, it is necessary to add the important contribution of systematic syntheses, so popular in recent decades, such as Lausberg's famous manual. Nevertheless, we do not have to strain ourselves to see the disadvantages of this initiative, so obviously extreme (G. Ueding, 1976). Figured into my conceptions here, again, are both the present crisis of literary criticism and the past failure and petrification of traditional rhetoric (B. Vickers, 1988).

The same rhetoric which today offers so much promise, historically failed as a customary science of discourse, beginning with European Romanticism (R. Barthes, 1970; G. Genette, 1968). From our present analytical perspective, this defeat was the result of the convergence of many causes, the invalidating influence of which has not disappeared even today. Among these causes, the following are worth noting:

a) *Rhetoric loses its interpretative and normative value.* Increasingly, and especially beginning with the late rhetorics of the Baroque and Neoclassical periods, rhetoric lost its character, not only as a discipline dedicated to the interpretation of discourse, but even as a normative "corpus" of resources for textual synthesis (M. Fumaroli, 1980). This process of utopian degeneration was strongly intensified throughout Europe in the nineteenth century (Group μ, 1970, p. 8). At that point, rhetoric became a purely historical and monumentalist discipline, in which the connection between the inventories of devices and figures, learned by rote, and the interpretative reality of language was no longer sought.

b) *Rhetoric severs its ties with contemporary discourse.* In a certain way, this is another facet of the previously cited cause. The didactic transformation of rhetoric into a purely historical, archaic discipline favored inertia in the maintenance of examples, especially Latin examples (H. F. Plett, 1977, pp. 125—128). The absence of a new system of exemplification, submitting the canonical paradigms of Greco-Latin, medieval and Renaissance rhetoric to the pressure of critical thought and revision, was without doubt one of the determining factors in the petrification of these paradigms. In the long run, this translated into a feeling of frustration and a lack of interest.

c) *Modern discourse's new paradigms surpass the rhetorical model.* Romanticism's tension and its programatic attack on classical discourse in its use of vocabulary, syntactic and textual structures, figures, images, etc., created the first example of an anti-rhetorical text, or, better put, a set of texts relatively deviant from classical texts and, hence, from the rhetorical paradigm established *ad hoc* on the basis of that discursive model. But Romanticism signals only the first step in a whole series of anti-classical revolutions, through which a modern scheme of artistic discourse was gradually structured (A. García-Berrio and M. T. Hernández, 1988, pp. 54—57). The successive pressures applied to language by the *literary vanguards* and the corresponding phenomena in the evolution of the norms of practical, logico-communicative discourse definitively sanctioned the emerging crisis in classicist scholarly rhetoric. As a result, the rhetorical disciplines, upon not evolving doctrinally in a manner parallel to the evolution of the effective resources of common and artistic language, suffered for the first time a process of decline marked by the growing insufficiency of its doctrinal categories, both on the descriptive-interpretative and normative planes. From this situation — evident, for example, in the Russian formalists' feelings that traditional rhetorical categories were inadequate for their purposes (A. García-Berrio, 1973), that is, for explaining the tensions of futurist language and imagination — the early crisis of literary criticism in the first decade of the twentieth century begins to take shape.

d) *Final rejection of rhetoric as synonymous with a certain kind of ineffective discourse.* The didactic rhetoric of the schools specialized only one kind of figure of speech and one scheme of expressiveness: that representing the most overloaded and baroque extremes of hyperbaton, catachresis, spectacular cadences of the phrase, etc. — in short, the devices characterizing the most emphatic and unnatural kind of expressiveness. Thus, rhetoric was discredited stylistically in such memorable examples as that of Verlaine (H. F. Plett, 1977, p. 9; Group μ, 1970, p. 8). Everywhere, at the beginning of the century, a "rhetorical" way of speaking or of style became synonymous with a kind of exaggerated, emphatic and grotesque expressiveness (G. Ueding, 1976). The undesirability of the so-called "rhetorical style" inadvertently generated the general and irresponsible, but very effective and long-lasting rejection of all rhetoric.

This anti-rhetorical feeling characterized, for example, reaction among the Spanish writers of the last decade of the nineteenth century, the so-called *noventaiochistas* (ninety-eighters) against the generation that had preceded them, viewed as representatives of tendencies in prose and oratory belonging to the nineteenth century. Keep in mind, however, that this was a simplification. It can certainly be argued that nobody escapes rhetoric or, better yet, that every style has its rhetoric, to the extent that verbal style implies the stylization of that which we call expressiveness. All of the historical forms of expressionist stylization, the extreme as much as the measured, the Ciceronian as much as that guided by the influence of Tacitus or Seneca, the Asianist as much as the Attic, are examples and options for the development of expressiveness as an intentional and active feature in language. Classical rhetoric, like its present version, was a complete science of expression or, rather, of the intentional devices of expressiveness (E. Black, 1965, pp. 13—16), a true stylistics of verbal communicative expressiveness. Clearly, the rhetorical discipline, as the secular deposit of classical textual knowledge, had at its disposal the resources and foresight to incorporate any kind of expressive discourse, since, in effect, all of the possible options were fulfilled in human communication with the passing centuries.

Taking all of these circumstances into account, the rhetoric which would result from a substitution of formal poetics by traditional rhetoric, given these kinds of premises, is simply a trimmed hermeneutics of *elocutio*, attentive to certain features of *dispositio* only through the example of the textual interest of structuralist narratology and of textual linguistics. That is, more or less the same parcelled discipline the replacement of which motivated the inauguration of a productive formalist poetics. And it would not be a question of relapsing into the situation which gave rise to Bakhtin's central accusation that such poetics do not elucidate anything more than the *material* in the verbal work of art (M. Bakhtin, 1975 [1978, pp. 24—39]). Such a rhetoric could be destined to achieve no other purpose, and in this task would certainly not match the achievements of the old formalisms. The implementation of this option would leave certain opportunities undeveloped. The profound reimplantation of the many possibilities for aesthetico-thematic explanation from the perspective of *inventio* would not take place, and the necessary explanation of *actio* from the decisive possibility of a pragmatic orientation would remain unexplored. A rhetoric with this kind of scope can only be approached in the option I call complementation, and is only entirely fulfilled in a final moment of integration, in the deployment of a rhetoric related to the ideal algorithms of textual analysis and interpretation.

Having discarded the convenience of entirely substituting the system of formal analysis of literary texts with the traditional rhetorical system, we will consider the possibilities created by a second alternative, that is, attempting to reciprocally complete both systems. In this case, the first criteria, the adoption of which appears to me to be a top priority, is that in these operations of collation one of the two systems must constitute a base and the other a source of complementation (D. Breuer, 1974; 1977, pp. 29–30). For the previously mentioned reasons concerning the failure of the traditional rhetorical method in the face of the new modes of verbal expressiveness with an anti-classical vocation, it seems more expedient — and here, moreover, I am well within the most authoritative line of debate to be found in modern bibliography (B. Lüking, 1977, pp. 55–59) — that the doctrinal *corpus* of modern linguistic poetics constitute this base. The limits of the methodological scheme set forth by poetics would thus be complemented by the vast inventory of categories and hermeneutical strategies which traditional rhetoric can put at its disposal (B. Spillner, 1977, p. 102). In this task of complementation we can foresee two fundamental and opposing developments: in particular situations, either rhetoric will be deficient or linguistic poetics will be inadequate.

In the case of the first scenario, there are, without doubt, aspects in which linguistic poetics has surpassed traditional rhetoric in the accuracy and suitability of its consideration of the artistic text's verbal expressiveness. Perhaps the most outstanding example occurs in the area of reflections on fictional prose and, in general, narrative style (Group μ, 1977, pp. 30). If one considers the urgent motives the Russian formalists alleged for legitimating their nonconformist critical program, the validity of their observation of a total lack of analytico-interpretative instruments for the analysis of narrative texts in traditional criticism, itself fundamentally nourished as such by traditional rhetoric, is clear. This is certainly the case if we keep in mind that this complaint referred most strictly to narrative fiction and not to a rhetorico-doctrinal vacuum of categories and principles relating to other modes of artistic prose. On the other hand, we must remember that the different rhythmic organizations that could alternate in the organization of the clauses' *periodare*, or the broader schemes for the *dispositio* of argumentative texts — for example, the different modes of forensic or religious discourse (T. M. Charland, 1936; H. Caplan, 1934–1936), or even of epistolary argumentation (C. Baldwin, 1924 [1959, pp. 206–257]; L. Rockinger, 1863–1864; J. J. Murphy, 1974, pp. 194 ff.), and many other concrete specifications of the structure of artistic prose, were all perfectly foreseen by classical rhetoric. In fact, the mine of rhetorical materials dealing with the countless textual variants for the disposition or structure of the *case*, the sermon or the letter, are, in my judgment, one of the most solid sources for extending the more restricted concept of elocutionary expressiveness to the more developed alternatives of textual expressiveness which rhetoric has to offer, especially in view of the structural mechanisms it developed beginning as early as the Middle Ages (E. Faral, 1928).

The entire question of narrative expressiveness also suggests a second kind of consideration. Attention to narrative fiction and its textual structures, if effectively lacking in the rhetorical tradition, is not absent to the same degree within poetics. The relative modernity of the novel as a narrative genre, largely coinciding with the decline of classicist poetics and rhetoric beginning in the seventeenth century, surely explains this analytical and theoretical void in both disciplines (J. Spingarn, 1908, pp. 116—119; B. Weinberg, 1961, pp. 954 ff.; 1970—1973). But narrative fiction, as a mode of discourse, was given considerable attention in classical poetics from its very beginnings in Aristotle, in terms of his discussion of the succession of events in tragedy. The inherent value of these antecedents is very well substantiated in the fact that some of the most widely disseminated characteristics of narrative structures cited in recent narratology, such as the notions of processes of progressive improvement or deterioration (C. Bremond, 1966, 1973) or some even more general concepts, such as the basic structure of the distribution of actants in general and narrative discourse (A. J. Greimas, 1966, 1970, 1973), share more than obvious correspondences with Aristotle's descriptions of the textual mechanisms of *fabula* and *mores*, respectively, in classical tragedy (A. García-Berrio, 1975, pp. 110 ff., 161 ff.; 1979 a, pp. 34—35). Nevertheless, the significant advantage modern poetics has over classical poetics with regard to the investigation of narrative *dispositio* cannot be extended to include all other types of texts. Lyrical and poetic texts, for example, would have to be excluded from such an affirmation. Even with respect to dramatic texts, insofar as the very fact of dramaticity itself is concerned, classical poetics still has a great deal to contribute.

The *superiority of classical rhetoric* is absolute as compared to the experience of modern criticism, even without including what poetics has to offer as far as its attention to the artistic features of expressiveness is concerned, based on the infinite figures and schemes it has developed in the domain of *elocutio*. In this field the neoformalist structuralist trends have almost entirely abandoned the general lines set forth in the Russian formalists' analysis, including such notions as those of *zaum* or transrationality, the conflicts between logical and rhythmical syntax, the textual dynamization of isolated elements, polysemy, etc., thereby ignoring some excellent descriptive models of the formal design of expressive intentionality. The only corresponding notions adequately developed thus far, concerning isotopic (A. J. Greimas, 1966; F. Rastier, 1972; Group μ, 1977, pp. 30—73) or thematic networks (J. S. Petöfi, 1973, 1975), are small steps in comparison to the enormously rich mass of possibilities waiting to be explored (J. Klinkenberg, 1973). Perhaps neoformalism's shortcomings in this regard were adequately compensated for by stylistics, which created a fairly satisfactory system of the stylemes and mechanisms of eloquence, particularly those relating to poetic expressiveness, albeit linked almost exclusively to the syntagmatic-sentential domain; that is to say, exclusively relating to the microtext (D. Alonso, 1952; A. Alonso, 1955). In this respect, moreover, Spanish, German and French stylistics were all clearly following and continuing the rhetorical analytical tradition.

It is worth noting here that the concept of expressiveness I am working with as the proper object of rhetorical description and explanation cannot be reduced solely to the elocutive-verbal sphere. Nevertheless, this is the area classical rhetoric paid special attention to, in terms of said expressive stylistic intentionality. At present, we should extend the concept of expressiveness to its rightfully broad textual terms. In this way, in the composition of an extensive text, as for example in the structural calculation of the process of a discourse's persuasive argument, or in that of the fictional verisimilitude of the novel, we can truly see strategies of intentional expressiveness at work.

These forms of expressiveness, which we might call macrotextual, are the result of the same psychological and communicative causes as those underlying the strictly verbal or micro-syntagmatic expressiveness of elocution. In both cases, it is a question of creating the emotional and expressive emphasis in the message favoring the kind of special communicative effect in the receiver which we recognize as sentimental, aesthetic or artistic, an effect of a connotative nature which adds the extra sentimental or imaginative elements that serve to transform the denotative structure of the communicative expression into forms of emotive and artistic expressiveness.

In conclusion, there is no doubt that the doctrinal superiority of rhetoric over modern poetics turns out to be complete in regard to particular and concrete facts and questions relating to the verbal phenomenon of discourse's expressive intentionality. This valorization nevertheless should not appear scandalous to an ideology fed on the conviction of modern superiority and on the idea of the progressive perfection of human thought. In effect, what caused the break to occur, in its time, and has caused this recession, is the deliberate interruption of the evolutionary course of critical textual science as a rhetorical tradition, put into operation at the end of the last century by different formalisms. This rupture, as such, which in reality never came to be entirely consummated, has endowed critical postulates with an essential measure of depth which they lacked in the automated analytical methods of the rhetorical treatises (D. C. Bryant, 1967, p. 36). This was, even so, achieved at the cost of an unquestionable detriment to analytical categories dealing with the broad extension of the artistic devices of textual expressiveness. In short, it could be said that modern formal rhetoric has incremented, or at least revitalized, traditional rhetoric's capacities for textual interpretation, thereby reducing its own resources for textual analysis (B. Lüking, 1977, p. 59).

1.3.5. The Integration of Rhetoric and Linguistic Poetics: The Thematic Macrostructure of Expressiveness

The third way of relating rhetoric and linguistic poetics is by way of interdisciplinary integration. In terms of the advantages of this option compared to the two already discussed, which I have already hinted at, it should be kept in mind that the principal task of linguistic poetics over the past eighty years has not consisted in innovating aspects or contents unknown to traditional rhetoric, but in renovating doctrines insufficient in their potential for the analysis and interpretation of the text, and, especially, in extending and adapting these doctrines to the greater demands of new textual modes, particularly as concerns artistic texts.

Complementarily, this effort at scientifically adapting poetics has been realized with the intention of integrating and assuming the developments of closely related disciplines, especially linguistics, in the knowledge that its progress through those same years had been exemplary and its methodological leadership among the other so-called "human sciences" was unquestionable. Thus, linguistic poetics has taken an important step towards endowing itself with a doctrinal content autonomous from that of rhetoric. Proceeding with its back to the ancient science may well have initially favored the depth and reach of that autonomy. However, in view of the current crisis of formal poetics, amplifying the number of real objectives in the text subject to interpretation may prove to be an interesting alternative.

Still, we have to assume that the present relative crisis of formalization in human sciences should not be taken as an irreversible and definitive phenomenon. On the contrary, I believe this is yet another facet of the exhaustion by super-production affecting linguistic poetics, on which my previous considerations have been based. This slump will grow increasingly deep and insurmountable the longer linguistic poetics resists adapting itself to its new contents and demands. A more realistic and complete consideration of the text seems inevitable today. In such a conceptualization, the text's extensional aspects, its *pragmatico-social* and *individual-aesthetic* dimensions, necessarily including its imaginary meaning, urgently require placing the artistic text in a position adequately reflecting its true nature and complexity. For this reason I appeal to the need for rhetorical complementation, or the substitution of rhetoric, in the same way that, further ahead, I will propose the expansion of the concept of the text to include its imaginary space. Both proposals may really mean nothing more than the obvious and immediate fulfillment of this need for the true adaption of literary theory to reflect textual complexity, far broader and more general than it has been conceived of in the past (J. Kopperschmidt, 1977, p. 217).

However, we should not forget that, as deep as the present crisis in linguistic poetics may be, and as great as the deficiencies and limitations of these studies may be, compared to the objective complexity of artistic verbal texts, the efficacy with which formal poetics has dealt with its objectives cannot be doubted, be they many or few, partial or total. The fundamental key to this efficacy resides in post-Saussurean linguistics's profound examination of the formal nature of language and in its ability to articulate it, as opposed to classical rhetoric and grammar, as part of a general understanding of human faculties for the production of thought and language. To this, we may add a capacity for demonstration which, at the very least, can be compared to that of logical and grammatical thought's very best historical moments. By virtue of its association with this linguistic trend, modern poetics has more than satisfactorily achieved its foundational goal of revitalizing rhetorical categories (K. Dockhorn, 1968, p. 63) and has rescued them from the didactic automatization to which they had been condemned by a long scholarly tradition which restricted them from having anything to do with the real characteristics of the transmission, analysis and interpretation of language's productive texts.

From all of this, we may deduce that a program of collaboration between linguistics and rhetoric — with the aim of elaborating a complete general rhetoric — can only be outlined after the detailed examination of the great majority of existing rhetorical texts is completed. This means, at the very least, the exhaustive review of those documents which have proven decisive in the historical development of the discipline, as well as the suitable systematization of the resulting material. In this task it is important to always remain open to the surprise afforded by valuable discoveries and contributions, which will indoubtedly begin to emerge from the historical review of thousands of forgotten texts.

This starting point simultaneously serves to broaden our awareness of rhetoric's activities to the full and true domain to which they apply as it continues and extends the notion of artistic discourse's rhetorical expressiveness, revealing its definitive importance. In effect, this more active awareness of rhetorical expressiveness — including that which I have described in the initial pages of this chapter — is exclusively combined with the forced historical understanding equating rhetoric and *elocutio*. But literature's expressiveness is not restricted to conventionalized microtextual *elocutio*. Far more than that, it is the effect of artistic choices and selections of *inventio* and the macro and microcomponental processes of *dispositio*.

Neutral reality, historical and objective — that is, the mere inventory of extensional contents included in discourse's referential operations — is not, in itself, aesthetically expressive. The object of the historian or chronicler, the naturalist or technician, it only reveals its poetic-expressive illumination when it is taken on and channeled through the process of *intensionalization* (T. Albaladejo Mayordomo, 1986). This reduces the unconventional breadth

1.3. Artistic Modes and the Aesthetic Law of Expressiveness

of the text's extensional weight as a neutral, anodyne and imposing reality to its artistic and literary dimensions of textual insertion and *expressiveness*.

This process of "intensionalization" includes the entire set of rhetorical-artistic operations; only by appealing to its complexity and its ample dimensions is it possible to explain the secret of the poetic text's general and profound expressiveness, in contrast with the instantaneous and very concrete, precise expressive effect of the joke, the convincing advertising jingle or the active slogan which mobilizes political opinion. The central theme together with its deployment in secondary themes, spread throughout the complex semantic network of the text, is an unmistakable artistic element by virtue of its intensionalized stylization. This is how reality's neutral order, constructed by rules of truth and falsehood, becomes iridescent in literary themes, where the feature of rhetorical-inventive expressiveness gives the effect of a component inserted in its setting, of its focalization and reduction to the most biting, symptomatic and enlightening space, under the control of verisimilar rules.

But the expressiveness of the extensional referents of reality, in their insertion as artistic themes of the literary work, is not produced only as the effect of a process involving the expressive trimming and intensionalization of the text's mass of semantic contents. Semantic intensification is strictly linked to various structural manipulations of macro and microsyntax. From the text to the syntagm, rhetorical *dispositio* governs and explains the most striking achievements of literary expressiveness, which of course culminate in that final most immediate and visible element of eloquence.

The second problem to be addressed prior to the formulation of a rhetoric of literary expressiveness is the suitable articulation of the theoretical successiveness of the parts of rhetorical discourse with the simultaneity of the verbal utterance's operations. Closely related to the previously discussed inadequacy and of greater consequence is the habitual simplification in rhetorical treatises of the five parts of discourse production — *inventio, dispositio, elocutio, memoria,* and *actio* — as a general image of the production of the linguistic act. Amidst this confusion, the idea of the succession of the parts (H. Lausberg, 1960, § 255) was suggested beginning with Cicero's *De Oratore* (I, 31, 142) — in one of the passages selected by Lausberg — by means of subordinative-successive particles as explicit as: "*primum* quid diceret, *deinde* inventa non solum sed etiam momento ... *tum* ea denique vestire ... oratione, *post* memoria saepire, *ad extremum* agere". The generalization of this enumeration of the parts of discourse confused and simplified:

1. Discourse's *double onomasiological and semasiological perspective*, situating it since then preferentially in the exclusive perspective of production, against the traditional custom of rhetoric itself, which had paid attention to both production and reception in its consideration of the persuasive effects of discourse (*delectare, docere, movere*) in all of the three basic genres. In this

respect, recall, for example, the existence in ancient rhetoric of contrasting couplings of categories as significant as *inventio/intelligio*, used to represent the double perspective, creative and receptive, of one and the same activity of conceptual discovery.
2. The existence of a real plan for discourse's production and reception, not based on a fixed non-lineal-terminal order (J. S. Petöfi, 1973, p. 221), but on the principle of the simultaneity of operations, and of an order achieved by means of a system of macro and microcomponential transformations (T. van Dijk, 1972, pp. 139—156), operating as a "block of information" on the textual basis (J. S. Petöfi, 1975, pp. 8—15).
3. The "rhetorical order", both from the experience of linguistic awareness itself and of elementary competence, is shown to be contradictory, since it seeks to affirm itself as a planned structure of discourse, when in reality it is an arbitrary dis-arrangement or dis-ordering of the textual plan.

Considering the current general level of linguistic knowledge, it does not seem necessary to have to insist on the historical and theoretical consequences precipitated by an order of closed compartmentalization like that inspired by the stereotype of rhetorical production (B. Spillner, 1977, pp. 100—104). The enumeration and description of the parts of discourse popularized by rhetoric can offer, and in fact has offered, a secure and relatively exhaustive model for the conception of the mechanisms of textual production (D. Breuer, 1974; especially, 1977, p. 32). In this case, not only the developments and contributions of European textual linguistics, previously indicated, or of French semiological structuralism, but also the contributions of Chomskian generativism itself can corroborate and perfect rhetoric's traditional claims. Whatever their degree of concretion or of linguistic reality may be, there can be no doubt that productive concepts like those of deep structure, transformational hierarchies, stylistico-semantic transformations, lexical insertion, generalized, optative and obligatory transformation, etc., do serve to perfect, as perhaps no other grammatical doctrines until the present, the true reach and order of production of the old rhetorical paradigm's components (B. Spillner, 1977, p. 104).

In my judgment, the unforeseeable and spontaneous nature of the effects of expressiveness is, to a large extent, due to this neither discrete nor independent condition of rhetorical compartmentalization and operations. The reversibility of the three rhetorical compartments, their permeability and the indistinct flow of the processes of genesis are the source of the majority of the aesthetic effects of expressiveness. At times, the accidental association between close or highly contrasting signifiers activates the logical processes of ambiguity or lexical and conceptual analogy, expressive results progressing from *elocutio* to *inventio*. On occasion, what stands out expressively are the effects of parallelism or of dispositive contrast in the text's macrostructure.

There is no doubt that the poetic effects of rhetorical expressiveness have their best guarantee of quality in their unforeseeable spontaneity, their being,

1.3. Artistic Modes and the Aesthetic Law of Expressiveness

therefore, incompatible with a compartmentalized mechanism of rhetorical operations. Literary expressiveness escapes all foresight, appearing suddenly and from the most unexpected direction. It thus has its genesis, indistinctly, in any of the three great areas of rhetoric's theoretical divisions, mobilizing them simultaneously and in a disorderly fashion. By the same token, expressiveness is the harvest of the concrete and localized syntagmatic discovery, as it is the fruit of the flowering of distributions, calculations and representations of a longer and more delayed kind, generated in the macrostructure's syntax and semantics. Poetic expressiveness is an antagonist of the parsimonious, of that which is mechanically articulated, of temperate expectations. For this reason it does not escape rhetoric's dynamic models but resists and hides from its more rigid forms of organization, fleeing any excessive schematism.

Inventio was fashioned in classical rhetoric as a dialectical instrument permitting the discovery of the circumstances inherent in the question or theme to be debated, according to the famous basic questionnaire of interrogation, and only secondarily as an inventory of information and facts, pertinent to the knowledge of the "rhetor". Beginning with this rhetorical base, the poetic application of *inventio*, or at least of its corresponding section, is what served to fix a certain restricted type of thematism — suitable or decorous — corresponding to the verisimilitude of the kind of language proper to the character. The historical occurrence of this mode of rhetorically based rules and restrictions in the archetypal and topical constitution of texts has had very important consequences, rarely brought to our attention by modern literary theory and poetics. Moreover, as I will discuss next, in the establishment of a topic of modern discourse equivalent to the restrictive topic of classical discourse's rhetorical *inventio*, there lies an important task, at present largely unexplored, for social and psycholinguistics, as well as for critical psychoanalysis and social anthropology. Of course, I propose this program for fields, like those just mentioned, less familiar to me with all due prudence and caution. On the other hand, I can more categorically assert that, in the fields of poetics and literature, this task figures among the most important still awaiting, entirely untouched, the formulation of a literary theory of the modern artistic text (T. Albaladejo, 1989, pp. 73–82).

Quite possibly, in the most hermetic and irrational texts produced by modern poetry since futurism and surrealism, as in the thematic and structural varieties of modern prose and plastic arts, an infinite rhetoric of thematic and structural textual openness has not entirely triumphed, in spite of appearances to the contrary, as an *anti-retractatio* frustrated by the nature of the beast. Perhaps, what has prevailed in modern art is more a negativity as opposed to an effective productivity in the face of classical art, more an opposition than an alternative.

But the negation of a rhetoric serves only to establish a rhetoric of the opposite, without giving birth to a new rhetoric nor guaranteeing the definitive abandonment of other rhetorics. Perhaps by simply extending beyond the point of classical convergence the structural affirmation as a unit of the text's constructive intention, the rule of structural divergence of open, modern art would be delineated. Obviously, the affirmation of a rhetoric of modern "topoi", different from the classical, but analogously finite and economical, is a risky hypothesis. The existence of more than evident lines of continuity in the modes of textual, communicative and artistic production, which globally characterize the cultural spaces known as classical and modern (or, more extactly, anti-classical), allows us to reasonably surmise the accuracy and productivity of such a hypothesis. In any case, the establishment of a new *inventio* for the modern kind of discourse, which corroborates and typifies the finite nature of its lines of convergence in our hypothesis, or illustrates the infinite parallelism of the divergencies and their non-recursive nature, is one of the most urgent tasks facing the new rhetoric, which would thus be constituted, by the ambition and representativeness of the objects of its analysis (R. Lachmann, 1977, p. 169), in an authentic general rhetoric.

The poetic effects of rhetorical expressiveness are, of course, not foreign to the polarization between the closed and limited nature of classical art and the open and supposedly infinite nature of the art considered to be most modern. By definition, that dream of infinite renewal and renovation which governs the most open art, relies heavily in its aesthetics on the surprising quality of poetic expressiveness. Which, nevertheless, does not deny the weight of expressiveness as an aesthetic capacity, animatedly dynamizing classical art's discourses.

The topical nature of classical art, closed and economical, is, as I indicated before, certainly a fact, regulating the infinite variety of its results through the limitation of principles' combinations (R. Barthes, 1953). The rhetorical effects of poetic expressiveness are taken for granted among the variables of predictable animation. They surely are the least stable, the most fortuitous of the constituents, which nevertheless places them entirely out of the reach of the economy of convergence regulating the dialectic between the fortuitous and the agreed upon, the equilibrium of which defines classical art. The frameworks in which the schemes and rhetorical categories function guarantees their necessary economical limitation. The free play of a very free associationism, exercised from the perspective of a fairly extensive set of invariable elements, shapes poetic expressiveness in classical art, guaranteeing its perpetuation.

Under this same perspective, the genesis of the values of expressiveness communicated to language reinforces the multiple constitutive scheme of meaning I am proposing. The production of poetic expressiveness presupposes an author's value, linked to the textual deployment of an unusual proposal. It's true that expressiveness has to count on the effect of reception, like any other mode of aesthetic value. Expressiveness echoes in the effect of reception; reception is what, in the final analysis, confers expressiveness its

1.3. Artistic Modes and the Aesthetic Law of Expressiveness

stature and guarantees existence and survival. But to assert this is merely to state an obvious principle based on everyday observation. From the perspective of rhetorical expressiveness as a poetic value, the receiver, in his necessarily partial reading, is the one who establishes the excluded space of the text's meaningful genesis. The aesthetic effect of expressiveness relies on an unusual discovery of the transmitter, a liberty, a new find, still uncontrolled, in which the literary text's author exceeds the patrimony of the receiver's customary possessions.

To say that the reader constitutes the instance which measures and sanctions by means of criteria of intensity and novelty the expressive effect of a text from the perspective of the phenomenon of his or her response, is to ignore, by way of that purely theoretical and schematic proof, something more decisive about expressiveness as the creation of the author and as a sign immanent in the text. The reader's response to the unusual and brilliant note of expressiveness denotes, more than anything else, the receiver's surprised uneasiness when faced with that feature of novelty. Poetic expressiveness, especially that of traditional discourse, conceals itself in rhetorical and grammatical rules, but it is the exceptional capacity of the author that preserves the unusual and unexpected effect of novelty. The reader only confirms what the author has previously experienced within the text. In the face of the feature of poetic expressiveness, rescuing exhausted and automatic values in the reader's habitual discourse, the latter's initiative is minimal or null. In the poetic effect of expressiveness, the reader plays a purely notarial role, affirming with his active surprise the value of novelty which has activated an inert and dormant space in his experience of language or of the world.

Poetic expressiveness in the artistic text also, almost always, operates by means of rarely symmetrical and rational devices. Their very nature as incalculable features minimizes the role of the reader's participation, today very encouraged by the strength afforded it by some of the textual formulas of contemporary art. It especially contributes important arguments to the fund of differences separating the artistic text from logical discourse, reducing to a minimum the possible objections of rational argumentation, served by the infrastructure of categories belonging to the metaphysical tradition (J. Derrida, 1967). In this chapter, I will not enter the debate over the reason for the existence of the anti-metaphysical deconstructive method in philosophy or in literary criticism, except to observe that it can achieve little construction or deconstruction as far as poetic expressiveness in literature is concerned.

The general aesthetic effect of the Cervantine discourse of the captive before the walls of ill-fated Nicosia, the hilarious freshness of the jokes and verbal nonsense heard in Monipodio's patio, or the effects of the renewed dignity with which the first lines of Don Quijote's discourse on the Golden Age opens, are all products of active expressiveness which escape the grids imposed by a form of metaphysical conformity. Sometimes it will be the ironic elegance in the naturalist contrast, or the dignified sympathy in the deepening pathetic sense, sometimes the pure, instantaneous verbal effect of some utterance and, always, the non-asymmetrical, the unexpected, the non-conventionalizable, taking on aesthetic forms of expressiveness. Expressiveness, as with the other poetic components of literary discourse, dislodges art from the universe of metaphysical mediations, with its dualist traps and the requirements of craft, as proclaimed by Derrida. Expressiveness annuls the rational organization imposed by the *différence*, its poetic effects naturally recover the dissolved substance of the *trace* for artistic discourse.

Expressiveness as a poetic property of discourse is lodged in the reiterative sentimental mechanism of the familiar, of recognition mocked and broken by the values of novelty. The expressive effect of discourse exploits the new, the asymmetric and unexpected, as I have said. But as a product of communication it originates and ends in the awareness of its location with reference to the values of systematicity, of traditional constancy. With traditional conventionality — another one of the values I will address in the ensuing chapters — poetic expressiveness shares the common root of an anthropological system of meaningful economy. But poetic expressiveness distinguishes itself from the traditional convention, in particular, as one of the privileged procedures of defamiliarization or de-automatization, of a permanently renovated break with traditional schematism, in the form of a perpetual diffraction, of asymmetrical diversification.

Like fictionality, expressiveness is also *poetic*, and partakes of the fantastic activity common to fictionality and to the set of symbolic-semantic and syntactic-spatial constructions which shape the background of poetic density alluded to as imaginary construction. But among all of the other modes of literary quality, expressiveness is the closest and most dependent on the rhetorical support included in the literary text's verbal scheme, in which the density and breadth of imaginary participation is the most concrete and contracted. The literary message's features of poetic expressiveness adjust themselves to the schematism of rhetorical foresight.

Perhaps the greatest attraction in the expectations for the scientific modernization of rhetoric is offered by the possibility of restoring this discipline as a technique of persuasive expressiveness. On this point a variety of initiatives of differing origins coincide. Initially, this tendency has been led, perhaps because of the keenness and aggressiveness of its presentation, by a theory of communication oriented ideologically, like that envisaged by Joseph Kopperschmidt (1976, pp. 83—84). Kopperschmidt aspires to reimplant an authentic rhetoric — and not a mere "technological" mechanism, falsified in its literary specialization — as a "grammar" of "reasonable" discourse, through a communicative act which strategically breaks with *discussion*, culminating in the *consensus* between the protagonists of the communicative act. However, his objectives are not, fundamentally, as different as Kopperschmidt himself declares them to be, persuaded by the urgency of an orthodox theory of rhetorical communication, from the intentions of a large sector of rhetoric proceeding from the fields of philology, linguistics and literary theory. As an example, one might consider the exemplary work of Paolo Valesio (1980, 1986).

Bernd Spillner, to cite another example, confessed in 1977 that the aspects of rhetoric he called "scientific," that is, those oriented towards a theory of textual production and analysis, were then ascendent and primary over strictly ideological-practical elements in the readaption of a new rhetoric (B. Spillner, 1977, p. 97). In spite of this, he recognized in the final analysis the practical coincidence of these two kinds of interests. Spillner explained the neorhetorical boom as a simple result of the internal amplification of contemporary linguistics, once the *limited* model of linguistics, which functioned in preceding years in structuralist and generativist thought, was uprooted (B. Spillner, 1977, p. 99). Like the German linguist, the great Italian philologist Luigi Heilmann emphasized the coincidence between the development of the new rhetoric and disciplines like linguistic pragmatics, sociolinguistics and psycholinguistics, text grammars and the theory of communication's linguistic acts (L. Heilmann, 1978; A. Leoni and M. R. Pigliasco, eds., 1979).

In the presence and range of the rhetorical ideal of discourse as a process of *persuasive* expressiveness oriented towards *moral action*, individual or collective, one of the great centers of gravity of tradition rhetoric intersects with an important and expanding tendency among the current interests of neorhetoric (P. Valesio, 1980). I propose to dissect this process here in order to analyze it in two different sections dedicated, respectively, to a reflection on the exemplary character in this regard of the ancient doctrines and, secondly, the translation of the general principle of *persuasive* expressiveness to well-known terms of general and literary modern discourse, but from different perspectives of judgment.

I propose, in the first place, that what underlies the traditional enumeration of the objectiveness of rhetorical-poetic activity — *instruction* or profit as the final goal, *pleasure* as the vehicle or instrumental goal, and *to move to action* as the final pragmatic translation of the other two goals (A. García-Berrio, 1977–1980, I, pp. 331–410; 1975, pp. 86–108) — must be interpreted for its adequate contemporary understanding as a conscious and carefully graduated process of the exchange of values between the transmitter of the discourse — the rhetor, poet or any person in the general position to persuade — and the receiver of the same. The latter may be the judge or judges of the case, an audience, a jury, a collection of potential buyers or voters, a theatrical audience, the individual reader of a novel or a poem, equipped with his or their own values and beliefs coinciding with or in contrast to the *values* that are the object of the persuasive transmission, etc. It turns out to be useful to fix the voice or concept of *ethical value* as the initial terminal of persuasion assigned to the transmitter, thereby specializing a different concept and denomination, *appreciation*, as the result of the acceptance or rejection by the individual or collective receiver of the *values* that are the objects of the rhetorical-persuasive proposal and argumentation.

This vision of the performative efficacy of literature in valorative and ethical terms connects with very remote traditions of the *moral* interpretation of the artistic and, specifically, literary function. On the other hand, it has also produced one of the most profound and developed formulations of literary sociological theory in Bakhtin's doctrines on the social "polyphony" perceptible in the novel (M. Bakhtin, 1929). Still, Bakhtin almost exclusively emphasized aspects of the interpretation of social variety in the plurality of expressive registers ironically lodged in the great bourgeois novels from Cervantes to Dostoyevsky. The great Russian critic thereby translated his awareness of the systematic entelechy of *langue* as a purely speculative construct, compared to the concrete reality of *parole* as an act (M. Bakhtin, 1929 a).

However, it is important not to exaggerate the scope of key expressions in Bakhtin's literary ideas, placing them at the service of more or less *ad hoc* and casual interpretations, easily conformed to our own purposes. This would be true, for example, of the approach which Bakhtin denominates as the *ethical factor*, as the third component — together with the representative and aesthetic — of a social-aesthetic poetics, as opposed to the material poetics practiced in Bakhtin's opinion by the Russian formalists (M. Bakhtin, 1975, pp. 51—52). Note, still, the absolute lack of any rhetorical reflection connected with the dimension of the moral persuasion of the reader, the exchange of sentiments between the transmitter and receiver via the text, or simply the persuasive argument exercised in terms of ethics, as is embraced in my own proposal of the ethico-rhetorical register of literary discourse, in terms of *values and appreciations*.

The scope of the ethical component in Bakhtin's understanding of the novel refers precisely to none other than Aristotle's requisite "men in action", through which Aristotle made directly concrete the structural distinctiveness of tragedy (A. García-Berrio, 1988, pp. 55—59), and indirectly suggested his strict, didactic-social definition of literary function (A. García-Berrio, 1981, pp. 507—508). The novel's character, *character* or *ethos* in the poetical-rhetorical tradition, constitutes the vehicle or fictional support of a certain social mode of discourse, incorporated in the novel's polyphony as the literary equivalent of a general social order. The novel fulfills its aims and function through the incarnation of characters in the verbal expressiveness of language, according to the different registers of linguistic performance — or at least of the most characteristic and representative — carried as a simultaneous suspension in the social ideolect. The novelist's art, and, as a result, his merit, lie in his capacity for *ethical incarnation* through the convincing verbal expressiveness of his characters, and of the plurality of the registers representative of the concrete social situation (M. Bakhtin, 1929). As can be seen, with these considerations Bakhtin did not transcend the strict sphere of the structural description of the expressive peculiarities of the novel's text. His ideas moved exclusively within the same horizon of explanatory ambitions as those very logocentric poetics, centered on the text as a product and not as a vehicle of exchange, which he himself criticized, under the guise of other premises and experiences.

Nevertheless, from another perspective, Bakhtin's ideas on the "plurality of voices" easily transfer to the rhetorico-pragmatic interpretation of the literary text as a fortunate collection of forms of expressiveness. Any kind of text with characters incorporating the mode of persuasive-argumentative discourse to the verbal fiction of certain *voices*, which makes possible the ethical exchange between transmitter and receiver, is relying decisively on the artistic efficacy of the verbal expressiveness achieved by the fiction's author. The character's voices constitute, in my opinion, a first instance of expressiveness, through which the author not only collects and describes the elements present in the social situation, but also makes use of them, above all, to present his own interpretation of the world in intellectual and moral terms. The expressive veracity of the characters, their efficacious social representation, achieved by way of the success of the verbal forms of expressiveness, is the vehicle of the efficient verisimilitude required of the novelist by the reader as a necessary condition for closing the pact of fantastic enthusiasm, through which the system of the author's ideas, his capacity for social and moral judgment and valuation of the world, is examined. The author proposes his theses, permitting his preferences to be associated by means of procedures easily recognized by his audience, the most common of which is sympathy. The novelist invests his dearest ideas about the world with the features of semantic content and structural functional emphasis which are unmistakably profiled in the hero and the antagonist. This is done in a manner making the disagreeable representation of the counter-values of the villanous antagonist as successful as the exaltation of the attractiveness by which the hero's virtuous value is conventionalized in the typical bourgeois novel from Stendhal to Balzac, Dostoyevsky to Tolstoy.

An author's success tends to be attributed precisely to his capacity to enthusiastically involve his readers, to impose or infect them with his own valorative codes, by means of the suggestive effect of the various forms of rhetorical-literary expressiveness, both in the most directly expressive and microsentential elements of the discourse and, more generally, in the persuasive argument's macrotextual efficacy. In this respect, it matters little whether an author or a novelist in fact confronts a sector of his contemporary society or all of it, if he has set as his goal provoking it in the form of a generalized confrontational satire. This all-inclusive confrontational stance would be an example of the not infrequent case of the creation of a text with *values for posterity*, such as those that Sade's or Lautréamont's may have represented among the majority of their contemporaries. In such cases, persuasion, if it is really effective, is directed towards a future code, leaping over the contemporary system of values which repudiate it.

A much more frequent situation, especially in modern literature, is represented in the case of the partial rejection of an author's system of values by a near majority of his contemporaries. This was the case, for example, with the anti-clerical scandal involving Galdós in nineteenth-century Spain, or with the confrontation based on the conservative incomprehension of Borges in our own century. All of this points to the fact that the individual reader, or collective groupings of readers, are not passive and defenseless in the face of the system of values proposed by an author through the seduction of his sympathetic argument. Instead, they confront and examine it relentlessly, adhering to it or rejecting it in disdainful or even exasperated terms, given the mysterious, illusory mechanisms of verisimilar artistic fiction. On the author's part, the literary work cloaks the proposal of seduction as a set of values, which can even shape themselves, as Black indicates (1965, p. 150), as an intention of complicity in a system of prejudice. Correspondingly, the reader disposes of a field in which to maneuver which includes both adherance and rejection (E. Black, 1965, p. 161), solidarity and discrepancy. This exclusive zone of the reader's emphatic decisions regarding the theses offered by the author through the convincing and attractive forms of the text's fictional expressiveness could appropriately be called the sphere of *appreciations*.

The reader's *appreciation* can coincide entirely or partially with the writer's system of *values*. A broad agreement establishes what is required for *enthusiasm*, generally linked to the public approbation of literary success. On the contrary, a negative appreciation, in which values and appreciation differ, translates into the work's failure or *rejection*, be it momentary or definitive. Note that the extreme limits of appreciation, enthusiasm and rejection depend on a kind of persuasive ethical solidarity between the author and his audience, of a general argumentative character; they are not necessarily concerned with the work's formal artistic efficacy, which would be associated with more concrete and exact forms of verbal stylistic expressiveness. Nevertheless, it can generally be affirmed that the work's persuasive ethical solidarity is intimately linked to the degree of effectiveness in the expressive artistic representation of the moral thesis, as Bakhtin himself indicated (1975 [1978, pp. 52–53]), since certainly the soul of the general artistic argumentation of a work is the seduction of the reader at every moment by the sympathy evoked by the representation, which fundamentally depends on the capacity for literary effectiveness of the text's artistic structures of expressiveness.

This would explain the disorder of the moral code attributable to the capacity for subversion on the part of artists. With episodes that extend from Plato's well-remembered expulsion of poets from his republic or the condescending attitude towards the "rogue" in the sixteenth century novel to the satanisms of the Romantic heroes of Byron or Espronceda or even the sympathic characterization of the villain in certain genres of popular literature and in the comic strips of our own times. The correlation between the aesthetic efficacy of the text's stylistic-verbal and global-argumentative expressiveness and readers' appreciations does not necessarily place analogous factors in relation to one another, but is governed by generally fixed rules, easily established, although this is not the right moment to develop them.

1.3. Artistic Modes and the Aesthetic Law of Expressiveness 135

On the other hand, in relation to the mechanisms of the general macroargumentative rhetorical expressiveness which affect the interaction between value and appreciation, the immense historical casuistry which combines the variables of contemporary adherence and rejection with their subsequent reversal, or with their permanent maintenance, is well-known. Both of which may refer to the scale of the individual reader's life as well as to the case of social and collective success and failure. Without a doubt, it is a question of the game of accomodating the efficacy of the discourse itself to the requirements of the *implied reader* (W. Iser, 1972, 1976), which may or may not coincide with a more immediate and generalized type of reader, a possible reader, or even a future reader. Finally, we must take into account the most common assumption of the permanent process of vicissitudes and changeableness affecting a work's appreciation, singularly illustrated in terms of shifts in fashion and moral orientation over the course of different historical periods (H. R. Jauss, 1973a).

The concept of value proposed here implies, from my point of view, the three canonical objectives of rhetoric as partial components, to the extent that it proposes an ethically conceptualized object (*docere*), which is communicated attractively, effectively and adequately through the stylistic-verbal and argumentative-textual mechanisms of persuasive expressiveness (*delectare*). Finally, dealing with an ethical objective presupposes a movement of adherence or rejection (*movere*), establishing the solidarity between values and appreciations as a result of the communicative-rhetorical exchange, or discrepancy, as the result of non-solidarity.

The role of the poetic phenomena of expressiveness is very important within the general rhetorical-persuasive mechanism which I have just described, originating in a Bakhtinian stimulus, presupposing that all of it in its entirety is, in my judgment, extensively expressive-poetic, since it is based on the parameters of the standardized reaction of ethical and aesthetic reading to the text's proposals of challenging novelty. The responsibility played by the verbal *expressive-stylistic* conduction of these proposals, in Bakhtin's explanation, in terms of the expressive verisimilitude of the *voices* which constitute the *ethical* component of the novel's literary message, confers a decisive role on what I have been designating as the rhetorical-argumentative expressiveness of the text. That is, beginning with the most restricted and conventionally rhetorical elocutionary elements, which are without doubt the most easily perceptible, expressiveness as a general literary property of artistic discourse extends itself to and is affirmed in the most general textual mechanisms of persuasion and of rhetorical argumentation.

In the *aesthetic* design of the novel's discourse, in the very same component terms in which Bakhtin understood it, the evidence of expressiveness is decisive, together with those properly imaginary and those specific to poetic fiction. In the literary task of artistically composing the work's polyphony and its use of social voices, the literary successes of micro and macrotextual expressiveness are always revealed as fundamental factors. The singular expressive feature confers the definitive seal of representative liveliness to the descriptive choice of the character and thus contributes decisively to the effects of social mimesis which, in Bakhtin's opinion, are essential in the aesthetic constitution of novelistic discourse. At the same time, these concrete and exact successes of verbal expressiveness are added to the execution of the persuasive plan of the text's overall macrotextual and argumentative expressiveness, composing a discourse the persuasive values of which can be conceived, as we have seen, in rhetorical-artistic expressiveness' local and global terms.

In this new perspective, rhetorical expressiveness reveals itself as an increasingly powerful and extensive feature in the vast and complex phenomenon of literary aestheticity. It was not in vain that classical art trusted artistic intentionality to it, with the full awarenesss and responsibility for what it was thus doing. The values of expressiveness, almost alone and in themselves, encouraged and maintained the literary discourse of traditional art in its aesthetic dignity, governed by the Greco-Latin tradition of rhetoric. And, as we have seen, even the new genres like the novel also survive aesthetically under a partial dependence on the features of expressiveness.

The linguistic-rhetorical activity which I have been representing as specifically expressive in this chapter penetrates the universe of verbal art's discourse and lives in the novel, endowing it with animation, movement and verisimilar reliability, and is a basic ingredient in what is most characteristically aesthetic about its nature. It also governs the most recognizable registers of lyrical discourse, both classical and modern. Poetry, before being recognized at the most "infernal" frontiers, the most deep-seated and radical regions of its essential imaginary and anthropological constitution, is first sensed aesthetically in its expressive discoveries, in the dazzling play, never monotonous or foreseeable, of the rhetorical forms of expressiveness.

Rhetorical-expressiveness, when present, is recognizable as the most universal artistic phenomenon of discourse. And it also appears as a general structure of argumentation, acting as the foundation for the general rhetorical effects serving to move and persuade, thanks to the corresponding macroargumentative strategies. It is perceptible, in its most immediate and precise form, in the success of dramatic dialogue, in touches of the mimetic demonstration of narration in the novel, and in the immediate, startling and perfectly targeted insight of the word made immutable formula in the exceptional poem. All in all, the value of poetic expressiveness is so familiar to us that we even tend to forget about it as a concrete device beyond classical art, but, without any doubt whatsoever, it is so general and decisive that any other poetic value in artistic texts begins with it and is founded upon it.

Among the considerations currently occupying our attention, that is, those concerning the rhetorical-artistic structure of persuasive expressiveness, a classical and central question has focused on the debate regarding the aims and purposes of artistic discourse. This question constituted a basic part of the doctrinal *corpus* of rhetoric, and was quickly transferred to poetics. I do not believe it is necessary for me to dedicate any space to an extended account of the historical development of this question (A. García-Berrio, 1977–1980, 1975, 1988 b). Moreover, this question, in many different guises, is not entirely absent in some modern discussions centered on the essence and function of the various artistic discourses (R. Barilli, 1979). And it is also involved and implied in the current explanation of the workings of reception (R. Warning, ed., 1975; G. Grimm, 1977), and reading (H. Weinrich, 1967; M. Charles, 1977), under which indirectly and perhaps even involuntarily the attempt is being made to dodge in a definitive way the dead-end of reflections on poeticity, in its most concrete and positive equivalents, in terms of a factor of mediation (J. M. Klinkenberg, 1977, p. 87).

With regard to the first aspect of the problem, it is also evident that it has been almost entirely since the second decade of this century that the debate over the purposes of art has intensified between its main participants, Marxism and formalist vanguardism, with a series of already well-known vicissitudes (A. García-Berrio, 1973, pp. 267–404). Nevertheless, it seems these disputes have begun to be abandoned through a lack of interest in recent years, due to the generalization in the West of artistic ideologies substantially concerned with the entertainingly playful, counter-cultural, ecological, etc.

Greater technical interest, although with analogous root causes, can be found in other trends of recent methodological investigation on the pragmatic exchange of discourse. Among those of least literary dissemination, we may situate a set of initiatives of the most strictly pragmatic nature, largely linked to the theory of "speech acts" (M. L. Pratt, 1977), from which derived the general expression of a "pragmatic proposal" of literariness (A. García-Berrio, 1979, pp. 127–130), together with the already fully developed expression of an empirical theory of literature, founded on the hypotheses of a social statistics appraised by Siegfried J. Schmidt (1979). These initiatives do not differ very much in their fundamental aims, in spite of superficial appearances to the contrary, from the better known activities of the schools that have specialized the traditional investigation concerning the peculiarities of literary discourse in terms of a theory of reception and interpretation (T. Albaladejo Mayordomo, 1981, pp. 120–130; J. A. Mayoral, ed., 1987) and a rhetoric of reading (H. Weinrich, 1971 a; M. Charles, 1977; A. Jefferson and D. Robey, eds., 1986, pp. 122–144).

As I have already said before, the feature of rhetorical expressiveness which I am considering in this chapter as the first, most traditional and obvious among the signs of literary discourse's value, can serve to put to the test in a very critical way the excesses of the relativization of the artistic text's general and poetic meaning, insofar as it has been extending its influence since the pragmatic-communicative trends of poststructuralism (U. Eco, 1968,

1979; R. Barthes, 1966, 1970 a) and from the perspective of the aesthetics of reception (W. Iser, 1976) in the moments in which it most exclusively radicalizes its reasonable foundational postulates. I have already commented on how poetic expressiveness, a textual feature and activity corresponding to the author's initiative, has in its elements of surprise and even in its condition as an unknown to its readers the operative support which guarantees its existence and shapes its development and success.

In view of the questions examined here, we can proclaim the current scientific relevance of a general rhetoric as a theory of appreciation which, moreover, entails a very symptomatic example, as we have seen, of the rhetorical expressiveness of texts; and this, in the general dynamic of its argumentative representations, as in, above all, everything bearing on the exact literary procedures which fix the successes and the expressive achievement of the argument's mimetic-artistic execution (E. Black, 1965, p. 61). The next challenge presents itself in terms of exactly determining the principles and operations essential for carrying out the aspiration, evidently necessary and useful, of implanting a rhetoric of expressive persuasion as a constituent of literary theory.

On this point, it would seem inadequate to me to ignore the directive value which, in a general plan of rhetorical discourse — general and literary — as a process of persuasion, it is necessary to assign to the current theoretico-linguistic components such as speech act theory (J. Searle, 1969; F. Chico Rico, 1988, pp. 116 ff.), linguistic pragmatics (D. Breuer, 1974; 1977, p. 238; T. Albaladejo Mayordomo, 1983), the theory of communication (J. Kopperschmidt, 1976, pp. 45—49) or the theory of argumentation (C. Perelman and L. Olbrechts-Tyteca, 1958). A plan of this kind must also be concerned with an important segment of the aesthetics of reception, incorporating components like the reader's identification (H. R. Jauss, 1973 a) with the hero's values or the villain's anti-values, insofar as they reveal the least questionable aspects of the liberty of meaningful construction attributed to them by the method (H. R. Jauss, 1975). As concerns the judgment of this particular aspect (A. Rothe, 1978, p. 16; K. Maurer, 1977, pp. 268—271), H. R. Jauss (1975) discusses Th. Adorno's interpretation, which began with the reader's identification. Globally speaking, the rhetorical function of persuasion can perhaps now acquire its genuine physiognomy as a general procedure of literary expressiveness, as well as all of its original analytical and predictive potential, thanks to the traditional and customary procedure of perceiving its approach as one more among the pragmatic perspectives of linguistic exchange. In order to achieve this, it must function within the textual linguistic hypothesis establishing the adequate framework of the psychological (H. A. Murray, 1943) and expressive organization of the textual macrostructure.

But it is also important to keep in mind that, although it may seem most suitable to insert the facts and observations of traditional rhetoric into the

1.3. Artistic Modes and the Aesthetic Law of Expressiveness

framework created by modern linguistic descriptions, the specific doctrinal development of a pragmatic theory of influence or persuasion has not yet been sufficiently achieved. Perhaps in this aspect of the question, as in so many others, the collaboration of rhetoric with linguistics in the project of establishing a general literary rhetoric will on its own begin to slowly discover the proper stages within the very process of collaboration (G. Mosconi, *et al.*, 1981).

Complementarily, literary-historical experience may itself offer the safest and most concrete models for this aspect within the general program of collaboration between traditional rhetoric and the different modern disciplines of discourse in the formation of a general rhetoric, just as we have seen it conceived of in this chapter. The rich casuistry literary history offers, as far as the history of changes in the appreciation of literary works, yields excellent patterns of observation, both in general and as concerns very concrete texts, for elaborating this theory of rhetorical persuasion within the framework of a general rhetoric.

The detailed investigation of the structure of individual texts' *values*, and especially of the specific devices and mechanisms designed to impose their acceptance and positive appreciation, undoubtedly constitutes a task not yet fully developed by historians of literature as a conscious rhetorical operation. Nevertheless, the effort involved in this kind of examination would not be too great or very problematic. Knowing beforehand, as is the case with the works of the past, the historical results of the public's appreciation of authors, works and moral systems makes fixing the general constants of persuasive success and failure relatively easy and accessible to critics. The description of the specific procedures tied to positive results of the argumentation of a certain text, author or period can be formulated in the same terms. An intelligent selection from among the almost infinite possible observations of this kind, suitable to the experience or conclusions one is seeking to establish, would with all certainty offer a *corpus* sufficient for defining descriptive and predictive phases as well as the systematization of the pragmatic-persuasive component of the prospective general rhetoric. This component powerfully influences the establishment of a specifically literary rhetoric.

A privileged sector for mapping persuasive strategies within the formal plane of the rhetorical theory of argumentation is that consisting of the specific doctrine of the *loci*, a traditional doctrine related to the structure of the case, or parts of discourse: *exordium, narratio, argumentatio* — with its optative division into *probatio* and *refutatio* — and *conclusio*. The necessary prior condition, however, for its productive application to the kind of argumentative exigencies of literary rhetoric I am attempting to outline would be the attenuation of the traditional emphasis of these doctrines in the rhetorical treatises, customarily focused on the preferable methods for finding arguments. This explains the exceptional development of the *argumenta*, compared with the less comprehensive treatment of the *exempla* and *signa*, the other sources on the same level of *probatio artificialis* forming part of the *argumentatio*. The emphasis on the important persuasive dimension of rhetoric favors, as is known, its application to a fundamentally formalist rhetoric and implies ignoring the dimension more particularly belonging to *inventio* in the theory of the case's parts, and first paying preferential attention to the linking and succession of these parts, with their respective subcomponents, within an argumentative perspective clearly coupled with interests relating to *dispositio*.

The examination of the kinds of advice offered with regard to the efficacy of the *exordium*, as well as the perfect and exhaustive ranking of the subcomponents of *narratio*, defended and explained in many rhetorical treatises — *initium, digressio, transitus, propositio, expositio* (H.Lausberg, 1960, §§ 338 — 347) — can present us with sure and very illuminating models for the manner in which the attempt is made to link the attention and favor of the listener, judge or audience, in terms of *appreciation*, to the *value-laden* exposition of the point of view of the case itself by the orator, whether a lawyer or not. Within the *probatio artificialis*, the "arguments" themselves (H. Lausberg, 1960, §§ 366—409), more than is the case with the *exampla* or the *signa*, offer greater interest in the same respect. It is not a question of fixed pieces included as such in the structure of the text as a process of acquiring knowledge, as is the case with the other two models of evidence (E. Black, 1965, p. 125), or of the degree in which in its own structure the argument offers us a scheme organized in parts or generally ordered in its own terms for persuasion. Such a feature would be intensified in an exemplary way in the *enthymema*, and is similarly illustrated by the other two modes of *ratiocinatio*, namely, the *syllogism* and the *epicherema*. More unequivocally linked to the essence of *inventio*, the famous *loci communes* constitute, to cite Quintilian's celebrated characterization, *sedes argumentarum* (H. Lausberg, 1960, § 373). Thus, they are sources for argumentative schemes and the core of the *enthymema* (L. Bornscheuer, 1977, p. 210), which act persuasively, more than schematized organizations for verbally processing conviction.

The analysis I have set forth in this chapter concerning the formulation of a general literary rhetoric fundamentally consists, as can be seen, in an amplification of the classical and traditional concept of expressiveness as a source of aesthetico-literary experiences; that is, as the basis of a poetic emotionality. The classical tradition particularly linked expressiveness to the tropes and figures of speech and, more generally, to the rhetorical "schemes" of a restricted syntagmatic and microcomponential scope. A modern general literary rhetoric, which requires the extension of a literary rhetoric restricted to *elocutio*, such as it was in its period of greatest decline, to the domains of *inventio* and *dispositio* — recommended by dialectics, logic, general linguistics and textual theory — also implies the extension of the classical concepts of poetic elocutionary expressiveness. For its most adequate conception within a general literary rhetoric, that narrow and verbalist expressiveness needs to be shifted to a comprehensive textual understanding of expressiveness, which reveals and emphasizes macrotextual operations of a scope and complexity customarily unknown in the basic concept of rhetorical expressiveness.

In the two-way parallel analysis I have practiced in this chapter — dealing with the disciplinary constitution of a general literary rhetoric and, at the same time, with the phenomenon of expressiveness, annexed to this structure — I have in fact attempted to restore to the discipline and to literary value an exclusive range that both had been stripped of. In essence, it is a matter of becoming aware, from the broad perspective of macrotextual *dispositio* and *inventio*, of their rhetorical capacities for macrotextual expressiveness. The radically rhetorical and expressive nature of the argumentative mechanisms of persuasion has been increasingly blurred and lost over time, reducing the evident scope of rhetorical expressiveness to the microtextual domain of tropes and figures of eloquence, important but far too scant and exiguous for our purposes.

A contemporary thematic theory, which literary rhetoric has recently shown an active interest in developing (*Poétique*, special issue, 1985), together with a re-activation of textual and psychological theories of interest and reading, converging with the reformulation of Perelman's argumentative neorhetoric, are all important illustrations of the range of correct and useful ways of employing the classical concept of rhetorical expressiveness as a possible source of poeticity. Hence, the problem should be formulated, in my opinion, in terms of whether these novel extensions of the well-known and well-surveyed phenomenon of classical expressiveness should be constituted, as such, as poetic data owing their existence to rhetorical expressiveness; or, rather, whether it is more worthwhile to include them among other sources of poeticity of a more extensive textual scope, as, for example, mimetic fictionality or the poetic activity of the imagination.

In this respect, it seems to me there is a less urgent need for a drastic decision concerning exclusions or restrictions than for highlighting the common rhetorical-expressive roots of aesthetic functions, like those related to the argumentative operations in the novel's text encouraging or discouraging interest. I would, furthermore, extend this opinion to include the structural manipulation and disposition of the poetic text's material *scheme*, insofar as they are supports and catalysts in the communicative exchange of imaginary impulses upon which the communication of the text's fantastic symbolic-temporal elements and anthropological spatialization are constituted.

Perhaps, in the resulting dilemma, it is important to restrict the scope of the terms of rhetorical expressiveness in those extensive macroargumentative and imaginary operations to those aspects more closely related to the most proven conventionally traditional uses and stylistic and critical data. Thus, let us continue to consider as central the elocutive-rhetorical phenomena as the foundation of the features of poetic expressiveness in texts, which in fact is already a big step if we keep in mind the common disregard for rhetorical-expressive stylemes as the source of poeticity in modern literary theory. These stylemes, which less than a century ago were basic pieces of evidence for postulating the value of a literary text's literariness, are barely recognized today as such. All of which makes sense within the excessive hypotheses of a critical science hammered by an anti-classicist prejudice which mistrusts not only expressive-rhetorical schemes as sources of poeticity, but also any other immanent feature of the text intentionally assessed by the author in the work's creative genesis. The clearly critical problem of poeticity as an aesthetic value linked with the literary text is presently overwhelmingly denied by a complacent tendency towards relativist convenience, founded on the most obvious, straightforward evidence of reading theory, which disparages and rejects any objective poetic matrix constituted in the text.

Beyond the receptive positions which, in their most absolute forms, relativize the artistic texts's aesthetic meaning and ignore expressive-rhetorical, poietic-mimetic and structural-imaginary features as constitutive objectives of poeticity, I believe it is necessary to reassert philology's traditional certainties. These are nourished by the aesthetic experience of rhetorical expressiveness and can be extended from this foundation to the new areas incorporated in a general literary rhetoric like the one I have been outlining here. This will restore to criticism and literary theory that which has always been their most specific task and most appropriate to their nature: the determination of poeticity as an aesthetic value in the skillful, successful text. In order to escape in this effort the accusations of gratuitousness and the suspicion of caprice and fancifulness, it is necessary to link poetic value to precise, specific features. Among the traditional elements of rhetorical expressiveness and its neorhetorical developments, concepts like those of fictional interest and the expressive structure of the imaginary drive offer, without doubt, a legitimate and rich source of clarifications.

The examination undertaken here of the set of hypotheses for the formulation of a *literary rhetoric as a constituent segment of a general rhetoric*, leaves us with a balanced list of questions of sufficient complexity to provide that future rhetoric with a respectably ample framework. On the other hand, I am convinced that a more extensively detailed reflection on many of the points that I have outlined here, counting on the enrichment available from integrating the resources of linguistic theory and semiological poetics, would considerably amplify the development of said subjects (C. Segre, 1979, pp. 63–75). Such an approach, in turn, will give rise to new questions and will, above all, more fully fix the links and dialectical interrelationships between these various starting points, which at present still appear relatively autonomous, thereby establishing their interaction in an integrated rhetorical theory.

Second Part

2. Artistic Conventionality and Ambiguity

2.1. *The Pragmatic Relativity of Meaning*

2.1.1. *Objections to Meaningful Textual Construction: Conventionality and Arbitrariness*

The case for an autonomous poetic value is not easily made either by literariness nor the more specifically aesthetico-artistic properties of language, which we have been referring to generally as constituting literary specificity. The expressive features of literariness do not, when considered individually, yield a specificity of unquestionably poetic value, capable of qualitatively identifying and differentiating literary expressiveness from that exhibited by other successful communicative texts. Especially in the cases of successful jokes, advertising jingles, proverbs, witty sayings, etc., the line between the properly literary formula and the successful communicative act is difficult to determine, at least as regards linguistic behavior.

The lack of linguistic specificity ascribable to the distinctive features characterizing the literary text, compared to those associated with standard communicative texts, has for some years now provided the basis for a great deal of discussion concerning the *conventionality* of literary properties; that is, an argument was made for the absence of anything essentially and necessarily its own in the discourse we call literature. Current objections to the specificity of literature stem from pragmatic positions of disappointment and exhaustion in the poststructuralist speculation of poetologists like Barthes, Todorov, van Dijk and S. J. Schmidt, all of whom in their heyday had cultivated structuralist poetics. Following a path which ends up converging with that of this nucleus of poststructuralist critics are the advocates of the so-called "aesthetics of reception", together with the practitioners of deconstructive philosophy and criticism.

The overall result of these developments is the complex state of opinion we find in contemporary poetics, which has made a constructive contribution to literary theory by ushering in a fruitful epoch focusing on readers and reception after the previous structuralist moment's concentration on the role of the text and its structure. The negative aspects of the new critical situation may well consist in the radicalization of this shift in perspective to the point of embracing an overly universal attribution of the sources and causes of artistic specificity to the receiver.

We are simply stating a proven fact in saying that a literary utterance's reader or receiver closes the text's communicative circuit, a circuit which originates with the intentional constitution of meaning by the text's author. But if we reject or ignore the role played in this process by the meaning's "poietic" vector — that is, the author's codifying will and intention — we automatically begin denying the textual foundations of the aesthetic judgment of literariness, reducing it entirely to readers' free will — that is, to individually and collectively conventionalized opinion.

In effect, literariness is a principle of a conventional nature. Upon exercising the *option* to constitute a mode of discourse recognizable as literature, we signal our observance of cultural frameworks for discourse which enable us to identify it precisely as literature within the pragmatics of the verbal communicative act. I have already contrasted this foreseeable and optative characteristic of the literary pragmatic initiative with the unforeseeable and unconventionalized nature of the resulting *value* present in only certain literary texts, for which I reserve in this book the qualifier *poetic* and the name of *poetry*.

Still, although it is true that literature is a *conventional and optative practice in its cultural transmission*, this should not confuse us and lead us to the conclusion that it is also *arbitrary in its natural, essential foundations*. The selection and intensification of certain particulars in the human discursive construct — such as mimesis, acoustico-temporal or visual-spatial rhythms, or the principles of constructive proportion, recurrence and alternation —, obey the need to express certain anthropological structures of the human imagination and its organization and representation of the world.

The importance of these unconventional foundations and principles of literary structure lies behind the fact that their more or less artistic execution is responsible for the success or failure of their intense representation. Poetry as an experiential value consists precisely in this fact.

The explicit and conscious consideration of the pragmatic perspective in literature is not very old. The first formal references to it in modern grammars barely date back twenty years. Its introduction as an analytical parameter in the study of literature is even more recent. And yet what we generally take to be pragmatic positions on the question of literariness have carried considerable weight and have been extensively developed.

As is known, pragmatics proposes that every linguistic utterance's situation and, consequently, its meaning, should be considered from the perspective of its being a *speech act*. Meaning is the result of a communicative act proposed and codified by the text's sender and decoded by its receiver.

In the case of the "special speech act" of literature, the linear pragmatico-linguistic scheme is enormously more complicated and dense. For example, we have to keep in mind, at the very least, the normally deferred and indirect nature of literary communication. Very rarely do a literary text's receivers directly experience its sender's expressive proposition.

This first special circumstance, in turn, introduces very noticeable peculiarities in the pragmatic activity of the literary sender and receiver. Among authors themselves, the debate over the question of whom literature is written for is already ancient. And they have proposed many different answers. Some claim they have no model reader, others clearly express references to a given cultural or social type, while there have been some cases in which the author appears to or even confesses to be writing with the sole objective of his own singular awareness in mind.

The recently activated concepts of "implied reader", "potential reader", "implicated reader" and "reader in the story", demonstrate the urgent need to introduce the receptive variable in the conception of the construction of meaning. In particular, the attentive consideration of the "narratee", a concept put into circulation very recently in narratology, has allowed the structure of the complex narrative text to be focalized in terms of a set of strategies involving and implicating the reader in the story. Umberto Eco has, for example, proposed a conception of reception in these terms, adapting Petöfi's textual base to his own theory (U. Eco, 1979).

The due consideration of the reader's role in the construction of textual meaning is a reasonable and illuminating venture in and of itself. There is no doubt that every reader closes the circuit of signification opened in the course of the sender's textual codification. Moreover, literary messages, consciously originating as "literal messages" (F. Lázaro Carreter, 1976a), overcome and outline the limitations inherent in the necessarily contingent nature of purely practical verbal acts. The literary work, beginning its existence as a poetic communicative act in the absence of a precise receiver, nevertheless originates with a vocation to survive generations of ever-changing readers.

Literary meaning is formulated and lives in a multiple, uninterrupted tradition. The meaning attributed to a work by every reader in every reading is directly influenced by the multiple examples of simultaneous and previous reception, to the extent that it is possible to speak of an age's particular receptive *patterns*. Thus, the medieval or Renaissance reception of Horace's *Ars Poetica* or Aristotle's *Poetics* results in receptive patterns accomodated to the unique conditions and needs of each period (A. García-Berrio, 1977–1980). And this is still more self-evident when considered in terms of the patterns of fashion and "taste" or the particular configurations of aesthetic meaning contributed by certain periods or ages, such as Romanticism or positivism.

Hence, it is entirely reasonable to adopt a pragmatico-receptive perspective in the process of constructing and attributing the conceptual and aesthetic meanings of texts, like literary texts, which are so open to and dependent on the receptive tradition. Reconstructing the history of literature with an eye towards the "aesthetics of reception", something not consciously undertaken until recently, is a fruitful and necessary venture, particularly in view of the fact that traditional literary history customarily concentrated on the *poietic* factor of meaning; that is, it attempted to reconstruct only that segment of meaning which embraces the text, the author and his codified intentions (H. R. Jauss, 1982).

Still, I believe that, since the "aesthetics of reception" has until now focused far too insistently and exclusively on the polemical affirmation of its own needs and legitimacy, the most important task of justifying its claims "with deeds and facts" remains pending. That is, its principal and most urgent mission must be the construction of a satisfactory and representative history of receptive texts.

From my point of view, the pragmatico-receptive perspective, in outlining the physiognomy of the implied and implicit reader and transposing it to the special aesthetic constitution of artistic texts, involuntarily revitalizes the forgotten concepts of rhetorical persuasion and *movere*. The hermeneutical perspective of receptive implication proposes a theory of the text modeled on securing and maintaining the reader's interest and, hence, indirectly, on readers' shared moral sympathies. The very announcement of the task ahead reveals the procedures' rhetorical identity.

Current literary theory and critical practice have in recent years become more convinced than ever, as I have already had the opportunity to indicate in previous chapters with regard to other matters, of the conventionality of the values literature handles, as well as of the constitutive properties attributed to literary texts. Confronted with the difficulty of determining the aesthetic features necessary to artistic works, theorists and critics surrender to the simplifying tendency to consider the attribution of aesthetic values and specific features as a merely conventional phenomenon, essentially and substantially hazardous and gratuitous, linked only to historical necessity and dominated by momentary, passing rules of taste.

Were this scheme of things to prevail, conventionality would become the only and ultimate feature of literariness, which, as a result, could no longer be distinguished from poeticity as an aesthetic value. The rules of literariness would be governed only by the cultural accord which establishes and which modifies them in the course of an entirely historical dialectic, always in keeping with conventional reasons. These conventional principles would establish the constitutive characteristics and options of literary and artistic phenomena, unlimited except by the free initiatives and whims of arts' users. In this scenario, the theory of literary texts is deprived of all interest in inherent aesthetic essences (W. Iser, 1976, p. 67).

Similarly, literary history would no longer be oriented, as it has been until now, towards the formulation of the unvarying elements of creation. Nor would it attempt to set forth the successive relationship between texts on the basis of such elements. A literary history based on such an aesthetic of reception (H. R. Jauss, 1970), would ideally wish to focus on the interpretation of literary and artistic production, not in terms of unvarying creative features, but through the confirmation and explanation of the receptive demand originating and justifying the variables of historical differentiation.

A literary theory like the one I propose, which seeks to reconcile the tradition of investigation focused on authorial "poietic" with the variations of an "aisthetic" perspective emerging from receivers' historical contributions implies the following:

a) Adequately appraising the clearly decisive role of the receiver in the constitution of the general and aesthetic meaning of literary texts. This entails pondering the relative importance of the communicative nature of the artistic work's meaning compared to the work's fundamental genetic factor, the process of creating the text understood as an expression of the author's system of aesthetic and anthropological representations, both semantico-extensional and fantastico-imaginary, insofar as he or she is the producer of the text (T. Albaladejo Mayordomo, 1986, pp. 113 ff.).

b) Offering an up-to-date and explicit explanation of the concept of aesthetic universals in general through an explanation of poetic-literary universals in particular. In the face of the gratuitous scandal that in this respect the antimetaphysical fashion created in literary theory, I believe that, at this moment, the poststructuralist and protoanthropological critical experience is capable of suitably filling the abstract notion of aesthetico-literary universals with concrete contents, thereby endowing it with the references needed for its proper and precise location in the artistic text, both as a material scheme and framework for meaning and as a psychological structure central to the process of imaginative communication. The technical design of this textual-literary content of the universal is examined in the third part of this book.

c) Finally, the entirely relative approach to textual meaning, represented by the various proposals based on the concept of convention, is open to the mediation of the alternative concept of traditionality as the element forming a structure and system of aesthetico-artistic values. In the form in which I have considered it in my typological studies of Renaissance lyrical texts, the literary tradition is presented as the most immediate and active among all of the factors external to the text in the creation of its contextual frame. Within these limits, each individual text regulates its structure and originality. Decisions concerning value and poeticity are constituted and explained by each work's capacity to surpass this frame without exceeding or destroying it.

In general, there is nothing wrong or inappropriate in the initial proposals and claims of the various original schools and trends of receptive theory (W. Iser, 1972, 1976; H. R. Jauss, 1967; U. Eco, 1968; R. Barthes, 1970a; H. Weinrich, 1971a). In the act of communication which creates meaning, the receiver, especially in the case of the reader of literature, confirms or denies through either his agreement and comprehension or his disagreement and lack of understanding the meanings proposed by the texts' producer, who, moreover, always "implicitly" relies on the reader (W. Iser, 1972) as the person to whom the message is addressed and the one responsible for decoding its meaning.

To ignore or dismiss the phenomenon of reception, as was the practice, almost without exception, in theoretical reflections on literature, was in fact an error. Moreover, to the extent that aesthetic meaning is a more open and subjective matter than general denotative-linguistic meaning, the customary lack of references to the parameters of reading and interpretation point to a very obvious weakness of traditional theories.

Traditionally, critical practice and the suppositions from which literary history worked had always implicitly included receptive parameters. The desire to realize a more exact description or interpretation of texts and authors, which served as the inevitable starting point of every kind of traditional criticism, assumed the act of individual reading as a perfectionable principle. In this sense, every critic implicitly had been proposing himself as the text's ideal reader, the one who most closely approached, in his own interpretation, the *desideratum* of precise comprehension the original author had set forth. Furthermore, nobody wanted, on principle, to subordinate his own analysis to the general body of interpretations and readings of a given work, as though it were just one more effort among many, without transcendence. The invocation of Iser's proposed "horizon of expectations" as the basis of an aesthetics of reception really amounted to the theoretical recognition of the customary state of affairs in critical reading as a rule for the closure of the process of creating and identifying meaning.

In this sense, Jauss' proposals concerning receptive parameters seems far more adequately formulated for the creation of a renewed awareness of literary history capable consequently of influencing its future elaboration. In effect, our search within every past artistic age and trend for an aesthetic governing understanding and reaction, would not only enrich our historical understanding of periods of literary history, in which the literary texts analyzed, especially the great texts, would function invariably as touchstones, but also, complementarily, would enable us to measure those reactions characterizing the individuals of a period as well as the period itself in terms of their historical role in forming the current physiognomy attributed to great works of art. To which, in my opinion, we should add the privileged opportunity to register, through a broader, more historically objective perspective, the flexibility of the meanings tolerated as reasonable and possible within a given structure of meaning, insofar as it corresponds to the author's intentional construction, by means of observing and recording the vacillations and freedom of movement permitted these meanings. Hence, the problem with receptive theory is not the result so much of the inherent nature of its initial postulates and claims as of the deviations derived in their radicalization (E. D. Hirsch, 1967).

Working from the foundations laid by earlier structural semiologists like Barthes and Eco, the original current of receptive theory was very much

2.1. The Pragmatic Relativity of Meaning   151

encouraged to radicalize the negation, at first quite timidly, of the text's objective structure of meaning. In addition, though somewhat later, a convergence developed, driven by the efforts of a group of linguists and poetologists from whom communicative-pragmatic information and decisions relative to the nature and characteristics of the literary text began to take precedence over those derived from the textual knowledge — throughout the phonological, grammatical and semantic levels — available in formal grammars. Taken as a whole, such heterogeneous historico-methodological factors have turned out to be decisive in establishing the later, definitive form literary pragmatics and receptive aesthetics have taken; however, the usual studies and critical summaries of these trends do not usually take into account the fact that they are the product of so many converging factors.

Nevertheless, it seems that suitable reflection on the opposition between poetry and literature, deriving from Croce and previously common to Herder and Vico, a contrast based on their characteristic properties of poeticity and literariness, respectively, contributes powerfully, in my opinion, to help clarify this debate on the pragmatic realization of aesthetic meaning. There are structures in literary texts governed by mechanisms of cultural conventionality, be they, for example, the fourteen lines in iambic pentameter constituting the textual scheme we recognize as a sonnet or the rules of fictionality, strictly regulated by the "law of semantic maxima" (T. Albaladejo Mayordomo, 1986). The set formed by the various rules arrived at and perpetuated by cultural consensus can be seen as a collection of features of literariness which appear in the literary system as the objective of options structuring and realizing the texts and modes of discourse we recognize as literature (C. E. Reeves, 1986).

By this, however, I do not mean to deny that the system of conventional features which specifies the textual condition of *literariness* is lodged in areas involving man's deeply rooted expressive-communicative needs and his vision of the world. This is certainly understood to be the case, for example, in all that relates to the nature of rhythm and proportionality in texts, or with regard to that which composes the scheme of referential properties constituting the world model generating verisimilar fictionality. It is along those lines, which I will elaborate more fully in subsequent sections of this book, that the linguistic, sociological and anthropological foundations upon which aesthetic universals are modeled appear to me to be identified and justified.

Poeticity as a value should be understood as neither optional nor conventionalizable, but rather as a fortunate and unforeseeable effect found in the communicative expression of very subtle messages able to move beyond conventional logic and practical communication. It is a feature of certain literary realizations, an aesthetic property that asserts itself as an unexpected, unforeseeable and unconventionalizable effect. All of which is not to say that the value of poeticity characterizing certain literary messages cannot be explained *a posteriori*. The attentive observation of the poetic text's verbal scheme permits us to recognize the features of expressive success upon which the text's general fantastic effect is affirmed and dynamized — networks of symbols, of dynamic impulses exposing, in the essential coordinates of the self's implantation in space and time, elemental tendencies of the subconscious and sensations of an intimate, anthropological orientation. Our sense and explanation of poeticity unfolds through the expression of these profound states of being, the radical and essential expression of a set of operating principles governing man's sensibility and his contact with the world, in which we discover the affirmation of poetic universals. But the elucidation of the poetic, in the terms in which I have just outlined it here — and which I will explain and further develop in the third part of this book — is not an easy or immediately accessible task, at everyone's disposal. Rather, it requires an extensive formation and training in the hermeneutical techniques of traditional philology, rhetoric and literary criticism. It requires all of the formal knowledge about the text deposited from the Russian formalists to neoformalist structuralist poetics and textual linguistics, all filtered and explained by the critical channels of stylistics. And, above all, it requires a great effort from the formal analyst to understand the text's immaterial space, which is what truly completes the text as such in its expansion and communication of the psychological axis of its productive genesis and its transmission to the receiver. A shift of focus which, at the same time, implies an interest in and knowledge of the still imprecise and shifting disciplines of psychology, anthropology and psychoanalysis, insofar as they relate to literature.

2.1.2. *The Poststructuralist Crisis of Literary Meaning*

In a study in 1979 entitled "Lingüística, literaridad, poeticidad" ("Linguistics, Literariness and Poeticity") (A. García-Berrio, 1979, pp. 139—142), I discussed having noticed a pragmatic trend in a series of investigations recently published at that time (T. A. van Dijk, 1977; M. Corti, 1976; M. L. Pratt, 1977; S. J. Schmidt, 1980), a trend which took shape programatically in a collection of studies by various authors edited by T. A. van Dijk and published in 1976 in a volume entitled *Pragmatics of Language and Literature*. This group of poetologists and linguists presented a pragmatic solution, as a more fitting alternative with explicitly less radical intentions than had elsewhere been proposed, to the problems I have been examining here on the nature of meaning and the role of the creator (M. Hancher, 1977; J. A. Fanto, 1978; J. A. Mayoral, ed., 1981). More fitting because it incorporated a new linguistic and semiological perspective, until then not very well-represented in formal systems of textual description and for which these formal grammars had been very severely criticized (R. Posner, 1976). This had to be unsatisfactory and uncomfortable for authors as involved in the formal evolution of structuralist poetics as were T. A. van Dijk himself, W. Kummer and S. J. Schmidt among the Europeans, or S. R. Levin and W. O. Hendricks among the Americans.

As I mentioned, they put the final touches on their proposal by presenting less negative hypotheses with regard to the nature of meaning. Less negative, in effect, because they generally did not question, as pertains to the linguistic level of their analyses, the existence of a structure of meaning in the text linked to the productive proposal. Nevertheless, in the perspective of our ideas at the time on the nature of aesthetic meaning, the pragmatic alternative as a whole was still negative and relativizing.

What can be considered consolidated and disseminated since then among the influential group of linguists and poetologists I have been referring to is the resolution of textual problems inherent to and constitutive of the characteristics of literariness and the aesthetic values of poeticity to the pragmatic level (T. A. van Dijk, 1977). That is to say, without questioning themselves about the objective foundations of textual meaning in its production on the creator's side of the equation, they attributed all of the decisions pertaining to aesthetic meaning to the initiatives conventionalized in the text's pragmatic interchange (I. Fonagy, 1961; G. Mounin, 1969; S. Chatman, 1971). Because I believe this important distinction has not been sufficiently emphasized, I would like to point out in passing that the pragmatic proposal differs from the models of the aesthetics of reception in that it locates the zone where the conventional relativization of aesthetic meaning is generated in the broad pragmatic area incorporating the entire communicative exchange, including both the text's producer and its receiver (C. Bousoño, 1952; S. R. Levin, 1976; F. Lázaro Carreter, 1980).

In any case, I responded at an early date to these affirmations, which at the time appeared extreme to me (A. García-Berrio, 1977a; 1977b, p. 260; 1979, pp. 127–128); and to a certain extent, my activity over the course of subsequent years has been oriented towards reasonably justifying my first reaction, which was particularly influenced by the textual hermeneutical tradition in which I was educated. Thus, I have explored more deeply the reasons behind the aesthetic requirements and motivations of textual foundations: linguistic, in the material scheme, strictly defined, and imaginary, in the psychological space of communicative exchange constituting the text (A. García-Berrio, 1985). Taken together, these make the aesthetic effects of literariness and the perception and feelings that are identified as the poetic value or aesthetic meaning of the text a matter of objective necessity rather than arbitrary convention (S. Fish, 1973, 1980). In my judgment, the consideration of the complete inventory of all these textual features — linguistic, psychological and anthropological — can effectively orient us to the reach and specific physiognomy we attribute to aesthetic-literary universals (J. Searle, 1969; R. Ohmann, 1971, 1972).

By denying the textual-objective status of the poetic properties of aesthetic meaning, entrusting them entirely to the conventional arbitrariness of readers, I think literary theory and criticism, and even philosophy, to extend the question to a broader generic domain, reject and renounce the use and usefulness of some of their most refined and precise instruments. In fact, the majority of the critics involved in this pragmatic process have moved on to other tasks, not strictly philologico-critical, and they all, I believe, have systematically distanced themselves from reflecting on literary texts characterized by a high degree of aesthetic intentionality. As an example, we might point to Schmidt's current work examining informative texts. It is quite obviously pointless to discuss the textual nature of aesthetic universals in regard to these kinds of texts.

In his day, Siegfried Schmidt was one of the principal instigators of the poetological application of linguistic poetics and textual linguistics during the structuralist phase of European literary theory (S. J. Schmidt, 1973, 1974). His philosophical preparation had even predisposed him, still earlier, to reflect on the textual nature of aestheticity (1970). Nevertheless, like the majority of the European representatives of linguistic poetics, moved by the poststructuralist crisis, he joined the pragmatic "trend", pursuing in the first moments of the shift to pragmatism (S. J. Schmidt, 1976, pp. 161–178) an investigation into the non-conventional foundations of aesthetic value. In developing his initial theory in this area, he based himself on a few limited properties of the literary phenomenon, such as fictionality (1974, 1980). Viewed in these terms, the deceiving idea that fictionality is the only and exclusive poetic value inherent to literary aesthetics quickly vanished as a convincing argument as far as Schmidt was concerned.

Nevertheless, Schmidt's speculative tenacity almost immediately engendered a well-articulated, constructive alternative in the form of what he denominated *The Empirical Theory of Literature* (1979). The theoretical formulation of his ideas, which in essence took the principle of pragmatic conventionality as its starting point, presupposed a genuine effort, very suitable to Schmidt's own personality, to avoid being imprisoned within the fruitless and unprofitable pragmatic negation of the possibility of establishing a literary axiology inherent to artistic texts. As such, the affirmation of a well-modulated theory in the basic text of 1979 was preceded in the years before its publication by a laborious activity of newspaper polls dedicated to sampling readers' opinions and judgments about literature (S. J. Schmidt, ed., 1979; D. Hintzenberg and S. J. Schmidt, *et al.*, eds., 1980).

In its general principles, Schmidt's empirical theory is not substantially different from the instructions which regulate the method of the great German school of reception. For Schmidt, the literary text is replaced as the focus of poetological speculation by the notion of *literary* "Kommunikat", understood as the set of "social actions" relating to the verbal work of art (S. J. Schmidt, 1980a, pp. 542–545). The notion of the text underlying Schmidt's work also takes into account the "linguistic basis of communication", on which, as I demonstrate in this book, the aesthetic discriminative and communicative principles cannot be established. To the contrary, all of the communicative actions of the verbal work of art form the "system of literary communicative actions", which, in practice, Schmidt identifies with the system of literature. This system, in turn, is broken down in the general plan of empirical theory into a fourfold network of communicative action, namely, of "production", "mediation", "reception" and "elaboration".

Based on the principles of "radical construction" in cognitive psychology (P. L. Garvin, ed., 1970; H. R. Maturana, 1985; H. von Foerster, 1985, pp. 39—60; E. von Glassersfeld, 1985, pp. 16—38), the empirical theory of literature does not consider the literary work as an ontological absolute, having a meaning of its own and possessing a stable value (S. J. Schmidt, 1984, pp. 253—274; H. Hauptmeier and S. J. Schmidt, 1985, pp. 26—29). On the contrary, the literary work is contemplated solely in the center of a series of initiatives on the part of its receivers to attribute meaning and value, according to its own contextual situation and by virtue of a set of social conventions. That is, meaning and value are no longer attributes inherent to the text in its broad material-verbal and anthropologico-imaginary development, but have become fortuitous and uncertain properties linked to the cognitive process of interpretation (S. J. Schmidt, 1980, p. 542; 1981, p. 322).

As can readily be seen, at least in terms of its fundamental ideas, the empirical theory of literature does not differ very greatly from the aesthetics of reception. It is, perhaps, more radical, since the school of thought to which Jauss and Iser belong does not proceed like Schmidt from the frustrated experience of structuralist investigation, but from the very different perspective of certain reasonable claims based on historico-literary expectations. This explains the fact that receptive aesthetic's increasing trend towards relativist skepticism has been the result of a gradual, progressive, and accumulative process, with very significant individual differences, while, in contrast, Schmidt's method began with the negation of textual meaning, both conceptual and aesthetic, and not merely receptive and relative, an attitude that has remained unmodified up to the present throughout the development of his methodology.

The characteristic method adopted by Schmidt and his collaborators, whom together constitute the Nikol group, involves the systematic development of an elaborate inquiry, based on polls, into the social peculiarities in the constitution of individual and collective criteria establishing the attributions affecting the meaning and values of literary texts. Without doubt, this is an interesting aspect of the school's work, developing and perhaps perfecting the traditional methods utilized by the sociology of literature, including the use and usefulness of polling techniques. Nevertheless, on the whole, all of this seems foreign to the kind of matters of interest to a literary theory, which traditionally, as is known, works from presuppositions about the nature of literary meaning and value entirely contrary to Schmidt's. In effect, the task facing any effort to contribute to this literary theory, like my own, ought to be to discover and debate new explanations of artistic texts' literariness and poeticity.

The empirical work carried out by Schmidt and the Nikol group contributes very useful descriptive clarifications, similar to the historical reflections of the aesthetics of reception, at least when not insisting from the beginning on an absolute radicalism regarding the relativity of literary meaning and value. However, the passing moment of poststructuralist exploration and clarification which Schmidt's initiatives started twenty years ago has been perpetuated in his work as a dogmatic absolute. Through its concept of the *polyvalency* of meaning and aesthetic *convention* (S. J. Schmidt, 1983, pp. 57—58, 63—64), the empirical theory of literature mobilizes and moves within both possible avenues of radical skepticism.

First, it adheres to Derrida's protopragmatic negativity, falling short of proclaiming the linguistic fallacy (S. J. Schmidt, 1984, p. 264), but in practice denying the text the possibility of even a fundamental nucleus of unequivocal meaning. And secondly, by virtue of the concept of aesthetic convention, it attacks the traditional foundations of literary theory affirming the non-existence of artistic meaning as an inherent value, differentially expressed and recognizable in terms of texts' objective properties (S. J. Schmidt, 1979 a, p. 563; 1980, p. 543).

From my own perspective, Schmidt's general proposal is acceptable and useful above all for its codification and description of the pragmatic disturbances introduced in the manifestation of a text's meaning by its readers' circumstantial historical peculiarities and, in many cases, by their deficiencies. There is no doubt that each act of reading produces a deforming effect as concerns the meaning codified in a text's foundational act, that of the author with his immediate readers. But the radicalization of the power of these deformations to the point of attributing to them the capacity for absolutely abolishing the axiological and meaningful manifestations of the work of art constitutes an inexact exaggeration. In the aesthetic messages of texts it is necessary to distinguish between a periphery of meaning, accessible to connotative relativism, and a nucleus of meaning which remains constant and is clearly evident and absolute (G. Kerbrat-Orecchioni, 1977; B. Garza Cuarón, 1978; V. M. de Aguiar e Silva, 1967 [1984, p. 81]).

As distressing as Richards' famous classroom experiences were, or as relativizing as the results of Schmidt's newspaper polls may be, the interpretation of a text's nucleus of meaning — for example, the narrative argument of *Don Quijote* or even its proposal of a confrontation between one idealistic, visionary and crazy character and another realistic, sane and pragmatic one — as the nucleus of a different text — for example, Dante's voyage through hell, purgatory and paradise —, can only result from a deliberate, capricious joke, which criticism could not be expected to assume as serious. Not to mention the fact that the historical role of every generation of a text's readers has above all consisted in pruning the deformations peculiar to preceding generations' historical readings, particularly those of the *immediately* preceding generation. Consciously or unconsciously, this task is equivalent to the zeal for preserving the *original* nucleus of an artistic text's conceptual and aesthetic meaning.

We frequently forget the purely historical and circumstantial character of the preeminence currently granted the collective sociological variety of the group, dismissing the constituents of anthropological identity common to all individuals. Literary theory, after the initial fundamental efforts of structuralism and psychoanalysis, has lived through a period of disorientation in which it has hastily adopted methodological and philosophical stimuli — Gadamer's hermeneutics of psychological relativism and the anti-metaphysical skepticism of Derrida's deconstruction — very distant, if not entirely alien or inappropriate to the nature of its object of study. The consequence of which is that, as the occasional result of the deficiencies normal to its customary task of historically readjusting explanations on the nature of the artistic, literary and poetic, theory first fell, with a few exceptions (L. Doležel, 1979), into the rut of poststructuralist discouragement, which was then prolonged and deepened by the various representatives of pragmatic relativism (T. A. van Dijk, 1979), among them S. J. Schmidt and the other followers of the empirical theory of literature (S. J. Schmidt, 1983a).

I believe that, under the influence of this exterior confusion, the cultivators of literary theory have sometimes precipitously abandoned their most genuine instruments and methods, even forgetting fundamental reservoirs of specific experience. Schmidt's case is symptomatic of a feature generalized among many of the current protagonists of poststructuralist skepticism in the international panorama of the theory of literature. Undoubtedly, it is a matter of keen minds, living exclusively the questions raised by the crisis of philosophy that followed Heidegger's antimetaphysical revision. But it is also true that many also possess sensibilities fairly distant from and unaccustomed to the exploration of aesthetic experience. In such circumstances it is easy to expect art to live up to certain legitimacies of logical coherence, the lack of which it more than fully compensates for in the sentimental and imaginary suggestions of its nature as an *experience*.

Surely, this is the source of the confusion between literary structure and poetic value, and the failure to make this distinction has undoubtedly weighed down the speculations of the poststructuralisms, including Schmidt's "empirical" one. Literary structure must be verified in the artistic text's formal peculiarities and uniqueness, an entirely feasible and illustrative task, as demonstrated, on balance, by the results accumulated in the poetological experience of European structuralist neoformalism. Effectively, poeticity as a value is not justifiable on the textually immanentist hermeneutical scale which characterized the focus of the formal and structuralist stage. The aesthetic experience of poetic value, however, can be represented in absolute terms through the recognition and description of the anthropologico-imaginary mechanism organizing the psychological space of literary communication. In this space, as I hope to demonstrate in this book, the sources of a psychological, sentimental and imaginary unity appear, a unity underlying the universal structure of the imagination's behavior in its processes of anthropological identification and orientation in the universe of otherness.

By incorporating this psychological space into its considerations, literary theory does not fall into the undesirable and rightfully condemned territory of lucubrations on the nature of the "ineffable". It only reactivates the concerns that were its own field of development during the Romantic era, focusing on the undeniable psychological component of art as an aesthetic mode of knowledge, in the same way as, in its formalist and structural stages, this century's poetics modernized and readapted the interests in the text's material scheme which for centuries had characterized classicist poetics and rhetoric. Through these compensatory initiatives involving the legitimate recovery of the balance of its past thought and experience for the purposes of constructing an authentic general poetics, the literary theory I propose adds to the profound aesthetic reflections of Romanticism on the psychological structure of artistic experience the accumulated results of modern psychology and anthropology, cultural psychoanalysis and mythocriticism, in order to create a powerful and well-founded *poetics of the imaginary*.

From the perspective of these powers and capacities, a literary theory aspiring to justify itself in the end as a general poetics should not permit itself to be weighed down by the limitations represented by the arguments in favor of sociological criteria of *variety*, in view of the strength of those of universalist *identity* illustrated by the psychology of the imagination; such universal criteria proclaim the lived experience of art as an aesthetic experience, the well-founded, hardly chimerical alternative to the eroded credit of logical knowledge.

The negation of meaning in Roland Barthes' work covers a complete logical cycle, molded to his own productive trajectory and even his personal experience. It might be said that, having laid down his initial theoretical premises on the possible futility of meaning, Barthes' literary activity was carried out entirely within this domain, culminating in the attempt to produce a writing for pure pleasure, a literature about nothing, constituted on the meaningful pleasure of being a text. I should add that this cycle in Barthes' work does not respond to his own exclusively singular motivations, nor is it the result of any disagreement with his immediate surroundings, but, on the contrary, is an itinerary of writings intimately in touch with his intellectual environment. This is already the case with *Writing Degree Zero* where, although Barthes himself declared the absence in his text of the influence of the best-known thinkers of his time, with the exception of Sartre, which he attributed to his lack of familiarity with them, the technical term of the title was suggested to him by a linguist Barthes considered "second-rate", V. Brøndal. And, above all, the concept of writing in degree zero of style was imposed by his always keen and discerning vision of the stylistic uniqueness of modern writing compared to classical literature. What already stands out in *Degree*

2.1. The Pragmatic Relativity of Meaning

Zero, at least indirectly, is precisely his central intuition on the nature and function of contents in modern literature, a question which, developed later with greater explicit clarity as a contingency of meaning, will be central to Barthes' reflections on literature and art. The problem, then, is the definition of modern art as an open, free-standing and specific form; the problematic roots of that characterization begin already from the very start, when it is dealt with on the basis of its radical difference from classical art (R. Barthes, 1953), a claim historically never very well argued.

The contrastive characterization of the new art, which we should note was at that early point only a *desideratum* for Barthes, a project still rudimentarily glimpsed, from the point of view of its historiographical contribution, did not yet, in 1953, complete the rupture with the ideal of meaning, nor even with that of content: "This verbal form — that of modern writing —, *from which the ripe fruit of meaning will fall*, supposes a poetic time that is no longer a *fabrication*, but that of a possible adventure, the encounter of a sign and an intention". However, what is beyond doubt is that Barthes already at this early date had hit upon the features of a writing yet to come, that of his own final period and that of his own artistic generation, which in those years was taking bold and determined steps towards an absolute writing, a text on writing, pure Mannerist delight, but which ended up, in my judgment, producing a futile, barren effort.

The meaning in the writing to come, which I cannot see as that which Barthes then called "modern", in those terms, does not invoke any tactic of premeditated *inventiveness* or originality, but rather emerges from the "extensions of the word." An autonomous word, in pure liberty, which in "infinite liberty" develops "thousands of uncertain and possible relationships." Note that Barthes still speaks of thousands of relationships and, rhetorical and euphonic considerations aside, not of infinite possibilities, as will later be the case. That is, there is still no talk of an infinite text. Rather, he envisions a plural text, still not radically open, eternally and totally available. Lacking the historical profile of the intuited desire of the modern, Barthes already, in this first stage, accumulated powerful and attractive images. Barthes' ideas on this point will bear fruit especially in conjunction with other forms of the negation of meaning, like those of the American deconstructive critics, the most distinguished of whom, Paul de Man, in his first thesis as proposed in *Blindness and Insight* proclaimed his particular list of literary values, at the top of which would be the most plural and polemical texts in their suggestion of diverse readings (P. de Man, 1971).

Thus, in *Degree Zero*, the annulment of meaning as a specific task and essential feature of modern writing appears foreseen as a future development more than as a categorically conceived claim. In the brief pieces from the same period later grouped in *Critical Essays* and *Mythologies* this relativism as regards meaning appears frequently, thereby elevating it to occupy its position as a symptomatic feature of Barthes' thought. Thus, for example, he echoes the idea of the open nature of form, a *literal language* in its own terms, which achieves a meaningful role (R. Barthes, 1953). Here, from my point of view, the sincere desolation that Barthes foresees does not originate from having exceeded the conventional frontiers fixed by classicism for artistic writing. Rather, it seems to me these fears respond to the suspicion of an inconsistent area lurking under the insecure foundations of such a daring effort, founded on simple negation. A kind of apprehension which was lacking when, for example, in "Reading and Difference", with regard to the same texts and authors, the dimension of the "difference" is conceived of more modestly, in terms of the relative intensification of the mechanism of connotation.

The understanding of the connotative procedure or, in other words, of the autonomous power of the valencies of the signifier and its intransitive pleasure (A. J. Greimas, 1970, p. 93; J. Molino, 1971) as revenge against controlled classical meaning, is increasingly consolidated in this period, even affecting the values attributed to myths and, in general, the unwritten symbolism of images. The world of wrestling, one of the obsessions that most attracted Barthes' reflections in *Mythologies*, offers a perfect paradigm of this, where the falsified awareness of meaning does not hinder, for Barthes, the autonomous function of the form: "that extinction of the content by the form" (R. Barthes, 1957, p. 196). As a result, semiology, as a specific discipline, is not unitary, according to Barthes, except "at the level of forms, not of contents". In his final analysis on the actuality of myth, Barthes proclaimed the "alienation" of meaning in the "concept". An operation, basically, aborted by myth, the most characteristic property of which is the theft of language, consisting of "transforming a feeling into form" (R. Barthes, 1957, pp. 199, 208, 217).

Evidently, Barthes preferred betting — even fantasizing beautifully — on the nature of the future text, the signifier's form, to verifying and analyzing the content of classical texts. This evocation of the future text bore its best fruits in the powerful keenness and attractiveness of his critical brilliance concerning the texts of the new art, especially the fantastic foresight of the future text. On the other hand, the inability of such a fine productive spirit to ingeniously surmount the tedious analytical repetition of elementary categories learned in Propp and particularly in Greimas is very surprising, but this is what Barthes produces when he was faced with preparing an analysis of Balzac's story *Sarrasine* in S/Z (R. Barthes, 1970a), or the biblical result in "Jacob's Fight with the Angel" (R. Barthes, 1971). In his few exercises of analysis, prudently small in number, this brilliant cultivator of allusive synthesis never surpasses the most mediocre structuralist epigonism. And something similar occurs with his thematic analysis of Michelet's work (1969). An early commissioned essay, Barthes was unable to make anything out of it, as he himself recognized, beyond a mere organized grouping of thematic contents. In spite of the frequency with which this work is cited, it appears it had no greater ambition than any other practical work of editorial interest dedicated to a synthesis for university students.

The case of Barthes' studies on Racine is a different story. On this occasion, the circumstances of the commission were different and Barthes' own emphasis and maturity led him to tackle it with greater psychoanalytical ambition. Nevertheless, the most important aspect of this work for us was that it gave rise to the famous polemic with the distinguished Racine expert, Raymond Picard. A debate in which, as far as Barthes is concerned, what least mattered was how right he was, compared to the unsurpassable attractiveness, depth and brilliance of his writing about writing. Focusing his attention in *Sur Racine* on the narrow question of the nature of meaning, the work assumes as its goal the unequivocal search for the same in Racine's texts (R. Barthes, 1963), albeit at this point under the influence of a psychoanalytical liberty of inquiry undoubtedly far too scandalous for his detractors. Nevertheless, contents' reasons for being are not misrepresented, examined from the perspective of obsessive convergences in Mauron (C. Mauron, 1962).

The great general question of meaning is thus focused on centrally in this work, in terms of its relationship to the reader's freedom of reaction for selecting a level of particular interest to him within the overall plurality of the text's construction. Barthes expresses this conception in his preface in far more absolute terms than my own. The writer abstains from formulating a response to the questions indirectly raised by his own analysis: it is a response to the readers who contribute their own interests and language from the perspective of their own history. The multiplicity of responses, the fruit of historical change and the personal peculiarities of readers' languages and interests, determines the unstable variety of the original text's meaning. Barthes here no longer relativizes: "the world's response to the writer is *infinite*". But: "the senses pass, the question remains" (R. Barthes, 1963, p. 11). The rhetorical shift in the number of responses stands out here — from the multiple to the infinite — but also the control of content recognized as a permanence of the question.

The shift of interest this book reflects — from the objective question of meaning to the subjective one of readers' reactions and responses — is perhaps what is most important for the history of the evolution we are following: "Undoubtedly this explains the existence of a transhistorical essence of literature: this essence is a functional system in which one term is fixed (the work) and the other variable (the world, the time that work consumes)". Up to this point, the discussion is qualitatively correct in view of the fact that the proper appreciation of the receptive case was the great forgotten right, correctly demanded by all. Nevertheless, in my opinion, a quantitative lapse is produced with regard to the relative magnitude of the dialectical presences. The superior importance of a text is unknown in Barthes' scheme, precisely insofar as a work is not an objectively empty frame, but the stable assertion of a meaning by its sender, permanently exerting a control over the possible variety of responses, not infinite but adjusted to the bounds of that sense.

From this moment on it seems to me that Barthes' activity yields more beautiful and illusory results. His internal dialectic with paradox itself, with the trampoline of his own discourse, distances him from the truth about discourses which are not his own: "Allusion and assertion, the silence of the work that speaks and the word of the man who listens, such is the infinite spirit of literature". Undoubtedly, a very beautiful suggestion, whatever its consequences may be; though clearly, these will not be very reasonable, in real terms. Barthes has said before that the text is a permanent questioning; here we have a good starting point. Meaning does not change, nor is it *changeable*. What is true is that meaning can be approached from a variety of perspectives. The great work's powerful meaning, which Barthes himself imagined in terms of a geological metaphor as an immense vertical monolith rising through intertextual strata, possessing the peculiarities belonging to each of the strata it penetrates and borders. The variability of readers' responses is thus controlled by the essential unity of that great monolithic entity of meaning.

That Barthes can transform the anodyne opportunity of a brief polemical tract into a beautiful and transcendent reflection is proof enough of his inimitable talent, his great capacity to surpass himself. *Criticism and Truth*, published in 1966, collects in one volume Barthes' reflections of the previous ten or fifteen years on the nature of aesthetic meaning, tested in the light of polemical objections and transformed into a well-articulated and original body of work. With unsurpassable irony, Barthes characterizes the inflexible proposals of meaning as an absolute space, conceptually closed and unyielding to modulation. This unique and absolute meaning, applicable once and only once, cannot be anything more than a "triviality". The critic as Barthes represented and conceived of him, resists, with good reason, the institutional repetition of triviality. The possible and necessary freedom he claims already announces an attractive, but very dangerous deviation: the revalorization of criticism at the level of writing, that is, the famous definition of criticism as writing on writing (1966). An attractive idea that quickly becomes popular, reaching distant domains, like that of American deconstruction (G. H. Hartman, ed., 1979, 1980).

This ambitious project to gather and juxtapose two entities presumed to be identical — artistic writing and critical writing — was, logically, particularly artificial. And, when not artificial, it was clearly contradictory. Assuming an obligation to a text of reference, still worse in the case of having to consider a text to be analyzed, is awkward, an unnecessary hindrance, a stunt. Letting go of the orientation of the base text, forgetting it, Barthes would have found it easier and more natural to progress towards the autonomous text, written freely, motivated only by pleasure — *The Pleasure of the Text* (1973). By assuming an obligation to somebody else's text mediating his own writing, he took the road towards an impure writing, a goal he achieved in *Barthes by Barthes* (1975). Still worse when this course led him to a writing consisting of other's fragments, a Mannerist puzzle of aesthetic collectivism, as with *A Lover's Discourse: Fragments* (1977). In effect, criticism cannot excel by exceeding the very ample meaning of the text. A lesser activity? Who knows. After all, there are excellent critics able to fascinate us and mediocre authors able only to bore us. Modern critical writing should not renounce, of course, any of its conquests and freedoms. Perhaps its only limit is the distant meaning of the work it interprets, but this is a limit set by the nature of the object itself: that of existing or not.

The Fashion System (1967) does not raise the question of the nature of meaning. An unusually mechanical book for Barthes, it is an investigation of the writing of the fashion world, that is, the specialized commentary in magazines, written many years before its publication when Barthes had not yet even glimpsed the line of inquiry he would follow on problems of meaning. The destitution of the text's structural meaning is completed in *S/Z*. That is, *S/Z*, in J. Culler's quite correct opinion, completes a shift in Barthes' attitude. What Barthes fails to take notice of in his considerations is the extent to which his categorical affirmations are valid, expressed in universally abstract terms, and which I believe, as such, can only very tortuously be applied with interest and good sense to concrete works, be they classical or modern. Excepting, of course, that circle of writings closest to those of Barthes. Hence, Barthes' case reproduces a very similar situation to that which in Spain, many years before, had led José Ortega y Gasset in his *Ideas on the Novel* to proclaim, in vain, the immediate apocalyptic death of the genre due to the depletion of original themes, a claim made on the basis of the very real impression he had of the circle of novelists sorrounding him, as sharp as they were lacking in imagination. At least Barthes slipped in an important exception to his formulation to the effect that the concept of meaning changes quantitatively, if we are referring to classical literature: "Connotation is the path to the polysemy of the classical text, to that limited plurality on which the classical text is based" (1970 a, p. 14).

In my view, with the experience of *S/Z*, Barthes, centering his proposals regarding the infinitely ambiguous nature of textual meaning on the active role of the reader and the reader's definitive responsibility for the unlimited construction of meaning, had reached the point of no return. Motivated by his brilliant proposal of an alternative criticism and his confidence in the insistent effort of the tedious analytical method practiced in the book, practically all Barthes had left before him was the writing of pleasure, the writing, in any case, of the intertext, but independent from the concrete critical reference of a text as the object of mediation, be it through interpretation or analysis. Thus, in the years between *S/Z* (1970a) and *The Pleasure of the Text* (1973), a collection of interesting articles, *Sade, Fourier and Loyola* (1971), consolidates on theoretical ground the dissolution of meaning implanted in *S/Z*, without adopting the critical lack of differentially regarding the object of discussion which would become the chief characteristic of Barthes' independent artistic writing beginning in 1973.

Among Barthes' candid, direct and always illuminating responses in Jean Thibaudeau's interview, those related to *S/Z* contained particularly definitive assertions. Barthes already consciously formulates his old aspiration, which had long been unexpressed but clear to his readers: *"for my part, I don't consider myself a critic, but more like a novelist"* (1974, p. 49). The statement is, in itself, revealing, even ignoring its intention, as though it were just one more of the author's paradoxical pirouettes. Barthes does not yet clearly see himself as a novelist — just "more like one". But he is far more conclusive and forceful in his assertion that he is not a critic. And at this point in his conception of the literary work as an object and of the critical text as a mediation of meaning, there is no doubt in the end that Barthes has made a difficult but truthful confession. Naturally, Barthes' eternal sense of self-moderation as regards his own paradoxes immediately propels him into tortuous modulations of his statement, but all of these boil down to clarifying the reach of what he has said about his insecurities as a novelist. Thus, he quickly adds, "writings, not of novels, really, but of the novelesque. *Mythologies, The Empire of Signs* are novels without history. *On Racine* and *S/Z* are novels about histories, *Michelet* is a para-biography, etc. I like the novelesque, but I know the novel is dead". And he concludes: "that is, I believe, the precise place from which I write" (1974, p. 49).

As can be seen, Barthes has already entirely exceeded the critical problem of aesthetic meaning, the first purpose and starting point in this long itinerary of texts. Nevertheless, it is worth observing that the awareness of the meaningfulness of classical and modern works constitutes for him a fact he haggles with, but leaves intact. The work's general and aesthetic meaning can be presented by the force of Barthes' brilliant paradoxical writing, as a critical concept forgotten in the conceptual warehouse of lost objects, but not in that of non-existing objects.

The crisis of structuralist methodology in literary criticism has been channeled, above all, in the most outstanding and significant cases, within the process of the traditional negation of meaning, framed in the productive relationship between author and text. We could also rightfully allude to various other facets in the resolution of this same crisis (L. Doležel, 1979).

The debates over reader response theory can surely exemplify the hypertrophy of a dangerous understanding of literary theory (M. H. Abrams 1979, p. 587). The main danger in this case can be represented by the anti-economical banality of the type of discourses and metatheoretical dissensions which increasingly distance criticism from its appropriate objects and profitable objectives, with the aim of exhaustively consolidating it within their methodological pretexts. I repeat here, once more, that the relevance of taking into consideration the temporal-receptive vector in the constitution of meaning is a reality which nobody can reasonably deny. One could even justify historically the occasional use of a certain supplementary emphasis, in space and in time, by recent literary criticism, to awaken and reactivate the traditional critical awareness, "ignored and devalued", in Fish's own words (1980,

p. 158), of the receiver's role (R. S. Suleiman and I. Crossman, eds., 1980; J. P. Tompkins, ed., 1980; C. Di Girolamo, 1982; M. Ferraris, 1984; R. C. Holub, 1984). Beyond that, the prolongation of the debates and methodological arguments over supposed questions of principle, has contributed more to incrementing the confusion of the most sterile "professionalist" outskirts (S. Fish, 1986, pp. 89–108) in the present-day critical "Babel", than to illustrating and truly enriching a literary history of reception, fundamental to the perfection of literary theory through an adequate historical reference.

The problem is that one of the fundamental risks attached to considering critical documents as mere "self-consuming artifacts" (S. Fish, 1972) under the permanent foundational awareness of inexactitude and provisionality, consists in provoking the distancing and fatigue of receivers at the expense of the most fundamental evidence of the direct experience of literary reading. In this sense, Stanley Fish is not one of the least contradictory protagonists in this process, precisely starting from his reasonable and realistic denunciations of the sterility of the artificial debates of present criticism, encouraged by the powerful spurious factor of "professionalism". An observation, in turn, founded upon his idea regarding the differentiation between direct and unbiased "readings" of literary texts, which he recognizes as having the ability to reasonably assimilate an objective meaning of the same, and critical "interpretations", which, for unavoidable reasons never satisfactorily explained by Fish, tend to deform and compromise — universally and inevitably according to the polemical American critic — the reasonable immediacy and objectivity revealed as possible in literary communication; in other words, that which has not been deformed by the interpretative professionalization of criticism: "This, it seems to me, is a pseudo-problem. Most literary quarrels are not disagreements about response, but about a response to a response. What happens to one informed reader of a work will happen, with a range of nonessential variation, to another. It is only when readers become literary critics and the passing of judgment takes precedence over the reading experience that opinions begin to diverge. The act of interpretation is often so removed from the act of reading that the latter (in time the former) is hardly remembered" (S. Fish, 1980, p. 52).

Particularly with regard to literary reading, the affected and self-satisfied complexity of a type of critical argumentation nourished upon its "self-consuming" professional conscience has naturalized the phenomenon of an uncontrollable — and calculated — dispersion of critical viewpoints with regard to the nature of literary meaning. And I must add that, in my opinion, in the majority of useful and important cases one is not so much dealing with the by now often denounced Babel of critical languages, fruit of the marked linguistic emphasis of the criticism of the structuralist period, but rather with a sort of deassimilative confusion produced by the features of the real "face" itself, that is of critical motives, being forgotten. Often one can observe how the "professional" autonomy of individual critical discourses, so longed for nowadays, is fomented by a "misreading" not so much inevitable as deliberately cultivated. Along these lines attitudes are produced, which are discussed at various points in this book, such as those of Harold Bloom, who has had the courage — and the daring — to go as far so to recognize it as a programmatic starting point for his actual critical productivity, obsessed with originality. Similarly, in reader theories such as that of W. Iser himself, the alleged inoperativeness attributed by him to the intentional vector of the authorial production of meaning has been equally objected to, as a postulate which is difficult to reconcile alongside his polemical proposal of the concept of "reader implication". A proposal brought about mainly by authors' meticulous calculation mobilizing linguistic and potential communicative devices of the system in the construction of the successful literary text, as a structure and mechanism capable of capturing the interest of a reader who is permanently free to choose and optionally prolong alternative directions provided — and foreseen — by the text. The same situation of striving to maintain and augment a cultivated "difference", which is merely polemical, aiming for a "professional" tactical advantage can also easily be discovered in Derrida's indifference towards translating the logical negativity of his "différance" into aesthetic positivity regards his utopian concept of "writing", resorting inevitably to the generalized Romantic myth of original or "pure" language as the natural lodging of poetic potentiality. One resistance, which is recognizable, as can be seen in this very book, in the more familiar proximity to the literary aesthetics of his close follower, Paul de Man.

Stanley Fish's case becomes paradigmatic and exemplary. The model of progression of his writings — above all in those which are brought together in *Is There a Text in This Class?* — is closely tied to the progressive modification, influenced by the strategies of polemical pressure, of several perspectives on the role played by reading and the structure of the text and its objective meaning, confessedly rooted in the European tradition and that of I. A. Richards and forcibly brought into relation with M. Riffaterre's neo-stylistics. Such perspectives, however, are not initially differentiated in any substantial way from the most concise — and frustrated — textual hypotheses of the Barthes of *S/Z*; nor from the situation of the French neoformalist school at the end of the sixties (S. Fish, 1980, p. 21). To think of language "as an experience rather than as a repository of extractable meaning" (p. 67), ultimately does not surpass the general principles of the European poetics of reading in its earliest and most consolidated manifestations of twenty years ago (see other equally illustrative affirmations, for example, on pp. 28 and 47). It is a question of taking the demonstrably partial position — although in itself not a false one — of assuming meaning as stemming exclusively from its effects on the receiver, denying the possibility of doing so by taking its codified inscription in the textual entity as the starting point. That is, it involves Fish's repeated questioning of what the text *does* and not of what the text *is* or *signifies* (1980, pp. 3, 26—27, 66—67, etc...); or the similar

2.1. The Pragmatic Relativity of Meaning

receptive *temporal* perception of textual meaning being favored by Fish, over the spatial, structural and codified one (1980, pp. 147, 159, etc.).

However the gratuitously partial condition of such a radical hypothesis on the nature and constitution of meaning in the text creates great dialectical problems for Fish, which he himself — and this is the most peculiar aspect of this theoretician — takes no care to cover up or hide. On the contrary, he proclaims and exhibits them within a "self-consuming" conception of theory, which if it so radically obliged to do so, this is due to the exclusive limitations adopted in its origins. Thus Fish himself perceives his famous distinction between what the text "signifies" and what it "does", as an equivocation in order "to retain the text as a stable entity at the same time that I was dislodging it as the privileged container of meaning" (1980, p. 3). In other cases he openly confesses to being conscious of exploiting "loopholes" drawn towards identical effects of dialectic ambiguity (p. 9); meanwhile at different points in the dialectical development of his self-consuming theory, the reality of meaning as a form of codified stability in the text forcibly appears as a controlling reference to the obliged "obliquity" of reading. For instance, in one of the appraisals in the essay "Literature in the Reader": "the result will be a description of the structure of response which may have an oblique or even ... a contrasting relationship to the structure of the work as a thing in itself" (1980, p. 42). The text as a necessary point of reference for the reader is thus shown time and time again to be an indisputable reality. Although referred to an initial stage — and according to him one which has been overcome — in his theoretical development, Fish affirms it in the synthetist introductory chapter to *Is There a Text in This Class?*: "I felt obliged to posit an object in relation to which readers' activities could be declared uniform, and that object was the text (at least insofar as it was a temporal structure of ordered items); but this meant that the integrity of the text was as basic to my position as it was to the position of the New Critics. And, indeed, from the very first I was much more dependent on new critical principles than I was willing to admit. The argument in *Literature in the Reader* is mounted (or it is anounced) on behalf of the reader and against the self-sufficiency of the text, but in the course of it the text becomes more and more powerful, and rather than being liberated, the reader finds himself more constrained in his new prominence than he was before. Although his standard is raised in opposition to formalism, he is made into an extension of formalist principles, as his every operation is said to be strictly controlled by the features of the text" (S. Fish, 1980, p. 7).

Hemmed in polemically by the inherent weaknesses in the simplest and most direct basic affirmation of the structure of meaning as reading experience, Stanley Fish has developed more solid fundamentals to qualify — although without openly admitting it — the difficult consistency of reader theory in its absolute terms. In this task Fish has offered, in my way of seeing it, one of the most attractive and original solutions, via the concept of "interpretative communities" (1980, pp. 171–172). Defined in the first instance by Fish as groups of individuals sharing "interpretative strategies" with regard to the codification and reading — Fish prefers to speak, in conventional terms simply of "writing" — of texts, it becomes clear that this instance can guarantee the unsustainable atomizing weakness of the most individualist promotors of reader theory, with the well-known result of anti-economical paradoxes over the potential infinity of readings and interpretations and the negation of the codified and stable component of the text as an object of communication.

Disregarding as secondary Fish's dialectical efforts, always cleverly argued, to remain as faithful as possible to his intuition as an original theoretician (for example, pp. 11–14), here it seems to me more useful and illustrative to highlight the importance of that search for a generalizable support — if one desires to avoid using the word universalizable, due to its being, in effect, unnecessary in this case — to explain the fact backed by historical evidence which the reality of literary communication represents, substantially maintained, with regularity and loyalty, by the textual constitutive instances of authorial codification and reader decodification. Sharing common structures of linguistic, imaginary, cultural, ideological and literary competence, is what facilitates not only the reading and writing, separately, of literary texts, but also the total phenomenon of artistic communication — the codification and reception process — which is fixed and stabilized in texts, with every room for significative freedom and fluidity, enriching and perpetuating literary experience. By virtue of this fundamental and undeniable fact, all the efforts towards enrichment carried out by Fish preferably to qualify and illustrate the receptive conditions of artistic texts, can be well received, provided the more extensive and general condition of the totality of vectors producing literary communication is not radicalized by these same efforts, by virtue of the principle of belonging to "interpretative communities".

I believe, moreover, that on numerous occasions Fish does not fail to accept the existence of this continuity of communication via the text. Formulating it even categorically: "This, then, is my thesis; that the form of the reader's experience, formal units, and the structure of intention are one, that they come into view simultaneously, and that therefore the questions of priority, and independence do not arise" (S. Fish, 1980, p. 165). From this point on, as I have said, Fish's dialectical retouching qualifies only those questions of merely partial interest, no matter how necessary or even prior they might appear to his polemical conscience.

Proposing the concept of "interpretative communities" to introduce a standard guaranteeing the dissemination of interpretations and readings of the text, Stanley Fish's critical discourse is brought closer to the habitual space of the most universalist forms in the investigation of literary meaning. For this entails appealing to a series of stable and transindividual forms involving individuals' participation in terms of "competence", facilitating and permitting communication through the codification and decodification of messages in accessible and interchangeable texts. This awareness conveyed to readers as a common code is that which, furthermore, reduces both anomalous codifications and extra-systematic and unconventional readings to their status as allusive and incomprehensible entities. While the existence of stable and untransgressable conventions among members of the same community, will furnish, in Fish's own terms, the limitative support for the same conventionality, the latter would not reach the limits of the arbitrary without breaking the principles and limits of comprehension which regulate and are moulded in the agreed rules of communication in the community.

Stanley Fish has not described extensively and explicitly the functioning and content of the rules of any these "communities", nor has he even dealt with their enumeration and historical boundary marks. However the theoretical characterization of the same which he has established allows one to orient the aforementioned conventional principle in the same direction of universalist tendencies which regulates such constructions as the formation rules of basic structure in generative grammar, the deepest symbolical structure in the anthropological regimes of the imagination, or in more strictly sociologico-artistic terms — as Gallagher (1983) has so cleverly observed — such concepts as Bakhtin's "architectonic forms", or Goldmann's "genetic structuralism" in their contextual setting, Jameson's delimitative forms of the "political unconscious", etc. No matter how evident the differences in specific content may be among all of these proposals based on contextual support, all of them have in common, however, the same principle of transindividual movement justifying and regulating the need for meaning as an obtainable principle of communication.

There is no sense, furthermore, in limiting to the receptive vector of literary communication the principle of control which regulates the facts of intelligibility and conventional referentiality in the bosom of "communities". Neither is the group of senders who codify the texts serving as objects of interpretation exempt from this same competence, and consequently, texts need not distance themselves from the mechanisms of convergence which reach and regulate the communicative behavior of the total number of individuals of each community. Fish's persistent attempts to recuperate the unilaterality of his interpretative interests are frustrated — in spite of his undeniable dialectical capacities — when faced with the fact of this evidence, discovered and invoked with very notable brilliance and independence by Fish himself.

Neither do these attempts improve their results when Fish tries to save for himself the undesireable risk of approximating his concept of "interpretative community" to the parameters of artistic communicative universality — "interpretative communities are no more stable than texts because interpretative strategies are not natural or universal, but learned" (S. Fish, 1980, p. 172) — relativizing the stages or historical and cultural points in time which would establish the limits and constitutive boundaries of different communities. Apart from the fact that he himself is not in a position to carry out the historico-theoretical investigation in order to specify the frontiers and, consequently, to characterize the specific differential content of the different communities unable to communicate from one to another (p. 173), the objection in itself is of little substance when faced with the reality of artistic analysis. Once more, even regarding as incommunicable stages such as those of the tripartite Hegelian model — Oriental, Classical and Romantic — the limitative objection with regard to the generalizable explicative value, if one wants to avoid purely calling it universalizable, appears trivial, a value which fulfills the established functioning of rules — conventional or otherwise — which in turn assure the communicability of contents between the members of each of these large "interpretative communities". Once more the memory of Gombrich's idea of historical investigation definitively imposes itself, ultimately oriented towards guaranteeing the maintenance of rules of convergence and of communicative aptitude among texts and artistic protagonists of different periods, under Goethe's dictum that in the last analysis "they were all human" (E. H. Gombrich, 1986).

2.1.3. *The Relativization of Meaning in the Aesthetics of Reception: A Criticism of the Fundamental Concepts*

One of the main trends among the methodological tendencies appearing at the onset of the crisis in structuralist poetics is that which has been called the aesthetics of reception (H. D. Weber, ed., 1978; W. D. Stempel, 1979; G. M. Vajda, 1981; R. C. Holub, 1984). We consider it here as a *relativizing* position regarding meaning, since it does not deny it as a possibility and aim of language, as deconstruction has attempted to do. The aesthetics of reception, in the formulation of one of its main proponents, Wolfgang Iser, affirms the meaning of the *work*, that is, the set of meanings elaborated by readers in the reading process, but it denies the meaning traditionally attributed to the *text* as the objective product of the author and a simple storehouse of meaningful *capacities* (W. Iser, 1972a, pp. 279—280). In this conception, meaning is no longer the entity fixed by the text's codification, an idea which Iser had demonstrated his reservations about in earlier works (W. Iser, ed., 1969), but has become a relative variable, adopting a different form and valency in each reading act.

The fundamental ideas of Iser's thought and that of his school revolve around this difference between a relativized and a traditional conception of aesthetic meaning. Keep in mind that the text we have taken as a starting point is from 1972 and, therefore, reproduces the state of opinion formulated in *The Implied Reader* (W. Iser, 1972), one of Iser's key works, corresponding to a stage in the evolution of his ideas in which reading's preponderant and decisive role over the authorial utterance has not yet been radicalized to the extent that it will be later. For this reason, Arnold Rothe's review of Iser's claims in 1972 does not yet deal with the relativism of meaning (A. Rothe, 1978). Still, the predominance of the role of reading over the utterance is explicit in the text we began with: "*The work is more than the text*", (W. Iser, 1972a, p. 279).

As Iser's critics have indicated, fluctuations of opinion are apparent in the foundational formulations of his school. Moreover, the lack of analytical verification is particularly noticeable. This, in general, is the critical attitude adopted by one of the method's wisest proponents, K. Stierle (1975, pp. 345—387). In general, like Stierle, the group of critics who followed and developed Jauss and Iser's initial proposals have denounced the initial lack of clarity of their basic categories, and particularly the confusion obstructing their proper evaluation resulting from the continuous shifting away from these first opinions (among others, we might cite: G. Wienold, 1974; H. Eggert, H. Berg and M. Rutschky, 1975; W. Haubrichs, 1975; K. Maurer, 1977; and, particularly, the book by N. Groeben, 1977).

Anyone seeking to explain this unforgettable constitutive feature, belonging to a methodological proposal that has achieved such wide dissemination, should keep in mind the admittedly polemical roots with which its founders, first Jauss and, in his image, Iser, set forth their first claims. Jauss' famous discourse of 1967, preceded by an anxious tradition of displeasure with historicist weaknesses (H. R. Jauss, 1967), was significantly entitled "Literary History as a Challenge to Literary Science"; moreover, in 1970, Jauss published a book with a title as revealing as *Literature as Provocation*. Iser's attitude is similar. Like Jauss, he takes advantage of the opportunity presented by an academic inauguration to proclaim the provocative principles of "the appellative structures of texts" (W. Iser, 1975).

The polemical presentation of Jauss and Iser's theses really corresponds to the widely-felt desire latent among traditional historians of literature to make up for the decades of preeminence, not without its prepotency, of formalist and structuralist critics and theoreticians. A general situation which was made concrete in the polarization of literary studies between German universities, with two new experimental centers at Bielefeld and Constanza. Jauss himself admitted, years later, that the haste associated with taking advantage of a polemical opportunity had hindered the congruent reaches of his foundational principle of the *horizon of expectations* (H. R. Jauss, 1975). An attitude of self-criticism that, in any case, honors its author; nevertheless, beyond the provocative style of these first affirmations, as we will see shortly, the reality of the doctrinal and analytical development of the very limited principle of reception has in the end converted this methodology into a great historical claim (W. Kroll, 1977).

There is no doubt that Gadamer and Jauss' call to remember the value of the receiver in the definitive constitution of meaning is timely and valuable, as we will continue insisting throughout this chapter. Nor was the recovery of the role of historicism in itself inappropriate, considering that it had allowed itself to recede too far during the boom of structuralist criticism and theory. The distortions were produced when it sought excessively to exploit the new perspective's relevance for literary meaning, which, in any case, must be, even taking into account its own problems in establishing itself, complementary to the values and interests on which the traditional, authorial constitution of meaning were established. This, as we shall see, is already a fact in itself. Even as regards viability, the deduction of authorial meaning, with its traditional problems, is far more viable than the determination of horizons of expectations and reader responses — in rigorous terms, that is, empirically and not merely as deduced from the texts —, since it is hard to distinguish between this receptive meaning and the one which stems from the author's message.

On the other hand, we should not forget the antecedents for tracing the matrix of receptive proposals, since, apart from the immediate philosophical influence of Gadamer and Habermas, Jauss himself recognizes the impact of Paul Ricoeur (H. R. Jauss, 1975) and the precedents represented by the intuitions of Czech structuralism, particularly J. Mukařovský and F. Vodička's proposal of communication as the undeniable principle for constituting meaning (J. M. Pozuelo Yvancos, 1988, pp. 112—113).

Iser's initial concept concerning the receiver's activity, freely creating a variety of concretions of meaning and preparing the way for the attractive notion of the text's "dynamic", through which the aesthetics of reception would end up converging with the various currents of poststructuralist thought, is formulated on very limited and markedly literary-historical foundations (W. Iser, 1972a, pp. 280—281). He invokes the creative awareness of authors as characteristic as Lawrence Sterne in *Tristram Shandy* or of Virginia Woolf. In this regard, Iser's critics have frequently indicated the very restrictive and *ad hoc* slant of his literary models and objects for reflection, among which the exceptionally open singularity of Joyce stands out (K. Stierle, 1975; K. R. Mandelkow, 1974; K. Maurer, 1977).

In this respect, receptive aesthetic's initial intuition necessarily yields a broader program of objectives, which its followers have yet to cover in the theory's no longer brief period of development. Thus, they have yet to establish the public's influence on creation in terms of the adaption of creative freedom to the demands of contemporaneous taste, consciously converted by authors into a stance of positive obedience or negative rebellion. Another possibility for investigation is the formative value of subsequent readers and their aesthetic tastes, an effect I will address in the final section of this second part, considering the positive character of poeticity attributed to authors' traditional prestige. And the same is true, with a different aim, of the prejudices inherent in reception derived from the presumptions about a genre or artistic mode: the festive character with which we confront a comic work or the opposite attitude in the case of tragedy, etc.

As a deployment of receptive aesthetics' fundamental postulates, other possible objectives, still not sufficiently investigated, might be those relative to the possible modifications of the reader's experience as a result of his reading, or the more thorough examination of the still unclear forms of his self-awareness. In my rhetorical proposal of the concept of expressive argumentation in this book (A. García-Berrio, 1983, pp. 134—142), I have taken into account the role of the author's control over the reader's affective identifications (H. R. Jauss, 1973a), one of the fundamental areas in which the receiver's free initiative is exercized (H. R. Jauss, 1975, pp. 263—339; see especially the polemical notes of T. W. Adorno, and H. R. Jauss' response, 1975, pp. 268—269). All of which testifies to the ample areas for exploration still pending on the critical agenda of the aesthetics of reception (A. Rothe, 1978, pp. 99—101); in fact, the ground that still remains to be covered attests to the fact that the elemental concept of reception which has been popularized up until now constitutes only the very starting point for the in-depth study of the literary and psychological variety constituting the receiver's communicative stance (K. Stierle, 1975, p. 347).

Together with Iser's affirmations in *The Implied Reader*, which we have just examined in its initial claims, the other great foundational principle of receptive aesthetics is the concept of the horizon of expectations formulated by Jauss as a fundamental proposal in his polemical stage (H. R. Jauss, ed., 1967).

This formulation, which has been the object of profound criticism and corrections both from within and beyond the receptive current, is limited in practice to alluding as a whole to the constitutive factors of the *traditional context*, without delving any more deeply into the complex structure of the same. Traditional culture (A. García-Berrio, 1978, 1978a, 1979c, 1979d, 1980, 1980b, 1981b, 1983a, 1985b) thus establishes the horizon of expectations within which each reader is allowed to realize the work of complementarily filling the "gaps" budgeted to him as well as the strategies merely suggested by each text's "scheme of implication", to use Iser's terms. The work's deviation from that scheme of expectations allows us to measure the degree of originality or of literary value each new text produces (A. García-Berrio, 1982, 1984c, 1985a). Thus, the complementary concept of aesthetic distance is added to that of the horizon.

The fundamental objective of the method involves constructing a rich and detailed history of the receptive axis from the point of view of literary history. On the other hand, when it has maintained itself solely on the grounds of its theoretical proclamations, the method has fallen into a stage of occlusion in its development yielding a doctrinal disorientation which even the school's own most representative members complain about. Thus, Egon Schwarz denounced the existence of an "airless space" in the fading theoretical debate and demanded a "return to historiographical work" (P. U. Hohendahl, 1974, p. 11). For his part, Hans U. Gumbrecht pointed to the same situation when he alluded to the method's "stagnation in an unlimited theoretical debate" (H. U. Gumbrecht, 1975, p. 390). And, finally, in order not to multiply the observations of this phenomenon offered by its most qualified witnesses, K. Stierle called attention to the situation for constructing the history of the conditions in which reception was produced, declaring it practically inaccessible (K. Stierle, 1975, p. 346).

After the first stage of the new theses' polemical affirmation, the moment to articulate and consolidate them naturally arose. A second step, in Jauss' own terms, and one not without its problems, as we will see, all of which have not been resolved. We have at our disposal largely ungeneralizable, asystematic, and individual historical evidence. Dante's early *commenti* to the *Commedia* is a very exceptional case in this regard. As far as reader reactions in the Greco-Latin world are concerned, we have little or no explicit sources. Even in the case of a key text, like *Don Quijote* and the Cervantine canon generally, we do not and will never have reliable facts about its readers and their immediate readings, at least until fairly recent dates and, even then, only the recorded observations of such outstanding figures as F. Schlegel, Unamuno and Ortega y Gasset, which are not, by virtue of their originality and exceptional quality, applicable to more general levels of receptive expectations.

In the course of literary history, the specific outlines of cultural readings' conformative levels are sensed more as a general collective entity deduced from individual cases than as an event described in detail. Thus, we know a very specific example: the inevitable characteristic modification imposed by the European Romantic "reading", particularly among the French and Germans, for the contemporary physiognomy of Spanish Baroque art in painting, literature and customs. The most direct and appropiate task for a literary history of reception would be the exhaustive survey of the historical warehouses of scattered readings in order to construct suitable systematizing syntheses about ages, authors and generations of readers, the development of ages and modes of "taste", etc. All, naturally, in the field of historical recovery and restoration, quite apart from the very different aim of the current constitution — be it "empirical" or of any other kind — of the panorama and methodologies of investigation dealing with the reception of contemporary literature.

Jauss' proposals on the historiographical inquiry into reception point to two compatible possible paths. First, the study of the documented receptive history of concrete works and authors (P. Schunk, 1971; H. R. Jauss, 1973), leaving aside the risk of repeating the traditional histories of "posthumous fame", as Jauss himself recognized. Or, secondly, the exhaustive examination of very concrete moments — Jauss suggests that of truly key years — in the modification of literary, artistic and cultural tastes and mentalities (H. R. Jauss, 1975). Both initiatives are incomplete and preparatory although still necessary for undertaking general explorations of greater depth and illustrative power, such as Harald Weinrich's intuitive theses on the great stages in the history of reading (1967), or even historical attempts barely touching on specifically receptive questions, like Gunter Grimm's noteworthy effort (1977).

Faced with this problem, Jauss and especially Iser welcomed the dangerous expedient the thesis of the implicit reader presupposes (W. Iser, 1972). This involved the well-known proposal of resorting to the study of literary texts' structure in order to detect the sender's strategies to capture the reader's interest. In particular, the author achieves this, according to Iser (1971, pp. 1–45), by leaving sufficient "gaps", in the text for decision, permitting the activation and commitment of the reader' imagination in the cooperative construction of meaning (W. Iser, 1972).

From the perspective of the implicit reader the aesthetics of reception was forced to appeal to, it was possible to emphasize both the causal aspects of authorial activity, with the inclusion in the text of "gaps" and strategies "open" to the reader's initiatives for the construction of meaning. In the strictest sense, it is even true that the causal imposes a logical priority over the properly secondary and subsequent consequences of the reader's activities. Moreover, the knowledge of this causal factor, which establishes the conditions for receptive implication, can be approached in one universalizable explanation, while the singular descriptions of the different receptive processes for the construction of meaning, even if it is true that they are constitutively meaningful, would by definition never achieve an explanatory value of immediately generalizable discovery.

The new "phase" — the third step in this synthesis — in Jauss' methodological progression, identified by the author himself as a "rupture with Platonism", in part corresponds to the congruent but scarcely novel initiative to investigate the rhetorical structures of reader implication. The same return to the schemes of classicist poetics — *aisthesis, poiesis* and *catharsis* — which structures the collection of works leading to *Aesthetic Experience and Literary Hermeneutics* (1977), is symptomatic of a search for extraordinarily preliminary foundations for an object which will require mobilizing much more profound and detailed analytical categories and schemes, even at the disposition of the same classical system of rhetoric. Certainly the basic assimilation of the poetic categories that Iser combines is wrong and disproportionate: the two perspectives of action, productive or onomasiological — *poiesis* — and receptive or semasiological — *aisthesis* —, do not offer any purely doctrinal homology with classicist poetics enabling them to enter together in the same scheme of correspondences as those which link the "three fundamental *experiences* of praxis" to the famous *catharsis*.

Catharsis, as is known, is a modality specific to the final cause of the art form corresponding to a concrete kind of text — tragedy — just as "instruction", "admonition", "astonishment", "ridicule" or the production of "unpainful ugliness" belong to other genres. All things considered, all — including catharsis — are variations of the unique poetic articulation of rhetorical *movere*. Perhaps it would have been more appropriate on Jauss' part to invoke this general principle to achieve a more convincing degree of proportionality among the components of his famous scheme, especially given the fact that the other generic and textual varieties of the aesthetic effect mobilize schemes of reader implication identical in number and refinement, although of a nature different from that of the famous, and even more euphonic and peregrine, catharsis.

Considering the easy acceptance Jauss and Iser's foundational ideas have had in broad sectors of international criticism, it is advisable not to forget the severe corrections which the same have suffered among German authors very close to the methodological area of the literary historiography of reception, if not entirely representative of the tendency.

A critic like Hans Ulrich Gumbrecht, who is commonly assimilated and anthologized among the cultivators of the social history of reception, openly formulates his arguments in order to "support the proposal of adopting the construction of meaning conceived by the author — and not that of just any receiver — as the background for the comparison of constructions of historical meaning" (H. U. Gumbrecht, 1975). It is not possible to imagine a more open discrepancy with the basic principle of the "orthodox" aesthetics of reception as a "provocative" proposal of the reader's role in the construction of textual meaning.

Also representing the sector which marks the sociological and empirical differences with the "liberal" or structural-formalist evolution of reader implication, Bernhard Zimmermann has not trivialized the differences between his own critical stance (1974, pp. 13—14) and that of the group closest to it (K. R. Mandel, 1970; S. J. Schmidt and G. Henkel, 1972; and above all, M. Naumann, 1971) with the most characteristic ideas of the recognized leaders of the literary history of reception. Fundamental concepts, like that of Jauss' "horizon of expectations" are the object of criticisms similar to the faults I myself have indicated. Zimmermann's opinion, for example, about the imprecise and "abstract" nature of the concept of the public receiver, calls for a more precise definition along the lines of the more well-founded notion of social horizon in the terms concretized by Warneken or Naumann, with the help of all of the empirical evidence that is at hand. And he demands from Jauss a more cautious distinction between *addressee* and reader (B. Zimmermann, 1974, p. 48; M. Naumann, 1971, p. 166). In the pragmatic sphere, M. Pagnini (1980) has exhaustively systematized this set of denominations, often confused, distinguishing in general between the various modulations of *addressee* on the one hand, which includes, in turn the kind of "implicit reader" Iser speaks of (1972), the "ideal reader" close to the narrative specialization of the concept of G. Prince's "narratee" (1973), S. Fish's "informed reader" (1970), or M. Riffaterre's "archreader" (1971), and, on the other, the conception of the *receiver*.

2.1. The Pragmatic Relativity of Meaning

What the sociological school opposes to the concept of Jauss' "horizon of expectations" is equivalent to the radicalism of the differences to which the theoreticians of reading like Karl Maurer reproach in Iser's concept of the "implicit reader". My own previous objections about the traditional, rhetorical and formalist nature under which the textual concept of reader implication is construed, appear in Maurer's harsh criticism: "it is also clear that to determine the objective mode of the text's 'appellative structures' basically raises the same problems as traditional interpretation" (K. Maurer, 1977, pp. 472—498). In this line of the subjective evaluation of message's contents, Maurer opportunely compares the absolutely opposite opinions of Iser and Ingarden regarding divergence or convergence in the seried readings of a text. A highly symptomatic argument which I myself have echoed in the preceding pages.

Entering the concrete examination of the textual features of reader implication, Maurer proceeds with much more depth and detail than does Iser. Thus, for example, he examines the author and reader's degree of freedom compared to such decisive instruments for the constitution of the novel's meaning as "point of view". In order to illustrate his argument, he in fact does appeal first to the contrast between the ideas of Butor or Genette rather than to Iser's always prejudicial facts. On the decisive question of "identification", he reasonably emphasizes the readers' superior degree of freedom and emotional reactions, both sympathetic and unsympathetic, without slipping into the temptation to extract overly drastic conclusions about its role in the constitution of the text's meaning. One must keep in mind that, in effect, the possible alternatives for the reader's identification with historical "heroes" and villains — including the most anomalous ones — do not affect the consistency of the meaning produced by the text, but the success or frustration of the thesis in its rhetorical-persuasive objective, when the text has such a goal and emphasizes it in a marked way. In the cases of reader's anomalous identifications contrary to the author's will, the undesirable nature of the poor or good identifications are not confused in the message, but the reader's will produces a consciously ethical and elaborately anomalous identification.

In the examination of other mechanisms that are fundamental in reader implication, like that of the requirement of the textual constitution of the plot towards the coherent endings of classical stories — exceptionally open or intentionally incoherent only in certain numbered texts to modern poetics — (1977, pp. 271—276) or of the "orientation" in the possible complexities of the text (1977, pp. 276—277), Maurer completes an extraordinarily well-founded description of the broad field of authorial restrictions on the reader's illusory absolute freedom, superficially advanced in the most trivial disseminations of the method, or in the most uncontrollably "provocative" moments of Iser's polemical arguments. Maurer's reasonable conclusion coincides with our own identifications and discrepancies in the collection, commonly not sufficiently clarified, constituting the most general and disseminated concept concerning the degree of freedom — and thus responsibility — of the respective cases of production and reception in the construction of texts' meanings. In Maurer's opinion, the reader's liberty in this regard is much more conditional than that of the author, if not *illusory* according to the ideal of classicist poetics.

In my opinion, one of the most consistent and profound criticisms of the aesthetics of reception, as it was set forth, basically by Jauss and Iser, and as it has most commonly been circulated and disseminated, is that which Karlheinz Stierle formulated in his extensive article "What Does 'Reception' Mean in Fictional Texts?" (1975), calling attention to the irrecuperable schematism of the system's simplification in reception to an illusory pretense of an infinite freedom of legitimate individual readings.

Stierle, like Maurer before him, does not show any signs of equivocating his firm adherence to the principles and objectives that act as the foundations of the history of reception which, for him, "has become the principal problem of literary reflection" in the aftermath of Jauss' foundational lecture in 1967. Faithful to his recollection of those proposals, his syntheses cover the basic principles with precision and fidelity, those very principles whose most extreme versions illustrate the discrepancy between Jauss' proposals and our own ideas (K. H. Stierle, 1975, p. 344).

Nevertheless, the firm clarity of his fundamental convictions never carries Stierle, when attending to the constitution of the text's meaning, to in any way divorce himself from the most absolute evidence imposed by the structure of meaning in literary works (K. Stierle, 1975a). Analogous to my own conception of general meaning in very complex literary works, which distinguishes between a nucleus producing an untransgressable meaning and a connotative periphery of contents that is of a more fluctuating conceptual, sentimental and imaginary meaning, Stierle distinguishes between a text's "central axis of pertinence", a sphere beyond the reader's modification, and a set of secondary pertinences, in which the reader's undepletable associative freedom is exercised, a freedom Stierle characterizes as "infinite", undoubtedly in the customary concession of the historians of reception to unpremeditated excess (1975, pp. 370—371).

This recognition of the meaningful central firmness of the text produced by the author allows Stierle to attribute the reasonable objective space for these legitimate activities to the reader's variations. It is here that we see Stierle's disagreement with Iser's scarcely well-founded design for the structures of reader implication.

The text's meaningful identity is therefore recognized without diminishing the importance of this alternative freedom, bounded in its inexhaustible potential, which nevertheless recognizes an end in the strict limit of the meaningful will of successful production. The literary text, thus, is viewed as a consistent structure, in whose artistic complexion the signifier itself is already an indistinguishable element of meaning. The masterful intuition of a formalist, Lotman, is unexpectedly recognizable in the appreciable depth of this sociological historian of reception: "The *signifié* of the artistic text is the *signifiant* of its form" (1975).

In conclusion, the critical and detailed synthesis of the principles constituting the methodology of the aesthetics of reception, with the genesis of the same in the foundational work of Hans Robert Jauss and Wolfgang Iser, demonstrates that there is no lack of limits and even fundamental contradictions in the elaboration of a disciplinary modality of literary study which has known an overly broad and reductive dissemination over the course of the past decade. Its greatest merit, demanding the due attention which the communicative vector of reception deserves in the constitution of meaning, is impaired when the proposal is zealously exaggerated. An exaggeration which leads to the demand of meaningful exclusivity for the reader's initiative, followed by its almost automatic sequel, transforming by inertia the relativity of the "work's" meaning into the negation of the "text's" meaning.

A careful examination of texts allows us to identify, nevertheless, the fact that Jauss and Iser's gestures have been more "provocative" than consistently demonstrable in their affirmations, which has only contributed to a greater extent to the relaxed dissemination of the stereotype of an aesthetics of reception strongly implanted in negative convictions about the stability of meaning in the vector corresponding to the text's production. On the other hand, we have collected opinions of some of the methodology's distinguished cultivators which point to discrepancies over the method's two central concepts — the "horizon of expectations" and the "implied reader" — thereby demonstrating that the method's limited doctrinal nucleus — which nevertheless aims at presenting itself as the pillar for a paradigmatic change in the study of the literary — is full of considerable empirical difficulties, above all because of the internal contradictions of the effort to resort to formalist procedures in order to determine the behavior and nature of historicist reception.

2.1.4. *The Formalist Mechanism of "Reader Implication": Textual "Gaps" and the Work of the Imagination*

In the preceding section of this chapter we have seen how the empirical and historical problems for determining the "horizon of expectations" of literary works, above all those of the most remote past, led to W. Iser's fertile and widely disseminated recourse to the concept of an "implicit reader". Iser's efforts are a matter, as I have already discussed, of the disguised formulation, for reasons of fidelity to the receptive method, of a formalist initiative which locates the mechanisms of readers' implication and identification in rhetorical-formal procedures situated in textual structures. By invoking the concept of the "gap", the formalist twist of *The Implied Reader* attempts to rescue Jauss and Iser's old postulate viewing the meaningful predominance of the work, understood as a pragmatic result of readers' activity over the text, as a product of authorial or, according to the kinds of prejudices under which it is considered, authoritarian creation.

The "gaps" or "holes" in the text are, according to Iser, the spaces of inexpressive discourse. As detailed as naturalist art came to be in Zola's novels, for example, the description of landscapes, places, objects and people always proceeds through the selection of details. The artistic reproduction of reality in the description of objects or in the narration of events cannot be exhaustive; the constitutive complexity of real referents entirely surpasses the reach of artistic mimesis' referential capacity, be it in the plastic arts or, even more regularly, in the case of literature (A. García-Berrio and M. T. Hernández, 1988a). In the communicative requirement that these gaps in the text's expressed discourse be "filled", the reader's activity discovers and uses *fantasy*, which Iser — and in general all of the theoreticians of reception who touch on these doctrines — habitually denominates imagination. It appears that Iser attributes an uncontrollable freedom to imagination, entirely unstructurable and unforeseeable. From this it follows logically that the decisive initiatives to construct textual meaning reside in this work involving the imaginary occupation of the immense gaps left open in the text's structure, the result of either the author's calculation or the incompetence of the expressive system of human discourse. At the same time, the absolute freedom, diversity and infinite number of possible readings are rooted in the unstructurable freedom of the imagination and in the greater proportional number of "gaps" in the text.

That lasting form of life literary texts possess is produced by the interaction of the conceptually expressed and the *not said*, the space of the imagination's activity, being the case that the story's interest and identificatory animation respond to the action of this second component (W. Iser, 1972a).

In principle, the basis in reality of the verifiable evidence about the experience of artistic reading which Iser describes cannot be denied. It is particularly valid, or perhaps *only* valid in these terms, as we will see later, within a restriction he assumes as the whole of the narrative mode of literary discourse. Gaps do in fact exist, fantastic activity fills them, and, as a result, the communicative, sentimental and aesthetic interaction between the verbally expressed and the reconstruction or imaginary filling of the not said are characteristic features of all discourse. Up to this point, Iser is correct: these elements form part of the reflexive experience of any reader of novels, as the critic establishes in a reconstruction based on a fairly anodyne text by Virginia Woolf. The problem begins with the proportionality of meaningful reponsibilities which he attempts to attribute in the resulting general body of meaning to the expressed components or the fantastic reconstruction of textual gaps.

The discrepancy between my own experience and the modern trend towards the "openness" of artistic meaning, in Iser's position, needs to be put into its proper perspective. My own attitude responds to the "classical" understanding of meaning as a fundamental initiative of the text's authorial production, albeit true that today neither I nor anyone can afford to turn his back on the effective imaginary *iridescence* unique to individual readings (note that with the term iridescence I am alluding to the marginal secondariness of this element of "pertinence" pointed out by K. Stierle [1975, p. 121]). In this regard, my own experience leaves me neither "persuaded" nor "convinced" by Iser, but allows me to recognize that it begins, as is the case with Iser's experience as well, with the social diffusion of a reality which becomes particularly perceptible in the arguments recently raised in art, in current philosophy and, above all, in the inescapable system of political and social life and ideas determining the human environment in which we exist.

In fact, Iser himself takes as his starting point a text of classical understanding about meaning written by Roman Ingarden, the influential phenomenologist, in which he manifests the traditional concept about the discontinuities and gaps of narration as distorting limitations in artistic works (R. Ingarden, 1931). And Iser takes advantage of this in order to affirm the radical contrast with his own opinion about the dynamicity, aesthetic animation and role in the production of meaning stemming from the receiver's reconstructive activity (W. Iser, 1972a).

The key conceptual breakdown affecting Iser's views about the degree of the reader's responsibility for the construction of meaning in the text undoubtedly proceeds from his overly general and superficial understanding of the entities he denominates "gaps" and "holes" in the text (W. Iser, 1971, pp. 1—45). Surprised at having been caught in a linguistic problem typical of those facing the structuralist poetics of the text, Iser's intuition as a literary historian cannot make up for his overly general knowledge of modern linguistics and traditional rhetoric.

Jauss' general intuition of the "gap" as an unconstructed hole largely corresponds with linguistic structures perfectly recognized in their rule-governed predictability, such as ellipsis and the systematic control of the poetically sublime, the manifestation of elements in *zero degree*, and especially the broad and inclusive logico-linguistic concept of *presupposition* (J. S. Petöfi and D. Franck, eds., 1973). Not to mention the spaces of indeterminacy and ellision that appear in the scheme of rhetorical structures such as irony, preterition, simile and, in general, all of the metaphorical schemes (H. Lausberg, 1960). That is to say, the receiver's behavior in his "reading" of gaps is *almost* as explicitly foreseen and regulated by the linguistic norm as is the text's explicit extension.

If we thus apply all of these reductive conditions to the space of the receiver's autonomous initiative, lodged by Iser in the unforeseeableness of textual "gaps", we find that the concept of a regulated textual structure is considerably broadened, beyond what explicitly corresponds to the textual extension of *the said* (P. Macherey, 1974). In the same practical, normal and monosemicalizing conversation, linguists recognize an undoubtedly more important space, where the normative power of many implicit presuppositions is exercised, which are commonly more numerous than the regular consequences reflected in the structures of texts' terminal manifestations. Nevertheless, the linguistic activity of these "presuppositions" is not any less determined than that of grammatical and semantic rules that form the meaningful structure of the expressed. The theme is so elemental, that it doesn't seem necessary for me to go on at length providing more detailed illustrations of well-known linguistic questions.

A second type of textual "gap" of a non-automatic structural nature at the linguistic level of the implicitly and foreseeably obligatory is that which is *intentional*, that is, foreseen and calculated by the author, with very varied communicative, rhetorical and aesthetic aims: awaken and conduct interest and intrigue, calculatedly manipulate the ethical "implication" of the reader, experiment with and encourage the forms of playful freedom to which the aesthetics of reception and of the open work concede such importance, etc. In fact, with this second genre of intentional gaps, owing to the calculation of the textual production's intensity, we find ourselves within what Iser (1972) and Eco (1979) consider intentional structures of reader implication, according to the different selective behavior of the text. This gives rise to variables of meaning which are nevertheless itineraries entirely foreseen by the author himself, or at least not contradictory with the structure of production, with the author's foreseen meaning manifested in the work's message as a constructive act of volition.

Still another class of "gaps" results from the author's *lapsus*, a true nightmare of classical writers and theorists in the tradition of the "dormitat Homerus" (A. García-Berrio, 1977, I, pp. 310 ff.). According to this tradition, Cervantes corrects the argumentative omissions and lapses of the first part of *Don Quijote* in the preamble to the second part. Nevertheless, this type of gap does not produce an alternative meaning in line with Iser's intentions, since correcting or "fixing" a partially incorrect meaning is not, strictly speaking, an independent and alternative receptive activity.

In the fourth place, we still have to consider the genre of genuinely aesthetic "gaps" within implied reader theory. For the moment, we must indicate the important and meaningful fact that Iser's work has not generated the analyses that would have been necessary to adequately illustrate, inventory and typologize literary examples of this textual phenomena, so fundamental in the development of his theory.

In the case of these gaps, we are either dealing with intentional gaps, like those we have discussed earlier, set out by the author as a function of the established meaning, or with spaces of autonomous association. This is the case, for example, with the fantastic construction of the accessory details concerning characters or places not set forth in the text. Undoubtedly, here the receiver's initiative is given in complete freedom, resulting in different fantastic constructions; for example, each one of us will have a different finished image of Fabrizio del Dongo. But the well-constructed text will have explicitly adjusted the substantive terms to the meaning, in such a way that nobody can transform those that Stendhal felt were necessary to set forth for Fabrizio without falling into error. Recall in this regard Tomashevsky's invocation of Chekhov's observation regarding "compositional motivation", when he affirmed that if a novel mentions a nail in a wall at its beginning, the hero should hang himself from that nail at the end (B. Tomashevsky, 1965, p. 282).

There is no need to deny that a great novelist's art — and here we insist that, in the theory of reception, all of its examples end up referring exclusively to this genre — resides in large part, as Iser claims, in his capacity to provoke fantastic suggestions of the kind just mentioned. Barely two notes of conventional decor enable Cervantes to suggest the Atlantic in *La Española inglesa* and, as I've said elsewhere, the spatial poetic imagination is fundamental in the artistic value of *Don Quijote*, in spite of the concise economy of descriptive details which characterizes not only Cervantes' narrative art, but also that of the Baroque novel in general. Nevertheless, it seems sensible to think that that capacity for suggestion can be extracted from the author's inventive intuition and his capacities for thematic selection and narrative revolution. Only in this manner can we explain the obvious climaxes of sublime art, successful or not.

A hierarchy of quality in readings and readers can also clearly be invoked, in such a way that there exist very different levels of appreciation and particularly of sentimental and imaginary reaction, from the most trivial to the most poetic. But this does not imply at all the meaning which is codified in the text, insofar as the type of reader reactions *proportionally* attributable to the same. The greater capacity of the more cultured, imaginative and sublime reader will surely beautify any work on which it is projected, whereas a vulgar and insensitive reading will not produce responses more interesting than those of the reader suitable to the task, whose ideas, emotions and fantastic representations are enriched and stylized by the same works (W. Woolf, 1928, 1932; G. Poulet, 1970; and, more centered on the receptive discussion: R. T. Segers, 1975; H. Heuermann *et al.*, eds., 1975; G. Grimm, ed., 1975; W. J. Ong, 1975; L. Decaunes, 1976; H. Grabes, ed., 1977; J. Kamerbeer, 1977; R. de María, 1978; S. R. Suleiman and I. Crossman, 1980).

It thus seems clear that it is necessary to separate the level and meaning of texts from the content and level of their readings. We must especially distinguish between exact and inexact — faithful and unfaithful — readings, in relation to their attributions of meaning regarding the text's explicit and objective meaningful proposals. And then, in one and the other case, we can speak of readings enriched by peripheral conceptual, sentimental and imaginary associations, as well as of other drier and more impoverishing readings. In the optimal case of a faithful reading, rich in responses, we might even be able to consider it archetypal and interesting in itself, even removed from the original text that served as its basis. But in this extreme case, we would be judging two different phenomena and objects. The senseless hypothesis of an extraordinarily rich and creative reading should be judged, in order to be meaningful, as an independent production.

As one can see, it is not possible to follow the logic inaugurated by the principle of gaps in implied reader theory according to the terms and aims Iser initially proposes without reaching incorrect conclusions. In any case, it is important not to forget that narration and literary mimesis in general are regulated by principles possessing a very broad capacity for extension, such as those of *verisimilitude* and *decorum*. These should be considered as *extensive* rules, in such a way that the *textual indications* assumed by the mimetic selection of authors are extended under the logic of these rules to the set of situations and objects verisimilarly presupposable; they are *necessarily* logical and proportionally *convenient*. In this way the hypothetical autonomy of the reader in his reactions knows not only the explicit limitation of the text's elements, but also the more rigorous and comprehensive limits of the general system of implicit rules which inaugurate it as meaning.

One might think that I have mentioned only the principles corresponding to the classical and realist artistic system, fixed by Aristotle's *Poetics* and by the rhetorical tradition that begins with him and extends throughout the monumental works of Cicero, Quintilian, etc. In any case, if this is so, one should also not forget that the artistic products that obey this system of rules constitute the vast majority of Western literary art's products. In comparison to this great historical volume, the experimentalist alternatives of pragmatically open art did not for a very long time represent — in spite of some highly esteemed values — anything more than an anomaly. Not to mention that, as I have justified at various points in this book, anticlassical art of pure negation is largely absorbed by the same logic it works to defeat.

The second of the major questions Iser habitually activates in this theory of gaps in reader implication refers to a stereotyped conception of imaginative work (W. Iser, 1972a; 1976). Iser conceives the imaginative activity of filling the gaps of the explicit structure as a possibility that cannot be reduced to rules and norms of expectation (W. Iser, 1979, pp. 1—20). At this point in our knowledge about the artistic imagination's activity and its rules (J. P. Weber, 1960, 1963; G. Durand, 1960; C. Mauron, 1962; F. Pir, 1967; O. Mannoni, 1969; M. Mansuy, 1970; J. P. Sartre, 1950; J. Chassegnet-Smirgel, 1971; A. Clancier, 1973; S. Felman, ed., 1982; C. Castilla del Pino, 1984; A. García-Berrio, 1985), a simplification like that Iser regularly proposes is entirely inadequate and naive.

Moreover, on this point, the distinction between *imagination* and *fantasy*, already linked to Romantic antecedents, is perhaps not useless and may provide pertinent clarification. In the sense which I have been advocating (A. García-Berrio and M. T. Hernández, 1988, pp. 52—53), the imaginary activity which Iser customarily invokes can better be understood as the work of *fantasy*. According to the sense popularized since Coleridge, I understand artistic fantasy as that capacity to which the work of the imagination corresponds which goes hand in hand with the necessary correlation of facts and presuppositions of reality controlled by the logical principle of truth and falseness. It is, as can be seen, the specific work of filling "gaps" in structures of regulated verisimilitude, which has to be congruent with the rules of the support structure on which it acts.

The fantastic activity invoked by Iser, since it adjusts to the logical structures it pretends to complement, proceeds according to a norm of accumulative and associative activity; it is by nature associative in the maintenance of what is congruent. It acts upon preceding materials, formed by the spirit under a simple impulse of juxtaposition. In short, it is a form of memory of the marginal and alternative, disciplined by certain and foreseeable rules. In such circumstances, it is necessary to correct the hypothesis that this fantastic capacity's activity is entirely free and unforeseeable, filling the "gaps" of the novelesque text's structure, in the terms of Iser's proposal. To the same extent as with the conceptual activity of the presuppositions corresponding to the not said, the freedom of fantasy should be restricted to the estimate of a behavior of limited, regulated transfers, according to the verifiable norms for the anthropological structuralization of imaginative capacities.

Even imagination itself, in the freest subconscious sense in which I distinguish it from fantasy, has a structure determined by the regularity of its own regimes (G. Durand, 1960), although it is a capacity that really has little to do with the kind of imaginary work of associationism and verisimilar deployment conceived of by Iser, who never moves away from the artistic domain of narrative fictionality, the most immediately dependent on the realistic conceptual verification of the imagination's literary forms. In their creative involvement with poetry, the imagination's symbols respond to a surprising, highly congruent structure, distributed between the contradictory dialectics of the symbolization of temporal otherness — the positive-diurnal and postural and the negative, nocturnal, and digestive — the synthesis of which, the copulative, constitutes the regenerative power of eros. Similarly, the subconscious drives which induce the patterns of the imaginary representation of space are distributed with startling regularity in the same dialectic of the positive and the negative: between the dynamic — elevation and expansion vs. fall and collision — and the static — the environment as a favorable and protected space and the enclosure or fence as a threatening space of fearful expectation and pursuit (A. García-Berrio, 1985, 1987). Evidently, appealing to the imaginary in the terms of Iser's theory of the implied reader, in either its sense of fantasy or imagination itself, does not corroborate the dynamic, unforeseeable freedom which the proposal of infinite readings requires.

It appears that the aesthetics of reception and the theory of reading exhausted their usefulness to modern literary theory, having recalled a relatively derivative factor: that of the receptive case and its role in the critical and particularly historico-literary modulation of meaning. Personally, I believe the extensions of critico-receptive relativism that have been disseminated through the present are more obedient to critical handicaps, that presume themselves protected by a prestigious theory, than effective extensions and enriched articulations of a theory of reception assumed and stabilized as history. It is not enough, in this respect, to declare oneself in favor or against the aesthetics of reception. The advocates of this method should move on — and they do not usually do so — to the urgent task of reformulating the various histories of literatures, or significant chapters of the same, from their new point of view (G. Grimm, 1977). Nobody could validly object against the reasonable principle of the receptive perspective as a point of view complementary to the author's in the elaboration of meaning. I believe my own experience elaborating a broad chapter of the Renaissance reception of classical poetic "patterns" (A. García-Berrio, 1977—1980) offers a very positive, balanced lesson in this regard.

The receptive and pragmatic relativizations of meaning that were disseminated fifteen or twenty years ago, when the European protagonists of structuralist poetics — Barthes, Eco, van Dijk, Schmidt, etc. — were looking for a brilliant alternative to a path already surveyed, outlined and without surprises, do not fit together with the real experience of literary texts and their historical workings. This is the sensible understanding of the theory of meaning informing the thought of Michel Charles (1975).

The institutional confrontation unleashed by the aesthetics of reception has taken place, as is only logical, with the traditional methodological trend of literary hermeneutics (R. Warning, 1977, pp. 126—131; F. van Ingen, 1975), as a method and activity for the objective discovery of texts' meanings. In Gadamer's decisive model (1960), both passions are encouraged, with some confusion. Nevertheless, the hermeneutics of literary knowledge (E. Forastieri-Braschi, 1978) knows a long tradition of the textual discovery of meaning (S. Haugon-Olsen, 1978), well-founded on criteria of a congruent and strongly motivated nature, which allows us to speak of a perfectly well-constructed "logic of interpretation" (H. Göttner, 1973; P. Ricoeur, 1969).

From the constructive proposals of literary hermeneutics, the ideas on the receiver's initiative already underwent correction in the work of Erich D. Hirsch, *Validity in Interpretation* (1967), an exact, even minutely involved discussion of the key presuppositions regarding meaning's relativism and receivers' plural response. The starting point for debate, nevertheless, was not the opinions of the German theoreticians of reception and, even less, as is only logical, the corresponding ideas arising from European post-structuralism, but the important doctrinal block of Anglo-Saxon criticism, especially the familiar ideas of I. A. Richards and T. S. Eliot. Hirsch's conception of meaning as heuristic "type" implies on the one hand an exact notion of an entity of meaning, the type, formed by immediate features or constituents,

2.1. The Pragmatic Relativity of Meaning

produced by a meaningful "act of will" (1967, pp. 50—51). Two classes of features of characteristics define the concept of *type*; they establish the outlines of an environment and can be represented by more than one case or example. The first notion of *meaningful boundary* alludes to the possibility of defining attributions of meaning as concerning or not concerning the author's act of intention, constitutive of the text's meaning.

This solid and concrete concept of meaning corresponds with an equally univocal and enclosed understanding of interpretation, or of the attribution of meaning by the receiver, which is situated at the antipodes of the polysemical relativization placed into circulation by reception theory. Thus, the interpreter must distinguish between what a text implies and what it does not imply. He must give the text all of its expectation, but at the same time maintain norms and limits. The understanding of the text corresponds to the act of will constituting its meaning; for Hirsch, it is a particular operation that can be distinguished from other operations.

Obviously, Hirsch is not unaware of the common arguments on which the relativization of meaning is founded, although for him the question can be channeled through Frege's well-known opposition between *meaning* (Bedeutung) and *sense* (Sinn). Hirsch, who explicitly establishes the most immediate genesis of his ideas in Frege, also extends them to similar oppositions in Husserl, one of the most influential sources of his work (1967, pp. 217—219). In the Husserlian concept of *intention*, meaning is constituted only by the receiver's potential for participation. Nevertheless, compared to the intersubjective need for participation in the essence of meaning, this never appears for Hirsch as an open availability, but as a center of convergences constituted on the basis of the author's foundational intention.

Frege's notion of *sense* offers a space for the variable activity of focalizing the nuances or forms of a rich conception of meaning, in such a way that a text's *meaning* incorporates the accumulated partial references of the critical understanding of its meaning. The result of this is that "what changes (for the interpreters) is not the meaning of the work, but its *relation* with that meaning" (1973, p. 18). It is this critical modulation of meaning in which, in Hirsch's opinion, the set of individual or age-oriented critical focalizations of meaning are made to fit, without altering the fundamental base of the author's meaningful intention. For Hirsch, the strict and fixed condition of meaning is the guarantee of the variety of the partial complementary interpretations because, according to it, interpretative variety is controlled compared to the risk of irrationalist gratuitousness or capriciousness. And it is the concept of unity in the construction of meaning which is the base that controls and guarantees the reasonable diversity of readings, which would be senseless without it.

Affirming the control of "meaning's construction", the powers of language would not consist so much in encouraging open readings irreconcilable with the textual utterance as, according to Hirsch, in the potential of drastically contracting into a meaning with a powerful allusive capacity, such that no textual meaning could escape the meaningful possibility and the control of the language in which it is expressed. A conviction, as can be seen, fairly different from that which is customary in the currents of meaning's pragmatic relativization; thus, the variety of interpretations and readings result from the utterance's broad meaningful powers, from its unitary solidity as its author's affirmative proposal, rather than being the fruit of a supposed polysemical openness, as the advocates of plural reading, with Barthes in the forefront, claim. In this respect: "The standard answer to this question is that every interpretation is partial. No single interpretation can possibly exhaust the meanings of a text" (1967, p. 128).

Compared to the dazzling potential diversity of the text's readings and interpretations that the various advocates of pragmatico-receptive relativity feel, the consideration of the origin of this richness is turned by Hirsch towards the unitary principle of meaning, particularly modulated and intense in the case of artistic texts. But the spectacle of interpretative plurality which in fact demands verification, should not be extended. Otherwise, we rush headlong towards the production of a Babel of interpretations.

Hirsch's perspective reveals the double edged character, simultaneously optimistic and pessimistic, which is hidden behind the proposals of a Roland Barthes for freeing meaning from its link to the author's intention. A toss-up for criticism, the absolute freedom which facilitates and confirms readings with the guarantee of infinity free from convergences and without the steady anchor of meaning, also condemns them to an undesirable condition as unnecessary, infinitely erratic activities, without any possible reference and, thus, destined to the senseless horizon of absolute gratuitousness. Without the reference to meaning, fixed by the author's intentional will, readings become new utterances, entirely autonomous. Each reading re-establishes a new absolute meaning. Indifferent to the original meaning, readings inevitably propose a new stable meaning, born from the paradox of negation. The absolute freedom of reading is thus a frustrated effort; the reflection of a paradoxical deformity, it results in absolute contradiction.

Hirsch's text, exaggerated in the meaningful voluntarism and the rigid physiognomy of meaning's space nevertheless has, in my judgment, the value of having bound itself to the inveterate hermeneutical belief in meaning (P. Ricoeur, 1969), having possibly been able to serve as a model of common sense in times of multitudinous relativist fevers. The good sense of Hirsch's proposals has nevertheless been ignored more than answered in rigorous terms. His influence has surely been slight; and yet he was able to adequately explain, from the traditional categories of meaning as a process of intentions, the constitution of meaning's solid spaces and flexible openness in artistic works.

Validity in Interpretation proposes the notion of a "meaningful boundary" in order to establish a domain of reasonable control over the vacillations of meaning attributable to the author's unconscious, involuntary or indirect intentions (E. D. Hirsch, 1961, p. 51). This principle requires that these intentions find themselves represented in the textual structure's manifestations without obeying, like conscious elements, a voluntary impulse of construction. Nevertheless, the indirect requirement of the component of volition has always seemed to me to be one of Hirsch's excesses. For the North American critic, the involuntary constitutive nature of the unconscious drive must be limited in some degree within the control of meaningful volition which characterizes the construction of meaning.

Clearly, I believe that we find ourselves in the presence of one of those excesses of emphasis which characterize Hirsch's polemical position on meaning, which I nevertheless share in its broadest and most moderate aspects. I think that it is one thing to demand textual constancy from the impulse as the instrument guaranteeing the uncontrolled deviations of critical intervention, but it is quite another to forcefully impose the filter of meaningful volition on deep drives. Perhaps this requirement and limitation was sustainable — which I do not believe is necessarily the case — with regard to conceptual meaning, but it certainly was not for general and aesthetic meaning, as far as I conceive of this notion.

For example, the unconscious drives of spatial imaginary orientation seem to be very decisive elements in the constitution of the text's poetic meaning, creating a perfectly verifiable impression from the great range of material and verbal resources clearly present in the text. Such anthropological records, decisive in nocturnal poets such as Young and Novalis, or essential and diurnal poets such as Valéry and Guillén, form part of the frame of fantastic references which create the general poetic meaning of these authors; but they do not normally appear as voluntary elements of meaning. Nevertheless, as I have said before and believe to have demonstrated in the third part of this book, their role in the constitution of the work's aesthetic meaning, in terms of its poetic-imaginary construction, seems to me to be both fundamental and undeniable for the critical judgment of poetic meaning.

I believe, moreover, that in spite of the involuntary nature of these unconscious features, their link to the meaningful *boundary* of desired intentionality which Hirsch requires of meaning is fulfilled, because in the wider volume of aesthetic meaning said involuntary notes always turn out to be cooperative and integratable in the general direction of meaningful volition. That is, that *coherent continuity* exists between the components of the conscious surface and the subconscious or simply implicit depth that Hirsch expressed with his well-known image of the iceberg. Having guaranteed the requirement of continuity without discrepancy, Hirsch's reiterated insistence on the necessarily direct and voluntary nature of unconscious components seems to me to be an upsetting lapse.

Recognizing along with Hirsch the need to define the meaningful *boundaries* in the submerged zone of subconscious meaning, I believe that this need is achieved with the guarantee offered by the requirements of textual presence and congruence, without insisting on the particular aspect of the feature of voluntariness which, at this level, seems contradictory to me. This is what Hirsch demands in other cases. All of which, unless we understand the voluntariness Hirsch requires in such a broad way that it could be grouped with the unconscious reasons of the drives which travel through the subconscious categories of the imaginary constitution and their manifestation in the utterance's textual traces. But this would then merely amount to a contradictory exercise of unfit generalization.

2.1.5. *The Modern Itinerary of Meaning: Umberto Eco*

Among the foremost protagonists of structuralist and poststructuralist experience, the most complete and instructive, and, simultaneously, alert and versatile itinerary has been carried through in the work of the Italian semiologist Umberto Eco. To follow it in detail is equivalent to the moment by moment auscultation of the most directive pulses and silences of the progression of modern general aesthetics in the definition of its most specific objects — the works of art with the most experimental and open vocation — and of its own methodological working hypotheses: the initial concept (1962) of "openness" or "formativity", then that of "unlimited semiosis" (1975), and finally that of the "implied reader" (1979). I do not think it is trivial or idle to indicate here the importance played in this process by the initially geographically and scientifically peripheral position Eco has felt himself to be operating from in Italy. This experience of marginality must have been felt, first with regard to French structuralist culture, with his initial fascination with Barthes and his school, later and more tangentially as concerns Central European developments, including Petöfi's highly formalized canonic textual model, with its influence on *Lector in fabula*, and, simultaneously, the still ongoing "provocation" represented by Iser's receptive historicism, and, finally, with a certain academic fascination for North American trends, which has revived and reinforced his adherence to the Peircean model (Ch. S. Peirce, 1934–1938), ultimately responsible for the central notion of "unlimited semiosis" which has inherited, since *A Theory of Semiotics* (1977) and in *Semiotics and the Philosophy of Language* (1984), the role in Eco's theories played initially by the more polemical and slippery concepts of the "open work" (1962) and the "absent structure" (1968).

In any case, that bothersome initial feeling of peripheral cultural marginality — today presumably resolved, in view of Eco's international stature — with its adverse origins and its not always negative results, can be extended as a general symptom of postwar Italian culture, from which a certain scientific attitude, like my own in the Spanish domain, is not entirely foreign. But in its most positive aspects, this sense of marginality explains Eco's cultured attention — the greatest and most exemplary, in my opinion, in the panorama of modern semiology — towards the earliest symptoms, both European and American, of scientific and cultural novelty, a focus which registers itself as a singularly privileged constant in the permanent signs of readjustment and re-orientation present throughout his work. Which is not to forget, moreover, that these complexes of scientific "inferiority" and marginality so evident in Italian culture twenty or thirty years ago were surely inappropriate, and even unjust. By that time, the humanist culture and intellectual vivacity of Italian cultural and academic life were decisive differential factors, which certainly was passed on, as a substrate Eco easily bears within himself, in the overall result of his culture and irony, truly unique in the current international intellectual panorama of scholars.

This initial constitutive sensibility, open and quick to seize on every novelty, combined with the interesting originality of the ideas of his teacher Pareyson regarding the "formativity" of the artistic work's structure (L. Pareyson, 1954), endowed the first book of Eco's to be widely disseminated, *Opera aperta* (1962), with a nature which *inevitably* called attention to the most innovative and modern of its arguments: the concept of *openness*, founded especially on the most pragmatic and intentionally open modern model Eco could possibly have selected, the literary production of James Joyce. As much as Eco's recent protests are reasonable regarding the poor interpretation of the balance between stable structures and openness, unequally explicit in that work (1990, pp. 20—21, p. 6), there is no doubt that the title's most arresting and novel message — and therefore what was logically most noticed by the majority of his readers — was the concept of openness, under which Eco's thesis began to circulate provocatively throughout the intellectual circles of the new culture of international modernity.

What should never be forgotten with regard to Eco — although perhaps it may be what the author himself currently resists admitting — is the powerfully semiotic, even iconic nature of his excellent and ingenious titles and labels, through which his work as a whole has progressively made its mark internationally, often in spite of the true extent and detailed contents of its very own theses, articulated as a doctrinal corpus. Hence, we are faced with compatible truths when contrasting Eco's current complaints regarding the readers' habitual distortion of the true reach and contents of his messages since *Opera aperta*, and the almost inevitable nature of such "misreadings" in view of Eco's own instinctive communicative emphasis up until this point on the least traditional aspects of his ideas.

In a careful and attentive re-reading of his initial works from *Opera aperta* to *Lector in fabula* from the point of view which Eco currently holds, notably assured — or perhaps definitely driven to despair — by the international success of his intellectual project, it is possible to glean the fragments of balanced mediation between the stable and exemplary concept of meaning, as a finalist abduction in Peircean terms, and the space the work opens to a controlled but unlimited implication of readers in terms of "unlimited semiosis" (U. Eco, 1975, 1979, 1984, and especially 1990, pp. 38 and 325—338 [pp. 37—43]). Hence, the following review of Eco's work — which in large measure continues to reflect the arguments I set forth in the Spanish edition of this book in 1989 — has attempted to be attentive to the *incomplete* — and today we may add measured (after Eco, 1990) — progression in the "relativization" of meaning that has been characteristic of the Barthean and "reader response" trends in Europe and America, and that was the general tenor to be expected given Eco's proximity to those strongly relativistic currents, customarily identified as being the closest and most similar to his own attitudes.

Umberto Eco's past and current influence has been based, above all, on the brilliance of his keen intuitions. The novelty of his thesis in *Opera aperta*, his first work to be widely disseminated internationally, already appears manifested with restrictions, having achieved the easy divulgation of the most novel aspects of his arguments among his readers, consistent in their dazzling attribution of the artistic work's structural plurifunctionality and its dependence on readers' points of view (U. Eco, 1962). However, an attentive reading of the work yields many passages demonstrating the respect Eco shows towards the closed volition of the creative poetic intention. Moreover, we must not forget *Opera aperta*'s circumstantial nature as a diagnosis precisely focused on a very concrete group of modern works, both musical and plastic, all of which are programatically and intentionally open. Although this fact is almost always overlooked, an oversight Eco has complained of in his latest book (1990, p. 126 [p. 52]), *Opera aperta* is essentially interested in undertaking a critical reflection regarding the progressive "formativity" of the artistic work, focusing in particular on Joyce's *Ulysses*. As a whole, *Opera aperta* neither pretends to be, nor is it, a poetics of relativism, still less a poetics of the negation of meaning as an intentional entity of creation. In his most extreme affirmations, openness is a structural peculiarity of the artistic work which, without affecting the poetic-constructive unity of meanings the text aims for, is concretely fulfilled exclusively on the receptive level.

The second of Eco's most famous works, *Apocalittici e Integrati* (1964), almost exactly reproduces the idea on the nature of meaning the author had set forth in *Opera aperta*. The assumption of the same as the affirmation of a process of monosemicalization can be seen more forthrightly, flatly expressed in certain passages (U. Eco, 1964, pp. 86—93). It is true that ambiguity is invoked as a constitutive characteristic of the poetic message, an attribution which, by itself, is hardly out of place, nor particularly scandalous (1964, pp. 94—95). For Eco, the artist realizes a process involving the linguistic masking of the most objective values of the communicative message, skillful and monosemicalized. But this exercise of aesthetic ambiguity appears attributed and trusted in *Apocalittici* exclusively to the sender's controlling initiative; in contrast, for example, to what can be seen reiterated already by Barthes at the same time, the idea that the artistic labor of shading meanings reaches the infinitely polysemical, the totally and uncontrollably open, is never mentioned here by Eco. Rather, for Eco, the artistic text's ambiguity is a literary artifice of a quantitative nature, without a qualitative and essential reach. Moreover, at this point in the evolution of his thought, ambiguity is always invoked in the sender's role and produced within the author-text communicative segment.

In a pattern of this nature, the receiver's initiatives are powerfully "constrained", as Eco himself warns. It is Jakobson's model of poetic function which contributes the definitive outlines of Eco's formal scheme, as it stood in 1964. In his own words, the artistic work imposes a "continuous stream of meanings". Notice, however, that this continuous stream of meanings is "immobilized in only one direction" (1964, p. 98). In effect, we are dealing with a limited ambiguity as regards the monosemicalizing aesthetic certainty imposed by the author. For the reader, this amounts to a polysemy controlled by the poetic function in the text's set of self-deictic procedures.

We must situate these affirmations in the intellectual atmosphere of poetological euphoria (J. Culler, 1975) unleashed by the discovery of the receptive role in shaping meaning. Carried away by this enthusiasm, Eco responded to the severe and well-argued restrictions the semiologist Emilio Garroni had formulated regarding the most polysemical aspects of *Opera aperta*, recognizing that the message, "through its structure, tends continuously to coordinate its de-codifications" (U. Eco, 1964, p. 99). And, nevertheless, *Apocalittici* already shows the signs of the foreign stimuli which Eco, in 1964, felt an attraction towards: the Barthes of "Reading and Meaning" in *Tel Quel* and of the preface to *On Racine (Sur Racine)* (1964, p. 100, note 27). Still, Umberto Eco's writings in these years especially exhibit the outlines of an interesting conception of the nature of aesthetic meaning, which would later partially be altered. For example, he speaks of the notion of "organic" and integral assimilation — that is, not only intellectual and limited assimilation, as is set forth in the collection of articles entitled *The Definition of Art* (U. Eco, 1968a).

The Absent Structure (1968) fully affirms an interest in semiological methodology in Eco's work, with the result that affirmations on the concept of openness are restricted to the control of more nuanced and objectifiable formulations. Hence, the comparison between "singular semiotics" characterized as "closed systems" and "the proposal of the communicative model of an open process" is presented as a double-faceted process of reciprocal implication (U. Eco, 1968, p. 413). Nevertheless, on the whole, *The Absent Structure* shares the undeniable profile that all poetological criticism at the time shared: the distance and disproportion between its ambitious theoretical speculations and the real, very limited confirmation provided by the texts submitted to the analytical process. I believe *Forms of Content* (1971) completes, through a constant process of self-restrictions (U. Eco, 1971, pp. 31 and 179), the impossibility of the relativizing theory of meaning to absolutely impose itself in view of the forthright affirmative will of structural organization, which is made patently obvious in the presence of the architectonic works examined in the book.

The *Trattato di Semiotica generale* (1972) definitively affirms, in the system of international ideas coined by Eco, the importance of the concept of "unlimited semiosis". A formula of Peircean origins, like the earlier ones of formativity and even openness which were originally coined by Payerson but which Eco's disseminative abilities have inserted with definitive vigor in the construction of modern semiology. The concept, initially welcomed, by and large — once again —, as a new reinforcement to the most disproportionate theses of the modern work's structural "openness", associated the new sensibility extended since Iser (1972) towards the receptive vector of literary semiosis, the "intentio lectoris". To which we must add, moreover, the fact, always scarcely noticed, but highlighted already by Eco in his polemical response to Luciano Nanni in 1981, that it is in the *Trattato* where his speculation regarding the openness of the artistic work stops referring exclusively to modern works insofar as they are "ad hoc" structures, as he had done until this point (U. Eco, 1962 and, especially, 1968), and takes the definitive step — and in my opinion perhaps not yet sufficiently detailed and explicit — to elevate the structural concept of openness, through the receptive concept of unlimited semiosis, to the general set of classical and modern artistic works (U. Eco, 1990, p. 126). According to Eco, all of his later production has worked within this new parameter, a fact which is particularly visible, in my view, beginning with the five essays which compose *Semiotics and the Philosophy of Language* (1984), originally written between 1976 and 1980.

Certainly, we must once again objectively recognize, also with regard to this new category of "unlimited semiosis", Eco's balanced impartiality as concerns the receptive relativization of meaning and, as a result, in the balance he strikes between the "abduction of sense", the channel of the ideal of meaningful guarantees, and the "progressive" plurality of readings; this is more noticeable after the alterations made to his expositions of the last five years and now collected in *The Limits of Interpretation* (1990, pp. 325–328 [pp. 24–32]). For example, according to Peirce, "the idea of meaning is such as to invoke some reference to purpose" (1934–48, 5.166). Eco cites this passage and then quickly makes clear his own conception of it: "A purpose is, without any shade of doubt, and at least in the Peircean framework, connected with something which lies outside language. Maybe it has nothing to do with a transcendental object, but it has to do with referents, with the external world, and links the idea of interpretation to the idea of interpreting according to a given meaning" (U. Eco, 1990, p. 334 [p. 38]).

With *Lector in fabula* (1979), the appropriate distinction between the work's *interpretation* and its *use* appears formulated, according to the slant towards rediscovery which Eco wishes to call attention to in the last decade in the apologetic revisions to his own previous work (U. Eco, 1990, p. 127 [p. 57]). Eco understands as "interpretation", for example, the kind of reading which Derrida makes of Poe's *The Purloined Letter*, that is, a paraphrase attentive to the constructive or deconstructive explanation of the concrete utterance; while as an example of "use" he cites the utilization of Poe's texts by Marie Bonaparte when she seeks to "connect textual evidences with aspects (known by extratextual sources) of Poe's private life" (U. Eco, 1990, pp. 32—33 [p. 58]). Interpretation supposes an effort to clarify the "intentio operis", while in use the "intentio lectoris" alone is imposed on any hermeneutical and semiotic use, now judged harshly by Eco as marginal divergence. To this end, it is true that, in effect, once again, it is possible to discover in the 1979 text passages which vouch for this important distinction, which from the evidence emphatically presented in 1990 turns out to be supplementarily decisive as the simple and necessary dodge to the "fundamentalisms" and "heresies" of the uncontrolled fashionability of the "intentio lectoris". Nevertheless, the emphasis on highlighting this, without any obstacles to the addressees of *Lector in fabula,* has been largely insufficient in view of the scarce relief this decisive distinction has traditionally received in the readings of this work; at least compared to Eco's more obvious interest in that book — and at that time — in acquiring and correctly transmitting Petöfi's canonic textual algorithm — massively cited and used throughout the book —, as a definite and objective solution for registering the textual strategies of receptive implication.

From my point of view, Eco derives the greatest critical benefit in this book from freer and more capacious categories, like Ducrot's "not-said" (1972). The not-said, a universal mechanism guaranteeing the economy of communication, should not be identified with the non-existent, but rather with the foreseeable (1979, p. 51, Ch. 3). The textual not-said is always the immaterial moment of a convergence, of an intersection between the explicit constituents of meaning, calculated by the sender. Nevertheless, forced by all that this notion suggests to him under the influence of current fashion, Eco fires off towards the universe of reception and his favorite images of the all-powerful reader-cooperator. This is how the idea of the text which "wants to leave to the reader the interpretative initiative" or which "wants someone to help it function" is personalized and mythified (1979, p. 52, Ch. 3).

The dilemma confronting the author of *Lector in fabula,* in the midst of the full triumph of reader theory, is that he either capriciously moved towards the unjustifiable decapitation of the sender as generator and cause of the text, forgetting the producer's textual initiatives, and joined the novel propaganda of receptive aesthetics or, on the other hand, he insisted on the textual mechanisms of reader implication. This second option would have condemned him to follow the course of very well established traditional doctrinal experience, a path incompatible with Eco's tastes and aspirations in 1979. In my judgment, the best way out of this dilemma would have been to develop the explicit physiognomy and typology of the textual mechanisms of authorial foresight — the wisest and most originally balanced portion of Eco's entire book — and of the pragmatic activities of reader cooperation.

The difference which I have been insisting on between foreseeable crossings and empty slots with regard to the productive concept, assumed by Eco, of the not-said, appears decisive to me. The category of an empty slot generates the comfortable reflex of constructive and interpretative liberty, of the "use" of the text (1979, p. 59, Ch. 3.4). The alleged empty slots of the text which, with regard to artistic and particularly poetic texts, are viewed as spaces open to interpretation, give rise in the long run to the negation of meaning in the completely open work, by means of the intermediate stage of the infinite relativization and variation of meaning through the plurality of receptive volition. On the other hand, the concept of *implicit crossings* allows us to save the reader's initiative, since his cooperation perceives and constructs the meaningful reality of these associations of meaning, which do not consistently and explicitly figure in the material structure of the text's units. Moreover, conceived in this way, the not-said is composed in terms of textual positivity, since it encourages an initiative of meaning related to the most common experience of textual production. To proclaim the complete liberty of reception, the free play of patterns of associations in the paradigm, where contiguity is equivalent to a paradoxical dialectic among contraries, entails ignoring the author and his always problematical initiative in constituting and transmitting meaning. But, above all, it is to eliminate the evidence of the text itself, stripping it of its structures in order to construct capricious alternatives; all of which is a potential but artificial free creation from nothing. Or worse, impoverishing the reader's initiative, leaving him to the ghostly residual traces of a deceived and defeated text. Conceived in all of the immensity of its exaggeration, freedom of interpretation leads to a maddening, contradictory activity.

The supposed textual openness resulting from free interpretation does not end up being a way for the reader to cooperate in the construction of meaning, but a way of destroying the text, of relegating it to the unnecessary function of a superfluous pretext, of a deceptive and fallacious presence that, if it avoids becoming redundant, it can only be because it survives in reality as a pure simulacrum, without any referential capacity. When the text affirms its presence and reality, the reader's only possible activity consists in the *recognition* of its explicit elements of meaning and of its implicit associations and crossings. In the text's presence, in the presence of its meaningful rigor, the capriciousness of the receiver's deviatory readings condemn themselves as false rather than as generous amplifications. Free receptive construction represents the destruction of the text as a principle of communicative exchange; it is, in another sense, the mediated formulation of different, alternative texts.

On the other hand, as we have seen, Eco's attitude in this work, and in the whole of his production, never turns its back on the manifestations of

2.1. The Pragmatic Relativity of Meaning

meaning. His brilliant allusive capacity leads him to formulate under paradoxes full of contagious vigor the realities referring to the cooperation of the reader and his foreseen space in the structures of the text. What can make Eco's formulas dangerous for the absolute nature of meaning is their very brilliance more than their radicalism, which is never overly extreme. For Eco, for example, the nature of the thematic *topic*, as a meaningful reality generating the text, in a pattern in agreement with that of van Dijk (1972, 1972a, 1977), is an unforgettable reality. With this, the principle of the unity of meaning, upon which the non-relativizable meaning of the text essentially depends, appears assured. In Eco's opinion, the principle of unity as a "trajectory of meaning" shaping the textual entity is not undermined by the multiple structure of the text's topical isotopies, ingeniously conceived of as an "umbrella term", a single category incorporating a variety of forms and procedures.

With the recognition of the topic as a controlling principle of the meaning of multiple isotopies, the universality of the open work is limited. Only an either purely senseless or artificially and laboriously maintained initiative opens the discourse, removing it from the organizing control of the topic. In the structure of the narrative text (the object of interest in *Lector in fabula*), the structural opposition between *fabula* and *intreccio* signals, on the one hand, the pragmatic level of receptive cooperation in the *intreccio*, as a place for the exploration and accomodation of variable isotopic strategies. On the other, the structural proclamation of the *fabula* is emphasized as an exigency of textual necessity, "a fundamental scheme of the narration" (U. Eco, 1979, p. 102, Ch. 6.1), which narrative meaning remains intentionally linked to, insofar as it is a fixed structure controlling the imaginary activity of fiction.

The basic textual strategy of fictionality, the "writing of worlds" in literary narration, which Eco explores as a fundamental novelty in *Lector in fabula* (U. Eco, 1979, pp. 122–123, Ch. 8.1), appears also as a structure of receptive cooperation, where the narration's addressee must know how to orient at every moment his own references to the reality or hierarchical variety of possible worlds in which the peculiar verisimilitude of the narration is articulated (T. Pavel, 1975, 1980; L. Doležel, 1976, pp. 524–533; 1979, 1980; T. Albaladejo Mayordomo, 1986, pp. 113–136). But, at the same time, it is constituted by the precise initiative of the author, who constructs the story as a closed diagram of references structured in a network of worlds. The aesthetic meaning of narrative fiction is thus linked to the implication and inference of the reader and of his organization of reality in a series of scaled worlds; but the essential reason for the existence and control of that activity, in order not to get lost in deliriousness, corresponds to a hierarchy of proposals made by the story's creator, stimulants in the text's network of references.

As can be seen in the different sections of *Lector in fabula*, in order to ponder the decisive role of the activities of reading in the constitution of meaning, we find the semiotic activity of the text's producer invariably recognized as a preliminary and generating initiative. He is the one who creates with foresight the textual mechanisms that will involve the reader in the story. Meaning, therefore, is closed by the reader, who would limit himself, in the thoughtful model Eco sets up in this book, to following the instructions foreseen by the author in the natural pragmatic trajectory of literary communication. Thus, meaning as a communicative will of a message is produced and achieved — or determined — by the text's author.

Obliged by the popularity and brilliant evidence of his partial diagnosis of the "open work" as a specific sign of a determined modulation of modernity, and plagued by the wave of fashionable studies on the receiver's role, Eco may have let himself get carried away towards an easy excess in his formulas. But in his understanding of the construction of literary semiosis none of the extremisms which de-naturalize and discard the meaningful initiative in reading are detected. The mobility and roominess of the aesthetic content as a process of agreement between the structuralization of the message in a literary utterance and the interpretation of the receiver, should proceed between the limits set by absolute identification and senselessness. The flexible and fixed nature of meaning constitutes literary semiosis.

A licit limit is offered, nevertheless, in the attribution to the author of the semiotic initiatives which form meaning: the conscious intentionality in all the features which constitute it. Eco opportunely raises this essential question in the section on "The Limits and the Possibility of Deep Structure" (1979, pp. 178–184, Ch. 9.3). He begins with a suitable distinction between "interpretation" and "use", attributing to the disproportionate use of the text those hypotheses of communicative will in the author that do not appear reasonably reflected in the explicit structure of the text. The Freudian interpretation of Sophocles' *Oedipus* seems to him to be a model case, with respect to which "neither Sophocles as the subject of the enunciation nor Sophocles as textual strategy could remit to such an encyclopedia". In spite of this, "the Freudian reading constitutes a legitimate operation of textual cooperation", and for this reason "the model reader of *Oedipus* was not the one Sophocles thought of, but the one Sophocles *postulated*". In the constitution of the deepest structures of literary meaning, the reader's cooperation would presuppose, according to this, transgressing in a certain way, by means of interpretation, the conscious control of the author over his text (1979, p. 183).

Perhaps this difficult limit to the discernment between the critic who interprets and the one who uses the text, is established in the verifiable record of the utterance itself (E. D. Hirsch, 1973). Such references in many cases translate realities which escape the writer's consciousness, but which the structures of the text make transparent. For example, the transcendental facts about the spatial imaginary representations, or rather flowerings, witnesses, of the subconscious symbolism that crystallizes in obsessive images. These and other symptomatic indications of the unconscious personality of an author and his implicit vision of the world appear almost always, without the conscious intention of the sender, in the structural forms of the utterance. What Eco denominated "deep drives" form a part of the meaning of the text and even its decisive components in the constitution of aesthetic meaning. The critic's exploration has a right to concentrate on them in order to establish meaning; what's more, it is necessary to lift them from the utterance's transparent traces.

This activity of searching for textual indications in the involuntary phase of meaning, which Umberto Eco appealed to, is far from being equivalent to the free exercise of reading which would utilize the textual facts to constitute associative developments which exceed, consciously and deliberately, the meaning of the work. The critical frame for the unconscious facts of the texts attempts to close aesthetic meaning and to complete the examination of its convergences, corroborating the textual trajectories of meaningful consciousness with the convergent support of subconscious indices. But all of this within the text and without the volition, necessarily, to exceed it, especially when we are dealing with brilliant messages of an inexhaustible objective depth. All in the meaningful indices of the utterance, attentive to the vector of the enunciation, to the path from author to work, which establishes meaning; and without nostalgia or the temptation to transcend the text with eccentric alternatives of reading.

With *Lector in fabula*, Umberto Eco brought the process of semiotic discussions about the nature of literary meaning and the reader's methodology for obtaining and constituting it to their culmination. Eco's intellectual curiosity, which led him to momentarily dazzling discoveries in the past, with occasional adherences — never with unconditional surrenders — to the most prestigious novelties of pragmatico-receptive relativism, find in this last phase of his work the precise and ingenious way of rescuing their own coherence. With the brilliant formula of the "reader in the story", Eco is able to maintain the decisive status of modern reading, but attributing the absolute primacy in construction of the work's message to the progressive abduction of meaning. The formula of transaction was worthy of Umberto Eco's superior genius: the greatness of the artistic work as a result of the extraordinary author's capacity for brilliant foresight, able to grasp by intuition and formulate in the text the variegated set of mechanisms determining the reader's involvement.

The recent appearance of *The Limits of Interpretation*, almost simultaneously in Italian and in a revised English edition, definitively clarifies many previous ambiguities, fed by the circumstances particular to the international circles in which Eco has been moving. From the introduction's amusing initial anecdote from John Wilkins' *Mercury* (1641) and its reduction to absurdity of the most extreme theses of deconstruction and the relativism of "reader response", we are in the presence of Eco's most categorical declaration of the undeniable nature of the "literal meaning" which reasonably guarantees communication among men: "Every discourse on the freedom of interpretation must start from a defense of literal sense" (U. Eco, 1990, p. 26 [p. 45]). A statement usually taken as obvious; but to have arrived at this point, Eco certainly must have had to surpass a widely-disseminated set of professional biases, including those he warns us about in his introduction: "I admit that in order to make such a statement one must first of all assume that sentences can have a 'literal meaning', and I know that such a point is controversial. But I keep thinking that, within the boundaries of a given language, there is a literal meaning of lexical items and that it is the one listed first by dictionaries to say what a given word means. I thus assume that Everyman would first say that a fig is a kind of fruit. No reader-oriented theory can avoid such a constraint. Any act of freedom on the part of the reader can come *after*, not *before*, the acceptance of that constraint" (1990, p. 9 [pp. 5–6]). Really, what this involves for criticism is the admonition to begin with this adaptation to reality in its most undeniable but not always well-remembered foundations, to adopt, in short, a correct and reasonable starting point before moving on to the specialized subtleties of technical debate. Thus, Eco justifies his affirmation: "I feel sympathetic with the project of opening readings, but I also feel the fundamental duty of protecting them in order to open them, since I consider it risky to open a text before having duly protected it" (1990, p. 27 [p. 54]).

In this task, Eco moves very cautiously to avoid degrading his technical discourse to overly elementary or banal levels and producing abusive simplifications, such as those committed in a sphere similar to his own by critics dedicated to relativism and receptive skepticism such as Richard Rorty (1982). Nevertheless, the weight of neglected evidence invariably leads Eco to the most direct criticism, which I share, of those whom he denominates "incontinent readers": "Before a text is produced, every kind of text could be invented. After a text has been produced, it is possible to make that text say many things — in certain cases a potentially infinite number of things — but it is impossible — or at least critically illegitimate — to make it say what it does not say. Texts frequently say more than their authors intended to say, but less than what many incontinent readers would like them to say..." (1990, p. 107 [p. 148]). And one should not forget that such assertions are formulated with regard to nothing less than receptive economy before such a programmatically diffuse and polyhedrical text as Joyce's *Finnegans Wake*, to which Eco adds his respectful reservations regarding certain readings like those of G. Hartman (1985, p. 145 ff.), based on hypothetical excesses of phonic and meaningful analogies, proposing the surprises and reversals afforded by readings in the example of Leopardi's composition *A Silvia*, as well as in many criticisms of his own novels (1990, pp. 110–122).

The predominant standard he takes advantage of, and quite correctly, in my opinion, to oppose to the errant plurality of readers' excesses is that of *economic control*; dealing with the excesses of these "heresies", he is not so much trying to determine and describe what the good or best interpretation would be, as he is trying to "delegitimize the bad" and economically erroneous, invoking J. Hillis Miller's guiding principle to support his arguments (1970). These ideals of reasonable economicity and common sense converge with Eco's treatment of very diverse questions, like the interpretation of metaphor (1990, pp. 142−161), emphasizing its intentional nature as a "connotative phenomenon as a result of its semiotic mechanism within a given language at a given moment of its existence, and not because of the commentator's intentions" (p. 155); and, hence, for which there "exist limits of interpretation" (p. 161). The same ideals are to be found in a study with such an apparently diverse objective as that regarding the criteria for establishing the authenticity and lack thereof of documents and artistic objects (1990, pp. 162−192 [pp. 174−202]), or, again, in his analysis of the theory of narrative worlds (1990, pp. 193−212 [pp. 64−82]).

Underlying Eco's resolute decision to emphasize the limits of interpretation is his ability to draw on the traditional and popular awareness of the existence of meaning which has customarily nourished the intersubjective certainties regarding verbal communication. An awareness supported by common sense or conjectural sense, to which Eco adds a measure of technical dignity by means of his well-known reference to the Peircean concept of "abduction" (1990, pp. 325−338 [pp. 152−162]); but which nevertheless serves to assure a serious and economic interpretative activity in comparison to the aberrant "drift" of critical writings of pleasure and the uncontrolled game of the alternative infinite readings of a "nihilist relativism", the legitimacy of which Eco drastically checks, alleging that, in the end, it "annuls all discourse about art" (1990, p. 140). Without ever falling into the opposite form of extremism, Eco denounces the impatience which so many earlier, barren debates regarding the statute of meaning has inspired in otherwise useful and economic critical work. The result is to be seen in the categorical assertions included in the brief section on *interpretation* and *conjecture*: "The initiative of the reader basically consists in making a conjecture about the text intention. A text is a device conceived in order to produce its Model Reader. I repeat that this reader is not the one who makes the 'only right' conjecture". And here Eco makes a strategic concession: "A text can foresee a Model Reader entitled to try infinite conjectures". But he moves on to point out that the reader's conjecture, to be proven, must be checked against the text: "How to prove a conjecture about the *intentio operis*? The only way is to check it against the text as a coherent whole". In these terms, he concludes: "any interpretation given of a certain portion of a text can be accepted if it is confirmed and must be rejected if it is challenged by another portion of the same text. In this sense the internal textual coherence controls the otherwise uncontrollable drives of the reader" (1990, p. 34 [pp. 59−60]).

There can be no doubt that, for many of Umberto Eco's usual readers — foreign to the narrower circles in which during the last decade, and especially in the past four or five years, the articles which make up *The Limits of Interpretation* have been being produced and divulged — these postulates regarding the "intentio operis" must come as a "surprise". Not to mention the effect produced by the serious consideration he gives the "intentio auctoris", universally ignored by most of the fashionable theories of the past twenty years. To this we may add the shock these same readers must feel when Eco affirms in a section of the Italian edition entitled "When the Author Doesn't Know He Knows": "I do not consider the study of the psychology of the author unfit for attention" (1990, p. 122). Even to Eco himself, beyond his own formal allegations to the contrary, this sense of surprise in the face of an apparent shift of position must be predictable; in contrasting his most recent book with *Opera aperta* — a task undertaken when writing a recent English introduction to the latter work — he notes at the end of the introduction in the Italian edition of the former that "it would not be bad to confront the possible objections of the Italian reader" (1990, p. 13). All of this in spite of his attempt to justify the lack of incongruity in his trajectory, based on an understanding of his own intentions, and supported by reference to certain claims which are not among those his readers have been most attentive to, though no less important because of this.

What is certain is that, with affirmations like these, the most "incontinent" defenders of the theories of infinite readings, not to mention deconstructive readings, have been left without one of their, until now, surest and most prestigious fellow travellers: "In *Opera aperta*, even though stressing the role of the interpreter ready to risk an ideal insomnia in order to pursue infinite interpretations, I was insisting that to interpret a text means to interpret *that* text, not one's own personal drives. Depending as I was on the aesthetics of interpretation of Luigi Pareyson, I was still speaking of a dialectics between fidelity and freedom. I am stressing this point because, if during the 'structural sixties' my addressee-oriented position (neither so provocative nor so unbearably original) appeared so 'radical', today it would sound pretty conservative, at least from the point of view of the most radical reader-response theories" (1990, pp. 13—14 [p. 50]). And, in the original Italian version, he goes on to add: "In the course of these thirty years some have leaned too far towards the side of the interpreter's initiative. The question now is not to unbalance the equation in the opposite direction, but to underline once again the uneliminatable nature of this oscillation" (1990, pp. 13—14).

I for my part leave others to their possible surprise — or indignation — regarding these last timely and necessary clarifications by Eco regarding the stability of his balance on questions of meaning. I do not count myself among those who must reorganize or re-balance my previous stances, to the extent that Eco has believed it necessary. My frequent calls to the critical order, issued to the most ardent supporters of infinite structural polysemy, be they receptionists, or deconstructionists (from A. García-Berrio 1977 to 1989) have always been balanced by my awareness of the artistic text and the interpretative needs which its aestheticity imposes. Faced with such pressing literary proof, all of the disquisitions regarding the previous procedures of interpretation have seemed to me to only be legitimate "ethical sitting-room debates", appropriate to those most given to philosophizing, but very far removed from the "legality" and the pressing questions artistic texts give rise to, especially the most sublime texts, if one is in frequent and direct contact with them and their interpretation. On the other hand, my own previous analyses and pronouncements concerning Eco's position (A. García-Berrio, 1989, pp. 210–219) outlined, with some contradictory surprise, the line of constant fidelity to the "intentio operis" which he adopted, at a time when he was commonly invoked by the majority of critics as an authority supporting the exclusive "intentio lectoris".

In spite of all of this, nevertheless, it is clear that for the most superficial — or biased — readers of *Opera aperta, La struttura assente* and even *Lector in fabula*, Eco's new book is a surprise, and it will be interpreted — for a short time only, I hope — as a radical change of course, or even worse, as an act of desertion and a change of party. The sense of defrauded indignation, which I personally do not wish to see, will be more strongly felt and expressed to the extent that critics have relied on the authority of those opinions which the Italian semiologist now believes it necessary to repress in their excesses. Still, my own opinion is that the re-establishment of the interpretative balance is indispensable at the present time; and Eco's own attitude, like that of Gombrich in 1986, does not differ — except qualitatively — from what I have been sustaining for years, set forth most fully in my *Teoría de la literatura: La construcción del significado poético*, in 1989. What is happening in all of this is that, as has been said on more than one occasion, the intellectual inertias of scientific debate tend to radicalize in an opposite direction those positions which were initially appropriate and timely corrections, both exact and necessary; as was the case, in effect, with the historicist corrections imposed by taking into consideration the parameter of reading in Jauss and Iser's first claims. The collection of relativist attitudes — even deconstructive warnings, at their most propaedeutic level for the exercise of literary criticism, as philosophical preconditions regarding the nature of language and reference — in literary criticism, lodged during the immediately preceding years in a diffuse and uncontrollable triumph of epigonous dissemination, have assumed such a high degree of dogmatic confidence that any call to the reasonable restitution of the interpretative balance, like Eco's or my own, runs the immediate risk of counting on "misreadings" which discredit them as given to the contrary extremism: traditional, conservative, authoritarian, etc.

Umberto Eco finds himself in the uncomfortable position of having to prepare excuses and to avert the immediate movements of those who will feel most defrauded by his stance, and who will try to lodge him at the opposite extreme. It is interesting to note in *The Limits of Interpretation* the frequent rhetorical "occupatio" directed at anticipating this kind of opposing argument. Hence, for example, the emphatic fragment I just cited (U. Eco, 1990, pp. 13–14 [p. 50]) defended against the foreseeable accusation, still not produced, that after having occupied progressive positions — "revolutionary" it indirectly notes — in the past, Eco is now esconced in a conservative one. Analogously, further ahead, in the section entitled "An Apology of the Literary Sense" (Chapter 1.3 of the Italian edition), Eco seems to believe himself again in the position of needing to justify his position with a new "captatio": "I admit that this principle *may sound* (I, for my part ask, "to whom?"), if not conservative, at least banal, but I do not attempt to avoid it at any cost. Today, much of the debate about meaning — the plurality of meaning, the freedom of the interpreter, the nature of the text — in a word, about the nature of semiosis, revolves around this" (1990, p. 28). This situation repeats itself with each unpopular correction; for example, in his legitimate and well-argued criticism concerning "the falsifiability of misinterpretations" in section 3.7. Once again one feels the presence of Eco's conciliatory modesty: "I understand that from the point of view of a radical deconstruction theory such an assumption can sound unpleasantly neopositivistic..." (1990, p. 36 [p. 60]). Still, the author's polemical contentiousness reacts immediately by turning the "occupatio" towards its true dialectical terms: "The provocative self-evidence of my last argument suggests that we can prove it only by showing that any of its alternatives is self-contradictory" (1990, p. 36 [p. 61]). And so on. Consider, for example, the correct and continuous efforts Eco makes in this book to avoid appearing personally provocative, such as in his nuanced examination of some of Hartman's deconstructive exaggerations (U. Eco, 1990, pp. 104–105).

The invariably impeccable and commendable tone of sincere respect which Eco demonstrates towards the distinguished critics implicated in the positions he believes it necessary to redirect towards more reasonable terms changes only when he faces the extremism of the arguments he is considering. Hence, even though Eco's arguments become more subtle with the refinement of Peirce's theory of unlimited semiosis (1990, pp. 325–338 [pp. 32–43]), or in the analysis of the interpretations by Black or Ricoeur concerning the systematic foundations of metaphor (pp. 142–161), or with the most advanced logical and theoretico-literary investigations of Hintikka or Doležel regarding the theory of possible worlds (pp. 193–212 [pp. 64–82]), his impatience with regard to what he judges the growing spiral of inordinate extremisms explodes with irony in the most attention-getting and devastating formulas of common sense. Consider the following passage, regards Wilkins' story about his servant and the basket of figs in the Italian edition: "If in the sphere of hermeneutics or the theory of literature it may appear provocative, but in the final analysis arguable, that the initiative of reading belongs completely to the interpreting subject, it seems even more dangerous to affirm this with regard to those other processes which lead us to identify a person or an object, distant in time or in different situations, to distinguish a dog from a horse, to find the way home every day. In these cases, to assume that the decision depends entirely on the interpreter has only one name in the history of thought: magical idealism" (U. Eco, 1990, p. 12).

Eco's respectful prudence has its foundation in his figuring among the names of those that have, directly or indirectly, contributed in the history of recent criticism to the general result he refers to in acknowledging that "undoubtedly the universe of literary studies has been *haunted* during the last years by the ghost of the reader" (1990, p. 18 [p. 46]). In this same section, ironically entitled "Archaeology" (3.1), Eco traces the fundamental inventory of the protagonists in the critical erosion of the "intentio auctoris": Barthes, Todorov, Genette, Kristeva, Lotman, Riffaterre, the negative polemic of Hirsch, Corti, Seymour Chatman, van Dijk, S. Schmidt, Weinrich, etc. These he separates from the line of those who, in his judgment, have predominantly favored the "intentio lectoris", beginning with W. Iser, who according to Eco assumes W. Booth's formulas, adjusting them to the poetological tradition of Ingarden, Gadamer, Mukařovský, Jauss, Stanzel, and in general the critical tradition specializing in Joyce. It goes without saying that these "archaeological" lists include the vast majority of the main influences responsible for the scarcely placid voyage through modern criticism Eco himself has taken. Which explains the respectful caution and, in effect, the balanced self-discipline and rigorous self-censure which characterize *The Limits of Interpretation* as a whole, this rounding off and settling of accounts with all critical extremisms, which perhaps could only have been accomplished, in order to be massively operative and efficient, by someone with Eco's talent, cultural authority and ironic versatility.

Perhaps the most forceful impatience which Eco exhibits in this book — apart from the devastating but nearer and more circumstantial criticism to Luciano Nanni's book (1980), a radical example of the relativist extremism of theories of reading (U. Eco, 1990, pp. 126–141 [pp. 32–43]) — was directed at Jacques Derrida, in his double role as a participant in the greatest "drift" of the relativization of meaning through the skeptical renewal of deconstructive negation, and also for his sociological responsibility in the massive, unnatural — that is, incoherent — displacement of a debate of metaphysical cares to the factual terrain of the interpretation and analysis of literary works. Therefore, faithful to his claimed personal attitude of respect towards the intellectual hierarchy of individuals, Eco reasonably distinguishes between Derrida and Derrideanism. And the distinction appears to me to be more than mere courtesy, but necessary and essential in these allegations against the "drift", which are always in reality against the looseness of epigonous developments in comparison with the rigor of foundational claims. In so doing, Eco directs his most severe and necessary censure, not at the initial "philosophical game", but at the very different and disproportionate "decision to apply this method to literary criticism, or to make of that method the criteria for every act of interpretation" (1990, p. 38).

Faced with Derrida and deconstructionism in their most radical principles, Eco has no qualms about putting into play the arguments of congruence and common sense most directly linked to the relevance of critico-interpretative work regarding literary meaning. Persuaded that, at this stage of the international confusion raised by the critical "drift", it is only the conviction of these decisive arguments, and not the raising of internal and byzantine arguments in the rarified and unnatural frame pursued by critical Derrideanism, which can rescue interpretation, Eco claims not to agree. Although he does not avoid the literal reproduction of the figure of "preterition", with Searle's direct and strongly-worded opinion of Derrida — "Derrida has a distressing penchant for saying things that are obviously false" (J. Searle, 1977, cited by Eco, p. 204 [p. 36]) —, he does nothing to dilute the potency of these objections in his own assessment: "But frequently Derrida — in order to stress nonobvious truths — disregards very obvious truths that nobody can reasonably pass over in silence" (U. Eco, 1990, p. 332 [p. 36]). And in this same tone of very direct argumentation Eco ironically alludes to Derrida's request for his written support for the creation of an Institute of Philosophy as valid evidence in favor of the argument that Derrida, in practice, must have had some confidence in the assertive objectivity of certain texts.

This gallery of allegations based on the reduction to absurdity of the opposite extreme — similar to those I have produced from time to time negating, in the potentially infinite series of readings produced by its licit readers, the possibility of reading the *Divine Comedy* as the ravings of a gentleman driven mad by the tales of knight-errantry or as affirming the true and uncontestable fact that Bologna does in fact exist right now — motivate Umberto Eco's serious jokes, like that regarding Derrida's letter, or his refusal to criticize any teacher who would fail a student for claiming that Hamlet was married to Ophelia (1990, p. 193 [p. 65]). And, nevertheless, only the relativist negation of the most evident facts — for example, the "technical" superiority of Cervantes or Shakespeare over the mass of minor figures of his age or our own, or that of Velázquez over his father-in-law Pacheco — explains and justifies the need to have to argue in such emphatically categorical terms against what has carried us to the present epigonous "drift" with regard to readings and interpretation. Recall, as a final example, the exemplary nature of Eco's argument against this "drift" and its claims regarding the equal validity of readings. Referring to the argumentation alleged by one of his opponents regarding the variety of readings of the *Divine Comedy* produced by Croce or Eliot, Eco asks himself: "If it is interpretation alone that legitimizes the object, why should I continue interesting myself in Dante? It suffices that I interest myself in Croce or Eliot" (1990, pp. 134–140).

The predominant argumentative structure in the initiative towards Eco's balanced realignment of the three "intentions" which the perfect hermeneutic act must consider — that of the author, that of the work, and that of the reader — is, as has been mentioned before, that of *economy*. In its name Eco censures the extremisms of the infinite "drift" of readings above all as a "waste of hermeneutic energy". Granted, of course, that nowhere is it explained why this should be the only human activity choosing to obey the general operational law of minimal effort. Still, on this subject, Eco is conclusive: "If these criteria may appear founded solely upon the appeal to common sense and to the principle of minimal effort, I want to recall that no other methods exist for determining the *intention* of a text, when the text is simultaneously the object and the parameter of its interpretation". It is understood that what Eco proposes is the intervention of a common sense and some principles of economy of effort guided by the more refined articulation of the Peircean concepts of unlimited semiosis and of his term "abduction". In these terms, Eco adds the following nuanced observations: "this minimal effort is what might be accepted by a community of interpreters attempting to reach some agreement, if not regarding the best interpretations, at least in the rejection of those that cannot be sustained" (1990, p. 11).

With this same great sense of theoretical balance, Eco issues his programmatic calls in favor of the principles of common sense and reasonableness, and against the antieconomical excesses which the abusive radicalization of the theoretical urge for complete "legality" at the expense of meaning can lead to. Thus, in his discussion of forgeries, Eco warns us: "even though no single criterion is one-hundred percent satisfactory, we usually rely on reasonable conjectures on the grounds of some balanced evaluation of the various tests" (1990, p. 191 [p. 200]). The paradigmatic condition of Eco's reflections on the criteria of authenticity and falsification, extrapolatable to deconstructive demands regarding the legitimacy demanded of the text, gather all of their forcefulness and paradoxical urgency when faced with the reality of the objective situation of contemporary criticism, when by extension Eco places us in the impossible situation in which every person viewing the *Mona Lisa* would have to verify for himself if what he is seeing is really the same canvas he was looking at the day before or the same canvas that left Leonardo's hands. An unreasonable situation with regard to the analogous experience of reading, which could be compared to the maximalism of certain readers who aspire to the exhaustive verification of the criteria for evidence in the case of the verisimilar fictionality which narrative worlds play with (L. Doležel, 1989, p. 233; J. Hintikka, 1989, p. 58; B. H. Partee, 1989, p. 118). A kind of relationship of a conventional economic basis, governed by the practical principle, according to Eco, of "goodwill" (1990, pp. 211–212 [p. 82]).

Eco's call for an ideal of academic control over interpretations is founded on principles governing the strict semiological regulation of the textual order. One of the most outstanding of these is that which Eco denominates the principle of *relevant semantic isotopy*; the common sense approximations through which the common speaker can block, discarding them as antieconomical, certain abusive demands tending towards the utopia of a "maximalist deconstructive" legitimation, or the inappropriate and senseless readings for the same reasons of the economicity of semiosis, are just mere intuitive reflections of this general principle. Even with regard to a text as experimentally open as Joyce's *Finnegans Wake*, so familiar and favorable to the history of Umberto Eco's critical speculation, itineraries exist hidden in the construction of unlimited semiosis, since, as Eco understands it, if semiosis permits the establishment of theoretically unlimited modes of interpretation, the movement among them must obey the conditions of congruence demanded by an economic ideal of communication: "*Finnegans Wake* is a satisfactory image of the universe of unlimited semiosis just because it is a text in its own right. An open text is always a text, and a text can elicit infinite readings without allowing any possible reading. It is impossible to say what is the best interpretation of a text, but it is possible to say which ones are wrong. In the process of unlimited semiosis it is certainly possible to go from any one node to every other node, but the passages are controlled by rules of connection that our cultural history has in some way legitimated" (1990, p. 107 [p. 148]).

In *The Limits of Interpretation*, Eco has not abandoned, in favor of a mere immediate intuitionism no matter how sensible it may be, the task of carefully and prudently laying the scientific groundwork for his ideas about semiosis and interpretation. He is at every moment aware of the fact that the current historical oscillation of the problem ranges between two equally disposable extremes: on the one hand, that which reduces itself to the reconstruction of hypotheses regarding the meaning intentionally attributable to the author and, on the other, that reflected by attitudes in which "it is assumed that texts can be interpreted in infinite ways" (1990, p. 325 [p. 24]). Eco knows he should surrender to neither extreme, but instead must move between them under an ideal of absolute balance. His adherence to the Peircean semiotic ideal imposes on him a faithfulness towards the principle of the *perfective progression* of representations in the semiosic chain, together with that of the *control of the shift* according to the fulfillment of rules of progression — and not of cancerous deviation, in the image Eco uses to illustrate the "hermetic shift" (1990, pp. 326—329 [pp. 27—32]).

The ideal of the perfective progression of unlimited semiosis also allows for, beginning with confidence in the capacity of orientation towards congruent conclusion in the chain's first impulse, the experience of transindividual historical enrichment of the representations about objects of knowledge, texts and reality: "there is a sort of growth of the global content, an addition of determinations, since every new interpretant explains on a different ground the object of the previous one, and at the end one knows more about the origin of the chain as well as about the chain itself" (1990, p. 329 [p. 32]). It is in this manner that the ideal of unlimited semiosis effectively formulated by Peirce as tending towards an "ad infinitum" movement (Ch. S. Peirce, 1934—1938, 2.303), is articulated in Eco's hermeneutical interpretation in a

2.1. The Pragmatic Relativity of Meaning

different way, a much more positive — and optimistic — version than Derrida's skeptical one, in which Eco tries to defend what he judges to be the correct interpretation of Peirce's hermeneutical ideal (1990, pp. 329–333 [p. 32–37]).

In the Peircean conception of reality as a "continuum" (1934–1938, 6.170), Eco finds his response to the skeptical orchestration of unlimited semiosis in deconstruction. In effect, in the chain of cognitive semiosis we move as individuals in part under the conviction that this contributes to the total perfectability of semiosis, but in part we feel reassured by the principle that Peirce called "fallibilism objectified" (Ch. S. Peirce, 1934–1938, 5.166). A collection of Peircean references which lead Eco to the following well-grounded conclusion: "A purpose is, without any shade of a doubt, and at least in the Peircean framework, connected with something which lies outside language. Maybe it has nothing to do with a transcendental subject, but it has to do with referents, with the external world, and links the idea of interpretation to the idea of interpreting according to a given meaning" (1990, p. 334 [p. 38]). Regarding the nature of this last object — a *dynamic object* in Eco's Peircean denomination —, in spite of the fact that nothing "objective" may be said about it, it nevertheless affects the set of representations deposited as the "habitual" experience of wisdom (1990, p. 335 [p. 39]).

Agreement among members of the community is based on the principle of *habit*, understood by Eco as a disposition to act. This agreement, in spite of the fact that it is unable to constitute a new chain of signs, nevertheless already contemplates *something* that is at the origins of the semiotic process. From this, it follows that this habitual object guarantees for Eco the cognitive positivity of semiosis: "In textual terms, to establish what a text speaks about means taking a coherent decision in terms of the successive readings we will make of the same. A decision of this type is a *conditional habit* (1990, p. 335). The habitual semiotic and communicative experience of the formation of interpretative representations is thus rigorously grounded by Eco in a possible and non-deconstructive interpretation of the Peircean model of "unlimited semiosis": "The Habit is a disposition to act upon the world, and this possibility to act, as well as the recognition of this possibility as Law, requires something which is very close to a transcendental instance: a community as an intersubjective guarantee of a nonintuitive, nonnaively realistic, but rather conjectural, notion of truth" (1990, p. 334 [p. 39]).

The Peircean constituent of *community* (Ch. S. Peirce, 1934–1938, 5.356) thereby clarifies the foundation of habits of confidence in the interpretations of common sense which assure a reasonable and necessary semiosis, faced with the unrealistic maximalism of deconstructive distrust. The *common habit* is therefore configured from Eco and Peirce's perspective, not as a degraded "bricolage" assuring error, but as the natural "transcendental" principle, beyond the particular intentions of individual interpreters, in such terms that interpretation is not produced by the structure of the human mind but by the constructed reality of semiosis. The communal consensus is founded and guaranteed in this *intersubjective* reality, a communal agreement which as a "universal inquiry toward a common core of ideas", providing a sufficient and absolute basis for the legitimacy of interpretation. Hence: "the transcendental meaning is not at the origins of the process but must be postulated as a possible and transitory end of every process" (1990, pp. 336—337 [pp. 40—41]).

By lodging the hermeneutical object in the intricate labrynth of Peircean semiotics, Eco distances himself from the urgent requirements of immediate proof created by the critical situation of the unlimited and reductive "shift" propelled by deconstruction and the other more "incontinent" sectors of the theory of reader response. It is also true, on the other hand, that he musters the technical rigor needed for rescuing what are, in any case, precious critical demonstrations of common sense saving them from the immediate accusations of banality, purely tactical and defensive compared to the depth of the problem. In any case, with his opportune last-minute plea, Eco has sought to put an end to the scarcely productive and even tortuous consequences of what might have started feeling like a children's game with revolutionary appearances. Common sense — I would say with the full and undeniable weight of interpretative responsibility — and hermeneutical culture demand, without complexes, their right to regulate, without scares or suspicions, the normal workings — which is to say collectively useful workings — of their interpretative tasks. We can, finally, agree with the words Eco has chosen: "But, even though interpreters cannot decide which interpretation is the privileged one, they can agree on the face that certain interpretations are not contextually legitimated. Thus, even though using a text as a playground for implementing unlimited semiosis, they can agree that at certain moments the 'play of musement' can transitorily stop by producing a consensual judgment. Indeed, symbols grow but do not remain empty" (1990, p. 337 [pp. 41—42]). And thus, for now, Eco closes his vigilant journey through aesthetic modernity.

2.2. The Deconstructive Lodging of Poetic Experience

2.2.1. Deconstruction in Literary Criticism: The Intensified Undermining of Meaning

Deconstruction is, as is known, a philosophical development originating in a tendency of thought propagated by Jacques Derrida. It has known a certain following in the literary criticism of the United States, which nevertheless is beginning to show, in recent times, signs of divergence from this "fashion". As Jonathan Culler, one of the most familiar divulgers of this movement, has shown, the peculiar style of the American critical tradition favored the positive reception accorded Derrida's ideas (J. Culler, 1982). Evidently, the

2.2. The Deconstructive Lodging of Poetic Experience

detailed tendency of the analysis Derrida called his own, which deconstructive analysis demands and advocates, fits in well with the Anglo-Saxon critical tradition, almost entirely predominating in the literary theory of the United States. Said analysis particularly abounds, as is known, in the paraphrastic transposition, profoundly and interestingly motivated in the best cases, of the manifestations of the artistic text's utterance, which are transferred to the peculiar reorganization of each critical commentary.

According to the founder of deconstructive philosophy, Jacques Derrida, language, such as it lies at our disposal after centuries of being impregnated by metaphysical thought, is a negative vehicle for the rigorous expression and communication of meanings, such that logocentrism comes to mean the fundamental obstacle for direct and pure 'thought'. The key contamination which characterizes metaphysical thought consists in its not having been founded on pure, free and exclusive categories, but rather on the binary nature of *differences*. The most solid and frequently invoked metaphysical categories, such as existence and essence, substance and accident, potential and act, moral categories such as good and evil, or meaningful ones like meaning and signifier, etc., all display this impure, differential and dualist nature in their origin, excluding, in Derrida's opinion, the possibility of recovering the *trace* of reason and meaning as a *predifferential* space (J. Derrida, 1967a, pp. 142, 260 [1976, pp. 93, 183—184]).

For Derrida, the concept of *trace* is therefore constituted in a manner very similar to that in which the preromantic thought of Vico and Herder proposed the *percorsi*, dislodged from logical space in the genesis of language. A kind of lyrical moment of oral expression in a pure state, preceding the later stage of its communicative specialization. The trace introduces the great difference, the radical, solid and alternative difference from logical thought characterizing Western philosophy (J. Derrida, 1967a, pp. 92—95 [1976, pp. 62—65]). Derrida has dedicated fundamental pages of his work *La dissémination* to delving into the concept, fundamental to him, of the trace as a space defined by this radical difference, *différance*, which extracts any singular meaningful capacity from categories of thought before, as I have already stated repeatedly, the current logocentric and metaphysical stage characterized by the dualist distinction of *différences* (J. Derrida, 1972, pp. 11, 194, 238 [1981, pp. 4—5, 168, 210]). A space or moment of meaning, the pure differential, intimately fundamental categories (J. Derrida, 1967a, pp. 342—344 [1976, pp. 240—242]; 1972, pp. 118—124 [1981, pp. 103—109]) —, in which the very richest contributions of Derridean "poetic" thought may be lodged, by means of the potential positivization of the concept of poetic meaning, which the critico-literary transfers of deconstructive philosophy have unfortunately not systematically known, in my opinion.

Trace and *différance* imply the great referential shift in the nature of meaning which results, in Derrida's case, as with Blanchot earlier, from exposure to Emmanuel Levinas' ethical thought (J. Derrida, 1967, pp. 123, 154—5 [1978, pp. 82—83, 104—105]). Derrida's early assimilation of Levinas' ethics is fundamental for his reflections on "Violence and Metaphysics", in *L'écriture et la différence* (J. Derrida, 1967, pp. 117—228 [1978, pp. 79—153]). Levinas' central proposal of a *philosophy of the other* involves the pure assumption of otherness as a total, radical alternative to egocentric thought. Proposing a space of total otherness as an *outside* (1967, pp. 165—167 [1978, pp. 112—113]), which does not necessarily refer to an *inside* of dualist difference, yields a search, significantly and basically Heideggerian in nature (1967, p. 132 [1978, pp. 88—89]), to dispose of customary differential logic, which may be identified in some sense with poetry's capacities for communication and discovery, as I will explain shortly. On the other hand, deconstruction destroys any structure received as unitary and "monadic", in Paul de Man's terms (1979), on the basis of inquiring into the implicit and truncated associations wagered on any resulting unitary interior. But it also is able, on the contrary, to reveal the "hidden fragmentations" covered by the most superficial work of the fulfillment of discourse's logical deterioration (J. Derrida, 1967a, pp. 139—140 [1976, p. 92]).

In the philosophical foundations laid down by Derrida, deconstruction presents itself as a general practice, required by all categories and notions, that has its origin in the *logos*, beginning with the opposition between signifier and meaning within the basic question of writing and poetic meaning. The all-embracing problem of "logos" in the constitution of meaningful discourse determines the fixation of a universal *logocentric* key, bound together with the determination of *being as presence* (J. Derrida, 1967a, p. 23 [1976, p. 12]). A manifestation of being which could constitute itself thus as a rule and law of meaning; however, deconstruction eats away at and undermines the unquestionable foundations of presence, denouncing its differential dualism. Together with this, meaningful certainty is linked to a *predifferential* age of meaning, historically linked to the hypothesis of a stage belonging to the *original trace,* which can be illustrated presently by recovering the writing properties of an *arch-writing*, which Derrida relates to certain literary properties, and which I believe is identified very particularly with the most intimate and essential imaginary segment, the unique construction of an anthropological spatiality, in my own understanding of poetic meaning.

The differential logic of rational meanings is founded, in reality; on a theological conceptualization of the sign, in which divinity and sign occupy an analogous space and have the same origin (1967a, p. 25 [1976, pp. 13—14]), being objects protected by the book, as an expression of a natural totality, which is, for Derrida, alien to the meaning of writing (1967a, pp. 30—31 [1976, pp. 17—18]). The rehabilitation of the domain of absence as a predifferential space of indestructable meaning, in the manner in which Derrida practices it here as an antitheological philosophy, has its greatest stimulus in the discredit inaugurated by Heidegger of metaphysics "as the limitation of the sense of being within the field of presence" (1967a, p. 37 [1976, p. 23]).

But deconstruction concentrates above all on being an exercise of censure and differential disassembling, at least in the sense in which it has been exercised epigonously in Derrida's case.

Deconstruction customarily avoids and is suspicious of its own extensions, bordering on the poetic, which I, from my own point of view, consider its positive dimension. Born from the observation of a generalized set of deffi-ciencies — difference, graft, etc. — in the logocentric system of metaphysics, it avoids the risk of falling into the contradictions of any constructive hypothesis. As a result, it practices a kind of systematic and *ad hoc bricolage* on the defects and forced symmetries of texts. It denounces the traditional and structuralist philosophical presumption, which Lévi-Strauss' anthropology proposes (J. Derrida, 1967, pp. 418—423 [1978, pp. 284—289]), that a superior scientific "engineering" exists, which could recondition and revalorize the system of deconstructive bricolage's accurate discoveries, as ideological and false.

In my way of seeing things, every theoretico-literary reflection which, starting from the strength and topicality of American deconstructive criticism, proposes approaching Derrida's system, ought to make the effort to emphasize in it, as in Blanchot's poetics (C. Norris, 1982, p. 18), those positive aspects by virtue of which the negative and asystematic activity of deconstructive bricolage is legitimated. I am referring to the numerous signs arranged in the space of meaning without the differential fissures or vices that the deconstructive doctrine denounces and which its philosophical and critical practice attempts to disassemble. The starting point for this pure space of meaning is constituted in Derrida's representation by the *fissure*, which "is not a fissure among others, but the fissure par excellence: the necessity of the interval, the hard law of spacing" (J. Derrida, 1967 a, p. 286 [1976, p. 200]). Fissure is established insofar as it begins to trust in the need for a different focus on logical meanings, undermined by the deconstruction of logocentric fallacies in metaphysical thought.

Access to this pure space of meaning makes us assume the awareness of *suplementarity*, a difficult step which Derrida equates to the "threat of death", but under the desired incentive of an "access to life without *différence*". That is, to the reintegration in an entirely free domain, the sphere of radical *différance*, unpolluted by logocentric erosion; a total space in which it is possible to dissolve the insurmountable distances between the precincts of logical meaning, falsified by the differences, and the space of original meaning, where categorical dualism would impose an unrepresentable instance. Supplementarity actually supposes a state of consciousness where "the game of presence and absence" is played out, which, more than being particular to man is *what is particular to man*: "it is the very dislocation of the proper in general: it is the dislocation of the characteristic, the proper in the general, the impossibility — and therefore the desire — of self-proximity, the impossibility and therefore the desire for pure presence" (1967 a, p. 347 [1976,

p. 244]). Supplementarity imposes, with the radical *desire* which founds it, the necessity of an *original* place, the foundation for the myth of meaning.

The originating domain is established by what, under the awareness of the logocentric perturbation of meaning, we would contemplate as a space of *différance*, or of the radical and unique difference, which Derrida offers one of his most rigorous and precise characterizations of in *La Dissémination*: "*Différance* also designated, within the same problematic field, that kind of economy — that war economy — which brings the radical otherness or the absolute exteriority of the outside into relation with the closed, agonistic and hierarchical field of philosophical oppositions, of the "differends" or "difference": an economic movement of the trace that implies both its mark and its erasure — the margin of its impossibility — according to a relation that no speculative dialectic of the same and the other can master, for the simple reason that such a dialectic always remains an operation of mastery" (J. Derrida, 1972, p. 11 [1981, p. 5]).

The fallacious proposals of the metaphysical *logos* are fulfilled under *différance*, where the untrue is true and absence is presence (1972, p. 194 [1981, p. 168]). The meaningful space to which the *différance* refers to proposes itself as the corroboration as presence of a set of incursions carried out on the categories of logical discourse dislodged by deconstructive criticism.

The *différance* is a property of the space Derrida denominates as that of the *trace*, or the original domain of pure meaning, eroded to the point of its complete subversion by the implantation of logocentrism as a structural construction of differences. The original trace is therefore the principle of constitutive, real opposition, the last-first of the system, before projecting itself in the written, in the linguistic or in the cultural. The pure trace is identified with its constituent, at the point where Derrida can affirm that the pure trace is the difference, constituted beyond any pretension towards perceptible plenitude. The entity of discourse's customary meanings cannot be proclaimed as an existing form, a "present state"; and yet it is the legitimate antecedent of every sign (J. Derrida, 1967a, p. 92 [1976, p. 62]). A fundamental peculiarity of the trace would therefore be its nature as something irreducible to description by metaphysical categories, even though it is "the absolute origin of sense in general" (1967a, p. 95 [1976, p. 65]). Conditions, in effect, which proclaim the peculiar consistency of artistic meaning in general, and especially poetic meaning, as the most faithful representation/copy of the meaningful mode in the original trace, which is possible and in some ways transferable to the positiveness of actual experience, simultaneous with the structures of logocentric and metaphysical discourse.

Within the aporistic if not contradictory characterization of the trace in terms of categories founded on or besieged by logical erosion, it is clear to me that Derrida finds at the disposition of his hesitant activity almost exclusively those principles — and especially all of the spatial references combined with time — which are constitutive of the more intimate nature

2.2. The Deconstructive Lodging of Poetic Experience

of the poetic, according to the terms of the description I myself have proposed (A. García-Berrio, 1985, 1987). The trace therefore offers itself, in its most successful and immediate form, as the category which articulates the distinction between space and time, returning from the continuum of its spatial imaginary consistency to an absolute past outside of time (1967 a, pp. 96—97 [1976, pp. 65—67]). In it, every image of progression and displacement is exhausted in the radical "passivity" of the continuous space of the trace. The trace, in short, is clearly identified only when it is pondered in the absolute differential, beyond any full lodging of semantic truth (1967 a, p. 103 [1976, pp. 70—71]).

Clearly, the greatest perceptible certainties about the trace are those which refer to the process of its abstraction from philosophy. Derrida thus follows, in the most radical and explicit way, the same path Heidegger travels in his general consideration of the manifestations of essential truth. The history of metaphysics, Derrida affirms in one of the most brilliant and animated fragments of his *Grammatology*, would be the process of the trace's reduction, through the constructed structure of logical dualisms and "spiritualist or materialist, dialectical or vulgar" monisms (1967 a, p. 104 [1976, p. 71]). The trace disappears when it is subordinated and sacrificed to the principle of obviousness, of clear immediacy, according to which speech is located as the necessary and logical antecedent of writing, with time and space playing their role.

One of the most active and enthusiastic followers of Derrida in America, Paul de Man, has exceeded the very limits of the former's thesis, fixing the maximalist impossibility of exceeding the game which inevitably opposes the principles of truth and falseness. In the same way, the historical certainty of exemplary critical interpretations is surpassed, in which the reality of a higher capacity for illumination and proximity to the truths of the mediated text is recognized. Since his claim that the great and masterful artistic works allow us to see the great degree of interpretative maladjustments in criticism is true, his paradoxical proclamation of the same as an exemplarily constitutive part of artistic history's "aberrant tradition" seems to me exaggerated and inexact. That there is a history of these partial errors and maladjustments in the interpretation of artistic texts is certainly a fact, as de Man would have it. Nevertheless, the process of positive illustration and improvement which the critical tradition has contributed to the general understanding of literary and artistic phenomena, at least compared to the absolute vacuum posed by the alternative of forgetting works, seems to me a certainty beyond question. Not to mention its contribution to the more complete and plural understanding of individual texts.

Faced with the surprising negative insight de Man's presuppositions exhibited in their day, one cannot help feel that his words of scarcely five years ago have proven to be yet one more promising contribution that has in fact yielded little, another contribution to the futile "quarrels among theologians, at the furthest remove from any reality or poeticality", to quote de Man's own criticism of the futility of the traditional debates in literary theory (P. de Man, 1986, p. 27). I think the origins of the radicalness of his most negative claims can be glimpsed precisely in those moments in which he most closely approximates Derrida's skeptical analytical philosophy, as, for example, when he adopts the view of consciousness' misleading nature: "Consciousness (*here* and *now*) is not *false* and *misleading* because of language; consciousness *is* language, and nothing else, because it is false and misleading" (1986, p. 41). Or, to cite another example, when he yields to the paradoxes regarding creation and culture characterizing the French tradition of the literary essay, from the model of the least positive Blanchot to that of a Barthes progressively irreducible to positiveness. It is an attractive but unrealistic metaphoric style, well-characterized by the following comparison to fencing: "a battle of wits between author and reader in which they try to outdo each other, parrying, feinting, and setting traps in a sequence of attacks and defenses somewhat like a fencing match". Ultimately, the result of this battle is determined by the modern, paradoxical fashion of reading: "the smart reader always outwits an author who depends on him from the moment he has opened a dialogue that is never entirely gratuitous, that is always a battle for mastery" (1986, pp. 112–113).

Traces of Derrida's propulsive influence on de Man are clearly evident from his very first articles in 1970 (P. de Man, 1989, pp. 214–216), and serve to illustrate what is, in principle, the tempered adherence to Empson's traditional concept of ambiguity, still active within the general critical framework of *Blindness and Insight* in 1971 (P. de Man, 1983, p. 236), but progressively intensified towards the fully deconstructive thesis, already recognizable in the revised edition of 1983, concerning the supposed aporias of critical paraphrase in regard to the unstable structure of textual meaning. It should be noted that some of the most emphatic formulations of the deconstructive thesis appearing in that book were set forth in the chapter dealing with Derrida's readings of Rousseau. For example: "not only does the critic say something that the work does not say, but he even says something that he himself does not mean to say ... The work can be used repeatedly to show where and how the erratic diverged from it" (1983, p. 109). In the end, the most radical claims concerning the fungibility of textual meaning, advanced in the initial essay of *The Resistance to Theory* (1986, pp. 5 and 7), can be attributed to the moment of the greatest euphoria over Derrida's ideas in de Man and, in general, in North American criticism.

The problem of *unity*, the guiding textual principle of meaning, abounds in the absolute solvency of its reality as a positive and stable reference, and even as a stimulus which propitiates its own negation. In the Derrida of *Writing and Difference*, tenaciously opposing the model of structuralist schematization which reduces the immediacy of the fragmentary to the theology of a conventional unity governing the image of structure itself, the arguments

2.2. The Deconstructive Lodging of Poetic Experience 217

about the principle of fragmentary discourse manifest themselves in reasonable terms, referring to the impossible simultaneity of reading the entire contents of a book (J. Derrida, 1967, pp. 41–42 [1978, pp. 24–25]). The work's real volume, a space irreducible to simultaneous acquisition, is, in Derrida's opinion, the greatest objection to a superficial structuralist concept of synthesis. The idea of the "graft", which he subsequently develops, as aporias of meaning based on the peculiar manner of incorporating concepts through reading, already has a clear antecedent in these early texts; the same applies to his criticisms in *Of Grammatology* of the unrealistic and prejudicial fiction of the center, indispensible in the intellectual constitution of structure (J. Derrida, 1967a, pp. 139–140 [1976, p. 92]).

In particular, the basic structuralist notion of *centrality* is criticized by Derrida as one of the dualist fallacies, which opposes it to marginality or peripherality, making meaning a question, really, of centering, that is, of the arbitrary selection of a fundamental principle working among heterogeneous materials, a principle around which the plurality of different entities conform through convergence. These entities would nevertheless find themselves homogenized by the superimposition of the centering principle. Hence, centrality, meaning's constitutive foundation, would not depend, according to Derrida, on any factor of objective necessity materialized in the text and able to be deduced from it, but on an act of will, of *desire*, which focuses and privileges one given point as central. Thus, "the concept of centered structure is in fact the concept of a play based on a fundamental ground" (J. Derrida, 1967, p. 410 [1978, p. 279]). Note, however, that this Derridean notion of centered meaning, which appears to solidly vouch for the concept of meaning dominant in the poetics of reception and even the conceptions of infinite polysemy and absent structure in Barthes and Eco, does not by itself contradict the idea of meaning which I maintain, understood as an initiative of the text's sender or creator. The desire Derrida alludes to does not differ in principle from the author's focalizing or centering intention of meaning.

We do find a discrepancy when the conviction is affirmed that, within the universe of meaning, the author's *desire* is not entirely free. The materials of meaning are regulated by certain channels of necessity and coherence with the awareness of reality's objective organization, which sets the limits on the free initiative of the volition to signify. Notwithstanding this, the possible combinations of meaning which are available to the sender are enormously rich and open, with which the meaningful feature of desire as a focus and election is in fact highly perceptible. Something similar might be said about the initiatives for the construction of meaning in the operations of reception, in which not only the set of principles and factors proper to the general communicative system are attended to, but also the sender's desire, manifested as a meaningful will to organize and center.

What Derrida discards in the structure of meaning which he describes is the licitness and necessity of what I denominate the objective system of desire's structural limitations. Said system, the existence of which in practice Derrida recognizes, is the unnatural result of an architecture corrupted by metaphysical reasoning. Hence, deconstruction in the textual plane of the organization of meaning leads to the concept of *dissemination*, the first constitutive theses of which refer to "precisely the impossibility of reducing a text as such to its effects of meaning, content, thesis or theme". Even more than impossibility it is necessary to speak of the *resistance* of writing allowing itself to be reduced to this thematic or meaningful centering (J. Derrida, 1972, p. 13 [1981, p. 7]). The book, which exemplarily transfers, for Derrida, the logocentric volition of organizing centered meaning (1972, pp. 61–62 [1981, pp. 53–54]), can be contemplated similarly as a tenacious space, capable of authorizing and sustaining infinite grafts, as multiple anchors in its body for various diverging readings.

Every textual and compact proposal of meaning presents itself to Derrida as a positive volume that cannot have any reasonable organization foreign to the undeniable reality of the blank space or emptiness which surrounds it, and on which that affirmation is imposed. The margins of the utterance must be, therefore, the most important real space of meaning (1972, pp. 290–291 [1981, pp. 257–258]). We are seeing here, not so much the negation of meaning's manifestations which the most extremely deviated attitudes of the poetics of reception practice, but perhaps a displacement of the sphere of discussion. On the one hand, Derrida's disseminative proposal denies meaning's licitness from the evidence for a *marginality* which should not be ignored; but, at the same time, he drastically opposes the gratuitous relativism of a polysemy which, when it ignores the meaningful nature of the text's margins, loses all of its reason for being, restrictedly affirming itself only in the utterance's interior as a structure of meaning: "the text is no longer the expression or representation (felicitous or otherwise) of any truth, that would come to diffract or assemble itself in the polysemy of literature. It is this hermeneutic concept of *polysemy* which must be replaced by the notion of *dissemination*" (1972, p. 294 [1981, p. 262]).

Derrida's criticism in *Dissemination* of the concept of polysemy should suffice to at least warn against the easy assimilations currently practiced, as in Culler's manual, between deconstruction and the poetics of reading (1982). For Derrida, the text's infinite polysemy does not originate from any hermeneutical practice of meaning which is interior or homogeneous in the final analysis with the meaningful system which has founded it. If we proceed in this manner, Derrida seems to concede, the sender's desire to center meaning always ends up imposing a richness of plurisignification acceptable and compatible with a reasonably unitary space of meaning. What Derrida denies, as we have seen, is both the licitness of a monosemic reading and that of a reading based on relativist polysemy, insofar as both are corrupt hermeneutical forms (J. Derrida, 1972, p. 285 [1981, p. 253]).

But in the final analysis, Derrida's negative peculiarity on this point can be fruitfully shifted to the range of clearly positive consequences for the

2.2. The Deconstructive Lodging of Poetic Experience

affirmation of unique poetic meaning, as can be deduced from his work and that of Blanchot. It will seem, in fact, that the text's positive delimitation within infinite margins of blank space and emptiness manifests itself to Derrida not only in the restraint of meaningful deduction, but also as the reason which radically questions, in his judgment, meaning's logical and logocentric process: "the infinite flows from the finite, according to a non-Hegelian identity". But this infinity of the margin and of the text which for Derrida inhibits and prevents the logical determination of meaning, is on the other hand, from my own perspective, the necessary space where the great meaningful resonance of poetry is impelled in freedom, a resonance which "enriches itself with zeros as it races breathlessly toward the infinite. 'More' and 'less' are only separated/united by the infinitesimal inconsistency, the next-to-nothing of the hymen" (1972, p. 294 [1981, p. 262]).

Hence, we also see the negative and deconstructive concept of dissemination converted, by virtue of its own power of transference, to a dimension of positiveness, proposing and guaranteeing the space of otherness absolutely necessary for expressing the nature and condition of poetic meaning. From it, the arbitrary pretensions of polysemical relativism in the most radical theories of reception and reading are, in my judgment, adequately de-authorized. At the same time as the reasonable proposal of the margin is contributed from the most purely deconstructive and restricted negation of centrality in meaning, a more interesting explanation, in my opinion, is opened up and articulated about empty space, margin and hymen as fundamental manifestations of otherness in the differance. All of which contributes decisive intuitions for the suitable preparation of a theory of poetic meaning.

If deconstruction on balance characteristically offers us what we have just summarized, and if we consider it taken as a whole as relevant, the most genuine of its proposals nevertheless are open to being reinterpreted in their negativity — or, if one prefers, "deconstructed" in their negativity — towards transcendental aspects of the understanding of the artistic fact and initiative, as a search and illumination of the truly communicated intuition of artistic texts' aesthetic meaning. In this sense, Derrida immediately and Blanchot in a more distant way, offer the path towards a very enlightening reading about the reach of artistic nature and truth. This positive recovery of deconstructive negativity has always been superficially avoided by its followers, the American deconstructionists, according to Leitch's correct diagnosis: "many American deconstructionists tend to begin with Derrida and distance themselves from him" (V. B. Leitch, 1983, p. 101). In the next section of this chapter, I will attempt to demonstrate the possibility and even the positivity, with regard to poetry's aesthetic meaning, of "deconstructing" many of Derrida's critical paradoxes.

2.2.2. From Deconstruction as an Aporia of Meaning to the Poetic Space of Original Experience

To leave the judgment of and initiative for the text's meaning to the reader is one of the premises the tendencies of receiver relativism and deconstructive criticism share. In its origins, however, this final convergence has very different starting points. But in a certain sector of criticism, especially in North America, the emphasis is currently being placed more on the fortuitous coincidence of results than on the profound differences in origin (J. Culler, 1982). For the evolution of a thinker like Barthes, as well as for the already mentioned members of the pragmatico-linguistic and reader-reception schools, the negation of the literary text's objective, general and aesthetic meaning is the result of an evolution towards paradox, encouraged by many indiscriminate contagions, which — as we have just indicated — ignored or contradicted the starting point and first presuppositions of that same evolution. This is not the case for the purest deconstruction, Derrida's philosophy, which begins with a natural and radical negation of objective meaning from its foundational texts of 1967, *Of Grammatology* and *Writing and Difference*, a collection of essays, the earliest of which stems from 1963.

In this case, I am not implying a positive appraisal of Derrida, but rather a negative assessment of the contradictions, confusions and disorientation which the other tendencies reveal. In effect, a strong antecedent for Derrida's precocious posture has been indicated from America (D. G. Marshall, 1983, pp. 135–155): Maurice Blanchot. To which I would add the direct mediation of E. Levinas, familiar at both ends of this interesting process of contact (J. Derrida, 1967, pp. 117–128 [1978, pp. 79–86]). Gradually, the possible original merit attributed to Derrida will see itself, if not discarded, certainly reduced by the preparatory "steps beyond", taken by the brilliant Blanchot. The impotence of writing before the secret of "the beyond", which the interesting existentialist thinker adheres to, together with his final decision to focus on the text's blank space or silence in his criticism of the word's plenary space as a radical falsification of the void after the initial meaningful wager (A. García-Berrio, 1984a, pp. 383–384) — add up to place a great deal of pressure on discourse's constitutive insufficiencies, from which the subsequent negative criticism of Derrida will not differ.

Not only in Derrida, but also in the writings of many other representatives of North American deconstructionism, the traces of Blanchot's influence must always be searched out to justify those claims that are apparently overly radical and are the product, in fact, of similar judgments attributable to Blanchot himself, destabilized when removed from their original context of aesthetic positiveness. This is also necessary to explain the underlying sources of the viability, with regard to these same theories, of the non-deconstructionist inversion of these ideas towards the differential emplacement of the poetic entity. This is the case, for example, with the most attentive North

American exegete of Derrida, and of Blanchot: the Belgian-born critic, Paul de Man. Many of his most ambitious claims, made at the height of his deconstructionism, reveal traces of their origin in a decontextualized Blanchot; recall, for example, his well-known and widely-disseminated distinction between the author's greater degree of blindness with regard to his own utterances, compared to readers' greater distance and clarity (P. de Man, 1986, p. 75). In the passage I'm referring to, de Man attributes his affirmations to a Heideggerian genesis, mediated most immediately by Gadamer; nevertheless, the archaeology of these notions, such as they appear in *Blindness and Insight*, endorses the inevitable conclusion that Blanchot is to be found among other valid antecedents, such as G. Poulet and S. Fish (P. de Man, 1983, pp. 97 and 288). Recall: "The impossibility of a writer's reading his own work sharply distinguishes the relationship between work and reader from that between work and author. Reading, as well as criticism ..., can grow into a genuine interpretation, in the deepest sense of the term, whereas the relationship between author and work would be one of total estrangement, refusal and forgetting" (P. de Man, 1983, p. 66). One remembers such a text as being characteristic of de Man and of North American deconstruction generally; it is, however, easy to forget that it appears in a crucial chapter of the work, one entitled "Impersonality in the Criticism of Blanchot" (1983, pp. 60–78).

De Man even uses Blanchot to defend himself against the impact of the aesthetic, constructive sensibleness of his favorite, W. Benjamin. The strongest arguments regarding the pure sacredness of language, "which does not exist except as a permanent disjunction which inhabits all languages as such", are evidently touched and influenced by the paradoxical, transhumanized vision we know from the Blanchot of *Faux pas*: "Now it is this notion, this errancy of language which never reaches the mark, which is always displaced in relation to what it meant to reach, it is this errancy of language, this illusion of a life that is only after-life, that Benjamin calls history" (P. de Man, 1985, p. 92). As in earlier works, Blanchot's presence is diaphanous in its origin, sometimes even intertwined with the similarly paradoxical estimation of literary temporality in Georges Poulet, another one of de Man's pre-deconstructive sources (1983, p. 82). Paul de Man's unmistakably literary and aesthetic vocation continues and grows under Blanchot's early guidance. It is possible to look to this remote figure as the ultimate foundation of the poetic intuition's *consistency* and substance, a notion the Belgian-American critic never totally abandoned in the course of his literary experience, preserving the aesthetic convertibility of his artistic conceptions about literature, under the cover of the advantages required by a theoretical and philosophical *resistance*. In this way, just as is possible in the case of Derrida, and even presupposing a greater degree of awareness of this on de Man's part, it is feasible to deconstruct de Man's deconstruction in favor of the radical, preconceptual linguistic emplacement of poetry.

2. Artistic Conventionality and Ambiguity

A new intersection between deconstruction and the critical and linguistic relativist trends is signaled by their insistent refusal to consider the text as a structure of objective meaning. The various plural meanings constructed in broad freedom for the text by a reader who is not governed by any objective structure, according to Derrida and the relativist critics, stem from the lack of valid structures of meaning attributable to the text. Nevertheless, again here, the original differences return to impose important nuances. Barthes or Iser, in the most advanced positions of their respective claims, present that reader's activity as a rigorous alternative of subjective construction which remedies the text's insurmountable structural-objective defficiency. Neither Barthes nor Eco — much less Iser — delved deeply into the meaningful legitimacy of readers' constructions. On the contrary, they attributed to each reading act a constitutive legitimacy of its own. In this sense, Derrida's radical negativity seems to me, within the commonly advanced presuppositions, much more consequential.

In *Dissemination*, Derrida leaves a clear testimony of his belief that the proclaimed polysemical and polystructural nature of the text, because of its interior consistency, should not be traced in any form to the free associationism of its components, as Barthes conceived of it in his most extreme positions, a notion entirely foreign to the decisive regulation of the sender's meaningful intention. In effect, Derrida affirms the infinite nature of the text's meaningful polysemy (J. Derrida, 1972, p. 285 [1981, p. 253]), but attributes it more to the text's outside lodging; never to reasons stemming from the utterance's interior constitution, never based on the possibility of escaping the author's wishes to manifest meaning. Above all, the poetic text is naturally lodged in the desire which projects it towards a radical otherness, shaping the network of unlimited divergences of final meanings, but only to the extent that it can be projected to that exterior volition, never for internal reasons linked to the capricious combination of structural convergences.

The concept of polysemy, pushed to the void of meaninglessness by the poststructuralist readings of the text, came to be substituted, already in 1972, by that of dissemination, suggested to Derrida by the experience of the infinitely exterior resonance of Mallarmé's poetics. Compared to the always additive process which precedes the plurality of polysemical options, dissemination is governed by the opposite impulse of subtraction: "a kind of multiple division or subtraction which enriches itself with zeros as it races breathlessly towards the infinite" (1972, p. 294 [1981, o. 262]). The dispersion of meaning in the text's unreachable unity, as Derrida's "disseminating" explanation conceives of it, is thus produced in terms of a plural current of divergent forces of meaning, which multiply the suggestions from the text to the reverse exterior of an infinite, undeterminable periphery. An effect and property that therefore tends perhaps more towards the suggestive and exciting of the poetic than towards the opaque and skeptical.

From my perspective, it is not possible to deny the text as a construction of the author the possibility of meaningful closure which is granted, by itself, to any of the partial, momentary and individual readings of the same. Derrida is more coherent on dealing with the principle of meaning's relativism, denying it equally to the text's proposal of meaning and to any initiative constructed by the reader. In Derrida's familiar formula, what fails at its origin is the linguistic system that creates the text as a reflex of a metaphysical order corrupted by dualism. These antithetical formulas for understanding and explaining reality deny the synthetic possibility of tracing truth's objective unity, such as it existed in the stage which manifests the intuition of the "trace", and which is previous to the development of metaphysical thought and the formulas of linguistic expression which it institutes. And that initial defect reaches every form of absolute textual construction, that is, of original texts themselves as meaningful proposals, or of relative construction, with regard to texts in which meaning has been relativized by readers' interpretations.

What deconstruction could contribute more actively through its radicalness to the literary theories of meaning is precisely the manifestation of the contradictions implicit in an extremely relativist theory of reading. As for the remainder of Derrida's hypotheses, in their analytical and negative aspect, they scarcely affect literary theory. The kind of *legitimacy* Derrida demands from language (Paolo Fabbri, conversation with the author) is not located on the horizon of meaning which affects the critic in his examination of the meaning and value of literary texts. The theory of the literary text, scientific in its understanding of its objective, knows itself to be lodged within one of the margins of partiality, to which it resigns itself; not unlike, it seems, metaphysics itself. I for my part recognize without any qualms that I practice a kind of investigation regarding textual messages which will never approximate an absolute level of certainty with regard to its objective validity in comparison with the absoluteness that great poetic texts naturally possess as brilliant aesthetic instruments.

In light of this modest recognition of my own limitations I am encouraged by the fact that my views are shared by figures as relevant and experienced in the analysis of art as Ernst Hans Gombrich, and that others are beginning to return from the path toward excessive illusions to share this position, definitively replicated in the realism of observers as keen as Umberto Eco, in the pages of his most recent book (U. Eco, 1990). Just a few years ago, Gombrich bravely denounced, before an audience presumably consisting largely of relativist and deconstructionist philologists, the unrealistic fallacy of the "all or nothing" option that some time ago nurtured the scientist mirage of structuralism and the formal grammars, most closely approximating Wittgenstein's inhumanly explicit canonical ideal. Gombrich confesses: "the idea that to err is human is not new and, in my opinion, is not advanced so that we despair when faced with the problem of the progress of knowledge. Desperation only comes when we are overly demanding. The adult must oppose, in the spiritual sciences as well, the demand of *all or nothing*, perhaps natural to youth, with the conviction that we must learn to be modest". And, ironically invoking the testimony, beyond suspicion, of his friend and academic colleague, the philosopher of science Karl Popper, he adds: "He was the one who convinced me that neither in the natural sciences nor in those of the spirit do we have to look for total solutions, but that — in spite of this — we have a right to continue to ask ourselves questions and to continue investigating, because we can also learn from our mistakes" (E. H. Gombrich, 1986, p. 20).

The commonly rooted modesty invoked here by Gombrich — and by myself — against the fallacies of the *all or nothing* approach of radical humanistic scientism and of philological-deconstructive skepticism relies on the experience of the human foundations of the anxiety to know as well as, to a large degree, the individual and empirical knowledge each one of us possesses with the undeniable enrichment of experience, favored by the observation and communication with artistic objects. For this reason, Gombrich laments: "I am thinking above all about the demand, strongly rooted in recent decades, to throw overboard not only the effort to explain, but also that to understand... Cultural relativism has come to do without the most valuable legacy in any scientific activity, the determination to search for the truth" (E. H. Gombrich, 1986, p. 19). Whatever the degree of certainty of deconstruction's philosophical analysis, its theoretical resistance to the experience Gombrich and I am speaking of, the unquestionable positiveness of the substantial *consistency* of poetry and artistic objects stands out. Aesthetic experience communicates a degree of imaginary, sentimental and, to some extent, cultural approximation to the absolutes of the full understanding of the world. Exploring the structure and constitution of those artistic objects, of the artistic work, has revealed itself for centuries as a feasible and progressive task, with unquestionable historical results, even within its biases, its empirical relativism.

Deconstruction presents itself as a legitimate activity, of course, but as an inadequate one. From what we can deduce from its own unity, no better expectations for total certainty await deconstructive practice beyond the relative certainty about the reality which initiatives to construct meaning assume and acquire. Derrida's hypothesis regarding the predualist "trace", even in the case — which it has not objectively realized — of producing the total discredit of expressive-representative textual instruments, suffused by metaphysical organization, does not by itself introduce any objectively solid alternative for establishing investigatory activity in that hazy space of pre-cultural thought (J. Derrida, 1967a, pp. 92—105 [1976, pp. 62—72]). In this sense, Derrida's vigorous appeals to the objective insufficiency of our discourse sometimes reduplicate the impotent moral tone of the various "memento mori", or of the "vanity of vanities", which, beginning with the necessary humility of its discovery, prudent humanists have repeated since the beginning of time. Taking into consideration the unsurpassable limit is a principle inseparable from any sensible humanism, be it tormented like that of Blanchot or Juan Ramón Jiménez, or even agonized, like that of Sartre or Unamuno.

However, the degree of relative certainty which is viable for a critical or theoretical discourse about meaning in literary texts, as a communicated expression of their author's meanings, seems to me an undeniable and practiced reality. I certainly believe it is healthy to recognize the principle of the plural, nuanced reading of the text's meaning in the open, polysemical nature characteristic of artistic messages. But I also believe, disregarding as a general and philosophical evil the aporias the philosophy of deconstruction implies and proclaims, that the critical activity construing textual meaning as an intentional reality of the author possesses an intrinsic degree of validity and an undeniable basis in historical experience.

To the extent that deconstruction not only proposes itself as an ideal of theoretical negativity, but also as a principle with the potential for analytical projection, I think it is even possible to accept the usefulness of the best deconstructive analyses, paradoxically, in their role as critical enrichments on the deep structural constitution of literary texts. There is no doubt that Derrida's own analysis of the writings of Rousseau and Saussure, Husserl and Freud, are far from being useless for framing, in theses cases, the contradictions — though not all of them, nor always — of these authors' thought, conveyed as their texts' meanings. The same can be said for the brilliant, more strictly literary analyses of de Man. The true problem arises only when the purity of the deconstructive "urge" prevents the work of analysis and ends up consuming itself in the sterile task of denying itself any voice and meaning. Even so, I make no secret of my curiosity regarding what may result from deconstructive analyses of great literary figures, such as Dante, Shakespeare, and Cervantes, when they are written, as I believe they have not been.

And it is that in its transfer, almost always overly accelerated, to the terrain of literary analysis, Derrida's method — much more rigorous and respectable in my opinion than the vast majority of its critico-literary developments — has yet to survey the meaning of artistic texts in the light of the distinction between their general or conceptual meaning and their aesthetic meaning. In this book, I prefer sacrificing the inconvenience of monotonous repetition to the need for precision, which seems to me absolutely necessary; always discriminating, in the case of literary texts, between these two manifestations of meaning, the conceptual and the aesthetic; a distinction all the more necessary when speaking of works which achieve poetic values and qualities. In my opinion, however much the deconstructive method is ambitiously inclusive due to the universally radical nature of its negations, it seems, relatively speaking, to ignore questions of aesthetic meaning.

To distinguish between these two forms of meaning is relevant in the case of artistic literary texts. It seems very clear for any kind of understanding of verbal art that general denotative meaning is not an absolute component of artistic meaning. On this question, linguistic poetics has already pronounced itself to the point of satiety, and I do not believe it is necessary here to repeat already overly familiar doctrines and opinions. Roughly, we can say that the *how* of meaning is, in general, much more important for literature than the *what*. And this is even more acutely emphasized in texts of high poetic value. In that specifically poetic *how*, poetry above all finds a differential *what*; that is, poetic connotation — to use a common term — constitutes at the same time a form of special artistic denotation, to which very uniquely communicative contents are linked, especially those of a sentimental nature, which is never the case with the expressive and communicative instruments of denotation (J. Molino, 1971, pp. 9—10; V. M. de Aguiar e Silva, 1967 [1984, p. 81]).

It is precisely the special aesthetic nature of texts' poetic meanings which makes them invulnerable to the subversive reach of deconstructive analyses. Because literature, and particularly poetry, originates a manner of persuasion analogous to that of the deconstructive method about linguistic denotation: literature perfects and pushes to the limit the tensions in the structure of meaningful discourse, in order to rescue intuitions of meaning unfeasible even in the deepest communicative-verbal schemes. Literature, and especially poetry, systematically mocks, when it views it as necessary, every customary rule of proportionality in metaphysically-rooted thought.

Of course, poetry can enter into convergence with expressive, deconstructible schemes, but in itself it is a form of meaningful-aesthetic rescue, permanently transgressing every stable form in the communication of thought and language. The rhythmical features, the intratextual deictic value of disymmetric figures, the continuous license taken with conventional semantic extensionality in the number of alternative worlds shaping fiction — all suppose a subversion of logical meaning, a permanent exceptional break with any principle of proportionality or of accepted and imposed symmetry. It is possible that the usual mechanisms — I will not say canonical to avoid further provocation — of deconstruction may be extended to poetry, especially to those poems framed within the procedures of classical discourse. However, it would then be necessary to keep in mind that they would simply be attacking a symptom, an isolated exceptional fact, whose unique ways of delimiting meaning will have been refuted immediately by the nearest new poem, the great poem; and so on infinitely.

If I am making the effort here to avoid a critical stance entirely opposed to deconstruction, it is because, as can be seen, the critico-literary orientation long exercised in a form of analysis that is by definition irregular, imaginative and always non-conformist, can benefit from understanding the causes of deconstruction, though perhaps not from the results of its fatal antilogical constitution. The deconstructive intuition of antidualist disymmetry can be accomodated without great effort, as I have just indicated, to the old tests of "deautomatization", "transrationality", and the "practice of exception"; all recognized as basic mechanisms of literary systems. By the same token, that final deconstructive *desideratum* — the discovery of the "original trace" by a kind of archaeology of knowledge — does not differ, as an initiative, from the re-installation of lived experience poetry pursues, at the cost of an analytical logic, whose principles, instruments and goals poetry is the first to discredit as useless (J. Derrida, 1967a, pp. 342—345 [1976, pp. 240—243]).

Poetry seeks, from its very origins, to exceed the rational image of the world served by logical communicative discourse and protected by the categories of metaphysical thought. The constancy of this reality is law for literary critics. Perhaps for this reason the French philosopher's cause, his idea of an original writing, preceding an already insurmountably eroded writing (J. Derrida, 1967a, p. 64 [1976, pp. 43—44]), has found a warmer reception among literary critics and theoreticians concerned with poetry than among philosophers themselves. Certainly, this helps explain the ease and enthusiasm with which it has been received among the influential Yale Critics (H. Bloom, ed., 1979; J. Arac, ed., 1983; M. Ferraris, 1984). For the literary critic's current habits, deconstruction proposes an itinerary in search of the mysterious sources of poetry as "trace" that has already been explored. The preromantic intuitions of Herder and Vico that poetry is "pure language" are in my judgment to be found as the basis underlying Derrida's obscure concept of "writing". Derrida's notion would require an extensive and complex explanatory excursion in order to less than entirely fruitfully clarify it and shed it of its ambiguities; this, compared to the precise outlines of Vico's discourse, filtered through Croce (1907, Ch. XVIII). Shadows and ambiguities are, moreover, of an obligatory nature for establishing the exact outlines of the premetaphysical contents denatured by the instrument which ought to clarify them: discourse.

It is also not hard to understand on this basis how deconstruction, as a critical fashion, has had such success, rooted in the renovated popularity of Romanticism in current critical fashion. The fact has already been pointed out that in America the critics who have registered the warmest adherence to the deconstructive stance are recognized specialists and historians of Romantic literature, such as Paul de Man (*et al.*, 1984), Harold Bloom (1964) and Geoffrey H. Hartman (1975, 1980). The current popularity of Romantic *freedom* is foreseeable as a pendular alternative to the past age of structuralist *rigor*. As is evident, the spiritual movement is of a social and general nature; hence, it is much more complex and broad than its corresponding artistic and particularly critico-literary results. But it is also clear that these are better explained if they are linked to it.

After years of the tenacious effort of structuralist analyses and formal grammars, exerted at the service of an ideal of exactness, founding the eternal expectation of depleting truth on the rigorous exhaustiveness of canonical and formal metalanguages, it was natural that there would be a shift to either the skeptical reaction of relativism, patently obvious in the pragmatic evolution of poetology and the aesthetics of reception, or to the total and absolute radicalizations of deconstruction. But afterwards, once the new age of renewed expectations was normalized, the failure — absolute or relative — of structuralist limitations and of formal exactitude was channeled into the uncertain desire which the Romantic intuition of the absolute possesses. Thus, the past certainty of the intellectual discovery of everything there was to discover was transformed into the eager hope, desirably uncertain, of the sentimental or aesthetic discovery of the negative: the impossibility of absolute truth as a form of approximating meaning and experience.

Romanticism represents, as is well known, the image of instability and vacillation, of the unattainable epiphany of truth as a plenary lived experience; a state of "uncertainty" which reaches the indefinition of self-awareness, as G. Hartman characterizes the Romantic spirit (G. Hartman, 1970, pp. 298—310). The consistencies of reality are scarcely inscribed as sudden illuminations when they transmigrate to the shadowy space, destabilized as sure, secure forms (H. Bloom, 1975, p. 85). In his famous definition of the symbol in Romantic rhetoric, Paul de Man plays constantly with the decisive form of the pessimistic attitude towards achieving the consolidation (P. de Man, 1979, pp. 298—303). In de Man's interpretation, the discouragement with the universe of certainties which Romantic melancholy peculiarizes is transformed and generalized into a universal state of impossible verbal communication (P. de Man, 1979), with which his famous formula of interpretation as *tergiversation* corresponds.

This conception of the Romantic attitude, which the North American representatives of deconstruction share as a paradigm that can be transferred to the general capacities of language and the construction of meaning, is nevertheless still contrary to the well consolidated historical evidence of the Romantic spirit. In general, the sentimental affirmation of a necessary uncertainty is confused here with a form of skeptical constancy, which was unknown to the powerful desire of the Romantic imagination. In any case, a review of Romanticism's aesthetic sources, from Herder and the Schlegel brothers to Leopardi and Coleridge, clearly demonstrates the contrary (A. García-Berrio and M. T. Hernández, 1988, pp. 32—53).

In Romantic aesthetic thought, the same antimonial evolution is reproduced, to a certain extent, as has characterized current criticism, a development which deconstruction welcomed as one of its most extreme symptoms, compared to structuralism's textual and immanentist poetics. The Romantic aesthetic reacts, in effect, against classicist poetics and rhetoric, which had focused on the exhaustive exploration of texts' structural immanence. But this reaction, adverse to the positive consistency of poetic truth, does not lead to the skeptical radicalization which, in their current form, would be equivalent to the pessimistic relativism or deconstructive destitution of meaning. Rather, Romantic aesthetics and philosophy affirm their illusory and

2.2. The Deconstructive Lodging of Poetic Experience

resigned confidence in the approximation to the most inaccessible spiritual and ideal traces of any form of absolute reality. This explains the confidence the Romantic spirit places in the aesthetic illumination of poetry, which we cite here, paradoxically contravening the skepticism of the deconstructive critics, as an opening which naturally enriches structuralist investigations on the material nature of the poetic.

Therefore, one must remember that it is Paul de Man himself who has exalted, perhaps in its best terms, the autonomous power of the Romantic imagination to create, since Coleridge, an alternative "intentional" space, one which is not a reflection of natural space (P. de Man, 1983, p. 28). This alternative space is a space of imaginative experience which surpasses and sublimates, from our current structuralist perspective, the diminished domain of structuralist certainties, such as Doubrovsky (1966) moulded them, interpreting Merleau-Ponty's phenomenological image in his own manner with regard to the physiognomy of the literary work (P. de Man, 1983, p. 34). Recall that de Man had already invariably and with the greatest care sifted through all of the analyses concerning the alternative power of the imagination's irrational message to be found in the pages of Bachelard and Sartre (1940), highlighting its nature as a valid alternative to the insufficiencies associated with the conceptual design of the world (P. de Man, 1989, pp. 36 and 155).

Faced with the phenomenon of poetry, critical thought finds itself freed from the kind of logical fetters Derrida announces. Critical reflection on poetry — obviously the best or only possibility for approximating the object of its contemplation — meets with the imprecise space of the nocturnal, or the fleeting efficiency of diurnal forms. It is digestively enveloped in a chaos of massed intuitions, of transient and brilliant illuminating flashes, or, posturally, it is urged into the attentive observation of the most inseparable and unusual forms of the uncommon affirmation of reality (G. Durand, 1964). It means little to poetic intuition, to this kind of deep knowledge, always risky, difficult and fragmentary, whether or not the critic collaborates or not by "grafting" his own discourse onto that of the text. In this case, the critic's collaboration is between well-composed experiences, identified by their disproportionate elementality in the high-flying search for an unboundable object. The wager is on the aim, the communication of the other, of the something more beyond the self.

The highest poetry represents above all a symbolic and referential exercise of anthropological imaginary orientation. A universe of references, moreover, which, although it begins in a deconstructable dimensionality, based on the difference between the diurnal and nocturnal, the positive and the negative, the static and the dynamic, the ascendant and the profoundly abysmal (A. García-Berrio, 1985), ends up diluting that differential posturalist positivity in an objective space of unconstructable emptiness as it integrates the anthropologized symbolico-spatial relations with their most natural, cosmic and subconscious lodgings. And this unconstructable emptiness is the space of the Derridean trace, the volume of poetic weightlessness, governed by inertias and meanings surely taken in very different directions than those configuring the sphere of the "difference's" manifestation.

The lacerating reality of the "grafted" thought is a strong objection to important aspects of literature's theoretical ideology, even more definitive than it can be for the historical constitution of thought in general. In effect, ideas about literature are conserved and transmitted purely only with great difficulty, insofar as they are not technological reflections on the verifiable and utilitarian. The history of literary theory and of critical thought by definition belongs to the realm of the "graft", of the inevitable simplifications, of arbitrary mutilations. Awareness of this "graft" would be an aporia for man's aesthetic thought before the responsibility of recovering the threads of a millenial tradition of critical reflection about literature and art. On this point, my basic constructive agreement with the notion that "something is better than nothing", at the service of the reasonable awareness of limitations in man's activity and experience, plays an important role. Skepticism should not play a role in any approach to the artistic phenomena of poetry, and nihilist skepticism even less than pure uncontrolled gratuitous irrationalism, that "sad and conceited city" of entirely free readings.

In any case, one would think Derrida's harsh denunciation of grafting would logically have discouraged those defenders of receptive pragmatics who understand reading as the only controllable initiative establishing meaning. Readings which assume the arbitrariness of the author's textual orientations, particularly the most capricious of such readings, are equivalent to the savage consecration of the graft as an operation. Derrida's philosophy, which presents itself or allows itself to be presented so close to the most radical stances of pragmatic theory and of relativist reception, aspires to the absolute of the certain deconstruction of meaning (J. Derrida, 1967 a, p. 21 [1976, p. 10]). Deconstruction assumes the aim of purifying the language of all of the contradictions of "difference", in the remote, desperate attempt to discover some certain participation of the original "trace". Note, then, how the obligatory appeal to Derrida's reading to establish the practice of deconstructing textual meaning, hypothetically corrupted at its very origins, is in itself a fatal contradiction of Derrida's system. A trap into which the most radical theoreticians of reading have allowed themselves to stray, with all of the ingenuous precipitousness of fellow travelers, overwhelmingly dazzled by the defiant firmness of Derrida's thought.

In conclusion, the notion generalized in the recent manuals and syntheses on contemporary literary theory (J. Culler, 1982) regarding the links shared by critical deconstruction, the theory of reading and the pragmatics of reception, is the result of an automatic obedience to the most superficial resemblances, like the generic reference to the receptive method of analysis and the ultimate negation of textual meaning. What is forgotten, however, is that the reach of deconstructive negativity is absolute. It globally questions both the text's capacity for codifying objective meaning and the reader's own linguistic exercise. The result, naturally, is that meaning is best considered at the very opposite pole from receptive confidence.

In its positive aspects, deconstruction's aspirations to a remote "predifferential" space of objective reality lodged in the univocal domain of the "trace", for which the instruction of an original reading would constitute the source of homologies, powerfully approaches its utopian aim to the certain purposes and uncertain objectives of critico-poetic practices (J. Derrida, 1967, p. 47 [1978, p. 28]). Nevertheless, this proximity is more convincing when it is affirmed on the basis of contents which are relatively more concrete and accessible for criticism and the experience of poetry than is the case with the aporias on which deconstruction is built. Beyond the brilliance of some concrete contributions, deconstruction can expect far more from the literary attitude and experience of poetry than the latter can expect from deconstruction.

2.2.3. The Poetic Concept of "Writing" in Jacques Derrida

From the point of view of the theoretical reflection on literature and poetry, Derrida's thought, particularly that of his first works, less deconstructively executed, is far more interesting, as I have just said, in what it offers for a positive orientation towards the situation of poetic meaning, than in its most strictly deconstructive, explicit immediacy as a philosophy against the metaphysical formation of logical meanings. A perspective, therefore, analogous to that which can be observed in the case of Blanchot's literary thought which, although it is customarily approached from the angle of being an aesthetic of existential negativity, can perhaps better represent, as I attempt to argue here, an unsurpassable approximation to the ultimate and most radical truths about poetry as an experience.

It is already symptomatic that the first essay of *Writing and Difference*, "Force and Signification", which is really a very detailed and clever discussion of Rousset's famous book *Forme et signification*, deals with the defense of "force" as an instrument from which to negate the construction of meaning, under the rigorously structuralist sign, from the geometry of textual convergences. "Force" is an early Derridean intuition, which recovers a principle by which Liebniz is opposed to Descartes in the construction of meaning; it is equivalent to the poetic of the expressively beautiful, and it is offered as a meaningful alternative to construction insofar as it is "a geometric or morphological model, 'cinematic' in the best of cases" (J. Derrida, 1967, pp. 28−29 [1978, p. 16]). Thus, the opposition to meaning inherent in Derrida's early work, still far from the anti-structural maturity which will characterize his later notion of *dissemination*, is rooted in the alternative affirmation of a structurally unadaptable sense, the force, in which nevertheless we can catch glimpses of the written elements forming the more universal conception of the poetic and its specific meaning.

The forms of meaning which need to be deconstructed are, as a result, those which are linked more to the structural "rule" than to poetic exception, the "force" constituted as the axis of language oriented towards mysterious and unreachable otherness, irreducible to the fixed nature of structure and differential dualism. This first identification, in the still primitive terms of the "force", of the domain of radical otherness which the predifferential *différance* establishes — "writing is the moment of this original Valley of the other within Being" (1967, p. 49 [1978, p. 30]) —, indicates the stature, the unstable but accurate desire which underlies poetic experience, not only as an illumination alternative and complementary to the concept, but as an opposite and plenary differential experience of meaning. The Levinasian direction of otherness, the experiential ethic of the other as a space of difference closed to the corruption of identity, is soon constituted, in Derrida and Blanchot, as a lucid reflection of poetry's ultimate consistency.

But poetic meaning as the experience of force meets with the same general historical exclusion which introduced the violence of differential meaning of the "episteme" in the general process which spatialized writing as *pharmakon* or mediator, detracting from its possible role as a poetic sign. This is how Derrida's analysis recognizes in Foucault's work the impairment of insanity as a Dionysiac hyperbole of the force's exceptional meaning, excluded by the regular and tranquilizing *cogito* (1967, p. 96 [1978, p. 62]). Writing as a privileged modulation of meaningful force must have imposed itself as a poetic form within the asphyxiating tradition of differential philosophical thought, determined, according to Derrida, to construct a corrupted system of impossible meaning.

The ideal of poetic writing as force, mocking the meaningful circuits of the "episteme's" mediatory writing in a claim without a precise objective of pure externality is found by Derrida in exemplary form in Antonin Artaud's theatrical writing. Here the screamed value of the pure transmission supplants every previously concerted plan of customary meaning. Thus, for the Derrida of *Writing and Difference*, Artaud's word supposes the same imperious invitation towards an outside of unrealizable possession which Blanchot's novels offer in his more recent reflections in *Parages* (J. Derrida, 1986). Having escaped every logical game of differential meaning, Artaud's writing appeals to the meaningful beyond the *différance*, adhering to the powers of suggestion of the original trace. A poetic word that tries to be a pure expression of life, "extracted" from the differences in order to be lodged in its essential value (1967, p. 260 [1978, p. 174]).

The most surprising feature of this predifferential writing is its impotence. Its' force is the disseminated force of emptiness, not the power ordered by the accumulations of elements forming an obvious structure. A writing, therefore, of diffuse and formless origins, from which it receives its poetic

2.2. The Deconstructive Lodging of Poetic Experience

strength but which, at the same time, purely escapes any previous responsibility, that is, escapes the foreseeable calculation of the author or the addressee (1967, p. 266 [1978, p. 179]). This level of writing, which Derrida believes he discovers in Artaud's senseless scream, is never denominated poetry by the French philosopher, at least not usually. And nevertheless, the configuration of the word's hazardous impotence, joined to writing on the original trace's waves of formless oscillation, explains the kind of extraconceptual "volume" (1967, p. 287 [1978, p. 191]), the inaccessible nocturnal space in which poetry is founded and where it acquires its most rigorous principle of meaningful vibration.

Poetry thus supposes a regeneration of writing beyond its most current appearances. The most perceptible poetic quality of writing, its feature closest to evoking the trace, is to be found for the Derrida of *Writing and Difference* by that same suggestive capacity of *spacing* which he also pointed to as the utmost characteristic of poeticity. Writing spatially patterns the temporal flux, it consolidates it, it represents it as concrete and constructed. As Artaud himself felt was the case, poetic writing establishes the "visual and plastic materialization of speech" (1967, p. 354 [1978, p. 241]). From the critical tradition explaining poetry, we recognize it as a necessary "plus" of meaning superimposed on — and inaccessible to — the logical meaning of discourse. With Derrida and Blanchot we recognize the insurmountable space between both discourses, the unbounded difference between identity and otherness as the origin of poetic writing.

With *Of Grammatology*, Derrida establishes what could be — certainly I consider it to be so — his theory of poetry as a reflection on the predifferential nature of writing. The earlier vague Liebnizian notion of poetic expression as force is adapted in this work to a much more specific and concrete referent, writing. And nevertheless, over the monumental predifferential and logocentric history of writing, the licit and immediate transfer of writing in purity or of regenerated writing as a poetic property is not made explicit. The thesis of *grammatology* as a semiotics of the "trace" (J. Derrida, 1967a, p. 74 [1976, p. 51]) turns out in this book to be a mere project, outlined in its most external aspects, for a systematic treatment of the plurality of critical approaches to writing disfigured as a *pharmakon*, the intermediary of a discourse dominated by logocentrism. The same thing happens, even more so in this case, with the other great critical system of negativity, that of Blanchot, with regard to the polemical emphasis of Derrida's philosophical thought, focused on the deconstruction of meaning elaborated by a logocentric philosophy and a theology of presence, prevailing in the attention, both of the author and the readers of this work, more than on the clear lines of positiveness in his philosophy of absence and of predifferential reconstruction. And nevertheless it is these latter ideas which are of interest to me here and which can be equivalent, insofar as I have been transferring them without deforming them, to the poetic sector of a theory of the literary text.

2. Artistic Conventionality and Ambiguity

According to Derrida, the privilege of the *phoné* would consist of images of the world and of its origin beginning with the differences between the interior and the exterior, the inside and the outside, or any number of other dualisms, including the spiritual and the material. This explains how writing had been limited to being a purely secondary and instrumental practice, a mediation, an interposed and impoverished *pharmakon* to phonic discourse (1967a, pp. 17−18 [1976, pp. 7−8]). Hounded by images of totality exercised like that of the book, as unitary constitutions of meaning, the original fragmentariness or natural continuum of writing falls victim to the exigencies of logical sense, constructed and imposed from "the encyclopedic protection of theology and of logocentrism" (1967a, pp. 30−31 [1976, p. 18]). And in this way, linguists from Saussure on assimilate and perpetuate this exterior and foreign nature to the interior of the linguistic system, under the image of "exteriority which lends itself to these instruments".

Having announced the degraded impropriety of writing as an instance not of re-edification, but a case not even potentially equivalent with the phonic discourse in which the differential logos is expressed, it is necessary to call attention to the faithfulness which Derrida shows in continuing to maintain the denomination and concept of writing, both so decisively corrupted and eroded by the logocentric deformation. This is the category that might end up more than any other meaning as the content of otherness which would be properly characteristic of the original predifferential trace, of that pure moment of meaning lodged in the outside of identity as presence, in the absolute condition of the *différance*. Derrida will find himself needing new categories, even to justify the faithfulness of his choice, beginning initially by speaking of *arche-writing*, as an original writing from which we wanted to indicate the need to design a new concept, "and which I continue to call writing only because it essentially communicates with the vulgar concept of writing" (1967a, p. 83 [1976, p. 56]).

This degraded concept has dislodged the original essential reach of writing, which he now seeks to call arche-writing. But writing preserves, thanks to the powers which communicate it, particularly its poetic use, a potentially unique capacity for radical imaginary suggestion, which resists being reduced to any need for accomodation and temporal restriction. Writing is above all a spatial sign (1967a, p. 105 [1976, p. 72]) which reveals itself in poetry, a scheme of the subconscious pulsational pathways, a pattern of space that translates the respective fields where fantastic entites are compartmentalized, by which man's essential cosmic orientation in space is regulated. Thanks to this poetic value, writing still preserves the cryptic sphere where the mysterious echoes of unknown and necessary meanings resound. This is the reason why I believe Derrida persists with the concept of writing, beyond all of its undeniably uneconomical risks. It seems clear to me, as we will see, that the French philosopher viewed it in this manner, in spite of the fact that he almost never formulated it explicitly (exceptionally in 1967a, pp. 139−140 [1976, p. 92]).

2.2. The Deconstructive Lodging of Poetic Experience

The justification of writing as a characteristic dimension of the "trace" is always maintained in *Of Grammatology*, adjusted to the strict terms of its most accessible and immediate properties, as though Derrida were suspicious of entering on a genre of poetic and aesthetic considerations, which in a presupposition I should not adopt, are those which nevertheless end up legitimating his conception of the trace. Thus, he evokes the pluridimensionality of the hieroglyphic as a possibility for writing which establishes the counterpoint for the linearity of common writing, a writing of phonic secondariness. Its potential would appear only if one were able to remove the deposits of four thousand years of lineal writing (1967 a, p. 128 [1976, p. 86]), with which one would consecrate the definitive rejection of pluridimensional symbolic thought. In the second part of the work, he is moved to denounce the "violence of the letter", practiced from Rousseau to Lévi-Strauss, although Derrida is particularly vehement in his denunciation of the thought of the founder of structural anthropology. In Lévi-Strauss, the conception of writing as purely opposed to and duplicatory of the oral responds, according to Derrida, to an ideologization of language with Marxist antecedents, corresponding to the general system that opposes the cooked and the raw, as the technological is opposed to the natural or oppressive power to innocence. Writing is thus improperly lodged in a series of cultural-technological arrangements and results, developed as copies of the most natural instance (J. Derrida, 1967 a, pp. 151–174 [1976, pp. 102–118]). An irremediably injurious appreciation, as can be seen, for the Derridean intentions of writing's original rehabilitation in the representation of the structure of the "trace".

It is not at all a matter of being unaware of the similarities which exist between what Derrida calls arche-writing and poetry, as exercises of meaning in the supplementary space opened up by *différance*. What must be spoken about in this case is a decided will to avoid approximating his reflections on structure, insofar as meaning in the space of the original trace, to the kind of aesthetic hypotheses and lucubrations about the subsconscious and imaginary behavior most characteristic of poetic meaning. Nevertheless, Derrida had no doubts about alluding to poetry as the exclusive initiative executing the *displacement* and dismemberment imperative to the focused concept of logical meaning (J. Derrida, 1967 a, pp. 139–140 [1976, p. 92]). In this regard, he recalled how Fenollosa's works on Chinese writing were reflected in a kind of poetic writing as markedly original and antilogocentric as that of Ezra Pound, a case which also explains, by analogy, the poetic reach of Mallarmé's discourse.

But even in these cases, Derrida's discourse, in my opinion, lacks the will to commit itself to a more immediate and profound exploration of poetry as the original source of arche-writing; let it be understood that following writing and poetic experience would certainly have yielded him illustrations of the consistency of the original trace's space of otherness.

Nevertheless, inscribed in this differing destiny lies some not entirely trivial explanation of the philosopher Derrida's approximation to the experience of literature, as well as of the reasons for the fascination his ideas elicit among literary critics. There is no doubt that the Derridean prefiguration of the original trace's pre-differential meaning contributes a sign of incomparable brilliance, which orients and legitimizes the experience of the literary critic investigating the nature of poetic meaning. And this is even more so given the fact that Derrida, to a greater extent than Blanchot himself, recedes before the immediate analytical corroborations of poetic writing. He is simultaneously moved by the differential prejudices of professional slangs, coupled with a certain fear, to which I have already repeatedly alluded, of falling into some immediately deconstructable aesthetic trap.

And yet the poetic analogies provide, in the cases in which he appeals to them, the most diaphanous notes for the Derridean conjectures of pre-logocentric writing. For example, Derrida, upon considering the metaphor of passionate origin as a non-supplementary foundation of language, exalts "the relation of truth and property" characteristic of the poet with what he expresses, authentically reporting the origin of his speech (1967a, p. 392 [1976, p. 277]), which radically differentiates it from the kind of deconstructable relationship characteristic of the logical thinker. Poetry, in its dislocation of the text's immediacy, shifts writing from its dampened meanings, evoking the supplementary disassociation which the *différance* introduces as a lived awareness imposing itself from a pre-logical, original otherness (1967a, p. 397 [1976, p. 280]). Hence, poetic writing incorporates the exemplary dimension of writable supplementarity.

With the concept of *inscription* we achieve the most decisive assimilation of poetic experience for characterizing the mode of being specific to original writing, to the extent that both rest on the firm ground of spatiality. When Derrida exalts the manner in which Rousseau intuited the space of writing linking the nature of social space, he indicates the origin of "a new transcendental aesthetic", which should not allow itself to be led by "mathematical ideals", but rather "by the possibility of 'inscription in general' ". This would not take place as an accidental contingency of an already constituted space, but rather as something producing the spatiality of space. Moreover, Derrida warns that he understands inscription to refer not only to "the notation of a word, sudden" and ready, but also to "the inscription in the word" (1967a, pp. 410–411 [1976, pp. 290–291]).

The poetic word is thus outlined as a vehicle for the assimilation of an intimate space, many-shaped and anthropological, in the extensive trajectory of its own spatial consistency within the text. Derrida reaches formulations of this notion, which seem to me can be approximated without any exaggeration to the conception of imaginary spatiality as the key origin of poetic meaning which I advocate in this book: "A transcendental question on space concerns the prehistoric and precultural level of spatio-temporal experience,

2.2. The Deconstructive Lodging of Poetic Experience

which furnishes a *unitary and universal* ground for all subjectivity, and all culture, this side of empirical diversity, as well as the orientations proper to their spaces and their times (1967a, p. 410 [1976, p. 290]). That is, that common, universal and essential space grounded in poetic experience.

With Husserl, and with his criticism of Kantian geometry, Derrida undoubtedly discovered early in his studies the possibility of an original alternative to the immediate and logocentric conception of space (1962). The peculiar handling of spatiality, essential and constitutive of poetic meaning, provides a direct illustration for the alternative constitution of spatiality, to which the Derridean calculations regarding the constitution of the original trace are applied. Compared to time dominating space in the lineal formulation of logical and substitutive writing, the multi-shaped domain of poetic writing explodes the linear successiveness of time in the poetic dissemination of meaning, a pure space of infinite polysemical superposition. In this way, the Husserlian project of a coenesthesis as a transcendental aesthetics, as a "restoration of the logos of the aesthetic world", illuminates the spatio-temporal physiognomy of the original trace in Derrida, coinciding in what is essential with the basic structure of poetic writing.

Of Grammatology thus marks the crowning moment in the assignment with poetic writing of the most positive aspects on the constitution of the originating trace in the womb of the space of *différance*, within the general negative and aporistic philosophy of deconstruction. From this work on we can see only simple retouchings, like the more profound examination of the Platonic model in the concept of writing as pharmakon or double (J. Derrida, 1972, p. 118 [1981, p. 103]), or the illuminating considerations about original writing as an absent form of the true, and thus of poetry as one more moment of its most contrastable deployments and manifestations (J. Derrida, 1972, p. 193 [1981, p. 167]). Poetic writing and original writing, as a privileged form of the trace, would be, as a result, formal arguments for denying the logocentric prejudice which makes the present synonymous with the true, the absent equivalent to the false. By virtue of their alternative awareness of the *différance*, original writing and poetic writing subvert this differential assimilation, revealing the absent echoes of original and poetic meaning as the most profound forms restoring us to meaning's supreme truth. Beginning with these foundational works, Derrida has moved on to pursue, together with his prevalent deconstructive aporias, though unfortunately without any prospect for success, some essays of pure writing as a deconstructed form in the origin of meaning.

An itinerary almost parallel to that we have just observed with regard to Derrida is similarly visible in the case of his foremost American interpreter, Paul de Man. The claims of the American literary critic regarding the autonomous, non-referential and fictional nature of language are well-known, faithful in their resemblance to the French philosopher's basic postulates. The author's struggle with form testifies, according to de Man in his comments regarding Lukács' theory of realism, to the constitutive asymmetry existing between reality and its frustrated representation by language (P. de Man, 1983, pp. 42—43); reformulating Richards' old scheme of meaning, de Man claims that "instead of containing or reflecting experience, language constitutes it" (1983, p. 232). An assertion that, of course, while not entirely untrue, is exaggeratedly reductive.

What is most assimilatable with the experience of literary messages about affirmations like this one is indicated precisely by de Man's most direct familiarity with literary texts, together with the kind of critical references acting upon his ideas. In this sense, one should not forget when considering de Man's assertions that his books largely consist of glosses and outlines of other authors, the majority of whom are literary critics. Hence, Michel Riffaterre is the author lying behind and encouraging de Man's occasional assertions about the fictional and unsymmetrically referential nature of language. As a result, rather than a skeptical and philosophical reach similar to Derridean discourse, what ends up being most important here, under the influence of his familiarity with Riffaterre, is the consideration of the poetic word's nature as devoid of centrism (P. de Man, 1983, p. 138). Thus: "Literature is fiction not because it somehow refuses to acknowledge 'reality', but because it is not *a priori* certain that language functions according to principles which are those, or which are *like* those, of the phenomenal world. It is therefore not *a priori* certain that literature is a reliable source of information about anything but its own language" (P. de Man, 1986, p. 11). And it is on these fundamentally aesthetic terms that de Man's provocative claim regarding the "destabilizing", "unsettling" nature of literariness appears incarnated (1986, p. 14).

Riffaterre's well-known commentary on Victor Hugo's poem "Écrit sur la vitre d'une fenêtre flamande" (M. Riffaterre, 1979, pp. 175—178), illustrating the external non-referentiality of the text and its nature as the "expansion of a hypogram, matrix or cliche that functions in a purely verbal way" (1984, p. 46), serves de Man as an opportunity to proclaim from this aesthetic perspective the non-referential verbal nature of the text and of literary language. Moreover, he supplementarily encourages, once again from his experience of Riffaterre's *Essais* (M. Riffaterre, 1971), the ultimately "deviated" nature of literary language by way of a rebellion against that other "presumption of reference" which is customarily sustained — misleadingly according to de Man — regarding standard language (P. de Man, 1986, p. 35). All of which, in the end, serves only to link the most radical appearances about language's deconstructive frustration with a background of aesthetic experience customary and habitual in stylistic and formalist literary criticism.

The irreducible "residue of indetermination" which de Man attributes necessarily to the grammatical decodification of texts (1986, p. 15) is oriented towards positively underlining the inaccessible condition of the "figural dimensions of the text", affirming thereby the informative feature of its

2.2. The Deconstructive Lodging of Poetic Experience 239

rupture compared to the insufficiency of rational discourse (1986, p. 39). And even such relatively radical and briskly deconstructive affirmations in *The Resistance to Theory* appear more inclined towards the aesthetic side of their valency in the genesis of his previous books. This explains, for example, the spontaneous surge of final reservations in the 1970 review of *Of Grammatology*, alluding to the deviated analytical framework of Rousseau's most poetic texts (P. de Man, 1989, p. 217); or even how it is his reflection on a poem by Paul Celan or Hölderlin that inspires one of his more profound solutions, in this case regarding the accepted "luminous blindness" of the lyrical text "not caused by an absence of natural light but by the absolute ambivalence of language" (P. de Man, 1983, p. 185). More than the deconstructive emphasis on the insufficiencies of "standard" language in its representation of the world, what often triumphs in the most inspired critical moments of *Blindness and Insight* is the most enthusiastic and conventional proclamation of the extraordinary powers of art in its task of acting as a referential supplement to reality: "The world of the imagination then becomes a more complete, more totalized reality than that of everyday experience, a three-dimensional reality that would add a factor of depth to the flat surface with which we are usually confronted. Art would be the expression of a completed reality, a kind of over-perception which, as in the famous Rilke poem on the *Archaic Torso of Apollo* would allow us to see things in their completeness and so *change our lives*" (P. de Man, 1983, p. 34).

In his continuous encounter with a fairly restricted group of theoretical sources of inspiration, de Man's conservative cultural antecedents regularly force him to confront fairly constructive conceptions of the nature of literary meaning. Under such conditions, the deconstructive torque that de Man subjects such authors as Poulet, Riffaterre or even Walter Benjamin to, is not sufficient to oust them from their more stable meaningful foundations. In view of which, the Yale critic's own discourse rarely transcends truly irreversible deconstructive limits. In analyzing Benjamin's essay "The Task of the Translator" (P. de Man, 1986, pp. 73–105), de Man encounters a substantially classical and constructive conception of reception and reading. Recall Benjamin's own words: "In the appreciation of a work of art or an art form, consideration of the receiver never proves fruitful" (W. Benjamin, 1969, p. 69). In view of this, de Man's deconstructive tension, normally oriented towards favoring the mode of plural openness as regards reader reception, is forced to redouble its emphasis on the supposedly sacred condition of poetic language, inaccessible precisely for this reason to translation (P. de Man, 1986, pp. 83–85). In the end, behind the conceptual sword-play of the deconstructive paradoxes mobilized in de Man's brilliant argumentation — for example: "What the translation reveals is that this alienation is at its strongest in our relation to our own original language, that the original language within which we are engaged is disarticulated in a way which imposes upon us a particular alienation, a particular suffering" (1986, p. 84)

—, what appears are solutions normally rooted in the traditional and Romantic mythology regarding the poetic sublime.

Recall how Benjamin's famous solution regarding the faithfulness of a translation to its original was argued solely in terms of a parallelism of both texts to the general spirit of language considered as a general and superior entity in the well-known metaphor of the vessel and its fragments — both as "fragments of a greater language". Surprisingly, de Man summons this myth of language in the purity proper to poetry, in the tradition of the sublime running from Longinus to Croce and passing through Vico and Herder: "Then we can think of any particular work as being a fragment of the pure language, and then indeed Benjamin's statement would be a religious statement about the fundamental unity of language" (P. de Man, 1986, p. 90).

In this manner, once again, we see that, in the case of de Man's literary deconstructionism, the same itinerary has been followed as we have seen with Derrida. Considering a great literary critic like de Man, we reach, earlier and more directly than with the philosopher Derrida, the appeal to the preconstructive condition of pure language, of the general original language, as the source of poetry's autonomous powers of referentiality. In this unconscious restoration of poetic meaning, which according to my analysis affects the major representatives of the critical and philosophical schools of deconstruction, we should not see any contradiction which in and of itself undermines the operative results of deconstructive literary criticism; rather, to the contrary, the sort of poetic construction of deconstruction which I have proposed here comes to serve as proof that in the now old philosophical journey, inaugurated by Nietzsche and Schopenhauer, the nature of the great systems of modern ontology was never definitively resolved. In fact, with Heidegger and Derrida, consciously in regard to the former and implicitly in the latter's work, Metaphysics has been displaced by Aesthetics, and logical knowledge has been displaced by poetic experience.

2.2.4. *The Experience of the Poetic as Space and the Limits of Meaning. The Paradoxical Inscription of Writing*

The great potential of implicit meaning in the "margins" of literary writing presents it as a radically *paradoxical* entity, whose forms of plenitude would correspond, according to Blanchot, with the textual manifestations most dispossesed, most dislodged of material entity. The exemplary formula of the blank page, thus liberated of the associative limits of positive language in its formulation of verbal material, would constitute the furthest point of a constant paradox. Blanchot began to approximate the blank page's deepest resonances of essential truth through a progressive siege in his successive books, revealing a glimpse at the limits of destiny, writing as an experience of death, a central and essentially unique theme, plural and insistently enclosed, deepened, approximated, delimited in its condition as center of absences. In

2.2. The Deconstructive Lodging of Poetic Experience

Faux Pas, the first of the great collections of essays (1943), the paradox was still concentrated on accessible contents in the existentialist experience: *the work is useful because it is not useful for anything* (M. Blanchot, 1943 [1975, pp. 13—14]). The existentialist reformulation of the secular paradox of pure art, without objectives, of art for art's sake; that is, of art successful in its aesthetic meaning precisely under the most certain forms of its abdication of meaning.

The presence of the paradoxical design is diversely multiplied in the infinite cases of the experience of writing. In Eckhart's mystical thought, which "maintains, to its very limits, the exercise of reason in the study of a reality which is confused with nothing", the form of paradox appears in its most emphatic and pure lines. Mystic thought's approximation to its object most visibly denotes the cipher of an unsolvable disproportion; the finite and the infinite are contrasted in the insurmountable confrontation of a pure dialectic: "This ambition, which pretends to unite the uninterrupted movement of finite thought to the acquisition of an infinite, which does not correspond to any category of thought, is the mark of the dialectic" (1943 [1975, p. 32]). In the mystic process, the soul, "created essence", has to win the space of the archetypally eternal, which is "uncreated essence", but "this movement which transforms each affirmation into a negation ... which moves towards the negative though the positive and does not stop except in the affirmation of an absolute negation, is not possible except through *paradox*" (1943 [1975, p. 33]).

For Blanchot, the *absurd logic* of general human activity finds one of its privileged manifestations in art. Art offers the purest example of the intuition of an end which surpasses the means of a contradictory positiveness. This is the basis, for example, for the greatness of Leonardo, whose painting "appears rich not only in the most rigorous and broad knowledge, but also in what surpasses knowledge and questions it" (1943 [1975, p. 90]). The artistic text's material structure refers, on the one hand, to its positive consistency, to all of its potential for being and referring, but also simultaneously supposes the consolidation of its failure as an absolute, insurmountable limit. And yet the word, the relentless principle of poetic meaning, confirms itself as the only instrument of mediation with the pure pursued symbol, a lesson recorded in Mauron's reflection on Mallarmé (1943 [1975, p. 129]).

Poetry's positive consistency establishes the support for its meaningful disappointment. For Blanchot, aesthetic meaning is constructed not as an added element beyond the positive meaning of the expressed in the poem, but *against* the poem's positive meaning. In this way, pure art reveals itself as an impossible aspiration insofar as it is an art of language (1943 [1975, p. 142]); and, according to him, this is how Baroque art establishes the principle of its paradoxical superiority over classical art, trusting more in the meaningful reaches of the artistic periphery of the utterance (1943 [1975, p. 148]). To brandish art's essential, intimate contradiction is what every poet is absolutely dedicated to; this form of fixing "the essence of art as an object" appears in the Mallarméan dream of the perfect work, where "language is an absolute, the very form of transcendence, which can, nevertheless, be welcomed in a human work" (p. 192). With Blanchot, we are always faced with the hidden face of the myth of a dispossesed word, of the live form in its dislodged state, of the ideal of the blank page.

The poem above all denounces the risk of conformity which is involved in words' constructed and positive meanings. On the other hand, aesthetic meaning is composed of inaccessible transparencies, of the hints perceived within the rigid forms of verbal meaning. The poetic text mobilizes the word to denounce its historical imprecision, its nature as a forcibly frustrated and deceptive form. A subversive exercise, permanently controlled, therefore leading to *silence* as a block of unquestionable affirmation. And with the invocation of silence, Blanchot has discovered in *Faux Pas* the exact location of poetic questioning (1943 [1975, p. 193]). But the great difference between Blanchot's silence, as a paradoxical absolute of verbal meaning, and the ideal of the trace deconstructed in Derrida, is marked by the former's plenitude. For Blanchot, silence expresses the ideal accessible in the progressive purification of the word's historical and positive meaning, a space lodged to a large extent in language's traceable flip side.

The expectation of meaning positioned in positive terms of language is maintained from this space of silence; it is enough for the permanent and progressive operation of pondering its limits, which designs a strict capacity of emptiness, wherein a glimpse of pure and absolute meaning is lodged. Blanchot's contemplation of language does not ever lead to the limit of sad and tortured mistrust which appears inevitable in Derrida's never absolutely deconstructed readings. For Blanchot, it is enough to wander, abandoned in suggestion, in the exercise of echoes: the ineffable yields itself, submissive, as silence. In Derrida, the ideal of the imaginary trace dawns always as an unlimited positiveness, and the denunciation practiced by deconstruction on the traps of meaning provokes an apocalyptic consciousness, very different from the clean purifying ascesis of Maurice Blanchot's reading towards silence. The ideal of meaningful silence surely marks a much more feasible and immediate hope than the deconstructive utopia of attaining access, behind absolute negativity, to a chimerical trace, always threatened by new positiveness under the promise of its absolute being.

The block of exterior thematic consistencies in the deep debate of *Faux Pas* is purified and made more subtle in the next step, in 1949, with *La part du feu*. The absolute of silence, announced in the previous work as a result and final way out of a paradoxical process of affirmation from negativeness, now explores the profound symbolic implications of the phenomenon of artistic writing. The final and culminating essay of the work, "Literature and the Right to Death", is undoubtedly a contribution, from the ethical periphery of the humanist reflection on existentialism, to the consideration of literary writing's symbolic space.

2.2. The Deconstructive Lodging of Poetic Experience

Literature begins precisely, as Blanchot had already suggested in *Faux pas*, at the moment when it offers itself as a problematic question and object (M. Blanchot, 1949 [1972, p. 293]). In this way it is not only an illegitimate entity but even a null one, coinciding at a certain moment with nothing, and gaining its nature as everything at that hour of absolute inconsistency (1949 [1972, p. 294]). The culminating writing, the integrally transcendental writing, is that which affirms from nothing and in view of nothing or, following Hegel's expression, as nothing acting in the womb of nothing (1949 [1972, p. 305]). The poetic word's power consists in giving itself emptied of its own meaning, previously suppressed; it contributes the being deprived of being, and every act of unfrustrated poetic language requires having previously consumed discursive meaning's conventional formulas, in an enormous hecatomb (1949 [1972, pp. 312–313]).

Literary meaning supposes therefore, from the perspective of negation the erosion of objectivity by paradox yields, the radical destabilization of discursive affirmations. The ideal of language transfigured in poetry consists in annihilating its powers of mention, in volatilizing the nourishment of meaning which constitutes and chains it. Literature thus reaches the symbolic space of death; it configures itself in reality only beginning with the annulment of life, the instrument from which it is uselessly represented and estimated in its objective meaning. The existential experience of death is insurmountably disturbed by the living support from which it attempts to constitute itself; in the same way, the ultimate power of poetry as an essential glimpse is ballasted and blocked in the customary meaningful space of language from which poetry begins and in which it is consolidated.

The meaning saved by the limit, as Blanchot expresses it, particularly involves the manifestation of the objectivized word, with its powers of sensorial suggestion not limited to simple stylistic and sensitive effects, but restored to its original capacities of autonomous expressiveness, to its highest symbolic powers, to its inheritance purified in centuries of imaginary and cultural experience. The poetic word's pure meaning, successfully lodged in its capacities for aesthetic suggestion, begins by emptying conventional meaning from its origin. To a certain extent, it renounces meaning without deconstructing it; it transcends it from the limit of its own consistencies, without distrusting it, without denying it as a useless and untruthful obstacle, as deconstruction proclaims it.

The parallelism between the awareness of the poetic word and the existential experience of death opens up the possible calculation of a space of essential meaning. The feeling of death, an intuition inaccessible from existence, encloses the same paradoxical mechanism as poetic meaning, glimpsed only from the density of language's objective meanings. Such is the paradox of the final hour, ... to die is to lose death (1949 [1972, p. 328]). Before the most sublime poetry, like that of Hölderlin, Blanchot achieves those forms of essential nakedness which surpass the signs of mediation: the silence behind the rumor, the depth of meaning which implies, as a negation of the most immediate delivery of meaning which is disdained as trivial, because flat. Silence's association with the sacred (1949 [1972, p. 131]) which by the force of tension towards that which is difficult to express, begins to acquire volume as a positiveness of emptiness; hence, in the poetry of René Char "the poem moves towards absence, but it does so in order to compensate total reality with absence".

The transcended word — constant in its presence — exists to undo itself, to evoke, in absence, the presence of the remote and inaccessible. But once it has been consumed as a power of evocation, the word's material evidence remains as a remnant and testimony in the body of the poem, which lends it consistency and continuity against total loss and the absolute abolition of the poetic fact (1949 [1972, p. 55]): the text as constancy of aesthetic being. In the artistic work, language and thought do not exist isolated, but in relation to one another. As discontinuous terms they both have a different value for Blanchot than that represented by their respective identities, as constituents of the poem's solid unity. And the cement of this union is the unlimited lack of fit, the abysmal disproportion that exists between their components (1949 [1972, p. 59]).

With this infinite distortion between its elements, poetry seeks language's complete corrosion; but that destruction is also the only form in which poetic meaning acquires potential. The ruin of language opened by poetry stems from its continuous mobilization, from the annihilation of its controllable inertias and of its static supports; the poem, for Blanchot, forswears the definitively consolidated and fixed, attenuated and extinguished form of meaning. It seeks the paradox of a genesis which it wants to be interminable, the perfect form of aesthetic being, continuously maturing.

Blanchot learned, especially from Mallarmé, about the word's deconstructive reach, its capacity for erasing the most immediate and direct entities of meaning, to win the poetic space of the negative. The word's "material potency" is tied to this special transcended meaning, at the cost of the omission of the most obvious meaning (1949 [1972, p. 37]). This silent emptiness created from the word's material power is not the antithesis of verbal presence, under which it is commonly considered, but rather the plenary emptiness filled with the meaningful tendency presupposed from the words' positive entity (1949 [1972, pp. 41–42]). Silence means the sublime consolidation of absence, manufactured from the distant immediacy of textual constituents as mediated, inert and remote witnesses. It is channeled by the invading disposition of the poem's blanks, of the general emptiness which compresses the poem's voices, converting them into an oscillating and threatening presence and dislodging them of their most placid and stable meanings, in order to urge them on, with the destabilization of their most essential aesthetic valencies.

Kafka's writing would be, in this paradigm of literary meaning, a quintessential example of the "search for an affirmation which it attempts to reach

2.2. The Deconstructive Lodging of Poetic Experience 245

through negation" (1949 [1972, p. 14]). The transcendental tendency constitutes the objective that does not allow itself to be embraced except by way of the negative divestment of objective and immediate presences. But "the ambiguity of the negative is linked to that of death ... the death which ends our life, but which does not end our potential for dying". *The Metamorphosis*, the great Kafkaesque theme, offers Blanchot the consumated cipher of the poetic reverse as the terminal of a tendency, similar to the inaccessible limit of death in Kafka's story.

If *Faux pas* in 1943 and *La part du feu* in 1949 involve the discovery and location, respectively, of poetic sense in the inconceivable confines of a dimension of meaning like death, which is reached from life wagering on clearly manifest meanings, *L'espace littéraire*, of 1955 — after the relative parenthesis which *Lautréamont et Sade*, of 1949, represents —, was Blanchot's positive and mature effort to illustrate and represent this inaccessible space of the imagination. Beginning with the clearly successful intuitions of this work, Blanchot's direct critical allusiveness will have matured definitively in the clear awareness of the ineffable. In spite of all that has been said, Blanchot here exhausts himself, exhausts his powerful capacities of thought and writing before the limitless extension of a region of meaning more prospective and neutral than nocturnal. The intuition about the constitutive nature of the nocturnal is glimpsed with great difficulty from the perspicacity of his sensibility; or even more so, from the dense indications of the barrier establishing the limit between the day's lived positiveness and the nocturnal negation of the unexperienceable.

As I have said before, *The Literary Space* represents, from the moment of its culmination, the end of direct and representative writing. From this work onwards, and after the clear announcement of a transition by *Le livre à venir* in 1959, the organization of Blanchot's own critical discourse is irreparably marked by the echoes of the powerful silence of its object in *L'entretien infini* (1969), extinguishing itself in the barely accessible writing of his last work, with the significant title of *Le pas au-delà* (1973). Blanchot achieves a destiny frequently sought in modern criticism: Shakespeare's soft silence, Hölderlin's silent madness, Juan Ramón Jiménez's laborious final achievement of the myth of the silenced and blank page, and Larrea's non-existent poetry. All of them examples, chosen at random, of the inevitable itinerary followed in the experience of indefinable truth, of poetic consistency, a truth observed in silent ecstasy before the final comprehension of destiny itself.

Beyond the title of the work itself, *The Literary Space*, Blanchot was not excessively generous with poetic experience's explicit spatial representations, a moment of the negation of emptiness, of the unfrustrating null and negative. Still, with temporal reference formally denied (1955), the spatial support of meaningful negativity, of the absent emptiness, is invariably made transparent as the most certain form of sensing the negative. Poetic experience as literary space is one of the most powerful ways of characterizing it. An ultimate and essential image, transcending the text's most immediate and limited forms and consistencies; its nature as inconceivable "otherness," foreign even to the negative emptiness and the pure form of neutrality, finds nothing but the symbol of space as duration, as support for an emptied, supposed capacity for excluded forms. Constituted as a manifestation of flux, a "murmur" carried along, which survives in the text as a surface, the experience which literary writing engenders — the location of poetic meaning as image, as a tendency towards the final image of neutrality —, is lodged in an ultimate consistency perceivable as a pure image of space, necessary and previous to the opaque configuration of the neutral.

The spatial premonition of poetic experience in Blanchot, unable to be anything but an emptied capacity and extensive attempt, appears nevertheless, beginning with *The Literary Space*, under the form of thoughtful wandering, one of the favorite notions of this profound philosopher of art. In its mythical trajectory, an image from Hölderlin's elegy "Brot und Wein" appears as an appropriate suggestion of poetry: "I don't know. And why poets in the *time of abandonment?*" — "in durftiger Zeit". Poetic experience would occupy the necessary space dislodged by the god's absence, by "the disappearance of the historical forms of the divine". An exciting, frustrated anxiety of emptiness, language which proclaims only the lost feeling of an absence, the peculiar disorientation of a loss. And this incessant fluttering of anxiety takes on a unique awareness of its wandering in emptiness.

In experience, the ultimately spatial consistency of the image and of poetic meaning, being the purest previous form of the unreachable truth of the neutral, represents the truest and simplest expression. Under the allusion of this literary space, on which all of the positive and consistent limitations of artistic production evaporate and are annulled, Blanchot's preoccupation with the characterization of poetic meaning as experience reappears once again. A decisive and final obsession which we have already seen developed until *L'entretien infini*, where it reaches its most complete density as a central and radical formula. The impotence of the coarse word, ballasted by the weight of its material condition, the contagious limitation of the meaningful evocations of the image, the text's positive defficiency as affirmation, demand the foreseen awareness of the neutral's absolute satisfaction. Therein lies the reason for the existence of poetic emotion, of the positive search for images of radical lack, of the absence which guarantees plenitude.

The literary experience which underlies poetic meaning is above all the non-existent place in which a *tendency* is fixed, an unformulatable anxiety of discovery of a nature based in its own exclusion, in absolute exclusion. The nearest literary space, the text's language, already clearly indicates the settled frustrations of every discovery alien to the undermined pattern of absence (1955, p. 45). But the tendency, the tentative attempt at discovery confirmed by the text's language, is seen first and necessarily as pure inertia, without any greater end or object than the constant corroboration of a lack, of an essential form of radical emptiness, which constitutes the glimpse of the absent, the absolute plenitude of the *neutral*. Blanchot found in Rilke some of the most flourishing examples of the form of unrealizable tendency which experience consists of.

The literary work as a more conclusive and sensible instrument of the underlying tendency presents itself marked by the most radical evidence of insufficiency and yet pierced by eager signs of an exciting promise in the cases in which it consolidates under meaningful glimpses of negation, of excluded forms in the unique plenitude of the neutral. The work realizes the movement of the tendency, but it never accompanies the tendency to its end; what is more, it does not even promise to do so. The accepted condition of its final frustration is part of its being and an essential form of its capacity to achieve by limiting itself, to discover splendor from the negative. The aimless movement towards this end which the work implies, as a radicalization of experience, always moves from art towards what is manifested as the neutralized appearances of the world. Whoever submits himself to the inertia of this inexorable volition completely realizes the "deep emptiness of inaction in which the nothing of being was made".

The development of the question of poetic meaning in terms of experience and a tentative effort to seek origins, in *The Literary Space*, marks a crucial point in the development of Blanchot's critical thought. In this work, concretion as a literary activity of the tendency, achieved much more metaphorically in his previous books, is proposed as an unsurpassable image of that fundamental component of poetic meaning. Unsurpassable, in my opinion, not only because it summarizes all of the possible cases and illustrations about the tentative nature of literary activity, but also because it clearly fixes the untransgressable limits of negativity, in which the exclusion of forms of experience are consolidated as a plenitude of absence. The meaningful premonition of the neutral, which is achieved beginning with *L'entretien infini*, clearly makes its presence felt within *The Literary Space*, as the abandonment of the insufficient forms of dialectic negativity; a negative, nocturnal background, pursued in earlier works as an inaccessible content in the definition of the poetic.

Perhaps on this point, nevertheless, we have to distance ourselves from Blanchot and the fascination of his depth. The extreme lodging of poetic meaning in forms of absence, the insurmountable differentiator of the literary word and image, seems to me in effect to be a realistic effort. Moreover, it was necessary to define the positive statute of this mysterious excluded power, and I think Blanchot achieved this already in *The Literary Space* with his insistent delimitation of the positive meaning of absence as the constituent of the neutral. A poetic value the explicit proof of which was developed even more fully in subsequent works, but which is already present in *The Literary Space* in very convincing and characteristic forms.

Henceforth in Blanchot's thought, the neutral and the excluded will no longer be empty formulas which hide his critical impotence before the poetically ineffable, but rigorous terms for describing the negative reality of experience which, as tentative, lived experience, translates what we denominate as poetic meaning. The absolute center, the rigorous neutral value of experience, is of course constituted as an unattainable reference, but with strains very close at hand and well defined, which are not more certain, possible and familiar, more concrete and recognizable, than the tentative effort underlying experience. In Blanchot, the negativeness of that absolute center, final principle of the forms, effects and values of the poetic, is only its nature and form of definition; in no case, as happens with Derrida, is it a deconstructive obstacle, an exclusive proposal of aporia. The negative nature of the sources of poeticity in Blanchot is radically essential and productive and does not induce any form of the insurmountable denial of poetic meaning.

On the other hand, the extreme and final nature of the literary experience of absolute negativeness, together with the various radical forms of the positive presence of absence and exclusion, do not cease to express their own nature as sources. It is a matter of constitutive principles, whose potential for poetic challenge will be invested with possible and very varied forms of literary consistency. Blanchot's radical search for the origin of poetic meaning should not be confused with or interpreted as excluding the most positive and concrete forms of literary poeticity.

Blanchot throughout his work progressively inquires with greater and greater emphasis — and perhaps also with an increasing skill and brilliance — into the most profound and hidden depths of the literary experience of the neutral which underlies poetic meaning and value, ignoring the textual and positive forms which realize them in the text. A poetics of literature does not have to examine the origin and foundations of poeticity, but should fix the literary forms in which the hidden genesis is fruitfully reflected. Moreover, this has been what has customarily been done in the history of philology and literary criticism. Nevertheless, these convincing records of poetic evidence have habitually lacked any precision regarding the lodging of poetry as an unforeseeable value. Still, in the course of time, the majority of critics have looked to philosophers in order to orient their attributions of value and meaning regarding the poetic evidence available to them. Almost in our own times, and with a validity which he did not yet believe to be eroded, Blanchot has discovered some of the most convincing and fundamental conditions upon which poetic experience is aesthetically founded.

In Blanchot's last works, and particularly beginning with *L'entretien infini*, a deeper examination of the general question of experience at its furthest limits is perceptible. More than any new concrete development of his unique and by then reiterated ideas, what is noticeable is the insistence on certain aspects possibly compressed in his previous treatment of these questions. With the marked and progressive deviation of the theme of experience, from its most specifically literary aspects to those of a more properly anthropological and philosophical nature, the most appreciable advances made in these

2.2. The Deconstructive Lodging of Poetic Experience

works belonging to Blanchot's final period are those which explore the peculiarity of the *neutral*. By bringing this category into play, he begins to extract the traditional reflection about the negative nature of experience from its primitive outlines of dialectical negativity in order to lodge it in a new space of difference, in which it gains, of course, by the acquisition of that inaccessible radicality of experience under its condition of otherness.

Of course the principle and starting point which mobilizes Blanchot's reflections continues to be the source of artistic and particularly literary experience. As Emmanuel Levinas has established, the neutral manifestation of the *other*, which Blanchot pursues, never stems from logical and objective thought, but from the dissymmetry which is naturally a property of the poem's unique language. A revelation which does not consist in moving towards knowledge objectively, but which manifests itself "without giving itself away". Not giving itself over to any power whatsoever, it can not even be a form of the extreme human power of negation: belonging to the "domain of the impossible", it always dispels that which attempts to unveil it. Rather, it is an experience of extreme loneliness "in the desolate field of impossibilities irreducible to being constituted in worlds". It is equivalent to speech, but of the model and kind of speech specific and particular to poetic writing. A speech without interlocutor, without a *you* or *other*, and hence without being required to adjust itself to any meaningful postural coherence (E. Levinas, 1975, pp. 14—15).

The continuity characteristic of philosophical language, a continuous ontological discourse which gains its power from this fact of its nature and which also owes its limitations, from Aristotle to Hegel, to the same fact, contrasts with poetic language's characteristic "discontinuity". In Breton, Blanchot recalls how the inexhaustible "murmur" of poetry substitutes the closure expressed by the absolute continuity of the language of reason. This is the discontinuity of poetic writing, trying the awareness of every form of security dearest to man; faced with poetic writing, the condensation and unitary continuum of this security are revealed as superficial guarantees of its consistency and continuity. Hence, artistic discourse belongs to the kind of natural search that knows no end (M. Blanchot, 1969 [1971, p. 35]); that is, to the genre of "vanities" that Pascal characterized as being "without justification", the kind which are fulfilled in their very nature as unfinished efforts (1969 [1971, p. 140]).

Levinas himself has furnished Blanchot with one of the fundamental concepts for the unique configuration of discontinuous poetic discourse: the notion of the "curvature of the universe", which adequately and plastically explains the differences befalling any consideration of poetic writing in comparison to the genre of continuous utterances belonging to traditional ontological thought. This is the case to the extent that a kind of decline in the peculiar relation acquired by writing between the literary sender and the poetic interlocutor is produced, in contrast to the exact correspondence suiting the *I* and *you* of ontological dialogue. The communicative distortion unique to poetic discourse establishes that curvature where, between the author and his readers, initiatives are taken without any expectation or hope for symmetrical responses. This is how, particularly between men committed to the poetic dialogue, the peculiar relationship of infinitude is introduced between them, a relationship which characterizes the poetic conversation as a privileged manifestation of *L'entretien infini*. The poetic dialogue is a conversation in which "to speak is to locate the other in the search for a mediational word, but it is also above all to attempt to 'assimilate the other as other' and the strange as strange, another in his or its irreducible 'difference', in his or its infinite otherness, an (empty) otherness such that only an essential discontinuity can expect the appropriate affirmation" (1969 [1971, p. 115]).

The singular poetic search for the other in its irreducible otherness, which is characteristic of poetic writing as an infinite dialogue, privileges the power of one word, the poetic, on which it bestows every unlimitable dissemination of its radical liberty. Thus, the completely free dynamicity of words in the interior of poetic discourse crystallizes in their most recognizable property of continuity; that is, the continuity arising from poetic discourse's productively fragmentary nature, in which each entity constitutes its own cell, from which it migrates to contiguous spaces and relates itself to them in an unforeseeable plurality of movements, through itineraries so irreducible to thoughtful calculation that they appear to us to be infinite (1969 [1971, pp. 115–116]). The power of writing, as a material rupture with the sure dialogue of the word conventionalized in the relational equivalents of an overly immediate and asphyxiating, radically deceptive *you*.

Poetic experience, as Blanchot has progressively approached and besieged it, echoes familiar notions which I myself have not suitably welcomed in other systems and authors. The infinite nature of the poetic dialogue Blanchot proposes does not, in my view, either support or approximate the Barthean ideal of supposedly infinite polysemy, which opens the poetic text to any attribution of meaning whatsoever. It also seems clear that Blanchot is using the essential notion of *difference* in a way distinct from that of Derrida. The fundamental presupposition of Blanchot's poetic infinitude is precisely that which he roots in the space of exceptional meanings, in which the supposedly infinite polysemy of Barthes' plural text moves. Barthes' speculations would never exceed level space, where meanings of truth and falseness are constructed or mocked; a positive space in which the number of uncertainties always compete with homogeneous certainties.

Blanchot's infinite is the result of the lodging of poetic meaning in a different space, the space of the neutral, never foreseen by Barthes' mechanical structuralist positivism and his notion of the text. The infinite sliding of poetic meaning in the terms which Blanchot proposes, alludes to a different aim from that of the annihilation of meaning in the peculiar pragmatic model of poetic communication conjured up by the French essayist. The source of

2.2. The Deconstructive Lodging of Poetic Experience

the values of poeticity can be said in effect to be plural and even infinite by allusion to the neutral's innumerable spaces of origin, where poetic experience is constituted, and which is above all the awareness of its own exceeded reality. The infinite validity of poetry in Blanchot thus means the attribution of power, a necessary condition, and not, as in Barthes, the mark of impotence and gratuitousness.

By the same token, the notion of *difference* which Blanchot demands alludes to the neutral's space, where the experience gestates and knows itself to be excluded. Derrida's timely differential notion alludes to a principle of categorization, in his opinion deceitful, which has become classical in philosophy, and which is extended and generalized to the construction of thought in the space of experience which we denominate, with Blanchot, flat geometry. This face of the other as neutrality, exceeding dialectical thought, has nothing to do with the Derridean category of *difference*. Nevertheless, there are many productive similarities regarding that zone in which the common lodging of writing is produced, both in the prelogical sphere of the Derridean *trace*, as in the infinite experience of the spatial curvature where space is inscribed in Blanchot's neutral space, the domain of poetic writing's differential constitution (M. Blanchot, 1969 [1971, p. 6]).

The written word is, therefore, unique in that it exists in a peculiar relation to its entities of reference, a different reference from that constructed by vision, supposedly direct and homologous. To speak is not the same as to see, as Blanchot says in the title of one of the dialogues in his book: "To speak is to reach the manifest presence, as a procedure of the other, the presence inaccessible to sight and irreducible to the contact of light" (1969 [1971, p. 82]); in spite of the philosophy of vision, which trusts in reaching the self as the visible. But the generalization of the philosophy of vision contaminates our ideas about the referentiality of the word. To speak is to walk blindly and discover the sense of space different from the neutral, without light or form, where experience is constituted as an opaque revelation, a discovery which writing neither discovers nor entirely illuminates, but, on the contrary, is always consolidating as a luminous form of keeping watch (1969 [1971, pp. 40–41]).

For Blanchot, as for Derrida, writing offers itself identically as a principle of excelling, of overcoming, which if in Derrida's case means overcoming the defficiencies of a discourse modeled on the oral and linked to the forced rhyme of difference, in that of Blanchot it refers above all to overcoming a visual theological experience of flat space, where the forced convergences have created the illusion of correspondence and have stripped away any awareness of the outside and the other (1969 [1971, pp. 383–384]). By overcoming, the literary word proposes above all its own excess; it leads to the experience of the neutral, but on the condition that it, the literary word, disappears behind silence (1969 [1971, p. 387]). Writing ceases being a mirror and is consolidated as *an absolute of writing and of voice*, uniting space and time, and being "successive simultaneity" where space is constituted. The necessary outside space de-naturalizes the book as a possible past; the task of writing, its work, is always consumed in the ideal of an effort never able to reach a concrete end, towards the neutral. The work of that writing is always the *book to come*, which "does not affirm anything that is not of the *outside*; that is, it itself, not as a plenary presence, but in relationship to its absence; the absence of the work or its *un-working*" (1969 [1971, p. 388]).

The descriptive notion of a continuum, whisper or murmur, applied to poetry as the unformed appeal which does not know strategic segmentations, the divying up of the language, which normally works towards a kind of message of converging and homologous contents, is a notion we have known since *The Literary Space*. Now it is converted into one of Blanchot's most expressive references about the manner in which experience shapes itself, in *Le livre à venir*: "Something which speaks, something which does not stop speaking, is like the emptiness which speaks, a light murmur, insistent, indifferent, which without a doubt is the same for all". Nevertheless, it will above all be *L'entretien infini* where the profound characterization of the murmur is revealed in its most powerful forms. The whisper of the poetic voice is proof of how the brief space of sudden movement and activity between silences returns almost immediately to that silence, submerging itself in silence's insurmountable density (1969 [1971, p. 385]).

The poetic suggestion of the murmur begins to play an important role in *L'entretien infini* not only in its explicit and exterior characterization, but also in the neutralized dialogues between interlocutors, on which the work is largely constituted. Gertrude Stein's line, "A rose is a rose is a rose is a rose", symbolizes the repetitive exercise of the whispered nature of the poetic utterance as an evocative nomination of being. The terms thus "uprooted, fall into the multitude of whispering, the chatter which arises as the manifestation of every profound word, speaking without beginning and without end" (1969 [1971, p. 504]). In the same way, Blanchot finds the most interesting affirmation of Samuel Beckett's entire work in the whisper's uncertain suggestions, neutralized echoes of a nothing in which the nature of existence is affirmed.

Poetic writing, the unceasing murmur which, as an expectation in silence, does not only de-naturalize the hypotheses regarding its own cells, in the temptation of affirming some construction of unity as an entity, a form, but even erases any solid initiative to identify itself as its beginning or its end. The nature of that writing for Blanchot is absolutely foreign to every manipulation of its visible body, which would privilege any way of structuring or destructuring its meaning. Once again, we see Blanchot's incompatibility with the negative relativisms of meaning, held before him nevertheless by the necessary limits which in the end they are condemned to by their own spirit of positiveness regarding the text. In contrast to Blanchot's thought, deconstructive pessimism could be characterized by its inability to posit the origin of the poetic as a form of value or a form of meaning which escapes the experience, positive or negative, of the immanent material dialectic.

2.2.5. Otherness as a Reference Forming Experience's Essential Emplacement

One of the fundamental aspects in Blanchot's process of describing experience is constituted, in my judgment, by the gradual discovery of the neutral as a specific consistency. In effect, in his first approaches to the basic notion of experience, Blanchot emphasized the dialectical feature of its negativeness, founding the perceptible mechanism of paradox. Yet, slowly, Blanchot can be seen detaching himself from the dialectical weight of negation, more proper to the regimes of understanding of the *over here*, in order to opt for the neutral as a reference of the entities which belong to the experiential limit, as an impossible awareness of the *beyond*. In *L'entretien*, Blanchot collects and consolidates the hints present in previous works, especially in *Le livre à venir*, and contributes an image of neutrality as a content of the object of experience. Without contradicting it, he surpasses every negative notion of nihilism, in which even the word which expresses it "is one of those words which are not enough to hand over what they indicate" (1969 [1971, p. 590]).

The neutral is reserved for the impossible characterization of the contents of experience, but first, in the course of the tentative movement, the forms of negations continuously appear. This is the case, for example, with the word as "an object of dispersion", an instrument which "propitiates flight and becomes flight in flight"; with language as an "extension which manifests the movement of subtraction" (1969 [1971, pp. 30–31]). This is the language of poetry which excludes, in the act of constructing itself, every form of presence: "that previous presence which it is necessary for me to exclude in order to speak, in order to say it" (1969 [1971, p. 50]). It is the poetic attempt understood as "a passion of excess", of the departure from ourselves towards impossible outsides, proof of the negation of every power of affirmation.

Any experience of presence is nothing more than the intimated awareness of the dispersion of the Outside, of a necessarily foreign Outside, felt under the pressure of the negative as one's own intimacy (1969 [1971, pp. 65–66]). Measured from the passion of the tentative search, the radical insufficiency which experience proposes as an Outside is the positive form of negation: "It is not the impossibility which would be non-power: it is the possible which alone is the power of 'no' ". The weight of negativeness as an element of poetic language manifests itself in the radical paradox of its insufficiency. The poetic word means the exterior, the inaccessible, precisely from the very proposal of its insufficient presence (1969 [1971, p. 68]): the radical decline of the poetic word's power, which only under the awareness of its defficiency compared to the response which contracts, can give us the awareness of the outside as a positive presence.

The negativeness of the process of experience therefore converges as a result of a dialectical inequality with our link to the instruments of linguistic affirmation. The poem's linguistic immediacy as an affirmation locates the disproportional answer of experience over the free space of the Outside; a different region, radically unequal, corresponds to the region of the poem as a space of power (1969 [1971, p. 273]). A negative awareness, therefore, of the Outside as a necessary exclusion from the text's power, awareness that always expresses itself, from this perspective, in the negative terms of *emptiness*, as horror and as death (1969 [1971, p. 275]). An awareness that coexists with all of the forms of exclusion, as forgetfulness (1969 [1971, p. 289]) or madness, expressed by Michel Foucault in the terms of a space of rejection, an excluded and inexplicable zone, of a neglected Outside.

But the awareness of impenetrable otherness which experience reveals, does not suppose the necessary amputation of the tentative effort to estimate and know which begins this experience's movement. Thought does not capitulate, immolating itself in not being; it is on the contrary the plenary principle of the other and of the constitution of the neutral as a possibility and *measure* of the impossible (1969 [1971, p. 62]). In the plenary experience of the other, the impossible can be defined positively in the absolute reach of negativeness and not, as in our purely differential habits, under the positive attribution of a simple negation of power. In this manner it would be possible to reach, by itself, the absolute space of a darkness without any shadows of clarity, and of an absent and neutral time as "an unstable perpetuity, a halted time, incapable of permanence" (1969 [1971, p. 63]). The impossible is the other as possible.

The premonition of the *other* as a successful way out of the self is the basis for experience. Access to the other as an absolute awareness is the positive impossibility of our weight, of the un-deracinating of the self, the I, as the same. Emmanuel Levinas' philosophy of the other has turned out to be fundamental here for Blanchot (1969 [1971, pp. 72 ff.]). The corresponding scheme of the dialogue which Blanchot mobilizes as an appeal towards the other and the principle underlying and founding the dialogistic hybrid notion of *L'entretien*, has never seemed to me an entirely necessary or profitable instrument, without feasible alternatives. From the poem, as Blanchot himself experiences those of René Char, the transcendental erotic appeal appears, with powers of self-sufficient proof, of the one to the other, of the familiar which wants to uproot itself in what it does not recognize as its own. An erotic consciousness of poetry as the nostalgia of one for the other, as a tentative exploration of the spatial limit to the point of its dissolution in the without-space of the integral (1969 [1971, p. 76]). The poem's destiny, its only reason for existing, we know, is to break the bounds of identity, actualizing domestic space, and giving itself to the necessary passion of the different, of the absolutely other.

The poem exemplarily radicalizes, of course, language's most sublime and natural power: its effective appeal to the other as proof, as manifestation.

2.2. The Deconstructive Lodging of Poetic Experience

Here Levinas appears again in Blanchot's thought. In language, the other is welcomed as a natural manifestation and as a foundation. We speak in the awareness of the not-I; we communicate with whom we know to be different; a discontinuous awareness of space covered by the I: "If there is a relationship in which the other and the self, still maintaining itself as a relationship, are absolved, being terms which are maintained as absolute in the relationship itself, as Levinas says, that relationship is language. When I speak to the other, I appeal to him. Above all else, the word is that interpellation, that invocation in which the invoked is beyond reach ..., he who always remains beyond and outside of me" (1969 [1971, p. 79]). Language thus naturalizes a very complex and almost inaccessible awareness as absolute, that of the other as an absent space of one's own self. But poetry always "remembers" (1969 [1971, p. 89]) the impossibility of an absolute awareness, the emptiness of experience, which naturalizes the word made flat operation. Poetry is thus the absolute awareness of language's simple divinity.

In Blanchot's memory, Levinas' ideas act on the dialogue as a limit and a distancing warning of the absorption of language or writing under the function of the self's expressive continuum when they are de-naturalized (E. Levinas, 1975, p. 32). The presence of the other, naturalized manifestly in language in dialogue's effect and strategy, breaks the intimate perpetuation of the self as a pure and plain expression, without obstacles. The other, present in dialogue as an object of references and as a source of answers, spontaneously proposes the limit of the self, the impenetrable opaqueness which imposes proof of its strangeness, of its foreignness, on the self. The dialogical experience of the other erodes and cracks the self's self-absorption, breaking it into a thousand pieces. The dialogue imposes the other, and it imposes it as manifest, it naturalizes it as otherness, simply exposing experience.

In this way, the substantial space of the *difference* between the self and the other is thereby filled. In Blanchot, this is a radical and positive difference, an exact and first certainty; not, as in Derrida's claim, the foundation of every adulterated category. Between the self and the other, the difference substitutes the distinctive emptiness of nothing for the differential space in the use of language. A differential interval which creates what Blanchot denominates "the relationship of third genre" (1969 [1971, pp. 94–99]), a function which originates in the constellated consciousness, the pure contemplation of the possibility of appealing to the other, without any other contact. An other which the self can approximate in the certainty that "he" will never draw closer to "me", because "he" is irreducible to the subject of any action (1969 [1971, p. 100]). Its condition is the neutral, and like the *other*, that which is naturalized in language, *the other*, that which is supposed to be an impossible aim in experience, the poem's object.

The awareness of the other, manifestly consolidated in speech and writing through dialogue's differentiating effect, opens the intuition of the neutral as a non-dialectical entity. The neutral here means the peculiarity of an inaccessible and, in a certain way, inhuman space; unexperienceable experience, a peculiar condition of the space of the other, "the deepest question" (1969 [1971, p. 21]). The neutral, neither positive nor negative, only names the space of exclusion in the experience of the self; an imperceptible answer of a being and of a condition which are denied us because of the self's self-absorption: "All of the mystery of the neutral passes through the other, and returns us to it" (1969 [1971, p. 102]). An experience in no way impersonal, which approximates and naturalizes us only in the linguistic similarity of the dialogue, where the self and the other maintain their reciprocal constellative independence as a never superimposable entity, unmixable. In short, an infinite awareness of difference, which Blanchot reactivates in *L'entretien*, from the renovated light, the old theme of death as a space of exclusion (1969 [1971, p. 103]). Nevertheless, at this stage of his own proof, death's inaccessible aporistic space is more impotent and opaque to me as the lodging of the notion and consistencies of poetic experience than this evolved awareness of the other as the space of the neutral.

In writing, in language, under the dialogical presence of the other as a subject without possible action, pure constellative reference without functionality with my own awareness of action — a relation "of third genre" —, the neutral appears as an attribution of a purely foreign, unrepresentable space (1969 [1971, p. 104]). A space sheltered from every form of actual accessibility by the doubly dissymmetrical nature of the dimensions in which the impossibility of the relationship between the one and the other would be represented. A distance never reciprocally equivalent because it is produced in the space of the curvature, where the interval between A and B would never coincide with the inverted distance between B and A.

And it is that, as Blanchot himself indicates, the other is not exactly even one of the terms of the constellation of the third genre constructed by the awareness of the self. Its nature, absolutely foreign to the self's own awareness, leads it to escape and to disappoint every dialectical attribution. A consistency which is depleted in the proposal of the relationship itself, a relationship of the one to the other which demands *infinitude*. The linguistic presence of the other, a naturalized and functionalized experience, deepens our estimate of the neutral in its space, the intuition of the infinite. Poetic experience as an end which guarantees the life of writing is expressed in Blanchot's final vision as a purified and possible form of participation in the consciousness of the neutral. The other as "the infinite of a relationship without ends and as an infinite termination of an end without relation" (1969 [1971, p. 105]). The neutral, therefore, as the excluded; but excluded under the awareness of its inevitable presence, as Levinas has simply represented it: "That neutral is not someone, neither is it something. It is an excluded third which, speaking properly, cannot even be said to be. And nevertheless there is more transcendence in it than any other world has ever begun to open" (E. Levinas, 1975, p. 52).

2.2. The Deconstructive Lodging of Poetic Experience

Awareness at the neutral's limit, insofar as it is an inaccessible and infinite consistency of the other, always reveals itself as an act of language, as I have been repeating: the awareness of the other in the first place as a plural word, an expression multiplied under the estimate and the doubled reality of a dialogue (M. Blanchot, 1969 [1971, p. 320]). But language, which naturally includes a dialogical appeal to the other, implies the other also, especially as a neutral consciousness of the self. Blanchot offers his experience of Kafka's narrative as a privileged model on this point, beginning with *Le livre à venir*, for the acquisition of the consciousness of the other as a neutral space, irreducible to the self. Here Kafka's discovery of the narrative *he* as a substitute for the author's *I* as an awareness of the *self* comes into play: "What Kafka teaches us ... is that narration puts the neutral into play" (1959, p. 563). The narrative third person naturally distances itself from the first of the *I*, without easily converting itself into an absolute equivalent of impersonality, of the abandonment of the I from which it proceeds. It is a *he* which "dismisses every subject" to the extent that it affirms itself as a representation of an *I*, in which the structure of the language has broken any exact symmetry.

Under the neutral consciousness of the narrative *he*, with the dissymmetric projection of the consciousness of *self* which the *I* identifies as its own, the radical otherness of the other is deepened, established as a pure, infinite relationship without a stable term of reference. The other, nearer the *I* under the immediate appearances naturalized in dialogue, reconquers its space of otherness to the extent that the new narrative *he* is recognized in its absolute divergence from the author's *I*, from which it proceeds; and precisely because it is an other proceeding from the *self*. For us, this is the poetic essence of writing as an experience. Levinas has unsurpassably interpreted the difficult simplicity which characterizes it: "The mode of revealing what remains other in spite of its revelation, is not the poem's thought but its language... Its way of being consists in being present without giving itself, in not offering itself to the powers, since negation has been the last human power, in being the domain of the impossible, to which power does not accede... Solitude in the desolate field of the impossibilities incapable of constituting themselves into a world" (E. Levinas, 1975, p. 14). The poem as an inexhaustible *fund* of experience, as a reserve of otherness and proximity, never realizable, to the essential awareness of the neutral.

In Kafka's substitution of the *I* by the *he*, Blanchot, interpreted by Levinas, infers the fundamental character of poetic writing: to participate in a language of nobody, construct the space of an "absolute exteriority", of the "plenitude of emptiness" (E. Levinas, 1975, pp. 16—17). The poem amiably participates, therefore, in the beneficial naturalness of language in order to designate the consciousness of otherness, being itself, however, the source of the infinite frustration of its end as an object. The poem's verbal utterance locates it under the exceptional condition of the expressiveness of language as a natural tendency of experience. But the poem for this very reason makes itself emptiness, being the inexhaustible source of capacities moving towards the different experience of the neutral; an enigma nevertheless reveals, in its name, the greatest potential for suggestion, as Blanchot communicates in *Le pas au-delà* (M. Blanchot, 1973, p. 97). The poem as the privileged incorporation of the neutral would achieve its finished form by occupying "language's silent side". The poem, an absolute form of the neutral, registers the tendency which "designates difference in indifference, opacity in transparency, the negative excision of the other, which cannot be reproduced except by the exorcised — omitted — attraction of the self... The neutral which would mark being would not enclose it in the vulgarity of not being, but has already precisely dispersed being as that which, not ever giving itself, neither for this nor for that, also refuses to present itself as a simple presence, accessible, except in a negative way, under the protective veil of the 'not'... The neutral exorcises (being), dissolving it slowly, ridding it of every presence, even negative, neutralizing it until it impedes being from declaring itself in the neutral" (M. Blanchot, 1969, p. 106).

The poem expresses the pure tendency towards experience at the limit, the infinite experience which surpasses and moves beyond the bounds of possible knowledge. Its potential consists in proposing itself as the limit of the accessible in the wave of accepted impossibility. The neutral is the object of the poetic tendency, its premonition, the substantive without substance, a name without a name, a demand without an answer, except for that of failure accepted beforehand, an end fainting towards a beyond which it will never realize (M. Blanchot, 1973, p. 162). The poem, a failure of intentionally constructed language, turns out to be the revelation of pure language, dispersed, a-intentional, freed to its own capacities of involuntary remembrance: discontinuous language, in one of Blanchot's favorite formulas beginning with *L'entretien infini*.

In his approach to the neutral as a space and content of experience, Blanchot erases all of the consistent and solid forms of the intentional construction of meaning; for the neutral, the future book is the absence of the book: "The book winds and unwinds time and stalls that development as the continuity of a presence, where the present, the past and the future are actualized". The book's absence represents its outside, its exteriority; writing which does not confine itself to the book, which avoids that continuity adhering to presence, is an activity of un-working, an absence which is produced through its presence (1969 [1971, p. 622]). A writing which corresponds, then, with a poetic reading that undoes presence and welcomes what is fragmentary in language as also being exterior to language; poetry constructs a special book, which is not undone but which vanishes through its negation (1969 [1971, p. 630]). The future book, a book of fragmentary language, conspires from the beginning against every possible center of convergence; a work of *between-two*, it exalts dislocation and divergence as a movement of the radical exclusion of the center (1969 [1971, p. 235]). A

2.2. The Deconstructive Lodging of Poetic Experience 259

dionysiac tendency in which *flux* reveals its relationship with the discontinuous, a fragmentation is deified and replaces the constructive power of the old convergence in unity, now impotent.

I do not think it is necessary to make clear that language's fragmentary power, which Blanchot proposes beginning with *L'entretien infini* as a capacity, tendency and poetics of writing, is far removed from the plurisignification of the relativist thought of subsequent structuralisms. Blanchot's notions of the fragmentary and the absence of the book derive from Nietzsche without necessarily leading to Barthes. Language's dispersive power, for Blanchot as for Nietzsche, resides in the capacities for resonance of its nature as a tentative tendency towards the neutral. A neutral which is apart from any structural arrangement towards meaning's affirmative or negative dialectic, which is the space where Barthes would linger, as do all the relativisms of reading. The fragmentary in Blanchot is modulated in the old Nietzschean ideal of the aphorism as "a form of eternity" (1969 [1971, pp. 228–229]), with the radical reservation that that eternity, with those teachings Nietzsche dreamed, is the inaccessible eternity of the neutral for Blanchot.

It is true that Blanchot categorically denies the stable meaning of poetic texts as an intentional construction of meaning (1969 [1971, p. 502]). Such an understanding, according to him, would respond to an ancient order of the literary interpretation of the world as an answer; in contrast, Blanchot suggests the understanding of literature as a question, which leaves any answers suspended, and which makes the vehicle for this essential questioning a matter of insistence and not development (1969 [1971, p. 503]). But the insistence of poetry's unceasing questioning does not de-naturalize the unique, although neutral, entity of meaning. It proclaims it as inaccessible; but it does not supplant it with its multiplication in the same space of dialectical contingencies, in which the logical construction of meaning with a unitary and rational vocation does not work either. The object of univocal meaning as the participation in the text of the divine ideals of the one and the creator's authoritarian legality (1969 [1971, p. 635]), does not presuppose an order of certainties less acceptable for Blanchot than that of the plural certainty of the various in the democratic validity of individual reading options.

The borderline experience of the poetic, its aesthetic meaning, is infinitely univocal but inaccessible; it rests on the neutral's nature, towards which the successful poem is always the valid tentative effort. The neutral truth of the experience and meaning of poetry lies in the region of the step beyond, not to be confused with the game of the relativist multiplication of meaning, always in the same logical space of the "over here". Thus, in the appendix of his endless *Entretien*, Blanchot proclaims the value of *obstinacy* towards the neutral fund of experience, even given its vain destiny (1969 [1971, p. 637]). For me, the greatness of Blanchot's poetic thought lies here: in the belief that poetry is an aesthetic meaning, both in the tangible space of the literary text as an initiative and tendency, as well as in the experience of the neutral as a reality that can be intuited as a hidden object, but as one naturally participating under forms of language.

The delimitation of the neutral — if it would not be contradictory to propose its characterization — reaches a final brilliance in the thought of *L'entretien*. The neutral is a symbol of the "divine excess over meaning" (1969 [1971, p. 448]). The neutral is "an exclusion which manifests", like placing parentheses, "by a singularity of erasure, which is more effective to the extent that it is not indicated" (1969 [1971, p. 449]). The neutral is a substantive without substance, the proposal of a problem which has no answer, a form which allows itself to be traversed by questioning without retaining it, and without allowing the affirmation of the right to a response... The neutral, in short, is the un-emplaceable, exterior to every and any emplacement, even a negative one (1969 [1971, p. 450]).

Blanchot's thought rescues much more than the aesthetic meaning of writing as an experience of the neutral; it especially consecrates poetry's greatness, based on its infinitude. Misunderstood by many followers, near and far, from the poststructuralist reaction to the most literal deconstruction, as the first nihilist, modern aesthetics, under whose umbrella all of the possible, even senseless forms of receptive relativization, negation or deconstruction of meaning would seem to fit, the existentialist exploration of poetry as a borderline experience, which Blanchot tenaciously carries out for many years, with a reiterated and lucid insistence never identical nor repetitive, has traced an exemplary program insisting on the meaningful roots of the aesthetic experience which underlies and establishes poetry.

Beyond this, everything is accidental, and everything can be so when it serves that central coincidence of the dissemination of the neutral as an expectation of poetic meaning. Blanchot does, certainly, go far beyond the customary levels of reflection on the space of poetic meaning; he prolongs this space in the term of the infinite and he confines it in the dialectical exclusion of the neutral. But he does not deny it; and if it is true that he declares it inaccessible, it is no less true that he contributes considerably towards characterizing the emotions of its recognition in the neutral as a form arising casually, suddenly, unforeseeably. Is it that Blanchot has denaturalized the emotions by which poetry manifests itself?

Blanchot's fundamental insight, the depth reached in his diagnosis of the emplacement and nature of poetic experience justifies, as I have been indicating, his being considered one of the peaks of modern criticism. As a general norm, we have observed that Blanchot's thought is deeper and more universal when it approaches the positiveness of hermeneutical criticism than when it defines — based on authors like Mallarmé or Lautréamont — a poetics of anxiously existentialist negativeness. In the latter case, his critical opinions, which are immediately more verisimilar and comprehensive with regard to the texts they propose to explain, are self-restricitive in a universal sense, since they cannot be elevated as diagnoses to the high poetry of all ages — the optimal, the impulsive, the happily invasive of funds of confidence.

2.2. The Deconstructive Lodging of Poetic Experience 261

For similar reasons, Blanchot is just as limited when he indirectly associates himself with the well-known theses about the erosion of meaning in his diagnoses of avant-garde art. In his brilliant chapter on the "Ars nova", included in *L'entretien infini* (1969 [1971, pp. 506—514]), Blanchot amuses himself criticizing Thomas Mann's limitations, when negatively assessing the musical modernity of the dodecaphonic aesthetics. In effect, this is a matter of the customary phenomenon of the uncomfortableness and rigidity of personal taste with regard to novelty, which can be seen in the majority of the great theoreticians of contemporary art — Lukács, Longhi and Ortega y Gasset, to cite just a few. But, in the case of Blanchot, the maladjustment is produced, in my judgment, because of his extreme generalizations about the nature, which today we would call "open", characterizing the modern musical aesthetics. The voluntary destitution of the dodecaphonic work's structural unity, its radical abandonment of the principle of composition, is what configures it as a fragmentary work. This therefore consolidates its capacity as a more valid alternative, constituting it as the investigation of a new form of writing (1969 [1971, p. 510]).

The "Ars nova" obviously presents us with a space of crisis. Walter Benjamin's concept of *catastrophe*, with its exaltation of the aesthetic hypertrophy of the fragmentarily residual, of the surviving mutilation, of the cultural relic's productive incompleteness, moves Blanchot to adequately characterize the art of an age of perplexity and vacillations, compared to the classical constructed forms of enthusiasm (1969 [1971, p. 512]). The nostalgia for the "good" culture, that "familiar tug of everything and of unity", which has consecrated, in Theodor Adorno's terms, the difference between the center and the margin, between essence and accident, is transformed by the art of crisis into the target to be knocked down, patterned exactly as an anticonstructive effort, eroding the concept of the center, condemned as an unnatural form, as an interpretative trap.

Blanchot brilliantly knows how to set before us the best arguments of the apology for modern art's "painful demands". Schoenberg and Paul Klee, "dreaming a space where the omission of any center should suppress any trace of the vague and imprecise", provide him with excellent arguments. The problem, however, lies in not confusing this concrete diagnosis about a re-concentrated and circumstantial art for that which the questioning about the nature of the poetic becomes an exclusive object, with which it would universally correspond to the traditional and classical creative activity; an expansive art realizing in Shakespeare, Cervantes and Hölderlin, with the greatest ability known until now, and under capable formulas for expressiveness, the mysterious resonances of absolute otherness, the experience of the Outside, of the Other and of the Neutral, in the more familiar terms we owe to Blanchot.

That his keen circumstantial diagnosis of the art of the crisis apparently enables Blanchot to be linked — as in fact many interested in the question have done, including Derrida himself — with the subsequent poetics of the negativity of meaning, should not de-naturalize nor stir up confusion about the service which his work has offered aesthetics, situating and describing the infinite impossibility of language as an absolute power of poetry. Françoise Collin has hit the nail on the head in his evaluation of the fundamental potential of this author's aesthetic thought: "Blanchot's philosophy is not a philosophy of the absurd, a denomination by virtue of which it has before been approximated to that of Camus or to that of a certain Sartre, to the extent that it does not deny the order of meaning, but instead undermines it" (F. Collin, 1971, p. 227).

The solid steps Blanchot has brilliantly taken towards the definition of poetry's aesthetic meaning, ageless and universal, are many: representing the limits of literary writing, the disproportion of its structures of representation with the aesthetic effects which provoke and lend it proportion; defining its tendential condition as a tentative effort of writing, the only eligible form for evoking the accidents of experience; lodging the dazzling experiences of artistic revelation in the general space of borderline, existential lessons; identifying the awareness of otherness, which defines the familiarity of the same and marks the glimpses of the other and the outside as a form belonging to experience; defining the neutral as a faithful characterization of the deepest revelations of artistic knowledge, lodging themselves in the powers of naturalness which belong exclusively to language. To confuse all of this with some concrete power of historical characterization, be it existentialism, the aesthetics of the absurd, or deconstructive poetics, is to blindly detract from Blanchot's greatest aesthetic contributions.

2.3. *The Aesthetic Capacity of Cultural Conventionality*

2.3.1. *The Aesthetic Structure of Traditional Conventionality: The Historical Relativity of Artistic Meaning and the Non-Arbitrary Foundations of Cultural Conventionality*

The historical nature of literary facts and values is a variable which cannot be ignored but which also should not be exaggerated, much less restricted and deformed, as is so often the case. The claims of the aesthetics of reception concerning the relativization of meaning suited to individual readings, and above all of those which we might call collective readings or readings of an age, are actually a variation of the notions of contextualization first circulated years ago, particularly by sociologists of literature.

Literary sociology, especially that of ideological and Marxist roots, considers the establishment and recognition of contextual "conditions" to be the fundamental task of the historical and critical study of literature. For the same reason, the context is the decisive, most profound and relevant part of meaning. As a result, meaning is reduced to and identified with so-called historical or, more commonly, *social* meaning.

Establishing a work's social, historical and aesthetic context adjusts to the poetic or creative perspective for inferring the conditions determining the author's constitution of the text. But it is also basic for the history of reception, allowing one to measure and adjust various "readings" to the modifications of the same, both individual and general.

Within its incidence in the first — the poetic and creative — of these perspectives, the conditions of the historical context are obviously influential and we may even say decisive for textual meaning. For many years now this concrete point has been the object of debate between the partisans of contextual criticism and those of individual and personal poetics. It is in fact an ancient polemic, the exhumation of which would scarcely be interesting or novel here. Today nobody can either deny the definitive role of context in the formation and interpretation of the aesthetic and general meaning of texts or argue with the wide margin of freedom which great artistic creators have historically been conceded. Even the materialist sector of the aesthetics of reception admits this is the case, at least in its keenest criticism, as in the debate between P. U. Hohendahl (1974, 1974a) and R. Weimann regarding the interliterary context (R. Weimann, 1973, pp. 5—33; and especially K. Stierle, 1975).

The question which seems less obvious and more novel to me is that which would involve correcting the customary identification of the historical context with the social context or the context of material historical conditions. The explanatory historical context of literary texts includes the social and economic context as one of its parts, but not one of the most important. In the case of literary or artistic works, the most influential factor in a text's general or historical context is the most immediate and relative, which we might denominate the *traditional context*, that context internal to the artistic "series".

The traditional context of literary meaning refers to that formed by the broad collection of its nearest models for execution. For example, in the case of Spanish Petrarchism at the end of the sixteenth century, the traditional context would be imposed by the series of texts with equivalent *structural forms* — sonnets, songs, etc. — and similar *thematic forms* — amorous, the positive song, the negative song of suffering complaint, etc. In effect, one can discuss the character of the historico-social or economic *mediational* determination of the historico-material "conditions" through the artistic modelization of the same in antecedents (A. García-Berrio, 1985). However, there is no doubt that the traditional artistic context, as a reference for imitation or even for rejection, is the *immediate* and most attractive context bearing on the resulting texts.

From the perspective of reception, it is clear that, for new readers, works consecrated as exemplary, traditional or classical promote prejudices not easily considered separately in the reflecion on their value or their aesthetic meaning. This is one of the central arguments in the radical pragmatic stance on the relativism of meaning; and to deny this fact is to resist a proven and clear truth. Fame as a context of value regularly precedes the reading of works like Manzoni's *The Betrothed* or Stendhal's *The Charterhouse of Parma*; and, more generally, we can say the same about the imaginary and sentimental setting produced by the set of receptive references about these works, which precede each new individual act of reading.

An author's prestige or the fame of a classical work makes it hard to entirely twist the evaluative tradition of the same; similarly, it makes it difficult to accede with neutrality to the representation of its fantastic constitution and its aesthetic meaning. The cultural context of reading which accompanies a work as a part of the literary tradition of the *cultural series* in which that work is inserted, forms a part of the *poetic* properties of the same, both in terms of value and in terms of the sentimental structure of its general and aesthetic meaning (F. Jameson, 1981).

But this undeniable and positive fact should not then reasonably give cause, as in fact happens, for arguing against poeticity as a universal property, absolute and independent from any contextual influence in those artistic texts which achieve this level of value as an inherent property. In my judgment, there are natural features and qualities in great classical works which are particular to the formulation of their textual and pragmatic structures, and which qualifies them as poetic and of a singular and sublime meaning. Moreover, the traditional consolidation of the social awareness of these same properties adds to their poeticity on the one hand, although anticipating the knowledge of the fundamental aspects of these properties' aesthetic meaning on the other.

The roots of poetic meaning in great classical works reveal themselves in every case. Poetic meaning is supported by the work's textual properties, in which *incisions* and features of the text's *material scheme*, dynamizing forms of fantastic construction, are evident. These work to complete the sentimental and imaginary *space* of the artistic text as a general anthropological construct.

The work's contextual historical value forms a part, like expressiveness, of the literary mechanisms of aestheticity, which is why we have mentioned it in this chapter. However, it should not be proposed as a component of radical poetic value, which is substantive and universal and therefore absolute and independent from any form of context. Traditionality as a positive aesthetic mark, influencing value, and above all — insofar as it interests us here — as a structural cultural formative component of aesthetic meaning, helps to shape the sentimental and imaginary representation which we denominate poetic meaning, but it does not fundamentally determine it.

If these facts are customarily cited in order to reinforce pragmatico-receptive hypotheses about the contextual *relativism* of aesthetic meaning, they can just as forcefully underline the conjunctural and therefore secondary

2.3. The Aesthetic Capacity of Cultural Conventionality

nature of the historico-receptive factors which create cultural, traditional and historical contextuality.

In contemporary art, the value of the traditional context is strongly questioned. To a certain extent, the most visible symptom of the aformalist and abstract variants of so-called "modern art", or for the avant-garde in painting, music or literature, consists in their rupture with the system which creates art's traditional context. The classical philosophy of "minimal innovation", of the *retractatio*, compatible with the traditional imitation of models, has been replaced by the artistic myth of complete change and absolute novelty. For modern art, traditional context appears to be an excluded principle.

Nevertheless, the negation of classical art practiced by the modern artistic avant-garde has not yet created the real alternative of a different, radically "open" art. The central concept which presides over the classical work's constitution as a unitary affirmation of meanings has not yet been replaced. In my opinion, the rupture of the principle of the unitary affirmation of meaning is an almost "inhuman" possibility, which art as a system cannot achieve; nor, for that matter, is it desirable that it should.

For modern art, with its ideal of rupture, the constancy of the classical system, intuited in its calculated traditional context, continues to be valid in any case as an excluded block and starting point for negation. In this way, if a definitive poetics of modern art is to be formed as an absolute alternative, it would have to begin with the awareness of meaning shaped by the traditional context of the classical cultural system.

Traditionality forms a part of the most fungible constituents of texts' poeticity, undoubtedly contributing to their historical formation. As such, it is one of the properties which forms aesthetic meaning's conventional context, although that meaning is still not exhausted either by this conventional context or by similar features, such as expressiveness. Examining poetic values solely in light of their history, they surely are culturally arbitrary, which does not imply that, more radically, they are not essentially motivated. Aesthetic conventionality is thus a verifiable historical process, but only subsequent to the non-arbitrary structure of poeticity, the justification for which is rooted in universal, anthropologically based aesthetic properties.

What we understand as cultural conventionalism, which underlies the system of consensual principles as literary discourse, has an ample, explicit and conscious foundation of objective norms and exclusive materials. All of this functions in literary production as a contextual frame of references internal to the artistic series. The principle of *literary tradition as a conventional context* is thus formulated, the mechanisms of which I first referred to in 1977 (A. García-Berrio; E. Forastieri, ed., 1980, pp. 95—137), and which I have later amply illustrated, especially in the traditional context of a class of texts particularly conventionalized and topical — Spanish love poetry of the courtly and Petrarchist tradition.

In my opinion, the course represented by the typological and formal investigation of traditional cultural facts, in which each new text gestates, designing its own space of originality among its most immediate literary antecedents, is an illustrative way of defining and delimiting literary conventionality with regard to novelty and poetic value. Naturally, any such study begins by making clear the great complexity of the mechanisms which govern cultural convention. It is not only a matter of the conventional universe of reception and readers, the non-producers of the text, which is how the aesthetics of reception appears in our own time to understand the nature of cultural convention. The author of traditional works is the first receiver of the tradition; he is its most attentive and prudent reader, to the extent that it encourages his aspiration to inscribe a new piece in the chain of traditional texts, in a full space with little room left for novelty. As Harold Bloom indicates in his fundamental thesis on *misreading*, every text *confronts* another text as a reference for constituting itself (H. Bloom, 1973, 1975). Of course, here we want no part of the negative aims of these affirmations, according to which the textual confrontation is born from the condition of this interpretation or "misreading", to use the term Bloom has canonized.

A careful typological examination of thousands of literary texts very close to a conventionalized and topical tradition, as in the example I have offered of my typologies of the lyrical poetry of the Spanish Golden Age, illustrates above all the limit which exists between the conventionalizable and the space open to the creator's tutelary free initiative. The first sphere, the domain of topical convergences and the system's reiterative identities, would define the conventional, assumed under the texts' condition of literariness. The second space, the field belonging to the free initiative of the differential, successful choice, establishing the unique poetic reason within the topical current of discourse, defines and illustrates the processes of unconventionalizable singularization from which poetic value arises.

This is so, however, only in certain absolute terms which work well, as I will make clear further ahead, with regard to a conventional *corpus* of texts — brief and highly topical — like those in the set I have examined. In broader utterances, like novels, poems or longer literary works, poeticity as a motivated feature of originality lies to a greater degree in the text's inventive and dispositive macrostructure.

Up to this point, I have spoken of poeticity as a value of non-consensual originality, which is undoubtedly the clearest form, in a negative manner, for articulating and combining the conventional feature with that of poetic value. Nevertheless, the positive poetic effects of conventionality do exist, and we do not have to discard them, although their concrete manifestation is more complex and problematic. Classical literature consecrates the known value of *retractatio*. The classical spectator of Greek and Latin tragedies found himself before themes, characters and conflicts which were familiar to him beforehand, in the sentimental situation of a poetic expectation. Conventionality, then, was a condition of aesthetic meaning in classical art (A. García-Berrio, 1981, pp. 501–527).

Still, note that *retractatio* is founded on the limitations of imitable material, by virtue of a fundamentally thematic cultural conventionalism. The advice of the classical treatise writers, crowned by the Homeric model, focus, as is well known, on lodging the conventional constancy of traditional themes in the free variability of the artistically formal. In their dispositive and elocutionary inventories there undoubtedly were greater spaces of combinatorial freedom for escaping the artistic sensation of the conventionalized. It could be argued that the powerful doctrinal foresight of rhetoric's dispositive and particularly elocutionary schemes and inventories in practice eliminates any possibility for spontaneous innovation. Yet all of these affirmations ignore the obviously non-predictive nature of these complete preparations regulated in relation to the literary situation in which they originated (A. García-Berrio, 1977, pp. 127–162). That is, since Aristotle, poetics, and especially rhetoric, create and nourish their paradigms on the basis of an earlier artistic elaboration of expressiveness.

On the other hand, one should avoid crediting the conventional-predictive reach of the elocutionary-rhetorical paradigm with too powerful an influence, in contrast to what is customarily done. If we consider, for example, one of the most conventional and familiar kinds of figures, like metaphorical catachresis, the extensive classical use of this resource, culminating in Martial, did not stop the Baroque treatise writers, including Gracián and Tesauro, centuries later, from considering the art of conceptual wit, based essentially on the development of the mechanism of catachretic metaphor, as not having been addressed before. Moreover, once tipified and exposed in enormous numbers of readings and modes, including *Agudeza y arte de ingenio* and *Canocchiale aristotelico* (A. García-Berrio, 1968; M. T. Hernández, 1986), "wit's" innovative capacity for discovering the novel "concept", even when the effect was produced in the domain of some conventionalized structural rule, as the generic frame within the broad generality of its universalist formulation, remains always free and unforeseeable.

Thus, there is a general and paradigmatic system of language and competence in the exercise of artistic practices which can be constituted historically, in effect, at the level of conventional origins. However, the distance mediating between the paradigmatic consensual rules governing competence and the diverse and unforeseeable area of their concrete execution in each artistic "speech act" is, as is well known, enormous. And even more so in the case of connotative artistic language, than in that of the competence required for the realization of communicative-practical speech acts. At least of some use in this regard is the familiar experience of the insufficiency of modern linguistic theory in illustrating the parallel phenomenon, not well known in current times, linking classical rhetorical theory with the artistic practices from which it stemmed and which followed it (V. M. de Aguiar e Silva, 1967).

In conclusion, we have argued up to this point for the inadequacy of conventionality for excluding the poetic value of literary texts. Literary space, as a specific sphere of verbal artistic practice, offers a vast area of freedom, beyond the general conventionalized paradigms. In this framework of alternatives, macro and microstructural stylistic options are exercised. These choices do or do not — that is, they unpredictably — result in verifiable aesthetico-communicative values, sanctioned in the consideration of poetic value.

The characteristic of complexity figures among those which are most unanimously accepted and cited in the artistic text by recent criticism. Notions like those of "polysemy" and "polyvalency" are derived from this feature. And through the former, critics have attempted to explain the essence of literariness in its two different modern understandings, linguistico-poetic and pragmatico-cultural. However, it is important to note that the conception summarily denominated pragmatico-cultural, which I have discussed earlier, means a "devaluation" of the objective foundations of literariness, at least insofar as they are traditionally understood (A. García-Berrio, 1979).

Just as notoriously, the option of textual complexity, together with its correlates of polysemy and polyvalency, supposes the projection over the same of two different parameters: on the one hand, that of the text itself as a concrete linguistico-cultural object produced by the author in a dialectic with his own historical present and past and, on the other hand, that of the reader, who is not only the theoretical addressee, the author's contemporary, but also the set of future readers and readings of the work. In my judgment, however, what has all too frequently happened in contemporary poetics — though in a fatally justifiable way —, is that the glitter of the new fashions of relativism, skepticism and negation have cast exaggerated shadows on traditional evaluations. Thus, sometimes because of polemical pressures, sometimes because of the limitations of personal effort, and on still other occasions because of a poor cultural formation or for snobbish reasons, a very limited and partial description of the cultural complex called the literary text is constructed, at least incomplete with regard to that other interpretation of classical art founded on a semantics of certainty (R. Barthes, 1966).

In the past, I have occasionally warned early on against the danger of these new goods or benefits (A. García-Berrio, 1977). In my opinion, the most drastic affirmations of the plurality of readings represent the greatest risk for the scientific and functional stature of the critical operation. Similarly, I feel that common sense demonstrates that an interpretation based too partially on the criteria of receptive relativism cannot replace, in the final analysis, the objective description of the text's reality, not even in the case of the most experimentally modern art (C. Segre, 1969). But it does not seem worthwhile to me for contemporary literary criticism to bury itself, once more, in purely theoretical accusations and general metatheoretical discussions. Along the general lines of my previous proposals, I would rather

2.3. The Aesthetic Capacity of Cultural Conventionality 269

undertake, in concrete terms, the description of one of textual complexity's facets: that which derives from texts' topical or traditional-literary conventional nature, an aspect I have been examining for many years now.

For reasons which are easy to understand, I have proposed observing a classical textual set which fulfills minimal conditions of representativeness or objective historico-literary importance at the same time as, because of its very textual form, it facilitates the operations of intertextual comparison in situations of adequate homogeneity. My reflections on the complexity of utterances derived from the traditional topical integration of literary works have focused particularly on Spanish love sonnets of the Petrarchist tradition, from the sixteenth and first half of the seventeenth centuries. I have studied the entire production of Garcilaso de la Vega, Fernando de Herrera, Lope de Vega, Quevedo and Góngora, which leaves little doubt that the sample fulfills the requirements demanded by scientific standards of representativeness (A. García-Berrio, 1979, 1979 d, 1980, 1980 a, 1981 b, 1982, 1983 a, 1983 b, 1984 c, 1985 b). My previous experience with the topical workings of cultural renovation and progression had centered for the past fifteen years on the domain of theoretico-literary ideas contemporary to that of the sonnets which I am now discussing. In an extensive collection of books and articles (to cite only some of the first: A. García-Berrio, 1968, 1975, 1977—1980), I have been examining the gradual flow of literary ideas through that great "Renaissance Age" of European theory between the years 1500 and 1650, which includes a set of gradual and progressive corrections to the topical doctrinal block of Renaissance poetics, resulting in the articulation of a well-outlined Mannerist poetics and a poetics, or perhaps more accurately, a rhetoric of the Baroque.

The philosophy of cultural progression which has governed the focus of these investigations is linked to the age-old tradition of cultural topics examined by E. R. Curtius (1948), albeit with the logical modifications and the advantages afforded by a more limited textual sample. In contrast to the great Swiss scholar, I have examined the evolution of a topical system, perhaps, in greater detail, to the extent that I have not pursued the evolution of generic stylemes, but that of a set of theoretical axioms and principles which constitute a closed system, like a topically restricted grammar: the set of rhetorico-poetic literary ideas which nourished the Renaissance aesthetic ideology (A. García-Berrio, 1981). The historical period taken into consideration for studying this evolution has, moreover, been much briefer in my case than in Curtius' study and, thus, more given to systematic condensation.

The key conclusions about topical evolution in the Renaissance poetic system refer in the first place to the disassembling of prejudices concerning the singularity or unique success of an author or a more or less personalized, organic intellectual group. According to my observation of thousands of individual facts, the originality of an author as a singular person, which literary history has frequently exalted, is none other than the "crystallization" in that case of a set of tendencies — or of anti-tendencies, according to the situation — operating previously, and simultaneously organically derived, by positive deduction or contrast, from the systematic set of laws regulating and organizing the topic — in this case, a theoretico-literary topic.

The personalization of the antitopical evolution is, as I have just said, the fruit of understandable and even economic simplifications of reality, establishing chronological limits between ages and currents of taste — such as Renaissance/ Mannerism/ Baroque —, though often even more drastic and inexact. Here the image of cultural "crystallization" is at work, a notion I will explain by citing a concrete example: the evolution of aesthetic ideology from the Renaissance to Mannerism is not produced in a single step nor at any one time. Consider that in speaking of the Renaissance aesthetic we are alluding to a very complex system of *topoi*. And, in the same way that diachronic phonology has already illustrated, in my opinion, the differences of behavior between the evolution of an element of the system and of the system as a whole, so too Mannerism as an aesthetic complex is the general *result* of a precise set of changing elements, which evolve at different rhythms, but in a parallel manner. Thus, at a certain moment, the arrangement of elements cannot be assimilated to previous and successive paradigms.

Focusing on our example and my own experience, we can see, basically, an evolution from content-oriented, didactic artistic consciousness to another formal-hedonistic one, defined within the polarities of the three great and most important topics of Renaissance aesthetics — *ingenium/ars, delectare/docere*, and *verba/res* —, which at a certain moment allows us to speak of a largely evolved and Mannerist aesthetic in Aristotelean treatise writers like Ludovico Castelvetro, or in Horatian commentators like Francesco Luisini. However, in none of these authors do all of the system's topics, nor even the simple relation involved in the great dualities, present a homogeneous and clear dividing line (A. García-Berrio, 1980, II, pp. 248—335).

In the literary theory of the period I have been considering, the minute study of each one of the concrete documents of poetics and rhetoric greatly complicates the clean lines of the great culturalist categories created by that History with a capital "H", at least as important and necessary as the philological verifications which test, tighten and adjust it, channeling its reflections to the current object of traditional conventionality. The text is formed as an example of minimal topical entities in a very gradual evolution, in which the features of brilliant innovation should be viewed with suspicion and valued as such in their exact dimensions as components of a topical system (J. S. Petöfi and A. García-Berrio, 1979, pp. 311—366). All of this does not mean, as we will see shortly, denying the values of literariness or poeticity, nor the hierarchies of creative novelty or successful innovative realization.

This historical verification of the topical nature of the ideas forming the system of literary theory does not imply, in my way of understanding it, the corroboration of a cultural structure of arbitrary conventions, which limit and relativize the values of artistic creativity. In any case, reflection on the theoretical system of literary topics deepens the decisive value of the literary space which accompanies each singular contribution, gestated between received conventional paradigms and the individual affirmation of modifications. This sphere belonging to the personal initiative of creation is undoubtedly reduced when it is considered isolated from the global dimensions of the general artistic system — this is exactly what is understood when a topical conception of the great cultural systems among which the literary is to be found is assumed, as I have done; nevertheless it is certainly of sufficient weight and magnitude to be able to locate in it our emotions and feelings about the singularly poetic.

Creative initiatives are inserted in the space created by this differentiation between the *individually poetic*, as the product of unconventional novelty, and the *generally poetic*, as a *relatively conventional* paradigmatic frame, nourished as novelties by their topically shaped nature. A distinction which can contribute to clarifying the double-sided understanding of another pair of distinctions — simultaneously the opposite of each other, yet not contradictory —, which I have been illustrating in this chapter; I am referring to the difference between the *negatively conventional*, understood as a restriction of the initiatives creating poetic novelty, and what we would understand as the *positively conventional*, in terms of the traditional intuition of a framework of rules and paradigms about the literary and the poetic. The individual creator assumes all of these preceptive norms, which for their part are, as I will attempt to demonstrate, a systematic expression of artistic universals, understood as principles of aesthetic necessity which are not constitutively arbitrary but which may be historically conventional. In this respect, it seems to me important to emphasize once again here the differences between the conventional and the arbitrary, since the majority of the shortcomings and confusions that have resulted from the radicalization of the literary feature of conventionality by the aesthetics of reception and the pragmatic theories of reading are, in my opinion, due to the failure to distinguish clearly between these two concepts.

To unequivocally identify the conventional with the arbitrary is in itself a form of theoretical arbitrariness, which in the best of cases confuses historically causal reasons as necessarily equivalent to the causes of essential requirements. To affirm that the author assumes a system of conventional principles and norms, which is historically true within the cultural understanding of the literary system, is not automatically equivalent to having proved that artistic initiatives, beginning with this principle, escape every non-historical system of values and categories. This way of thinking ignores the decisive space mediating between the paradigmatic and the singular realization of the text, between the generally poetic and the individually poetic which I alluded to before. Above all, it omits any reflection on the constitutively necessary reasons which determine the basic genesis and causality of the rules and principles which shape the literary system as a human instrument of privileged expression and communication. On this point I do not attempt to oppose my own convictions to those of others. On the contrary, the contents of this book attempt to set forth my justification of certain aesthetically necessary reasons, which *motivate at their source* the set of expressive-communicative options which constitute literature and poetry.

To be precise, a reflection on the Renaissance's theoretico-literary system, the experience of which has yielded our current considerations, reveals and illustrates, in the astoundingly systematic skeleton of its structural complexity, the orderly genesis and reasonable necessity with which the classical literary system proposes itself as a monumental expressive and communicative arrangement, which completes and surpasses the analogous potential of the non-artistic verbal system. Knowing the anthropological causes of poetic operations, the representative-active reasons for mimesis, the symbolico-imaginary capacities of rhythms, the natural — inventive, dispositive and elocutive — order of the constituents of discourse and, as desired, the accomodation to the aims of its intentions ... etc., the natural, non-arbitrary genesis of the set of historical rules which constitute a literary system is illustrated with undeniable clarity in the historical investigation of literary theory as a causal system of expressive-communicative necessity.

2.3.2. *Literary Tradition as a Typologizable Conventional Context*

The experience of the European classical love lyric as a systematic collection of texts elaborated according to a limited block of traditional themes, expressive structures and pragmatic conventions, points first of all to the necessary refinement of the notion of context. As I indicated before, in our own times we can justifiably speak of a certain sense of overwhelming stupor suffered by contemporary criticism after the initially enriching effort to take the social notion of context into consideration (E. Forastieri, ed., 1980). For decades, if not centuries, artistic facts had been excessively "purified" in the conception of critics and historians; literary creation presented itself as a pure dialogue, without historical contaminations, between the inspired artist and the abstract universals of poeticity and literariness. The indispensable entry of the social parameter has more adequately than ever illuminated important motifs and aspects of that metaphysical whim of intra-artistic creation. Thanks to sociocriticism, then, the notion of context has been filled with precise contents.

However, since every novelty engenders excess — or at least this is a risk many novel ideas expose themselves to —, it is worth remembering, together with social facts, the fundamental importance that the intra-literary contextual component exerts in the general historical context of a work of verbal art, serving as a conventionalized and central element of the social context. This precaution, which might seem obvious and superfluous, has nevertheless led to a collection of voids, of situations in literary historiography in which the lack of a rigorous and precise description of the literary context condemns any individual analysis of a text to lamentably bask in ignorance and simplifications. At the same time, it makes other critical functions, as necessary as decisions of assessing value or judgments regarding novelty and originality, impossible or irresponsible (A. García-Berrio, 1978 a, 1984 c).

In the case of the classical lyric, even for the period which in the different Romance literatures would stem from Petrarch to Góngora and Marino, that historical void seems too important. There is an abundance of individual studies and collections on genre, there is no scarcity of works tracing sources and influences, and perhaps the number of atomistic analytical essays could even be described as excessive. My own intention to explain the evolution of the genre in this period has made it seem necessary to realize typological catalogues, which originate in the awareness that there is no rigorous, exhaustive description, at least to the degree scientific economy would advise, of literary context. In my opinion, after stylistics in its role as a modern rhetorical hermeneutics has depleted every possible resource for finding and making clear formal stylemes in the immanentist analyses of traditional discourse, it becomes necessary and urgent to have available an adequate theory of context, before moving on to speak of each concrete lyrical text strictly in terms of novelty and value.

Such a description of the context, which must be "rigorous", requires the descriptive-formal refinements of a linguistic poetics belonging to the structuralist tradition, of a well-organized semiology, and of the contributions of formal linguistics in those concrete areas most directly relating to the explanation of the text, as corresponds to textual grammars (W. U. Dressler, ed., 1978; J. S. Petöfi and A. García-Berrio, 1979). But above all, the most fruitful assistance comes from a healthy critical attitude of confidence in the capacity of self-organization the materials of reality possess. All of which, after so many years of empirical caution, of metatheoretical speculation and of extreme parsimony in the real verification of models, will naturally help locate a path for beneficial enrichment, an exterior form of guidance and a source of literary security. Which will in turn clearly establish the concrete objective support for illustrating the physiognomy and reach of the argumentative and thematic schemes playing a role in literary tradition, which the poet *conventionally* has to accept as the starting point for elaborating texts which can be pragmatically recognized as artistic literary objects.

Normally, a classical sonnet appears to the reader, critic or historian of literature in terms of an anthropological simplification. Even well-informed readers are surprised to learn that the number of love sonnets published and attributed to Herrera far exceeds three hundred, or that those by Lope de Vega exceed a thousand, given the case that there are perhaps a hundred or so sonnets by these authors that have truly been remembered. A surprise which is even greater when, placing some of the more uninteresting sonnets of these great creators next to other contemporaneous compositions created for purely social consumption, such as the "relations" of poetic festivals and competitions, written by minor figures or even by mere local amateurs, the thematic and even constructive differences between the two sets of poems are sometimes not so noticeable so as to reveal with absolute clarity, in the case of the great writer, particular "features of his genius". Finally, even within the general work of an author, the famous, genial and anthologized sonnet — Quevedo's famous poem beginning "Cerrar podrá mis ojos la postrera", for example — is usually thought of as a uniquely effective text, with the source of its success materialized in a collection of microtextual compositional decisions, among other utterances of an objectively lesser literary value, in which, nevertheless, almost entirely identical themes and even very similar paradigms of macrotextual construction appear (F. Lázaro Carreter, 1956, p. 145).

Every literary work and therefore every classical sonnet in the example I have been developing, seems constituted as one more impulse within the organism of incalculable complextiy which literary tradition is. The classical artist at the moment of creation fixed, consciously or not, very determined traditional models. And as strong as the unconscious pressures of the concrete contemporaneous social mechanism may have been, there is no doubt that at the moment in which Góngora, for example, prepared himself to write one of his sonnets, the immediacy of his sources as models — Petrarch, Tasso, etc. — represented a degree of direct responsibility in the physiognomy of the concrete text he produced much higher than any of the biographico-social incidents affecting the author on that same day. This, I insist, does not attempt to lessen the importance of the social circumstances for Góngora's individual personality and artistic creation, nor for those of any other writer; on the contrary, it works to emphasize the importance of the facts of literary tradition as a very important part of that complex, until now not exhaustively described, which is denominated as literature's social context (A. García-Berrio, 1985 a).

Two basic aspects of textual organization seem to me to be initially relevant for establishing the general typological framework of classical love sonnets, within which the uniqueness of each text can be explained in terms of its relationship to the set. The investigation of questions of novelty or of conventional acceptance must begin, just as is the case with every text, with the necessary break-down of its structure into the set of components of *semantic* contents and into those elements which correspond to the textual organization and disposition of these semantic contents in argumentative, *syntactical* structures. Since in fact there are differences and influences independent one from the other in these two spaces of textual constitution, we are obliged to speak of two types of considerations or two different classes of influences, semantic and syntactical. This distinction seems to me, in addition to being obvious, entirely pertinent and worth stating explicitly, in view of the failure, generally, to make the distinctions observable in traditional and contemporary positivist studies and investigations of sources and influences explicit. Still, almost immediately new distinctions become necessary, since, upon considering the semantic dimensions apart from syntax, we quickly discover important aspects of the general problem of the limits between both constituents of the semiotic scheme.

However, this new reality to be distinguished in the text's linguistic structure in practice helps explain, paradoxically, many difficult decisions, the necessity for which is rooted in the problem we have just raised. In order to clarify matters, it is helpful to refer to a distinction customary in textual linguistics — but also easily linked to analogous or parallel categories in the rhetorical tradition, European structuralism and generative grammar — between *textual macrocomponent* and *microcomponent* (A. García-Berrio, 1980 a, pp. 453—454; 1981 b, pp. 148—149). Upon having to distinguish in both components the syntactical and semantic domains, the *thematic* content is much more clearly outlined as a correspondent part of macrocomponential semantics as opposed to microcomponential semantics, which in practice covers the area traditionally attributed to syntagmatic semantics. Analogously, in the domain of macrotextual *construction*, or in certain kinds of texts, textual argumentation (A. Naess, 1975; J. S. Petöfi, 1980) clearly manifests, perhaps with greater clarity than is possible at the sentential level, the distinction between syntax and semantics, hence opposing *thematics* to *construction*, and each in turn to semantics and syntax, according to the following scheme:

	Contents	Organization
Macrocomponent	Thematics	Construction
Microcomponent	Semantics	Syntax

Clearly, the practical decisions adopted in the process of formulating the typology involve a great many linguistic problems currently being debated (A. García-Berrio, 1980a, 1984b, and especially, 1983a). In my judgment, however, the intricacy of most of these questions results from their theoretical purification, which still does not impede, along general lines, the typological processing of texts prior to the configuration of a table of topical currents.

To give examples here with perhaps the most difficult and unstable point in this set of theoretical presuppositions, I will simply allude to a problem relating to the thematic level: the process of determining a text's theme. A question which has been approached almost exclusively at sentential levels (O. Dähl, 1973; P. Sgall and others, 1973), and only occasionally in its textual dimensions (Chi Ni Li, ed., 1975; L. K. Jones, 1977; J. K. Scheglov and A. K. Zholkovskij, 1979), and, even then, in a way which seems quite preliminary. The problem, however, is noticeably simplified in the kinds of texts we are focusing on, since sonnets are by definition compositions constituting a generally argumentative and unithematic textual model. Already Dante, in the debate over the lyric, called attention to the sonnet's unithematic peculiarity when he indicated that the *concept*, that is, the theme, the poem's basic semantic content, is the composition's *fabula*, equivalent to the plot in tragedies or novels (A. García-Berrio, 1975, pp. 381—382, 416). Normally, moreover, the expression of a sonnet's central theme is located in the text by a kind of *metrical rule* of composition, either in the middle zone in the most balanced Renaissance sonnets, or, in the Mannerist and Baroque sonnets of clever conceptual "ponderation" and wit, in the final terzet, forming an implicit synthesis which re-emphasized the theme developed in the rest of the poem, either manifestly or indirectly through "suspensions" or "witty ponderations", in the terms of the age (A. García-Berrio, 1983a).

The process of *determining* the text's theme, or rather that of *hierarchicalizing* the themes in the sonnet's semantic structure, is a theoretical problem which has not entirely been resolved, and is assumed in my thematic typologies, and which does not in any way invalidate the possibility of provisionally moving ahead in typological efforts (A. García-Berrio, 1978a, pp. 25—26; 1983a). In general terms, the selection of the textual topic involved in typologies of contents is based on intuitive and customary decisions routinely carried out in normal discourse, decisions which are rarely wrong. The thematic summary of a text's contents has been secularly practiced over the years in many literary operations, or in less formal contexts, as in suitably entitling a book, formulating the synthetic title of informative sections in an article or book, the successful summary in a conversation, etc. On various occasions I have had to argue against the unacceptable proposition that poetics should suspend its activity and wait before realizing any of its operations, even those bound up most closely with linguistics, until all of its theoretical problems have been adequately resolved. If this were the case, then poetics' "patience", as one more of the disciplines applying general linguistic theory, would condemn it to an unnecessary silence.

On the contrary, what I have called reality's intrinsic capacity for organization can, I believe, yield brilliant and unexpected solutions to the theoretical debate about the linguistic formulation of the problem of determining textual themes. Keep in mind that a content-based typology like that which is attempted here is basically realized as an integration of thematic classes, corresponding to previous comparisons among texts, to which a thematic identity has intuitively been attributed. Such comparative operations undoubtedly objectively reinforce the central semantic identities which were intuited to exist, and remove the marginal thematic adherences of intertextual discrepancy. Moving from this level of observation to the following one of formulating the corresponding results as systems of rules has been facilitated in my own case by the deductive method I have adopted (A. García-Berrio, 1981b, p. 169).

2.3. The Aesthetic Capacity of Cultural Conventionality

For obvious reasons, relating to the subject's very nature, and above all to the concrete circumstances of its exposition in this book, I cannot furnish a description, however summarized, of the contents of my thematic typologies. Their schematic results are to be found in the first diagram (see Figure 1; also, A. García-Berrio, 1981 b, p. 157). Basically, the chart illustrates the general procedure for any typological organization, in which the entry level, I, represents the general formula fulfilled by all of the texts in the sample, in this case the formula of the courtly love lyric.

Following the successive application of conditions at lower levels — of predication on the second, actantial conditions on the third, and thematic ones on the fourth — a pattern is produced of homogeneous groups of texts with identical thematic contents, until one arrives at the chart's terminal slots. Beyond this level of typological explicitness, it does not seem to me to be profitable or informative to manifest in the scheme subsequent thematic subclassifications, which would, in the final analysis, reach to the level of the individual text's microstructure. Still, this is a task needed in other studies in order to fully define the typological relationships of groups of texts which are thematically similar, until reaching, if that is the intention, the detail of the individual text. For an example of this kind of analysis, see my explanatory development, among other terminals, of that corresponding to *carpe diem* (A. García-Berrio, 1978).

One of the main advantages the systematization of the text's macrostructural semantic contents offers is that it permits a more explicit and developed concept than we normally have about the important literary and linguistic notion expressed by the technical term of *theme*. The formative conditions and rules corresponding to the general level of the basic predicative-actantial formula in the higher ranges of the scheme determine what, in principle, we could call the *thematic genre*. In this way, when we say that a sonnet, or any other literary utterance, is a love poem, we are not, strictly speaking, referring to its explicit contents, but to the set of rules and presuppositions which enable us to recognize it within a "genre of contents", which is different from that of religious, moral and satiric compositions, for example. The successive insertion of actants and circumstances in the next row down the diagram determines the level of specificity I call *thematic class*. At this level, the structural thematic development, beginning with the initial formula, is added to the global generality of the thematic genre. For example, in the case of love sonnets, the specification of the terminal actant in the predication of the "complaint" introduces optional thematic possibilities — love's complaint, lady's complaint, poet's complaint —, according to a trend enabling the determination of the general theme within the thematic genre. In turn, each of the terminal forms created by the actantial insertion establishes alternatives according to the specification of *complementary* actants and circumstances: confident, place, time, etc.

Finally, a specific thematic content is added to the general thematic content resulting from the previous operations; this level determines the final con-

2. Artistic Conventionality and Ambiguity

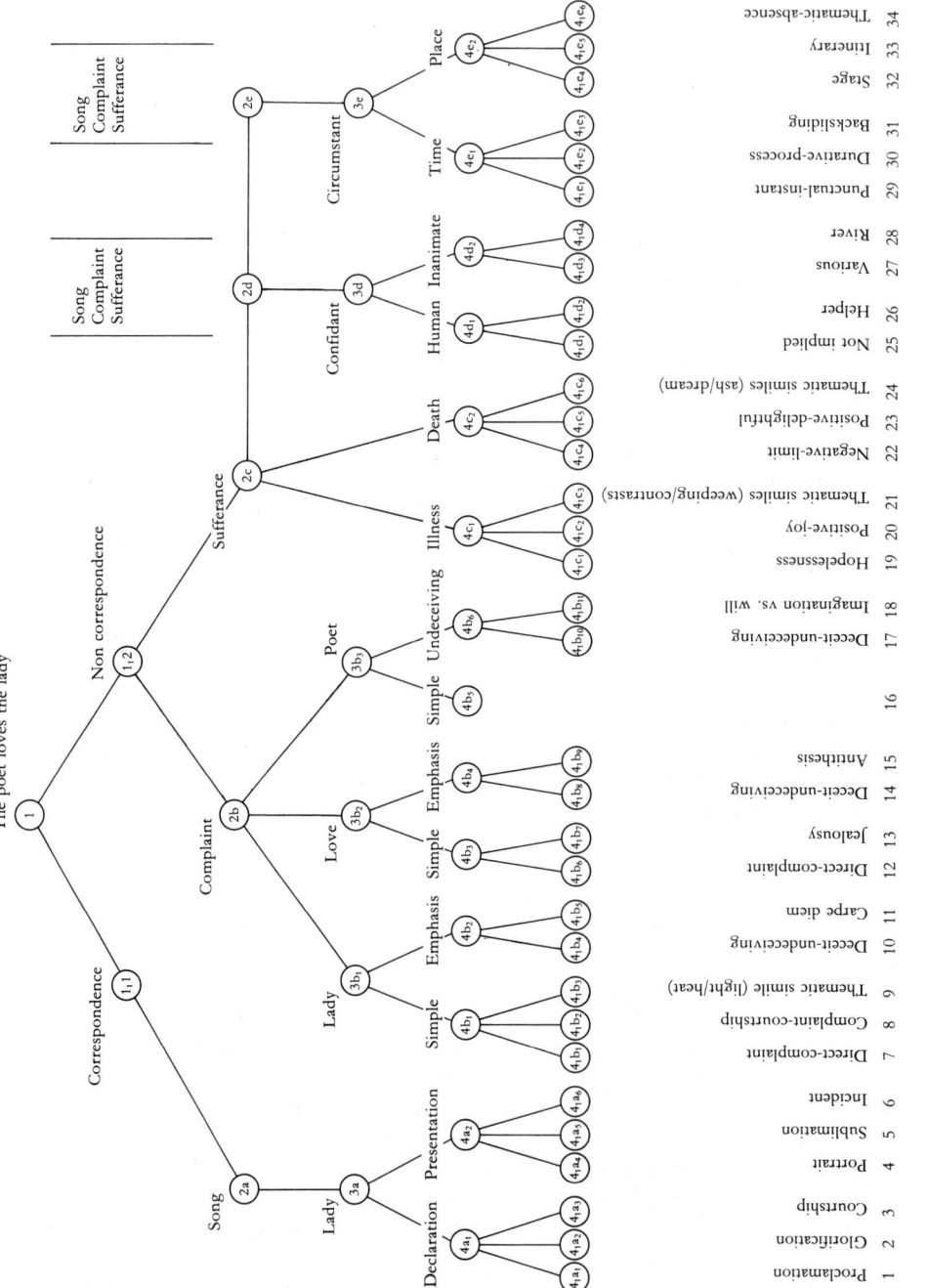

Fig. 1

stitution and appearance of the *theme*, strictly speaking. Hence, we speak of themes such as that of the lady's "portrait", or that of "declaration", both within the thematic class of the "song", a positive form of the utterance within the thematic genre of love poetry (A. García-Berrio, 1984 b, pp. 267—280).

What is truly relevant among the lessons which the thematic typology offers in our current theoretical considerations regarding the topical tradition's conventionality, derives from the undeniable fact of the surprising limitation of the thematic topics involved in a textual system of such complex appearances as that of the love lyric. In effect, the potential thematico-syntactical combinations which shape each individual text, not to mention the microtextual differences of lexematic, microsyntactic and other formalizations, contributes to present it to us — especially if we are deprived of an adequate level of typologico-topical information — as a single and unique piece. In each sonnet's textual structure the features of singularization are more obvious than the basic, shared structures. This is not to say, however, that in the process of textual construction the latter do not turn out to be highly operative and entirely decisive.

Nevertheless, the typological systematization of the thematics of classical love sonnets, for a fairly representative sample — initially (1978) of five hundred sonnets, extended without important modifications in the scheme to almost two thousand currently (A. García-Berrio, 1983 c) —, is organized around thirty four terminals. Moreover, what is even more surprising is that, in the inventory of marginal thematic features, deduced from the definition of all and each one of the sonnets, new themes do not appear. That is, the little over thirty topics determining the central thematic terminals are also distributed for other texts as secondary thematic features. In short, the general inventory of themes in the love sonnets of all of the great Spanish writers of the Golden Age is limited to a little over thirty topics.

From this perspective, each text appears to us as a complex network of elements, which is the logical result of the relative simplicity of the inventory of the system's basic components. The examination of this limited semantic repertory proves that the existence of a larger number of fundamental thematic components is not necessary for the general *corpus* of texts constructed from said inventory, with its minimal circumstantial variations, to guarantee the literary system's productive, effective and flexible operation. In this way the poet finds himself on the one hand comforted, safe in his understanding of the pragmatico-cultural prejudices of literariness, operating within a relatively restricted and definable universe of thematic arguments. But at the same time it is obvious, even from the reader's own experience, that such a thematic restriction does not ever become distressing or impoverishing.

On the contrary, the combination of such minimums and maximums in the system of the classical lyric is congruent with a certain equation of communicative economy in the literary system: thematic restriction yields textual diversity. As in so many other cases of immanent structures of semiotic systems, as recorded in various analyses (V. Propp, 1928; A. N. Samarini, 1979, pp. 309—315; I. Rezvin, 1979, p. 316; J. M. Lotman et al., 1979, pp. 191—224), this principle, which I have called communicative economy, reinforces the complexity of the system's products, which are complex precisely by virtue of the potential combinations of a basic and limited inventory.

These potential thematic combinations involve not only the association of secondary themes to the central theme, but also all of the formulas of textual construction; that is, it encompasses the macrosyntactical structure of textual argumentation, through which the macrostructure is organized, down to the boundaries of the microstructure. In effect, the typological investigation of the love sonnets' macrosyntax should occupy a similar space to that dedicated to the study of thematics (A. García-Berrio, 1979 d). As with the thematic typology, I do not believe it is useful to synthesize in this book the development of the macrosyntactical typology in all of its details. I will limit myself here to providing the general outlines and basic principles in which the real variations of the argumentative arrangement of singular texts are channeled towards rhetorico-dispositive structures, within a highly economical organization which constitutes, as with the macrosemantic thematic typology, the object of macrosyntactical typology.

In a first stage, the fundamental organizational principle of the macrosyntactical typology with which we begin is determined by the fact that lyrical compositions and especially sonnets are a special kind of text in which two different and simultaneous organizations of clauses and cæsuras, metrical and syntactical, are superimposed. When the entities of textual construction and the delimitative framework of the text's syntactical macrostructure — the sonnet, for example — coincide with the strophic cæsuras (the principal one between quartet/terzet and secondary cæsuras between the two quartets and the two tercets) a construction of textual metrico-syntactical *isodistribution* is established. I have labeled structures as *antidistributive* when the principal cæsura is not observed, and the syntactico-semantic continuity of the textual expression surpasses the limit of the terzets. In turn, isodistribution can be dual or multiple, according to whether the syntactico-textual clauses are organized in only two units around a principal cæsura or in four autonomous clauses coinciding with the four stanzas of the sonnet and its cæsuras.

The explicit or non-explicit nature of delimiting and connecting marks plays a decisive role in dual isodistribution. And, in the case of explicit marks, whether they are emphatic (imperative, exclamation, vocative, interrogation, rhetorical, etc.) or not emphatic (discursive with connectors) is important. The combination of the two organizational principles already presented raises the possibility of elaborating a basic diagram of the sonnet's textual construction, of a reach similar to that of the thematic scheme. It also constitutes the basic instrument of macrosyntactic textual classification (see Figure 2 for an example of the typological distribution of Lope de Vega's sonnets according to their macrosyntactic textual components).

				Appeal			Symptom	Representation
				Lady (Main Object)	Confidant	The Poet himself		
Exposition	Isodistribution	Dual	With explicit marks	Emphatic	Vocative Imperative	46 58 *121* 125 140 152 171 189	36	136 145 *150* 190		
					Vocative Exclamative	81 *147* *163* 195 *197*	130	63		
					Emphatic Discursive	39 83 144 164	28 173	70 101 156	2 7 11 20 *22* 33 40	
					Discursive Emphatic					
					Mixed	41 62 72 135 143	1 10 45			
				Not emphatic	Discursive	15 43 67 153 *165* *169* 184	8 *51* 47 119 120 197	141		*107*
			Without explicit marks	Intratextual Groups		17 59 60 74 *85* 88 *104* 105 *111* 133	66 82 115 129	158 161	29 48 *182* 185	
				Parallelism		25 34 44 49 53 *76* 87 113 *168* *178* 180	50 *54* 89 114 *128* 138 162 183 188	93 97	23 123	*196* *197*
	Antidistribution	Multiplex	Climax			38 62 71 106 *159* *193*	55 73 92	103	75 78	24
			Various			146 *157* 168 *176* 179 200	42 79	151 154	*149* 191	86
		Plurisentential				3 32 96 99 117 *131* *137* *142*	*198*	102	27 *76* 110	
		Unisentential				14 69 155	9 12 160		6 13 52 56 61 126 127 132 134 149 170	
Narration	Dual	Dramatized							19 68 98 148 175	39 57 87 *118* 174 181 186 187
		Narrative							4 5	41 70 *84* 87
	Multiple	Dramatized							64 166	16 30 91 *116* *172* 194
		Narrative							21 26 124	18 35 90 *122*

Fig. 2: Example of typological distribution of texts according to their text macrocomponent. It corresponds to Lope de Vega's work *Rimas* (1602–1609). Each text is indicated by the number of ordering of the edition. — The numbers in italics stand for texts of non-love contents.

The observation of macrodispositive topical convergences, which would constitute the metrico-syntactic typology of the conventional schemes of lyrical expression, must be completed with the introduction of a second *argumentative* parameter. In effect, I have already illustrated the limited nature of the number of thematic variables, and the similarly limited basic schemes of macrosyntactical distribution, between the order of the metrico-strophic clauses in their corresponding cæsuras and that of the syntactical clauses, distributing themselves in the discourse and organizing it, yielding categories that are neither numerous nor disperse. The economical nature of the argumentative schemes is both surprising and very useful, since it is more probable that the poematico-rhetorical organizations which characterize sonnets' argumentative structures would be able to be transferred with better explanatory potential to more extensive and open poematic structures like the song. Consider, for example, the very common kind of conditional-reflective argumentation organizing, among others, the structure of the discourse in Garcilaso's song "A la Flor de Gnido". The text's beginning marks the exposition of the unreal conditioner, followed by the result, the conditioned, which in turn organizes its interdependent link with the rest of the song. And the scheme of this example is repeated in constructions of many forms of argumentative types: concessive, causal, consecutive, temporal from various perspectives, etc.

From all that I have said, one may perhaps think that I am proposing an argumentative typology imitating the scheme of logical organization for the integration of simple sentences in a discourse (A. García-Berrio, 1970). In effect, I believe that the traditional schemes of neogrammatical origin contribute a good working model for characterizing some of the important and frequent structural rhetorical schemes of macrotextual argumentation. However, for this as yet unverified part of my typologies, together with the grammatical schemes, those of rhetorical origin should be taken into account, such as those organizational schemes belonging to irony, omission, etc. It is not hard to foresee that the initially grammatical schemes could be reconverted to the inventory of strictly rhetorico-argumentative schemes, in a certain stage of the future elaboration of this macrosyntactical sector of the typologies.

What the typologies in their various sections fundamentally illustrate, in view of the theoretical problem which we are interested in here, is the great complexity and strict economy of a complex literary system. Thus, the system's economy might persuade us that the supposed prejudicial and topical basis on which the system would be produced is an automatic matter, leaving no room for the kind of free options which our concept of aesthetic value and poetic quality would seem to require. However, the dense complexity of concrete textual results which that economical system produces argues to the contrary in favor of the unforeseeable freedom of the writer's literary initiative. To the simple combinatorial potential of the already numerous thematic

2.3. The Aesthetic Capacity of Cultural Conventionality

forms at the macrostructural level, expressed in each text in constellations varying between the central thematism and the marginal themes, we need to add the possible combinations introduced by the two macrodistributive parameters, metrico-syntactical and syntactico-argumentative. Moreover, it is important to indicate that the uncontrollable fund of outlined variations, relating only to the macrotextual structural order, indicates the limits on which, in turn, important microtextual stylistic decisions *begin to act*; this being the level of the traditional objects sufficient for allegations of value and poeticity in the traditional elocutive analyses of formalists, rhetoricians and stylisticians.

I believe that only from the orderly and complete determination of the rules shaping the content and appearance of a concrete literary subsystem, like the minimal one which I have sought to illustrate here with my typologies, can the structure and limits of traditional conventionality be projected. The evidence provided by this concrete example helps clarify the generic prejudicial proclamations about conventionality, poetic inoperativeness and arbitrariness, questions, along with all of those which have occupied us here, the answers to which are found to be adequately outlined in the rules governing the composition of the lyrical love sonnets we have examined. With regard to the notion of the author's creativity, I believe that the careful observation of the systematic behavior of hundreds of texts from different authors, ages and countries, forming a unitary literary and cultural system, leaves very clear the compatibility of a reduced economical space of literary conventionality with the notion of creative variety. The author's free decisions are generated in this domain of variety, linked to the estimation of the optionally contingent from which the aesthetic values of literary quality follow. But above all, the attentive and close examination of literary traditionality's contents dispels completely, in my opinion, doubts about the important role the creative vector linking the text and its author plays in shaping general and aesthetic meaning. The importance of the reader's responsibility in the construction of that universe of meaning and of the systems of cultural conventions by which the text's receiver closes the author's propositions of meaning will always play a relatively secondary role in comparison to the initiative for proposing meaning reserved, by the very nature of the matter, to the text's producer.

Of course, to the complexity of the texts of the classical love lyric we must still add the action of a very rich diversifying component, responsible in the final analysis for the most plausible appearances of individuality. The set formed by the semantic and syntactic typologies presented until now explains and allows us to measure the parameters of the textual macrocomponent's complexity. The differentiating action of the microcomponent begins here and is, more than important, decisive.

We already possess a complete inventory of stylemes for the microcomponential level, which has been, perhaps since stylistics and traditional textual interpretation, the best known textual level, the inventory of which has not been systematized in strict terms (A. García-Berrio, 1983 a). However, the microcomponent's domain represents the zone of the text's individualization, and therefore the area in which the interest and potential for typologization appear most doubtful.

Although I am aware of the need to introduce important nuances here, it still seems true to me along general lines that the text's poetic effectiveness, in the case of the Petrarchist sonnet, is very clearly entrusted to its microcomponential realization. It was at this level that the classical author could set forth the necessary corrections to the topical conditions of the cultural-literary system; that is, corrections to those conditions which are verifiable and measurable in terms of the macrocomponent's topicality. In this sense, the set of cultural conventions which the recently developed pragmatic theory of literariness has demanded — as I alluded to at the beginning of this chapter — would become obvious, in my scheme, through the economical restriction of macrocomponential syntactico-semantical manipulations, and above all in the extreme limitation of the system's thematic and constructive structures. But, as I indicated earlier, that same economical and conventional organization offers sufficient alternatives and potential combinations for corroborating the essential complexity of the textual results. The principle which provides the necessary nuance and opens the doors of conventionality to the valorizable freedom of the author's farsighted and fortunate aesthetico-poetic decisions is to be found in this area of free macrostructural options, exercised on the potential combinations of the conventional system.

As a pragmatic starting point or cultural value, literariness, then, was guaranteed within the universe of classical art by the macrocomponential level of a merely initial option; that is, any culturally experienced person knew intuitively the thematico-argumentative "literary type" which a *carpe diem* sonnet adhered to, and therefore knew it to be within the domain of an activity conventionalized as literature. But, starting from there he entered an imcomparably richer and freer universe, suggested by that very same "starting" point, of individual stylistic decisions affecting macrostructural combinations and the textual microcomponent; aesthetic value, by definition not conventionalizable, was shaped in the domain of individual options, those very options which do not force the creator towards basic structures, but to norms of realization that have not been agreed upon beforehand.

In conclusion, the classical text's complexity could therefore be defined, at least as far as the Petrarchist lyric is concerned, as a combination of the factors integrating the topical tradition. Said tradition would act in two clearly distinct blocks, imposed by the text's very linguistic nature: the system of topical instructions of literariness, more restricted and responsible for the textual macrocomponent's conventional economicity, and the set of options of poeticity, projected on the combinatorial complexity of various thematic and dispositive macrotextual and especially microtextual structures, interpreted according to very free formulas of expressive effectiveness and individual value. These formulas allow the concretion of a text's artistic value in terms of a rigorous dialectic between discovery and recognition, governed by the topical tradition.

2.3.3. *Traditional Conventionality as a Poetic Principle of Cultural Recognition*

Considering conventionality in light of the typologies I have just set forth, the universal assimilation of the feature of poetic quality or value to the condition of innovation itself should not be followed, either in the macrotext's thematic and argumentative sphere, or in that of the optional stylistic operations realized on the microcomponent. This may seem to be the case with the concrete texts the typology examined, in which the degree of topical proximity was very high as a result of similarities, be they structural (sonnets), of thematic genre (love poetry), or even of the concrete traditional mode in which they were inscribed (Petrarchist and courtly tradition). To analyze the concepts of pragmatic conventionality and topical traditionality in relation to the decisions of literariness and poeticity necessarily implies broadening the area of observation to include a much greater range of literary objects.

Not every innovation, microtextual or macrotextual, which breaks the cultural pact of the consensually agreed upon implies the incorporation of value in and of itself. As a general norm, literary novelty does not automatically yield the attribution of poetic value. In spite of everything, a certain kind of aesthetico-literary quality seems customarily to refer to the feature of innovation. This does not imply, however, that we should stop identifying cultural recognition, or the sentimental delay in the deeply familiar poetic effect of the previously known, as another potential source of poetic effects. The sentimental repetition of aesthetic values conventionalized as a cultural system can be a source of aesthetic value. I will now examine, in contrast to what in an opposite sense I have already examined and argued in this chapter, the conditions under which conventionality can be the basis for literary quality.

Before I begin, though, I would like to correct the second mistake I alluded to before, that which can follow from the current theoretical reflection on my typological analyses. Poeticity in texts of greater length and greater structural freedom than the sonnet, like the novel for example, or, in lyrical poetry, the less strictly fixed stanzaic forms like the *silva* or *romance*, can be attributed, as is only logical, to successful and aesthetically productive decisions in the inventive and dispositive spheres, thematic and structural, of the text's macrostructure.

Assimilating poeticity to novelty strictly conceived is therefore the most immediate and even conventional — if the paradox is valid — way of conceiving poeticity. This is the way modern art has commonly pursued its search for aesthetic values. This aesthetic of complete invention, which is dessired and sought in a permanent rupture with established forms, perhaps in the long run is nothing more than the simple and poor solution of escapism, or the most elemental and lazy negation. Negating form, or stylizing it in the chromatic or geometric expressionisms of a plastic abstraction which cannot in the final analysis escape some form of mimetic referentiality, is only one example of the limited nature of the alternative practiced in modern plastic arts. Negation, the formulation of the purest contradiction, does not offer a really novel alternative, but only follows the opposite direction from that of traditionality, a direction already foreseen, conceivable and discarded by custom (A. García-Berrio and M. T. Hernández, 1988 a).

Even so, I am not denying the expressive-poetic effect of supposedly anticonventional negation, which is the basis and raison d'être for the most disjunctive phenomena of modern poetry, novels and plastic arts. Nevertheless, in the anticonventional *acceleration* which has plagued modern art, the delightful balance between agreed upon traditionality and anticonventional modification or change is no longer understood and valued. The very nature of artistic *poiesis* as a constant, a certain guarantee against the risks of each age's fashions of taste and poetic variation, has been identified with this balance, up until the so-called "avant-gardes". Classical *retractatio*, in the terms we have already discussed it, constituted an exceptional source of aesthetic possibilities. But this *retractatio*, which includes by its very nature the principle of conventional permanence and the never implausible modification of the system, demonstrates an animated and plurivalent articulation between aesthetic merit and the principle of conventionality, understood not only in its usual restrictive sense of poetic value, but also dialectically open and positive as a *tradition* and a firmer guarantee of artistic poeticity.

The artistic phenomenon of the necessary and positive inclusion of traditional conventionality as a source of poetic feeling is a reality which the theoretician, perhaps due to the sheer force of current circumstances, is in the position of having to revive and restore among the fundamental and most productive literary aesthetic mechanisms. Northrop Frye has dedicated many farsighted pages to emphasizing the unforgettable role traditional conventionality plays in shaping aesthetic feeling (N. Frye, 1957 [1968, pp. 125—137]). A conventionality which we do not perceive in the majority of our reading acts, but which nevertheless forms the nucleus of our aesthetic understanding (N. Frye, 1957 [1968, p. 127]). In a way which coincides with my own analyses, Frye links the principle of conventionality with tradition, affirming that human beings do not create *ex nihilo*. In so doing, the great Canadian critic takes note of the Mannerist and transtextual basis of all poetic creation in its most positive terms: "poetry can only be caused by other poetry" (1957 [1968, p. 128]). Certainly, Frye's positive conception of the relationship between conventionality and tradition differs from the negative point of view inherent in Derrida's "graft" and Bloom's "misreading" (1973, 1975).

2.3. The Aesthetic Capacity of Cultural Conventionality

But in my opinion the single greatest insight in Frye's extensive examination of the phenomenon of conventionality consists in his lodging the question in its proper problematical place: indirectly he proclaims conventionality as the sequel to the "universal spirit", most exclusively expressed by poetry. Through this generalized encouragement, poetry can be sublimely communicative. The poetic universal takes its literary form as a conventional archetype, "a typical and recurring image", acting as the glue binding the great variety of poetic realizations together, forming the general unitary force of literary expression (1957 [1968, p. 130]). Naturally, the feature of traditional conventionality appears in differing degrees from one work to another, while remaining clearly visible in its minimal expression. Frye recognizes this in his own distinction between "completely conventional" art, present only in Eastern dances in their pure archetypal state, and "relatively conventional" art, such as we know it in the Western tradition and which, at the same time, appears with a greater archetypal density in so called "naive" or "spontaneous" poetry than in strongly individualized and personal poetry.

The principle of traditional conventionality appears therefore as one of the most inevitable and decisive frameworks shaping art; hence, the importance of its role in the phenomenon of literature's poeticity. In conventional convergences that identification of the roots of taste is produced which can be particularly productive in the feeling of artistic aestheticity. Frye also indirectly emphasizes the inevitably conventional nature of every artistic work, even those animated by the most radical spirit of novelty, when he recalls Coleridge's notion that literature which tries to escape conventionality only ends up falling back into it (1957 [1968, pp. 136−137]). A phenomenon which I recognize, identically, operating in the exaggerations of programatic negativeness in the art which proclaims itself anticlassical, but which never, in my opinion, achieves the complete eradication of classical art's conventions (A. García-Berrio and M. T. Hernández, 1988 a). Perhaps this is the case because the essential conventionality which underlies art's classical mode, joined to the artistic structure of universals of human feeling, is the aesthetic's necessary and eternal essence.

The feeling of traditionality dislodges the purest emotions concerning the artistic from the negative shadows of arbitrary gratuitousness which conventionality projects in its most recent echoes. It is reasonable to assert, as has been proclaimed since Jakobson, that the notion of recurring parallelism acts decisively in shaping literary emotions. The phenomenon has been restricted until now, however, to being more easily perceived at the phono-acoustical and formally grammatical levels. But the same recurring mechanism governs what has customarily been understood as conventional and repetitive on the thematic level. It is a repetition, we know, which is pure and never identical; but a reiteration, the traditional, which rescues innovation and exploits the sentimental inertias of well-known and poetic material. Within traditionality as a legitimizing level of the literary-conventional, a common and general feature extending to the entire textual entity, the literary phenomenon of the recurrent acquires the nature of a consubstantial element.

Contrary to superficial appearances, I have just indicated that a critical awareness of the feature of reiterative semantics — or representative semantics — is older than the formal recogition of this, only brought to the attention of contemporary theoreticians after Jakobson's poetological reflections. It suffices to recall any of the Horatian pronouncements on *retractatio* (A. García-Berrio, 1977—1980, I, pp. 135 ff.), which are not, in turn, anything more than successful literary formulations of commonly accepted knowledge. Even the most ancient texts give very satisfying explanations of the intimate, anthropological causes of the mechanism. Hence, in the first of them all, Aristotle's *Poetics*, we have the familiar passage about *mimesis* as the cause of poetry. There, Aristotle (*Poetics*, 1448 b, 15—20), like Lukács and Bakhtin in our own century, characterizes mimesis' poetic gratification in terms of the pleasure of *re-cognition*. Therein lies the radical difference between scientific knowledge as the total discovery of an enigma and poetic knowledge as the special and pleasant illumination of a previous objective knowledge (A. García-Berrio and M. T. Hernández, 1988 a, pp. 112 ff).

Clearly, the Aristotelian explanation — along with that of the two excellent modern theoreticians of realism alluded to before — refers to recognition within the wider sphere of the artistic representation of the phenomena and events, beautiful and even disagreeable, of reality. Traditional — or conventional — literary recognition only affects the effects of mimesis already formulated in texts which are objects of convention. We are thus dealing with the chain of recognitions of a Mannerist kind, interior to the works of the literary series. However, I see a common causal-affective root underlying both forms of recognition: the pleasure of the familiar, of "terra cognita", as a unique defense against the intellectual acceleration of scientific knowledge.

It seems that what is unique to artistic knowledge consists of an effortless and very natural capacity for installing itself, as a starting point, in customary spheres of experience, in which experience itself feels safe and protected. This is the situation which, nevertheless, is propitious to the dazzling lightning bolt of foreseen abysmal experience, which is laboriously grasped in the procedures of poetic expressiveness. A starting point, then, which has to do with the certainty provided by our safest surroundings, precisely because it has to make possible the most hidden and deep modes of illuminating the abyss of our own symbolic and referential forms of essential orientation.

The conventional familiarity of the literary universe and its values, when founded on the propulsive naturalness of great texts of art, seems to include the obligatory registering of the peculiar manifestation of the poetically sublime. The renovated itinerary of great works, and the network of familiar references in which they are lodged, create the poetic situation yielding the best fruits of our aesthetic knowledge of literary experience. Cultural conventionality in literature, as a familiar and recognized situation, is, from this point of view, one of the most positive factors of the general poetic effect. Thus we see the kind of protective guide tradition offers as a sentimentally and imaginatively ideal situation from which the highest experiences of poetry originate. Traditional conventionality, positively conceived, need not be defended from the accusation of de-naturalizing the poetic, but rather held up, from our own point of view, as one of its most capable formative features.

However, it is worth differentiating this traditional poetic value of literature and art from the conventional conceived as a purely arbitrary feature of literature's constitutive system, to zealously rescue it from the conceptual contamination this latter view represents, being the allegation normally made by those proposals seeking to relativize or negate general and aesthetic meaning. Feelings about the poetically unique, the new, the different or anomalous in the artistic system, appear controlled and aesthetically powered because they are defined and singularized on the basis of their inclusion in the complex sentimental and familiar gears of the traditional and the conventionally artistic. The literary system founded by tradition is not, as I have already said elsewhere, absolutely unmotivated. Its raison d'être rests on the fact that it nourishes the aesthetic form of experience. A structure of recognition shaped in the image of man and his systems of representing the world. The literary system founded by tradition materializes a necessary, expressive and communicative aesthetic organism, through which man is able to define and testify to his deepest questions and answers about the anthropological structure of his own universe.

The compatibility between the far from trivial feelings of anthropologically affective emplacement which constitute the conventionalized space of literature and the superficial and immediate constancy of conventional recognition, is made possible by the "everyday" nature revealed by the fundamental anthropological depth of the literary universe. The fatal confusion between well-founded tradition and gratuitous convention can only be attributed to precipitousness and analytical weakness. Which is not to deny that it is very true that historically one always begins with the conventional assumption of the rules and principles which constitute the literary universe.

Nevertheless, we must recognize the great responsibility conventionality has in the production of the cultural-poetic effect: not capricious or intranscendent, as it is often understood today, but possessing a powerful capacity for aesthetic genesis; even in the case of recognizing, in its origins, a radical basis in gratuitousness. But, what is more, that causal capriciousness does not in fact exist, since, as we will see in subsequent chapters of this book, the literary system lodges and links the text's formal mechanisms within a recognizable complex of principles of anthropological and fantastic communication, which provide man with the best instruments for his most intimate expression. These formal mechanisms of the text — artistico-verbal, plastic and purely sonorous — themselves constitute forms incarnated in the space of the signifier in order to channel symbols and impulses in which the human being translates, recognizes and communicates his poetic knowledge, the deepest and most unstable, the most necessary and instantaneous.

The old Bakhtinian requirement — ignored until now — of elevating material formalist compositional poetics to the general aesthetics of "architectonic forms" is perceived exclusively in this outline of the essential motivation of the historically conventionalized literary system. In the first place because this system registers, as in Bakhtin's reasonings, the analysis of the causal connection between the text's "compositional structures" with the physiognomy of the outlines, projected from them, of the architectonic forms Bakhtin called for. The homologous but inverse insertion, the projection of the architectonic's theoretico-artistic paradigms on texts' compositional elements, recognizes in anthropologico-aesthetic universals the raison d'être of its mechanisms of progression and expansion. The aesthetic universals overlie the architectonic forms, lending them a concrete nature and physiognomy, analogous to how expressive anthropological requirements underlie and provide the reason for texts' material forms.

The literary universe is thus constituted as a system endowed with four levels of harmonious and homogenous resolution: the expressive factors of anthropological symbolization, the verbal representation in the artistic text, the paradigmatic structure of the architectonic forms of the literary system and, finally, the set of aesthetic universals. In such an extensive network, with such coherent and necessary correspondences, it does not make sense to treat the historical phenomenon of literary conventionality as entirely arbitrary and capricious.

The importance of the traditional context in the constitution of aesthetic feelings regarding literature and art turns out to be such an undeniably decisive factor that its influence is felt both in my own typological analyses of classical *retractatio* and in the considerations and interests of the great American critic, Harold Bloom. Bloom's focus on the intertextual concept of *influence* at the heart of his critical preoccupations is well-known; in fact, it has become so central that it has come to be formulated in terms which displace the existence of texts as autonomous entities. Recall, in this regard: "Influence, as I conceive it, means that there are *no* texts, but only relationships *between* texts". Thus, we inevitably receive and read a text filtered, consciously or unconsciously, through other texts (the principle underlying Bloom's concept of "misreading"). Hence, the reader's reception does not differ in this respect from the phenomenon of the contamination and filtering of influence in the act of writing by a text's creator or first codifier: "The influence-relation governs reading as it governs writing, and reading is therefore a miswriting just as writing is a misreading" (H. Bloom, 1975 [1980, p. 3]).

The chief difference between Bloom's traditional concept of influence and that which I have set forth in these pages lies in Bloom's placing such an emphasis on the negative condition of *anxiety* and rejection through which

2.3. The Aesthetic Capacity of Cultural Conventionality

the Romantic poet, according to him, defends himself from the influence of his poetic forefathers, through the famous process entailing six stages or movements (H. Bloom, 1973 [1975, pp. 14–16]). This continues to constitute, in my judgment, the most enriching and substantial critical *map* which the widely debated and distinctive critic has contributed to literary historiography, especially that specializing in the period of antithetical Romantic poetry. Compared to the willing submission to the principle of "imitatio" proclaimed formally as decorum by classical artists after Homer, the modern poet, under Milton's shadow, fears tradition above all as a threat against his own autonomous consciousness: "The poem [Bloom here is describing the situation of the "ephebe" in rebellion] is *within* him, yet he experiences the shame and splendor of *being found by* poems — great poems — outside him. To lose freedom in this center is never to forgive, and to learn the dread of threatened autonomy forever" (1973 [1975, p. 26]). But, certainly, the traditional context is to be found *active* and *influential* in both senses: the positive and synthetic adherence of my typological examinations, and the negative, anguished one of the antithetical defense mounted by the Romantic and modern poets favored in Bloom's analyses.

As a result of this first differential factor — in my opinion a distinction only rhetorically irreducible — a second important component can be invoked. My consideration of tradition as an element of conventional poeticity is based fundamentally, as we have just seen, on an examination of the highly topical system of classicist poetry of the period from the Renaissance to the Baroque, a poetry dominated by the technical ideology of *convergence* in "imitatio"; Bloom's theses, on the other hand, are nourished by the historical sense, also very real and proven, of *resistances* and asphyxiating feelings of radical independence and originality perceived in "strong" modern poetry, from Wordsworth, Blake and Shelley, to Whitman, Stevens and Ammons. And while my schemes show the channels by which Homer, Virgil and Petrarch are constituted as referential foci which the classicist poets sense as authorized and benevolent protection and *shelter*, the gigantic figure of Milton raises the symbol of antithetical provocation for Bloom's analyses of English poetry. A thesis which, since *The Visionary Company*, has been increasingly powerful in Bloom's thought, according to which, for example, all of Shelley's poetic production from "Prometheus Unbound" to the unfinished "The Triumph of Life" is governed, like that of Blake or Wordsworth, by that "ambition to replace the Paradise Lost" (H. Bloom, 1961 [1987, p. 283]).

According to this theory, one can accept as a general principle, of course, that the great symbols of poetic "strength" Bloom habitually invokes, from Homer to Dante (H. Bloom 1989, pp. 27–50), Shakespeare to Goethe, move in a different age — an "antediluvian" age, in the myth Bloom avails himself of to characterize Shakespeare's poetic power in *The Anxiety of Influence*. A diverse poetic age nevertheless formed solely by the transfiguring, unique strength of Shakespeare's genius. In these terms, Bloom may correct A. D.

Nultall, in the sense that "the difference between the world that Shakespeare saw and ours is to an astonishing degree Shakespeare himself" (1989, p. 56). In any case, we are faced with this proposal of two radically different worlds. But, nevertheless, the contextualizing power of literary tradition is equally decisive and formative on each side of this never well-defined frontier of transition separating classical art from modern Romantic art. "Strong" poets owe their greatness to the intertextual stimulus whether they produce texts under a program of imitative adherence, or antithetical rejection.

Moreover, it is worth noting that not even the radical, central opposition between these two contradictory dynamics of tradition appears so neatly profiled historically. In the first place, one could invoke, to de-radicalize Bloom's theses of the "anxiety of influence", the detailed empirical arguments which the historians of Romanticism and modern English poetry have used to sharply object to his claims: the unassimilative and antithetical attitude which Bloom, almost without exception, applies to any creative movement of his favored poets does not always appear as clearly and explicitly in these author's works, in the judgment of many of the specialists on the individual poets concerned. I for my part can add the detail that the often proclaimed tendency toward the positive approach to the models which, along general lines, appear to govern the topical universe of classicist poetry, must be recognized as a general program or rule of principles against which profound individual transgressions were innumerable and subtly insinuating. For example, my historical analyses document the frequency with which, in the literary theory and artistic practice of the Renaissance and Baroque, the most substantial and immediate sources were concealed behind the massive use of ostentatious and false erudition and the citation of merely conventional and even purely decorative "authorities" and antecedents (A. García-Berrio, 1973). Even in the case of the great sources of tradition, like that opened up by Petrarch's *Canzoniere*, one can clearly observe how the initial model is progressively depleted. In the long run, Petrarchist intermediaries are more active, subtly but tenaciously modifying the originality of the Petrarchan textual models, having a greater influence than the direct impact exercised by their original source. Hence, often many of the most conspicuous followers of the amorous lyric of Petrarch's *Canzoniere* can be justly described, to use an expression I have often employed elsewhere, as "Petrarchists without Petrarch".

Undoubtedly, the faithful obedience to models and authorities as required in the classical program of *retractatio* and *imitatio* clashed with narcissist individualism, whether repressed or not, in the case of many if not all of the great classical creators. Without a doubt, the strong "poets", as Bloom himself recognizes in the sample and elastic space of the classicist myth, pursued the egocentric defense, without complexes, of their own independence, eagerly seeking originality as an ostensible value. What we can also affirm simultaneously is that the art of antiquity as a whole does not historically demonstrate the hysteria of antithetical independence that is programatically visible in Romanticism and, as an essential constitutive principle, in all of the "strong" and "weak" artists of the artistic avant-garde. Both that which is displayed in the one case and that which is avoided and passed over in the other are extraordinarily active traditional stimuli, which leave the contagion of their conventional evocation on the most proven poetic valencies of new texts; in such a way that the responsibility of the conventionalized traditional context cannot in any way — neither positively nor antithetically — be denied when the time comes to set forth the most decisive factors in the sense and judgment of poeticity and literary dignity.

In Bloom's case, moreover, it is worth arming oneself against personalist excesses which may easily result from the truly unique fascination and vigor of his critical discourse; because his historical diagnoses deliberately confuse the objective motivation — unobjectifiable according to his universal principle of "misreading" — of the authors read or criticized, grouping them together with the critic's own passions and ambitions. Hence, as examples of this tendency we might cite the tormented ambiguity of the Yahwist J and of the other biblical authors, defined Bloom through a Freudian filter as "a contradictory stance mixing love and hate" (H. Bloom, 1982, p. 58), or the other general principle of the "defense against the text" which Bloom attempts to insert in the historical attitude of the defensive retractions of the Hebrew agnosticism of the kabbalists from Cordovero to Luria and Scholen (H. Bloom, 1975a). Also one notes his provocative claims concerning the limitations of criticism, for example: "Criticism is not going to discover the truth any more than philosophy is going to uncover any truth" (H. Bloom, 1982 [1983, p. 42]). All of which exudes the singular personal passion of Bloom's character, of his incoercibly obsessive passion for originality and the defense against the contagion of any other, foreign, external discourse; all the more dramatic in a personality possessing the "total recall" of Bloom's critical genius. In many cases Bloom does not attempt to conceal his discovery of the dramatized trope of his own desire in the texts read, as at the end of the first chapter of *The Breaking of the Vessels*: "Poetry and criticism alike usurp strength only by invoking the language of desire, possession, and power, and such language, to me, seems inevitably the language of Gnosis". And, in conclusion: "I end this chapter by openly confessing an aestheticism, which is the only justification of our readings and unreadings, of the poets and ourselves" (H. Bloom, 1982, p. 140).

Personal inertias are stirred up in Bloom's powerful modern and universal culture, anxiously trying to define the space of an independence bound by time within the continuum of his convergence with the startling revelations of traditional Hebraic culture, orthodox and kabbalistic — recall Cordovero's "behinot" projecting itself on the scheme of six basic movements in the revisionist stance, or Isaac Luria's influence on the legitimate activity of "misreading" —, with the intense affinities with all of the great poets of

Anglo-American modernity, from Shelley to Stevens, with the recovery of Emerson's pragmatism, and particularly with the revisionist solidarity felt with Freud and Nietzsche. The current legitimacy of his independent modernity is intimately linked with the total assault of his personal critical independence, in terms not externally different from the desire for the creative, hedonist independence of critical discourse that encouraged the pursuit of critical writing and reading in Barthes' "pleasure of the text", or de Man's deconstructive "resistance". Still, the license taken with the textual entity and its meaning are always positivized in unexpected and extraordinary ways in Bloom's case; because his defensive maneuvers aim at antithetically surpassing the text's presence, his desire to programatically "misread", does not weaken his inevitably penetrating intuitions of the textual entity as certainty.

Bloom's antithetical conception of a literary tradition dominated by the anxiety of influence, like the underlying concept of "misreading", articulate the defensive needs of a powerful cultural memory nourished by the indelible presence of Harold Bloom. It is not that he, like his favorite tormented poets, Keats, Shelley or Whitman, cannot assimilate the meaning of the texts read; it is that he does not want to: he avoids it. In this manner the attempt is made to combat the anguished ghosts of a faithful and total recall, which would block, with the weight of their historical experience, any path towards the affirmation of oneself as an individual. In any case, both the antithetical tradition governed by Bloom's set of defensive strategies — from the Clinamen to Apophrades — and the basic mechanism of "misreading" do not clearly constitute an objection to the historical workings of traditional intertextuality, modulating and cooperating in the constitution of poetic meaning, as underlined in their negative inversion of this phenomenon.

2.3.4. Artistic Ambiguity as a Poetic Property

Ambiguity is a familiar resource (W. Empson, 1930), described and typologized by literary critics long before it was welcomed by and linked to the hypotheses of the open work's infinite polysemy which have circulated in literary criticism for the past twenty or thirty years. The obvious and verifiable phenomenon, consisting in the tendency to accentuate the referential polyvalency of meaningful elements, has for years now brought about, as I have demonstrated in previous sections of this book, a current of exaggerated affirmations concerning the value and role of polysemy in art.

Up to this point, I have attempted to control this overly capacious inertia, with its scarcely positive effects on the critical exercise's usefulness and rigor. On the other hand, it is worth affirming polysemy's true and positive role as a fundamental factor in the poetic effect. Until now, when I have sought to correct the exaggerated affirmations of the polyvalency of the meaning of artistic utterances, I have been particularly opposed to an understanding of ambiguity as playing a basically negative and limiting role in poetic meaning.

That is to say, according to this view, the artistic text lacks the capacity to induce and control the reader's meaningful associations. These products of reception would be legitimized, in that exaggerated hypothesis, by the utterance's radical weakness. And although the argumentative reduction which I propose may seem unrealistic, it seems nevertheless true that this is how those who, like the more essayistic Barthes and his more submissive followers, have in practice affirmed the unverifiable legitimacy of any attractive reading whatsoever.

The phenomenon of positive ambiguity, which has its antecendents in concrete classico-rhetorical practices as illustrious as the use of equivocal words and expressions, irony, omission, amphibology, metaphor and even allegory itself, is one of the artistic text's fundamental powers for achieving poetic effects and values. Ambiguity is formed in language's regulated and historical capacity and develops and is extended through the regular space of the licit conceptual associations of fantasy and its laws; in short, in the unchaotic, orderly space of the imagination's constructions.

Artistic ambiguity and its poetic powers always emerge from a background of positive individual or collective activity and never from the text's absolute void, from a space of emptiness. The meaning deduced by a reader from the gaps of a work is that reader's *ex novo* creation, independent from the original text. It is a new text weighted against any voluntary authorial meaning. To represent new meanings created from the text's voids as linked to the reference of the text in question is a senseless, sterile or simply fraudulent effort. And this is basically the kind of mistake which was sometimes made to pass as valid by receptive criticism a few years ago, and which it is perhaps not right to refer to anymore, strictly speaking, as modern and contemporary.

The calculated construction of ambiguously meaningful figures is among artistic talent's most positive capacities in authors of any period. Semantic polyphony as a plural form of associative resonance, as the expansion of the powers of suggestion, is a feature of literary talent in classical and modern art alike. But the recognition of this fact implies the very opposite of the text's displacement as the source for the formulation of artistic meaning; rather, it reaffirms the responsibility of creative authorial talent.

Muddling the explanations of this textual capacity for polysemy invariably results in confusion. Sometimes the reader, faced with a range of possible meanings, believes he has found — as certainly may often be the case — the author's intentional, conscious calculation. To suppose an author, even the greatest such as Cervantes, Horace or Shakespeare, is conscious of all of the possible alternatives foreshadowed in the text, of each one of the potential combinations that can be extracted from the network constituting the text's meaning, would be to attribute to him an almost inhuman ability for associative prediction.

But the authorial talent for foreseeing alternative receptive interpretations, which has nourished the most stimulating hypotheses of the aesthetics of reception and which also justified, in its time, the attractiveness of Eco's thesis of the "reader in the story", does cease being the author's responsibility, creating meaning even when it is not necessarily a consciously foreseen mechanism. The subtle ability to ponder the poetic utterance's meaningful resonance, figures as one of the psychological secrets of every great artist's innate talent. A very rare talent for surmising or foreseeing the powers of suggestion of a word or a poetic utterance certainly forms part of what is most unique to the great creators' talent.

In short, among the constitutive parts of a unique poetic talent is the ability to consciously foresee a multiplicity of meaningful suggestions and the intimate ability to sense potential echoes and resonances of meaning. The best proof of this is provided by the meaningful opacity of artistic texts by authors deprived of any such brilliance. Only the undue generosity of an extravagant reader can involve him in the task of combining alternative meanings with the pieces of a dull text; only the autonomous genius of that capricious reader — who, in such a case, cannot be considered purely as a reader — could infer interesting meanings from inane texts. A principle and system not different, in effect, from those which the notions of infinite readings put into play with regard to the author's itineraries of textual meaning. A legitimate task of the "pleasure of the text", undoubtedly a metalinguistic action, a creative and even philological literary activity, but essentially not a *critical* one, unless one strips literary criticism of all of its consolidated and specific hermeneutical contents. A fairly unfruitful sacrifice that Humanism surely has no reason to accept. We would lose a great deal, in my opinion, by renouncing the tradition that has been consolidated of interpreting literary messages as critical mediations, in favor of this modern genre of artistic writing, of free paraphrases; with a very uncertain future and tolerability. I simply believe that we currently are not obliged to pay excessive attention, in the critical field, to the extravagant amusement of playful capriciousness.

The capacity for the conscious authorial foresight of alternative meanings in fact is inferior to the exponential potential meanings deposited and treasured by artistic texts; this being, moreover, the essential characteristic of the great classical or eternal work of art. The origin of this mysterious capaciousness is rooted in the nature of the instrument literature works with: language in its dialectical relationship with history (A. García-Berrio, 1989a, p. 124).

Every linguistic form the speaker acquires and possesses is a provisional loan, a token of a historical cultural inheritance rooted in the past and destined for the future. In such a way that, when we mobilize the linguistic forms at a given moment with the intention for meaning to which the circumstances of their formulation destine them, we are aware only very partially and very limitedly of the meaningful and referential potential we are actualizing. All of the other submerged valencies, especially the sentimental and aesthetic values which tradition has deposited in that form, are not commonly abolished in the concrete pragmatic stamp of our occasional use. And the same is true in the case of great authors, privileged users of that historical aesthetic accumulation.

Because it is a historical form, the verbal utterance survives any speech act; it surpasses it — already, in turn, forming part of the diachronic fund for subsequent experience —, and lies at the mercy of the contingent nature of its future contexts. This is how the reader of contemporary and past literary works discovers at his disposition *closed but suggestive* utterances. The metaphor of the open work is fulfilled only as regards the text's potential for openness to suggestion; the open text, at least in the case of texts of language, is, as practice demonstrates, a purely hypothetical desideratum. The existing text is delimited, closed, by the very nature of its necessary formulation at the margins of emptiness and silence. In the unique space of artistic formulations, the singular tension of poetic texts *distends* them more towards meaningful capacity, towards ambiguity as a form of *openness*.

Confronted with the suggestive metaphor of the "open work", the truth emerges: the solid and affirmative block of the verbal utterance possesses a necessary structure of meaning. Everything else is playing with paradox. The modern experimentation with the potential referential combinations of verbal meanings in surrealism's vanguardist writings and in the futurist's phonic or graphic combinations, of Apollinaire, of visual poetry and the conceptual plastic arts, is neither wrong nor excessive. But behind all of it the most immediate question of the problematical nature of these productions and the true extent of their radical rupture with the canonical and classical systems of creating meaning always remains open. In particular, consider the already demonstrated aesthetic inferiority of Vassarely or Schoenberg compared to Michelangelo or Beethoven; together with the as yet undemonstrated superiority of Joyce over Cervantes or Boccaccio.

It is not my intention to deny the legitimate need for progress in the arts and, as such, the need for modern art. I count myself among those persuaded of the validity of the latter's raison d'être, and among those who believe that the pure fascination of the basic meaningful forms and entities of informalism and abstraction contributes a necessary and decisive revitalization to the mimetic period's masterpieces, which in occasion find themselves impoverished by the anecdotal nature of their most conventionally referential faithfulnesses. The essential magic of El Greco's ancient saint, presiding over the living room of the Frick mansion in New York, is produced by the symphony of Venetian purple in the reddish robe and the snow white of the disordered hair and long venerable beard. This is the visual impact of the aesthetic representation as I recall it, more imposing than the anecdotal iconography or the symbolic references denoted by mimesis. Which is not to say that the symbolization of the most elemental constituents of artistic imitation is not symbolico-expressive or even mimetic. I am only affirming that the unavoidable mimetic content of every artistic production, reduplicative of the real, is rooted in the most essential and necessary anthropological expression (A. García-Berrio, 1991).

Meaningful polyvalency, ambiguity, polysemic capacity — call it what you will — it is one of the fundamental characteristics of artistic language; perhaps, as Empson, Jakobson and Lotman, among many others, have claimed, its primary characteristic. This has been the case since art and literature were founded in the West as procedures for constructing mythical models of experience alternative to the hypothetical constructs of scientific reason and philosophy. But circumstances make it necessary to add that in recent times the objective recognition of this fact has been subjected to fairly inexact and sterile critical exaggeration. The artistic work's ambiguity, that ambiguity which is worth proposing as a legitimate and necessary space requiring critical explanation, is controlled by the text's responsibility as an initiative of the author lodged in history. Useful critical reflection on the variations of meaning located in the text's proposals must travel the rich range of alternatives authorized by the text as presence, and not those which a reader's own marginal initiative might suggest based on the text's emptiness.

Today as always, to affirm the feature of ambiguity, of meaningful polyvalency, as a positive and fundamental condition of artistic language, implies assuming and making all of these points very clear, an effort of clarification motivated by the polemical exaggeration of a true principle, excessively and inexactly enlarged and deformed by some critics. Literary criticism as a recognized and recognizable discipline is based on and limited by the nature of its *volition* for exegetic mediation, stemming from the historical *interest* of human beings in a series of complex, passionate messages codified under agreed upon conditions of artistic communication. In our own times, under the general stimulus of the modern myth of "writing" (R. Barthes, 1957a), a paraphrastic kind of writing, with an integral artistic vocation, which has only its metalinguistic paraphrasis in common with literary criticism, has nevertheless begun to approach and be incorporated into the traditional body of literary interpretation. It is not a matter here of approving or rejecting these serious modern forms of paraphrastical writing; rather, we are only concerned with providing the necessary nuances and distinctions to avoid confusing the objects, methods and aims of criticism as a discipline emerging from a theory of literature.

Up to this point, I have been considering the phenomenon of artistic messages' ambiguity and meaningful polyvalencies in an absolute way. In so doing, it is necessary to avoid the limitations of the traditional-rhetorical approach, which has customarily used the microtextual framework for considering the questions of language and meaning. In general, there is a tendency to focus the ambiguity of artistic forms under the individualist, lexico-semantic consideration of the word's polysemy. Nevertheless, in the pragmatics of general and artistic communication, ambiguity, like any other microstructural characteristic, originates and is reflected in macrostructural correspondences.

2.3. The Aesthetic Capacity of Cultural Conventionality

Modern critical debate has frequently demonstrated the double level into which the problem is broken down; although it has not always proceeded with very meticulous discriminative farsightedness.

That is to say, the traditional lexico-semantic feature of artistic polysemy, limited by traditional rhetoric to the space of individual lexical forms, is obviously a general linguistic phenomenon, necessarily extending to the text and the global dimension of the utterance. Under this macrostructural reference, the phenomenon of the artistic ambiguity of literary messages reveals one perspective of observation which tends towards zero and another, quite the opposite, which theoretically tends toward its exponential amplification. On the one hand, the author's communicative will, creating constellations of meaning in the text, outlines and defines the erratic plurality of polysemic valencies of the isolated component pieces and units. But, in the opposite sense, and above all — lacking the decodifying vocation centered on the author's integrative will — if one plays more with the speculation of the potential combinations of objective initiatives at the disposition of the readers' semasiological game, the sum of the utterance's optional constituents of meaning as a global text far surpasses any calculation of the literary text's ambiguity, due to the plurality of individual combinations its components make possible.

In the classical text's general construction, the author's communicative and monosemicalizing will almost inevitably plays a role in the valencies privileged and displayed by the text as a message. In the same way, in "modern" texts, at least, since Mallarmé and Joyce, in those in which the opposing desire for absolute meaningful openness abounds, authors search for and exploit all of the meaningful combinations which the polysemical capaciousness of each one of the text's constituent entities leaves open.

Fundamental mechanisms in the artistic text's poetic constitution, a message's ambiguities constitute an essential ingredient of its poeticity. It follows from this that, in the various arguments presented in this chapter, I have been making the effort to "positivize" for aesthetics that which remains distant and useless within the skeptical and negative tendency of the analytical technique of Derridean deconstruction, or that which is verifiable in the dogmatic fragility in the experience of a Romantic criticism like that of de Man.

Poetry, and particularly high poetry, approaches its aims through the skeptical glimpse of the uncertain, through the "ruin of sacred truths" (H. Bloom, 1989). However, it does so by means of a perfectly evident plan of conflicting signs, in Shakespeare as in Dante. To speak of a poetic message, of a communicative volition of essential truth, such as we are doing here with regard to great poets' intentions, is not to proclaim reading's most obvious truth to the letter. We will try to illustrate this later with an example drawn from Cervantes' art. The challenge of the great creators, classical and modern, is above all the absolute as a form of experience announced by language. This explains the fact that brilliant artists are obliged to appeal more to all of the resources of ambiguous approximation than to those of direct designation. For this reason, exemplary works of art are perfect plans for the exploitation of uncertainty.

2.3.5. *Cervantes' Irony as an Instrument of Poetic Ambiguity*

It cannot be denied that the classics' greatness lies in the inexhaustible nature of their messages. Each new generation of readers rediscovers the relevance of the classicaly exemplary message over the changing course of the enigmas and crises of their own individual destiny and the historical destiny of the age in which they live. Always of great importance in that permanent availability of the great poetic works are the spaces of ironic indeterminacy foreseen by their authors, more so even than those safer zones, filled with absolute personal plenitude. I do not know if we could claim of any one of the brilliant spirits which we consider classics of art, that his is the classicality of imposition. In any case, one should speak of degrees; thus, we may think that the powers of a Van Dyck or a Rubens, or the direct and radiant ingenuity of a Zurbarán are more absolute and consistent than El Greco's igneous splendors, more immediate than one of Vermeer's scenes, enveloped in a mysterious yellow light, and more explicit than the sacred reserve of Velázquez, the chiaroscuro ochres of Rembrandt's materials or Titian's uncertain crepuscular promise.

Speaking of the total lack of ambiguity is perhaps more difficult with regard to literature than is the case with the figurative arts. This is certainly not possible with the heroic Virgil, who was able to survive centuries as a numinous poet/prophet, nor with the urbane Horace, overly given to Rome's patrician obligarchy. To claim this of direct and powerful authors like Dante, Boccaccio or Goethe is always dangerous, if it is done as a broad affirmation, without leaving room for exceptions and distinctions. And, in general, the assessment today of a writer as direct and clear tends to leave one feeling more disinterest and indifference than the sure, gripping fascination we feel for the things which intrigue us: a difference in attitude illustrated in the archetypal opposition between the art of Lope de Vega and that of Góngora. Cervantes, along with Shakespeare, is one of the archetypal monuments of poetic ambiguity. The ironic distance of his messages always moves the entire universe of Cervantine reality towards the interest of the indeterminable, and thus of the many-sided and plurally valid.

As in Velázquez, in Cervantes everything is enigmatic. The question of his literary culture has divided critics by sections and ages, between those who are astonished by the brilliant intuitions of the "uneducated genius", and those who, after Américo Castro, have tended to find themselves dumbfounded — with far too much zeal, I believe — in the face of the culture that the author of *Don Quijote* must have acquired; where and how nobody

2.3. The Aesthetic Capacity of Cultural Conventionality

will ever know. A culture, moreover, which Cervantes himself simultaneously praises and mocks. In Europe and perhaps even more artificially in Spain, the age in which Cervantes was writing marked the peak of the prejudices regarding the confusion between poetry and science: the topic of the poet as an "ocean of knowledge" circulated everywhere to the point of excess (A. García-Berrio, 1977–1980, I, pp. 300–310). A degenerated Baroque culture was beginning to codify in manuals the best of a formal, vague and artificial erudition, without which geniuses could not think of ascending Parnassus. Everywhere there was secret studying and copying going on; plagiarism ceased being a vice and was consecrated as a form of Baroque knowledge in Quevedo and Lope de Vega. Bakhtin is credited with recalling that Cervantes, with Rabelais and Shakespeare, figured among those who brilliantly foresaw a new sense of literature as a hybrid of the educated and popular, the cerebral and digestive, the courtly and carnavalesque.

The integral nature of Cervantes' literary culture, won from the educated reserve of the "medieval clergy", is demonstrated above all in the iconic, distant and ambiguous treatment of the themes of "knowledge" in his work. Recall the often cited mockery of the cultural sham, the false scholar, in the prologue to the *Quijote*: "... a tale as dry as a rush, barren of invention, devoid of style, poor in wit and lacking in all learning and instruction, without quotations in the margins or notes at the end of the book; whereas I see other works, never mind how fabulous and profane, so full of sentences from Aristotle, Plato and the whole herd of philosophers, as to impress their readers and get their authors a reputation for wide reading, erudition, and eloquence? And when they quote Holy Scripture! You will be bound to say they are so many St. Thomases or other doctors of the church" [M. de Cervantes, 1950, J. M. Cohen translation, p. 26]. The appearance of this theme here is far from exceptional. Cervantes successfully distances himself from all of his age's conventional dogmas by the simple introduction of his ironic note. He does not hide the fact that his greatest sympathies in his tribute to reason and kindness are for the marginal being par excellence, the Renaissance madman, the outsider in a culture which, as Foucault indicates, amputates the differential. And this is not only clear with Don Quijote, but also with the mad protagonist of *El licenciado Vidriera*, or the irrational two dogs, Cipión and Berganza, censuring the behavior of rational characters in *El coloquio de los perros*.

The parody of serious and educated cultures recorded in the *Quijote* ironically destabilizes every system of values, beginning with that of literature. This is most visible and familiar in the ambiguous inversion of chivalrous notions; but the corrosive effect of irony weighs on the very notion at the heart of literature as an illusion, on its supposed capacity for imaginative movement. Cervantes recreates the scenes of pastoral and sentimental literature in the scenery of the eclogue of the preparation for Camacho's wedding and in the deceitful stagings at the Duke's palace of the fictions of Altisidora and of the grove beside the Ebro; and he insinuates his adherence to the adventurous fantasy of the travel narrative in the navigation against the watermills or in Clavileño's aerial gallop. The way out of it all, the disillusion, always turns out to be ambiguous itself. Nostalgia and sentimental adherence to the impossibility of a desirable and worthy world is coupled with the realistic verification of its unviability, the sarcasm in the descriptions of the bloody pranks, the falls, the beatings, the poundings, the broken bones ... and, worst of all, the corrosion of illusions.

Cervantes' messages are oriented in many directions; his sanction of truth and lies, justice and crime, always appears permanently unstable. Each character and each mode of discourse assaults the stable forms of certainty and unity. Sancho's simplicity is the source of stupidity and ridicule, but also of honorable prudence and wisdom; and not only in the effective discharge of his duties as a judge and governor, but also frequently as the realistic correction to Don Quijote's hallucinations and extravagance. But, at the same time, Don Quijote, in his lucid moments, corrects and teaches Sancho, pruning the meanness and egotism of his positivist values. And even in the foolishness and nonsense of the knight's madness, Cervantes always leaves uncertainty as to which state is best, whether the universe of the ideal wherein the master's hallucinations lie or the base reality made to measure for the adaptable morality of the repressed fantasies of innkeepers and peasants. Occasionally, even the narrator intervenes to introduce another subversive note against any stable norm of certainty, as when he asks himself who the true madmen are, poor Don Quijote and Sancho, prisoners caught in the nets of their own fantasies, or those mean Dukes and their courtesans, anxious over the complex preparations for the continuous ridicule of their guests.

Don Quijote's certainties destabilize the certainties of Sancho Panza's universe, and vice versa; and both taken together permanently test the stability of the entire system of simple dualities, deconstructing conventional morality and the rules of the good-real and the bad-fictitious, the beautiful and the ugly, the absolute-moral and the relative-immoral. Cervantes scholars long ago observed these two halves of the world, of man and of reason, the two Cervantine creatures of *Don Quijote*, not only complement one another but interpenetrate one another as well. In effect, the process of identification and fusion which progressively elevates/sinks Sancho's positivism into his illusory phantasmagoria towards the end of the book is obvious, as is the analogous and inverse process of Don Quijote's liberation/imprisonment within the truth, a process which can only lead to his melancholy death. And once again, Cervantes stands with everything and against everyone, upsetting every truth without giving into the proclamation of skepticism, desacralizing every dogma without ever pronouncing a single unorthodox formula, subverting every value of the moral life without adopting licentious behavior. Man and truth in the end fit into one book in *Don Quijote*. Transcended dualisms, dissolved contrasts, broken complementarities; man and truth finally in the shadow of an irony which transcends all urgency, all provisionality, every part.

Cervantes scholars have customarily despaired over this, disputing among themselves whether Cervantes is to be considered "reactionary" or "progressive"; a Cervantes who has his Little Gypsy pronounce cynical discourses on the conservation of virtue, or who will dismiss the triumphant Basilio with the advice that he should become rich, like his rival, instead of continuing to cultivate the attitudes and abilities, fun and liberal, by which he has just won over the object of his affections. A Cervantes who has no doubts about reflecting on the virtue of a pair of adolescent lovers, Ricaredo and Isabela in *La española inglesa*, describing them as being as "prudent as the elderly"; but who knows at the same time how to drop in a disconcerting note of irony, having the dogs of the *Coloquio* correct themselves in the midst of the euphoria of their virtuous indoctrination, contending they do not wish "to appear to be preachers". Nothing more than a game, the intersecting and very complex game of the destabilization of any moral example and every verisimilitude and fictional license, but one which appears everywhere in Cervantes, creating the ironic counterpoint in which everything is taken to the limits of a given convention, because nothing is sustained once it has been surpassed. Recall the ironic — whether cynical, skeptical or deconstructive I do not know — ending of the novel of juvenile pranks called *Las dos doncellas*: "They lived many long and happy years in the company of their wives, leaving illustrious descendants, who to this day still live in these two places, the best of all Andalucia, and which, if they are not named, it is only in order to show respect for the two maidens, for evil and foolishly scrupulous tongues might criticize them for the weakness of their desire and their sudden change of clothes; I implore those so inclined not to censure such liberties until they have asked themselves if they have not at some time been touched by what are called Cupid's arrows, the effect of which is, if it can be so described, unlike anything else in its power, devouring reason".

Cervantes proclaims and defends, effectively, an "official" system of virtues, but he does so with such constant affectation that, by its very forced rigidity, it presses the tension of the ironically unprobable to its limits. Thus, his *Exemplary Novels*, more than being a program of exalted virtues, under the relativist distortion of the pure game of artistic illusion and the ironic shifts in a narrative point of view very wisely doled out, ends up seeming like an altar to Cervantes' liberal relativism, the trying experience of which would drive any dogmatism into crisis, even to the point of being tempted to subvert the official system of values in praise of some unorthodox alternative. Cervantes' irony is always pleasant and civilized, tempered and relentless.

There is no social dogma which is not treated with a respect ridiculed by irony, beginning with the deeply entrenched question of "castes" and "lineages". Preciosa in *La Gitanilla* is improbably keen and virtuous because in reality she is a false gypsy, the lost daughter of nobility. The boy, born the offspring of a rape in *La fuerza de la sangre*, can give examples of a dignity inappropiate to his nature because he was "engendered by some noble parent"; but Cervantes, in the same story, provides a strong message as to the kind of advantages such a background seems to offer when he sanctions the way in which "the liberal rich always find someone to excuse and canonize their vices". *La ilustre fregona*, an archetypal novel dealing with the issue of lineages, offers a model enabling Cervantes to put a matter which aroused the most serious interest in his social environment to ridicule and irony. And the same can be observed regarding the most controversial questions of that historical moment, like the thorny debates about the legitimacy of secret marriages, the multi-faceted object of Cervantes' ironic consideration in *La fuerza de la sangre, La ilustre fregona*, and *Las dos doncellas*.

Occasionally, Cervantes' irony makes itself felt even at the cost of breaking the most stable pacts of the narrative convention. Few examples are more illustrative of this than the curious story of the Moor Ricote in *Don Quijote de la Mancha*. Cervantes' decision to tackle the tricky task of dealing with the subject of an official government act, the expulsion of the Moors, which it was impossible to publicly dissent from, inevitably tinges the characters of the exiled Moor and his daughter with sympathy. The most hidden historical tensions created by the sociological convulsion of the expulsion find a place in Cervantes' informative narration, in the estimates and conjectures regarding the possible ways to corrupt the relevant officials in order to hide the presence of the Moor and his family in Spain. A narration in which the hurried Cervantes of these final chapters does not resist measuring out, quickly and keenly, the corresponding ironic correction:

> 'No,' said Ricote, who was present at this conversation. 'There's nothing to hope from favours or bribes, for no prayers, promises, gifts or compassion can avail with the great Don Bernardino de Velasco, Count de Salazar, to whom his Majesty has entrusted our expulsion. For though it is true that he tempers justice with mercy, since he sees that the whole body of our race is contaminated and rotten he applies to it the burning cautery and not the soothing ointment. And so by prudence, sagacity, and diligence, as well as by terror, he has borne the weight of his vast project on his strong shoulders to its due execution; and our arts, stratagems, pleadings and frauds have had no power to dazzle his Argus eyes, which are ever on the watch to see that not one of us remains or lies concealed, to sprout like a hidden root in times to come and bear poisoned fruit in Spain, which is now clean and free from the fears with which our number inspired her. What an heroic resolve of the great Philip the Third, and what unheard-of wisdom in entrusting its execution to this Don Bernardino de Velasco!' [M. de Cervantes (1950 edition), J. M. Cohen translation, pp. 894—5].

> — No — dijo Ricote, que se halló presente a esta plática — hay que esperar en favores ni en dádivas; porque con el gran don Bernardino de Velasco, conde de Salazar, a quien dio su Majestad cargo de nuestra expulsión, no valen ruegos, no promesas, no dádivas, no lástimas; porque aunque es verdad que en él mezcla la misericordia con la justicia, como él ve que todo el cuerpo de nuestra nación está contaminado y podrido, usa con él antes del cauterio que abrasa que del ungüento que molifica; y así, con prudencia, con sagacidad, con diligencia, y con miedos que pone, ha llevado sobre sus fuertes hombros a debida ejecución el peso desta gran máquina, sin que nuestras industrias, estratagemas, solicitudes y fraudes hayan podido deslumbrar sus ojos de Argos, que contino tiene alerta, porque no se le quede ni

encubra ninguno de los nuestros, que como raíz escondida, que con el tiempo venga después a brotar, y a echar frutos venenosos en España, ya limpia, ya desembarazada de los temores que en nuestra muchedumbre la tenía. ¡Heroica revolución del gran Filipo Tercero, y inaudita prudencia el haberla encargado al tal don Bernardino de Velasco!'

Cervantes plays with a distancing irony at this complicated step in the narration. Once more, the astute Cervantes deliberately forces the emphatic tone of the artificial "excusatio" at the price of the verisimilar decorum of the story itself. A two-faced attitude, in which it is as worthwhile condemning its artistic impropriety as it is admiring it for the subtlety with which it protests a repugnant order of reality.

At its furthest extreme, Cervantes' ironic deconstruction lodges itself in the final limits of being and seeming, in those journeys in which it is difficult to distinguish between the real and that which has not occured, between the true and the false, which lodge all of the *Quijote's* discourse in the sublime validity of the absolutely superhuman. Don Quijote, in the final analysis, is a madman who never lets himself be fooled. He pursues and cherishes, at the price of the loss of prestige and the act of folly, the delight of living in his illusions. He lives endless days of enchanted visions in little more than the half hour, in the objective estimation of Sancho the witness, which passes during his descent into the cave of Montesinos; and we even end up discovering, after all is said and done, that he is aware of his squire's lies regarding Dulcinea's enchantment, and of the real truth behind Sancho's story. Recall his answer to the Duchess: " 'There is much to say on that score ... God knows whether Dulcinea exists on earth or not, or whether she is fantastic or not fantastic. These are not matters whose verification can be carried out to the full' " (1950, J. M. Cohen translation, p. 680).

Anchored in his characters in these brilliant pages of the Second Part of the *Quijote*, Cervantes, the realist narrator, has surpassed the references useful for the construction and preservation of difference. Lodged in the agony of his own frustrated experience, he writes in these final moments of his life in complete awareness of the existential chaos that has befallen him. Sweet fictions and undesirable truths intersect one another, as in the life of his own hero, in these final measures of his false history. With the final blow of the publication of Avellaneda's false *Quijote*, Cervantes and his creations become even more hopelessly entangled in the indistinction between fiction and reality, which leads them to sometimes know themselves to already be historical characters, a reality created by their public history, while at other times, they obediently return to being the puppets on the stage of a false history.

Towards the end we even know that only the uncontrasted recognition of his own imagination, on the occasion of the jokes preconceived in the Duke's house, begins paradoxically to raise the suspicion in the tested Don Quijote that in reality he may be an authentic knight-errant. We perhaps only now discover that the relentless resistance to disillusionment in the misadventures of the Knight of the Sorrowful Countenance had him always on the edge of awakening from his alienation. Only his firm will not to condemn himself to live in the heavy reality of sane reason has maintained him, immune to painful ridicule, in the constancy of his illusions.

Cervantes feels the need to make his exemplary figures, Don Quijote and Sancho, travel through the difficult region of consciousness where the abdication of every certainty has already taken place. The axiologically ideal — the true, the good, the just — is distorted so that truth and justice coexist with great difficulty. Cervantes' heroes briefly occupy the just truth which, as such, must always be the real truth or the truth of ironic paradox. Having dislocated the vital axis of certainty, everything is relativized in the truths of the *Quijote*. Cervantes' irony, creating complete alienation, the absolute otherness of reason, has set out for all eternity the animated setting of deconstructed truth.

But Cervantes' artistic procedure, in making use of the ironic deconstruction of the absolute, is far from having surrendered to the weaknesses of the relativism of meaning in the text. The poetic capacities of *Don Quijote* are absolute powers. The work's ironic relativism is not lodged in the text's meaningful tabulations; on the contrary, the work is a classical piece. That is, it is categorical. The text of the *Quijote* is able, through the exemplary univocality of its unambiguous and perfectly executed narrative plan, to face the unsurmountable uncertainty of our destiny. The *Quijote* is thus a perfect construction of meaning which, for that very reason, succeeds and is capable of effectively lodging us in the startling and overwhelming surprise of the *différance*.

This is, once again, the brilliant paradox of the *Quijote*, exactly suited to the theme of our own time: ambiguity. The instability of man's truth lies in the ironic stature of his destiny, in the insufficiency of his abilities to know and measure the known. A deep truth, that of human destiny's ambiguous instability, represented in a literary form — beyond explicit statements and in the always conservative appearance of Cervantes' reliance on his strongly differential axiology and his logic of the expressed —, in the ironic speculativeness of his discourse. A language, however, powerful in the explicit strength of its capacities for affirmation, a power that is made and legitimized by itself, by virtue of the text and its message's unambiguous capacity for meaning. An eternal strength, that of the text of *Don Quijote*, which maintains itself unalterable in the permanent faithfulness to its exact meaning regarding the ironic ambiguity of the status of the truth and the real, beyond the unstable agreements of comprehension and interpretation contracted with that nucleus of meaning by the risky variables of historical and circumstantial readings.

It is possible to make the claim about every great classical text, and therefore clearly about Cervantes' work, that the ironic flexibility of its message regarding the instability and ambiguity of any of man's affirmations about reality, of any conclusive assertion concerning his absolute awareness regarding the nature of his destiny, figures among the first elements shaping its poetic value. Nevertheless, the new paradox of the brilliant work of art consists in that it discovers the negative through a solid affirmation; from which perhaps the neutral, inaccessible and inexhaustible nature of the classical affirmation stems. The *Quijote* installs the radical nature of relativism as a necessity, through the rigorous textual formula of a block of meaning, perfectly constructed and controlled by the author's designs. Cervantes' ironic foresight is not, in any way, a modern mode of capriciousness regarding supposed voids — foreseen or involuntary — in the space of the text. The artistic encounter with the ironic manifestation of the absolute ambiguity of reason and truth in *Don Quijote* stems from a series of affirmed categories and of perfectly constructed and closed narrative situations. The open and inexhaustible nature of man's experience of his own natural enigmas, communicated in the poetic emotions which brilliant works of art transmit, constitutes the absolute message only achieved by plenary, full and textually guaranteed constructions.

Third Part

3. Poetic Universality

3.1. Fictionality: The Imaginary Forms of Fantastic Activity

3.1.1. Introduction. The Imaginary Structure of the Material Text: From the Immanence of the Material Text to the Poetics of the Imagination

At present, the poetics of the imagination makes it possible for us to definitively break with the past mistrust many critics have displayed towards traditional psychological literary speculation, an approach viewed as external and irrelevant to the rightful concerns of literary theory. As will be recalled, literary psychoanalysis from Freud to Marie Bonaparte initially focused on the so-called psychoanalysis of authors. Within this orientation, literary texts acted as clinical protocols permitting the in-depth examination of the psychological intricacy of complex souls like Kafka, Proust or Edgar Allan Poe (A. Clancier, 1973).

The debate over the propriety and usefulness of this psychoanalytical approach now forms part of an accessible and closed chapter in the critical adjudication of poetics (S. Freud, 1976). Objections were first raised concerning the literary text's suitability and propriety as an authentically personal and reliable manifestation of authors' psychological compositions. On a less obvious level, the case against this method is supported by the clear evidence of the author's "segmentation" into various mimetic "roles" corresponding to the autonomous nature of his or her characters as voices, props or protagonists of referential discourses different from and inconsistent with his own (A. García-Berrio, 1983; H. R. Jauss, 1973a). There is also the well-known fact that the artist is influenced in the formulation of his accounts by the dialectical expectations raised by the point of view he budjets to his "implicit readers" (W. Iser, 1972).

We may accept the claim that the psychoanalytical approach managed to break through to great testimonial depths of the creator's psychology, to the regions underlying the more immediate forms of artistic mimesis, the deep areas which are therefore most symptomatic and authentic — and free from literary manipulation (M. Bonaparte, 1933; C. Badouin, 1972; G. D. Painter, 1959). However, with this claim we are surely approaching other more recent and useful efforts involving the critical application of psychological data: C. G. Jung's study of psychic archetypes and especially C. Mauron's outstanding study of the forms of latent symbols and "obsessive metaphors" (1962). Still, without a doubt the greatest failure of the psychoanalytical approach to authors as criticism is its insignificance, which is to say, its lack of interest to literary theory and criticism insofar as it represents a purely personal diagnosis of an author. In this respect, it runs the same risk of irrelevance plaguing many literary biographies or even autobiographies (P. Lejeune, 1975).

Knowledge of these facts concerning authors' external and historical, intimate and psychological, conscious and subconscious biography may perhaps serve to satisfy our most superficial curiosity as readers about the circumstances surrounding the lives of people we admire and find interesting. But it is clear that little benefit accrues to literary theory from the satisfaction of this kind of curiosity, be it through exterior or psychoanalytical biography. In any case, all of this biographical and psychological information ought to be brought to bear to explain literary works, the final and universal objects of poetics' interest, rather than to focus attention on aspects of an author's character or life irrelevant to the understanding of his texts (J. Kristeva, 1979).

Only by deepening and widening the obvious or latent psychological data manifested in texts to the level of universal archetypes, in the direction Mauron has so precociously indicated, can a degree of interest be obtained which is sufficiently generalizable for it to be suitable for poetics' uses. The critical discovery and description of the products of anthropologico-imaginary activity, as manifested in literary forms, is of interest to poetics because these products form a part of artistic activity's communicative process. The psychoanalytical approach to authors produces data which, while offered to the reader as curious or useful information, nevertheless does not immediately address the text's receivers and their role in textual communication. The discovery of the existence of prototypical imaginary structures in the text, in contrast, does not only concern the author as the person who puts them forward. It also *involves* the audience of receivers to whom these universal anthropological structures are destined and implies the recognition of their psychological, sentimental and fantastic capacity to accede to what they receive (A. García-Berrio and M. T. Hernández, 1988, pp. 100—108).

The poetics of the imagination is most solidly grounded in the principles of Jung's archetypal psychology (C. G. Jung, 1950) and possesses a clear and exemplary model for their literary mediation in Bachelard's poetics of symbols. It is a poetics which reveals its greatest capacity for poetic explanation when it seeks and achieves the expressive and communicative generality of anthropological universals. Gilbert Durand (1960) has elaborated his exhaustive symbolic atlases guided by this aim and method. The literary forms materialized in the text's verbal substance, both the most predictable forms common to poetic conventionality and those unforeseen forms of protopoetic expressiveness, are positioned so as to serve as the expressive channels for that other, more universal level of the poetic imagination which, in the best of cases, achieves the poetic transfiguration of the expressive message into an interesting, unknown and exemplary revelation.

3.1. Fictionality: The Imaginary Forms of Fantastic Activity

Up to this point, I have referred to two levels or textual forms of literary aesthetics: expressiveness in general, and that deployed in mimesis or fiction in particular. Both partake in a more limited way of the principle producing a third form, which I will discuss in this chapter, namely, the imaginary structure propelling *poeticity*. The more conceptual realizations of expressive poeticity, above all those which combine metaphoric components and those which appeal to what rhetoric generally recognizes as "images" have recourse to the imagination's fantastic mobilization. Nevertheless, the articulation of the expressive paths of imaginary reconstruction is in these cases concretized in direct forms of conceptual representation. As Bachelard understands it, the image which is "fabricated" and lacks deep roots contrasts with the rooted product of the unconscious image which, according to Jung, suddenly and unexpectedly manifests itself in the realm of personal experience in a hallucinative and non-pathological manner. Its subject and producer, being able to discern it as something different from the sensorially real, identifies it as an intimate production. Of course, the imagination's work in the case of mimetic poeticity is even more important and visible. Even in fiction, a rational, intellectualized control is felt to be exercised in the realist verification of the level of "fictional saturation" (T. Albaladejo Mayordomo, 1991) of its imaginary semantics, contrasting with the case of the unconscious image.

The condition of the imaginary process and construct as poeticity's definitive and genuine source alludes to the imagination's poetic work of symbolic stylization. In these reaches, poeticity installs itself in its most absolute constituent depths, in the region where the "unanswerable" conundrums of reason are answered by myth (S. Vierne, 1980, pp. 204–205). Symbolic structure, resorting to the mythic representation of the most radically essential and ineffable subject matter, is ultimately inherent and natural to the poetry of different periods and modes of poeticity (J. Burgos, 1982, pp. 149–154). Correctly sought, the imagination's symbolic structure is usually to be found pulsing beneath the surface of poetic expression or mimetic fiction.

The poetic symbol's anthropological effect begins to organize itself and take hold at the conscious level of poetry's elaboration or reception, deepening further in the conceptually inaccessible zones of the subconscious' teeming activity (C. Mauron, 1962, p. 28). By naming this space, critical poetology does not slide down some unknown slope of the "abyss" towards the ineffable, but simply recognizes and more adequately locates the "transrational" component of poeticity. Already formulated in the methods of Russian formalism (Y. Tynjanov, 1924, pp. 52–53, Ch. I.8), this "transrational" constituent has since been accepted in poetic theory under various modulations as a competent, albeit inconcrete formula for situating one of poeticity's basic properties, more perceptible in its results than in the ascription of its causes.

Nevertheless, the direct and conscious literary exploration of the deeper strata of poetic material was not generalized in artistic practice until relatively modern times, beginning with the definitive consecration of a symbolic and anti-mimetic aesthetics, the first uncertain manifestations of which were already to be seen in the Romantic revolution (M. H. Abrams, 1953). But the artistic consolidation of this Romantic will was not essentially achieved until the triumph of the so-called artistic "avant-garde". Symbolism, futurism and surrealism deepened the modern manifestation of aesthetic ideals, unalterable but drastically in need of reconstruction (G. de Torre, 1966, pp. 311–314).

Numerous modern poetic systems, as diverse as those of Baudelaire and Juan Ramón Jiménez, undertook by common consent the task of *radicalizing* the most superficial images — meaning, naturally, the most textually obvious images — collected in the traditional rhetoric of classical expressiveness, a tendency towards seeking the essential which has carried through to contemporary poetry. The general result of this effort can be represented as a poetics of the imaginary. It is founded on the deep examination of texts, delving into that which is most schematically constitutive. This does not necessarily mean that it ignores the historical differences which mark each concrete appearance of the essential myth (J. Villegas, 1973; 1976, p. 27). However, by becoming thus absorbed with the radical, the verbal adherences on the textual scheme's surface are weakened in order to represent the symbol in its most pure structure, the symbol translating in every possible way the uncertain forms of anthropological desire.

The relationship between the text's material verbal structure and the imaginary activity on which this structure is based is important, although both entities, linguistic and psychological, must be distinguished as very different components. The text as an integral whole requires both: the material scheme, dynamizing conceptual, imaginary and psychological activity, which in turn acts as a unique way to produce the content and meaning of the conventional entity called the text, itself by nature unforgettably expressive and communicative. Privileging the material, verbal dimension of textual analysis has been, as is known, an exaggerated tendency of poetic linguistics and formalist criticism throughout this century. The result has been that the text-as-object was examined, but irreparably amputated from its more immediate immaterial dimension. Thus polarized and ignored by these methods, the psychological constructions linked to the verbal product's more inert material received no critical attention and were unknown. But, as anyone can see, although it turns out to be difficult to assume explicitly in practice, the text retains in its material structure, in its verbal scheme, the physical *trace* of an imaginary symbolic activity ultimately very complex and extensive in its expression and communicative exchange.

In my own analyses, I have always tried to pay attention to these relationships between the special stylistic structures of the literary text's verbal utterance and the psychological, intellectual and imaginary activities in which the text's most immanent compositional forms are revealed and elucidated (A. García-Berrio, 1983, pp. 282–303). Based on its nature as a model or exterior pattern, I believe it is suitable to denominate the materialized structure

3.1. Fictionality: The Imaginary Forms of Fantastic Activity

of the textual complex as its *scheme*. In effect, all of the tracks laid down and paths followed by the author's fantastic and conceptual activity remain imprinted in the material utterance, at least in the case of a linguistically and artistically successful product. Running between the text's ideal, pure form and the communicative material scheme's verbal formula are the conflicts well-known in artistic histories concerning the powerless disproportion and magic of the autonomous resonances, involuntary and incalculable, of a poetic word lodged in a fertile tradition of artistic culture and carrying with it ancestral anthropological echoes. Still more clearly, the immanent text offers schematic slots about which the utterance's receiver, the literary work's reader, deduces his own meaningful constructions, completing the text's definitive space in terms of its inevitable pragmatic-communicative nature. The materialist fetishism of the object ought not to lead us to confuse the verbal scheme, supporting these traces, with the text's general meaningful-pragmatic unity.

However, it is no exaggeration to claim that in practice the critical initiatives are rare which, with respect to literary texts, have proceeded according to this order of relationships. I believe that, as in most similar cases, the reason for such a flagrant discrepancy between what is recognized in the theoretical representation of the text and what is applied in practice is due both to the prejudicial inertia exerted by the choice of one or another aspect as one's starting point and, above all, the inability to simultaneously understand both of the two great fields involved. Linguists and poetologists, on the one hand, and psychologists and theoreticians of the imagination, on the other, have not had available, in my judgment, much more reciprocal knowledge of each other's fields than what is necessary in order to misunderstand one another and exchange impatient accusations concerning unproductive questions of principle.

Reducing this rift to its most characteristic and easily discerned manifestations, criticism of linguists is a starting point common to the two well-differentiated modes of the poetics of the imagination proposed by G. Durand (1979, pp. 85–114) and J. Burgos, respectively (1982, pp. 56–57). Further ahead I will examine in detail, with regard to J. Burgos, the argument that the position which he takes scarcely differs in its analysis from the constructive principles and textual data of syntactical linguistics. As for Durand, he has more than enough reason for denouncing, as he has insistently done, the insufficiency of linguistic analyses, choosing instead to bet on the ability of a "symbolic reading" to determine the complex meanings of mytho-poetic texts (G. Durand, 1979, p. 92). Nevertheless, when it comes down to the concrete case of correcting a famous — and clearly trivial and insufficient — structuralist analysis carried out by Lévi-Strauss and Jakobson (1962), his own symbolico-imaginary examination of *The Cats* is neither more satisfactory nor particularly different from what a strictly syntactic and semantic analysis of the text's linguistic evidence would yield. This is not to say that Durand fails to produce a stimulating example of his theoretical and analytical intentions. In fact, he does indicate and describe the direction in which criticism could productively proceed. Still, in view of Durand's diacritical and methodological aims, his results do not invalidate the undesirable proximity of his mythic and symbolic paraphrases to the well-known structure and characteristics of traditional semantic paraphrases. In any case, we can concede that Durand proceeds with a better sense of what is interesting than was the case with Jakobson and Lévi-Strauss (G. Durand, 1979, pp. 85—114).

At the present stage of the development of a literary criticism open to the artistic text's imaginary dimension, I consider the most urgent and most specifically literary task to be that of explicitly and exhaustively illustrating the system of transferences and communicative connections between the textual scheme's linguistic evidence and the mythic and dynamic activity of the text's fantastic space. Mythocriticism, as the most mature subdiscipline of the poetics of the imaginary, must clarify in the most categorical manner possible the differences which specify, define and limit the verbal meaning of imaginary symbols and myths in the double dimension of their formal expressive context and their linguistic and semantic meaning. In this regard, I should clarify, in passing, that the concept of *scheme* in the sense in which I am here proposing its use, following the manner in which I have employed it in the past in my own concrete analyses of poetic texts (A. García-Berrio, 1985, pp. 257—263), differs from Durand's notion of the term. The figure which Durand "metaphorically" denominates *verbal* — "because in natural languages the verb expresses action" (1979, p. 19) —, refers to the pattern of structures of imaginary representation, with the "symbolic imagination" understood as an overall plan in which interactions are framed.

Another example of the difficulty arising from the failure to clearly distinguish between the text's material scheme and its fantastic space, very different from those previously indicated — namely, the analytical approximation to an elementary semantic paraphrase in Durand's examination of *The Cats* and Burgos' analytical exercises with the imaginary syntax of modern French poetry — is represented by Charles Mauron's well-known system of literary psychoanalysis. Although, to my mind, his is the most coherent and pure technique within the critical form of literary psychoanalysis, the distancing between the text's mythic results — the ballerina, Deborah, the beautiful Dorothea, etc. — and the utterance's expressive context manifests itself suspiciously prone to critical capriciousness. The specific density and independence of Mauron's mythic analysis is worthy of admiration and imitation, but his deductions, coded in psychoanalytical terms, seem to me nearly always far too pat and comfortable to be applied to texts whose semantic proximity and homogeneity do not guarantee the licitness of the contrasts Mauron's method demands (C. Mauron, 1962, pp. 30—31).

The critical analysis of imaginary forms — propulsive symbols and schemes — ought always to find in the text's verbal scheme the grounds upon which the fantastic inference or the definitive imaginary construction are legitimized. It is true that in the transfer from one textual dimension to another it is necessary to apply rules of transformation and equivalency codes, regulated by principles and laws from the field of psychology. Such a system of displacements and transformations must necessarily be explicit and its consequences proportionally and steadfastly fixed. Any other attitude will always be suspicious to the mental habits of literary criticism. Perpetuating and multiplying Mauron's attractive style will never help assure the adoption and use of psychoanalytical analyses and diagnoses in criticism.

The verbal text refers sufficiently to the symbol, often even by way of a direct *mention*; that is, through the most transparent archetypal lexeme. In other cases, the fantastic impulse's symbol or conceptual sign — of ascent, fall, balanced center, open and expanding space, etc. — is *suggested* in a preliminary and proximate semantic representation, broad and mobile enough not to reduplicate the transposed fantastic image without novel variations.

In the text, many elements come together to constitute the range of linguistic, acoustic, grammatical and semantic signs which legitimately favor a fantastic reading aspiring to be an authentic hermeneutic of intentional meaning, one which is extremely complex but rigorous and constitutive nonetheless: explicit deixes, different verbal systems of anaphoric and cataphoric orientation, expressive rhythms, alliterations and various forms of phonic coloring, among others (A. García-Berrio, 1985, pp. 282—303). Respect for the literary utterance's purity of meaning defines and conditions critical operations. In contrast, gratuitous and autonomous interpretations, governed by creative capriciousness, yield largely irrelevant results beyond the initial effect of surprise. The sublime revelations and messages communicated by the great creators of the past, now only accessible to us by way of the hermeneutics of literary meaning, demand and deserve a rigorous and conscientious approach.

3.1.2. *The Structure of Fictionality: The First Traditional Feature of a Poetics of Fantasy*

In the poststructuralist crisis of absolute thought concerning the essential universality of specifically literary and poetic properties, some poetologists, like van Dijk, Schmidt and Kuroda, pointed to fictionality as the most characteristic and certain property or feature of literariness. In so doing, they were resorting in the second half of the decade of the seventies to a traditional opinion dating back to the Aristotelian ideal of mimesis. And the concept of art as mimesis (or the artistic reproduction of reality) implies the imaginary concept of fictionality.

What is particular to literary realism is the semantic and pragmatic awareness of the fact that reality's artistic "double" represents a *stylization* of the same or, as T. Albaladejo denominates it, an "intensionalization", which is the result of the projective and cooperative effort of the author's and reader's imaginations. The *illusion* of artistic realism, including the plastic or literary products of naturalism, is nevertheless a product of conventional relativism (A. García-Berrio and M. T. Hernández, 1988a, pp. 135 ff.). Many years ago, before Bakhtin's rich critical notion of the "vocal" physiognomy of characters spread through the West, my teacher Baquero Goyanes showed how, in the realism of the nineteenth-century Spanish realist novel of authors like Pardo Bazán and, above all, Pérez Galdós, rather than a meticulous plastic or prosopographic description of things, landscapes or characters, what the text actually contained was scattered notes or brushstrokes forming true literary still lifes. In these still lifes, what was most meticulously and solidly set forth was precisely the various characters' voices as modes of speech (M. Baquero Goyanes, 1970, p. 125).

We scarcely have available a hasty sketch of the physical appearance of most of the Dickensian creations which we believe we know in such visual detail: Pip, David Copperfield, Fagin, etc. In contrast, as Baquero Goyanes showed, the realism of a Galdós or a Dickens bends over backwards and takes particular delight in the verbal characterization of such heroes. And the trait may be generalized in my opinion to the vast majority of great novelists, including Balzac, Tolstoy and Dostoyevsky.

The realist text's literary stylization is in part an obligatory feature of literary communication's economy. The accumulation of descriptive details in order to achieve an exhaustive plastic representation of a discourse's true referents would be exhausting, undesirable and, ultimately, not even viable. Based on the succinct selection of characteristic features the text supplies, readers *project* an imaginary reconstruction of fictional objects, spaces and characters to correspond with their perception of the elements of their own lived experience.

The broadly-accepted case of realist fictionality confirms and illustrates the necessary nature of the process of collaboration between textual scheme and fantastic space. That is, the facts and propositions of the verbal material, organized as a *scheme*, suggest and stimulate the development of the sentimental and imaginary *space* produced as a psychic process of fantasy. The very complex poetico-aesthetic entities which we conceptualize as artistic texts are constituted in this very way.

The experience of realist fictionality as an activity regulated by the imagination's conventional course is equally perceptible in the case of painting's referentiality. In the plastic arts, the "intensionalized" or stylized nature of realism's visual illusion reaches its most extreme form when the imaginary assimilation of the facts of the bidimensional, flat textual base of a painting are translated into effects of tridimensionality, of volume and perspective. I allude to these initial and clearest consequences of the realist illusion in painting in order not to linger on more subtle and detailed considerations concerning the multiplicity of effects implied by semantics and pragmatics in

3.1. Fictionality: The Imaginary Forms of Fantastic Activity

the visual arts, which I have discussed in great detail elsewhere (A. García-Berrio and M. T. Hernández, 1988 a, pp. 67—145).

Literary fiction's aesthetic effect cannot be reduced to the realist game's most immediate veneer, the result of a stylized duplication of true referents which is therefore impoverished and limited communicatively. The uniqueness of the imagination's role in literary imitation is implied in the Aristotelian formulation of the receptive process of mimesis as a form of *re-cognition*, therefore differentiated from the simple, direct or logical activities of imaginary consciousness (A. García-Berrio, 1988, pp. 55—60). Literary mimesis adds as a characteristic feature a perspective of discourse as consciousness, establishing the broad frame of differential references which are the most immediate consequences of the imagination's work in painting the objectively real, proper to literary fiction.

With no apparent breakdown in its communicative or aesthetic efficacy, fiction's realist effect permits the interference in the objective referential process posed by the author's narrative adjustment and focus, as illustrated by the employment of perspectivism, point of view, and the various phenomena of "skaz". Thanks to these explicit disturbances, which reveal the narrator's conscious processes, informative approaches corresponding to referential space are made possible. Cautious, fictional imaginary transactions also serve to powerfully increase narration's possible depth in the processes of consciousness pertaining to the literary referent's space.

In literary reflections, fiction is presented as one of the key elements of the literary act's structure, especially due to its capacity to organize the literary work as representation and the fundamental connections between text and world that such a conception implies. Literature, to the extent that it is the artistic-verbal materialization of imaginary reality, cannot be understood without an explanation of the concept of fiction. In this respect, Aristotle's *Poetics* establishes a tradition enduring to our own times in which general theories of literature where fictionality is seen to play a predominant role succeed one another (K. Hamburger, 1957; F. Martínez Bonati, 1972; B. Gray, 1975), with an abundance of studies specifically dedicated to the characteristics of fictional texts.

Although fictionality is not an exclusive property of narrative texts, it has received the most attention in the study of narratives. For this reason, the growing interest of literary theory in fictionality is absolutely related, in my opinion, with the development of narratological studies. The hypertrophy of narratological analyses made fictionality one of the most representative elements examined in the formalist "crisis of superproduction" (A. García-Berrio, 1977, 1984), more than satisfying the need and possibilities for analyzing narrative discourse. Given this situation and since, for the most fertile formalist poetics (A. García-Berrio, 1973, p. 34), the referents themselves are already formal constructions directed towards representation in the literary work, a decisive shift has occurred in the study of the novel towards the domains of its extension, that is, towards theoretical reflection concerning its referents, in the sphere of semiotic semantics, and towards studies of communicative structure in the sphere of pragmatics (T. Albaladejo Mayordomo, 1984). The explanation of literary fiction is founded on research in these directions.

Nevertheless, this strong reactivation of the theoretical literary treatment of fiction does not depend solely on the internal evolution of literary analysis. Contributions have also been made by logic and philosophical semantics, as well as by pragmatic semantics, which have found in literary fiction an excellent field for analysis and theoretical comparison. At the same time, this collection of philosophical and linguistic contributions has been articulated in an exhaustive explanation of the questions, though important perspectives are still open to further investigation. These factors, in recent years, have made literary fiction a focus of attention within literary theory, an interest which has translated into the appearance of numerous studies. In fact, much of the specialized bibliography on this theme has been generated very recently.

The oldest and most traditional conception of literary specificity links it to fiction's artistic products. The intimate cause and effect relationship which contributed to the conception of fiction and poetry as sources and of fictionality and poeticity as their results, products or properties, emerged from the Greek consecration of the name "poetry" as an effect of *poiein*, the manufacture or duplication par excellence of the natural. Obviously, the notion of the poetic as a value and property of artistic and literary discourse which I argue for differs appreciably from this traditional understanding, diverging from it without necessarily contradicting it. Nevertheless, as I understand it, the poetic effect implies a pragmatic assent, wrenched from the appropriate patterns in the text, patterns resulting from the author's skill and success in proposing meaning. As such, fictional *poiesis*, in turn, constitutes a communicative literary operation which also establishes the reasons for its functional efficacy, of its poetic success, with the plenary communicative participation of both producer and receiver in the imaginary act of fictional production.

We thus find ourselves before a decisive aspect in the construction and definition of literature, the text and the literary act. In an important number of cases, critics have attempted to resolve literariness by arguing it is a characteristic of the literary text equivalent to fictionality, insofar as fictionality is a fundamental mode of literary construction. The fictional construct, although based in the sphere of the literary work and specifically in the connection between text and referent, nevertheless affects the entire literary act in all of its semiotic dimensions — syntactic, semantic and pragmatic.

The same affirmation I have made regarding literary discourses applies to fictional discourses: every poetic effect is founded on the literary and, in this case, fictional text's pragmatic adequacy, but not every text in which expressive properties of conventional literary intention converge is automatically assured poetic value. In effect, fictional discourse possesses certain well-

3.1. Fictionality: The Imaginary Forms of Fantastic Activity

known conventional locutionary, illocutionary and perlocutionary properties and characteristics which have recently been analyzed and formalized by speech act criticism (J. Searle, 1969; W. Iser, 1975; T. van Dijk, 1976; S.-Y. Kuroda, 1976; S. Levin, 1976; M. L. Pratt, 1977, 1986; F. Martínez Bonati, 1978; S. Reisz de Rivarola, 1979; J. Ihwe and H. Rieser, eds., 1979). According to this theory, the fictional consists of an alternative but similar duplication of the discourses inherent in reality, formulated and received under conventional conditions of consciousness as *double discourses*. This presupposes that, in terms of their referents, these discourses could be real, but in fact do not appear inscribed in the existing universe.

In part, the pragmatic organization of speech acts explains fictional construction, since the fictional literary text's conductor locutionarily represents and illocutionarily expresses a referent that does not exist in reality. At the same time, the text convinces the reader in a perlocutionary manner to accept the work as a reproduction of an alternative reality to the one which truly exists. I consider the role of convention in establishing the fictional construct entirely valid (C. E. Reeves, 1986), since literary communication of a fictional kind would be impossible without the agreement which it establishes (S. J. Schmidt, 1976, pp. 172 ff.; S. Reisz de Rivarola, 1979). Still, with regard to the pragmatic accord, all of this is not sufficient to establish fictionality, understood as a characteristic, and the fictional construct, understood as a textual literary structure, as this agreement's principal sources. Rather, the convention is produced and maintained precisely because it is established as a function of a literary text, the extension or referent of which lacks truly real existence. The characteristics of the text and the referent it represents are the conditions for the existence of said convention which, once generally constituted and realized in each of the concrete cases of the text's composition and communication, contributes to fictionality.

The distinctions between the existing, the real and the possible, between the true, the credible (verisimilar) and the false, and between the fictional and the imaginary, have been fruitfully reiterated since Aristotle in order to explain this unique poetic property of imaginary fictionality (*Poetics*, 1451 b, 27—29, 1451 a, 38). Logic and philosophical semantics, being particularly interested in reference to the extent that it constitutes the fictional work's semantic basis, also have an important role to play in explaining fictionality (W. V. O. Quine, 1960; A. Bonomi, 1975, 1979; J. Heintz, 1979; R. Howell, 1979; T. Pavel, 1979; J. Woods and T. Pavel, eds., 1979, 1980; L. Doležel, 1976, 1979, 1983; J. C. Moreno Cabrera, 1985). The kind of beings and events fictional discourse presents emerge as the basis for its unique ontological status. Specifically, these beings and events are interpreted in terms of whether or not they exist. And their existence is tied to whether they are true or false as compared, not to the objective world, but to *world models* which differ from it.

The fictional utterance's referent only exists because it has been intentionally created upon the production of the fictional construct and, therefore, of the text which is the representation of this referent. Considered as a fictional world, the referent is an authentic "poietic" reality. That is, it is constructed artistically and its existence is linked to that of the other poietic product, the fictional work. Referents are fictitious elements; that is, they represent them (F. Martínez Bonati, 1981a, pp. 82 ff.), they acquire the existence given them by the text which they form part of. Consequently, the beings and events which compose the referent of a work of fiction are fictitious elements. They have a mode of being which is that of appearing to exist, of being accepted as appearances of reality. At the same time, these elements acquire their fictional character when they are placed in relation to an expression (J. Landwehr, 1975, p. 180). According to this scheme, it is the global construct consisting of the world model, referent and text which fixes the fictitious referent as a poietic, fictional reality, sustained by its relationship with the fictional text. We are dealing, then, with a complicated creation, complexly related to reality: its linguistic materialization by means of the construction of an expression identified with the world is essential (F. Martínez Bonati, 1960, p. 72; 1981; K. Hamburger, 1957 [1973, pp. 139 ff.]; I. Crosman, 1983). The desire to have the receiver recognize certain essential forms intervenes in the intentionality constructing this poietic reality, as I will explain shortly.

The relationship which is established between the referents of fictional discourses and objective reality receives singular attention within the study of fiction, insofar as fictional works express referents which do not form part of that reality. This objective reality is understood as the way human life is (K. Hamburger, 1957 [1973, p. 9]) or the combination of elements and relationships, of beings and events, with an objective existence we are conscious of (S. J. Schmidt, 1984, p. 267; F. Gaillard, 1984, p. 756); it maintains a simultaneous relationship of opposition and complementariness with fiction. In this way the comprehension of a fictional work can be explained as the discovery of a satisfactory connection between the fictional world created by the author and the real objective world (R. Scholes and R. Kellog, 1966, pp. 82—105).

Without doubt, fictional construction is rooted in the referent's space. Starting from the referent's ontological characterization, the fictional construct is fixed and organized by virtue of the connection between text and referent; in turn, the referent depends on the world model (J. S. Petöfi, ed., 1979; T. Albaladejo Mayordomo, 1983, 1986). That is, the referent depends on the semantic construction consisting of the series of instructions that govern the referent represented by a text, meanwhile, the producer and receiver establish the world model. The component constituting the world model is formed with respect to both perspectives (T. Albaladejo Mayordomo, 1983, 1986), corresponding in the case of the producer with his own communicative intention and, in the case of the receiver, with his knowledge of the textual class to which the discourse received and interpreted belongs.

Thus, the construction of the world model is a prerequisite for obtaining the referent, which is at the same time the result of the materialization of the instructions which compose it.

There are three types of world model in which the referents of concrete texts may be inserted. Tomás Albaladejo has classified them as *real, verisimilar fictional* and *non-verisimilar fictional*: "The world models of the real are formed by instructions which belong to the real world; the referents obtained from them are real. The world models of the verisimilar fictional contain, in turn, instructions not belonging to the real world, but constructed in accordance with it. Finally, the world models of the non-verisimilar fictional are composed of instructions which neither correspond to the real world nor are established in accord with the rules of said world" (T. Albaladejo Mayordomo, 1991; also, J. S. Petöfi, 1979). As a result, fictional texts have referents which depend on world models of the verisimilar or non-verisimilar fictional, involving in both cases world models which imply the construction of a world different from the real one (K. L. Walton, 1978).

Fiction's semantic basis is also tied to the pragmatic sphere. In order for the fictional text's communication to be realized, it is necessary that the producer and receiver have at their disposal identical models, belonging to the same class; these repeated models constitute the semantico-extensional code in which the producer and receiver participate (T. Albaladejo Mayordomo, 1986, p. 63). As can be seen, semantic and pragmatic elements co-exist in fiction's fantastic and conceptual structure (H. Fricke, 1982).

The pragmatic perspective, given the previous consideration of its connection with the semantic point of view, appears necessary to the study of fiction, provided it is not elevated to the point of being the principal or exclusive object in the explanation of the fictional construct. We have already seen how fictional functioning requires the proper placement of the pragmatic perspective in a communicative scheme in which authors and readers fulfill the requirement of extensional agreement, made possible when both parties possess literary competence with the resulting understanding of the characteristics of fictional discourses (I. Crosman, 1981). Therefore, the pragmatic perspective should be applied taking into account especially the fact that fiction's nucleus is located in the semantic sphere. Nevertheless, along with studies in which fiction is dealt with from the starting point of speech act theory, all those analytical points of view in which attention is focused on the narrator or the receiver must also be kept in mind as being linked to the sphere of reflection concerning the pragmatic.

The narrator's function is fundamental in the pragmatic explanation of fictionality, since the narrator's mimetic — that is, narrative-descriptive — expression is decisively important for the text's referential and discursive constitution (F. Martínez Bonati, 1960, pp. 70 ff.). This is the case even though the narrator's ontological status presents us with many problems of a pragmatic nature (W. C. Booth, 1961; M. L. Ryan, 1981; K. Kuiper and S. Small,

1986; K. Hamburger, 1957 [1973, pp. 139 ff.]). The textual presentation of beings and events is accepted in verisimilar-mimetic fiction thanks to a broad convention, without which the status of the omniscient narrator, for example, would be neither comprehensible nor possible. On the other side of the communicative scale, that corresponding to the receiver, the presence of the receiver in the text (P. Rabinowitz, 1977; U. Eco, 1979) also contributes unavoidable and necessary perspectives to the pragmatics of fiction.

Perhaps the most characteristic aspect of this matter is that the interaction of the semantic and pragmatic elements in fiction necessarily introduces a relationship between the real and fictional worlds, which involves the separations and connections existing between both (K. L. Walton, 1978). According to this link, the fictional world is constructed beginning with the necessary presence and contrast of the real world, the universe inhabited by authors and readers and with respect to which they establish world models for the construction of referents and texts. Consequently, knowledge of the real world turns out to be inevitable for onomasiological or semasiological participation in the construction of fictional products.

In this context, I will concentrate here above all upon considerations relative to the properly imaginary structure of fictions (J. P. Sartre, 1950), because it ought to be kept in mind when speaking of literary fiction that, ultimately, it is composed through the adequate or inadequate achievement of a system of conventional expressive norms, capable as such of associating and producing the type of imaginary representations that determine fiction's unreal illusion.

In the first place, we may assume the poetic value of a fictional discourse lies directly and immediately in its capacity for imaginary mobilization and rests on the receiver's degree of enthusiastic adherence to pragmatic effects. In this sense, we would find our proposal for considering the poetic as an aesthetic value on an equal footing with the realist and Aristotelian conception of the poetic as a productive activity of the verisimilar fictional effect. Indeed, the traditional realist understanding of fictionality which has dominated literary and artistic poetics from the classical age to our own century in practice identifies the specifically realistic effect, founded upon credible artistic and literary appearances, with the type of imaginary representations of the truthful reduplication of what exists. Above all, these imaginary representations have been the foundation for the aesthetic effects of paintings and novels, narrative and theatrical.

As a quality of mimesis, verisimilitude (G. Genette, 1969; VV. AA., 1970; A. Gómez and K. R. Gürttler, eds., 1980) maintains the literary work's fiction within the limits which constitute true objective reality, creating the illusion of reality and of fiction as verisimilar fiction's referent, a poetic reality susceptible to being confused with natural, true reality. In effect, the verisimilar is not something similar to the true or real but, as Ricoeur characterizes it, is also the *appearance of reality* (P. Ricoeur, 1983–1985, Vol. II, p. 26,

III,1,1). And so great is the importance of credibility as a regulative principle in the construction of discourses that it has even become an element of rhetorical *narratio*.

Nevertheless, the incorporation within the fictional-imaginary category of the entire vast collection of possible extra-verisimilar formations, singularly empowered by the modern consideration of fantastic literature (T. Todorov, 1970; A. Zgorzelski, 1984; D. Suvin, 1979), necessarily obliges us to amplify and revalue the traditional identification of the fictional-imaginary with the realist-verisimilar in keeping with the semantic possibilities of fictional construction contained in world models.

In general terms it may still be said that the pragmatic efficacy of the fantastic fictional mobilization constitutes a reasonable indication, on its own, of the poetic value of fictional discourses. The human imagination's decisive ability for involving itself in artistic kinds of representation, both of the mimetic-verisimilar and of the illusory and unreal varieties, establishes itself as a fundamental peculiarity of the aesthetic functions of literature and art. Although I now propose to relativize fictionality's poetic value, which I judge truly to play only a partial role, in contrast to some critics' recent deforming excesses, this does not mean, however, that I am ignoring or trying to subvert the central importance of the just, although incomplete, Aristotelian attribution of poetic significance to the artistic operations of fiction.

The model of fictional narrative, the only operative genre in a strict sense in Aristotle's description of *poiesis*, does not actually exhaust literary discourse's fictional capacity. Literature's general expressive fiction — for example, the fiction of the lyric voice — cannot be ruled out, in rigorous terms, as an expressive model of fiction. Its primary discursive-expressive role is becoming clearer, in my judgment, in the imaginary mechanisms which form the foundations of general literary discourse. In lyrical discourses the continuous appeal for the imagination's cooperation, contributing, as we shall see, the most important textual manifestations of poeticity, contaminates and disturbs the elemental schematism which contrasts them as realistic, or representations of the existing, to the narrative fictionality of the dramatic or novelesque, insofar as these are fictional representations lodged in the universe of the non-existent (A. García-Berrio, 1989 b).

It is true that historically it has been the epic-narrative and dramatic genres that have been most directly linked with fictionality. Lyrical discourse was foreign to an explanation of fictional construction as the representation of alternative referents. This conception of the lyric is not unrelated to the absence in Aristotle's *Poetics*, at least in that version of the *Poetics* which has survived, of any treatment of the lyrical genres that compares with that given to tragedy and the epic. Moreover, the late inclusion of the lyric as a unitary genre integrated within the tripartite organization of genres (A. García-Berrio, 1975, pp. 370–378; 1977–1980, I, pp. 94–113; A. García-Berrio and M. T.

Hernández, 1988, pp. 121–127) is also related to the consideration of the lyric text as lacking in imitation or, more precisely, in mimetic representation. Nevertheless, Dante's doctrine in *De vulgari eloquentia* concerning the song, ballad and sonnet, according to which these forms express a unique thought, contributed to equate the lyric with the epic-narrative and dramatic genres, at least as concerns mimetic representation. This initiative has been developed exhaustively by the modern theory of textual macrostructures, from which may follow decisive consequences in the extension of fictional status to include lyrical discourse (A. García-Berrio, 1988, pp. 407–415).

Epic-narrative, dramatic and lyrical discourses all contain macrostructures which, provided with comprehensiveness, are textual representations of complex referents formed by the configuration of imaginary worlds. The *theory of possible worlds* (A. Baumgarten, 1735, § LII; S. A. Kripke, 1959; A. N. Prior, 1962; R. C. Stalnaker, 1976; U. Volli, 1978; T. Pavel, 1975, 1980; U. Eco, 1978; A. Bonomi, 1979; L. Doležel, 1976, 1979, 1983a, 1983b; C. Segre, 1985, p. 220, Ch. II, 2.4; T. Albaladejo Mayordomo, 1986, 1986a), by permitting an explanation of the literary text as an expression of the organization of imaginary worlds and subworlds, demonstrates that narrative, dramatic and lyrical fiction are all included in the unity of general fictional construction. The existence of desired, feared, dreamed and intuited subworlds, among others, within the referent of lyrical discourse and thus within its macrostructure shapes the imaginary organization of fantasy upon which the fictional character of the lyrical rests.

As is true in the case of narrative and dramatic fiction, so also with lyrical fiction we find ourselves presented with a configuration of worlds that do not belong to that of concrete objective reality, with which they undoubtedly have much in common. The same Aristotelian conception of poetry as a mimetic representation of the general supports the consideration of poetry in terms of the expression of essential universals in a fictional configuration. In this manner, the lyrical is linked to the literary manifestation of the essential and the true (D. Rasmussen, 1974, pp. 64 ff.). If we return to the notion of "true fictions" in Baumgarten (1735, §§ L, LI), we could even insert the fictional constructions of lyrical discourses among them. It is worth observing, in conclusion, that although the classification of world models is especially appropriate to the case of epic-narrative and dramatic fiction, it is also largely valid for lyrical fiction. However, in this regard we must add the important qualification that among the world models of the first type, that of the real, some may be found which govern referents of fictional lyrical discourses, so long as these contain an imaginary configuration of worlds and subworlds.

The argument which assimilates the degree of aesthetic poeticity to the fantastic effect of involvement must, after all, be relativized. Consider, for example, certain subliteratures — mystery or crime novels, sentimental novels, etc. — that link their success and broad commercial dissemination to the powerful imaginary effects of identificatory involvement they provoke (H. R.

Jauss, 1975; A. García-Berrio, 1983). It appears obvious, nevertheless, that in these cases we run up against a type of pragmatic efficacy that is fairly ephemeral and linked almost exclusively to psychological and artistic properties which exploit "context". After all, to cite one well-known case, James Bond novels clearly do not propose new situations, the evolution of which could not be foretold from the historic observation of the most interchangeable contextual frames of literature, such as the Renaissance sentimental novel, the novel of chivalry, the serialized story, etc. Evidently, there is no literary text, vulgar or otherwise, which cannot be inserted into one of those great *contextual frames* which to a large degree underlie much contemporary interest and that will continue always to animate, to some extent, fictions' sentimental and fantastic involvement. Still, considering the very different fortune befalling the *Decameron* and the decamerons, *Werther* and the werthers, we may point to the poetic structures and capacities of such texts in order to explain and recognize the aesthetic elements inherent in the general poetic effect of certain privileged texts.

The notion of fiction's "contextual frames" also enables us to explain the fictional fervor great myths possess. The successful literary myth always offers a handy slot at the disposition of fictional construction. It may be thought that it is the great closed historical text which inaugurates the myth's space, if one thinks of the "quixotism" of Cervantes or of Goethe and the myth of Faust. However, we know from historical investigation the scarcely successful artistic antecedents of Faust's diabolical pact or of the Celestina's solicitations. I believe that today, nonetheless, there is little doubt that myths represent and shape anthropologically necessary imaginary spaces, linked to necessary and universal domains of the representation of the world (G. Durand, 1960). Without having to descend abysmally — or excessively, according to how one wishes to represent it — through the levels of myths' imaginary structures, it has repeatedly been noted that some of the most universal and notable among the more artistically defined and characteristic myths, as for example that of Don Juan, are not founded upon any great literary text having originally given them form.

The example of the Don Juan myth and its diffusion (Gendarme de Bevotte, 1929) confirms the universal affirmation of a great literary myth which, in contrast to similar myths, is not founded on the singular aesthetic quality of any one great work of art. Neither Tirso de Molina's Don Juan, nor those of Molière, Mozart or Byron, to cite only the best known works, appear equivalent to the brilliant quality of the works which incorporate the great classical myths, like that of Oedipus, or of such modern myths as those of Quijote and Faust. But the collection of traits of rebelliousness and disorder which is included in the Don Juan myth represents one of those "contextual frames" of interest by virtue of which authors and readers of certain circumstances and ages feel themselves attracted and interested by the general subject matter or genre, almost without paying attention to the concrete artistic text in which it is offered (H. R. Jauss, 1977).

This is confirmed by the receptive phenomena of the survival and decline of interest through time on the part of readers and viewers. Observing the evolution of the Don Juan myth in Spanish literature, for example, one notes how each successive social moment requires the modification of those components of the myth that no longer arouse interest or excitement, with the logical addition of new elements or the development of constituents which were absent or compressed in the initial versions of the story. Hence, the hypertrophic development of the sentimental and amorous components of the myth in José Zorilla's Romantic version at the expense of the social and theological dimensions focusing on rebellion against God and the subject of infamy, which are the basic ingredients constituting the myth in seventeenth century society. And the mutations of the Don Juan myth are even more surprising when, with the development of a modern mentality, the peculiarities of the character begin to lose their appeal for new receivers, either because of the myth's loss of credibility or its lack of interest (A. García-Berrio, 1990a).

In my study on the modern evolution of the Don Juan myth in Spanish literature (A. García-Berrio, 1967), I had the opportunity to describe the modifications which, as opposed to classical and Romantic interests, signal the presence of the industrial age's belief in rationalist society and positivism. The explicit criticism of Romanticism throughout Clarín's work sets the stage for the positivist Don Juan of his Álvaro Mesía, lodged in all the awkward circumstances of a provincial dandyism and, at the same time, "deconstructed", under the pressure of external reality, to the extent that Mesía lacks the characteristics most consubstantial to donjuanesque amorous fascination, such as youth and erotic power (M. C. Bobes Naves, 1985). Galdós' numerous Don Juans offer analogously diverse perspectives on the dismantling of a myth incompatible, more because of its lack of credibility than its immorality, with the interests and possibilities of contemporary society. Thus, Don Juan de Urries in *España sin rey* represents a political kind of Don Juan, experiencing the seductive possibilities of what has later been called "the eroticism of power". And Don Lope Garrido in *Tristana* shrewdly sets forth the impossible topicality of Don Juan as an expired myth, already unchangeably lacking credibility in the society of the times. In Don Lope appear, in times now gone by for him, all of the fascinations and rebellions of the rake now definitely withered and unrecoverable in the face of old age and decrepitude.

The various intellectual theses about the waning virility of the conventional seducer, from Pérez de Ayala, Unamuno and Marañón, appear incarnated in numerous novelized recreations of Don Juan, among them Pérez de Ayala's *Tigre Juan* and Unamuno's *Nada menos que todo un hombre*. Authors' different views of the Don Juan myth's viability at different moments in various situations facing contemporary society originated Jacinto O. Picón's *Juanita Tenorio*, Álvarez Quintero's *Don Juan Buena persona* and Jacinto Benavente's *Rosas de otoño*. Finally, the conflicting archaism of a modern Don Juan inspires

Dionisio Ridruejo's drama and Torrente Ballester's novel. Only by way of the literary transformation of Don Juan into an "ugly, Catholic and sentimental" Bradomín does Valle Inclán make possible the modern assimilation of a myth already unrecoverable and uninteresting in its pure original forms.

Just as the degree of the receiver's interest in the literary imitation may depend, as we have just seen, on other strictly contextual factors apart from the exemplary perfection of the artistic text's fiction, we may also affirm that the play of pragmatic fictional complicity between the textual instant and its reader appeal does not represent the only level of quality to which the literary and artistic text may adjust itself.

3.1.3. *The Rules of Verisimilitude in Realist Fictionality*

The feature of fictionality is one of the most certain properties of literary *poiesis*, as has been emphasized in recent times by a radical sector of the new literary pragmatics (S. J. Schmidt, 1976, 1980, 1983; S.-Y. Kuroda, 1976). It is even more decisive if the understanding of fictionality, in keeping with my proposal, is extended, not only to fantastic narrative, but to any product of literary *mimesis*, understood as the deferred deployment of some segment of reality's language to artistic discourse; a case which would thereby, for example, include the discursive reflection of lyrical poetry as fictional. In these terms, and only in these terms, the fictional and the literary are of course identified with one another. In any other case — including the position which the above-mentioned representatives of the pragmatic initiative adopt — it appears obvious that fictionality seen as a realistic mimetic discourse of unreal characters and events cannot be generalized as a global characteristic of literature, but rather of several kinds of texts, especially narratives, from among those commonly grouped together under the broad heading of literary works.

Even so, the poetic feature's axiologico-aesthetic nature, which I claim as a specifier of value, cannot be identified with fictionality as a constituent, general or restricted, of literary discourse. That is to say, from the point of view of poetic value, the majority of the fictional-literary discourses recorded in literary history do not achieve poetic quality, or do so to a minimal degree. As is the case with any of the unvarying imaginary features of verbal artistic discourse, the simple fictional stance of literary articulation does not guarantee the achievement of that ultimate sublime and essential level of the expressive messages which receive the most positive aesthetic judgment. It is the organization of the literary text's worlds, the imaginary configuration of worlds and subworlds that underlies the determination of the aesthetic value of the fictional-fantastic text, corresponding to essential human constants, binding receivers to the work.

The poeticity of fictional discourse as such thus depends on the degree of imaginary absorption which the text elicits permanently and not circumstantially; that is, not for reasons based on what I have previously denominated contextual circumstances. Notice that, ultimately, we are assimilating the literary value of unreal narrative texts to the general value of the literary discourses of expositively and discursively real contents, such as lyrical texts or oratorical pieces with great powers of emotional mobilization. With regard to the poeticity of fictional discourses, we are dealing with, in all cases, the essential experience registered in the most profound symbolic regions of imaginary activity.

Consequently, it is advisable to begin adequately appreciating the fact that the most common and traditional understanding of fictionality as realistic *mimesis* represents only one circumstantial historic model of imitative *poiesis*. Certainly, the perfect initially Aristotelian formulation of the model and its many repercussions in Western artistic practice oblige us to consider it with preferential attention. But we should avoid the great error of considering mimetic-narrative fiction structured in terms of realistic correspondences as the only possible direction which the fictional constitution of discourses can take. In short, the trait of fictionality needs to be extended and generalized not only to fantastic fiction of an unreal nature but also as the model of the fictional constitution of every deferred literary discourse. Analogously, the degree of perfection of the mimetico-realistic fictional text, understood as the adaption of the recorded discourse to the real references of existence, represents only one of the historical parameters of value which the aesthetic judgment can and should adopt with regard to the poetic perfection of narrative discourse (A. García-Berrio and M. T. Hernández, 1988a).

Traditionally, literary theory has paid more attention to fictional realizations of a verisimilar nature, which have come to be identified with fiction in general, by way of the weight of realistically-tending mimetic poetics. A conception of literature so strongly rooted could not embrace fiction's fantastic realizations without polemics, like the debates engendered by Ariosto's *Orlando Furioso* (A. García-Berrio, 1975, pp. 269 ff.). As with the fictional proposition considered in general, the semantico-extensional code, shared by the author and his receivers, makes possible the pragmatic acceptance of the non-mimetic and non-verisimilar fictional construct, which seems alien when not confronted with predictable fictional possibilities in accord with concrete reality. The world models of the fictive non-verisimilar, constituted for the elaboration of non-mimetic fictional texts — therefore implying the rupture of the hegemony of imitative poetics — and based on world models of the verisimilar fictive, have achieved their implantation in history only insofar as non-mimetic fictional praxis has been accepted, thereby qualitatively extending fiction's outer limits. This has made it possible to detect diverse classes of non-mimetic literature in the complex field of fantastic fiction (A. Zgorzelski, 1984).

The expressive modes of fictional narrative-realistic texts clearly diverge, at least considered from the perspective of the most material and discursive textual evidence, from the other unreal and non-narrative modes of fictional literary discourse. In this divergence their specification with regard to those other forms is to be discovered. However, when the common content of imaginary conduct raised by artistic texts is examined in depth, all of these differences begin to merge and fade away. In the remainder of this chapter I hope to adequately demonstrate how the personal consolidation of symbols, by which process the fictional, dramatic and novelized characters of the "imitation of actions" are differentially concretized and restricted, substantially converges with the semantico-symbolic consolidation of lyrical ideas. Ultimately, both processes translate different semantic versions of one, final organizational impulse; for example, the impulse of the fall in the cases of Icarus, Phaëthon or mortal depression. That is, the mythological-narrative symbol conceals in its semantic sheathing or incarnation a structure of the spatial system of anthropological orientation.

It is always advisable to begin with the terms in which Aristotle composes his scheme defining the realist current of mimesis. Compared to the scientific amplification of experience as *cognition*, fictional artistic contents are unique in their mode of *re-cognition* (M. Bakhtin, 1975). Through fictional literary discourse we recognize or rediscover forms of reality. These real forms are patently obvious in verisimilar and non-verisimilar fictional constructs, although their presence is greater in the former (A. García-Berrio and M. T. Hernández, 1988a, pp. 127–130).

The relationship between fiction and reality is so close that reality, in addition to constituting the axis opposite to fiction, also becomes a part of fiction as one of its most prominent features. Objective reality is one of the limits of fiction (T. Pavel, 1983), established as an ontologically separate but contiguous sphere to that of fiction. On the other hand, reality is converted by its presence in the fictional construct into a decisive and necessary prop for fiction, especially in the case of the mimetic-verisimilar class which, within fiction in general, constitutes the principal axis of literary representation's articulation as a *poietic* activity due to its intermediate and connective position between concrete reality and the aggregate formed by verisimilar and non-verisimilar fiction. The relationship between reality and fiction is thus established as a form of mutual communication (W. Iser, 1975, p. 7 ff.).

Verisimilar fictional constructs differ from the non-verisimilar in that they are based on mimesis, to which they owe their elaboration, while non-verisimilar constructs, realized according to a fantastic imagination, are not mimetic. Precisely for this reason, the rich and complex concept of mimesis ought not to be understood as a simple imitation of true reality by the artistic text. Mimesis needs to be understood broadly as a representation of an alternative reality of a verisimilar nature.

In a brilliant interpretation of the Aristotelian notion of mimesis, Paul Ricoeur explains mimesis in terms of a representational operation, discarding the idea of the reproduction of a pre-existing reality. Of the three moments which Ricoeur distinguishes in mimesis, the second is the most fundamental, producing a break with true reality and thus opening the space of fiction (P. Ricoeur, 1983—1985, Vol. I, pp. 76 ff., I, 2.4; I.3.II). But the operation of mimesis, strictly associated, as is well known, with the concept of *mythos*, is first and foremost the comprehension of human action, of the world of action (P. Ricoeur, 1983—1985, Vol. I, pp. 87—100). And in its final moment, mimesis establishes, as the culmination of the mimetic operation directed towards the text's interpretation by the receiver, the intersection between the world of the artistic work and the receiver's world (P. Ricoeur, 1983—1985, Vol. I, pp. 109—129; I.3.III).

Corresponding to Ricoeur's ideas, mimesis presents itself as an activity creating reality and directed towards artistic communication, producing in its reception the recognition of the real forms included in the representation, by virtue of the special connection between reality and fiction. Mimesis is fulfilled in the constitution of world models of a verisimilar nature, with instructions in accord with the rules which govern the organization of the true, real word. Thus, receivers' access to textual and world model referents is made possible by the establishment of literary referents corresponding to said world models and the production of artistic texts expressing these referents.

Since mimesis involves the creation of world models and of referents close to the real world, mimetic fiction tends to be realistic, oriented towards reality. In this manner, by way of the role played by reality in fiction, realism is revealed as an important phenomenon in fictional constructs. Still, mimesis is a more general, far-reaching and developed operation than the production of realistic fictional texts, which represent one particular mode of imitation. Hence, mimetic activity is not sufficient to stand alone as the foundation of literary realism, although it is a necessary condition.

As opposed to non-mimetic fiction, realist fiction is inscribed in mimetic-verisimilar fiction. For this reason, realism is required to comply with the exigencies of general imitative construction, in addition to which it must comply with others of a strictly realist nature. Within mimetic fiction, it is necessary to distinguish various modes with differing degrees of verisimilitude. Hence, mimetic fiction with a high degree of verisimilitude is differentiated from mimetic fiction of little or restricted verisimilitude, without the latter entering the compass of non-imitative fiction (T. Albaladejo Mayordomo, 1991).

Once the distinction between mimesis and realism is thus established (J. Bruck, 1982), realism can be characterized as a singular mode of realistic mimesis. Realism demands, of course, a very high level of verisimilitude which, moreover, implies a great proximity of the realistic fictional construct to true reality, which is nevertheless not to say that it merges with and becomes one with reality. Properly speaking, it is true non-reality. In artistic practice, realistic mimesis in those texts characterized by the presence of this

3.1. Fictionality: The Imaginary Forms of Fantastic Activity

feature is carried out thanks to the author's constitution of mimetic world models with a high degree of verisimilitude, in which instructions included by a process of selection from all of those possible within the ample field of extension occupy a prominent place. Beings and events of an everyday nature depend on these instructions. Upon the constitution of the referents, these instructions, if they are considered in the aggregate, make these beings and events into semantic constructions with the appearance of being true reality. However, they are not real in the strict sense, nor do the author or the readers pretend they are. In the activity of conforming the world to the fantasy of their artistic texts, the referents of the constructions of realist fiction are the results of intentional selections among beings and events (R. Wellek, 1963; J. P. Stern, 1973), the goal of which is none other than a maximal approximation to the real, true world.

True reality is present in fiction, especially in fiction of a realistic nature, as a collection of elements and relations the organization of which in part determines the mimetic construction, which in turn remains differentiated from reality even in the cases of the greatest degree of verisimilitude and of the greatest approximation between the fictional and real worlds. But this reality is also to be found in fiction in another way: as fragments of the real world included in the fictional text's referent. This is what occurs when truly existing beings and events accompany those of fiction, supporting the appearance of the mimetic fictional construct's reality and becoming impregnated with the fictional nature of those elements with which they are joined in order to form a referent which is, both generally and in particular, of a fictional nature. Recall for example, the powerful novelesque unity which incorporates even historic figures and events in Baroja's *Memorias de un hombre de acción* or Galdós' *Episodios Nacionales*. Both are examples of how the combination of true reality with fiction (B. Gray, 1975, pp. 117 ff.; M. L. Ryan, 1980, pp. 415 ff.; T. Albaladejo Mayordomo, 1986) permits, inversely, the fictional to be anchored in the real world (B. Harshaw, 1984, pp. 241 ff.), contributing powerfully to the reader's recognition of what is represented.

This conjunction of opposing and complementary spheres is what is produced in fictional texts with historical realities, mimetic fictional discourses mixing historical and fictional beings and events as referents. In this class of texts, the inclusion of characters and facts from history reinforces the appearance of reality, contributing to the observation that, in regard to their organization, history and fiction have a lot in common (P. Ricoeur, 1983–1985, Vol. III, pp. 264–279, IV, II.5, 1–2; A. Wright, 1987). However, in spite of the strong appearance of reality obtained, mimetic fiction and realistic mimesis clearly remain unreal.

All of which contributes to explain the necessarily fallacious and repetitive nature of the poetic "lie". The artistic simulacrum necessarily constitutes an unproportionally abstract and stylized form of reference, interchangeable only by virtue of conventions inherent to the language it practices and the artistic system of representation in which it is inscribed. As has been repeated ad nauseam, every painting, even those with the strongest vocation towards realism, is by nature conventional and abstract (A. García-Berrio and M. T. Hernández, 1988a, pp. 77—83). This certainly holds true when it is necessary to explain the volumetric imitation of forms or the proportional parcelling of spaces and perspectives. Moreover, the most realistic literary paintings always and inevitably incorporate methods of representative focalization, the selection of traits and foreshadowing, scarcely corresponding to examples of reality. Do we truly have, from the descriptions of *The Red and the Black*, all of the features of its characters — Julien, Madame de Rênal, or Mathilde de La Mole — which we would immediately acquire with the real and direct knowledge of these individuals if they had existed? Isn't the most accomplished and realistic literary portrait always a diminished form representing a symptomatic selection of objective facts?

Clearly, this selection of semantic elements (E. Gombrich, 1959, Ch. II, V), in spite of the appearance of reality, produces a limited presentation of beings and events deprived of the complete integrity of their features through their dependence on the focalization exercised by the author in the constitution of the world model he realizes, searching for the most representative and significant aspects of the mimetic reality which the artistic text can express. I consider such a selection to be associated with the first of the moments in which, in Ricoeur's opinion, mimesis appears compartmentalized.

In contrast, perhaps the only features truly representable in literature with regard to characters of realistic fiction are their characteristic discourses, their most particular forms of speech. As already mentioned, Baquero Goyanes has made this point in reference to the realistic art of the majority of Spain's novelists. What complete prosopographic paintings of Galdós' characters do we have? Are their descriptions more often than not expressionist stylizations of literary still lifes? (M. Baquero Goyanes, 1956, 1963, 1972). Are we not always more familiar with the modes of speech of Galdós' principle heroes than the visual peculiarities of their physical appearance? Or what amounts to the same thing: don't we usually believe we are seeing these characters when in fact we have only "heard" them?

Unknown to Baquero, Mikhail Bakhtin had already disseminated the notion of the novel's fundamentally polyphonic nature, together with the idea of the expressive and verbal quality of the portraits of beings in novelesque fiction (M. Bakhtin, 1929, 1975). What the realistic novel offers, be it Dostoyevsky's, Flaubert's or Balzac's, is not, as is customarily claimed, a portrait gallery, but rather a graduated and dialectical collection of individual and social "voices". On the other hand, the idea that the role of characters' discourses is fundamental in realistic mimesis is an ancient element in literary theory regarding the novel (E. Auerbach, 1946; G. N. Leech and M. N. Short, 1981, pp. 160 ff.).

In the mechanism of recognition particular to fictional realistic mimesis, we are primarily interested in *generalization* or archetypal universalization more than in the complementary literary mechanisms of realist *singularization* and *individualization* (G. Lukács, 1954; 1963, III, pp. 199—275, Ch. 11.V). Generalization is the result of the abstraction of features by which the author attempts to have those characteristics he wants to represent occupy the predominant place in the world model and the referent (E. H. Gombrich, 1959, Intro., Ch. VI). This abstraction leads in many cases to the conventional representation of *stereotypes* (R. Amossy, 1984; Z. Ben-Porat, 1986) and stylized versions of portions of reality (V. Nemoianu, 1984, p. 293).

The generalization in mimesis fits in perfectly with Aristotle's well-known conception of poetry as a representation of the general, while also serving as the basis for the possible extension of fiction to lyric. On the other hand, detailed description contributes to individualization, which is not, however, exclusive to mimesis or sufficient for its production (E. Auerbach, 1946; J. P. Stern, 1973, pp. 129 ff.; N. Schor, 1984). The ethical and imaginary mechanisms working to produce our interest and involvement in fictions reside only at the point of osmosis where the common and opposed origin of these two divergent senses is diversified within the novel's unique and identical directional path, according to the form in which the Marxist theorists of novelesque realism have commonly succeeded in identifying and representing it, especially since Lukács (G. Lukács, 1920, 1955, 1958; E. Fischer, 1970; P. Chiarini, 1983).

In the art of classical tragedy the abstract consistency of mythic archetypes, scarcely detailed in naturalist terms, permits the recourse's roots to be considered in terms of their schematic perspicuity. This is classical art's didactic-archetypal conception, which all "Romantic" art has later striven to confuse and camouflage, superimposing its own poor attempts at detailed plastic representation. In the most recent period of determined novelesque naturalism the multiplication of singularizing facts has almost always failed in its efforts to entirely individualize and singularize the "character". Even if it had completely achieved its aims, it surely would have ruined the character's literariness, in a manner similar to what has occurred with the photographic excesses of hyperrealism in recent painting. Only through readers' *recognition* of the identificatory generalization of the type as model, is the interest of the moral and imaginary adherence of our true needs and demands ignited and propelled in the fictional flight towards an irreducible irreality, which is the very flesh and bones of fiction's fantastic creatures.

If before I recalled that there is no painting, nor literature for that matter, that is not conventional and abstract, I can now declare similarly that there exists no unreal fiction; that is, there is no unrealistic fiction that does not base its sustained interest on essential forms of realist necessity (R. Arnheim, 1954; E. H. Gombrich, 1959). In other words, the intranscendent game of literature, which the poetics of pure fiction always comes down to in some form, constitutes an unsustainable entelechy. Fictional space suggests literature's playful domain is a distinctive feature of the imagination, an explicit tribute and sublime recognition of an indispensably essential existential dimension: that which posits possible alternatives based on the rigid, narrow scope of the real. But this alternative dimension does not impair the necessary anthropological questioning of the nature of being and the principles of existence; rather, it empowers the explanations and makes them flexible, communicating and confirming them in the convergent expansion of the univocal space of "reality" in a series of alternative "worlds". Both fantastic/imaginary fiction and realistic fiction consist in the representation of referents shaped by different worlds and subworlds forming complex imaginary patterns, according to the theory of possible worlds previously discussed. The oppositions between the mimetic-real world and the worlds of desire, dream, hope, fear, etc., establish a tension (T. Albaladejo Mayordomo, 1991) in which the reader recognizes constants of his experience of the world, to the extent that they are also constants of general human experience.

The mimetic fiction of realism superimposes individual creatures on a symbolic archetype, establishes the trajectory of the realistic event's actions in a simple anthropological geometry of spatial designs and of subconscious drives, constructs its physical spaces in the essential fields of anthropological representation (A. García-Berrio, 1985; R. Ronen, 1986), and multiplies essential time into a succession of causal moments. But underneath its volume of natural consistencies and of representations of a realistic tendency, fiction affirms that which is essential and necessary, the causes which sustain its frivolous, interchangeable and intranscendent appearances, above and beyond its nature as an inexplicable game.

Don Quijote and Sancho, as has often been repeated, fictionally embody two essential spaces of reality, as the fundamental contrast in Cervantine narration between open country and the inn also places essential forms — closed and open, unlimited and finite — in opposition: forms of the comprehension and representation of time in terms of space and space in terms of time. Without their reduction to forms of reality of the archetypally essential, the circumstantial and multiple manifestations of the unreal in fiction would undoubtedly be incapable of forming the rigorous space of necessary convergences which are the very reasons for the existence of man's interest in art. Literature's fictional component implies the supplementary artifice of imagination, to which it contributes the unique mechanism of artistic recognition, a cheerful recognition of dispensable forms which soon discovers, as we have seen, its essential substance's reason for being.

The fascination and appeal of the fictional story is thus constituted through the mediation of fantastic operations of external mimesis which make up the playful surface of *poiesis*, under the essential guarantee of an internal system of imaginary convergences which translates the conventional symbols of the *fabula* into fundamental structures of the fantastic representation of the universe. The action of fantasy in the fictional story is powerfully and highly complex. Normally, one thinks only of the imagination's capacity to communicate the conventional forms of mimetic discourse through the real referents that said forms introduce between the text's transmitter and receiver. That, of course, is the fictional space corresponding to the most superficial dimension, innocent and external to fiction. But the imagination's work does not end here; on the contrary, it lodges immediately recognizable forms in spaces not always present to exterior consciousness, but which are nevertheless those definitively operating in the most committed and demanding activity of artistic mimesis.

3.1.4. *The Realist Control of Fantasy: The Law of Semantic Maxima in Fictional Production*

Tomás Albaladejo has formulated the set of rules that operate to create and govern the fantastic fictional illusion (1986). The "law of semantic maxima", as he denominates it, regulates the levels of indispensible saturation of objective and real references required for fiction's unhindered construction, according to the fiction's intended place among the set of possible worlds, at the service of the communicants of the fictional verbal act. It is the *law of semantic maxima* which propels non-fictional beings and events capable, as we have seen, of forming part of discourses of a fictional nature, towards fiction. These non-fictional beings and events are integrated as components of fictional discourses and contribute in large measure to sustain the fictional illusion thanks to the semantic shift which unhinges them from the objective reality they form a part of.

The fictional construct is the result of a semantic elevation with respect to the real objective world, wherein the semantic level which we ought to consider as normal resides, corresponding to the field of direct human experience. Once located in fiction, when a fictional construction with a different referent from true reality has been established, fantasy, which has already been active in the elimination of the objective world's boundaries, deploys all of its creative energy for the creation of alternative worlds; that is, of substitute worlds. The tendency towards fantastic representation is so strong in *poiesis* that fiction, located at gradually ascending semantic levels according to the scale of world model types differing from actual reality, dynamically attracts the reality integrated in the referent, which emerges as entirely fictional. The inclusion of verisimilar fictional elements in non-verisimilar fictional constructs also responds to this fantastic tendency, resulting in the transformation of verisimilar elements into non-verisimilar fictional elements by means of their integration into non-verisimilar fictions.

The law of semantic maxima, the theoretical literary formulation of a device for the constitution of fictions, also controls the fictional hypertrophy or saturation in the referents of fictional texts corresponding to different types of world models. The only limit to imaginary progression at the maximal level of fictionality is set by the requirement that the general lines of imaginary representation feeding the connection between the fictional artistic text and the most profound human reality be maintained, even in the least mimetic and most fantastic fictional constructs. The law of semantic maxima is active in those texts in which the referent is governed by a world model of the non-verisimilar fictional, thus avoiding a semantic hypertropy which would produce a fictional text uprooted from the imagination's constants.

In fictional mimetic constructs, with referents depending on world models of the verisimilar fictional type, the law of semantic maxima prevents the production of a fictional saturation which would exceed the maximal semantic limit of realist fiction. Exceeding this limit would mean the frustration of the aesthetic will which sustains the creation of mimesis, resulting in a non-verisimilar fictional construct, which in this instance of poietic activity we would not have desired. The law of semantic maxima also insures that mimetic fiction does not depart in its imaginary configurations from the anthropological constants of an essential function, constants of man's profound and intimate reality.

The whole collection of details of realistic convergence guarantees the fictional illusion. In painting, the genre which is currently called realistic or even hyperrealist annoyingly multiplies the trajectories of convergence at the nearest and most evident surface of its referents, in a fairly ingenuous exercise of technical virtuosity (P. Sager, 1974). All of these innocent efforts at realism would cease to be valuable without the structural appeal of the painting's dispositive background, a combination of elementary plastic and visual forms and successful exercises in the harmonic organization of space. This explains our appraisal of the current efforts of a sector of hyperrealist painting as a step back in the history of the plastic arts (A. García-Berrio and M. T. Hernández, 1988a). Abstraction represented the definitive acquisition of the immediacy of what is essential in painting, albeit self-evident that in the practice of abstraction, as in everything, there is some essential success and a lot of repetition, ineffectiveness and failure. In this respect, the development of the modern abstract plastic arts does not differ from the history of Western realism, with its few numbered museum-quality successes and its infinite factional recapitulations, which turn out to be both useless and inexpressive.

Artistic mimesis' realistic effect has always moved us, in painting as in literature, not by virtue of the simple exercise of exact duplication, but precisely because of what in the artistic replica is unattainable in its model, in reality: the deforming "stylization" of the objectively real and the "spiritual" contagion of the most silent and inexpressive material in the historical presence of the model. Even in the most naive form of the artistic marvel in painting there comes into play the consciousness of the unavoidable difference between the multidimensional object belonging to reality and the compulsory bidimensional nature of the representational base. Painting's fictional surprise, as with literature, necessarily requires the previous assumption of the unreal difference between artistic objects and the being of reality. This *difference*, indispensable in the constitution of artistic fictionality, is implied in Leonardo's famous notion that painting is an "idea" or "mental object" (E. Panofsky, 1976 edition).

As we can see, everything converges on the consideration of the powerful undertone of imaginary activity in fictionality. Until now, in literature as in the plastic arts, attention has been focused on the design of the rules patterning fiction as a realistic illusion, fixing the maximal and minimal levels of saturation which effectively constitute or mar it. The conventions of fiction in the plastic arts are known as rules of chiaroscuro, perspective, of the dispersion of volumes, etc. Up until recently, the corresponding rules of mimetic economy in literary fiction have been less often proclaimed, in view of the fact that they are not as clearly evident.

The problem in question really involves the rules of discursive efficacy, a concept already well-covered in the conventional artistic representation of the unreproducible infinite discourse of historic reality, reproduced and reimplanted at a scale accessible to literature, according to certain proportional criteria of semantic convenience. Nevertheless, what interests me more here is to emphasize that less familiar part of the fantastic activity in the mechanisms of fiction; that is, that which expresses the principles of convergence between narrative mimesis and every other instance of mimesis in literary discourse. What is involved is the dynamic of the imagination which reproduces in artistic texts the universal convergences reiterated in all acts of anthropological experience.

Only from this perspective can the Aristotelian principle of mimetic *recognition* acquire its greatest capacity for universal explanation. Through artistic fiction — the realistic as well as the abstract, for at the least immediate level of imaginary activity the two are identified — man recognizes and rediscovers the deep revelations of his most muffled historic experiences. What is unique to recognition refers to that simple realist activity functioning in order to distance or de-automatize art beyond the absolute novelty of the communication of knowledge, of "cognition". But, at the same time, the depth of the anthropological space in which the imaginary resonances of artistic recognition explode, presents us with this activity as an acquisition by no means trivial, but rather as an essential and irreplaceable form of experience (E. H. Gombrich, 1959).

The most profound imaginary reconstruction guarantees the fundamental nature of the play of rules of fictional mimetic convergence, rescuing pure forms of prelogical and premetaphysical space which Derrida has referred to in particular as the area of the *trace* (J. Derrida, 1967a, pp. 92—95; 1976, pp. 62—65).

This explains why artistic fiction since Aristotle has not been identified with the common forms of logical knowledge and cognition, but with the subtle and special mechanisms of a kind of discovery produced in the area of the purest, most logical and objective knowledge, amounting to a subjective recovery, a flowering of the imaginary encounter's most intimate personal experiences. Obviously, in acknowledging this aspect of the imagination's activity, I do not mean to invoke or encourage any adherence to the risky hypotheses of Derridean philosophy in its least verifiable zones.

Rather, my aim is only to relocate the least controversial suppositions of artistic and poetic experience, indicating their fundamental irreducibility to logical reasoning. The depth of artistic communication, its unique and irreplaceable ability, resides in the necessary contents that it is capable of contributing to anthropological experience, a universe of converging forms, expressing the most solid principles of man's cosmological orientation, rescued by the imagination from the unreachable density of the subconscious through, among others, the instruments of literary fiction.

The set of verbal mechanisms and imaginary activities mobilized by literary fiction in its mimetic-reproductive stage fulfills the role of motivating and unleashing the poetic imagination in ways very similar to those of the fantastic provocation in rhetorical expressiveness. In a strict sense it can be affirmed without exaggeration that mimetico-realistic fictionality is part of the same system of expressive processes that I have already examined elsewhere with regard to rhetorical devices. Literary fictionality is the fruit of fantasy's primary conventions and activities, which are invoked and concretized in expressive agreements guaranteed by a strict system of artistic-communicative conventions, above all, by virtue of the fact that certain twists and expressive formulas of the literary text are projected to the representation of equivalent verbal forms belonging to the real universe.

From the point of view of the psychological and imaginary activity regulating the fictional operations of artistic mimesis, we find ourselves before a new demarcation of literary axiologies, which can be explained by reference to the difference between forms of *fantasy* and forms of *imagination*, already described and applied here to other dilemmas. As with the fantastic results of the connotative periphery of expressiveness, realistic fiction's unique constructions also act with the cooperation of conscious and associative facts of reason and judgment. Fantasy's regulation of fictional entities and decisions concerning their reality or unreality, the appraisal of whether they are verisimilar of non-verisimilar, possible or impossible, is the result of the joint use of the imagination and cognitive experience. *The semantics of fiction*, realistic or fantastic, traverses conscious experience's cooperative control over fantasy (A. García-Berrio and M. T. Hernández, 1988, pp. 52–53).

As far as *fictional syntax* is concerned, the same structure is evident. The constructive syntactic relationship between semantico-fictional entities in *mythos'* discursive body, whether it is realistic or fantastic, is regulated according to the same rules of conscious experience which discriminate, clarify and graduate the diverse constitutive entities of fictional semantics. The rules governing the interdependent, dependent or independent construction of narrative sequences of necessity, chance, congruence, non-verisimilitude, desire, fear, dream, illusion, etc., are also *nomical* products, that is, determined. Rational experience, historical knowledge, and the cognitive arsenal of observed and contemplated facts, among others, intervene in the form in which the rules are proposed and formulated.

Frequently the value of classical fictional narrative's construction is attributed precisely to the relevance, depth and rarity of the observed facts, which progressively develop in density to the detailed and exhaustive accumulation characterizing the poetics of the naturalist novel. In these cases, what is applauded or censured in the construct is the verisimilitude of the semantico-fictional discoveries and of the syntactico-narrative associations. Realistic *fictional pragmatics*, like that which distinguishes it from the different modes of fiction, acts according to a well established network of conventions which simultaneously feed and limit conscious fantasy, the general constitutive principle in the nature of mimesis, according to objective reason's set of rules.

As a poetic property of literary discourse, fictionality is a premise which does not by any means deplete all of the possible references available to the imagination's poetic activity for the constitution of verbal art. In the most recent renovation of the concept, the poststructuralist sector of linguistic poetics, as previously mentioned, did not seriously consider attending to the development of fantasy's artistic work in its natural and not strictly fictional realm. Rather, recent revisions of our understanding of fictionality have tended towards the exclusive incorporation of its manifestations in narration and the novel. There has been no attempt to establish broader connections with or differences from the evident modes of fantastic activity involved in the pragmatic production of the poetic messages of other not strictly narrative fictional kinds of literature such as the lyric.

When fictionality alone is invoked as literary activity's specific imaginary trait, the customary error of identifying literature with the novel, very characteristic of this century's critical reflection, is only perpetuated. As I have repeatedly indicated, fictionality, an illusion of realist or naturalist referentiality in verbal discourse, is only one of the imaginary activity's manifestations, all of which together complement the development of the text's verbal scheme, propelling it towards the general verbal and imaginary substantiveness which we identify with a work of art. The most recognizable aspects of realist fictionality cannot possibly encompass the varied elements characterizing the full domain of the imagination's textual artistic work. Nevertheless, the truly realistic and referentially mimetic work of fictionality most surely rest on more universal mechanisms of imaginary activity.

Considering its various modes, degrees and forms of effectiveness, what we have said about expressiveness is generally also applicable to the uniqueness of fictionality's poetic capacity: it is an insufficient *sine qua non*. The literary exercise of composing the syntactic and semantic textual conditions in a manner capable of satisfactorily reproducing the pragmatic effect of fictional illusion is more of an expedient mediating the process of achieving poetic value. The fictional effect's pragmatic capacity is an indispensable indicator of a novel's poeticity. By the same token, insufficient fictional credibility radically legislates against any poetic aspiration in those texts that have opted for fictional discourse as an expressive meaningful form.

The poetic effect and value of great novels, like *Don Quijote*, *War and Peace* and *Ulysses*, far exceeds the simple extent of their fictional credibility. The characters, events, times and scenery capable of persuading beyond the verisimilar possibilities and conveniences of their individual histories are merely convincing signs, the symptoms of the very successful individual animation of a few great movements orienting the human spirit, "architectonic" universals approximating Bakhtin's intuition, universals of anthropologico-imaginary symbolization and perennial forms of the fantastic orientation of time and space as coordinates of anthropologico-imaginary orientation. It is the deep strata of this *essential identification* where the great fictional texts coincide, undifferentiated, with other sublime manifestations of literary and artistic *poiesis*.

The special kind of *poiesis* in which the lyrical universe reveals its status as a particular variant in terms of a "possible world", as has been revealed to us from Leibniz to Doležel, is identified with its anthropologico-fantastic base. Upon this same base, fundamentally anchored in anthropological revelation, lyric's essential, intimate and personal confidence ends up becoming a "true fiction" for Baumgarten. In the final anthropologico-imaginary identification of symbolic values, the purely verisimilar forms of fiction and the true expressions of the lyrical are united in their common mediating condition as meaningful messages.

Fictionality, currently identified above all as the characteristic property of narration in the novel and theater, thus appears in the form of a modal variant of literary expressiveness. It is also, like literary expressiveness, an unpredictable form of wisdom, conventional in its textual and semantic origins but aleatory as a pragmatic result. Because of its unforeseeable pragmatic nature, the successful products of fictional expressiveness already share in the axiological status of the poetic in terms of *value* which I have attributed to poeticity. But, as is true for verbal and conceptual expressiveness as well, fictionality's poetic value is an elaborated value, an aggregate construct, obtained through mediation. As opposed to the fantastic nature of the fictional narrative's imaginary work, the fundamental value of the poetic stakes its reason for being in the deepest regions of the imagination's anthropological constitution, where the poetic experience takes the form of the purest prelogical intuition.

3.1.5. *Literary Fantasy's Conceptual Forms: The Cultural Imagination*

Both the fantastic constitution of fictionality's artistic phenomena and the unique periphery of literary expressiveness participate, as we have seen, in the universe of fantasy's forms. In this universe they demand and receive the

3.1. Fictionality: The Imaginary Forms of Fantastic Activity 343

psychological resonance which we link to the success or failure of a large number of verbal formulas' symptomatic outlines. Images and emotions, lively representations of fantasy and feelings of singular affective vibration are the result for literature and art of that common work of well-chosen and effective words, of novel concepts with powerful capacities for sentimental resonance and of the imagination's evocative and relational forms. All of which has already been emphasized; still, I must mention these first conceptual forms of poetic fantasy, the most available and perceptible, in order to fully set forth the imaginary foundations of poeticity.

I designate all of the fantastic phenomena bound to the psychological space of expressiveness and artistic fictionality as the imagination's conceptual forms in order to differentiate them from the imagination's anthropological structures, which are phenomena which underlie the establishment of the aesthetic sense of poetic value and significance, generally unnoticed or even subconscious. All of the considerations up to this point regarding the fantastic periphery of the successful artistic effect of expressiveness and fictional illusion constitute the space of those conceptual forms of the literary imagination, those most familiar and most immediately detectable in the dense block of emotions which we identify with the aesthetic entity. Until now little attention has been paid to what I have denominated the imagination's anthropological structures; and only the recent work of sectors of artistic psychology, anthropology and mythocriticism, extending from Jung and Bachelard to Durand and his school, has made it possible to gain analytical access to these terminal — and for this very reason essential and basic — zones of the poetic phenomenon's constitution as a value of anthropological responsibility.

In this book, given the novelty of the questions implied in the imagination's anthropological structure and the importance which I attribute to them in the genesis of poetic emotion, I will proceed to examine them in detail in the following chapters. On the other hand, the clear and doctrinally well-known nature of the imaginary forms associated with the artistic expression of conceptual contents persuades me not to embark upon a more detailed consideration of these topics beyond the discussion already presented in the chapters concerning expressiveness and poeticity.

The differential nature of the poetic concepts amplified by the imagination may reach the most vital depths of personal experience, even transfiguring the most resistant emotions — often because they are objectively trivial — into conceptual formulations. For example, the sense of solitude experienced as a difference from "others" predominates in a book by an excellent Spanish poet of my own generation, Carlos Piera's *Anthology for a Parrot (Antología para un papagayo)*. Piera's poems exhibit a keen observation of reality tempered by the elegant and precisely correct positioning of feelings of anguish, an anguish impeded from overflowing entirely at the last possible moment by an ironic feeling of identity. Only the comprehensive impulse of the fantasy is capable of making difficultly identifiable emotions recognizable. This is evident in the poem "Gusto en verlos", ("A Pleasure to See/Meet You"), which also plays with the polyvalent meanings of the title's conventional expression of greeting:

> Se me han ido empañando los cristales.
>
> Depositado en una Arcadia, compro
> felicidad de otros en sus tiendas.
>
> [The windows have been steaming up on me.
>
> Deposited in an Arcadia,
> I buy others' happiness in their stores].

In order to sentimentally appraise the moving effort of solidarity compelled by the deep imperative of ethical reason in this "different" solitary man, our own fantasy must actively strive to frame and define the infinite similarities and differences in men's behavior. And above all, in the case of this formulation and in my own act of reading, the imagination must activate innumerable differential frustrations of "dis-identification". Analogously, although focused on other contents, the succeeding allegory of a "distanced" urban mass is activated in the description of the pleasant existence of a society of squirrels and badgers:

> En paz con los castaños y las lluvias
> dejan el bosque y su cobijo a veces.
> Se congregan al paso, se sonríen,
> desaparecen como los tejones.
>
> [In peace with the chestnut trees and the rains
> they leave the woods and their burrows sometimes.
> In passing they congregate, exchange smiles,
> vanish like badgers].

The imagination, sentimentally reactivating the habits of conceptualized experience — divided and apportioned in the cultural memory's mass of associations — is ultimately responsible for the sentimental and valorative focus. It announces a restrained anguish in terms of an impotent awareness of difference inseparable from its essential being:

> Yo, que no sé guardar para el invierno,
> con mi indulgencia desde mis rendijas,
> yo, el tipo de detrás de las ventanas,
> quería ser normal.
>
> [I, who do not know to save for winter,
> with indulgence from my crevices,
> I, the fellow from behind the windows,
> wanted to be normal].
>
> (Carlos Piera, *Antología para un papagayo*, Madrid, Hiperión, 1985).

Fantasy diligently rummages through memories of the animal life of badgers, La Fontaine's fable, the ethical appraisal that might be made for compassion for oneself, the esteem for disciplined control, the ethical and artistic admiration of exact limits, through its own memories of the desolate vision of Anglo-Saxon cities, deserted on Sundays, with observers perched behind windows, and through the tender reaches of an ingenuous and impossible refusal of all differential identity. These and many other simultaneous associations are necessary in order to transform the rigorous allusivity of an expressive account of the reality and feeling of "difference", as consciousness of an impossible identification, into the attractive sentimental groundwork for a successful poem.

When culture's communicative economy elects to adopt the frequent literary expedient of cloaking rationalizable concepts and experiences under a mantle of poetic allusivity, it is conscious of seeking the support of verbal expressiveness, capable of mobilizing fantasy's imaginary activity in order to achieve complex and hidden aims with the intention, above all, of exemplarily perpetuating them. The poetic expressiveness achieved in definitive forms, fantastically coined and materialized, externalizes notions and indelibly seals feelings. Recall, as regards the latter, the best examples of didactic poetry. In this sense, for example, the high value of Horace's *Literary Epistles*, especially the one directed towards Pison's sons, illustrates the capacity for the doctrinal fixation and perpetuation of the literary imagination's expressive forms. It is a proven fact (C. O. Brink, 1963—1982; A. García-Berrio, 1977—1980) that the ideas which Horace reduces to poetic expression's exact discipline in this work were commonplaces circulating in the fungible imprecision of classical technical, rhetorical and poetic texts. Horace's contribution amounts only to the poetic inscription of the same, achieved in terms of a rigorous expressive economy and an exact capacity for imaginative perpetuation. Nevertheless, no one doubts the definitive achievement in his historical rendering of that personal literary assimilation.

Expressive success and the capacity for imaginary and sentimental mobilization of exquisite emotional registers are characteristics equally unique to poetry. The sentimental itinerary of amorous passion in Salinas' *La voz a ti debida* enriches the common experience of recollected love, on which the human capacity for memory scarcely reflects, with infinite circumstances and nuance. An excellent poet like Jaime Gil de Biedma is able to represent in the series of "Poemas póstumos" ("Posthumous Poems") in *Las personas del verbo (The Persons of the Verb)* abysmal forms of the self's splitting and entering into conflict with itself, as expressed in the poem "Contra Jaime Gil de Biedma" ("Against Jaime Gil de Biedma"):

> De tus regresos guardo una impresión confusa
> de pánico, de pena y descontento,
> y la desesperanza
> y la impaciencia y el resentimiento
> de volver a sufrir, otra vez más,
> la humillación imperdonable
> de la excesiva intimidad.

> [Of your returns I have a confused impression
> of panic, of grief and unhappiness,
> and the desperation
> and the impatience and the resentment
> of returning to suffer, once again,
> the unforgivable humiliation
> of excessive intimacy].

In cases like these, the imperfect and lazy fantasy of souls foreign to the profound discovery's happy trance are opened to the total perfection of a dazzling lightning-bolt of absolute truth:

> ¡Oh innoble servidumbre de amar seres humanos,
> y la más innoble
> que es amarse a sí mismo!

> [Oh the ignoble slavery of loving human beings,
> and the most ignoble
> of loving oneself!]

The poet's imagination deepens the examination of the most profound feelings and the possibility of giving verbal form to conceptual images. In successful cases it is capable of carrying the soul of the reader most distanced from those emotions to the warm measure of their exactitude. Recall Gil de Biedma's "Pandémica y celeste":

> Yo persigo también el dulce amor,
> el tierno amor para dormir al lado
> y que alegre mi cama al despertar
> cercano como un pájaro.

> [I also pursue sweet love,
> the tender love to sleep beside
> the one that cheers my bed upon waking
> close as a bird].

(Jaime Gil de Biedma, *Las personas del verbo*, Barcelona, Seix Barral, 1982).

The poetic discoveries of this kind of imagination, coating the concept's worn neutrality with feeling and uncommon images, constitute, among forms of poetic phenomena, the most prevalent and the first to be recognized, identified and conceived. It is what appears in the moral and emblematic reflections which activate the judgments of Greek tragedy, and continues through to the most direct and profound sanctions on the human heart's contradictory nature in Shakespeare's plays. It does not matter that in Homer or Dante, Cervantes or Goethe the analysis of their poeticity also reveals — as will be demonstrated here later — deeper and more radical underpinnings to the imagination's structure. From the beginning of the reading of their works and surely even from the conscious origins of their own psychological representations, the most evident and active task of poeticity proclaimed in the labors of these great artists has been located in these forms of conscious experience's imaginary and sensible overlays.

3.1. Fictionality: The Imaginary Forms of Fantastic Activity

Along with poetic fantasy's vital, essential and existential discoveries, literature has fostered and nourished another special form of the non-anthropological imagination, which I call the *cultural imagination*, an endogamous activity of artistic fabulation in which poetry feeds on the poetic imagination crystallized in privileged mythical moments. The Grecomania of Roman literature and even of Greek decadent literature already composed the first products based on this structure of poetic imagination. The Renaissance also, from its very beginnings, experienced a poetic attraction to the archaeology of a "superior" and idealized age. In Florence and Rome, the rediscovered ancient statues were adored and, as Dante exalted Virgil, so Alberti exalted Vitruvius and Lorenzo, and Poliziano exalted the classical Aphrodite appearing on Botticelli's panels.

Nevertheless, with the total imposition of mannerist fashion, the cultural imagination began to enjoy its most absolute affirmation. The mannerist painter perceived the image mediated through Raphael Sanzio's retina rather than in the objective naturalism of the real, and poets from Bembo to Chiabrera and Garcilaso to Góngora adjusted the poetic scheme of their passions to the sentimental itinerary conventionalized by Petrarch's *Canzoniere*. The cultural imagination unfolds the modern phase of its integration with poetic emotion's productive scheme, affirming the classical notion of *retractatio* and imitation and, above all, discovering in "mannered art" literature's own successful objects and creations as mythical pillars of imaginary activity.

In this way, the "echoes" of earlier voices and gestures begin to become poetic ingredients explicitly mobilized in art's game of aesthetic suggestion. From the point of view of the imagination's poetic work, a third path for the construction of aesthetic images is opened, that of the cultural imagination, in addition to the two others addressed in this book: first, that which I have characterized until now as fantastico-expressive, fictional and involving the sentimental coating and deepening of conceptualizable experiences; and, secondly, that which in subsequent chapters will be defined as anthropological universal. The cultural imagination deepens the powers of poetic resonance of previous literary discoveries, consolidated in their dimension as artistic myths. It is, therefore, a poetic form entirely rooted in the sentiments of the aesthetic and cultural tradition itself (H. Bloom, 1973, 1975).

Every age or historical mode of artistic aesthetics has preferentially delved into one of these two forms of conceptual poetic inspiration, the extroverted and existential or the autoreflexive and mannerist, to such an extent that the entire history of art can be written by following the pendular swings of these alternative forms of fantastic creation. In the case of recent Spanish literature, we have at hand a particularly intense and monographic representation of the mannerist manifestation of the cultural imagination in the poetry of those who, since José María Castellet's anthology, have become known as "novísimos". Authors like Pedro Gimferrer and Guillermo Carnero on the one hand, and José María Álvarez and Antonio Martínez Sarrión on the other, exalt the deliberately stereotyped representation of the old classical myths — Mediterranean, Venetian, Orientalist, etc. — or of the new musical and cinematographic culture as objectives for the inspired crystallization of the imagination's poetic caress.

Influenced by the canonic technicalisms of the prestigious linguistics of the seventies, this mannerist mode of the cultural imagination is often referred to as "metapoetry" (C. Bousoño, 1952, pp. 27—30). And, in reality, it has been just that in at least two senses. First, as a metalinguistic reflection on the process of everyday language's transformation into poetic language, it has been exemplarily cultivated by authors like Guillermo Carnero or, almost monographically in his book *Columnae*, by Jaime Siles. Secondly, we can also speak of a *mythic metapoetry* in the preferences of these "novísimos", which delights in the sentimental iridescence of aesthetic history's culminating moments, generally decadent, or is given to deliberately cultivate scenographic splendors. The latter is exemplified in two works by José María Álvarez, *Museo de Cera (Wax Museum)* and *La edad de oro (The Golden Age)*, and the former in Guillermo Carnero's *Dibujo de la Muerte (Drawing of Death)*.

The most characteristic aspect of this postmodern aesthetics in Spanish literature is obviously not its originality, representing, as we have noted, one of the poetic imagination's classic resources, but maybe only the obsessive insistence of its predominance in the work of a group of poets that, beyond this pact of working with the cultural imagination, do not share a homogeneous aesthetic and, above all, have not yet succeeded in establishing, any one of them, the autonomous expression of a recognizable individual voice with which they may be identified. Of course, their critics and the poets themselves look for and propose other consistent stylistic features of the imagination and of certain shared sensibilities, attempting to find some common ground in otherwise intrinsically different aesthetics, but I believe all of these solutions are still very far from finding any more apt formula beyond this mannerist passion for the artistic monumentalism of various themes, which I have been characterizing here as a form of the cultural imagination.

I propose to illustrate this with one of its most representative examples: Guillermo Carnero's exquisite and dazzling poem "Embarque a Citerea" ("Embarkation for Cythera"). To begin with, a flood of cultural resonances belonging to both the plastic and literary arts is already produced with the title's evocation. Among the less obscure we might recall the insular idyll of Hölderlin's "The Archipelago", and the contrasting and sinister image of "Un voyage à Cithère" ("A Voyage to Cythera") from *The Flowers of Evil*, in which the imaginary construction of the cultural idyll is thematized as a vehicle for interested reflection, contrasted with a fierce and degraded realism, characteristic of the book's essence:

> Île des doux secrets et des fêtes du coeur!
> De l'antique Vénus le superbe fantôme
> Au-dessus de tes mers plane comme un arome,
> Et charge les esprits d'amour et de langueur.

3.1. Fictionality: The Imaginary Forms of Fantastic Activity

Belle île aux myrtes verts, pleine de fleurs écloses,
Vénérée à jamais par toute nation.
Où les soupirs des coeurs en adoration
Roulent comme l'encens sur un jardin de roses.

[Island of sweet intrigues, and feastings of the heart! / Of ancient Venus, most magnificent of ghosts, / Over your swelling seas glides a bewitching scent / Enrapturing the soul in languishing and love. // Sweet isle of greenery, myrtle and blooming flowers, / Perpetual delight of men in every land, / Where sights of adoration from the hearts of lovers / Roll as incense over a rose bower (Baudelaire, 1985 edition, p. 137)].

Another reflection on the Cythera theme, resembling Carnero's in its inspiration, is Jaime Gil de Biedma's "Desembarco en Citerea" ("Disembarkment in Cythera"). But here the mythic presence of the cultural imagination's repercussions ends up absorbed by a lover's sentimental experiences, coded in terms of a bloodcurling decadence: "Porque le apremia el tiempo / y en amor — él lo sabe —/ aunque no tiene aún que dar dinero / tiene ya que dar inteligencia" [Because time presses him / and in love — he already knows it —/ although he does not yet have to give money / he must already show intelligence].

Carnero's evocative talent, abundant even in its detailed documentation, without doubt has composed the most suggestive classical picture of all the imaginary reconstructions the theme has given rise to. He relives the melancholy instant of the animated embarkation, recreating the scene's fantastic details, his allusive success dazzlingly furnishing the power of evocative conviction:

Hoy que la triste nave está al partir
con su espectacular monotonía,
quiero quedarme en la ribera, ver
confluir los colores en un mar de ceniza
y mientras tenuemente tañe el viento
las jarcias y las crines de los grifos dorados
oír lejanos en la oscuridad
los remos, los fanales y estar solo.

[Today, as the sad ship is about to depart
with its spectacular monotony,
I want to stay on the shore, see
the colors of an ash sea converge
and while the wind tenuously strokes
the rigs and manes of the golden griffins
hear the oars and great lamps distant
in the obscurity and be alone].

Here then is the dialectic of a man full of foreboding, of the self guessing at itself before the golden age of myths, with the imaginary representation of the dream, a pure sea of sensations and colors joining together to test a purely aesthetic reality. The poem portrays a state of mind, the nostalgia for a lost age, sensed by an imagination nourished on historical accounts, on anonymous decadent Greek poems, and on the evocative engravings of some

Romantic dreamers. Carnero's cultural imagination serves, above all, as a stage-setting for manifesting his elegant *spleen*:

> Y no guardo rencor
> sino un deseo inhábil que no
> colman las acrobacias de la voluntad,
> y cierta ingratitud no muy profunda.
>
> [And I hold no grudge
> but rather an unfit desire which
> the will's acrobatics do not satisfy,
> and a certain not very deep ingratitude].

(Guillermo Carnero, *Ensayo de una teoría de la visión*, Madrid, Hiperión, 1979).

The cultural imagination is, as I have already said, an important domain of poetic inspiration. Its presence has always characterized literary schools and tendencies, commonly in artistic times, and particular personalities brushed by the bittersweet overtones of elegant decadence. We have just seen this confirmed in the case of the recent Spanish *novísimos*, but, as I suggested, it is an entirely historical recourse. All of the poetry of homage frequent in Machado, Aleixandre and García Lorca, for example, directly exploits this method. In the Spanish tradition, it is worth highlighting Jorge Guillén's *Homenaje (Homage)*, in which the poet records his own cultural dialogue with the best figures of the past. All that which in *Cántico* involves the diurnal recording of present reality, animated by eros' regenerating effect and pressed out of the encircling void of nocturnal shadows, in *Homenaje* is the historical exploration of reality as cultural space. And the same may be said for Rafael Alberti's *A la pintura*, a dialogue the author sustains in the present with the artistic tradition's affective forms.

I have already insisted on the classic antiquity of this cultural form of metapoetic imagination, finding its plenitude in the sentimental exercise of archaeological resurrection for which the Renaissance is recognized and with which it is identified, and in which Mannerism is created. But the current form in which postmodernity explores these mythic creatures of the cultural imagination has without a doubt its strongest precedent in the sentimental experience of this facet of poetic imagination inaugurated with Romanticism. Recall the power of the classical myths in Hölderlin, sustaining his unshakable ethical serenity.

"The Archipelago" is, for example, primarily a passionate epic song in which the evocation of Hellenic places, personalities and events is rigorously adjusted to the themes' customary associations in terms of history's successive chronology. This is so, above all, in Hölderlin's narration of the process of invasion, ruin, victory and reconstruction, which presupposes his lyrical poetization of the narration of the historical events in the Greek wars of the fifth-century (B. C.), one of the poem's most extensive segments. On the other hand, the elegiac theme of "The Archipelago" necessarily provides entry to the imaginary sense of the Greek age's collapse, of Athen's ruin, of the disappeared and buried forms of heroes beneath present fields, all emotional themes visible in the spatial mythology which I will set forth in the upcoming paragraphs dedicated to Hölderlin. With Hölderlin, we are especially familiar with the spirited enthusiasm of his odes, in which man projects himself in his arrogance towards divinity and contentedly roams about the familiar plane, impenetrably establishing springlike fantastic itineraries.

The first noticeable traits of the cultural imaginary structure of "The Archipelago" derive from the mythic nature peculiar to the spatial protagonist, the archipelago itself, formed by the glorious peninsular and insular lands of heroic Greece. In Hölderlin's poetization, the Archipelago, the object of a personalizing mythification, is converted into a semidivine entity. This fact determines, as a result, the very unique forms and circumstances of its imaginary character: a cultural myth of felicitous space, at the same time above and mediating between the human earth and the ethereal domain, the imaginary location of Hölderlin's Pantheon.

The plasticity of the imaginary representation, stylized in deeply felt cultural stereotypes, utilizes globalizing procedures in panoramic space and time, from which the verbalized observation of lands, cities and islands is produced. The poet positions himself in the ancient hero's abode, in the privileged shade of the sacred mountain: "Immer, Gewaltiger! lebst du noch und ruhest im Schatten / Deiner Berge, Wie sonst," ["Even now you live on and, mighty as ever, untroubled / Rest in the shade of your mountains" (Hölderlin, 1966 edition, p. 213)], from which the poetic enunciation of the otherwise too vast collection of real spaces is made both possible and very solemn.

The altitude at which the point of view of the poet's heroic discourse is positioned in "The Archipelago" recognizes the persistent sublime superiority of ethereal space, abode of the gods, and the supreme stage for the diurnal and nocturnal mutations of light in the spatial uniqueness of Hölderlin's mythic cosmology. Everything here is characterized according to the habitual functioning of the author's olympic myth: the benefactor gods dwelling in a place of eminence from which gifts fall, like fine rain, upon mortal heads:

> Auch die Himmlischen, sie, die Kräfte der Höhe, die stillen
> Die den heiteren Tag und süssen Schlummer und Ahndung
> Fernher *bringen über das Haupt* der fühlenden Menschen
>
> [And the heavenly, too, the powers up above us, the silent, / Who from afar bring the cloudless day, delicious sleep and forebodings, / Down to the heads of sentient mortals (Hölderlin, 1966 edition, p. 213)].

A question opens up a glorious period for the "gloomy hills" of this sad and desolate hour, with the vivid presence of the cultural imagination's mythic motifs masterfully determined in the movement of symbols and voids, of questions and fantastic evocations:

> Stiegen *dort* die Säulen empor und leuchteten *dort* nicht
> Sonst vom Dache der Burg *herab* die Göttergestalten?
> Rauschte *dort* die Stimme des Volks, die stürmischbewegte,
> Aus der Agora nicht *her*, und eilten aus freudigen Pforten
> *Dort* die Gassen dir nicht zu gesegnetem Hafen *herunter*?
>
> [There did not columns rise high, and there on the citadel rooftop / Did not shining figures of gods once gaze down at the people? / And the voice of the people, did it not roar like a wind-lashed / Forest from the Agora, and there, to a prosperous harbor / From the joyful gates did the streets not come hurrying down to meet you? (Hölderlin, 1966 edition, p. 217)].

Rhetorical questions corresponding to the plastic dream of the archaeological caves of animated urban activity, which serve as their anachronistic answer, through the abrupt introduction of the exclamation, "*Siehe*! da löste sein Schiff der fernhinsinnende Kaufmann" [Look! the distantly scheming merchant unmoored his good ship there" (Hölderlin, 1966 edition, p. 217)], and by way of the descriptive resources contributed by the vigorous pattern of deictic deployment.

Something similar occurs with the startling epic presentation of the Persian invasion. The text's expressiveness is achieved and reinforced by poetic notes of powerful expressive coloration. It revives the cultural chronicle of the unwinding of the great Persian army from Ekbatana on its invasion, likened to the column of "terrible lava" which descended from Etna "Wenn er furchtbar umher vom gärenden Ätna gegossen, / Städte begräbt in der purpurnen Flut und blühende Gärten, / Bis der brennende Strom im heiligen Meere sich kühlet" ["as the flames of the torrent, / Horribly spurted and poured from Etna's ebullient crater / Buries towns in its purple flood, and blossoming gardens, / Till the glowing effusion cools in the holy sea's waters" (Hölderlin, 1966 edition, p. 217)]. Or we discover, in the imaginary stereotype of Enlightenment culture, the animated picture of the Olympic gods, weighing the destinies of the burned ships of Salamis: "*es schauen die Götter des Himmels* / Wägend und richtend herab" ["weighing and judging, the eyes of / Heaven's gods now gaze down" (Hölderlin, 1966 edition, p. 219)]. Similarly, the marvelous lyrical strains which exalt the *Polis*' emergence, its victory and salvation, are implanted as the response of a universal current of elevation; as if mortals' space projected its compass towards the heavens' eternal immensity, under the architectural symbol of the temple of Olympus: "Göttertempel *entstehen*, ein heiligkühner Gedanke, / *Steigt*, Unsterblichen nah, das Olympion auf in den Äther" ["Temples are built for the gods and, near to the immortals, a thought as / Holy as it is bold, the Olympion rises to Aether" (Hölderlin, 1966 edition, p. 225)].

Evidence necessary for establishing the physiognomy of Hölderlin's cultural imagination is also to be found in that part of the poem which could be considered as reflecting the denouement of its elegiac content. Myth, as I try to argue here, is a decisive component of the general poetic feeling of Hölderlin's work and a genetic element responsible for his artistic creation. Seen from the perspective of our "age of iron", the elevation of the Greek golden ideal indicates the source and location of the imaginary uniqueness of Hölderlin's telluric foundations.

Essentially, the poet's classical cultural myth is but the representation of an existential activity implicating all of the filaments of Hölderlin's personality. The excited pull towards the supreme dignity of the golden age's classical symbols was maintained, perhaps until the definitive collapse of insanity, as the testimony of his complete detachment from the trivial convictions of a bothersome, troubling present. And this enthusiasm is translated in the fluid mobility of an imaginary activity of dreamy evocation, more historical than actual, a fantasy paid for at the high cost of a hopeful spiritual tension, which will hardly permit an inflection of enthusiasm until its strength is entirely exhausted.

The revision of golden antiquity's *evocative* myth as a form of balance and harmony which Hölderlin offers us in his great odes and elegies has few parallels, in terms of its poetic quality, in European Romantic literature. But the imaginary constitution of the evocative procedure which characterizes the Romantic illusions we do find universally registered in the vast majority of its historic novelists, from Walter Scott to Manzoni, and its poets, from Leopardi to Byron. The exhaustive analysis of this historical process is unnecessary here, having fixed the general nature of the cultural imagination's procedure for literary transfiguration. As a final example, among the purest and most definitive, recall the delicate evocation of the same Hellenic myth, without Hölderlin's solemn grandeur, in the melancholy murmur, animated nevertheless by the same suggestive evocative fragrances, of John Keat's "Ode on a Grecian Urn":

> Thou still unravished bride of quietness,
>   Thou foster-child of silence and slow time,
> Sylvan historian, who canst thus express
>   A flowery tale more sweetly than our rhyme: ...

The reliefs of this urn are an open story for the heart of this ecstatic contemplator. Absolute truths in their immutable eternity, more certain — though extinct — than any manifestation of heavy contemporary reality:

> Heard melodies are sweet, but those unheard
>   Are sweeter: therefore, ye soft pipes, play on.

Keat's idyllic dream is projected in the sentimental suggestion of the country urn, rising by way of imagination to an absolute state of pure beauty. The historic monumentality of the past does not tear the vigor of historic evocation from the English poet's delicate spirit, producing inspired forms of realist incrustation. The cultural imagination tinges its objects with the color of the souls engendering the dream. Keat's evocation serves his unique capacity for feeling the serene beauty of languid sentiment, verging on mortal reflections on eternity, the inert and necessary extinction of the animate and living:

> O Attic shape! Fair attitude! with brede
>   Of marble men and maidens overwrought,
> With forest branches and the trodden weed;
>   Thou, silent form, dost tease us out of thought
> As doth eternity: Cold Pastoral!

The objects which play the roles for fantasy's mythic construction, the rustic urn in this case, are like mirrors of eternity held up to capture mortals' reflections in the transitoriness of their lives. Myths, forms of persistence, indifferent and beautiful, survive the melancholy of those who contemplate and recreate them. Like the man or woman without anguish — collective humanity, not the individual troubled by the inexorable awareness of his own end — myths constitute the eternal region of absolute beauty, the only undepletable reality imagination uncovers:

> When old age shall this generation waste,
>   Thou shalt remain, in midst of other woe
> Then ours, a friend to man, to whom thou say'st,
>   Beauty is truth, truth beauty, — that is all
> Ye know on earth, and all ye need to know.

The forms of the cultural imagination, like those of fictionality, are constructions of fantasy, close to reason and its aim of explaining objective reality. They do not, therefore, move in the essential psyche's terminal zones, where the anthropological and unconscious knowledge of absolute poetic imagination is produced. Their favorite action consists in a labor of divinatory transfiguration, of the sentimental coating of objects and myths, symbols and examples. Fantasy's fictional constructions, the peripheral images of literary expressiveness, and the products of the cultural imagination make up the system of manifestations of the nomical imagination, still accomodated to the conceptual rules and principles of reality governing reason and history as an objective myth. Like Coleridge, I will call the imaginative segment which intervenes in the manufacture of this vast arsenal of artistic products "fantasy" *(fancy)*. In this book I will always reserve *imagination* to refer to the autonomous capacity of history's logical realities which propitiates the least conscious structures and drives of essential poetry, those in which men and women perceive the fundamental patterns and designs of their anthropological constitution, origin and destiny.

3.2. Poeticity: The Imaginary Structure of Symbols in the Temporal Domains

3.2.1. On the Imaginary Structure of Poetic Value: Traces in the Text's Material-Verbal Scheme of Temporal and Spatial Orientations, Anthropological Symbols, and Patterns of the Imagination

Literary entities, the text's fictions and characters are all mimetic or conceptual jackets enveloping pure symbolic forms and narrative myths. In my judgment, the explanation of the poetic effect's most important constituents and processes is to be found following a trajectory of essential anthropological radicalization. In this manner, the great anthropological symbols are responsible for forming the terminal space to which all literary myths are conducted. Myth is, as is known, the temporal and narrative development of a pure and atemporal symbolic intuition. It is a history which develops the understanding of the symbol.

Therefore, symbols are, like the characters and settings of narration, the components of a *semantics of the imagination*. They consolidate the meaningful values of the text's fantastic construction. Symbols are embedded in the text's imaginary depths, in the impalpable space inferred from the material scheme's forms. Nevertheless, we must avoid the tendency to conceive of this imaginary depth as a purely hypothetical and unrealistic fictitious space. On the contrary, what I have called the imaginary depth, space or density of artistic texts bears the greatest responsibility for texts' general organization and significance as aesthetic, sentimental and imaginary messages.

By means of symbols, which dominate in the semantic incarnations of literature's fictional and most symptomatic characters and circumstances, art offers an essential structure for the representation of the world (C. Bousoño, 1952, I, pp. 21–30). The formal-playful activities of artistic, poetic, and literary texts' material constitution achieve transcendental importance through their deeply rooted anthropological commitment. In those favorable cases in which the imagination is capable of establishing, through truly brilliant and novel symbolic coordinates and fantastic spatial references, a convincing and attractive representation of the real universe, we experience poetic communication as an unexpected and dazzling illumination. We *re-cognize* something we had previously ignored.

Mythocriticism has elaborated typologies and functional formulas describing symbols' articulation in mythical narratives. The efforts of an anthropology of the imagination have culminated in Gilbert Durand's tripartite classification of symbols according to regimes of imagination: myths and symbols of the diurnal universe, myths of imaginary nocturnal exploration, and, finally, symbols of eros' mediational activity.

The imagination's three regimes as I have just enumerated them correspond to the three *basic dominants* designated by psychology since Betcherev as the fundamental forms of perinatal behavior. The diurnal imaginary representation corresponds to the *postural dominant* establishing the perceptive awareness of otherness through the tension between the self and its environment. It fulfills the *function of relation* between the individual and the reality which constitutes his or her cosmological and vital context. The tree, the spear and the sword are elemental symbolic forms expressing this consciousness of identity as situated in the world as an environment. The extroverted dynamics of power, luminosity and discernment constitute the emotional forms linked to all of these symbols.

The nocturnal universe represents the *digestive dominant*. Experience of the internal cavities is a kind of interiorized sensing of unexplorable spaces, not reducible to postural verification. The imaginary representation of absolute night as the exclusion of any measure of light is analogous to the experience of one's own digestive intimacy as a chaos not capable of being explained or appreciated through one's postural experience. The shield or cup are the guiding symbols representing this dominant. The imaginary understanding of eternity as the complete expulsion of time is the goal offered under these attitudes of imaginary representation. Fiery forms of the "wager" are suitable to the digestive dominant as a metaphoric projection of the structures of diurnal experience. The dazzling luminosity of daytime and reality, when they involve absolute formulas, feeds a skepticism as to the deprivation of the capacities of imaginary calculation in the darkness of night, exemplified in Unamuno's anguish and Jorge Guillén's unyielding restlessness.

The imaginary constitution of the anthropological system of symbols is naturally equivalent to the body of *sentimental experience* which they themselves arouse. In fact, quite frequently the imagination's most perceptible and immediate anthropological work may be perceived in the form of emotional resonances. In this same way the pantheistic euphoria of Saint Francis' *Song to the Creatures* involves the sentimental coating of the pure intellectual indices of postural manifestations' precise development. Or, on the other hand, the aesthetic of the sentimentally terrifying which Ezio Raimondi has shown to exist in Alfieri's theatrical poetics (E. Raimondi, 1985), represents the most reliable form in which certain anguished vacillations of the nocturnal imagination are passionately manifested.

Of course, by pointing to this essential set of symbols constituting artistic texts' imaginary semantics, I am aware that I am indicating just one direction or one terminal form in the explanation of what constitutes the poetic. The unforeseeable as a sign of the unconventionalizable continues, even here, to be the characteristic guaranteeing, with mysterious uncertainty, the poetic. There are no *a priori* recipes or formulas indicating the artistic itinerary that must be followed to attain the substantial depth of anthropologico-imaginary symbols. But beyond the open and experimental condition of these journeys of literary activity, poetic value is manifestly and securely lodged in the responsible verification of the universe of imaginary representations which are essential to vital anthropological orientation.

The great elemental symbols lodged in the most pure forms of anthropological representation, are therefore only the final guarantees of poetry's

3.2. Poeticity: The Imaginary Structure of Symbols in the Temporal Domains

anthropological interest. But in the body of artistic texts these elemental symbolic regimes tend to appear transformed into myths which *intensionalize* them. That is, the anthropologico-imaginary base which is the ultimate reason for the power of vital implication of great poetic works is presented in texts transformed and interposed among other symbols together with which it forms symbolic systems and constellations of extremely varied complexity, coherence and interest (J. Burgos, 1982). The symbolic construction of artistic works has its poetic quarry in the anthropological foundation of the universe of imaginary regimes and of the terminal symbolic formulas which express and consolidate these regimes. Still, this anthropological basis is expressed and communicated well or poorly in each authors' *personal myth* (C. Mauron, 1962), according to the general law of artistic *intensionalization*.

Tomas Albaladejo Mayordomo has successfully elevated the process of intensionalization to a general index of literary construction (T. Albaladejo Mayordomo, 1981, pp. 117 ff.; 1986). The work's symbolic volume is thus subject to the general process of the transference of forms from the universe of the real to the unique referential construct of the verbal artistic text. It is in this "trajectory" that the essentially exemplary capacities of the great anthropological symbols are empowered or diluted, an itinerary which includes the representative accuracy and success of symbolic forms as such, the functionality of the strategies integrating them in myths, and the expressive success of the verbal forms which translate them from language to artistic discourse.

In the most immediate physiognomy of the work as an instrument of communication, the symbolic components of the personal myth take on progressively familiar existential forms. The literary process of intensionalization concretizes them. García Lorca's symbolic universe is one of the richest in modern literature. His greatest success surely lies in having incarnated his symbols in a lively way without stripping them of their mythic transparency. *Yerma*, the inhabitants of *La casa de Barnarda Alba*, and the nocturnal creatures of the *Romancero gitano* simultaneously live their anguished lives as tragic characters and retain the essential play of their pure imaginary meanings.

The variety of literary forms orchestrating the intensionalization of imaginary symbols is very great. The plastic correspondence of painting's myths achieve effective modulations in naturalist techniques, in the phenomenology of cubism and even in the absolute blurring of informalism and abstraction. Analogously, poetry lodges its capacities for symbolic representation in the direct imitations of intense plasticity of Machado's *Campos de Castilla*, in the essentially cubist still lifes of Guillén's *Cántico*, or in the abstract confident of Vicente Aleixandre's *La destrucción o el amor*. Still, if carefully attended to, in every case the literary process of symbolic components' intensionalization must necessarily pass through the same conventional trajectory of antinaturalist stylization which demands the transference of symbols and representations to the material forms of verbal expressiveness.

Two signs are indicative of the poetic value and interest of the symbolic universe of a work and of its author's personal myth, apart from the artistic fidelity in the process of intensionalization I have just referred to, which produces the experience of essential immanence and symbolic veracity. In the first place, the relative completeness of the universe of symbolic representation. The great essential poets like Dante, Cervantes and Shakespeare are precisely those who vigorously rescue the symbolic vivacity of all three anthropological spaces of the imaginary: day, night and eros.

The second condition for symbols' poeticity may be located in the medullarity of their imaginary construction; that is, the transparency of their folkloric or literary semantic flesh, which permits us to glimpse the more essential foundations of their imaginary consistency as anthropological universals. Under the temporal and narrative structure of mythic corporeity, great symbols always point to the scheme of their essential equivalents, sensed as designs of pure space, reduced to dynamic or static emotions, pure positions of the spatial myth.

The constructive system of the imaginary structure of certain poetic texts I have examined organizes the manifestation of symbols. First, by virtue of the association of solidarities which the most linguistically enclosed imaginary syntax proclaims, and above all as a result of modes of fantastic spatial design translating the structure and disposition of the general system of symbols in the imagination's anthropological construction to the terms of textual organization, manifested as subconscious drives or impulses establishing poematic, imaginary rhythms.

In poets' confidences and the stated intuitions of sentient readers, sensations situating a poem's genesis in a particular rhythmical profile are frequently cited as initial poetic experiences, before any form of conceptualization or imaginary symbolization appears to take place (C. Bousoño, 1952, I, pp. 381–385). Explanations which link this initial impulse, generative of the text, to a determined form of spatiality, to the fantastic pattern of an impulse's dynamic design, are also not entirely unusual. The translation to spatial images of the temporal phenomena of rhythm is not so much the result of a secondary schematization, but can be seen rather as an alternative expression, simultaneous and even anterior to the shaping of the impulse in poematic rhythms. In this way, the design of the poetic text's imaginary construction embeds the set of drives and models of the fantastic situation in the poem's universe. These drives and models enable man to define and become aware of his situation and postural references in the world. Thus, poetry channels spatio-temporal rhythms, conforming them to the most necessary and fundamental forms of existential affirmation.

The patterns of imaginary spatialization suggested by the unique channeling of subconscious drives in artistic texts constitute above all forms of the imagination's *anthropological orientation* at the very core of its own explanation of the universe as otherness. I do not wish to get ahead of the

3.2. Poeticity: The Imaginary Structure of Symbols in the Temporal Domains

expositive order I've set out, according to which I will deal with the syntax of imaginary space in the next chapter; nevertheless, I want to underline here certain peculiarities in the poetic-imaginary treatment of spatial consciousness, because of their relationship to the structure of temporal symbols, which I am now addressing.

As I frequently repeat in this book, the feature of psychological depth or anthropological medullarity is particularly important for characterizing the schematic conformation of spatial imagination resting on the structure of temporal symbols. The basic spatial designs, as procedures for anthropologico-imaginary orientation, constitute primary schemes with respect to which the semantic-temporal incarnation of symbols and myths appears as a derived and secondary structure. For example, I've indicated frequently how the linear and spatial, positive and negative forms of the spatialization of semantic realizations schematically dominate as a whole the plurality of their symbols and their mythic incarnations: hence, for example, Icarus, Phaethon, etc. are seen as variations of the drives of spatial orientation of ascent and fall.

A second feature which relates both systems of imaginary representation, spatial-schematic and mythico-temporal, is their absolute *constitutive homogeneity*. The structure of the symbolic system of anthropological and temporal orientation originates in a binary organization of contrasts: positive and negative. This is equivalent to the structure of symbolic constellations corresponding to the temporal regimes, diurnal and nocturnal. Analogously, the configuration of the schemes of spatial orientation is structured according to the same binary principle of antithetical contrast: ascent and fall as geonegative and geopositive forms of linear conception, while expansion and collision represent the same antithetical dynamism in three-dimensional space.

This basic dualism of imaginary constructs is easily traced in various mythic constructions, a task already realized by the systems of imaginary anthropology, folklore studies and mythocriticism. I will limit myself here to indicate its appearance in classical literary forms, which we already possess as eternal archetypes of poeticity. Day and night, ascent and descent, constitute the underpinnings of the imaginary-symbolic orientation which regulates the structure of parts, Paradise and Inferno, in the *Divine Comedy*. Also worth mentioning here is the role of synthetic temporal suspension played by Purgatory among the collection of temporal symbols and that of the structures of imaginary spatial orientation in the series of immobile balance.

Another of our culture's literary systems, forming the block of two synthesized histories by Homer, also exemplarily organizes the imaginary coordinates of extensional spatiality. *Expansion* as infinite domination or exploration takes shape in *The Odysses'* myth of the voyage or the quest. The contrary tendency in spatial symbolization represented as contrasted reality is concretized in the forms of polemic convergence and conflictive collision present in *The Illiad*. Day and night, voyage and sojourn, country (open space) and inn (carnavalesque sphere of refuge) are also themes of the antithetical homogeneity of spatio-temporal imagination, explaining, as I will demonstrate in detail further ahead, the most extreme and essential forms of Cervantes' capacity for poetic suggestion.

The poetic value of the great classical constructions of literature and art achieves transcendental form when, upon mobilizing all of the active textual resources of expressiveness and fantastic verisimilitude, they vigorously reach the immense temporal and spatial depths of consciousness' anthropological orientation, in which identity acquires unusual glimpses of the prevailing vivacity of otherness. The most decisive phenomenon of poetry consists, it seems to me, in this recognition of the self in the other, of the center in the circle.

Before discussing the imaginary semantics of poetic symbols, it seems necessary first to exemplify the important mechanism which puts the textual scheme in relation with the imaginary effect, by way of an examination of several compositions from Jorge Guillén's *Cántico (Canticle)*. Those readers who wish to examine more extensive considerations of these examples and Guillén's text as a whole may refer to my book-length study of *Cántico* (A. García-Berrio, 1985).

The examples are numerous. We will look at only a few cases: the emotion of plenitude in the elevation and centering of imaginary space which "Elevación de la claridad" ("Elevation of Clarity") tries to suggest, succeeds in seeing itself expressed in a very direct way at the height of said text, precisely by way of the two lexemes "center" and "zenith":

>   Y se *centra* el vasto
>   Deseo en un punto.
>   ¡Oh *cenit*: lo uno
>   Lo claro, lo intacto!

>   [And the vast desire
>   Is centered in one point.
>   Oh zenith: the one
>   The clear, the intact!]

In "Plaza mayor" ("Main Square"), the elements of wandering about, conductors in fantastic deixes of the disperse itinerary towards the center of general convergence, are alluded to directly: "Decid, muros de altivez, / Tapias de serenidad, / Grises de viento y granito, / Ocres de sol y de pan" ["Speak, walls of arrogance, / Walls of serenity, / Gray from wind and granite, / Ochre from sun and bread"]. A dense web of suggestions by way of the most abundant and detailed references induces the mobile aerial impulse which dominates "Árboles con viento" ("Trees with Wind"): "Aquel otro en un *vaivén* / Muy leve ... ["That other one in a light / Swaying ..."]; "Se eleva aceptando a quien / Lo domina todo ¡Viento! / Por estas frondas ya es / Una marea que ondula ..." ["Wind dominates it all! / It already is a tide undulating / Through the palms"]; "De las hojas que *no pasan*: / Álamo siempre recién / *Erguido*, recién *excelso*" ["Of the leaves that do not stop / Poplar, always just

3.2. Poeticity: The Imaginary Structure of Symbols in the Temporal Domains 361

/ Erected, just elevated"]. In the same manner, in the following poem, "Las doce en el reloj" ("Twelve O'Clock"), the dense system of references distributed in the text suggests in all of its necessary and possible extremes the fantastic feelings of midday as a plenary convergence and instantaneous center. In that vein, the movement of the old dance evoked in "Aire bailando" ("Dancing Air") is more effectively suggested by the textual references to winged movement than by its own reasonable and proper mimetic suggestions, which could have been better associated with the rhythm and movement of the verse:

> Parejas ... y *prorrumpen*.
> Del aire *en conmoción emergen*
> — No de mágica nube —
> Los cuerpos de la música,
> Y por su gloria *alzados* y ya ilustres,
> Pisan, *giran fugaces*.
>
> [Couples ... and they *burst forth*.
> In commotion they emerge from the air
> — Not from a magical cloud —
> The bodies of the music,
> And for their glory *elevated* and already illustrious
> They step, they *swing fleetingly*].

In the case of some of the longer poems, where different fantastic drives and emotions coincide and follow one upon another, a series of well distributed references orders the development of the texts' actions and moments appropriately. One of the clearest examples is that of the shared itinerary in "El diálogo" ("The Dialogue"). Even with regard to the grammatical particles lacking the referential-symbolic content essential to objects or actions belonging to reality, it is possible to speak in all propriety of the impulse's direct mention, which being of a pre-objective nature, is seen to be experienced and alluded to in its intimate, subjective and pure genesis as *impulse* or drive, previous to its being channeled into the concrete content of a real *action*. This is the case with the often analyzed particle *más* ("more", "most", etc.) (M. C. Bobes Naves, 1975), a symbolico-classematic representation of the permanent impulse of plenary ascesis towards the culminative splendor and certainty which predominates in *Cántico*, or even towards the centering and concretion of a process of convergence, which could be invoked as an illustrative example.

As is natural, the mentions of pulsation do not always appear in an absolutely explicit and categorical manner. There are many cases in which the allusion is produced in an *indirect* way, not by means of an explicit lexeme, as in the previous examples, but by way of associative verbal formulas, contributing unequivocal cultural references. Thus, in "Sábado de gloria" ("Easter Saturday") the text is filled with constelled forms of illumination and ascent, provoking as a whole the unexpressed sensation of joyful plenitude:

> Sábado
> *¡Ya gloria aquí!*
> Maravilla hay para ti,
> Si tu *primavera* es tuya
> *¡Resurrección*, aleluya!
>
> [Saturday
> *Now glory here!*
> There is wonder for you
> If your *spring* is yours
> *Resurrection*, hallelujah!]

Confirmed by successive references to an accelerated plenary dynamic: "*Explosiones* de esperanza. / ¡A su forma se *abalanza*!" ["*Explosions* of hope. / It *rushes* to its form"]. Or: "Se arremolina *impaciente* / La verdad. Triunfe el presente" ["It whirls *impatient* / The Truth. May the present triumph"]. These references combine with unequivocal luminous flashes: "Aleluya en esa *aurora* / Que el más feliz más explora" ["Hallellujah in that *dawn* / Most explored by the most happy"], "Todo a tanta *luz* se nombra. / ¡Cuánto *color* en la sombra!" ["Everything is named in such *light*. / So much *color* in the shade"] and, finally: "*Alumbrándome fulgura* / Ya hoy mi mente futura" ["*Illuminating me it flashes* / Already today my future mind"]. We are moving here entirely at the heart of the culture of the image, with full awareness of the automatisms of imaginary constellations and with the cultural associationism of a whole system of presuppositions. The direct and explicit mention of fantastic movement is understood, unexpressed, yet very alive in the forked branches of presupposition.

Indirect reference is produced by means of the explicit collaboration of all of the constituents of fantastic representation, lacking only the expression of a global lexical formula, an appeal to the imaginary result. For example, in a poem like "Aquel jardín" ("That Garden"), the spatial myth will perhaps not be alluded to in its strictest terms, namely, the protective circle of the center or of the most favorable sphere, but the collection of elements constituting the impulse are in fact represented. To begin with, the frame or enclosure: "*Muros*. / Jardín bien gozado / Por los pocos" ["*Walls*. / Garden much enjoyed / By the few"]. Following immediately is the mention of the positive, joyous feeling: "*Buen sosiego*. No hay descanso. / Tiembla el agua en su *remanso*" ["*Good calm*. There is no rest. / The water trembles in its puddle"]. Walls, the symbols of exclusion, enclose and isolate the aridity of dogday dessication, and this sensation is alluded to, in contrast with the interior memory of vegetal freshness and the fountain:

> Tan blanca está la pared
> Que se redobla mi *sed*.
> En más *agua* la blancura
> De la cal se transfigura.
> Fresquísima perfección
> La *fuente* es mármol y son.

[The wall is so white
That my *thirst* is redoubled.
The whiteness of the lime
is transfigured into more *water*.
Very cool perfection
The *fountain* is marble and murmur].

Agreeable interior shade, private joy, sensual delight translated into relaxed plenitude, an awareness awake to the fire and water: "Huele en secreto y me embarga / Con su olor la hoja amarga." ["It smells in secret and overcomes me / With its odor of bitter leaf"]. A specific reference to the center is missing here, although not in other similar poems such as "Jardín en Medio" ("Garden at the Center"), where it is designated by the explicit perfection of the enclosure, in the final synthesis, rhythmically graduated, of the constituents and their pulsing effect:

Muros.
 Jardín.
  Bien *ceñido*,
 Pide a los más el olvido.

[*Walls.*
  Garden.
    Well *encircled*,
  Asks forgetfulness of most people].

The consideration of the indirect references to the anthropological impulse should also take into account the intimate, personal parameter of the author's *imaginary uniqueness*. The path of that "anthropological trajectory", as Durand has called the image's circuit (G. Durand, 1960 [1969, pp. 37—39]), in this case relies on the intervention of the autonomous and singular fantastic constructions belonging to the subject. Most metaphors and allegories function in the midst of this accumulation of the author's singular presuppositions. For example, the euphemistic transfiguration of the female body in the landscape symbol, regularly present in *Cántico*'s amorous poems like "Salvación de la primavera" ("Spring Salvation") and "Más esplendor" ("More Splendor"), is not a universal of imaginary understanding. On occasion the density of these interposed fantastic constructs, of these subjective shortcircuits, is deposited in conventional allegory.

Here it becomes necessary to resort to even more interiorized correspondences, not always founded on the properties of the general sensory and associative constellations of the imagination's universal and standardized workings. On the contrary, we need to appeal to a profound knowledge of the imaginary deflections of sensation. In Guillén's case, being Castilian, these detours determine the symbolic pertinence of straight ascendent trees, tree-lined avenues, river banks, inviting gardens and groves, the preference for pure snow-bound winter with its capacity for sharp transparencies, contrasted to the fervid and disquieting summer and the experience of the very short transitional seasons of spring and fall, etc. Still, nothing beyond Guillén's most intimate fantastic universe can explain symbols of anguish like the overflowing invasion of yellow in "Noche del gran estío" ("Great Summer Night"), much less the brilliant serrated glimpse of the dreaded dry night, or the imaginary circumstances and necessity of the appearance of the fertile touch of freshness with "la más pomposa hortelana" ["the most splendid gardener wife"].

On the other hand, the constancy and stability of such singular subjective interpositions in the path of fantastic construction consolidates them into systematic permanence. It thus creates that kind of restricted universal symbol associated with the idiosyncracy of personal fantasies, stocked with correspondingly typical images. The great poets, above all, set forth truly alternative universes of extraordinary complexity, the interpretation of which requires great effort on the part of the reader, requiring him or her to become definitely familiar with that block of fantasy set in the universal and standardized circuit of the general imaginary system. In certain cases, the most immediate suppositions of the image's fantastic foundations totally fail, and the reading may then attend to the author's habits of specific imaginary suggestion. Only those references relating to the pure indirect mention of the fantastic impulse are to be found in poems like "La Gloria" ("The Glory") or in the dream of incorporeal vibrant ascent, suggested by the very subtle, colorful morning sky in "Galán temprano":

> Notorio garbo de la camarista
> Toda real en las apariciones ...
> ¡Oh dulce seno tan amanecido!
> Hacia la gloria del galán temprano
> Van en volandas blancas algazaras

> [Notorious grace and ease of the lady in waiting
> Entirely real in her appearance ...
> Oh sweet breast so awakened!
> Towards the glory of the early suitor
> White din goes quickly, carried in the air].

Together with the cases of the imaginary impulse's direct and indirect *mention*, I also perceive in *Cántico*'s texts a second modality of *suggestion* and orientation of the impulse towards the text's receiver. As opposed to the preceding examples, we are not dealing here with a process of lexico-semantic correspondence. Suggestion operates through forms which channel the imaginary attention towards those textual zones revealing the image which, in the textual scheme, materializes the subconscious drive. Deictic verbal signs, onomatopoeic formulas, phonic reiterations, alliterations and a broad selection of schemes of rhythm and general textual organization, contribute in the majority of *Cántico*'s poems towards establishing an unmistakable pattern in the compositional scheme, which sheds light on both the imaginary drive's origins and the possible pattern of its reception. In what follows I will review

3.2. Poeticity: The Imaginary Structure of Symbols in the Temporal Domains

and illustrate each of these features with representative poems according to the increasing complexity of the devices of fantastic reference to be found in the textual scheme.

One of the simplest mechanisms to evoke the impulse is created by Guillén's habitual recourse to deixes. Keeping in mind that the imaginary drive, of whatever nature, is constituted ultimately in terms of a movement of spatial orientation, the role deixis plays in registering this imaginary movement can easily be grasped. Consider, for example, a poem like "La estrella de Venus" ("Venus' Star"), with a textual scheme clearly oriented towards the appearance of the first luminous point in the nocturnal sky, prepared for by the progressive demarcation of the space required for its appearance:

> Y en montón de horizonte
> Se *agolpan calcinándose*
> Las nubes de aquel soto.
>
> [And in heaped horizon
> The clouds of that thicket
> Swoop together and calcine].

Everything converges in this space in which hope and expectation accumulate. All that is left is the concrete sign, the aimed-for apparition, presented in the final deictic explosion:

> Hay siempre luz. El cielo
> Próximo brinda playas
> Sale Venus, ¡Allí!
>
> [There is always light. The sky,
> nearbly, offers beaches
> Venus comes out, there!]

What is suggested here is precisely the elevation and splendor of the center. The textual scheme does not mention it directly, but indicates it, signals it, *suggests* it, and thereby makes it evident.

In the focalization and channeling of the imaginary drive's *onomatopoeic gestures* and equivalent forms of emphasis, repetition and insistence play a very nearly equivalent role to that of the morphemic grammatical gestures of deictic adverbs and pronouns. It is not necessary here to highlight the importance of these features in the overall conformation of the stylistic will of *Cántico*'s poems. Concerning their concrete role in the imaginary scheme, they demonstrate a behavior almost identical to that we have just seen in the case of deixes. Onomatopoeic suggestion, typically closely associated with a concrete type of imaginary movement, is produced by the evocation of similarities. Thus, the two movements of avulsive tension and soothing tranquility referred to in "Arena" ("Sand"), are more easily deduced from the corresponding acoustic mimesis than from any lexical mention. First, recall the set of imaginary representations of the undertow's marine violence, induced by the alliterations and onomatopoeic voices at the poem's beginning:

> Retumbos. La resaca
> Se desgarra en crujidos
> Pedregosos. Retumbos
> Un retroceso arisco
> Se derrumba, se arrastra.
>
> [Echoes. The undertow
> Rips in rocky
> Grindings. Echoes
> A surly recoiling
> Collapses and crawls].

The textual scheme's structure yields a more complex degree of imaginary *suggestion* in its poematic *rhythm*. In this case, effects at the general textual and strophic level can be as suggestive as those particular to isolated rhythmic lines. I will begin by considering this scenario. As I have already indicated, in many cases the rhythm of the verse is the best instrument for driving the imaginary impulse, beyond — and in some cases entirely independent from — the semantic representations of the words themselves.

Considerations of this type could serve to explain the case of the rhythmic suggestions of the lively flames' agonizing and varied movement in "Las hogueras" ("The Bonfires"). The poem's thematic thrust — "El amor arde contento, / Arde el viento" ["Love burns happy, / The wind burns"] — is well served by the varied metrical practice, a combination of strophes and constantly modifying accentual rhythms, breaking the underlying octosyllabic meter:

> ¡Ese viento
> *Pintor de su movimiento!*
> Llamas remuevan tinieblas
> Donde se alumbran estrellas.
>
> [That wind
> The painter of its movement!
> Flames remove the shadows
> Where the stars are illuminated].

Here, the bisymmetric forms of hexameter are partitioned into trimeter — "¿Estrellas en caos? / Saraos" ["Stars in chaos? / Soirées"] —, and accentuated by the instantaneous pulsation of the trisyllabic groups in the refrain: "Estrellas. / ¡Son llamas / Tan bellas / Las damas!" ["The stars. / Are flames. / So beautiful, / The ladies!"].

As a matter of principle we may affirm that every option selected in the metrico-rhythmic scheme involves a clear desire for the expression of subconscious drives. Or, if one wishes to formulate it inversely — and perhaps this is not just a case of an indifferent and equivalent set of options — it could be said that, just as every representation of a subconscious content is

3.2. Poeticity: The Imaginary Structure of Symbols in the Temporal Domains

naturalized in a specific symbol, every subconscious drive or impulse engenders or selects some rhythmico-acoustical pattern and filters consciousness through a specific spatial design. Once again, we are dealing with Guillén's formula for creation as "din" resolved in rhythm, as chaos grounded in some profiled line, as digestive undercurrent purified in a pattern of open and luminous form. If one remains unconvinced, recall the solid correspondence possible between the very frequent rhythmic enjambement in Guillén's poems and the mode of pure recurrent movement, also so familiar in *Cántico*, as can be seen, for example, in the swaying movement in "Ahora" ("Now"): "Morosamente concierta / La lentitud invasora / De la siesta con el vago / Giro del gusto en el lago" ["Morosely harmonious / The invading slowness / Of the nap with the vague / Pleasurable swirl in the lake"]. Or, for another example, the abrupt continuity of the rhythm of nodding in the sweet abandonment to naptime dreaming in "Beato Sillón" ("Blessed Armchair").

The transition from the textual scheme to the imaginary drive, through these more or less explicit and immediate forms of mention or suggestion, is therefore a mobile space, very frequently working in both directions. First, the movement of the subconscious drive, more or less invisible or inexplicable to man's consciousness until articulated, ciphered in terms of spatial orientation, as an intimate metaphor of experiential desires and terrors stratified in time. An opposite process is observable running from the schematic interpretation of the textual universe to the movements and entities summoned and translated into equivalents of the subconscious drive of human beings to explore and express uncertain and difficult feelings concerning their destiny.

The practice of these critical transferences between the imagination and the textual scheme, accustomed to lodging the material concreteness of verbal utterances in the ample density of meaning's imaginary space, ought not to be restricted to examining only overly immediate and homologous levels of meaning. Still, the hyper-literalist attitude which literary critics have a tendency to be drawn towards can serve to illustrate another opposing perspective to which psychologists are inclined in their work of literary interpretation. The multiple signs the transformations induced by imaginary constructions inscribe in the sphere of meaning on the immanent text's verbal scheme should be apparent and established by the literary critic. Precisely because of this, I believe that it is necessary to proceed, confidently and rigorously at the same time, concerning those meaningful values of the immanent text which rest on its power to multiply meaning. A propagative effect of one of the text's most immediate and effective motifs is the kind of compounding contagion produced by the associative interaction of contiguous images, as Northrop Frye clearly recognized in vigorously alluding to the associative articulation of the poem's images as an unstanchable "prophetic rhythm" (N. Frye, 1957 [1968, pp. 270–272]).

In their contact with imaginary impregnation, the verbal components of the textual scheme exhibit their portentious capacities for aesthetic transfiguration, their singular powers of sentimental resonance. The unexpected capacity for suggestion relatively inert elements of the expressive system acquire when fused together in the body of the verbal or plastic artistic text, thus establishing their own objective meaning, simple and weak, distended in the elastic nets of poetic meaning, is well-known since ancient times among observers of artistic works' signifiers. The resulting poem, under the paradigm of the image, transcends and surpasses the data of objective sensibility (G. Bachelard, 1957 [1970, p. 15, Intro., VII]). In the poetic text, the meaningful unity, apparently cold and general to the most wary and foolish adherents of the objective urge, is multiplied and articulated by the imagination, fertile and lively, in associative, suggestive stimuli. Literary formulas' values of expressiveness, which I have referred to as the primary source of verbal aestheticity, fire the poetic word's associative mechanism, iridescing the unique form into many-facetedness, projecting it on the imagination, not as a hindrance, but as the most precise and efficient of catalysts.

There is no doubt that in that unforeseeable brilliance of the artistic work's results is where one must lodge some of the chief reasons for its poetic source as "indeterminate" suggestion (C. Mauron, 1962, p. 12). An indeterminate space, in effect, which according to Mauron guarantees a certain restrictive prudence as far as the general capacity of critical operations are concerned. For his part, Gilbert Durand assumes the same process of the aesthetic acceleration of uncertainties and surprises is at work when he denounces the impropriety of submitting poetic objects to a sterilizing "physical objectivity" (1979, p. 55), reiterating the arguments and experiences his teacher Bachelard brilliantly set forth at the beginning of a chapter on "The Phenomenology of Roundness" (G. Bachelard, 1957 [1970, p. 208, Ch. X, I]).

Considering the depth of the poetic text's imaginary work, focusing on the simple surface appearance of its verbal structure, its immanent textual scheme, constrains the extensive role fantasy plays in creating poetic meaning. In the history of its own tradition of imaginary resonances, each of the text's terms possesses a thousand suggestive promises; each image is brought to life, a "sudden salience on the surface of the psyche": stimulating surprises on which the text's imaginary powers have the opportunity to openly prove themselves.

That confidence in verbal components' capacity for meaningful aesthetic multiplication constitutes, basically, the philologist's most solid legacy, the literary critic's most serious and sensible contribution. Before them they will always have the jealousy and indifference of those who lack that confidence because they are deprived of the kind of technical knowledge, humble but indispensable, bestowed by formal and philological criticism. For the literary critic it is necessary, at this time, to progress responsibly towards the depth and complexity of the textually imaginary, surpassing his restrictedly material and immanent understanding of the artistic work's beauty. But it is highly advisable that in this new path he should not forget his precious sense of the textual utterance's intrinsically poetic nature, with its profound capacity for aesthetic suggestion.

3.2.2. The Anthropological Roots of Temporal Regimes' Symbolic Semantics

An unremitting tendency towards extensive universalization is unique to imaginary poetic meaning, compared to the more immediate and direct forms of linguistic semantic meaning. The explanation for the individual symbol's poetic value, and even more so that of the mythical sequence and the exemplary object or figure representing it (the spear, Oedipus, the tree, Prometheus, the chalice, the shield, etc.) lies in very deeply rooted zones of human personality and behavior. As a result, these symbols, sequences, objects or figures are able to represent very broad aspects of anthropological behavior and reality. Man discovers and expresses his fundamental myths in imaginary meanings, the "profound dream" hidden from the most lucid gaze under this elaboration (C. Mauron, 1962, p. 23). These are the most intensely representative symbols of man's primary motives, the most deeply rooted and secret, symbols of the most universal schematic forms of his cosmological orientation in time and space. As Eliade indicated, these meanings are evoked in order to escape the anxieties and anguish of time through the special expression of the lyrical (M. Eliade, 1963, pp. 95—96). The simple mention of these facts relative to the imaginary poetic conscience corroborates, in my opinion, its transcendental importance and value in the aesthetic entity of literature and art.

It is not, moreover, necessary that these myths, symbols and spatializing tendencies be discerned in a conscious manner by the literary receiver; nor even that the text's producer formulate them with complete awareness. It only matters, in both cases, that they intuitively perceive them as deeply rooted forms of intimate expression, of global representation out of the reach of more minute and concrete processes of objective and realistic meaning. To identify the symbolic bundles operative in concrete structures of mythical schematization, fixing and specifying them under conscious symbolic labels, is not a relevant objective for the pragmatic processes of symbolico-artistic communication. Rather, it is the reflective task of critics, a content of *a posteriori* analyses.

The expression of imaginary meaning and its communication begin in and are directed to the most automatic zones of the subconscious. They are its only expression and the objects the effects of which enable us to fathom its identity. As Gilbert Durand notes, the poetic symbol, because it is concrete, optimal, and imperceptible to intuition, imposes itself on us beyond the limits of the verbal material which expresses it. The symbol, in Durand's words, "annuls the opacity of the signifier" (1979, p. 18). A product and message of the subconscious, it assumes, in its flow through the text, structural forms within the reach of consciousness. Nevertheless, these patterns never shed their differential condition with regard to the semantic conceptual constituents of the message's representation.

Through symbols we perceive the nominal entities of the imagination's mythical constructs (G. Durand, 1979, p. 20). Hence, symbols are constituted in the text as the most consistent nuclei and mainstays of imaginary meaning. The delicate modernist swan or the revolutionary star of the sub-literature of slogans, Dali's supple watches, Hölderlin's ethereal space, metamorphosis, or Electra and the complex she personifies (P. Brunel, 1971, 1974), all constitute the immediate symbolic representations of much more diffuse and powerful aesthetico-imaginary contents, themselves the particular objectives of artists' respective aesthetic messages. This fundamental aspect of the imaginary criticism of poetry is perhaps the most well-known, given the symptomatic emphasis placed on it by Freud and Marie Bonaparte (1933). From a different methodological articulation, it has been well-explored by the fitting and discerning extension of symbolic representations and their aesthetic-imaginary contents to the mythical forms constituting the "collective unconscious", under the guidance of Jung and his followers. Still another well-known contribution in this area is Charles Badouin's exemplary effort aimed at tracing the heroic myths represented by the literary tradition's protagonists (M. Bodkin, 1934; C. Badouin, 1952, pp. 1–25).

The anthropology of the imagination has arrived at the very threshold of producing tables and atlasses of the imagination's symbolic firmament, having in fact gained possession of the most necessary and integral materials required to accomplish this task. Gilbert Durand has disseminated among us a well-known and valuable systematization of myths and symbols. As a result, symbolic criticism already can count on the elements needed to travel safely, naturally, with ease and without unexpected setbacks through the space of methodological and analytical application (M. Eliade, 1961). As I noted before, the greatest caution is needed in adjusting the pattern of the immanent scheme to the text's imaginary construction, scorning capricious excesses.

The great critical systems of the anthropological organization of myths, like those realized by Durand and Northrop Frye, not to mention the commendable pioneering efforts of Maud Bodkin (1934), have set forth both ambitious and committed schemes of mythical cosmovision. The grouping of symbols in broad congruent series of regimes, *diurnal* or *postural* and *nocturnal* or *digestive*, objectively corresponds, I believe, to the most deeply rooted and natural form of perceiving and calculating the conditions of human existence. The diurnal attitude with its acquisitive posturalism reflects human beings' uncertainties concerning any given which is taken as objective. Daytime constitutes the space of luminous certainty, the discovery of true and real support, of the forms of cosmic otherness arising before our senses and revealing themselves, always unexpectedly, to reason. Day is the space of known and possible dimensions, and its symbols are lodged like stable

3.2. Poeticity: The Imaginary Structure of Symbols in the Temporal Domains

and verifiable milestones in schemes of elevation and fall. Symbols are forms serving as horizons to the intimate desire for immense expansion (G. Bachelard, 1957 [1970, p. 169, Ch. VIII–I]). They populate the surfaces of our itineraries as deep and dear references, never indifferent. We recognize them in the polemical clash or in restless effervescence. Finally, they propose and create the references to our intuitions of centered, circular and spherical equilibriums.

The symbol's meaning is fundamentally substantival, nominal, although it is capable of adapting itself textually — as has been pointed out (G. Durand, 1979, p. 20) — to adjectival or verbal manifestations. Symbols are therefore the imagination's *semantic* constituents, relatively static, at least with respect to the currents of textual meaning incorporating subconsciously oriented drives. This characteristic of symbols makes them above all suitable for demarcating and structuring the diurnal and postural imaginary consciousness. In the silent density of the night, poetic symbols decrease. We record existence in terms of the postural, acquisitive and sentient consciousness of diurnal symbols, which create its relative dimensions and its reciprocal spaces and divergences. In the nocturnal space of the imagination — without existence, without a singular, clear context — the symbol collapses and is dissolved. The night is the total sum of undiscernable addends, the tonal emulation of a continuous achromatism, a space without dimensions, lodging lost trajectories, without any possible reference. Even the tenuous glimmers sustaining our consciousness of nocturnal space are illusory; they are metaphorical contaminations projected from the reminiscence of day, of the postural habit of orientation and symbolic construction.

Nocturnal poetry, with that of the mystics and Romantics standing out as exemplarily characteristic, does not represent anything more than the paradox of a day unextinguishable in its hopes and nostalgia. The mystic denies night in view of the unique illumination of his expectation of the unitive trance with divinity. The flames of living love in Saint John of the Cross cleave night's tenebrous density, implanting an awareness of the dimension in which the dream of divine symbols flourishes. The mystic's poetry, like that of visionaries in general, is not, strictly speaking, nocturnal poetry, but its negation. It is a projection of diurnal representations. As an extreme example of this phenomena, consider the rabid chromatism of the nocturnal passages Jean Paul and de Tieck offer us in their poetry (G. Durand, 1960 [1969, pp. 256–258]). It is a privileged and very real, concrete space which, as Blanchot foresaw, vanishes with the word, the backbone of positivity, even in its most intentionally negative forms (M. Blanchot, 1949 [1972, pp. 293–331]).

Recall how in his fervorous voyage towards God, Saint John of the Cross explicitly expresses the projection of his own heart's light over the tenebrous space of total, impracticable density. For example, in "Noche oscura del alma" ("The Dark Night of the Soul"):

> En la noche dichosa,
> En secreto, que nadie me veía,
> Ni yo miraba cosa,
> Sin otra luz ni guía
> Sino la que en el corazón ardía.
>
> [On that happy night — in
> secret; no one saw me through the dark —
> and I saw nothing there,
> no other light to mark
> the way but fire pounding in my heart.
>
> (Barnstone, 1968, p. 39)].

Not even the mystic's illuminated sensibility is able to extract glimmers of light and clarity from the impossible forms of nocturnal imagination. Given the absence of anything hostile in this space — "Oh noche amable más que el alborada" ["Oh night, more kind than dawn"] —, its fantastic impenetrability is absolute. The poet himself confesses this to be so in his prose paraphrase of the preceding verses:

> La segunda propiedad que dice, es por causa de las tinieblas espirituales de esta noche, en que todas las potencias de la parte superior del alma están á escuras, no mirando el alma, *ni pudiendo mirar en nada*, no se detiene en nada fuera de Dios, para ir a él; *por cuanto va libre de los obstáculos de formas y figuras y de las aprehensiones naturales* ...
>
> [The second property spoken of is caused by the spiritual shadows of this night, in which all of the potential of the soul's higher parts are darkened, and not looking at the soul, nor being able to see anything, he does not pay attention to anything but God, in order to go to Him, freed from the obstacles of forms and figures and natural comprehension ...]

In Novalis' *Hymnen an die Nacht (Hymns to the Night)*, another climax of nocturnal ecstasy, this time represented in terms of the unitive Romantic theology of transcendence through love, the dream is also linked to an interdicted space requiring construction. Premonitions of the luminous and diurnal calculation ballasted on the infallible "dream of revelation" or the "deep distances", about which one can only predicate the negation of the categories constructed in the diurnal calculation of enlightened reason: "aber zeitlos, und raumlos ist der Nacht Herrschaft" ["but timeless and spaceless is the Night's dominion" (Novalis, translation by C. Passage, 1960 edition, p. 4)]. In the largest and most conventional monument of European nocturnal poetry, night is no more than a void wished for from the context of diurnal light — an impenetrable, unspeakable space. Every reference to liberation is diaphanous — "du Nachtbegeisterung, Schlummer des Himmels kamst über mich — die Gegend hob sich sacht empor; über der Gegend schwebte mein entbundner, neugeborner Geist" ["Night inspiration, slumber of heaven, didst come over me: the region gently rose aloft and over the region hovered my released and newborn spirit" (Novalis, 1960 edition, p. 5)] —, every nocturnal construct is lodged in the postural coordinates of luminous experience — the Redeemer, the Mother, the Lover: "Es war der erste, einzige Traum — und

3.2. Poeticity: The Imaginary Structure of Symbols in the Temporal Domains

erst seitdem fühl ich ewigen, unwandelbaren Glauben an den Himmel der Nacht und sein Licht, die Geliebte" ["It was my first and only dream, and since then only have I felt everlasting, immutable faith in the heaven of the Night and in its Light, the Beloved" (Novalis, 1960 edition, p. 5)]. And, as with the Spanish mystic, we find the curious coincidence of the heart's interior light in fervorous ecstasy, projecting itself as the only form capable of occupying the space negated by Night (see the comparative analysis of both poems in G. Durand, 1960 [1969, pp. 247–249]). Here, we see one of the fragments where the fantasy constructing the images subsequent to the transition turns most plastic (and, hence, most plausibly impotent):

> Getrost, das Leben schreitet
> Zum ewgen Leben hin;
> Von innrer Glut geweitet
> Verklärt sich unser Sinn.
> Die Sternenwelt wird zerfliessen
> Zum goldnen Lebenswein
> Wir werden sie geniessen
> Und lichte sterne seyn.
>
> [Have cheer! life steps at last
> Into eternity;
> By inner fire made vast,
> We are changed utterly.
> The star-world melts, dissolving
> To golden living wine,
> Which we shall drink, resolving
> To stars that clearly shine.
>
> (Novalis, 1960 edition, p. 13)].

The great paradox in Novalis' monument to the artistic fantasy of the nocturnal dream consists in the fact that its best moments are to be found in his affectionate farewell to the diurnal space. His enthusiastic entrance into night's unitive liberation is clearly distanced, first, from the valley of tears of those who exist entirely concentrating on their postural experience:

> Auf ewig nun von allem abgeschieden,
> Was hier das Herz in süsser Wollust regt,
> Getrennt von den Geliebten, die hinieden
> Vergebne Sehnsucht, langes Weh bewegt,
> Schien matter Traum dem Todten nur beschieden,
> Ohnmächtiges Ringen nur ihm auferlegt.
> Zerbrochen war die Wage des Genusses
> Am Felsen des unendlichen Verdrusses.
>
> [Forever parted now from all that taught
> The sweet sensations that the heart may know,
> Bereft of loved ones who on earth are wrought
> By futile longings and by lengthy woe,
> Within a languid dream the dead seemed caught
> And strengthless struggle there to undergo.
> The wave of all delight was shattered, spent
> Against the rock of ceaseless ill-content.
>
> (Novalis, 1960 edition, p. 9)].

But the nocturnal space remains unrevealed between the urgent parenthesis — in Novalis, a joyful one — that opens before an unpassable space: "Doch unenträthselt blieb die ewge Nacht, / Das ernste Zeichen einer fernen Macht" ["Unriddled still remained eternal Night, / The solemn sign of a far-distant might" (Novalis, 1966 edition, p. 9)]. Impotent formulas of approximation at the untransgressed limits of the expressable, overloaded with the undeniable constancy of luminous experience. It becomes clear how the most effective tones of *Hymns to the Night* are those which sing without resentment the song of a radiant life. The Olympic poet, in order to bid farewell in the trance of a change of fortune, captures in fresh images of classicist stylization, related to Klopstock or Hölderlin, but resolved in a delicate, subtly Romantic kind of naturalism:

> Welcher Lebendige, Sinnbegabte, liebt nicht vor allen Wundererscheinungen des verbreiteten Raums um ihn, das allerfreulichste Licht — mit seinen Farben, seinen Stralen und Wogen; seiner milden Allgegenwart, als weckender Tag. Wie des Lebens innerste Seele athmet es der rastlosen Gestirne Riesenwelt, und schwimmt tanzend in seiner blauen Flut — athmet es der funkelnde, ewigruhende Stein, die sinnige, saugende Pflanze, ...
>
> [What living man and sense-endowed loves not, above all the wonders of space spread out around him, the universally gladdening Light with its colors, its rays and waves, its gentle omnipresence as awakening day? As inmost soul of life it is breathed by the giant-realm of the restless stars and floats dancing in its azure flood; it is breathed by the glittering, everlastingly reposeful stone, by the sensuous, suckling plant ... (Novalis, 1960 edition, p. 3)].

The absolutely fantastic intuition of the nocturnal regime is thus revealed, even in its most unrivalled approximations, as alien to symbolic representation and, of course, irreducible to verbal expressiveness, confirming the prelogical nature of the imaginary drive (N. Frye, 1957 [1968, p. 140]). But the nocturnal symbol is not ever a frustrated falseness. It is recognizable behind any form of fervorous vision in the diurnal imagination. The drastic awareness of its dry, clear, pure limit increases the intensity of the day's poetic confirmations. The solemn reality of the shadow outlines, necessarily, the projection of luminous forms. Novalis has created, from the Night, one of the most tender formulations of the myth of encapsulated day, forms of light conformed maternally to the bosom of immense obscurity:

> Hat deine Sonne freundliche Augen, die mich erkennen? fassen deine Sterne meine verlangende Hand? Geben mir wieder den zärtlichen Druck und das kosende Wort? Hast du mit Farben und leichtem Umriss Sie geziert — oder war Sie es, die deinem Schmuck höhere, liebere Bedeutung gab? Welche Wollust, welchen Genuss bietet dein Leben, die aufwögen des Todes Entzückungen? Trägt nicht alles, was uns begeistert, die Farbe der Nacht? Sie trägt dich mütterlich und ihr verdankst du all deine Herrlichkeit. Du verflogst in dir selbst — in endlosen Raum zergingst du, wenn sie dich nicht hielte, dich nicht bände, dass du warm würdest und flammend die Welt zeugtest.
>
> [Does thy sun have friendly eyes that recognize me? Do thy stars take my desirous hand? Will they return my tender pressure and my endearing words? Hast thou adorned them with hues and with delicate contours? Or was it she who gave to thy adornment a loftier, dearer signification? What bliss, what sensual delight does thy life provide which would outweigh

3.2. Poeticity: The Imaginary Structure of Symbols in the Temporal Domains

Death's ecstasies? Does not all that enraptures us wear the color of the Night? She bears thee maternally, and to her dost thou owe all thy splendor. Thou wouldst burst asunder within thyself, in endless space wouldst thou crumble away, were it not that she held thee, bound thee, that thou mightest become warm and, flaming, mightest give birth to the world (Novalis, 1960 edition, pp. 6—7)].

The *semantic imagination* thus values its symbols and myths in the light of the human being's unique vital experience: diurnal posturalism. For this reason the collection and paraphrase of myths and symbols we know in literary criticism correspond in their positivist unities, from Jung to Bachelard, to the imaginary universe of the diurnal (L. Cellier, 1971). Myth-making man, "preponderant ruler" and demiurge of reality (G. Gusdorf, 1952, p. 146), is in another sense the prisoner of the only symbolic expression available to him in his existential experience, lodged between space and time. I will not elaborate any more here on the semantics of the diurnal imagination, a further discussion of which is comfortably within the reader's reach in the bibliography of mythocriticism found in these pages. If I have dwelled somewhat more on the consideration of the inexpressably nocturnal, it is not only because of its more interesting and unusual nature, or in order to satisfy a simple whim of contrariness. Rather, the examination of the poeticity of this fantastic space of the night, irreducible to a verbal description and, precisely, to imaginary exploration, is a decisive and important cause. The wave of silence in which the poetic word vibrates, creating the literary space (M. Picard, 1948; M. Blanchot, 1955; P. Valesio, 1986; L. Terracini, 1987) is at root nothing more than the sensitive compensation for the fantastic resonance of the nocturnal imagination, supporting the transcendental iridescence of diurnal forms — symbols and myths — of poetic fantasy.

Many of the nocturnal symbols collected in the catalogues and atlases of the imagination correspond to the limited space of night seen as a vital experience bound within two periods of postural activity. These imaginary constructions and these symbols are those which constitute the poetic representations of nocturnal peace and agony, of rest and insomnia. At one extreme, for example, we might cite Foscolo's famous sonnet, "Alla sera" ("To evening"). As much as this poem is committed to the same Romantic vision of annihilation which we have seen in Hölderlin — "Forse perché della fatal quïete / tu sei l'imago, a me sì cara vieni ... / Vagar mi fai co'miei pensieri su l'orme / che vanno al nulla eterno ..." ["Perhaps because you are the very image / of the ultimate quiet, you are so welcome / ... you make me roam with my thoughts along the way / that leads to eternal nothingness ..."] —, the nocturnal space is woven out of daytime auroral symbolic motifs alone — "... E quando ti corteggian liete / le nubi estive e i zeffiri sereni" ["and when the summer clouds / blithely court you along with the mild breezes"] — and is finally resolved in the everyday experience of repose, as appeasement and palliative for the polemical tension: "e mentre io guardo la tua pace, dorme / quello spirto guerrier ch'entro mi rugge" ["And while I contemplate your peace, there slumbers / in me the warlike spirit, its roars hushed" (U. Foscolo, translation by Cambioni, 1980 edition, p. 344)]. In the end, there could be no more clearly active and conjunctive temperamental example of the possible reach of the night as a potential image of the definitive abdication of existence.

Diurnal and nocturnal existentially vital experience are, in short, two sides of the same coin, the most deeply rooted of man's anthropological experiences, a familiar space, "terra cognita", and a distressed, inaccessible dimension, respectively. From its illusory confidence, poetry assists the creation of hypotheses on the closed night, on the chaotic feeling of a digestive interior and a cosmically inapprehensible exteriority, irreductible to the reckonings of experience or to formulas of expression capable of concretizing and subverting it. Pure and total symbols, like that of water are not very numerous in the nocturnal regime (G. Durand, 1960, ed. 1969, pp. 250–254). Space and time are positive limits which hinder equally the negative consciousness of the void and of the night. Immenseness and eternity, the radical dimensions of nocturnal existence, transcend any descriptive formula of characterization: words betray and subvert them.

Time as a peculiar perception of diurnal extension, of its mobile plurality, vanishes before the scarcity of effective symbols for dusk, the entrance to the night. Nocturnal eternity is at the most a feeling, a premonition of the negation of the seriated spatiality of work and daytime. A third type of symbols and poetic myths — the lunar cycle and the seasons, the androgynous (M. Eliade, 1965), the wheel, the swastika, the yoke and chariot, etc. (G. Durand, 1960, ed. 1969, pp. 410–433) — express the experiences of succession and of eros as unique diurnal forms participating in the peculiarly atemporal nocturnal dimension: the freezing of the present, that annihilation of time, the eternal plenitude of pleasure at its delicious climax. The symbols and myths of the three regimes of the imagination are fantastic formulas for exploring anthropological experience, incorporated into direct poetic expression in myths and to the almost always oblique formulations of literature's greatest artistic syntheses.

Through man's appropriately growing awareness of the poetic capacity to formulate and express his most intimate and decisive anthropological coordinates, we can come to understand what I consider to be the most transcendental and eminent revelations of poetry, the imaginary instrument of man's self-recognition in the elemental symbols and crucial designs of his fantastic orientation. Thus, at this level of poetic texts' imaginary activity, the most distinguished and decisive aesthetic components of their meaning are revealed. Through the operations of anthropological synthesis, when adequately channeled by poetic expressiveness, the artistic text recognizes the third decisive component of value and of the nature of the aesthetic: *poeticity* as the fantastic expression and communication of man's radical anthropology, orienting him and identifying him with the space of otherness.

3.2. Poeticity: The Imaginary Structure of Symbols in the Temporal Domains

The imaginary level of poeticity's aesthetic configuration which, due to the decisive importance of its effects for self-comprehension and anthropological communication, designates the most genuinely constitutive feature of the same, can explain the incomparable precedence achieved by the Jungian understanding of the psychology of artistic production. This Jungian conception deals with the poetry which Bachelard, following P. J. Jouve's usage, denominates "absolute creation" and identifies as "rare", in other words, that privileged formula of the collective unconsciousness' expression by means of universalist imaginary symbolization, as contrasted to the localizing emphasis of Freudian interests. To highlight, under the Freudian influence, the singular poetic case as an individualizing psychological diagnosis contributes in every case to closing the flow of the most sublime forms of poetic communication. These forms are constituted through mythical identification in experiences of anthropological communication, the poetic specificity of which is exclusive to artistic messages. As Bachelard has so plainly seen: "The psychoanalyst ... is not prepared, because of his permanent stance in the passionate region, to study poetic images *in their climactic reality*" (G. Bachelard, 1957 [1970, p. 14, Intro. VI]). In these terms, the European philosopher's psychological experience coincides in every respect with that derived from literary practice by the great critic Northrop Frye (1957 [1968, p. 111]). Myths, symbols, images, designs of imaginary structuralization in space — they all constitute the deliciously delicate space of a productive poetic affluence. Through it, we attend the revelation in the text of the most sublime forms of meaning; an experience, as is known, beyond the reach of the reflective and objective products of reason.

The feature of imaginary poeticity of certain singular artistic texts — both literary texts and those produced by other arts — lodges poetic value in the most specific cells of universality. The poetic — and especially mythical — communicative convergence, in a "center" of certain symbolic entities, proclaims that "group of universal symbols" Northrop Frye speaks of as the true nucleus of human experience, less direct and simple the more they are essential, synthetic and accumulative.

The chapter of Frye's *Anatomy of Criticism* dedicated to the study of the "symbol as monad", constituting what he calls the "anagogic phase" of his ambitious theory of literature (N. Frye, 1957 [1968, pp. 115–128]), offers us one of the most outstanding moments of comprehension that can be found in the entire critical corpus of our century as far as the proper valuation of the imaginary component of poetry with an anthropologico-universal reach is concerned. That is, a universality that bases the forcefulness of its poetic consistency on the highly non-material purity Frye achieves in his concept of the mythical and symbolic component.

The previously alleged existence of a "center of archetypes" postulates, by itself, "the possibility of a literary universe closed within itself" and constituted by "universal symbols" as instruments of comprehension and contact common to all, with a potentially unlimited capacity for communication. The symbols related to the world of food and drink, or others like the images of the voyage or the search, of night or day or those related to the universe of erotic creativity, guarantee a convergent community of symbols for human communication and man's understanding of reality, the content of which is not accessible to any other forms of knowledge or recognition. The principle of *desire* as the drive of man's infinitude figures at the very outset of this convergence and serves as the elemental basis of its nature. As Frye indicates with regard to Blake, poetry in this manner reproduces and perpetuates impulses and drives in terms of a "total ritual", with which the unique initiative of the artist is multiplied and universalized as "the action of an omnipotent human society that contains within itself all natural powers".

Until this point, Frye's explanation constitutes a lucid summary of the process of universalization visible in high poetry, the outlines of which I try to offer and validate in this chapter as absolute creation, implanted with the value of poeticity in its highest and most extensive degree of solemn and sublime implications. Nevertheless, from this point onward, Frye strays from his conclusions considerably, in my judgment, at least to the extent that he elevates the universalizable poetic property to the condition of a pure essence, an absolute *logos*. At this point, the *dianoia* of art is no longer a *mimesis logou*, but the Logos, the formed subworld (N. Frye, 1957 [1968, p. 120]). This amounts to a very daring leap, inclined to confusionism, on which it seems to me theoretical-literary speculation does best not to comment, as it addresses a question clearly foreign to its concerns and capacities. Moreover, in order to articulate his final proposals, Frye also falls back on his well-known forced re-implantation of the *triad* of Aristotelian categories — *mimesis, dianoia, ethos* —, which he introduces as the central pillar of his ambitious and, even given the restrictions and criticism which in my opinion it deserves, beautiful theory.

The reason for these final unnecessary tensions in his brilliant analysis is no doubt related to the great Canadian critic's religious commitments, linked to a poetic word encumbered with the divine reality of the "Verb" (1957 [1968, p. 164]); a speculative domain in which Frye's confessed beliefs garner my deep personal respect more than they correspond to the nature and rules of critical-speculative interests.

Through its encounter with these sublime resonances and their communicative recognition in the artistic text's structure, poetry achieves its identification with *aesthetic universals*. In poetic experience, the vital transcendence of art and poetry rests, in the final analysis, on these forms of conscious or intuited imaginary communication. Man discovers in the myths, symbols and designs of poetry's exemplary texts the most luminous vision of his nature and its horizon, the principles which link his erratic and crushed individuality into a general cosmic destiny. It could be said, playing precisely with these terms, that poetry collectivizes the individual conscience lost in a sublime

3.2. Poeticity: The Imaginary Structure of Symbols in the Temporal Domains 379

universal identification. By means of the aesthetic universals discovered in the imaginary explorations of strong poetry, the individual identifies his plural universality. The anthropological message vigorously announced through the artistic text's fantastic entities is the culmination of literary meaning's sublime condition.

Myths are cultural variables, symbolic-narrative lines along which different cultures and mentalities channel their *mythologemes*, transcendental objects, limited in number, of universal human questioning: "questions about life and death, the place of man in the universe and in society, the relationship between the sexes, the sacred and the profane, the problems of autochthony (relations with the Earth-mother), the historical and the atemporal" (S. Vierne, 1980, p. 204). Up to this point, I have generally attended to symbols as semantic products of the imagination. Nevertheless, it is also necessary to refer to the complex structure of the imaginary's semantics, which mythocriticism, folklorism, psychoanalysis and the poetics of the imaginary have satisfactorily explored. Although not widely applied in specifically literary analysis, we are dealing here with questions widely disseminated in books within these disciplines, reason enough for explaining why I do not believe it necessary to examine the issue at great length in a book of this kind. Recall only that, in Durand's school, the "mytheme" constitutes the basic and elemental unit for the construction of the myth, and the myth, by the same token, presupposes the serial, dynamic and narrative result in which symbols converge and are articulated (G. Durand, 1979, p. 34). In different senses, Durand also proposes the concept of the "archetypal image" as "the first and universal image of the species", which would thus correspond with the level of mythologemes. Durand distinguishes it from the strict symbol, which functions in the dimension of the myth, constituting the level of "cultural" affirmations and differences (G. Durand, 1979, pp. 20–22).

Restricting ourselves to the poetic and literary perspective, which is what I prefer to deal with here, it is clear that, in the poetic text's structure, we can identify a series of concrete symbolic entities which govern very well-defined spaces of the textual scheme. The set of these symbolic constituents, traditionally identified and grouped as *images*, establishes the general, global symbol, the text's imaginary theme or mythical meaning. Hence, the structure of imaginary semantics and its constitutive dynamic, as I have just described it, do not fundamentally differ in the physiognomy and organization of syntactico-semantic processes from logico-conceptual meaning as it is produced in traditional linguistic analyses.

As concerns the foregoing, I have already indicated, and soon will have the opportunity to repeat and develop in greater detail, that the critical effort most urgently needed for the vigorous structuralization of a contemporary poetics of the imagination is that which requires examining its object of analysis very deeply and defining the differences between conceptual semantics and imaginary semantics. Truthfully, not an easy task, but an urgent and necessary one for definitively raising mythocriticism's imaginary phenomena above criticism. To continue with the current degree of confusion, based on the lack of existing distinctions between fantastic images and logico-semantic representations, presupposes the inability to distinguish between mythical and linguistic analyses, realistically reducing the former to the status of linguistico-formal analytical exercises on texts' meaningful contents.

Nevertheless, what remains clear is that there exist two ways of approaching the symbol in mythocriticism's methodology. On the one hand, there is the kind of attention which isolates, scrutinizes and identifies individual symbolic constituents. An exemplary case of this kind of approach is that of Gaston Bachelard. His symbolic universe is constituted as a vast imaginary cosmology, a great imaginary planisphere implanted only in an ample possible text, the individual symbols extracted and individualized with an indifferent or even deliberate abstraction towards their concrete textual location. This system, in spite of Bachelard's occasional protests proclaiming the reasons for establishing a "philosophy of the dynamic imagination" (G. Bachelard, 1957 [1970, p. 180, Ch. VIII, IV]), acts on symbols entirely uprooted from their expressive context. It ponders them and submits them to comparison only in the general theoretical perspective of the anthropological universe's mythical configuration. This explains why Bachelard's vast imaginary writings, which have founded a satisfactory cosmology of the imagination, nevertheless turn out to be inoperative when the time comes to transfer his generic definition of symbols to the strategies describing and explaining their coexistence within the texts of myths, poems and novelesque narratives.

The desire to attend to the symbol's associative structure in mythical constructs has also appeared, in a different form, among those who have continued Bachelard's important pioneering initiative. Hence, Charles Mauron, following the Freudian example modified by Marie Bonaparte, was the first to address, perhaps inexplicitly, the access of symbolic semantics to the imaginary syntax constituting the myth and the literary text's fantastic topic (specifying here the customary notion of "topic" as macrostructure's dominant central theme, in the sense in which it is generally used in textual linguistic's systems; see T. A. van Dijk, 1977, p. 136). In effect, the statistical survey of texts' "obsessive metaphors" implies the consideration of unitary symbolic constituents, which are ordered as progressive subcomponents towards a higher and more comprehensive symbolic entity, the "personal myth" (C. Mauron, 1962, pp. 12–13).

It is true that Mauron's general theoretical scheme and the terms in which he expresses it are open to criticism, as well as to conceptual and terminological rectification. Thus, for example, his concept of "metaphor" in the denomination of "obsessive metaphor" is incorrect and reductionist since the imaginary-symbolic components of the obsessive trace do not always or necessarily, in their textual manifestation, appear characterized by a metaphoric semantic structure. Durand himself has proposed a correction con-

3.2. Poeticity: The Imaginary Structure of Symbols in the Temporal Domains

cerning Mauron's concept of the personal "myth" (G. Durand, 1979, pp. 168–169), calling attention to the fact that the personal symbolic construct or result betrays myths' primary collective and transindividual condition, as supported in mythologemes. I, for my part, believe that Mauron's complex analytical structuralization surely suffers from not having emphasized in an adequately explicit and organized way the intermediate steps and states of the progressive symbolic constitution serving to mediate between obsessive metaphors and their general mythical result.

I am convinced of the explanatory richness to be gained from the gradual genetic charting of any complex macrostructural space, a concept which includes myths, according to Mauron's terms. Still, in other respects, Mauron's convincing analyses are today faulted for their having lacked a necessarily ordered explicitness with regard to the structure of the broad generative development of the "personal myth". But, beyond the always inevitable corrections and adjustments, Mauron's now somewhat outdated book is still meritworthy for its insightful initiative in configuring the substance of elementary symbolic constituents in myth's extensive supratextual space. In short: Mauron's work has the merit of having been an introductory first approach to the syntactical configuration of meaning's imaginary space (C. Mauron, 1962, p. 25).

The most explicit and orthodox attempt to elaborate an imaginary syntax of the literary text, at least the most recent, is Jean Burgos' effort (1982), which develops the principles of Piaget's genetic epistemology (1950) in the terrain of imaginary *dispositio*. Identifying the symbolic entities constituting the text with images — an attitude that is not without its terminological problems —, Burgos studies the constitution of networks of interselective association among the text's images, which determine its syntactical-imaginary structure.

In *Pour une poétique de l'imaginaire*, Burgos not only sets forth a rich theoretical exposition of his methodological initiatives, but also illustrates them with detailed analytical examples, to which the interested reader is referred. I will, however, transcribe a powerfully synthetic fragment, in which the author indicates the six tasks and objectives of his syntax of the imaginary, understood as "the specific syntax which governs the relationships between full forms inclined towards possessing their own meanings, specifying and particularizing symbols which make the schemes which guide them in their regroupings flower and which they, for their part, nourish; which permits us to discover the convergence of these schemes, in spite of the heterogeneity and polyvalency of the images which they attract; which allows us to attribute this convergence to the permanency of great organizational schemes proceeding directly from certain vital tendencies, which are also the creative imagination's own tendencies; and which, finally, establishes the coherence of imaginary writing" (J. Burgos, 1982, p. 155). Burgos' syntactical, macrotextual effort is also not lacking in important semantic-imaginary aspects: in effect, the symbolic entities, considered individually and in the abstract, offer a very rich plurivalency, within which the selective interaction of the syntactical function isolates certain fantastic valencies and excludes others from each individual image, at the service of global meaningful cooperation in the symbolic result (J. Burgos, 1982, p. 83).

The syntactical-imaginary initiative conceives the text's structure, not as a state emerging from the simple accumulation of images, but as a general dynamic effect, gestated in the duration of the imagination's associations. The identification of the poem's fantastic organization with the macrosyntax of its images presupposes the existence of the linguistic category "text" and its role as a reference point. An implicit inference without doubt, but perhaps not made sufficiently explicit; and, in any case, certainly not with the frequency and depth necessary for filling the general characterization of the imaginary with a definitively clear and rich content.

This feature of insufficiency and relative lack of concreteness, which for the moment can be charged against Burgos as the principal fault with the literary application of his syntactic theory of the imaginary, derives from the drastic marginalization of linguistic speculation (J. Burgos, 1982, p. 11). Obviously, the notion of the imaginary itself entails, as I have been asserting, a resolution of the question of poeticity totally different and today more promising and decisive than the formal-linguistic level. This does not mean, however, that it is reasonable to establish this syntax of images with our backs turned on the text's linguistic macrosyntactic and macrosemantic models (J. Burgos, 1982, p. 12).

With regard to Jean Burgos' proposals, it is impossible to avoid foreseeing the same kind of disappointment which other well-known methods of linguistic poetics or semiology produced in their day, like that divulged by Barthes' *S/Z*. I am referring especially to the obvious imbalance existing between the ambition and attractiveness of the preliminary theoretical and methodological hypotheses compared to the fairly unsurprising nature of their analytical achievements (J. Burgos, 1982, pp. 360—361). Burgos' emphatic and vigorous argument for the independence of the poetic analysis of the imaginary from "linguists'" customs and objects of analysis appears to be exaggerated, considering the associative examples of imaginary syntax often purely and simply coincide, as I already indicated, with the most clearly superficial syntactic connectors of the text's inter-phrasal structure. This phenomenon does not argue against the reality of the isomorphy of levels, but rather against the author's prejudices of methodological exclusion. These exclusions, in addition to not being reasonably sustainable, only deprive the method of the clear advantages inherent in its strategies for establishing the text's symbolic network.

I believe, on the contrary, that the association of this poetics of the imaginary with the facts of the text's linguistic structure, long known to the various currents of linguistic poetics, yields excellent results. I have, at least

3.2. Poeticity: The Imaginary Structure of Symbols in the Temporal Domains

partially, developed an analytical method suitable to such a decisive task in a work that by its very nature and volume is far more adequately specialized than this one (A. García-Berrio, 1985). Hence, I do not here wish to go beyond sketching the method's prospects, all of which I believe to be quite reasonable, for those who do not find the combination I recommend exaggerated from the outset. In any case, when the time arrives to put this collaboration into practice (which I have carried to concrete analytical terms), I believe as always in the selection of the most formalized and rigorous linguistic doctrines. In the textual domain, this includes the efforts of the group of collaborators working with the rigorous Greimas (for example: A. J. Greimas, ed., 1972; A. J. Greimas, 1976; F. Rastier, 1973; J. C. Coquet, 1972), as well as the more autonomous work by G. Genette (1966, 1967, 1972) and C. Bremond (1975).

Of course, before being crystallized in a formally-based *critical* methodology — totally or partially, as in our case, relative to the structure of the text's linguistic material —, any analytical instruments of this kind must pass through a rigorous phase of strictly linguistic speculations (J. Burgos, 1982, p. 48). This does not always imply that the priority in raising the problem does not proceed from a preliminary and partial discovery, obtained from a critical-literary exercise, as in the current example. On the contrary, it seems to me this is the most frequent case to be found in the history of modern linguistic poetics. This "ideation" of linguistic spaces, especially at the textual level, is previous to and the cause of the subsequent "canonical formalization" in the disciplinary conglomerate linguistic poetics establishes (A. García-Berrio, 1977, pp. 190−209).

As a result, I find conceptual and methodological categories put into circulation by the poetics of the imaginary very interesting. This assessment is certainly not diminished in the least by the fault I have just found with some of Burgos' points of view, which after all does not amount to more than a positive correction, "from within", of those auto-restrictive prejudices which are, in my opinion, unjustified. The critico-analytical invocation is especially valuable, not only as the pure and necessary complementation of one more level of poeticity's textual structuralization, entirely ignored in linguistic poetics, but also as the invocation of a decisive instance in the construction of the literary text's meaning. I suspect that this — the imaginary articulation between the poem's spatial concreteness and the failings of human temporal conjecture — ends up explaining the mysterious poetic transcendentalization of language's material deployment in the body of the poem (J. Piaget, 1950, I, pp. 16−18).

In the poem, the imagination's spatial organization of feelings concerning time must be conceived, of necessity, in broadly general terms (J. Burgos, 1982, pp. 86−87). Burgos basically speaks of three types, reflecting Durand's tripartite system of imaginary regimes. The first type consists of structuralizations "which organize chronological time's sheath in space". The next, those constructs which "attempt to immobilize time" and which tend to resist or elude it. Finally, a third type utilizes the cyclical repetition of time in order to "better occupy and open the text's privileged space" (J. Burgos, 1982, p. 126). The first class of the imaginary's organization appears governed, in Burgos' words, by a drive "of *conquest*", manifested in the poem's spatial propensity towards a "total occupation" of the textual scheme. It pursues the effect of "arresting the chronology", freezing time in a kind of eternal present. Here, the general *schemes* for structuring the imaginary foreseen by Durand operate to organize the text. These include, for example: extension, expansion, ascent, enlargement, growth, multiplication, abduction and domination.

The fantastic macrosyntactic identification of this type in Burgos is partially equivalent to Durand's group of diurnal and postural symbols and representations. In effect, within posturalism the most emphatic and affirmative attitude is the active and dynamic one, the textual effects of which are those which Burgos describes in the distribution of images. The impulses of elevation and flowering (G. Durand, 1979, pp. 117–136) are the most appropriate forms for translating our lived consciousness of the reality which surrounds us. The imagination of elevation implies and assumes as its paradigmatic sign a set of movements reflecting reality's manifestation and epiphany. The fantastic sensations of immersion, illumination, concreteness, manifestation, consolidation, etc. (A. García-Berrio, 1985, pp. 304–334) are only derived forms of a great ascentional directrix. Analogously, expansion assumes the intimate conjecture projected over a determined space, which is felt to be possessed (G. Bachelard, 1957 [1970, pp. 177–178, Ch. VIII, IV]; J. Burgos, 1982, pp. 166) under the clarity of diurnal illumination. Overall, a diaphanous experience of the diurnal which outlines the objects doubled and multiplied and assures the selection of subjects appropriate to expansive domination (A. García-Berrio, 1985, pp. 354–364). Finally, only the spatial familiarity of the diurnal meaningfully fixes the space in which the vehement movements of polemical contrast and forceful abduction are unleashed.

Notice how the simple juxtaposition of Burgos' syntactico-fantastic categories, implanted in the text's scheme, with Durand's organization of substantive symbols in regimes requires a new type of dynamic feature with which to characterize the structure of the imaginary. Neither of these authors has sufficiently emphasized this third, dynamic component, which is nevertheless decisive in imaginary representation. I will soon focus on a discussion of this element, since we are dealing with one of the systems of texts' fantastic expressiveness which best describes and measures the imaginary effect of poeticity as a power of anthropological representation.

In Burgos' formulation, the impulse of *withdrawal* constitutes the second type of dynamic structuralization: "The rejection of time's passing finds in this impulse a response to the anguish in the construction and preparation of fantastic refuge; in the creation of spaces in the interior of these havens, as though the erection and multiplication of privileged domains, each one

3.2. Poeticity: The Imaginary Structure of Symbols in the Temporal Domains

more restrictive, will finally permit us to situate ourselves such that we are protected from the degradations of time" (J. Burgos, 1982, p. 127). The innate tendency towards perpetuity attempts to affirm itself by way of this fantastic structuralization, not, as in the preceding case, by means of the spatio-temporal occupation of the text, but rather through the elision of every chronological image. This impulse is textually particularized in the schemes of flight or escape, interiorization, descent, collapse, confinement, and in those of reduction by erasure and fusion.

Burgos' enumeration reflects, to a great extent, the symbolic contents which Durand groups within the nocturnal tendencies of imaginary regimes. The symbols of the fall and the textual schemes of dissolution, as is natural, are closely tied to the desire for the disintegrative annihilation and erasure belonging to nocturnal space (G. Durand, 1960 [1969, pp. 225—268]). A situation always inchoative, well understood, initiative or of symbolic-metaphoric approximation, since the objective plenitude of the absolutely nocturnal escapes, as I said before, pure imaginary representation, or, to put it another way, it contradicts any positive effort at description. The fantastic feelings of descent and collapse, along with the symbols and images which represent them, nevertheless assume the most advanced position in the abdication of the postural experiences which make up the patrimony of positiveness. They are more like representations of the negative desire with which the images of the diurnal sacrifice themselves for the sake of the impossible experience of the nocturnal. The schemes of dissolution and erasure which Burgos alludes to represent the last step in the process of nocturnal annihilation, the "black collision" of the postural vestiges of the concentration of images.

The third of the basic impulses is constituted by tentative and optimistic *progress* opposite to that of the two preceding impulses, rather than, as might be expected, their synthesis, as Burgos himself indicates. It involves the exorcism of chronological anguish by means of the "insertion in the very sense of chronology". In short, this amounts to the resolved acceptance of anguish in order to transcend it, under the fiction of a reconciliation with time. As in so many other magical artistic initiatives, the simulacrum, the euphemism or the conventional dimension of the feared object here has the force of an exorcism. The specialized constructions of time's fantastic flow — such as cyclical reiterations, repetitive anaphoras, the effects of the modulated reappearance of images implacably populating the text, without allowing any empty gaps — aspire to the production of their own space. The schemes of imaginary construction which attempt to establish their corresponding correlates in the space of the text would be those corresponding in Durand's anthropology of the imaginary to images and representations of journey, return, progress, relation, review, germination, fructification, periodicity, alternation, afront, overflowing and the exceeding of limits (J. Burgos, 1982, pp. 127—128).

The repeal of time through the cyclical schemes expounded by Burgos as a correlate to the formulas of associative construction of this third genre, corresponds entirely to the symbolic expression of the copulative regime in Durand's anthropologico-imaginary systematization. The seasonal succession of the calendar, the unfailing successive rhythm of the days and seasons with their own work and rites implies the guarantee of survival through the permanent and periodic replacement of its individuals. Individual time, measured in the anguished consciousness of origin and final decline, is saved and preserved in the unextinguishable duration of the species, which recognizes its survival in the identical and punctual return of the cycles and seasons. The very myths of procreation and of succession, of perpetuation in offspring as the final objective of amorous fusion, are variants of the cyclical materialization of the species' survival.

The nocturnal regime's symbols and the textual structures of imaginary construction which represent them presuppose a precipitation towards the fatal annihilation of time which, nevertheless, is unable to realize itself except as a foreseen intuition; the effort is merely a pure inertia, a trajectory without an objective. But the true annulment of the temporal is converted into an accomplished reality in the perpetuation of the species beyond the succession of individuals, and especially in the experience of erotic ecstasy, a compromise in time between the instantaneity of day and the unextinguishable eternity of night.

The value of time converges in anthropological symbols and textual structures of imaginary construction as the constitutive sign of this synthetic regime of the copulative imagination (A. García-Berrio, 1985, pp. 413–456). Between the postural experience of day, measured in the fatal precipitation of inexorable time, and the imaginary evocation of definitive night, annulled in the totality of the void of successions, the imaginary experience of eros consecrates postural constancy, the luminous experience, without sacrificing itself to the anguish of the measurement of a time inflexible in its course.

In the subsequent specification of each of these three basic impulses and in the corresponding exposition of the schemes which develop them, Burgos makes many aspects of this notion of imaginary space concrete. It seems to me that of particular importance here is the concretion of the concept of imaginary syntax in six aspects (J. Burgos, 1982, p. 155, note). In the first place, it is necessary to characterize the forms with a tendency to isolate their own meaning, which according to Burgos are checked by imaginary syntax. We have already had occasion to comment on this particular when highlighting the analytical transcendence of the progressive monosemicalization of images, as with any meaningful and autonomous entity, upon being constrained within textual networks of meaning.

Also worth noticing is the polarization between both points of view — the autonomic isolationist and the textual — with respect to the opinions in conflict enveloped by the concept of the infinite plurality of readings, favored

3.2. Poeticity: The Imaginary Structure of Symbols in the Temporal Domains

by textual polysemy; or even of the search for a unitary meaning for the text as a principle of communication (see the ample and insightful treatment of the subject in J. Burgos, 1982, especially, pp. 96, 124−125, 170−172). The obvious result of this constellation of images for the syntax of the imaginary serves to establish this second mission, while the evidence that the "schemes" conduct symbolic groupings, as well as the record of their convergence, would be the two developments automatically following from the syntactic dynamic of the imaginary. I, for my part, break them down within Burgos' program as the third and fourth stages of its development.

But the truly transcendent value, in my judgment, of this syntactical process is reached with its two final phases or objectives, following Burgos' order. Precisely in those stages the induction of the properly textual process is produced, lodging it in its extensional context. Here the literary critic's analytical experience is finally assisted by the anthropological and psychological universals established by the tradition of Freud and Jung, Bachelard and Durand. What is correctly proclaimed by this tradition, as a development of the textual syntactic tendency, is its testimonial rootedness in the great human forms of constructing the universe of imaginary experience, in terms of truly "vital tendencies" (J. Burgos, 1982, p. 56). It is in this manner that the coherence between writing and the imaginary finally shines forth, a coherence which, to my mind, is the ultimate raison d'être of every literary process.

The syntactical associationism of images constituting the text's global meaning is, according to Burgos, subject to "universal laws" (J. Burgos, 1982, pp. 15−16). That is to say, the figures of imaginary aggregation are not absolutely free, but are characterized by certain natural conditions which act to limit them to certain forms of association; excluding, of course, the textual structures of infinite combinations. Burgos has perceived this fact — and in this respect my own observations coincide with his —, linking it to the Kantian notion of the "transcendental scheme" (J. Burgos, 1982, p. 117). Nevertheless, invoking Albert Mouloud's opinion, he appears to resign himself to the mere verification of this "schematism", considering it inscribed in the depths of the soul, without making any attempt to present, much less to systematize, the associative operations motivated by these "hidden laws". Nevertheless, his preliminary approximations are brilliant and convincing: "These powerlines are not vague echoes, uncontrolled and uncontrollable, inevitable products of words' blooming, resulting in the revelation of scattered images. On the contrary, they are what give order to this blooming, recovering the images' energy, the constellations of which dictate and impose the path from image to image and from constellation to constellation, multiply the exchanges at all levels, and above all, give these different operations imperative directions, which are possible meanings".

In my own case, it would appear that with this particular syntactical sense of the integration of symbols in schemes of spatial-dynamic construction, to some extent the need to concretely identify and describe the constructive universals of the imagination has been resolved, something which Burgos' work lacks. Under my approach, symbols' basic schemes of spatial organization in the text, as we will soon see, manifest a closed inventory of forms of associative organization, which coincide, moreover, with the most universal and basic motifs of the spatial schemes in which the anthropological tendencies of man's imaginary orientation in the world are materialized.

3.2.3. *The Structure of the Poetic Imagination: The Spatial Pattern of the Imagination's Anthropological Orientation*

The imaginary products which constitute the anthropological representation of the world are not limited to those which have been presented thus far, namely: the *individual myths* integrating narrative myths and cosmologies, which integrate what I have denominated imaginary semantics and, secondly, the *figures* which establish the textual syntactic articulation between symbols, integrating complexes of fantastic meaning such as the poematic textual symbol, the narrative myth or the great intertextual structure which Mauron denominated "personal myth" (C. Mauron, 1962, pp. 12—13). All of these elements of the fantastic representation of the world and of existential experience play the important role in establishing meaningful imaginary schemes which the theoreticians of the imagination have demonstrated. As a result, they are decisively influential in the deep construction of meaning in artistic messages and they are the basis for the configuration of the aesthetic effects of poeticity.

But together with semantic images and their syntax of reciprocal articulation in the construction of imaginary meaning, it seems essential to point out the powerful and obvious role of a set of fantastic representations present in the textual scheme and incorporating integral elements of the mythical cosmovision. I am referring here to those fantastic representations I have denominated (A. García-Berrio, 1985, p. 260) *schemes of imaginary orientation and spatialization,* fantastic designs with the ability to organize the lodging of symbolico-semantic elements in a scheme of orientation within fantastic coordinates. Glossing the experience of Henri Michaux, Jean Burgos has intuited, in his case in the image's effects, the "prolongation of the word in a pattern approximating the poet's pictorial trajectories" (J. Burgos, 1982, p. 36). Perhaps he thus correctly expressed poetic notions close to my own intuitions about the fantastic spatial pattern as a visualized spatial imaginary translation of the verbal and rhythmico-acoustical procedures represented in the text; or even as a content of poetic meaning genetically prior to the acoustico-material rhythms of the poem and, hence, one cause, among others, of these rhythms.

The schemes of imaginary spatialization are patterned in their most schematic and essential formulation according to the images of diurnal, dynamically vertical and positive sensations — *elevation and constitution* — as well as

3.2. Poeticity: The Imaginary Structure of Symbols in the Temporal Domains

of negative, nocturnal feelings — *fall and dissolution*. In the two-dimensional progressiveness of the plane, or in the three-dimensional progressiveness of space and volume, positive postural recognition is patterned in the euphoric feeling of *expansion* and the polemical sense of tormenting *collision*, both opposed to the corresponding nocturnal tendency towards *retraction* and *centering* in enclosure, which also recognizes its analogously tranquil experience in the balanced feeling of refuge of the favorable, comfortable *environment*, contrasting with the tormented recognition of seclusion as the enclosing, encircling *fence*, the threatening space. Finally, the compromise between the two great groups of forms of fantastic orientation is characterized by feelings of *fluctuation*, languidly engaging in a balancing act or conflicting in fervorous ebullience. Note that the positive tendencies of the diurnal spatial orientation establish *dynamic* postures of unstable vibration or of open ecstasy and movement, while those established by the nocturnal orientation seek the affirmation of an equilibrium which would have to be resolved in the annulment of all extensive spatial consciousness (A. García-Berrio, 1985, pp. 304–398).

At this point, it seems necessary to reassure those readers who may be harboring the suspicion that I have surrendered to an unwarranted *a priori* method or a capricious schematizing urge, due to the schematic symmetry of the preceding description. In fact, that summary is the analytical result of my analysis of an extensive poetic work, Jorge Guillén's *Cántico* (A. García-Berrio, 1985). Hence, this scheme of imaginary spatiality's patterns has emerged only *a posteriori*, reappearing as it does in the work of writers and poets of every age. Furthermore, it is always necessary to recall Bachelard's thought, exalting in appropriate terms the crucial importance of the imaginary processes of spatial construction in the symbolic representations of the world, not only arising from our conscious activity and evocations, but also from those "forgotten" elements of an unconscious "lodged" in the spatial (G. Bachelard, 1965, p. 31). If, in his *Poetics of Space*, Bachelard speaks in terms of a fantastic spatiality lodged in the symbolism of the room and house, he later, in extending his search to a more universal and abstract domain, ends up proclaiming the imaginary reality of "a philosophy of the cosmic imagination" analogous to that of the room and house (G. Bachelard, 1957 [1970, p. 213, Ch. X, IV]).

The degree of schematic clarity in the system of spatial coordinates of poeticity varies from one poet to another, as surely as it differs from one individual to another. An enumeration as complete, detailed and discerning as that which I have just outlined can only be deduced from a particularly "pure" poetry, a poetry disposed to the precise delineation of a tense postural awareness, like that of Jorge Guillén. Still, it undoubtedly should be readapted for different cases. The varied examples which are analyzed in the successive pages of this chapter prove the universal poetic reach of the artistic feelings of imaginary spatialization. Burgos himself, always concentrating his attention on the syntactical associationism of images in the text, could not avoid taking note of the reach of spatiality's global design in the text's rhythms. Certainly, he proclaims the fact in an offhand manner, but, nonetheless, with definitive clarity: "the poetic text is defined as that in which the imaginary plays with plenitude, and where writing *spatializes*, finding its significance in the volume which it simultaneously occupies and animates" (J. Burgos, 1982, p. 86).

The space of the text itself creates and incorporates the experience of a higher, immaterial extensionality, which does not exactly coincide with the immanent physical spatiality of the utterance's writing nor with that of its absolute and strict referentiality. It is the imaginary suggestion of a unique poetic space which allows us a more vital approximation to things, enabling us to sentimentally "anchor" ourselves in them, converting them to our own desire, our own needs or our own anguish. Poetry's imaginary space is Bergson's "lived" and affective space which, extended through Heidegger and Minkowski, reaches the existentialist need to install a felt space, "simultaneously physical and psychic" (G. Matoré, 1979, pp. 22–23).

In any case, the poetic operations of spatialization seem to me to be crucial in defining art's aesthetic effect. Behind the poetics of every great creator we can trace and deduce privileged distributions of intimate and exterior space, the preferential trajectories of fantastic dynamics and very unique forms of imaginary orientation constituting his personal cosmovision; to the point that I believe it would be proper to speak of the great *spatial myth* proper and characteristic to many great brilliant artists, complementary to and preceding, in general terms, the singular semantic myth.

The poetic medullarity of this artistic assimilation of the spatial universal also constitutes an object of obligatory reference on the part of critics, within the traditional consideration of the limits between the arts' temporal and spatial domains. Hence, Northrop Frye notes that poetry "presents a flow of sounds which are close to music on the one hand and, on the other, a complex pattern of images approaching painting" (N. Frye, 1957 [1968, p. 78]).

Certainly, it does not surprise us that a critic with such a rich openness to the imaginative as Frye should acknowledge the responsibility of the poetic representation of space in the construction of the diffuse aesthetic sensations of poeticity; far more surprising is to find this kind of appeal in the literary thought of Paul de Man, considered by the majority of his critics as a deconstructionist par excellence. Nevertheless, as in so many other aspects of his critical corpus, the heterogeneity and traditional nature of his most basic sources is reflected unexpectedly in the pages of his most widely disseminated books, which paradoxically are collections of essays and glosses about critical figures, most of them of French or North American birth, as is the case with Blanchot and Sartre, on the one hand, and Bloom and Hillis Miller, on the other. As concerns the imaginary space, it is Georges Poulet's work (1960, 1961), attentively studied by de Man (1983, pp. 78–119; 1989, pp. 107–115), which motivated his particular interest in this important aspect of the construction of poetic meaning.

3.2. Poeticity: The Imaginary Structure of Symbols in the Temporal Domains

As is well known, Poulet's concept of literary spatiality alludes to a notion of the text's extensive structure more in line with Blanchot's intuition than with my own, which concerns itself more with the imaginary structure of the reference. Nevertheless, Poulet's notions about space as representation in the textual continuum of personal experience over time, necessarily offer a rich storehouse of fertile intuitions regarding the metaphors of the extensive figural reference of Proust or Jorge Guillén, which, in my judgment, have not yet been sufficiently exploited by criticism. It is therefore, in any case, to de Man's credit that he paid attention so early to an imaginary element as decisive in the aesthetic constitution of artistic works. In examining Abrams' *The Mirror and the Lamp*, de Man already emphasized the way the literary imagination creates powerful impressions of spatial suggestion, "not founded on an analogy with nature", but absolutely "intentional", that is, corresponding to the intimate uniqueness of an anthropologico-fantastic representation (P. de Man, 1983, p. 28). A spatial orientation, the poetic one, of an intimate and intuitive nature, which surely conflicts with the supposedly objective space of the differential phenomenology of a Merleau-Ponty, for example (1983, p. 35). An alternative space to the logocentric presumption, the fantastic structure of which de Man, in 1955, began to approach through Sartre's *Psychology of the Imagination* (1940), and which, in his review of European criticism in 1965, opened the way for a sound reflection on the suggestive creation of fantastic space as explored by Gaston Bachelard (P. de Man, 1989, pp. 36 and 155).

In addition to which we should not forget the revealing fact that in 1964 de Man was already particularly attentive to the significant echoes of Poulet to be seen in decisive books of American criticism, such as Hillis Miller's *The Disappearance of God* and Joseph Franck's *The Widening Gyre*, both published the previous year. De Man's insightful review of these works (1989, pp. 107–115), significantly entitled "Spacecritics", explicitly underlined the great importance of analyzing the projection in the literary work's spatial structure of the representations related to the image of time: "Much was gained by separating the temporal and spatial organization of literary language, as it crystallizes in rhythm and imagery, from the experience of time and space. But even more was lost by ignoring the highly problematic and intentional nature of these entities" (1989, p. 110). As a result, de Man agrees with and follows every detail of Franck's consideration of the "aesthetic space as the fundamental project of the writer who transforms random experience into the order of spatial structure", even going so far as to discuss how such a model imaginary structure plays a central role, as Franck, directly influenced by Malraux, would clearly have it, in the constitution of art in our century; the reach of which de Man, *a fortiori*, extends to nothing less that all of Western art since the Renaissance. As regards Hillis Miller's book, which analyzed the diffuse, typically spatial sense of "proximity and distance" rooted in the world of premonitions about patriarchical or matriarchical power relations in Victorian poetry, de Man is capable of appreciating very clearly the non-immediate nature of the spatial reference and its symbols, noticing its latent nature as a differed and deep structure regulating the text's most circumstantial, immediately anecdotal and realistic references. Thus, "the Victorian effort to reconquer God becomes for the Victorian writer the aesthetic effort to reconquer space in the closed circularity of poetic form" (1989, p. 112).

A sensibility so alert to the problematic medullarity of imaginary spatiality in the aesthetic constitution of the literary work helps explain why the issue is raised in the central work of de Man's critical career, *Blindness and Insight*. If de Man had found it possible, through Hillis Miller's analysis, to schematize the structural foundations of Mathew Arnold and Emily Brontë's Victorian literature in terms of the diffuse feelings of the subject's proximity and distance with respect to the political and ethical center, in Ludwig Binswanger's critical approach to Hugo von Hofmannsthal's poetry in 1943, de Man is able to detect the dominant role of basic, complex spatial structures of verticality and horizontality — ascent and descent, expansion and collapse —, governing and lending depth and political interest to the semantic system of anecdotes nourished by the textual utterance: "The phenomenology of distances, which befits the behavior of the man of action, is replaced by a phenomenology of heights and depths; the horizontal landscape of plain and sea becomes the vertical landscape of mountains" (P. de Man, 1983, p. 46).

Note the fundamental agreement of de Man's intuitions with those that govern my own analyses in this book concerning Hölderlin's characteristic spatial myth, together with our agreement in the selection of illustrative authors — Baudelaire, for example, in both — and spatial symptoms, such as the "feeling of levitation" of the Romantic soul, which I refer to with regard to the German poets, especially Novalis, and which de Man detects identically, beginning with the Bachelard of *Air and Dreams* or with Binswanger himself, in the visionary English poets like Keats and Wordsworth, in whom "poetic transcendence is closely akin to the act of spontaneous ascent, which resembles an act of grace although it is only the manifestation of a desire" (P. de Man, 1983, p. 46). Nevertheless, my own position differs from de Man's in the kind of consequences — and in the emphasis placed on them — which each of us extracts from a phenomenon we both agree in considering fundamental. While in my conception all of this serves to indicate a basic structure of the artistic work as a constituted construction of the poetic ideal of experience, in de Man's early reflection, the role of the artist's spatial myth found itself blurred, confused among the kind of non-deconstructible intuitions that form part of the predifferential, non-logocentric message.

Overall, I believe that the decisive influence — not merely ornamental, plastic or secondary — which the spatial imaginary pattern has on fantasy, induced by the poem's acoustic and meaningful structure, has not been

3.2. Poeticity: The Imaginary Structure of Symbols in the Temporal Domains

emphasized sufficiently and persistently enough. To the extent to which the effect of anthropologico-imaginary discovery and orientation in space is found in certain texts of great symbolic value, it forms the most decisive component of poeticity's elements. Consider, for example, Leopardi's "The Infinite":

> Sempre caro mi fu quest'ermo colle
> e questa siepe, che da tanta parte
> dell'ultimo orizzonte il guardo esclude.
> Ma sedendo e mirando, interminati
> spazi di là da quella, e sovrumani
> silenzi, e profondissima quiete
> io nel pensier mi fingo; ove per poco
> il cor non si spaura. E come il vento
> odo stormir tra queste piante, io quello
> infinito silenzio a questa voce
> vo comparando: e mi sovvien l'eterno,
> e le morte stagioni, e la presente
> e viva, e il suon di lei. Cosí tra questa
> immensità s'annega il pensier mio:
> e il naufragar m'è dolce in questo mare.

[This lonely hill was always dear to me, / And this hedgerow, that hides so large a part / Of the far sky-line from my view. Sitting and gazing, / I fashion in my mind what lies beyond — / Unearthly silences, and endless space, / And very deepest quiet; then for a while / The heart is not afraid. And when I hear / The wind come blustering among the trees / I see that voice against this infinite silence: / And then I call to mind Eternity, / The ages that are dead, and the living present / And all the noise of it. And thus it is / In that immensity my thought is drowned: / And sweet to me the foundering in the sea (G. Leopardi, translation by L. Origo — J. Heath-Stubbs, 1966 edition, p. 187)].

Where does this poem's essential poeticity lie? Beyond its rich testimony to personal biography and its ability to communicate the sensibility of the age in which was written. Beyond its interesting conceptual and philosophical depth, which include exact alignments with the idealist Kantian scheme of the *a priori* formation of synthetic judgments (Ezio Raimondi), as for example in the passage "*io* nel pensier *mi* fingo". Even beyond the lyrical interest in the objectified communication of the poet's imaginary processes. In short, beyond any of the poem's conceptual and symbolic-substantive suggestiveness, its essential poeticity resides in the clear confidence of the spatial symbolism which effectively infects and transmits the plural mastery of the formal signs in the text's verbal scheme.

The spatial role of symbols appears clear and simple from the start with the local evidence, reinforced by the present deixis, of the immediate obstacles — "quest'ermo colle, / e questa siepe" — behind which the invisible space of the infinite, that favorite of the imagination, is constituted. With this, with the conjugation of rhythms and symbols, Leopardi achieves some of the most sublime accents possible in the representation of the vertiginous void of infinite immensity: "interminati spazi ... e sovrumani silenzi, e profondissima quiete". The fantastic movement, which Leopardi makes sensible and communicates at this point, is one of *unlimited expansion*. The accelerated dynamic in the free space of thought is felt, palpable, unbound from the seriousness of the material obstacles of presence. The confidential emphasis of the feeling — "ove per poco il cor non si spaura" — records and corroborates this expansion of the lightened soul.

From this point on, the set of descriptive symbols sustained in the poem's masterful lyrical tension prolong the vibratile sensation of fantasy's expansive exploration of infinite immensity. In the contrast between the penetrating voice of the present wind and the sonorous emptiness of imaginary vastness — "quello infinito silenzo" —, the fantastic manifestation of the eternal takes hold, that eternity where all of life's "seasons", be they present, past or future, are confused and annulled. What is more, Leopardi's imaginary expansion, lest we forget, has been produced in the intangible space of the nocturnal, of nothingness, in the insubstantial, unrepresentable region of the infinitely eternal. This goes a long way towards explaining the fact that Leopardi's first fantastic movement gives way quickly to other, new movements, contrary to the centrifugal fantastic feeling of sure domination which is commonplace in the concrete spatial expansion of the diurnal regime.

First, it is the accelerated acoustical rhythm of the ineffably extreme sensations at the poem's climax — "e mi sovvien l'eterno, / e le morte stagioni, e la presente / e viva, e il suon di lei" — that symbolizes this unstable ethereal vibration, this peculiar semantic mode of weightless suspension in the ether which, for example, essentially defines Novalis' symbolic uniqueness. But the exhausting weight of the difficult imaginary experience ends up imposing the natural logic of decline and fall on the sense of sudden expansion and vibrating gravitation. A third, definitive movement works to particularize the singular character of this descent into the density of the infinitely nocturnal, entirely lacking in referentiality, a slow, rhythmic immersion, the sweet, suffering asphyxiation of drowning among the waves: "tra questa / immensità s'annega il pensier mio / e il naufragar m'è dolce in questo mare".

It seems obvious that the symbolic scheme of the fantastic patterns of movement and imaginary orientation, to which I attribute such an important role in eliciting poeticity, aspires to transcend a rustic and elemental geometrical measurement of space, understood in the terms Bachelard used to forewarn us: "The space grasped by the imagination cannot continue being the indifferent space given to the geometrician's measurement and reflection. It is lived" (G. Bachelard, 1957 [1970, p. 27, Intro. IX]). Our consciousness of the transcendental uniqueness of the anthropological orientation in poetry must keep in view, in a "concentrated effort of the spirit" and in terms of its ambitious aspirations to master the poetic essence, all of the precautions against easily falling into the schematic inertias of "the physical model of existence" (J. P. Sartre, 1950, pp. 8—9).

The most phenomenological poets, those most focused on the marvels of diurnal exactitude, generally effectively adjust the schematic pattern of their

3.2. Poeticity: The Imaginary Structure of Symbols in the Temporal Domains

imaginary drives to the service of a spatiality of the most accurate and clear coordinates. In their case, the spatial translation of that sublime perpetuation of the diurnal postural experience registers a clearly directed geometry, as happens in the clearly delineated phenomenological spatiality of cubism. The sublime perfection of poetic value certainly fits well into such aesthetics; the pure line and exact space, perfectly vibrating in substantive agreement with the real in a present maintained before our eyes, constitute an unreachable objective for anyone with strained eyes or given to trivial formulations. In examining the work of Jorge Guillén, one of the creators of the most pure kind of spatial syntax, I had the opportunity to detect the purified anthropologically-oriented schematism of the certain and sure space achieved by his postural and diurnal phenomenology (A. García-Berrio, 1985).

Nevertheless, not even in such extreme cases of postural vigilance does the simple design of oriented direction exhaust the manifested reach of the poetic symbol's space. *Cántico* is characterized by the predominance of a privileged affirmation of spatial orientation, positive ascent, as an epiphanous and condensed blossoming of experience. In the majority of cases, the system of dominant symbols in a poet's imagination, his complex "mythologeme", finds itself translated into certain unique coordinates of anthropological orientation, into what I have previously denominated his own "spatial myth". Often critics have intuited these characteristic movements in their analyses. For example, Bachelard's keen instinct discovered the directive value of the fantastic sense of Baudelaire's most characteristic expressiveness, as an expansive movement of diffuse, undulating immensity through which the musical scores of Wagner and Liszt resonate.

This chance intuition by Bachelard is immediately confirmed when we review Baudelaire's greatest poetic production. In many poems in *The Flowers of Evil*, we have the opportunity to note the presence of symbolic variants of the feeling of vast, sinuous expansion, consolidating into one of the favorite active symbols of Baudelairean sensuality. Recall the dynamic signs of voluptuous undulation in "La Chevelure" ("Her Hair"), which appear in the phonico-rhythmical sinuosity of the form and in the semantic emphasis of the key terms in the poem's very first lines:

> Ô toison, moutonnant jusque sur l'encolure!
> Ô *boucles*! Ô *parfum chargé de nonchaloir*!
>
> [Oh fleece, billowing even down the neck!
> Oh locks! Oh perfume charged with nonchalance!
>
> (Baudelaire, 1985 edition, p. 31)].

It becomes more explicitly evident in the descriptive hyperboles of the hair, "forêt aromatique", a symbolic space where the poet's breath of expansive undulation gathers force:

> Comme d'autres esprits *voguent sur la musique*,
> Le mien, ô mon amour! *nage sur ton parfum*.

> [While other spirits sail on symphonies
> Mine, my beloved! swims along your scent.].

The braided hair is set up as a platform from which the pulsation of expansive ecstasy takes off — "Fortes tresses, soyez la houle qui m'enlève" —, while the unleashed hair will be transfigured, in a still more clear symbolic convergence, in a sea of murmuring undulations, vast and open to sailboats, rowboats and ships:

> Tu contiens, mer d'ebéne, un éblouissant rêve
> De voiles, de rameurs, de flammes et de mâts.
>
> [Yours, sea of ebony, a dazzling dream
> Of sail, of oarsmen, waving pennants, masts ...].

Everything moves toward the unlimited immensity of a unique symbolic universe implanted by Baudelaire's expansive fantasy: his soul will be satiated "a grands flots" with perfumes, sounds and colors, while the symbolic ships motivate the author's unvarying sense of infinite, silky expansion:

> Où les vaisseaux, *glissant* dans l'or et dans la moire,
> *Ouvrent leurs vastes bras* pour embrasser la gloire
> D'un *ciel pur* où frémit l'*eternelle* chaleur.
>
> [Where vessels gliding in moire and gold
> Open their wide arms to the glorious sky
> Where purely trembles the eternal warmth.].

Dominated by this kind of fantastic sensation, the poet does not achieve any deep submersion in his plunge, thrown down in a vertical fall; on the contrary, it will be a barely hinted at immersion, a cherished pretext to enjoy the infinite, the rhythm of a lazy rocking, of unlimited indolence:

> Et mon esprit subtil *le roulis caresse*
> Saura vous retrouver, ô féconde *paresse*!
> *Infinis bercements de loisir embaumé!*
>
> [My subtle soul that rolls in its caress
> Will bring you back, oh fertile indolence!
> Infinite lulling, leisure steeped in balm!].

Here, rhythms and sense cooperate in the synthetic representation of a pattern of expansion converted into feeling.

Under accidental differences in modulation, we find the expansive sign of the undulating inflection everywhere, from the rest of "Her Hair" to the sinuous shift, full of lazy voluptuousness — "chère indolente" — of the symbolic woman appearing in "La Serpent qui danse" ("The Dancing Serpent"), and the vibrant evaporation of the aroma of the flowers in the open space of a vertiginous dance in "Harmonie du soir" ("Evening Harmony"): "Les sons et les parfums tournent dans l'air du soir; / Valse mélancolique et langoreux vertige!" ["Perfumes and sound wheel in the evening air, / A mournful waltz, a langorous, whirling flight!" (Baudelaire, 1955 edition,

3.2. Poeticity: The Imaginary Structure of Symbols in the Temporal Domains

p. 60)]. Fugitive sea wings, penetrating perfumes and flowing melodies are the symbolic signs characteristic of the fantastic movement that accompanies the imaginary representation of the poet's dissolution in melancholy, united in the images of "La vie antérieure" ("A Former Life"). All of the symbols reveal that fantastic desire for the annihilation of limits in imaginative expansion, the "great vaults" under which he "used to live". Everything will be fluid, elusive and uncertain in the weak recollection of an evasive feeling without frontiers; the symbol of the flowing oscillation of the waves is distended in the sensation of crepuscular lights and harmonious music:

> Les houles, en roulant les images des cieux,
> Mêlaient d'une façon solennelle et mystique
> Les tout-puissants accords de leur riche musique
> Aux couleurs du couchant réflété par mes yeux.
>
> [In surges rolled the images of skies;
> With solemn, mystic force the sea combined
> Its harmonies, all-powerful, sublime;
> With shifting colors, glowing in my eyes.
>
> (Baudelaire, 1985 edition, p. 19)].

The poet's voluptuous languor is thus lodged, without fetters, obstacles or rigidity, in the vast dreamt domain of a diffuse and fleeting sensuality, of penetrating and inconsistent emotions:

> C'est là que j'ai vécu dans les voluptés calmes,
> Au milieu de l'azur, des vagues, des splendeurs
> Et des esclaves nus, tout imprégnés d'odeurs.
>
> [So there I lived, in a voluptuous calm
> Surrounded by the sea, by splendid blue,
> And by my slaves, sweet-scented, handsome, nude.].

And what ends up occupying the immensity of that lazy space is not, logically, any active power of domination, but a tenuous melancholy in softened, sentimental dissolution: "Le secret douloureux qui me faisait languir" ["The secret grief that made me languish so"].

In *The Flowers of Evil* this intuition of the vast and expansive is frequently confirmed, dominant as it is in Baudelaire's imaginary personality. Recall the kind of emotions in which the cursed opium-induced hallucination is translated for the poet in "Le Poison" ("The Poison"):

> L'opium *agrandit ce qui n'a pas de bornes,*
>   *Allonge l'illimité*
> Approfondit le temps, creuse la volupté,
>   Et de plaisirs *noirs et mornes,*
> Remplit *l'âme au delà de sa capacité.*
>
> [And opium dreams can roam and rove
> Past that which has no bourne,
> Can plumb eternity, and mourn
> The emptiness of love
> And satiate the soul with joys forlorn.
>
> (Baudelaire, 1985 edition, p. 62)].

The spatial image translates and supplants all other non-extensive feelings; the impassioned flight, the sentimental outburst invariably are characterized in *Flowers of Evil* by a predominantly conceptual bias towards a softened, penetrating space, responsive to the voluptuously languid diffusion of the poet's imagination. In "La Musique" ("The Music") the invading symbol is transfigured meaningfully by its association with some of Baudelaire's other favorite motifs for the fantastic representation of a spatial tendency which for him, as we have seen, is paradigmatic:

> La musique souvent me prend comme une mer!
>   *Vers ma pâle étoile*
> Sous un *plafond de brume* ou dans un *vaste éther*,
>   Je mets à la voile; ...

> [Music doth oft uplift me like a sea!
>   Towards my planet pale,
> Then, through dark fogs or heaven's infinity
>   I lift my wandering sail].

The decisive poetic importance which I have attributed to this type of phenomena of the imagination — fantasy's spatial flights — together with the emphasis and the relatively extensive attention which as a result have been given them in this chapter should not detract from the relative value of the same in contributing to the phenomenon of poeticity. As I have insistently repeated, the impulses and drives which create the imaginary spatial pattern in the artistic text are a decisive and, I believe, as yet insufficiently explored component in the constitution of the values of poeticity. Hence, my own insistence on them. My appraisal of them as decisive constituents of the aesthetic sense is justified both by the profound and medullar nature of the anthropological message of fantastic orientation and the failure of traditional critical analyses dedicated to the aestheticity of artistic texts to suitably recognize or acknowledge their value. As a communicative orientation of fantasy, the pattern of imaginary spatialization makes a profound and important contribution to this aestheticity, albeit one resistant to being easily discovered.

However, other factors are also involved in producing the difficulty and rarity of recognizing the role of imaginary spatialization. Not least among these is the traditional set of prejudices regarding the spiritually sublime nature of intangible poetry. For those committed to such ethereal myths, the claim that these apparently elemental structures of physical and geometrical schematism are a cause of poeticity — and hardly an irrelevant one — is immediately repugnant. Further ahead, with Aristotle close at hand, I will discuss the natural and physical dimensions of poetry's causes; for now it will suffice to point out that any explanation of poetry, insofar as it is an expressive and communicative human phenomenon, must necessarily take as its starting point the specific nature of man and his constitutive peculiarities, both physical and imaginary. Among these, there can be no doubt that spatial

3.2. Poeticity: The Imaginary Structure of Symbols in the Temporal Domains

coordinates, along with temporal ones, constitute the most radical forms of sensibility; and surely in the most profound and pre-conscious strata of the psyche, the former even more so than the latter (G. Bachelard, 1957 [1970, pp. 17—18, Intro., IX]).

Concerning the role of a single feature of fantastic movement or of a spatial scheme of imaginary orientation in yielding a unique materialization of poeticity, we must set forth one more restriction, in this case without abandoning the same aspect of fantastic spatialization. The unique sign defines a constant characteristic, but does not negate other possibilities in the network of spatial imaginary coordinates. Thus, without even moving beyond *The Flowers of Evil*, we can find clear examples of patterns of ascensional verticality in "Élévation":

> Au-dessus des étangs, au-dessus des vallées,
> Des montagnes, des bois, des nuages, des mers,
> Par delà le soleil, par delà les éthers,
> Par delà les confins des sphères étoilées,
> Mon esprit, tu te meus avec agilité.
>
> [Above the valleys, over rills and meres,
> Above the mountains, woods, the oceans, clouds,
> Beyond the sun, past all the ethereal bounds,
> Beyond the borders of the starry spheres
> My agile spirit, how you take your flight!
>
> (Baudelaire, 1985 edition, p. 9)].

Within this same poem, the clean rhythm of ascensional flight inevitably culminates in unique forms of expansive horizontal vibration, expressed through customary marine symbols: "comme un bon nageur qui se pâme dans l'onde" ["as a strong swimmer rejoices in the wavy sea"]. And the pure, always dominant ascensional signs now present themselves oriented towards the extensionality of open spaces:

> Envole-toi bien loin de ces miasmes morbides;
> Va te purifier dans l'air supérieur,
> Et bois, comme une pure et divine liqueur,
> Le feu clair qui remplit les espaces limpides.
>
> [Fly far above this morbid, vaporous place;
> Go cleanse yourself in superior air,
> And drink up, like a pure divine liqueur,
> Bright fire, out of clear and limpid space.
>
> (Baudelaire, 1985 edition, p. 9)].

On the other hand, the decadent and nocturnal nature which typifies the Baudelairean poetic of this work could not help but manifest its presence in the dynamic signs of the corresponding spatial orientation: the fall and digestive dissolution. In "L'Aube spirituelle" ("The Spiritual Dawn"), the defeated poet gives himself over to an abysmal attraction: "Des Cieux Spirituels l'inaccessible azur, / Pour l'homme terrassé qui rêve encore et souffre,

/ S'ouvre et s'enfonce avec l'attirance du gouffre" ["Above the stricken, suffering man there glow / Far azure plains of unimagined bliss / Which draw his dreaming spirit like the abyss" (Baudelaire, 1955 edition, p. 59)]. Analogously, in the tenebrous and fetid space of "Le Tenneau de la Haine" ("The Cask of Hate"), Baudelaire reaps exemplary and very rare images from the most abysmally nocturnal and desperate lyricism. Recall, moreover, the first fragment, "Les Ténèbres" ("The Shades") of the long poem "Un Fantôme" ("A Phantom"):

> Dans les caveaux d'insondable tristesse
> Où le Destin m'a déjà relégué;
> Où jamais n'entre un rayon rose et gai;
> Où, seul avec la Nuit, maussade hôtesse, ...
>
> [Down in the fathomless despair
> Where Destiny has locked me in,
> Where light nor joy descends, and where
> (Sole lodger of Night's dreary inn)].

Here we see the experience of a dissolutive degradation populating the same unreal spaces in the kingdom of pure fantasy, as in "L'Irrémédiable" ("The Irremediable"), where the nocturnal scheme of fall and dissolution is expressed in neatly plastic and schematic forms:

> Une Idée, une Forme, un Être
> Parti de l'azur et *tombé*
> Dans un Styx bourbeux et plombé
> Où nul œil du Ciel *ne pénètre*.
>
> [A Dream, a Form, a Creature, late
> Fallen from azure realms, and sped
> Into some Styx of mud and lead
> No eye from heaven can penetrate].

Or in images of startlingly realistic degradation:

> Un damné descendant sans lampe,
> Au bord d'un gouffre dont l'odeur
> Trahit l'humide profondeur,
> D'éternels escaliers sans rampe, ...
>
> [A lost and lampless soul descending,
> Within a gulf whose fetid scent
> Betrays its damp and deep extent,
> A railless staircase never ending, ...]

An impure, digestive dissolution, which also appears in the filthy degradation of so many poems in the series of "Parisian Scenes". "Brumes et Pluies" ("Mists and Rains") serves as just one example. Here, the immersion in the autumn of dirty urban fogs precipitates Baudelaire's morbid decadence in the dark depression of unstable limits:

3.2. Poeticity: The Imaginary Structure of Symbols in the Temporal Domains

> Ô fins d'automne, hivers, printemps trempés de boue,
> Endormeuses saisons! Je vous aime et vous loue
> D'envelopper ainsi mon cœur et mon cerveau
> D'un linceul vaporeux et d'un vague tombeau.
>
> [Autumn's last days, winters, and mud-soaked spring
> I praise the stupefaction that you bring
> By so enveloping my heart and brain
> In shroud of vapors, tomb of mist and rain.
>
> (Baudelaire, 1985 edition, p. 107)].

A call to immensity materialized in the invading tendency towards an expansion without limits and a tenebrous descent to which the pure itinerary of the fall and the nocturnal sojourn in the tumult of cosmic digestion respond. Here again we see the poetic emotions which characterize the author and his work, together with the imaginary symbols which, on the semantic contingency of the terms of verbal expressiveness, constitute their most faithful and penetrating representations. In the end, man, expression and symbol are schematized for the poetic imagination in a design of orientation. After all, is the portentous symbol of the decadent satanism of *The Flowers of Evil* in that "Don Juan aux Enfers" ("Don Juan in Hell") anything more than a spatial syntax, a gaze which prolongs the interminable marine wake without limits? Recall:

> Mais le calme héros, courbé sur sa rapière,
> *Regardait le sillage et ne daignait rien voir.*
>
> [But our calm hero, bent upon his sword,
> Stared at the wake, and gave his glance to none.
>
> (Baudelaire, 1985 edition, p. 23)].

The directive value that the imaginary spatial pattern has for poetic sensation and emotion is confirmed, as has already been said, at the level of the most important features and in the most decisive dimensions of the poetic and imaginary structure of long and complex works, to the point of being able to provide fundamental models of the aesthetico-fantastic circulation and constitution of an author's universe. For example, we might consider the symptomatic and directive nature of that special form of ethereal gravitation or fluctuation which, as we have already seen, has been cited by Novalis' critics as one of the most significant features in the construction of his poetic world.

Limiting ourselves only to the *Hymns to the Night*, we see this immediately confirmed in the work's opening lines, in the laudatory reflection on light as a singular balancing form in the stars' cosmic location: "der rastlosen Gestirne Riesenwelt, und schwimmt tanzend in seiner blauen Flut" ["the giant-realm of the restless stars and floats dancing in its azure flood" (Novalis, 1960 edition, p. 3)]. And it is so active that, analogously, it appears in his own psychic situation, as in the third hymn: "das kam aus blauen Fernen — von den Höhen meiner alten Seligkeit ein Dämmerungsschauer — und mit einemmale riss das Band der Geburt — des Lichtes Fessel" ["out of blue distances, from the pinnacles of my old blessedness, there came a twilight shudder, and all at once the bond of birth broke Light's fetters" (Novalis, 1960 edition, p. 5)].

This imaginary premonition of uncertain and ethereal fluctuation corresponds with an interesting poetic reflection, of powerful intuitive capacities, on that unique entity, nocturnal spatiality. Once again we are witnesses, even in the milestone of fantasy the *Hymns to the Night* represents, to the frustration of the powers of the imagination. The positive spatial images and darkest metaphors of night as "capacity" are reiterated in this inevitably fruitless attempt to express a sense of nocturnal density; an example springs to mind from the fifth hymn: "Die Nacht ward der Offenbarungen mächtiger Schooss — in ihn kerten die Götter zurück — schlummerten ein" ["The Night became the mighty *womb* of revelations; thereunto the gods returned, and fell into slumber ..." (Novalis, 1960 edition, pp. 9—10)]. And in the final hymn, on "Yearning for Death," this *womb* is identified as a remote, deep distance, the endpoint of a deadly though enjoyable fall, of a spatial descent — "Hinunter in der Erde Schooss, / Weg aus des Lichtes Reichen, // ... Hinunter zu der süssen Braut, / Zu Jesus, dem Geliebten" ["Down now in the dark earth's womb / From Light's domain away! // ... Down to the sweet bride come away, / To Jesus whom we love!" (Novalis, 1960 edition, pp. 13, 15)] —, which nevertheless must be lodged in an uncertain and soporific drift hinged to the hope of an undefined eternal nightfulness, womb and end, sustained by the Father's mercy: "Ein Traum bricht unsre Banden los / Und senkt uns in des Vaters Schooss" ["Dream bursts our bonds and sinks us free / To our Father's arms eternally" (Novalis, 1960 edition, p. 15)].

The emphasis which I have been placing in these pages on the decisive role of the phenomena of fantastic spatial design and anthropologico-imaginary orientation in constructing the aesthetic effect of poeticity, is not meant to minimize the decisive importance of other poetic constituents, beginning with the text's linguistic structures and the conventional systems constituting literariness. Nor should it in any way detract from the even greater importance of the features of expressiveness, fictionality and imaginary symbolism. Each of these, working in isolation or together as a set, is the source of unique and aggregate aesthetic effects. Moreover, as has already been indicated, the relative critical novelty of my current claim concerning the poetic role played by imaginary spatialization conflicts with some immediately evident facts. This kind of poetic constituent is far more limited or, at least, not exclusive in the role it plays or its' transcendence in the aesthetic systems of other great creators, and, of course, its' impact is quite diverse from one author to another.

Nevertheless, once we have admitted and pondered their relative basis within a complex reality, the existence of spatial structures serving to particularize the poetic being of different artists seems to me to be a highly plausible element of universal value. Consider, once again, the example of Friedrich Hölderlin, whose work is commonly characterized by the aesthetic success of its rigorous rhythmical and verbal expressiveness, which led him, to reiterate a point favored by his critics, to miraculous Olympic enthusiasm in his way of evoking the primaevil Hellenic myths, as well as the warm atmosphere of the German *lares*. And from that Olympic archipelago of the cultural imagination, he culls the most delicate forms of sensitivity to the amorous sentiment and the most detailed traces of essential lyricism. Of course, successful expressions and exact, vigorous symbols populate his poetics. But the examination of the spatial coordinates of his mythical organization of the world reveals hidden peculiarities which, by the same token, delineate constitutively poetic meanings important for this author.

In Hölderlin's case, the occasional exploitation of the general resources of the imaginary pattern is a characteristic feature of his poetic style, although not a decisive one. The poet frequently makes use of these effects in order to achieve sensations of vibratory agitation, as in the first fragment of the hymn to Diotima: "Wie in liebendem Streit / Über dem Saitenspiel ein tausendfältig Gewimmel / Flüchtiger Töne sich regt" ["His lyre produces a multiple *tumult* / of fugitive sounds, in amorous battle"]. Or those expressing disorder's destructive chaos in "Die Musse". They also appear frequently in the dynamic suggestion of spiritually or physically violent drives, as in the active turbulence of the torrent's restricted flow in "Der gefesselte Strom" ("The Fettered River"). As with so many other profound authors, imaginary spatialization is, in the final analysis, the most synthetic and fundamental expression of his poetic myth.

Further ahead I will have the opportunity to illustrate this at greater length in a consideration of what I consider to be the central myth of Hölderlin's cosmovision and the expression of his directive formula of fantastic spatiality: the patterns of elevation and descent between, on the one hand, the unextended ether serving as the gods' abode, of the highest compassion and beauty, a space of delightful amplitude for the spirit and, on the other, an inflexible earthly reality, without the refuge of any protective subsoil which might collect mitigating forms of abysmal flight. For now, though, I will invoke a less important and more accidental myth in the author's life and psychology, namely that of a pleasant and shaded space as a privileged and protected domain protected from the painful voyage through adverse reality. This is a spatial myth in which the passionate, mature sorrow belonging to the second stage of Hölderlin's amorous poetry is beautifully expressed. We are now far from the first conventional symbolic forms of emotional depression and exaltation, expressed by their common and customary coordinates of collapse and elevation.

In the first stanza of the extensive "Menons Klagen um Diotima" ("Menon's Lament for Diotima"), we find the privileged materialization of the amorous sentimental journey expressed in the mythico-spatial structure of the shackled search and the favored place: "... so flieht das getroffene Wild in die Wälder, / Wo es um Mittag sonst sicher *im Dunkel geruht*" ["so a wounded deer will flee to the forests / Where he used to lie low, safe in the dark towards noon" (Hölderlin, 1966 edition, p. 233)]. The description is of a consoling refuge filled with pain corresponding to the dream of an ethereal upper domain of union, already invoked in the third stanza, where it also appears configured symbolically as the ideal space of a favorable environment: "Denn sie alle die Tag' und Jahre der Sterne, sie waren, / Diotima! um uns innig und ewig vereint" ["For all these, all the days and years of the heavenly planets, / Diotima, round us closely, forever, conjoined" (Hölderlin, 1966 edition, p. 235)].

But the imaginary sense of place is not reduced in Hölderlin's poetics to the spatial equivalent of a particular symbolic situation, similar to what we have seen with regard to amorous sorrow. Rather, the fantastic spatial sensation of protected space and sentimental reservation is expressed in a wide variety of semantico-imaginary representations, the majority of which allude to the happy experiences of serenity linked to the concrete and placid space of the valley and plain, as the setting for the most pleasant and tangible daily activities. This, of course, is a fantastic spatial domain entirely opposed to that of the alpine peaks and the lofty solitude of the mountain ranges projecting the imaginary sense of ascent, and the space corresponding to a tremendous revelation. In "Der Rhein" ("The Rhine"), the pleasant atmosphere of the wild little forest is offered as a counterpoint to a mixed mode of suffering that lies between amorous sorrow and some higher form of heroic condemnation: "Wenn er den Himmel, den / Er mit dem liebenden Armen / Sich auf die Schultern gehäuft" ["When he considers the heaven / Which with loving arms he himself / Has heaped upon his shoulders" (Hölderlin, 1966 edition, p. 417)]. However, the spatial symbol at work here functions imaginarily with a markedly different idyllic shading:

> *Im schatten des Walds*
> Am Bielersee *in frischer Grüne* zu sein,
> Und sorglos arm an Tönen,
> Anfängern gleich, bei Nachtigallen zu lernen.
>
> [In the forest's shade, / By Lake Bienne amid foliage newly green, / And blithely poor in tones, / Like beginners, to learn from nightingales (Hölderlin, 1966 edition, p. 419)].

This more genuinely metaphysical situation will be ever increasingly accentuated in Hölderlin's poetic development, carried on through to its early end. Along the way, symbols are purified in their precise manifestation of an ideal space, as in "Wenn aus der Ferne ..." ("If From the Distance"):

> So sage, wie erwartet die Freundin dich?
> *In jenen Gärten, da nach entsetzlicher*
> *Und dunkler Zeit wir uns gefunden?*
> Hier an den Strömen der heiligen Urwelt.

3.2. Poeticity: The Imaginary Structure of Symbols in the Temporal Domains

[Then tell me how your girlfriend awaits you now? / In those same gardens where after horrible / And darkened years once more we're meeting, / Here by the holy primaevum's rivers (Hölderlin, 1966 edition, p. 573)].

We are in the presence here of an imaginary drive very deeply rooted in Hölderlin's poetics, one which was associated with the warm space evoked in "Der Winter" ("Winter"), and which always appears under that profile of universal destiny in which the powerful values of fantastic spatial schematization facilitate the most successful instruments of expressiveness:

> Wohl frommer ist, denn andere Lebendige,
> Der Mensch. Doch zürnt es draussen, gehöret der
> Auch eigner sich und sinnt und ruht, *in*
> *Sicherer Hütte*, der Freigeborene.

[But closest to the gods among all that lives / Is man. When angry elements rage outside, / The freeborn mind is more his own and / Safe in his house he reflects and pauses (Hölderlin, 1966 edition, p. 31)].

An always green and flowering space — "Der *Winkel* von Hardt" —, where the feeling of protection is perceived in terms of tranquil intimacy or of sweet marine harmony, as in "Reif sind, In Feuer Getaucht ..." ("Ripe, Being Plunged Into Fire"). Nor is the diurnal splendor of the Mediterranean and Germanic singer foreign to Hölderlin's spatial schemes, which echo the odes and their most successful and descriptive accent on the characteristic opposition between the great rhythms, diurnal and nocturnal, of imaginary existence. Recall, for example, the solemn extinction of the poetic melody with which the lyrical fervor of Hölderlin's hymn to the Rhine culminates and winds down:

> Bei Tage, wenn
> Es fieberhaft und angekettet das
> Lebendige scheinet oder auch
> Bei Nacht, wenn alles gemischt
> Ist ordnungslos und wiederkehrt
> Uralte Verwirrung.

[By day, when all / That lives seems febrile / And fettered, or also / By night, when all is mingled / Chaotically and back again comes / Primaeval confusion (Hölderlin, 1966 edition, p. 421)].

These effects become further intensified, streamlined and closely bound to a pure faithfulness to the rhythm in the last poems, the nearest to the faltering silence of madness. This is the case, for example, with the pure suggestiveness delineated by the "propitious hour" in "Viel tuet die gute Stunde", or in the rhythmical consecration of pure song embodied in the poem "Sybille".

But beyond the use of such universal resources, what I am interested in calling attention to here is the penetration of the concept of spatiality and of an exact and immutable scheme of imaginary spatiality in the construction of the poet's mythical universe. Basically, Hölderlin's space conserves and avails itself of a normal paradigm of presence and absence, of manifestation and hope, singularly divided between an earthly and material *here* and a divine, ethereal and elevated *there*; a structure we will see repeated and perpetuated in the different moments and periods organizing the poet's life and work. The youthful poem inaugurating the "Diotima" series already neatly reflects this imaginary organization of the world, from within a conventional tradition of the poetic presentation of amorous passion. Amorous recovery signals the transition from the disillusioned recesses of the skeptic's vision — "Lange tot und tief verschlossen" — to a vehement impulse, the vital strain of luminous extroversion:

> O, ich kehre noch ins Leben,
> Wie heraus in Luft und Licht
> Meiner Blumen selig Streben
> Aus der dürren Hülse *bricht*.

[Oh, I will live again, / like the happy effort of my flowers, / breaking their hard shell / and throwing themselves towards the air and light].

An ascent, an escape, that is very much aware of its opposite, the depressing experience of collapse, the intolerable experience of an exhausting luminosity. The absence of love's paradisiacal delights translates into a sense of unbearable spatial weight:

> Da die Last der Zeit *mich beugte*,
> Und mein Leben, kalt und bleich,
> Sehnend schon hinab sich neigte
> In der Schatten stummes Reich.

[When days' weight crushed me / and my cold and pale life / already wanted, in decline, the silent kingdom of the shadows].

In any case, here we may observe quite clearly the peculiar predominance in Hölderlin's imagination of the sense of depressive collapse, contrasting with the more commonplace spatial sense of an elastic plunge expressing the feeling of nocturnal fall. All of the conflict of the poet's anguish is present, set on solid ground, as the inflexible consequence of a certain cosmic destiny. An anguished sense which is depressively reiterated in the poems' successive images, as in the terrible formulas of "Menon's Lament for Diotima":

> Ach! und nichtig und leer, wie Gefängniswände, der Himmel
> Eine beugende Last über dem Haupte mir hängte!

[Oh, and futile and empty, walls of a prison, the heavens / Press, a smothering load heaped on my head from above (Hölderlin, 1966 edition, p. 237)].

Beyond this anxious space, hope invariably points the way towards the higher ethereal regions where gods and destiny dwell. Hence, ascent, in Hölderlin's mythical scheme, is the compulsory means for passing from misfortune and misery to perfection. We see it operative in the conventional amorous formulas in the "Diotima" poem:

3.2. Poeticity: The Imaginary Structure of Symbols in the Temporal Domains

>   Da, wo keine Macht auf Erden,
>   Keines Gottes Wink uns trennt,
>   Wo wir eins und alles werden,
>   Da ist nun mein Element.

[Henceforth, my element is / that where no earthly force, / no divine order separates us anymore, / there where we savor total union].

An element of one's choice, an immensity foreign to the postural experiences of light, without time or need — "Wo wir Not und Zeit vergessen" — the access to which is reserved to the ascendant enthusiasm of the spirit, the glorifying and arrogant rapture, as at the conclusion of the poem to Rousseau:

>   Kennt er im ersten eichen Vollendetes schon,
>   Und fliegt, der kühne Geist, wie Adler den
>   Gewittern, weissagend seinen
>   Kommenden Göttern voraus ...

[In seed grains he can measure the full-grown plant; / And flies, bold spirit, flies as the eagles do / Ahead of thunderstorms, preceding / Gods, his own gods, to announce their coming (Hölderlin, 1966 edition, p. 131)].

Or in the same longing for aerial sublimation in "Abendphantasie" ("Evening Fantasy"):

>   ... o dorthin nehmt mich,
>   Purpurne Wolken? und möge droben
>   In Lichte und Luft zerrinnen mir Lieb und Leid!

[Oh there now take me, / Crimson-edged clouds, and up there at last let // My love and sorrow melt into light and air! (Hölderlin, 1966 edition, p. 91)].

In Hölderlin's cosmic and spatial myth, an identification with ascendant tensions and with the best of the spatially sublime constitutes an undeniable constant; an aesthetic and moral category firmly implanted in the imaginary symbolization of space. The poem "Die Götter" ("The Gods") is, to put an end to our consideration of this topic, perhaps the most complete and synthetic formulation of this encounter of myth and space, the union of spiritual tension and ascent:

>   Du stiller Äther! immer bewahrst du schön
>   Die Seele mir im Schmertz, und es adelt sich
>   Zur Tapferkeit vor deinen Strahlen,
>   Helios! oft die empörte Brust mir.

[You silent Ether, always in pain or grief / You keep my soul untouched, and when, hurt, I rage, / Yet often I take heart, ennobled, / Helios, in the face of your nobler brightness (Hölderlin, 1966 edition, p. 137)].

The space between the two regions, ethereal and earthly, does not only imply, as has been shown thus far, the dimension of ascent and of human transcendence in an impulse of spiritual elevation. Hölderlin's spatial myth is also characterized by the opposite communicative movement: namely, the descent of the gods. A sumptuous orchestration of fantastic rhythms and forms accompanies the majestic divine voyage in his poetry. Although invoked on a limited number of occasions, the presence of this slow ethereal rain, of this pacifying and illustrious descent, adds a perfect spatial coherence to the symbolic harmony of the poet's universe. This is the exclusive condition reflected in "The Only One":

> Denn nimmer herrscht er allein
> Und weiss nicht alles. Und stehet irgend
> Eins zwischen Menschen und ihm.
> Und Treppenweise *steiget*
> Der Himmlische *nieder*.

[But He never rules alone / and is not omniscient. Something always comes / between men and Him. / And only gradually / the Celestial One descends towards us].

The favorable, charitable gravitation of the immortals towards the world forms an essential part of the poet's mythical comprehension of the latter's nature.

In this way, an ancestor raised to the heavens lets his presence be known in the home by means of a providential and silent invasion:

> Stiller Vater! auch du lebtest und liebtest so;
> Darum wohnest du nun, als ein Unsterblicher
> Bei den Kindern, und Leben,
> Wie *vom schweigenden Äther, kommt*
> Öfters über das Haus, ruhiger Mann! ...

[Silent Uncle! You also lived / and loved. For this reason you live together with your sons / as an immortal. And sometimes, life seems to / come from you, as from the silent Ether, descending on this house, gentle man].

What is important about the schemes of imaginary spatialization is not the type of symbolico-semantic associations with which they fill and concretize the functional diagram they implant. It is true that the spatial myth's semantic content is its most perceptible element, its most immediate and intuitively observable feature. Surely this explains why the semantic dimension of mythocriticism has been consolidated before the syntactic, without regard to the sense in which this syntactic dimension is understood: be it Burgos' more strictly grammatical conception, or my own notion of spatial schematism. Nevertheless, frequently — and it may even be generalized as the norm, although I do not yet count on sufficiently varied and numerous analytical examples to do so — the symbolic manifestation of any mythical construction is supported by a rigorous spatial scheme of imaginary orientation. It is in this spatial scheme that the most solid imaginary constants reside, determining the peculiarities of the poetic personality, almost always incorrectly attributed exclusively to semantico-symbolic associations.

The semantic level of mythical construction "explains" the temporal conception of the world, both diurnal and nocturnal, and "implies" the spatial conception, which thus manifests itself as an implied foundation, as a deeper

3.2. Poeticity: The Imaginary Structure of Symbols in the Temporal Domains

and more essential structure than that of temporality itself. According to all indications (M. Eliade, 1963, p. 30), the unique process of poetry's spatialization, like the narrative-symbolic domain of myths, manifests a will to "occupy" anxieties about space. For Jean Burgos, poetry's unique imaginary mechanisms offer a base from which "to spatially locate answers to the trials of existence in the temporal" (J. Burgos, 1982, p. 86).

The proof of all of this might be found in the description of how this same basic scheme of imaginary orientation circulates and is repeated among various symbolic paths. Returning to our concrete example, we may observe in Hölderlin's poetics the two-dimensional distribution of anthropologico-imaginary orientation between a superior ethereal space and an earthly base. This configuration manifests itself as the spatial skeleton supporting the myth of the divinities and is rigorously reiterated in order to affirm other key objectives of Hölderlin's cosmovision. In his early poetic maturity, Hölderlin most characteristically resorts to Germanic myths which go hand in hand, as is known, with the Mediterranean myths inspired by his enthusiastic Hellenism and rooted in his most radiant youth. The supreme elegy, "Heimkunft" ("Homecoming"), no doubt figures among the most representative of the poet's works. In it we find manifested the same mythico-spatial scheme of high and low, superior and inferior, displayed in Hölderlinean poems through the myths of love, gods and men. Heidegger himself intuited no less when he indirectly constructed his well-known commentary to this poem on the basis of the contrasting spaces which I have alluded to (M. Heidegger, 1951, [1971, pp. 9–32. Ch. I]).

Moreover, the piece is rigorously divided into six units of which the first three gloss the higher region, while the last three are dedicated to the expression of the most delicate and sublime sentimentality of nation and home. Hence, the scheme of sky and earth, of here and there, reappears. The initial presentation of the great chain of mountains, both a place of reflection and a starting point, is handled with grandiose fantasy, filled with vehement deixes of ascent and of penetrating interiority:

> *Drin in den Alpen ist noch helle Nacht* und die Wolke,
> Freudiges dichtend, sie deckt *drinnen das gähnende Tal.*
> Dahin, dorthin toset und stürzt die scherzende Bergluft,
> *Schroff durch Tannen herab* glänzet und schwindet ein Strahl.

[There in the Alps a gleaming night still delays and, composing / Portents of gladness, the cloud covers a valley agape. / This way, that way roars and rushes the breeze of the mountains, / Teasing, sheer through the firs falls a bright beam, and is lost (Hölderlin, 1966 edition, p. 255)].

The mobilization of this chaos — "das freudigschauernde Chaos" ("this chaos trembling with pleasure") — is reflected in the jubilant conflict among the peaks. Everything is there, in the remote heights, more vast and monumental with the first light at the break of day, in the accumulation of the idiomatic symbols of clarity and elevation, which Heidegger speaks of in regard to these lines (1951, [1971, p. 16. Ch. I]). Perpetuating the mythic path of descent, and falling as a vigorously fertile rain, which echoes in the immense natural workshop of the peaks:

> Wachstum ahnend, denn schon, wie Blitze, fallen die alten
> Wasserquellen, der Grund unter den Stürzenden dampft,
> Echo tönet umher, und die unermessliche Werkstatt
> Reget bei Tag und Nacht, Gaben versendend, den Arm.

[Growth it foreknows, for already ancient torrents like lightning / Crash, and the ground below steams with the spray of their fall. / Echo sounds all around and, measureless, tireless, the workshop, / Sending out gifts, is astir, active by day and by night (Hölderlin, 1966 edition, p. 255)].

But the invocation of the inaccessible physical mountain peaks only fulfills the function of fixing the fantastic reference, the visible testimony of celestial space, dwelling-place of the immortals. Above the most inaccessible heights — "die silbernen Höhen darüber" ("the silvery peaks lie aglitter") — transported in the most extreme clarity of light —

> Und noch höher hinauf wohnt über dem Lichte der reine
> Seelige Gott vom Spiel heiliger Stralen erfreut.

[Even higher, beyond the light, does the pure never clouded / God have his dwelling, whom beams, holy, make glad with their play (Hölderlin, 1966 edition, p. 255)].

God, delighting in his providence, perpetuates the Hölderlinean vision of the good harvest:

> Der ätherische scheint Leben *zu geben*, geneigt,
> Freude *zu schaffen*, mit uns, wie oft, wenn, kundig des Masses,
> Kundig der Atmenden auch zögernd und schonend der Gott
> Wohlgediegenes Glück den Städten und Häusern und milde
> *Regen*, zu öffnen das Land, brütende Wolken, und euch,
> Trauteste Lüfte dann, euch, sanfte Frühlinge, *sendet*.

[He, the ethereal one, seems kindly, disposed to give life, / Generate joys, with us men, as often when, knowing the measure, / Knowing those who draw breath, hesitant, sparing the God / Sends well-allotted fortune both to the cities and houses, / Showers to open the land, / gentle, and you, brooding clouds, / You, then, most dearly loved breezes, followed by temperate springtime (Hölderlin, 1966 edition, pp. 255, 257)].

All of the semantic characteristics of the poet's general myth of the providential rain regenerating life through the gods' paternal care return in the new scene, torn from the pure evocation of space and of elemental references to the myth of ethereal circulation among gods and men:

> Und *mit langsamer Hand* Traurige wieder erfreut,
> Wenn er die Zeiten *erneut, der Schöpferische*, die stillen
> Herzen der alternden Menschen erfrischt und ergreift,
> Und *hinab in die Tiefe wirkt*, und öffnet und aufhellt.

[And with a slow hand once more gladdens us mortals grown sad, / When he renews the seasons, he, the creative, and quickens, / Moves once again those hearts weary and numb

3.2. Poeticity: The Imaginary Structure of Symbols in the Temporal Domains 411

with old age, / Works on the lowest depths to open them up and to brighten all (Hölderlin, 1966 edition, p. 257)].

In the second part of the poem, the categorically immense resonances of the Olympic god, revealed in a poetic discourse on the pure light of icy alpine desolation, change and are amiably extended towards the warm images of patriotic and domestic tranquility. The poem deals now with the valley, happy under the poet's reencountering gaze, the spacious and familiar field flanked by the alpine lake, a welcoming, warm and friendly dimension which joyfully embraces the wandering son, who returns having conquered the secrets of the heights (M. Heidegger, 1951, [1971, pp. 18—19 Ch. I]): "Alles scheinet vertraut, der vorübereilende Gruss auch / Scheint von Freunden, es scheint jegliche Mine verwandt" ("All seems familiar; even the word or the nod caught in passing / Seems like a friend's, every face looks like a relative's face"). In the open space of the serene plain, the hospitable cities gladly open their doors, "happy Lindau", the emblem of the accessibility of the open valley, of physical expansion and intellectual diffusion, and of recognition:

> Aber reizender mir bist du, geweihete Pforte!
> Heimzugehn, wo bekannt blühende Wege mir sind,
> Dort zu besuchen das Land und die schönen Tale des Neckars,
> Und die Wälder, das Grün heiliger Bäume, wo gern
> Sich die Eiche gesellt mit stillen Birken und Buchen,
> Und in Bergen ein Ort freundlich gefangen mich nimmt.

[Yet, you door that are hallowed, much more strongly you urge me to / Make for home where I know blossoming pathways and lanes, / There to visit the fields and the Neckar's beautiful valleys, / And the woods, green leaves holy to me, where the oak / Does not disdain to consort with quiet birches and beeches, / Where amid mountains one place holds me, a captive, content (Hölderlin, 1966 edition, p. 259)].

This transformation of scenery into a state of mind appears, as can be seen, powerfully linked, beyond the immediate symbols, with the imaginary sense of spatial orientation — up and there / down and here. An intuition which is deployed at the same time in local dynamically contradictory patterns — elevation and the violence of collision / expansion and the calm brush of a familiar caress. The wanderer dreams of finding everything, at the end of a long voyage, as it was when he left; and he is ecstatic with the vision which accompanies his desire, which is his desire: "Dennoch sind sie es noch! ... Ja! das Alte noch ist!" ["Yet they are still themselves! ... Yes, it's all what it was" (Hölderlin, 1966 edition, p. 259). With this happy expectation, the fields open and the first venture in familiar and loved territory is distended into an idyllic exploration of rediscoveries and reunions: "Wenn wir gehen und schauen draussen das lebende Feld, / Unter den Blüten des Baums, in den Feiertagen des Frühlings ..." ["When we go outside, look at the living green field / Under the trees in blossom, on holidays due in springtime" (Hölderlin, 1966 edition, p. 259)]. What is recovered here are the spaces open to the friendship of the airy valley and the fields of flowers in the spring, which contrast with the craggy domains propitious to divine revelation — "Droben in Höhen erfrischt und waltet über Gebirgen" ["Wandering Time up above and governs the high mountain ranges"] —, the high space of silvery and inhospitable snow from which life descends as a celestial gift in the form of showers which make the lands fertile — "Der gewähret uns bald himmlische Gabe" ["Him who now will grant heavenly gifts" (Hölderlin, 1966 edition, p. 259)]. Thus, Hölderlin expresses the ecstasy of serene expansive delight in the presence, perhaps overly accessible, of the restrictive experience of a formidable revelation. Sensitivized poetically in the expression of heights and of ethereal raptures, the singer's languid lament finally appears. He knows himself to be the only elected one, the definitive solitary one, beyond salvation: "Sorgen, wie diese, muss, gern oder nicht, in der Seele / Tragen ein Sänger und oft, aber die anderen nicht" ["Whether he likes it or not, and often, a singer must harbor / Cares like these in his soul; not, though, the wrong sort of cares" (Hölderlin, 1966 edition, p. 261)].

The imaginary spatial schematization which the most complex and exquisite poetic feelings can lead to, as we have just witnessed, is constituted under a privileged personal structure into the permanent category of an author's poetic representation, into a genuinely universal aesthetic. Hence, we can see the imaginary structure of spatial orientation which organizes the decisive forms of Hölderlin's mythical horizon repeated, more or less in the same fashion and with slight modifications and variations, in many of his texts, and in almost all of his most fundamental texts — that is, in those where the materialization of the mythical poetic universe imposes itself as a broad and explicit exigency.

One system for cataloguing the imaginary behavior of texts and authors involves observing the prevalence and density of symbols and of what we have called schemes of spatialization. The case of symbolic density places us in the presence of forms of art considered most impure, more densely communicative and paraphrastic: the fertile poetry of an Unamuno as compared to the schematic lightness of a Juan Ramón Jiménez. In the cases of so-called "pure" poetry, the purity of which critics have until now explained as a "matter of words", what in fact produces and transmits this sensation of purity is above all the light touch of its symbolic content, the careful and exclusive selection of the text's symbols, their privileged ponderation.

So-called pure art does not multiply symbols in a poem; on the contrary, it lightens texts' semantico-imaginary space, it decimates fantasy's substantive representations, perhaps in order to individualize and customize them better, isolating them through the aesthetic dignity of their unrepeatable surprise. This genre of poems thematizes and makes explicit the concise precision of points, lines and moments in the schematism of their spatial designs. Recall Valéry's pure art, as in his unforgettable "Le Cimetière marin" ("The Graveyard By the Sea"):

3.2. Poeticity: The Imaginary Structure of Symbols in the Temporal Domains

> *Ce* toit tranquille, où marchen des colombes,
> Entre les pins palpite, entre les tombes.
> *Midi le juste* y compose de feux.
> *La mer*, la mer, toujours recomencée!
> Ô récompense après une pensée
> Qu'un *long regard sur la calme des dieux.*
>
> [Quiet that roof, where the doves are walking,
> Quivers between the pines, between the tombs,
> Justicer Noon out there compounds with fires
> The Sea, the sea perpetually renewed!
> Oh what a recompense, after a thought,
> A prolonged gazing on the calm of gods!
>
> (Valéry, 1977 edition, p. 269)].

Note the concise extension of sky and sea, without any symbolic adjectivization. Underlying the former, we find only the immaterial trace of an illusion of direction, the doves' flight; and, in order to emphasize the eternal reiterative density of the sea, there is only the euphonic repetition of the symbol: "La mer, la mer, toujours recomencée". Animating both symbols is their subjection to the midday hour, exact and punctually explicit: "Midi le juste". For their part, the pines and tombs represent the concise vertical contrast destined to animate those two "calm seas" of extension, over which the gaze wanders out and is lost.

Hence, imaginary schemes of spatialization predominate in "pure" poetry. In their breadth, these schemes affirm subtle hints sustained by the barely noticeable impulse suggested by the spatial sense, almost without any substantive symbolic presence. The sensation of subtle weightlessness and purity in Valéry's "The Graveyard By the Sea", for example, springs from this source. The lexicon in poetry of this kind is of course the most immediate and external testimony to the unequal distribution of imaginary emphasis; but the lexicon itself, in contrast to what is customarily affirmed, is not ultimately responsible for the fantastic sense of purity which stems, as has been said, from the predominance of spatial schemes. These schemes guide the drives of the subconscious spatial orientation beyond the semantic charge of substantival symbols.

Immersed with the poetics of the imagination in the depths of the symbolic constitution of poeticity, we may seem to be irretreivably beyond Aristotle's proclaimed belief in the *physical* nature of poetic effects (1448 b 5), which seems to me to be a definition not only worthy of consideration, but also an exemplary guiding principle. Hence, I believe that in fact we have never found ourselves so close to this principle as now, when considering the *imaginary* mode of poeticity. This imaginary mode is, as I have argued, the ultimate schematic basis for every manifestation of poetic value since, in Jung's formulation, the image constitutes the most concentrated expression of a psychic situation — and, hence, a "natural", global, general phenomena.

In this case, there is nothing more physical or "natural" than this poetic foundation, largely unexplored in its psychic role. It reveals its most accessible and concrete anthropological outlines in the light of the construction of the semantics and syntax of the poetic imagination. The most radical symbols of the diurnal, the nocturnal and the copulative, together with the imaginary patterns of spatial orientation, correspond rigorously to the constitutively physical evidence of our experience and instincts: the postural, digestive and reproductive. The pre-natal and immediately post-natal experience is, as has been proven, the domain where the anthropological nature of the world of our identity is organized (G. Durand, 1960 [1969, pp. 48–51]).

It is not difficult to reconcile the symbolico-semantic component of imaginary production with our understanding of the double causality, natural and physical, of poetry in Aristotle's own precise terms. This same physical nature is even more easily observed in the case of the imaginary component which I have conventionally denominated *syntactic*. There is no doubt whatsoever as to the strictly observable and physical nature of rhythms. The poem's acoustic rhythm represents only one reiterative-temporal expression of poetry, conventionalized as its most characteristic element. Aristotle's text (1448 b 20) speaks generally of the naturally pleasurable nature of rhythm for man, without identifying, perhaps with a deep awareness and penetration into the nature of the poetic phenomenon, the concrete mode of this rhythm. From our point of view, the conventionalized acoustico-temporal rhythm of the poem is linked, through its imaginary reflection, with corresponding forms of spatial rhythms. The psychology of artistic perception (R. Arnheim, 1954) presents no problems for the consideration of the genre of correspondences between the structural rhythms which serve to dialectically bring together the textual entity's various constituents, in addition to those corresponding to the visual trajectory operative in a work's recognition and comprehension, as among the most reasonable foundations of plastic aestheticity.

In the poem, the immediate and exterior temporal acoustic rhythm corresponds to the rhythmico-spatial structures of the fantastic drive, to the extent that both, individually, are nothing more than the perceptible representations of a common and intimate imaginary coenesthesis by which the subconscious expresses its most extreme articulations. Some here might wish to raise the question about whether or not, by mentioning the interpretation's physical, spatial and cognitive level, I am not detracting from the high spiritual character secularly attributed to aesthetic sentiment and enlightenment. Nevertheless, perhaps an appropriate response would be to appeal once again to the deconstructive position on the inevitably fallacious nature of the argument which attributes poetic excellence with greater ease and frequency to the loftily sublime, rather than to that which is abysmally deep. Though in the anthropological dimension unique to a universe without known centers or limits, the relations of meaning and sense which point in a certain direction should be indifferently discounted.

3.2. Poeticity: The Imaginary Structure of Symbols in the Temporal Domains

Nobody should feel defrauded by the fact that poetry appeals to these "infernal frontiers", to these final limits of conscious anthropological depth where it gains an advantage even over conceptual speculation (D. Romero de Solís, 1981), nor that it is in this respect that our universal interest in poetry is justified. In all of the paths he takes towards self-discovery, man perceives how the abundant combinatory complexities of the products of his behavior are only complex on the surface. Upon exploring more deeply the causes which create this surface intricacy, he discovers a quantitative simplification of active elements, corresponding to the economy governing human psychic activity. To discover, in the end, elemental and discernable anthropological motifs which, as a result, are "physical" in the Aristotelian sense, should not be construed as a superficiality or over-simplification of causal explanation; rather, on the contrary, such a discovery indicates that one has penetrated deeply into poetry's essential being.

To attribute the cause of poeticity, as we have done here, to an essential and profound anthropologico-imaginary structure, does not presuppose anything which would in any way contradict our understanding of the poetic as a *value*. That the subconscious drives and symbolic representations of the fundamental imaginary regimes exist in the individual, in a latent state preceding the poem itself, does not mean that they unconditionally surrender or reveal themselves in any structure of verbal representation whatsoever. In the area of imaginary construction, poeticity continues to be a *value*, a non-automatic result adhering to the successful and fortunate textual formula and denied to those which fail. Nevertheless, it is true that from the deep imaginary constitution common to every poem and to every artistic text it is possible to arrive at more convincing explanations of certain mysteries concerning the success or failure of poeticity in literary texts which are not explained to anybody's entire satisfaction through analyses which focus solely on their allusive expressiveness. Such is the case with "The Cypress of Silos", which is more a symbol or a trace of desire than a poem, or even with those *Exemplary Novels* of Cervantes least affected by a realist coloring, those which reveal the broad mimetic function of an imaginary structure.

Among the questions which occupy our attention in this chapter dedicated to the ultimate grounds for crediting the artistic text's imaginary dimension with a key role in the construction of poetic meaning, it seems very appropriate and convenient to mention and adequately locate the active component of poetic texts' meaningful gaps and voids. I am referring to that collection of empty spaces surrounding words and to those echoing cells in which poetic voices' positive resonances are relaxed, moderated and multiplied, a set of holes with a powerful capacity for attracting meaning, empty slots for accelerating suggestive polysemies and effects of emotional concordance in the poem, censured in regard to their aesthetic effects since ancient times in the most pure and esoteric poetics like that of pseudo-Longinus, but also known to Saint Augustine's educated taste. The product of the examination of the nature and role of all of these empty textual structures has been promisingly denominated, in Saint Augustine's own phrasing, a *rhetoric of silence* (G. Mendonça-Telhes, 1979, pp. 11−12; P. Valesio, 1986; L. Terracini, 1988).

The materials which compose this rhetoric of silence are more precisely perceptible, in my judgment, within the framework of a poetics of the imagination. At least this is the best approach if one wishes to avoid playing with the paradoxes of negativity which have been used in an unsuccessful attempt to characterize them through a set of paraphrases enlightened by an awareness of the existence and implications of a zero degree linguistics. Meaningful silences are spaces between the material forms of the text's verbal scheme, which are justified by the imaginary structure's unequal density.

The space of "sonorous solitude" in the poem's material body establishes the empty pause required in order to permit the sentimental vibration of the symbol to be heard, or to allow the fantastic introduction and deployment of the patterns of imaginary spatialization expressing the subconscious impulse or drive. The rhetoric of silence monopolizes meaningful elision, but also channels and brackets the most varied forms of meaningful imaginary expression. From the word to the symbol, from the semantic representation to the fantastic resonance; from the acoustical suggestion of spatial proportions and movements to the imaginary pattern of coordinates, of anthropologically-oriented signs; all resulting from or belonging to the subconscious impulse which bursts forth and is identified in the text's material structure. I have invoked here the poem's space, its poetic density, rich and substantial.

Verbal art's imaginary effects do not consist exclusively of the full, omnipotent substance of the word; the poem's sentimental identification is not simply the effect and result of an unechoed voice. Rather, the multiple sentimental and imaginary resonances of the verbal suggestions encountered in silence's porous domain are also responsible for convoking the unexpected echo. This echo, uprooted and multiplied by the voice, resonates in the subconscious cavities, unfathomable and unpredictable, of the individual anthropological constitution and of the remote experiences buried in profound and latent biographies.

Hence, we are in the presence of poetry seen as an echo, an unforeseeable sentimental murmur but not, therefore, poetry understood as an unfounded, capricious, integrally conventional effect. Keep in mind that the resonances arise from the voice, an entity modulated, in turn, by the silence of its own origin. This modulation is what produces powerful resonances, when the voice is successful, on target, and poetic. Only in the sublime poem or the moving story does the word, immersed in the deep latent domain of silence, yield its full resonance. In fact, in most cases the opposite occurs: the unsuccessful expression is deadened, muffled in the superficially mechanical operation of the adjacent words. The result is that the poem grates and grinds, without yielding a rich and substantial product, a poetic space, without the fullness of a revived, stirred up, activated, resounding and sonorous space. On many other occasions in this book I have striven to reveal the predictable and effective traces which point to the poetic word's productive activity.

It is not only that the word stems from silence, that it convokes and assumes silence as a foreseeable and necessary space. The mature poetic voice originates in a conscious awareness that the word is rooted in silence as its natural medium (F. Jessi, 1968, pp. 22−23). The confident foresight of seeing in the poetic word the environment with which it will combine to form a "literary space" (M. Blanchot, 1955), defines and establishes the unstable restlessness of creation, moving from the familiar suggestion of controlled voices towards a capricious and unstable poetic domain. The imagination later occupies these empty domains of the scheme, establishing around them the paradoxical contrast of the productive density symbols possess in the imaginary strata of meaningful textual production.

Silence prepares and completes the word's poetic value, its capacities for sentimental repercussion and for imaginary constitution. It does not present itself as a pure emptiness woven around resounding words, as a kind of "capacity" for the freedom foreseen as at the word's disposition.

The positive substance of silence is constituted in the busy density of the unconscious, in the region of the solid convergences of general imaginary, nocturnal, universal and cosmic experience. We participate in silence, but it surpasses us; it is left to the judgment and will of the imagination's intangible rules. It is a block irreducible to possession which communicates and joins: uncontrollable storehouse of deeply-rooted subversions, a natural and "physical" foundation and, hence, a trace of the unreachable experience of nothingness (M. Blanchot, 1969 [1972, pp. 41−42]).

The essential poetic stance before silence is to be on the lookout, to "listen" (P. Valesio, 1986). Force is of no avail with silence; only a cultivated patience. From listening-in, the reach of pragmatic conventionality is also understood. From poetic observation we learn the most productive postures for each of us, we sketch the familiar reoccurrence of productive intersections in our memory: we repeat the movements we have learned. We call this communicated and adopted experience culture. But do not confuse the customary with the true and definite. As great and hardened as our cultural experience may be, the poetic resonance of the voice in the silence will always surprise us: that is its necessary function and nature.

3.2.4. *Versions of the Personal Articulation of the Spatial Myth and the Universality of the Imaginary Orientation*

The individual modalities, in which we have been seeing how a diffuse and general sense of the imaginary is lodged in the unique space created by the imagination of each poet, are sufficiently clear now for us to be able to claim that this, which, considered in terms of the complexity of its substantial elements, we can call the *spatial myth*, is one of the most decisive foundations — and of course the most generic and profound — in the constitution of the collection of emotions we know as the aesthetic effect of the artistic imaginary construct. In certain essential poets, like Jorge Guillén, the spatial myth can be seen as the decisive factor in motivating the interest which attracts us to his poetry. In other cases, like that of Hölderlin and perhaps Valéry, Juan Ramón Jiménez, William Blake, or Wallace Stevens, we have seen that this mythical spatial support plays an indispensable role in the call to the reader's imaginary cooperation which all poetry encourages and implies. Of course, the analyses presented thus far in this book are in themselves quantitatively insufficient to elevate my hypothetical claim to a realized proof. This is a task still waiting to be accomplished, as a complement to the handful of other studies dedicated to this issue, all of them indirectly relevant to the poetic intention, like Abraham Moler and Elizabeth Rohmer's *Psychologie de l'Espace*, the lexicologist Georges Matoré's *L'Espace humain* (1976), those by J. Franck (1952) and R. Gullón (1980) on the space of the novel, and especially the diverse and profound contributions of Georges Poulet (1950, 1961, 1963). Not to mention, of course, the indispensable revisions to the philosophical tradition, from Heidegger and Husserl to Bergson and Merleau-Ponty.

What distinguishes my own appeal to the spatial myth as it is realized in these pages from the content and orientation of the studies I have just mentioned is my own claim of a large measure of responsibility for the spatial imaginary component in the production of the artistic aesthetic effect, in those cases where it is not absolutely definitive. In so doing, I begin by citing the decisive importance in the literary phenomenon of the exploration of the relationship between consciousness, identity, and otherness and the radical, basic role of space in this search, characteristic in poetry, even beyond that of the correlative coordinate of time, so widely emphasized in the idiosyncrasies of the present age. In this I fully agree with Matoré's conjecture: "It is as if, in our times, space were about to replace its competitor — time — or to take its revenge for the neglect it has faced in philosophical thought" (G. Matoré, 1976, p. 286). In fact, it seems that our own age is more propitious than those that have preceded it — especially in view of the nineteenth century's deification of temporal philosophical reason — for revealing the *temporal structure* in which the rational organization of the world in light of the spirit is cemented. Space, in effect, seems to be a category "more docile than time", as Matoré assured, "with regard to the rational demands of the spirit"; an element of objective existential realization, more suited than time to the stable and concretizable in images and in verbal terms, with a greater ability to "exorcise ... mysterious powers". Thus, "if time, while the material of our lives, is also and above all the promise of our death, space is the vital medium in which our activity is incarnated". From the models of verbal and imaginary representation of our culture induced by phenomenological

3.2. Poeticity: The Imaginary Structure of Symbols in the Temporal Domains

thought, space, in a role foreseen by Gabriel Marcel in the philosophical arena and Oswald Spengler in the historical, finally discovers its eternal nature as the "anchoring" dimension of stable consolidation, compared to the anguish of the temporal journey; space suggests to human consciousness the "milestones" — to use the term Matoré adopts from Merleau-Ponty — constituting "the only stable points which float across the moving magma of the real" (G. Matoré, 1976, pp. 286—287).

Therefore, to propose the poetic responsibility of the spatial imaginary within the very complex conglomerate of textual, contextual, sentimental and imaginary factors which compose the sense of poeticity, above all represents the mention of one of the most substantive means — if not the most decisive one, according to the social, cultural and anthropological urgency being felt in our times — by which human discourse lodges consciousness in reality. Moreover, there is no doubt that poetry contributes, through its singular capacity for imaginary mobilization, to bring about this situation, this imaginary orientation, and most assuredly with an advantage over logical and philosophical thought; at least, this is how it is expressed in the cultural "desire" of postmodern man. And within the initiatives poetry mobilizes, its spatial emplacement is perhaps the most solid, stable and concretizable of the imagination's symbolic coordinates. A concretion at times clear and explicit, at others expressed through indirect textual paths and with a more diluted referential effect in temporal symbolic intermediaries; but always necessary and essential.

Nevertheless, it already seems necessary to begin a more detailed description regarding the universal or personal nature of the spatial and poetic imaginary, as well as its extension to the restrictive and differentiated heritage of diverse ages, regional areas, cultural groups, etc. (G. Matoré, 1976, pp. 288—290). A first elemental question that emerges concerns the historical divergence of scientific conceptions of space — Euclid, Descartes, Einstein —, which point to different stages, according to the physicists, in its mathematical conception. This is itself a different matter from the question of whether such technical differences among scientists trascend the specialized sphere of knowledge and influence or determine the idiosyncracies of the masses' imaginary conception of the spatial myth. I believe this is an interesting area for further investigation, which I can only mention here in passing. In any case, the plastic arts, especially painting, exhibit different modes for representing space, volume and perspective, which, as Gombrich (1959), Arnheim (1954), and Matoré himself (1976, pp. 248—276) have already indicated, are not simply related to the technical coarseness or refinement in gestural representation of pictorial mimesis, but are representations of different visions and imaginary perceptions of space. The famous Hegelian division of art's evolution into three great stages — oriental, classical and Romantic — incorporates above all the different initiatives of human curiosity and imagination concerning space.

It seems obvious that human beings, and therefore poets, do not all agree and coincide in the final configuration of their respective spatial myths. That is, the imaginary emplacement of spatiality differs among individuals, both in the imaginary orientation of the wakeful state as in the interesting peculiarities with which the dimension flourishes in dreams. All of these differences, and many more that could be raised, would seem to negate the nature of the spatial myth as a poetic universal and a defining feature in the interest and value of artistic works. Still, the answers to this observation that immediately come to mind seem obvious. First, the different individual articulation of the spatial myth does not exclude its universal personal rootedness as a general and basic coordinate of the human representation of space and as an *oriented* organization of the imaginative estimation of otherness. Moreover, in the second place, evident modal individual differences abound in the possible axiological-aesthetic acquisition of the same, in the case of poets and, in general, of all artists: be it by its singularity and rareness in the case of William Blake, or by its generalized nature, as in that of Dante. In summary, the spatial poetic myth can be, in fact, a decisive principle of interest and curiosity — satisfied or defrauded — in artistic communication, the oscillations and peculiarities of which signal features of originality and attractiveness, of appreciation, adherence or indifference.

It must be kept in mind that the imaginary structure in which we place the poetic spatial myth is flexible in nature and that the referential system it implants varies greatly and is highly diffuse, which explains and guarantees the variety and originality of the possible personal articulations of the myth, without in any way implying it is fictitious or phantasmagoric. Matoré provides an accurate description of the nature peculiar to the psychological structure of the spatial myth in general in the following synthesis: "This *geometric place* of ideas and feelings has an eminently spatial character, and belongs to a typology simultaneously *fluid* and *elemental*, which lends space a sufficiently *immaterial* character for thought to be able to easily establish the different relationships among things. A *universality* and *transparency* is assigned to this space which enables the attribution of inert relationships at the highest level of generality and simplicity" (G. Matoré, 1976, p. 288).

The "fluid" — to repeat Matoré's term — nature of the spatial myth, which above all guarantees its generalizable universality, is that which consequently makes possible the liberty and variety of its concrete individual realizations, as is implicitly the case in the examples I have cited previously, and explicitly in those I will propose in this chapter. Matoré himself indicates, immediately following the preceding passage, the radical difference between the spatial universe testified to in the lexicon of the theologian Theilard de Chardin, populated with "excited presences as an uncertain and unbound space lodged in mystery, compared with the solid, closed coordinates of Sartre's universe". He concludes affirming his confidence, similar to my own, in universals and the generalizable nature of an identical basic consciousness

3.2. Poeticity: The Imaginary Structure of Symbols in the Temporal Domains

of spatial referentiality: "Such an apparent contrast (referring to that between Theilard de Chardin and Sartre) cannot but mask similar, less visible, but deeper contrasts" (G. Matoré, 1976, p. 289).

What my own ideas as I present them here add to Matoré's universalist confidence, in line with his own words, results from the different textual level of our respective verifications of intuitions about space. Methodologically, Matoré limits himself to the horizon of lexical realizations, albeit pierced — perhaps in spite of his efforts to escape it — by the involuntary contamination of intuitions of an imaginary kind which he, during the preparation of his book in the sixties, attempted to avoid. On the other hand, assuming the risks and advantages of placing my own considerations within the mobile structure of the imagination's mythic behavior, enables and obliges me to extend the limits of my reflections beyond the sphere of Matoré's considerations. The verification of the spatial imaginary myth in poetry has convinced me, as with Matoré, of the existence of "a common general denominator", of a mythic "collective" element of orientation. But this notion, which Matoré indicates in Gabriel Marcel's terms as an "inferior" substrate permitting the penetration of individual elements, constitutes a proven fact in the communicability of different poetic utterances, each of which rests on a different personal mythical base.

In the case of literature, it is worth keeping in mind, however, the first and greatest difference among artists as regards the representation of their spatial myth, is none other than its presence or absence in the text; or, rather, its explicitness or latent omission. Recall that in earlier chapters of this book, especially in its first part, I have paid extensive attention to the critical features derived from what can be denominated a *poetics of the literary utterance*. This implies the historical proof that literature, and poetry in many cases, even their extraordinary productions, have conformed to an embellished mode of the direct and logical formulation of rationalized messages of experience. In its most generalized explicit awareness, classical literature, even in Virgil and Horace's great poems, originated as an elegant and refined, rhetorically "skillfull", mode of the sapient — even philosophical — utterance. Such constitutive elements in Greco-Latin literature as the versified form of Parmenides' poetic treatise, the exemplary civic nature of, first, the Homeric poets, and later the social didactics of theater in Athenian society, all contributed to create the hybrid notion of the great poet as an "ocean of wisdom", the numinous and semi-divine prophet, forging the classical myth of Homer or the medieval Christian one of Virgil.

This classicist rhetorical ideal of the poetics of the utterance also establishes, of course, its own scale of aesthetic axiology linked above all to the rhetorical-fantastic virtuosity of style which largely governs classical and classicist taste, to such an extent that it yields us not only Cicero, but the Ciceronianism of Luis of Granada, not only Tacitus but the Tacitism of Malvezzi or Gracián, not only Horace but the Horatianism of Fray Luis of León, and not only

Virgil but the Virgilian idyll and pastoral of Sannazaro or Garcilaso de la Vega, thereby prolonging the classical predominance of this kind of utterance, at least until the definitive triumph of Renaissance literature. That same poetics of the utterance turns out to be permanently represented in every literary age; it has even extended in many ways to modern literature and poetry of our own times, as I have indicated elsewhere in this book. Thus, for example, in the Spanish poetry of this century, the *poetics of the lyrical utterance*, represented in great authors like Machado, Salinas or Cernuda, alternates with the post-Romantic and avant-garde aesthetic of the *poetic imagination*, orchestrated in various ways from Juan Ramón Jiménez to García Lorca, Vicente Aleixandre or Jorge Guillén. Even later lines of literary influence, beginning with the great poets of the Generation of 1927 and moving towards the culmination of Spanish modernism and contemporary trends, can be understood in terms of the alternation between these two modes of conceiving the nature of the poetic. For example, the poetics of the lyrical utterance justifies the differential physiognomy of the so-called Generation of 1950, in authors such as Gil de Biedma, Valente and Claudio Rodríguez, all of whom are indebted, especially through Cernuda, to the North American poetry of Eliot and Auden, while the later poetics of the *novísimos* like Guillermo Carnero, Pere Gimferrer, A. Martínez Sarrión and José María Álvarez corresponds to an evocative fantastic aesthetic under the influence of antecedents like Ezra Pound or, more explicitly, Cavafis. The fact that I focus my attention in these chapters of the book's third part predominantly on the *poetics of the imagination* rather than on the poetics of the lyrical utterance is above all due to the tactical organization of my own technical arguments, which has made it advisable to concentrate on the poetic and rhetorical questions of the aesthetics of the utterance in the book's first part, but also, in no small part, to the relatively more novel — and, hence, more in need of detailed discussion — nature, at the present time, of the anthropologico-imaginary roots of poetic emotion.

Nevertheless, having set forth the foregoing clarifications, I think I should also warn the reader of the schematic inaccuracies and deformations of reality that might result from a historical and theoretical explanation of literature in terms of the automatic and uncommunicated contrast of these two poetics of the utterance and the imagination. In this book I have insisted on and, particularly, tried to present the ways in which the psychological — sentimental and fantastic — resonances of the rhetorico-stylistic mechanisms of the classical literary utterance have been produced, including, moreover, those effects of the imaginary dimension of fictional mimesis. On the other hand, I have attempted to present, with the greatest possible detail and explicitness, the indispensable, essential mechanisms of aesthetic interaction between the literary work's "textual scheme", the field belonging to the expressive incisiveness of rhetorical enunciation, and the text's imaginary "space", where the fantastic effects of the conceptual suggestions of the utterance and the

3.2. Poeticity: The Imaginary Structure of Symbols in the Temporal Domains

symbolic, temporal, and spatial designs of the anthropologico-imaginary construct are produced. Having said all of this, on a historical plane, it is absolutely essential to examine more closely the role and degree of responsibility the imaginary construct plays in the poetic communicative-aesthetic results of great classical authors — Homer, the Greek tragedians, Virgil, Horace, Dante, Cervantes, etc. —, all of whom were until recently thought of and valued solely in terms of their expressive-rhetorical mastery, and in terms of an aesthetic of "amplificatio" and the image. The brief probes in this book into the spatial imaginary myths of Dante, Homer, and especially the Cervantine narration, offer unsuspectedly fertile perspectives for understanding the true importance of the imaginary construct.

This historical review of literature in terms of a systematic exploration that I am recommending, has no other aim but the restoration of the balance of artistic factors surrounding the poetic sublime, which the European theory of the Romantic imagination attempted to impose (M. H. Abrams, 1953; N. Frye, 1961). The alternative predominance of a rhetorical theory of literary enunciation was the classical compensation justifying the development of the curiosity of Romantic theoreticians and poets towards the essential labyrinth of the artistic imagination. But with the general counterpoint, first of positivism and, later, of its formalist extension in the critical stronghold of literature, we arrived at the anguished situation of exhaustive structuralist analytics, which — in spite of all of its merits — Frederic Jameson accurately defined, and not merely in its critico-analytical dimension, as a "prison-house of language" (F. Jameson, 1972).

The result of this historico-critical itinerary, which the theoretical position of this book attempts to indicate and, eventually, justify, will at least restore an equal, balanced sense of the importance of these two dimensions, the two "spaces", of the artistic, literary and, especially, poetic work: the expressive space of the rhetorico-stylistic verbal material, and the imaginary space, in which the suggestions of the expressive level are fulfilled and exponentially articulated. Only in this way will the complete structure of the artistic *text* be fully attended to; not to mention, obviously, its indispensable contextual (historico-social) and intertextual (historico-cultural) extension. In the final analysis, the full verification of the truth of the riskiest proposition of these theses, which locates the temporal and spatial mythico-imaginary structure at the highest level of genetic responsibility for poeticity as an aesthetic value, must be subordinated and deffered to the proposed readjustment of *literary history* in terms of a *historical poetics*, the perspective to be taken in my future expansion of this *theory of the literary text*.

Having attended to the first and most obvious differential parameter, that affecting existence or omission within the poetics of the imaginary, it will be most convenient and useful to move on to the consideration of the most concrete questions concerning the specifying generalization and differentiation of the imaginary construction and, in the final analysis, of what I have been denominating the "spatial myth". As I have said before, ultimately, each poet's spatial myth is a personal myth (C. Mauron, 1962), although if we seek out the general and dominant structures of these systems of symbolic orientation, without fail we find the constants, the common and general structures, which are precisely those which enable each of us to comprehend another's spatial myth, adjacently marking off the reactions relative to identification and foreignness. To illustrate the personalized spatial myth's specificity and generality, I will refer to two pairs of authors, from very different ages and genres. In the first place, I will examine two modern poets, the already analyzed Jorge Guillén, with whose poetic characteristics I have illustrated imaginary construction in previous pages, and Juan Ramón Jiménez, the initial teacher of the former's generation, with which he later found it difficult to maintain his personal and artistic agreement. In the second place, I will cite examples from the work of two of the greatest Spanish mystics: Saint Theresa of Avila and Saint John of the Cross, both Carmelites with similar doctrinal backgrounds, in personal and literary contact throughout their lives, and committed to the reform of their order.

Comparing the characteristics of Juan Ramón Jiménez and Jorge Guillén's spatial myths enables us to understand, if not explain, the roots of their personal incompatibility, usually, as is only normal, explained by criticism on the basis of their respective biographical data and external anecdotes concerning their literary relationship. The description of the imaginary construction of Guillén's poetry that we have already realized reveals it as of an immanentist, direct and positive nature, centered in the enclosed universe of the tangible and the palpable. For Guillén, the world is a space of "concrete marvels", bounded in its reach by what is visible, perceptible, breathable — "Our Air" is the final general title the poet gave to his collected works, articulated in a general construction of perfect, monumental systematism. The spatial environment created by the sky's dome and the planet's surface — a sky of an impenetrable, diurnal composition, an earth without subsoil, and a superficial sea without the attraction of any depth — constitute the space sufficient for the poet's admiring and amazed inspection, capable of discovering the sublime greatness of every common thing, and of each everyday detail: the first light of day, the nearest object in his own bedroom, the supreme perfection of the top of his desk. To avoid repeating a description I have already set forth at some length, I will only quote "Perfección" ("Perfection") from *Cántico (Canticle)*, which perhaps represents the best Guillenian materialization of his spatial symbology:

> Queda curvo el firmamento,
> Compacto azul, sobre el día,
> Es el redondeamiento
> Del esplendor: mediodía.
> Todo es cúpula. Reposa,
> Central sin querer, la rosa,

3.2. Poeticity: The Imaginary Structure of Symbols in the Temporal Domains

> A un sol en cenit sujeta.
> Y tanto se da el presente
> Que el pie caminante siente
> La integridad del planeta.
>
> [Curved, the firmament remains
> Densely blue, above the day.
> It moves toward that encircling
> Of magnificence: midday.
> All is a dome. Quietly
> There at the center rests the rose,
> Subject to the noonday sun. And
> So much does the moment lend
> That the traveling foot can feel
> The completeness of the planet].

On the other hand, as his best critics and exegetes have unanimously emphasized, the construction of a poetic space in Juan Ramón Jiménez's poetry characteristically revolves around expectation, the expectation of the soul's transcendental encounter with God; an unceasing and uncertain inquiry in all of his poetry until *Animal de fondo* and *Dios deseado y deseante*. A search which often takes on the conventionally ascensional sense, together with a psychic invasion, equally customary, of the descendant emanations of the longed-for divine epiphany, and other very varied forms of intimist spatialization, which illustrate the imaginary richness of this poet's spatial myth. Juan Ramón's sky is a permeable dome, almost always indeterminate and nocturnal, an elastic dimension, deeply inviting and rich in the premonition of lodgings and tentative paths, of half-open guesses. An always continuous contrast between up and down, here and there — *Piedra y cielo (Stone and Sky)*, to cite one of his titles —, explicitly makes up countless compositions in the poet's long poetic and vital itinerary, from the first verse of *Sonetos espirituales (Spiritual Sonnets)* in 1915 — "Como en el ala infinito vuelo" ["as in the wing infinite flight exists"] — to the final words of *Dios deseado y deseante*: "Tu sucesión no es fuga de lo mío, es venida impetuosa de lo tuyo" ["your passing is not a flight from what is mine, it is the sudden arriving of what is yours"]. And when the articulation of this irreducible duality of the essential coordinates of Juan Ramón's spatial myth is not explicitly stated, it is never difficult to find it, inevitably, suggested implicitly. For Juan Ramón, these dualities constitute the symbolic spatial foundations of his conscious and subconscious cosmography, on which the anthropological constitution of his personal imaginary and poetic myths are established. In this regard, composition 104 of *Eternidades (Eternities)* is archetypal:

> Cada estrella tranquila,
> está, para mis ojos con mi alma,
> sobre una frente de ellos.
> Cuando torno del mundo, ya cayéndose
> la sombra, *salgo al cielo*,
> *por mi balcón*, como a la casa mía.

— ¡Qué dulce anochecer, con sus estrellas! —
Dormido, luego, tengo abiertos
mis cristales al cielo, a ellos, que sueñan
más puras las estrellas de su frente.
¡Qué juntos así, todos,
tras el trabajo al sol,
con el cielo estrellado por memoria,
en el hogar celeste,
alrededor de lo infinito!

(Juan Ramón Jiménez, *Libros de poesía*, Madrid, Aguilar, 1967, p. 654).

[Each quiet star,
is, for my eyes and with my soul,
upon their brow.
When I return to the world, with the shadows
falling, I go out to the sky,
on my balcony, as into my own house.
— What a sweet nightfall, with its stars! —
Sleeping, later, I have
my windows open to the sky, to them, dreaming
more purely the stars on their brow.
That together like this, all of us,
After the day's work under the sun,
remembering the stary sky,
in the celestial home,
around the infinite!]

Sky and earth, contrasted, but in the hope of contiguity, of a communicated unity. Again, in *Eternidades* (p. 98): "¡Qué lejos, azul, el cielo, / de la tierra pobre! Pero / los dos son el día bueno" ["How far, blue, the sky, / from the poor earth! But / they both are the good day"]. Or (p. 46): "Me subí al cielo puro / y encendí mi velar en las estrellas, / sobre todos los sueños. / La tierra era una rosa abierta, ¡yo lo vi!" ["I climbed to the pure sky / and lit the candle of my vigil in the stars, / above all the dreams. / The earth was an open rose, I saw it!"]. Beyond moods, depressed or euphoric, beyond the object or feeling motivating the impulse — the beloved, the truth, God —, there is the consistency of this dual scheme, ultimately spatial, scrutinizing the concavity of the sky, with faith. We find the same scheme underlying the poems of *Diario de un poeta recién casado (Diary of a Newly Wed Poet)*; consider composition 36, entitled "Skies":

Un cielo cada día,
cada noche ...
Cóncavas manos cazadoras
de la fe de un instante por el mar.
Mas yo, pequeño, escapo, día
tras día, noche
tras noche,
como una mariposa ... (p. 253)

3.2. Poeticity: The Imaginary Structure of Symbols in the Temporal Domains

[A sky every day,
every night ...
Concave hands hunting
the faith of an instant by the sea.
But I, small, escape, day
after day, night
after night,
like a butterfly.]

Perhaps the most graphic illustration of the permeably transcendental nature of the celestial dome in Juan Ramón's imagination is denoted by the few cases in which the opposite feeling is concretized: desperation in the moments of greatest existential anguish, motivated by the anxiety of awaiting an answer that does not come, the suspicion of the impenetrability of space beyond the dome. An early example can be found in the metaphoric transposition, with powerful Romantic overtones, of the little bird locked "in the somber abandoned room" of composition 42 in *Sonetos espirituales*. Attracted by the possibility of free flight, of that "infinito, que lo está engañando / por su ilusión" ["infinite, tricking him for his delusion"], he finally "tropieza contra el bajo suelo" ["trips against the low ground"], to end up in the strangely degrading and pathetic scene at his bloody end: "... y por la sala / deja, pegada y rota, la cabeza ..." (p. 59) ["strewn about the room, / he leaves, hit and broken, his head"]. Or the anguish of a "broken elevator", unable to reach the sky, which overtakes Juan Ramón in New York, one 14th of April, in his *Diario de un poeta recién casado* (p. 340). Or, finally, the frustration he expresses, in *Eternidades* (p. 607), when the sky falls down in chaos, without any hope of transcendence:

¡Que se me cae el cielo!
¿Nadie? ¡Nadie!
— ... ¡Con qué trabajo trágico
pude medio ponerlo — techo triste — con su aurora

de grana y viento y oro,
medio clavado en sus columnas huecas!
¡Ay, el cielo se cae,
hombre de mí! —

[The sky is falling!
Nobody? Nobody!
— ... With what tragic work
I was half-able to place it — sad roof — with its dawn

of scarlet and wind and gold,
half-pinned on its hollow columns!
Oh, the sky is falling,
man of mine! —]

A radically contrary conception of the sense of transcendence and of the relation of man with the world and, consequently, of his imaginary spatial orientation, is what antagonistically differentiates the symbolic universes of the contemporary poets we have compared. However, all of these same aspects initially indicate the common ground shared by the two mystic Carmelites, Saint Theresa and Saint John; nevertheless, we are going to examine the contrasting spatial formulation exhibited in the literary materialization of the two, with regard to the common impulse of spiritual union, of identification and fusion of the soul with God, in mystical ecstasy. In the common culture of the two Carmelite mystics, all of their sources — from the most distant Muslim Sufies to the Christian tradition of German mysticism and the most immediate Spanish influences (Laredo, Osuna, etc.) — formulated the movement of the soul toward God under the common spatial myth of the itinerary, voyage or path: the ascent of Mount Carmel, the flight and rapture of the soul, etc. Within this shared spatial imaginary myth of the mystic impulse, however, we discover the visible effects of differential factors of gender and the unconscious reflex of somatic consciousness.

In effect, one should keep in mind that the general myth of the departure, of the voyage, as an ascent or as flight, had been minted historically by a fundamentally, if not entirely, masculine literary imagination. On the other hand, the erotic transformation of spiritual union, as the wedding or betrothal, had been universally established by the *Song of Songs*, a Biblical source easily accessible and predominantly used in the symbology of mystical union in Saint John of the Cross, Saint Theresa of Jesus, and generally in all of their doctrinal models, whether distant or near. For the structure of the imaginary process of union in Saint John, the feminine personalization of the spirit, as an inflamed soul or wife, counts for less that the assumed, intimate consciousness of the somatic sexual image. In the spatial myth of the departure and flight of this sublime mystic poet, the images which predominate are the masculine, active, aggressive ones of invasion, of the penetration of a space foreign to one's own identity. This is the basic structure organizing the sequence of search, entrance, encounter and fusion in *Cántico espiritual (Spiritual Canticle)*: "Buscando mis amores / *yré* por esos montes y riberas ..."; "*Entrado* se ha la esposa / en el ameno huerto deseado ...", "En la *interior bodega* / de mi Amado bebí ..." ["Seeking my love, / I will head for the mountains and the shores ..."; "The wife has entered / in the pleasant, desired orchard ...", "In the interior wine cellar / of my Beloved I drank ..."]. A spatial scheme of departure and entry which is reproduced identically in the same poem when, after the union, the pleasurable common voyage of the betrothed is related:

> Gocémonos amado
> y *vámonos* a ver en tu hermosura
> al monte y al collado,
> do mana el agua pura;
> *entremos más adentro en la espesura.*

3.2. Poeticity: The Imaginary Structure of Symbols in the Temporal Domains

> Y luego a las subidas
> *cabernas* de la piedra nos *yremos*
> que están bien escondidas
> y allí nos *entraremos*,
> y el mosto de granadas gustaremos.
>   Allí me mostrarías
> aquello que mi alma pretendía ...
>
> [Let us rejoice, beloved,
> And let us go forth to behold in your beauty
> To the mountain and to the hill,
> To where the pure water flows,
> And further, deep into the thicket.
>   And then we will go on
> To the high caverns in the rock
> Which are so well concealed;
> There we shall enter
> And taste the fresh juice of pomegranates.
>   There you will show me
> What my soul has been seeking
>
> (Saint John of the Cross, 1964 edition, pp. 414–415)].

In Saint John's other great mystical poem, *En una noche oscura (In a Dark Night)*, the materialization of this progressive scheme of the voyage as departure, ecstasy, flight and exploration is even more explicit. The detailed illustration of the spatial myth of the masculine erotic itinerary would involve quoting and commenting upon almost the entire song. But the first stanza will suffice to summarize it:

> En una noche escura
> con ansias en amores inflamada
> ¡oh dichosa ventura!
> *salí* sin ser notada
> estando ya mi casa sosegada.
>
> [One dark night,
> Fired with love's urgent longings
> — oh, the sheer grace! —
> I went out unseen,
> My house being now stilled
>
> (1964 edition, p. 295).

The poem moves on to describe the flame of love as light and guide in the soul's restless passage through an exterior nocturnal space without references, uniform, until the blind fusion:

> ¡Oh noche que *guiaste*!
> ¡Oh noche amable más que la alborada!
> ¡Oh noche que juntaste
> amado con amada,
> *amada en el amado transformada*!

> [O guiding night!
> O night more lovely than the dawn!
> O night that has united
> The lover with his beloved
> Transforming the beloved into her lover!

(1964 edition, p. 296)].

A spatial imaginary scheme which reappears identically, every time it is made explicit, governing the narrative design of many of the minor works. Recall the opening of the "Coplas ... hechas sobre un éstasis de harta contemplación" ("Verses ... written in an ecstasy of full contemplation"): "*Entreme* donde no supe / y no de esperanza falto / volé tan alto tan alto / que le dí a la caça alcance" ["I entered into unknowing, / and not lacking in hope / I flew so high so high / that I reached my prey"], a composition very apt for a gloss — nevertheless a risky task, especially given the limitations of this book — on the sexual scheme of the mystic imagination we are examining. The only exception in Saint John's work to the masculine spatial imaginary scheme is to be found in a poem known as "Llama de amor viva" ("The Living Flame of Love"). Note the expression of the intimate experience of a consummated union, of the kind that we find permanently established in Saint Theresa's work, and surely able to be explained as a moment of the inflection of the poet's habitual imaginary modes to the sublime circumstance of the momentary, complete plenitude of the mystical experience, and perhaps also to the thematic influence of his daily correspondent and spiritual teacher, Saint Theresa.

Compared to Saint John's images of rapture, flight or escape from oneself, Saint Theresa resorts to an image of the intimate itinerary. The same general allegory of *Castillo Interior (Interior Castle)*, which serves the narrative purposes of her most direct book of mystical experience, also symbolizes a space, described in surprising detail in the different chapters of the work. This woman of "anxious and wandering" vital activity, having scandalized many of her superiors to the point of censure, constructs the imaginary space of her spiritual vision as a voyage towards the interior of herself, from the outskirts to the center of her spirit, to the deepest mansion or dwelling place, where the ecstatic depth of her mystical union with the Beloved takes place. Recall the terms of withdrawal and *recollection* in the description of the passage through the interior castle, with which Saint Theresa projects an imaginary voyage, sustained unconsciously by the evidence of her own somatic projections, of an inverse sense to those of flight and escape Saint John imagines: "Pues tornado a nuestro hermoso y deleitoso castillo, hemos de ver como podremos *entrar* en él. Parece que digo algun disparate porque si este castillo es el ánima, claro está que no hay para qué entrar, pues se es él mismo; como parecería desatino decir a uno que entrase en una pieza estando ya adentro" (Santa Teresa de Jesús, ed. *Obras completas*, Madrid, Aguilar, 1966, 10th edition, p. 392) ["Well, returning to our beautiful and delightful castle, we shall see how we are able to *enter* it. It seems as though I'm speaking nonsense because, if this castle is the soul, clearly there is no reason to enter, because we are it; as it would seem foolish to tell oneself to enter a room one is already within"].

The Saint herself later refers to the model for this itinerary of interior recollection, indicated in the manuals and treatises of mystic meditation and perfection: "Ya habreis oido en algunos libros de oración aconsejar al alma que entre dentro de sí" ["You have already heard that some prayer books advise the soul to enter into itself"]. Nevertheless, Saint Theresa avails herself, as we are seeing, of only one of the two canonical paths of mystical prayer, that which is most readily identified with the nature of her own spatial imagination, obviously constructed according to her consciousness of her own somatic experience. She was very well aware that one of her most often read guides to meditation, Francisco de Osuna, had alluded in his *Tercer abecedario (Third Alphabet)* (IX, Ch. VII) to the double option of "entering oneself" or "departing oneself", but, faced with what is less familiar to her, the Saint, with her popular, simple frankness, disregards such doctrinal subtleties: "Dicen que el alma se entra dentro de sí, y otras veces que sube sobre sí. Por este lenguaje no sabré yo aclarar nada, que esto tengo malo, que por el que yo lo sé decir, pienso que me habréis de entender" (p. 417) ["They say that the soul enters within itself, and other times that it rises above itself. By this language, I cannot make anything clear, which I take as bad, but by that language which I know how to speak about it with, I think you can understand me"].

The language that Saint Theresa "knows", is that which expresses the intimate experience of the union with God as a reflex of the spirit symbolized through an allegorical itinerary served by the imagination of spatial withdrawal, that most in agreement with the structure of her own bodily intimacy. Hence, everywhere we find images of interiorization arising: "y nos muestra el camino, y da fuerzas al alma para *cavar* hasta hallar este tesoro escondido, pues es verdad que le hay en nosotros mismos" (p. 422) ["And it shows us the way, and gives the soul strength to *dig* until we find this hidden treasure, because it is true that we have it within ourselves"]. The focus of most of these images invariably flow towards the soul's *interior*, its intimate *center*. The examples are countless. In the second chapter of the seventh House, we read: "porque siempre queda el alma con Dios en aquel *centro*" (p. 481) ["because the soul always stays with God in that center"]. And just before, in the preceding chapter, she says with the divine voice recalled from a mystic trance: "sino que notoriamente ve, de la manera que queda dicho, que estan en lo interior de su alma" ["but rather he notoriously sees, in the manner that has been said, that they are in the interior of his soul"]. And she emphasizes: "en lo *muy, muy interior*, en una *cosa muy honda*, que no sabeis decir como es, porque no tiene letras, siente en sí esta divina compañía" (p. 479) ["in the very, very interior, in a very deep thing, which you do not know how to describe, because there are no words, he feels within himself this divine company"]. Further ahead: "en metido el Señor al alma en esta morada suya, que es el centro de la misma alma" ["the Lord, in placing the soul in its house, which is the center of the soul itself"]. Later: "Este centro de nuestra alma, o este espíritu, es una cosa tan dificultosa de decir, y aun de creer" (p. 483) ["This center of our soul, or this spirit, is something so difficult to speak about, and even to believe"]. And so on.

In any case, Saint Theresa is very careful whenever she believes it necessary to check and clarify the carnal release of the experience of union; these representations obviously correspond to the reflection essential for narrating what has been experienced in a written form: "Yo he dicho que, aunque se ponen estas *comparaciones*, porque no hay otras más a propósito, que se entienda que aquí *no hay memoria de cuerpo* más que si el alma no estuviere en él, sino solo espíritu; y en el matrimonio espiritual, muy menos, porque para esta secreta unión *en el centro muy interior del alma*, que debe ser adonde está el Dios mismo, y a mi parecer no ha menester puerta por donde entre" (p. 481) ["I have said that, although I make these comparisons, because there are no others that better suit my purposes, it should be understood that here there is no memory of the body as though the soul were not in it, but only of the spirit; and in the very interior center of my soul, that must be God Himself, and it seems to me there is no need for a door by which to enter"].

Nevertheless, in the places where the Saint's literary imagination is most rigorously evoked by the necessity of communicatively making the ineffable spiritual experience perceptible, we find the representation of intimate, almost physical experience reinforced in formulas of such fertile expressiveness as that of the *hondón interior* (interior depth). Recall, for example, the fascinating allegories concerning springs and running water in the reflection on the verse *Dilatasti cor meum* in the second chapter of the fourth House: "y no me parece que es cosa, como digo, que su nacimiento es el corazón, sino de otra parte aún más interior, como una cosa profunda. Pienso que deve ser el centro del alma, como después he entendido y diré a la postre" ["and it does not seem to me, as I said, that it is born from the heart, but from some other more interior part, as something profound. I think it must be the center of the soul, as I later understood, and as I shall explain shortly"]. Soon, she is forced to resort to accents and formulas of the most compact sensitive and corporeal awareness: "... como comienza a producir aquella agua celestial de este manantial digo ... parece que se va dilatando y ensanchando todo nuestro interior ... ni aún el alma save entender que es lo qué se le da allí. Entiende una fragancia, digamos ahora, como si en aquel *hondón interior* estuviese un brasero adonde se echaren olorosos perfumes; ni se ve la lumbre, ni donde está; mas el calor

3.2. Poeticity: The Imaginary Structure of Symbols in the Temporal Domains

y humo oloroso penetra toda el alma, y aún hartas veces, como he dicho, participa el cuerpo" ["When this heavenly water begins to rise from the spring I spoke of, our whole interior seems to be enlarging and dilating, not even the soul understands what it is that is given to it there. It understands a certain fragrance, let us say, as if in that great interior depth there was a brasier into which sweet-smelling perfumes were cast; the light is not seen, nor the place it is coming from; only the heat and sweet-smelling smoke penetrate the entire soul, and very frequently, as I have said, the body shares in this"]. And as though she immediately realizes the danger to the immaterialized perfection of the mystical experience that might arise from the imperfect corporeal images of her fantasy, albeit necessary to literary communication, she corrects and explains herself in the very next line: "Mirad, entendedme, que ni se siente calor, ni se huele olor, que mas delicada cosa es que estas cosas; *sino para dároslo a entender*" (p. 415) ["See that you understand me well, that no heat is felt, nor is any odor smelled, since it is something more subtle than these things; so that you may understand"].

The imagination, radically proscribed by all mystic authors as the principal enemy of the spiritual experience of union to the extent that fantastic images withdraw to the material and human dimension that which is experienced only as a spiritual and divine thing, is nevertheless constituted as the fundamental literary vehicle for the communicative perception of that experience. It is in this terrain where the differences and characteristics peculiar to different personal myths give way to different symbols and differentiated structures of spatial orientation.

A final example will suffice to indicate the different design of the spatial myths corresponding to Saint John and Saint Theresa. With regard to the source of Saint John's verse — "in the interior wine cellar / of my beloved I drank" —, that is, the fragment from *Song of Songs* 2.4 — "He put me in the secret wine cellar and ordered charity in me" —, I have already emphasized this passage's role in Saint John as a progressive device to describe the soul's activity. An intimate intuition that is recorded, perhaps even spontaneously, in the author's prose commentaries, formulated *a posteriori*. Consider the following highly representative examples of this emplacement: "Esta bodega que aqui dice el alma es el último y más estrecho grado de amor en que el alma *puede situarse* en esta vida, que por eso la llama interior bodega, es a saber, la más interior; de donde se sigue que hay otras no tan interiores, que son los grados de amor *por donde sube hasta este último* (San Juan de la Cruz, ed. E. Pacho, Burgos, Monte Carmelo, 1990, p. 793) ["This wine cellar which here the soul says is the last and narrowest stage of love in which the soul may locate itself in this life, which for this reason it calls an interior wine cellar, that is, the most interior; from which it follows that there are others not so interior, which are the stages of love which it ascends through to this last one"]. Later:

"Es de saber que muchas almas *llegan y entran* en las primeras bodegas ...; mas a esta última e interior pocas *llegan* en esta vida" (p. 794) ["It is known that many souls arrive and enter the first wine cellars ...; but to this last interior one, very few arrive in this life"]. Even in this definitive trance of union we see the persistence of the spatial emplacement of the itinerant soul, on the level of the representation of literary images, in its path towards the space of otherness, of God; but in these terms, not even at the supreme instant of identification between the soul and God is there an entry of God into the "depths of the soul", as in Saint Theresa, but rather an *absorption*: "Esta divina bebida tanto endiosa y *levanta el alma y la embebe de Dios*" (p. 796) ["This divine drink so deifies and lifts up the soul and it absorbs it from God"].

Compared to this formula of the active, progressive and invading imagination of Saint John's own masculine initiative, we see clearly affirmed, with regard to the same images from the *Song of Songs*, Saint Theresa's enfolding and passive feminine corporeal intuition. In the first chapter of the fifth House: "Ahora me acuerdo sobre esto que digo ... de lo que habéis oído que dice la Esposa en los *Cantares*: Llevome el rey a la bodega del vino, o metiome, creo que dice. *Y no dice ella que se fue* ... Esto entiendo yo es la bodega donde nos quiere meter el Señor, cuando quiere y como quiere; mas por diligencia que nosotras hagamos, no podemos entrar" ["Now I recall what I was saying ... about what you have heard the wife say in the *Song of Songs*: The Lord brought me to the wine cellar, or He put me there, I think it says. Which does not mean she went there ... This is what I understand is the cellar where the Lord wants to put us, when and how he pleases, but we can never enter by our own diligence"]. Until this point, she presents us with an image of passivity, of the opportune wait for the surrender to God. But, immediately, this less committed and more neutral image is diaphanously unbound in the text through the image of the passive assumption of God's entry into the soul: "Su Majestad nos ha de meter y *entrar Él en el centro de nuestra alma*, y para mostrar sus maravillas mejor, no quiere que tengamos en esta más parte de la voluntad, que del todo se le ha rendido, ni que se le abra la puerta de las potencias y sentidos, que todas están dormidas; sino *entrar en el centro del alma*" (pp. 424—425) ["His Majesty must bring us in, and enter Himself into the center of our soul, and to better demonstrate His wonders, he does not want us to have any more will in this than he who has entirely surrendered to Him, nor that we open the door to Him of our powers and senses, which are all asleep; but to enter in the center of the soul"].

As regards the same intimate experience of the soul's fusion in the Creator's being, Saint Theresa reaches an imaginary spatial resolution very different, perhaps entirely opposed, to that of Saint John of the Cross, indicating the very different spatial myths governing their compositions. As different as those of Guillén and Juan Ramón Jiménez in the symbolization of the physical domain and the intentional trajectories of their confrontation with the sublime. And yet all of these variations are in the end compatible, because they all definitely have recourse to a common spatial imagination, as a broad receptacle and device for their individual extension of these resources. In this way, the spatial myth emerges as the individual myth of space, based on the universal coordinates of common, shared imaginary orientation.

Surely the ultimate layout of the spatial myth escapes the sphere of the individual, being cultural, historical and universal in design. This is Matoré's sense of the issue when he sets forth his reflection in *L'Espace humain*, as a lexicological investigation of the space of modern humanity (G. Matoré, 1976, pp. 16—20), because certainly the need to lodge oneself in a solid, stable reality, to "transform the chaos into cosmos", to quote Max Scheller's expression, is a social, general need and not merely an individual whim or a personal artistic fantasy. The indubitable Romantic subversion which Harold Bloom has seen through Milton's eyes as an inversion of Satan's ethical role, does not deny, in the end, the same inversion of spatial terms with which Georges Matoré, certainly with less brilliance, contemplates the same question (G. Matoré, 1976, p. 15). And we must recall here that without doubt the shift of *Weltanschauung* between the Middle Ages and the proto-Renaissance that Huizinga outlines in *The Decline of the Middle Ages* can certainly be reduced to spatial terms, as can the substance of the stylistic characteristics Wölfflin so unsurpassably establishes for Baroque art.

In the final analysis, the examination of the transindividual foundations of the poetic spatial myth penetrates deeply into the unstable domain of the History of Culture and Minds. Recall how Spengler attributes the most important role, in his explanation of the great demarcations of European historical consciousness within the monumental designs of *The Decline of the West*, to the universal moments of the — imaginary — conception of space; even the culturalist concept of pendular oscillations is nothing more than a metaphor founded upon spatialization. Furthermore, it seems to me that the proposal, so often invoked here, of the Bakhtinian image of "architectonic" categories as ultimate forms for an aesthetics of literature is not distinctly local, under different assumptions; and, if we reflect on it more deeply, spatial equivalencies are not so very remote from the great seasonal periods set forth in Frye's cultural chronology. All of these great, stimulating examples, and so many yet to be put forward, at least since Vico and Hegel, do not in the end argue for the general cesspool of great unconcretizable formulas; but, on the contrary, they serve to indicate that the universalist explanation of art and of culture is the ultimate, most ambitious and, hence, most difficult stage for reaching the necessary, satisfactory explanation of the human sublime.

3.2.5. *Imaginary Poeticity in Narrative Prose Texts: Cervantes' Spatial Myth*

Up to this point I have limited the characterization of the feature of poeticity as a product of the imaginary activity constituting the text to the specific genre of poetry. Nevertheless, poeticity as an aesthetico-imaginary value can be present, obviously, in other classes of text besides poetry. In this section, I propose to attend in all the necessary detail to the effects of poeticity linked to the activity of the imaginary constituent in narrative works of fictional prose. The most concise definition of the imaginary outline of the poetic text does not exclude the feature of poeticity associated with the fantastic organization of artistic prose. In this sense, within prose, fictional narration, beginning with the verisimilar manipulation of the imagination, compensates for the primary role exerted by imaginary syntax in the poem.

In principle, the novel is the genre that, due to its textual constitution, with an explicitly textualized space and time, has traditionally received more attention as regards its spatial dimension. Of course, this has usually meant the description and explanation of its exterior, explicit space (R. Gullón, 1980; M. C. Bobes, 1985). The more complex process of textual interiorization, of the intensionalization of that space in the text, has received far less attention (J. Franck, 1952; G. Poulet, 1963; M. Baquero Goyanes, 1970). The imaginary perspective of the spatial myth in its application to the novel has not received the exhaustive and explicit treatment it deserves, at least as far as I know. Nevertheless, the possibilities for the success of such an investigation appear clear to me. It is enough to recall, for example, that reflection on the modern novel, especially on the authors of the "nouveau-roman", gave rise to the articulation of arguments for an exploration of the subject, albeit preliminary and limitedly lexicological, like Matoré's study of spatiality in modern society.

Beginning with Proust, who demonstrates according to Matoré "the fragmented and dissociated character of reality" in the modern perspective, followed by the brief evocation of the role the spatial plays in the work of Claudel and Misloz, for whom "under the thousands of ways of love, fear, pride and disdain, lies the eternal and unsolvable problem of space", the itinerary of this poll reaches the great peaks of the modern novel, like Joyce, creator of the "first of the itinerant heroes" in modernity, and Faulkner's unequalled modern aesthetics of the void, the Mallarméan basis of which Sartre himself believed he recognized. The invocation of interior space and its novelesque journey as an allegory of characters' intimate mutations and, taking this principle as its starting point, the infinite licenses regarding spatial observation, indicate one of the most characteristic features of the modern novel in Robbe-Grillet, Claude Simon, Beckett, Butor and Nathalie Sarraute. In this regard, Robbe-Grillet himself, without doubt the most lucid theoretician of this school, located the sign of the

3.2. Poeticity: The Imaginary Structure of Symbols in the Temporal Domains

new novel's most visible rupture with classical narration in a medullarly spatial concept, the "destitution of the old myths of depth" (G. Matoré, 1972, pp. 205—213).

By intuitive observation, I believe many of the psychic drives and impulses incorporated in the syntax of the imagination, starting with the synthesis which I have made ample use of before, coincide with archetypal narrative projections. An even greater similarity can be spoken of with regard to the schemes of these impulses' syntactical realizations, with narrative correspondences as familiar as those of the voyage, the progressive enclosure and collapse of an area, etc. The imaginary currents of narrative syntax are realized especially in the structuring of narrated events, and are concretized in terms of the disposition of themes and materials. But, beyond this, identical impulses and analogous structures are reproduced in an imaginary syntax of the processes of narration. The art of narrating can be summed up as the capacity to involve the listener in the story, to entertain, to carefully measure out the story's novelesque interest; a device which, like poetry, is finally schematized through the natural channels and orientations of the human imagination.

The effects of the subconscious' elemental drives, which in my opinion are similar in both lyrical enthusiasm and novelesque imagination, can also be traced in other prose modes, such as the persuasive-argumentative prose of generically rhetorical discourses. From Aristotle to Perelman, rhetoric has been the regulatory model for an entire genre of texts the structure of which, perfectly defined in the great lines of its performative canons and even in many of its most superficial details, is dictated by the need to persuade. In this rhetorical inflection of the judge's or jury's mind, a central feature shared by the majority of non-fictional genres of prose, the careful mobilization of irrational images is manifestly important. It is a matter of constantly operating with subliminally convincing resources, which leaves little doubt as to the important role played by the enthusiastic construction of the imaginary in said processes.

It remains to be seen, naturally, whether the mobilization of the imagination's elementary forms, as they have been outlined by Jung or Durand, is produced identically in lyrical, narrative and argumentative discourses. Or if, as appears reasonable in principle, each one of the major genres of discourse alluded to, or of their subgenres, privilege certain symbolic modes, fantastic impulses and imaginary schemes. The determination of such peculiarities would be of decisive importance in establishing typologically and genetically the physiognomy of the verbal artistic system, although the complex execution of so ambitious a program exceeds the possibilities of my current investigation.

Every mode of artistic expression constructed on the material verbal base presupposes a common differential attitude. Logico-communicative discourse, regulated by linguistics as a *science of expression* and tending towards the general communication of truths, adopts a relative neutrality in relation to the strategies of the imaginary (I. Gómez de Liaño, 1982). However, insofar as the aim of the discourse is to influence a receiver, the imaginary is noticeably manipulated. In this case, what is sought is not so much "universal truth" but "convincing truth", long-known in rhetoric as opinion.

The behavioral and rhetorical components of literary discourse founding different modes of persuasion — and even of the seduction of the public (R. Chambers, 1984) — on different argumentative strategies, commonly participate in some permanent and intersubjective conventions of the imaginary which convert general rhetoric, regulator of all of these kinds of discourses, into a truly *general science of expressiveness*. A different expressiveness, let me repeat, realized differently according to the requirements of each case: with argumentation and intellectual-sentimental progression, or through fictional structures and the marvelous suspension of disbelief, according to the discursive aim. But all of these different approaches act as one on the same anthropological fragment of the human imagination.

Focusing on the study of the aesthetic effects of narrative fiction, influenced by the activity of the imagination, a first type of phenomena is immediately obvious and familiar. The study of myths has broadened critical familiarity with the novel's symbolic constitution. This is undoubtedly the most important and fundamental aspect of the imaginary articulation of fiction, but also, as I have just indicated, the most commonly addressed in the mythocritical tradition (G. Gusdorf, 1952; M. Eliade, 1963; G. Durand, 1981) and, in general, in the psychological exploration of novelesque fiction (M. Bodkin, 1934; J. Villegas, 1973). In this book, I have already taken care of many of these questions in a previous chapter: in the study of fictionality as a particular mode of poetic expressiveness. All of which dissuades me from dwelling here on already familiar and scarcely novel materials, limiting myself to reminding the reader of their fundamental and primary importance in the construction of novelesque fiction.

Having first established that principle, it seems more interesting and in line with this book's structure to concentrate my attention on a singular aspect of imaginary fiction, the aesthetic consequences and effects of which are very important in the fantastic configuration of the narrative illusion, an aspect which has not received the critical attention that has been dedicated to mythical and archetypal-fantastic symbolization. I am referring here, as regards the novel, to the manifestation of the spatial category and its decisive influence, explicit and especially implicit, in the production of the aesthetic effect of the novel's poeticity. In fact, spatial patterns are present and operative in the novel in the same way as the spatial imaginary and semantico-symbolic patterns are essential constituents of the imaginary poeticity of lyrical texts.

3.2. Poeticity: The Imaginary Structure of Symbols in the Temporal Domains

The poetic effectiveness of spatial schemes in the novel is by no means a phenomenon that has not been observed before. It has traditionally been indicated from the external perspective of its configuration as space-scenery (R. Gullón, 1980; M. C. Bobes Naves, 1985, pp. 196–216). Recall that it was a classical typological category of narrations with a "spatial" character, differentiated from those governed by character or event. With an emphasis more specific to the strictly imaginary values of the spatial structuralization of the story, G. Durand himself has highlighted in a fine work of analysis on *La Chartreuse de Parme* (1971) the decisive role of archetypal space in a work's novelesque appeal. By the same token, the enumeration of the tradition of works, ranging from the *Divine Comedy* to *Don Quijote* and *Our Lady of Paris* to *The Name of the Rose*, where the poetic role of fantastic spatialization is exemplary, would be a task as endless as it is trivial and already overly familiar. Fantastic consideration and reflection on an affective spatiality undoubtedly turns out to be one of the most decisive keys in the aesthetic construction of the novel's meaning.

Hence, it is worth the effort to intensify and deepen investigations like those cited above in order to discover how they touch on or perhaps even are related to the impressive phenomenon of the novel's explicit or referential spatiality. Of the two great anthropological coordinates, time and space, the role of the first in the novel has already been exhaustively examined (M. Zeraffa, 1966; H. Weinrich, 1971; C. Segre, 1974; M. Baquero Goyanes, 1970, pp. 78–79 and 175–176; M. C. Bobes Naves, 1985, pp. 147–216).

The reasons for this critical attention are obvious. In the first place, the most specific features of narrative texts coincide with the causal chain of actions and events. Given that, what is unique to the novel, compared to other prose discourses also of an artistic nature, consists in the imitation of actions; as the treatise writers have been repeating since the first debates on the nature and legitimacy of the genre, it is immediately evident that the expression of this logical chain of actions is manifested precisely in its temporal measure and materialization. Moreover, as concerns the artistic and creative analysis of the feature, the varied range of games played with time, decomposing the historical logic of the *ordo naturalis* in artificial orders of an artistic nature, has been exploited as one of the most productive resources for innovative creativity and unexpected effects in the constitution of narrative texts (M. Baquero Goyanes, 1970, pp. 78–79 and 175–176; C. Segre, 1974, pp. 4–72; M. Bal, 1977, pp. 45–55).

The pleasure of narration, its mythical constitution as a discourse and framework for the inclusion of anthropological symbols, also relies on time as a natural coordinate of articulation (C. Lévi-Strauss, 1958, Ch. XV). More precisely, the rebellion against real experienced time is at the root of the narrator's controlled temporality, and is one of the most natural and recognizable sources of pleasure in the framework of the novel's craft.

Nevertheless, I believe the other coordinate of natural expressive orientation, the spatial, has not received, except in some isolated cases, an adequate critical treatment seeking to account for its decisive importance in the story's imaginary construction (G. Matoré, 1976).

The critical observations of space's traditional role in the novel inevitably demand, in my judgment, the immediate correction of the theory of narration to incorporate this decisive spatial component (J. Frank, 1952) and even the spatial as an imaginary construct (G. Durand, 1971; U. Eisenzweig, 1976). This is primarily due to the fact that temporal progression is necessarily linked, in the majority of cases, to its articulation in spatial domains, a principle foreseen and developed unsurpassably by Bakhtin himself under the critical notion of the "chronotope", which has subsequently not been very keenly exploited (M. Bakhtin, 1975, pp. 237−398). From my own experience, the "chronotope", restricted in the great Russian critic's theory to modes of spatio-temporal correspondence relative to the different modulations of social polyphony, should be emphasized more as one of the essential components in every story's fantastic articulation. This is especially the case as far as the most ancient and foundational phases of the modern novel's development, where the novel's more numbingly monological articulation impairs the plurality of "voices" and reduces the principle's suitability for critical analysis (M. Bakhtin, 1970, Ch. II).

I will cite Cervantes as an example because in the case of his narrations it seems to me that the critical effectiveness of the overly generic postulate of the polyphonic plurality of social voices in the constitution of the novel is weakened. In my judgment, perhaps the principle which best represents Cervantes' narrative fascination is his powerful capacity for the imaginary evocation of space, as W. Kayser, with other aims, has indicated. A spatiality, let it be clearly understood, that is schematic and exemplary, symbolic, removed from the naturalist descriptive space, from the naturalist still life or landscape. In the *valorative* dialectic of Cervantes' texts, the most attractive values appear linked to the inexorable fit between the imagination and the perfect geometry of a paradigmatic spatiality. The alternation of open and enclosed spaces, limited and infinite, unsuspectingly facilitates the narration's progress and yields fantasy's deepest and most suggestive aesthetic and sentimental solidarities.

Cervantine scholars have already repeatedly emphasized how the structure of *El celoso extremeño* represents the imaginary construction of a text consolidated as the quintessential thematic expression of space (M. Baquero Goyanes, 1976, I, pp. 51−62). The very emphasis given to the protective environment of the house-fortress sets up the first dimension of the novel's construction, already announcing and promising its transgression. The disarticulation of the surroundings, the environment, the initial space, thus turns into a necessary dynamic for the establishment of the novel's central

3.2. Poeticity: The Imaginary Structure of Symbols in the Temporal Domains 441

conflict. Moreover, space exerts an analogous imaginary role in the constitution of practically all of the narrations included among the *Exemplary Novels*.

It is also necessary to refer to the contrast between *the road* as a longitudinal dimension of open progression and the *lodgings* of the inn, house or palace as a domain of polemical and carnavalesque activity. Thus, a novel of spatial *anagnorisis* like *La fuerza de la sangre* does not violate the priority of space's role any more than the "labyrinth" of the *Celoso*. The set of novelesque scenes in open space, like the child's abduction and accident or the succinct references to the mobile narrative scenes which make up the heroine's secluded life in her father's Toledo home and the schematic mention of the Italian adventure of the defamer, barely serve any function other than to propose the logical setting required by the vigorous fantastic introduction of the bedroom. This place, the scene of violation and recognition, represents the privileged space to which every other temporal constituent or imaginary characterization of the novel is adapted and subordinated. Also, the contrast between the *voyage*, with its novelesque implications of "initiation", itself relatively marginal and propaedeutic, and the *interior* of the room, the building, the precinct, etc., as the space where the narrative intrigue originates and is developed, explains the structure of fantastic representation predominating in novels as attractive and full of the literature of manners' dense detail and embellishment as *Rinconete y Cortadillo* and *La ilustre fregona*.

Monipodio's patio and the Segovian's tavern, respectively, are *spaces of carnavalesque freedom* which define the imagination's expansive powers, permitting it to concentrate on the convergence of the characters' intersecting destinies. And if the elemental imaginary contrast is characteristic of these two novels, the simple multiplication of this one dialectical formula establishes the structure of the action in a lively story of voyages and adventures with a powerful capacity for imaginary effectiveness, *Las dos doncellas*. Here, the enclosed spaces, from the most common and easily recognizable to the lush oasis — the little forest of Igualada —, of fantastic evocative capacity in Cervantes, or the social solidity of the "home" in the Cardonas' aristocratic house, propose environments for the action's expansion which fulfill their possibilities for fantastic suggestion in their immediate contrast to subsequent places on the itinerary. A setting simply sketched in narrative formulas of very concise textual unity, which assume a surprising capacity to impel fantasy with their vibrant temporal swiftness and spatial schematism.

I do not believe it is necessary to continue insisting in detail on the decisive role of the formulas of spatial alternation for the imaginary structure and effects of novels like *La señora Cornelia*, namely, contrasts between the safety of houses and the dangers of streets and roads, so propitious to vengeful intrigues. A novel, moreover, in which the flow of characters between neighboring Bologna and Ferrara turns out to be important. Even in *El licenciado Vidriera* and *El coloquio de los perros*, the role played by spaces which introduce the respective "frames" play an important role in setting the "framework" for both stories. Precisely in cases like those I have just mentioned, the weight of the spatial imagination on the novelesque text reveals the depth and necessity of its literary possibilities through its very lack of explicit referential concreteness.

The role of spatial imagination in narrative poeticity, of course, constitutes a very deep structural level and surely one no less decisive than the sum total of all of the semantic data of characterization and setting which configure important novelesque entities, or even the very facts of local setting. In this way, a scheme of analogies is perceptible between texts of the novelesque type like *La gitanilla*, belonging to a genre of texts most respected for their realistic Spanish *costumbrismo*, and *El amante liberal*, a delightful example of a second kind of exotic, fantastic stories. It is interesting to note that this second type of novel was not to the liking of nineteenth century critics, precisely because of the lack of picturesque and circumstantial detail in its naturalist setting. And, nevertheless, the structural formula of the spatializing imagination discovers deep similarities between the two novels, which contributes in a very decisive way to fix the physiognomy of their style or, perhaps more clearly, to demonstrate the existence of what has traditionally been called traces of the author's "personality". In effect, *La gitanilla* and *El amante liberal* share an identical spatial structure, although, curiously, they completely invert the distribution of imaginary spaces.

La gitanilla can be summarized, from our current perspective, as a voyage across open fields between two enclosed spaces: initial and final, urban and domestic. The first of the flanking spaces, the court, is itself strongly structured by spatial forms. The narration of Preciosa's successive "entrances" into the city offers a clear scheme dominated by urban space, which progressively moves in very gradual steps towards centrality: the gambling den, the Lieutenant's house, and Andrés Caballero's house.

The departure to open country — where the idyllic scenes of forests and gypsy camps, merely suggested, always play a role of fantastic animation, not to be ignored, in contrast to the dangerous freedom of wandering in the open space of the roads — is also highly inflected. By virtue of this, the tale's structural center is folded over, an effect reproduced as clearly and symptomatically, as we shall see, in the domestic space of the Cadi's harem in *El amante liberal*. Finally, the colorful description of the carnavalesque procession entering Murcia carries the action, as before with Preciosa's initiation in Madrid, to the medullary setting of urban spatiality represented by the Corregidor's palace.

El amante liberal repeats an analogous scheme, inverting only the distribution of the initial and final scenes corresponding to the narratives of

3.2. Poeticity: The Imaginary Structure of Symbols in the Temporal Domains

open space. Each one, in substance, contains an adventurous itinerary of voyages, battles and shipwrecks which corresponds, respectively, to the story of the capture and enslavement in the novel's first half and the liberation and triumphal return to Trapani in the second. At the same time, the intrigues and the animated sentimental space where the two societies of captives and Turks devise their plans appear situated in the peaceful setting of an Arabian interior, always familiar and appealing to the exotic fantasy of Cervantes and his readers. The change of orientation in the character's destiny is produced in this environment; that is, we witness here the same novelesque sign establishing the story's principle central inflection as in the equivalent structure of *La gitanilla*.

The spatial-imaginary structure of these two novels — so very different in their critical reception, especially as regards realistic genres and techniques and procedures of setting — corroborates a substantial identity of action between them, which did not escape the notice of one clever Cervantine scholar, Casalduero, who included both among the set of novels he denominated as dealing with the amorous "test". In effect, the logical structuralization of the antecedents, development and denouement of the test imposes a *voyage* structure. On the other hand, as with those stories and scenes governed by the *interior* spatial mode, as in *Rinconete* or *La ilustre fregona*, the simple multiplication of recurrent spaces automatically establishes the genesis of new and more complex structures of novelesque action. Also, in this spatio-structural aspect of the test, the fantastic atmosphere's spatial duplication is repeated in all of its detail in the more complex *fabula* of *La española inglesa*. This text exhibits a broadened — doubled, in this case — test structure, also located in a double space: an Atlantic, English space, in which a schematic fiction with Byzantine antecedents predominates, and a national Mediterranean space, the representation of which emphasizes the most delightful Cervantine ability to evoke precise *costumbrismo* and local realist colorism.

Among the abundant variety of questions implied and raised by the imaginary sector of narratological criticism, those that refer to the *procedures for the textual incorporation of fantastic drives and impulses* are not among those with the least effect and transcendence. In principle, there is no reason to believe that the premises that govern this dialectic in the novel's space are substantially different from those that establish the complex relationship between the text and the imaginary effect in lyrical poetry. Nevertheless, the undeniable uniqueness of the construction of the imagination in the story imposes certain features peculiar to prose narration which, to continue with the examples I have been working with in this section, I will set forth in the course of examining some of Cervantes' procedures in the *Exemplary Novels*.

In the first place, I should emphasize the general importance of what we might call the principle of *disproportion* or of *variation* between the textual causes and resources and the effects and representations of the imaginary representation. The great novelist is particularly capable of multiplying his images with the elegantly economical and soberly precarious use of his meaningful textual resources. The spontaneous and inevitable imaginary collaboration of his readers — or "narratees" to cite a terminology that has been widely disseminated, albeit unsuccessfully and unclearly (G. Prince, 1973, pp. 178—196; 1982, pp. 16—25) — assures the nuanced multiplication and diversification of the general imaginary effect, from the highly concentrated and even humble reference of the textual stimulus. For example, it is frequently the case that a regime of correspondences of qualitative proportion produces the result of a *quantitative involution* between the text and its imaginary repercussion. The spatial experience assumed and transferred between the author and his audience almost always contributes to this effect. In essence, this is what facilitates Cervantes' animated narrative acceleration when, in *Las dos doncellas*, he designs the return voyage of the two couples from Barcelona to Andalucia, even fulfilling their vows to Santiago.

It does not matter, except that it perhaps helps to add some interesting element of powerful imaginary mobilization, that the two geographic spaces cited are situated in the relatively exotic atmosphere of an attractively distant land. This is the case in the outlines of Italian itineraries in *El licenciado Vidriera*, and, in *El amante liberal*, the evocation of a pleasant Mediterranean geography, filled with attractive and vague medieval echoes, both historical and artistic, of an Aegean, Berber, and Turkish space, a fantastic setting filled with brilliant references to the hero's ocean crossings, cavalcades and even maritime escapes, effective forms of imaginary evocation indeed.

But Cervantes' great narrative virtuosity allows us to illustrate situations of even greater and clearer disproportion between the nature of the text's material support and the effects of its imaginary representation. In this I believe Cervantes' extraordinary ability permits us to verify, due to their visibility, some of narrative art's universal procedures. I am referring to the use of devices for "variation" in which, unlike the previous case, the presence of an overall qualitative disproportion is evident. Recall, for example, the simultaneously majestic and vibrant tone of the discourse on the excellence and marvels produced by the enthusiasm of souls in love, which Cervantes invokes in *La gitanilla* on the occasion of the departure from Toledo to Madrid of the entire band of gypsies, including the young hero and heroine. Here, the narrator tells us the gypsies decamped, how Andrés and Preciosa chose to travel — she on a donkey with him serving as her footman —, then launches on the paragraph-long discourse on love I have just alluded to, before concluding his narration of the trip: "From there, in four days they came to a field two leagues from Toledo, where they set up their camp". Hence, in this particular scene, we can observe a

3.2. Poeticity: The Imaginary Structure of Symbols in the Temporal Domains 445

clear fantastic spatialization of distance, filling the textual space to delay the departure, substituting for the description of the voyage itself, and even successfully representing the characters' euphoric state of mind, with the resulting emphasis placed on the general image of the carnavalesque procession, an image which the novel does not abandon throughout the gypsies' wanderings.

The detailed descriptions of monetary minutiae, which in Cervantes come to constitute a constant, already indicated and interpreted in a variety of ways by specialists, serve the same spatial objective. In fact, this is a narrative vehicle, consciously or unconsciously used by the author, to efficiently introduce a textual space indirectly equivalent to the trip's physical distance, difficult to sketch in true verisimilar terms by direct artistic means. Archetypal examples of this delaying mechanism occupy extensive sections of the story recounted in *La española inglesa*.

In summary, the narrative genre is not an exception, in terms of the workings of its artistic mechanisms, to the general lines of the imagination's operation in the fantastic structure of verbal works of art. It is the case, however, that fiction involves a set of special efforts for the fantastic transfiguration of strictly linguistic materials, immanently inscribed in texts. These operations of fictional cooperation inherent to the novel and required by the respective points of view of the narrator and the narratee affect, in the most immediate and noticeable way, the imaginary representation of characters, events and settings of the most direct referentiality. But the deepest and most important structures are located beyond, or underneath, this immediate level of fantastic embodiments: those which support and make possible the interest and verisimilitude of the operations of fantastic adherence. This is the profound level of the temporal relations between the active pieces of the novel delineated by narratology and, together with it, the universe of axiological implications and their suitably interesting argumentation, which may provide a rhetoric of narration. Finally, it reveals the most abstract scheme supporting all of the possibilities for imaginary operation in novelesque fiction, expressed by means of references and critical equations of imaginary spatialization.

In these terms we understand the value of poetic aestheticity to be a principle of anthropological communicative experience, unattainable by any other instance of meaningful transmission. Underlying the irrationality of the artistic expression, contents of experience which are unviable for the conceptual consciousness of reason travel and are patterned in an accessible way. Such transfers, from this level to the textual surface and on to the reader, viewer and listener, are possible, in effect, because of the common physiognomy of the imaginary. Adequately interpreted, it is in these generalized structures of psychological homogeneity where we find the existence and nature of *aesthetic universals* confirmed, necessarily serving to pattern the nature and function of literary objects. I invoke them here without any nostalgia for some form of utopian idealism, but rather for specific reasons I believe I have made very clear and which have to do with the various structures, material and imaginary, which cooperate in the irreducible complexity of the literary text.

To reach the most efficient sources of this imaginary universality, of general and basic forms of fantasy at the service of the human explanation of the principal facts of our nature and destiny, of course requires us to recognize degrees of success and depth, of purity and essentiality. The powers of individual talent are revealed as variable and graduated in the identification of such drives, always mysterious, just as the ability to convoke them under textual forms of artistic expressiveness continues to be different and hierarchicalizable. The poetic axiology of artistic forms consists in the variety of those processes, from the startling assertion of the message of genius, to the frustration of the intranscendent and anodyne text. The intervention of the imaginary component does not detract from the axiological nature of poeticity as an element of value in literary meaning; on the contrary, it is what proposes the suitable textual spaces where the deepest and most suitable reasons for defining aesthetic meaning in terms of universal constants and constancy originate and are justified.

3.3. *Universality as a Property of Poetic Value*

3.3.1. *Textual and Anthropological Foundations of Poetic Universality: On the Frustration of the Arts' Diversity*

In the final analysis, the foundation for poetic value lies in its properties of *generality* and *universality*. What surpasses cultural convention, which merely enables us to easily and immediately recognize a text as artistic discourse or, more concretely, as literary discourse, is that which establishes a type of message illustrating essential structures of the human universal imagination's anthropological configuration. That is, those messages which do not affect us merely because they appeal to our particular individual experience or motivations, those which are not moving or revealing solely to isolated human beings. Messages reveal a poetic nature or attain poetic status when they are capable of constituting an object of deeply moving, essential revelation common to all human beings.

This first affirmation of poetry's universality conflicts with the principle that certain texts, which for the majority of readers or for historical reasons are considered sublime and poetic, such as those of Cervantes, Dante or Shakespeare, cannot move or interest some people because of their lack of culture or for whatever other reasons. The objection, however, answers itself. It appears clear that such people do not belong to the set of people open to the universe of poetic and artistic values, in the same way as there exist those excluded from normalcy in the moral order. Whether or not education and

3.3. Universality as a Property of Poetic Value 447

access to suitable information could develop in those individuals excluded from the aesthetic enjoyment of cultural objects a taste for them and an artistic understanding is clearly a different question, of little interest here.

More consistent and important are the objections which refer to the principle of poetic universality in terms of historic or synchronic inequalities in the consistency of artistic texts, which produce or have produced in different cultures or ages analogously different feelings of an aesthetic kind. One could cite, for example, the differences between traditional Chinese painting and contemporary European art. Or one could point to the powerful representative and perceptive differences that have come to exist simultaneously in one and the same poetic feeling in the case of Egyptian or Romantic European painting, a subject which has inspired curiosity and analysis from Hegel to Gombrich (1959; 1986).

Nevertheless, these kinds of difficulties do not deny the universal condition underlying the nature of the poetic. On the contrary, they reinforce and confirm it. The differences in perception in the plastic arts which I've just alluded to, or even those which might underlie the conflict between abstraction and figurativism in modern Occidental art, do not allude to anything more than differing modes, trivial or profound, of constituting meaningful texts (A. García-Berrio and M. T. Hernández, 1988 a). As extreme and clear as these textual differences may be, they are, in any case, attenuated or annuled in the psychological identity of the poetic effect. The distance separating the relativity of artistic structures and their anthropological constitution is clearly diminishing, to the point that it is possible to reduce and trivialize these differences, producing an absolute unity of the poetic in the activity of the imagination and of sentimental emotions.

I have frequently in this book resorted to the authority of E. H. Gombrich's testimony to indirectly illustrate, through his general experience and understanding of artistic works, the necessary aesthetic reasons which condition and hierarchicalize with spontaneous naturalness the sense and sanction of poeticity as a value and beauty of certain unique texts. Gombrich's work as a whole involves a plea of exceptional quality and authority against the temptations of relativism and aesthetic skepticism which have obnubilated approaches to art in our times. Recently, Gombrich even categorically declared himself against the relativist and deconstructive currents in the sciences of the spirit, which he characterized as a short-lived "fashion". What most interests me about Gombrich's declaration is not the absolute and conclusive terms in which it was issued, and with which I agree, but rather the openly *universalist* nature of his arguments.

The starting point for Gombrich's vast experience of art is sheltered in the stimulus of authority Goethe's cultural vision represents, as he recalled by beginning a recent address by quoting from the fourth part of the *Zahmen Xenien* the verses in which a reflection on Plutarch's remote texts yields the vivid record of the essential transtemporal identity of all human beings (E. H.

Gombrich, 1986, p. 17). That is, through the ages and even beyond individual differences, the universal basis of the need for and general rules of artistic construction are founded on undeniably anthropological roots which unify and universalize forms of perception and sensibility which aglutinate in interindividually similar feelings and passions, and which constitute, in the final analysis, the universal foundation for the imagination's operation. An anthropological base, wasted away and discredited by several decades of anti-idealist reaction, which Gombrich mentions by name: *aesthetic universals*. Consider his argument: "in ethnology there have been certain aspects which have worked so that relativism did not conquer everything with absolute power. Travelers have seen that foreign men laughed and cried, played and fought. Anyone who has had the good fortune to experience that can no longer doubt that universal human reactions exist" (E. H. Gombrich, 1986, p. 21).

In the course of justifying this principle, as valid as it is controversial, which Gombrich attempts schematically in the article I have just quoted from, itself a synthesis of his work and experience, the great art historian indicates general movements of the spirit which are at the source and are responsible for generating the textual structures we detect as constitutively artistic. Thus, for example, the idealist drive or ascesis of desire compared to the pragmatic retraction, adaptation or adoption — "that anxiety in search of satisfaction, and the contrary movement of cultural adaption" —, a symbolico-spatial contrast which everyone has always cited as an explanation of the universal reach of the two great Cervantine characters and one which Gombrich immediately illustrates with other dualist contrasts like that of Tamino and Papageno or the pairing of archetypal, antithetical figures in Hindu drama (1986, pp. 23—24). These are definitely natural forms, foreign to the life of civilization and the social education of the city, which, in Gombrich's view, produced Rousseau and Schiller's reflections, and Goethe's supernatural cry:

> "Zufrieden jauchzt hier groß und klein,
> Hier bin ich Mensch, hier darf ichs sein."

["In great happiness, the great and little rejoice here, / here I am a person, here I can be one"].

These personal, anthropological, natural roots are the fundamental constituents of human universality, the more obvious, according to Gombrich, the less conventionally refined they become: "as *creatures* we are all closer to one another than in the sphere of the highest refinement". At work here is the opposition, then, of the essentially radical to the historically variable, of fashion or *thesis* to nature or *physis*, as the Greek language assimilated this profound truth about the existence and nature of the universal and the constituent (E. H. Gombrich, 1986, p. 24). In this scheme, nature is understood as the universal record of behavior, which explains Gombrich's appeal for attention to be paid once again to psychology in explanations analogous to those I have called for here regarding the anthropological constitution of the imagination and feeling: "Whoever dedicates himself to the sciences of the spirit and is interested in such complex processes should direct his attention to psychology. For, as many schools and trends as that science may have, all of them share as a motto the words of Alexander Pope: 'the proper study of mankind is man'. Now then, since psychology wants to be a science, it cannot accept any dogma, not even that of the unity of humanity. And even in affirming this, I am on the side of those who, against relativism, take as their starting point the hypothesis that man's psyche demonstrates certain *constants*, which the scientific can depend on" (1986, p. 25).

Upon invoking the most immediate — far from the only — of these universal *constants* of human behavior having special implications for artistic communication, Gombrich finds himself in the tactical position of needing to warn us "not to expect much of them", and to alert us to the fact that they may even "sound trivial". In my opinion, this excessive caution results from Gombrich's concern when addressing, as he was on this occasion, an audience of German philologists, many of them strongly disposed to the relativist aesthetics of reception. The invocation of the universal condition of rhythm — "the inclination toward moving in a rhythmical form" — in terms of his understanding of this phenomenon as one of the natural and biological reasons determining the historical structure of the artistically universal, may not be novel, of course, but neither is it trivial. Rather, it is accurate; Gombrich here is in agreement with none other than Aristotle, when the latter, in his *Poetics*, indicates rhythm, together with mimesis, as the two *natural causes* — φύσικαι — of poetry and of all artistic imitations. A universal, that of rhythm, which is not only durational, temporal and acoustic, but which is equally characteristic of the spatial formulation and reading of visual artistic texts (A. García-Berrio and M. T. Hernández, 1988), and which is associated in the latter case, being Gombrich's favorite area for reflection, with the evidence for phototropic universals, constituting a fundamental biological component of man's nature and, consequently, of the structure of the artistically visual, as he affirms in his concluding remarks: "I am convinced that the plastic arts are also established on biological foundations. And if all of us share the tendency towards rhythm, which is expressed in the ornaments of all peoples, we also share an enjoyment of light and brightness. Man is a phototropic being; if we were photophobic like termites, we would have distanced ourselves from light. The mighty and the sacred have always made use of the brilliant and luminous" (E. H. Gombrich, 1986, p. 25).

It is interesting to note once again, even in the case of someone as keen and farsighted as Gombrich, the effect of the bias — this one certainly clearly "differential" — which has muffled the recognition and acceptance of the universal depth of the Aristotelian proclamation of "physical" causes as art's ultimate cause, a prejudice I have warned against on various occasions in this book. As his speech continues, we see how Gombrich feels the need to overcome — to "spiritualize", in fact — the biological elementality of the artistic causes just cited, considered in terms of their supposed material coarseness, in order to elevate the argument to the level of psychological mechanisms; mechanisms which are undoubtedly more sublime, but also diffuse and inconcrete and, in the long run, more questionable and evanescent, such as the *deferment* of pleasure and the overcoming of expectations. In this, Gombrich echoes, without necessarily being aware of it, the Schillerian ideal of the sentimental progress of epic narration, the old "deferment with love", which appears stated in his own apologetic urge: "Of course, it would be inadequate to explain human artistic activity in terms of such pleasant reactions, to argue that art is fulfilled between the deferment of satisfaction and the overcome expectation". To which a new culturalist caution is added, bringing to bear the most undeniable and positive of the artistic conditions Jauss contributed from the historical sphere of reception: "and what is especially needed for this is a tradition based on the time required and the prestige granted by the mastery in the use of such psychological effects" (E. H. Gombrich, 1986, p. 25).

In spiritualizing the most fundamental biological causes, which the historical-differential bias discredits as "base" in comparison to the "sublimity" of Art itself, Gombrich presents a structure of feelings and "taste" that is not hard to reconcile with the geometrical schematism of the synthetic designs of the spatial imagination which I term the radical reasons underlying the human interest in art as a privileged vehicle of the imagination's anthropological orientation. Hence, time and again, Gombrich's fine instinct leads him back to linking the final explanation for art's causes to the most radical schematic principles of the behavior of symbols and of human emotion. Thus, after making the dialectical concessions just discussed, Gombrich immediately recovers the train of thought most strongly linked to the initial insight of the basic principles he had set forth and defended in his speech: "Now then, as diverse as those effects, those structures and succession of levels may be, we cannot ignore the fact that it is always a matter of spaces of tension that arise from the primitive polarity of every human reaction".

What is unique to Gombrich's proclamation of the principle of aesthetic universals as anthropological constituents, compared to my own position, is that the great theoretician of art thinks especially in terms of a psychology of visual perception, such as this field was codified by Arnheim in particular, while I, specializing more in literature, tend to place these same roots in the context of the structure of imaginary behavior. Clearly, this is an emplacement of these two structures which is not in itself contradictory or discontinuous, but comparable and progressive. In my own search for psychological essentials, I rely particularly on the stimulus provided by the poetics of the imaginary and mythocriticism from Jung to Bachelard and Durand, and not, in the final analysis, on the English and German Romantic tradition of reflections on the sublime imagination. Gombrich, on the other hand, so deeply familiar with the visual contact of great works of plastic art, moves in his own dialectic between the luminous experience of optical perception and the sublimated projection of the Geistesgeschichte. Still, what matters most in this case, at least in my opinion, is not the disparity of origins or itineraries, but the common end results.

In the structure of its anthropologico-communicative causes, the poetic is universal. In previous chapters I have analyzed the imaginary configuration of the poetic's fundamentally anthropological roots. In the final analysis, artistic pleasures and delights are supplementary modes with regard to rational deduction. They serve the most natural human need for the *orientation* and location of existential references in *time* and *space*. Literature, like any other art form, also serves this human need to identify our essential anthropological coordinates. These operations of the imaginary activity are common, in one form or another, to all human beings. Some, or all at some time, understand them as rational forms of referential orientation and of the comprehension of otherness. Others "feel" them as intimate states of mind: an expansive, ascendant euphoria or a depressive feeling of dejection, fall or collision, the comfortable conformity of being lodged in the social and cosmic order or the anxiety of waiting, of feeling threatened or of an oppressive environment, etc.

Naturally, an explicit and concrete awareness of all of these essential foundations of the poetic has been fairly scarce in the artistic theory of this century; not only between the very subjects of artistic experience, creators and receivers, but also among critics, theoreticians and analysts of aesthetics. Nevertheless, the real nature of the anthropologico-imaginary foundations which support art's fantastic activity is what legitimizes and lends interest and essential seriousness to the artistically sublime experience. My analyses in this book are a relatively fresh effort to emphasize this transcendence. Without art's profound convergences with the essential forms of man's constitutive inquiry into his own *identity*, through the measurement of his relationship with *otherness* under the coordinates of time and space, it would be hard to justify the transcendence of this important historical and anthropological phenomenon.

The attractiveness of the most immediate and accessible sensory and imaginative pleasures in artistic objects has often captivated and almost monopolized reflections on the nature of literature, music and especially the plastic arts. The sensitive pleasure of the melody of certain rhythms, of the best-sounding verses or the most successful prose is a fact; the same is true for the wealth of images suggested to the imagination by verbal allusions and descriptions. Similarly, in pondering the revealing depths of certain poetic articulations and reflections at poetry's highest peaks of invention, it is certainly easy to think of all of those immediate phenomena as the poetic's reason for being. But we should persuade ourselves, nevertheless, of the fact that those sensitive and sentimental finds are only the most immediately verifiable *casings* for forms of time and space, the elements of final and unique interest in which the consciousness' anthropological stance and orientation are concretized.

In painting, the degree of sensitive delight and of perceptible referentiality is even more active and penetrating than in literature, or even music. The temptation to link the depth of aesthetic feeling to the most direct and perceptible values of plasticity, or to iconic images' capacities for referential truth, has historically been greater in the analysis of painting than in the explanation of literature's poetic mystery. The attractiveness of colors and patterns of design to the perceptive rhythms of the gaze and the representations of fantasy is so fundamental in the case of the great painters that the critical explanations of their value, from Leonardo and Veronese to Velázquez and Goya, almost always concentrate exclusively on noting their unequalled and unique talent for constructing the textual patterns of their paintings.

The sensitive and explicitly conscious delights of art in whichever of its manifestations, literature among them, are undoubtedly a component of their fascination which cannot be discounted. Often, claims as to a painting's merit are entirely based on this. However, with regard to a literary work or a poem, this kind of claim is more rarely made, in part because the conceptual depth of their contents tends to count a lot when the time comes for establishing their value. Moreover, one should not forget, in any case, that these successful surface forms of the artistic message's material representation are the peculiar guarantees of the effective reach of their interesting, anthropologico-imaginary depth. The poetic work transcribes in its form, and thanks to it, the unrepeatable vivacity of a vast reservoir of experience. I have attempted to give evidence of all of this in my description of the features of literariness and expressiveness.

Nevertheless, the explicit, perceptible and conscious beauty of artistic texts, at least surely with regard to literary texts, cannot of itself explain the passionate attraction of the same, as we have already said on numerous occasions. The formal beauties of poetic works represent only the effective instruments for the success of their symbols, in which the brilliant cosmovision which moves us is forged, explaining to us the irreconcilable secrets of our own nature. We perceive in the most sensitive and direct of these structures of artistic works the often subconscious depths of the symbolic plan which captivates us. But it is the essential radicality of the message symbolized and expressed, which induces us to be persuaded of the poetic's universal depths.

The poetic nature of literary texts is thus related to what they most necessarily and passionately express and communicate about the human condition. It is linked to those depths of our anthropological constitution which are not exclusive and singular; that is, those that affect all of us passionately. In these cases the universality which we claim here as a condition

3.3. Universality as a Property of Poetic Value

constituting the poetic is concretized: in the message's extension to all human beings, beyond the particular differences introduced by the uniqueness of meaningful artistic instruments. A conclusion arrived at thanks to the sublime text's capacity for the symbolic mobilization of anthropological structures. Beyond these deep imaginary levels, artistic devices, even the most ingenious and lively, flounder upon their intranscendent lack of essential necessity.

The traditional historical comparison between the arts seems to me, at this point, a decisive field for testing my hypotheses on the principle of universality as a cause and guarantee of poetic value. In effect, the often attempted demonstration of the unity underlying the arts' communicative system, a unity beyond their immediate material and textual differences, has frequently yielded, in the final analysis, proclamations of the existence of aesthetic universals, identified, as I have done here, with the anthropologico-imaginary principles involved in the process of artistic symbolization.

The institution of the notion of the arts' diversity results from the preferential contemplation of their material and textual differences. Observing the phenomenon of art from the perspective of its end products — paintings, symphonies, or poems — the impression of vast diversity among them immediately imposes itself. These are the grounds, since Lessing, for distinguishing between the instantaneous or *spatial* plastic arts and the sequential, *temporal* arts. In fact, the opposite critical tendency counts on no firm historical explanation beyond classicism itself. Plato and Aristotle, especially the latter, took an important step in arguing for the universality of the arts in considering them as expressive-communicative processes. It will be recalled that Aristotle's most transcendent observations in the *Poetics* on mimesis, or on the natural and pleasant condition of imitation and rhythm, approach these elements in a unitary manner. That is, they are considered as valid features, not only of literature or painting, but also of music and even the bodily imitations realized in the art of mimes and dancers.

Still, the kind of comparison which seeks to emphasize the similarities among the arts has historically been realized in a fairly superficial and gratuitous manner. In antiquity, after the occasional and topically repeated affirmations of Simonides, Plutarch, and Philostratus (R. W. Lee, 1964, pp. 8—10), Horace formulated the archetypal comparative formula *ut pictura poesis* in his *Epistola ad Pisones*. It is worth keeping in mind that Horace's inocuous comparison, only later converted by the humanists into the slogan which, synthetically, evoked a much more profound aesthetic reality, itself illustrates the history of one of the greatest interpretative "abuses" of the humanistic commentators, a process common in the aesthetic tradition (A. García-Berrio, 1977—1980). Properly contextualized, Horace's phrase refers only to the convenience of observing and describing artistic objects, in some cases in detail and in others in a more distanced and succinct manner (hexameters 361—365). On this point, Horace's thought has nothing to do with a profound exposition of the problem of the universality or specificity of concrete varieties of artistic initiatives.

Throughout the period stemming from late Humanism to the Baroque (A. Chastel, 1959), when it was most fashionable to posit resemblances among the arts, especially between painting and poetry, the resulting similes failed to delve deeply into the philosophical and aesthetic dimensions of the problem. Nevertheless, the formulas most topically cited by many authors, including Lope de Vega, who spoke of the art of painting as "mute poetry" and that of poetry as "painting for the ear", did touch in passing on the transcendental foundations of the question, although the topical nature of the affirmations rarely translated this into serious reflection (J. Schlosser-Magnino, 1924; M. Praz, 1975). The Baroque principle of synesthesia implied not only the more familiar and conscious problem of the simultaneous action of different arts, but also left the chief question open, as it is formulated and interests us today, of assuring the reality of that resemblance on the basis of some universal mechanisms of the artistic illusion's production and reception.

The well-known anti-Baroque reaction underlying French classicism and the German Enlightenment (R. W. Lee, 1964) ended for some time much of the speculation on the universal foundations of different arts. On the other hand, from Lessing to Kleist, a true crusade against descriptive literature was launched (H. C. Buch, 1972), which had the indirect consequence of delving ever more deeply and more markedly into artistic differences.

To once again raise and examine the old humanist simile *ut pictura poesis* might be useful and even definitive for demonstrating, against the grain of modern theory, that poeticity as a value is based on universal principles. These principles should be looked for, not in the inconcrete space of some new Pythagorean cosmic harmonies, as unverifiable today as in the times of Democritus and Leucippus, but in the perceptible reality of the imagination's anthropological and symbolic behavior. The question roundly affects the speculations of artistic semiology, a field dedicated to describing man's symbolic behavior in the phenomena of artistic communication, be they plastic, literary or musical.

Furthermore, given the predominantly linguistic and poetological advance achieved by contemporary semiology, it may be more appropriate and reasonable to invert the terms of the old Horatian simile, speaking instead of an *ut poesis pictura* (A. García-Berrio and M. T. Hernández, 1988a). This inversion reflects and signals the greater current explicitness of linguistic theory compared to the theory of the visual arts with regard to their capacities to describe the deep and surface structures of their respective texts. In addition to this debatable question of the current superiority of literary semiology — or of linguistic poetics — compared to the semiology of painting (L. Marin, 1978; O. Calabrese, 1985), the proposed inversion recognizes the cultural change of mind which serves to invert the terms based on the degree of hermeneutical difficulty of the respective objects under examination. In other words, it recognizes that the current assessment of these objects differs from that disseminated in Horace's times, when the order of the day called for the assertion of the greater simplicity and transparency of painting's material iconic objects compared to the poem's supposed hidden "spirituality".

Currently, the "reading" and interpretation of works of visual art, especially as regards the products of modern informalism, can be more complex and intricate than the accurate understanding of literary messages. But, in any case, the rigorous transfer of a theory of the poem to the analysis and interpretation of the products of the visual arts may serve, among other things, to illustrate one very important feature of the universal foundations that constitute the anthropological structure of poetic value.

It is necessary to reproduce these customary reflections on the material nature of literary texts, since a deformed consideration of the same has in the past attributed an absolutely immaterial nature to them, thereby portraying them as more abstract in the scale of things than they actually are. This same prejudice has invariably contributed to the perception of poetry as a more unstable and indeterminate entity when compared to the rest of the plastic and visual arts. Today, the material, sonorous and acoustical nature of the human voice is a reality about which debate seems unnecessary. Saussure himself addressed the material nature of acoustic representations and sounds in his famous definition of the linguistic sign. If, in addition, we do not exclude, in the case of literature and especially poetry, the definitive role attributable to the text as *material writing* and, thus, as a *spatialized* concretion of a process, a notion which has been suggestively proposed by authors like Blanchot and Derrida, the position emphasizing the text's material nature would seem to be strengthened even more, with the result of casting doubt on the arguments which favor the view that it is more abstract and inaccessible compared to the rest of the arts.

Similar consequences result when literature is considered in view of the set of physiological, psychological and imaginary mechanisms which concretize texts as processes of communication. Beginning with Aristotle's own claims in the *Poetics* for poetry's *physical* nature (1448 b 5), we are now better prepared to explain and describe its material-acoustic, rhythmico-synesthetic and anthropologico-imaginary mechanisms (A. García-Berrio, 1987, pp. 177–188). With this, we avoid having to resort to ineffective and false confessions of the "ineffability" of the poetic phenomenon, which weigh it down under the prejudices of its supposedly inaccessible nature and have historically hindered and detracted from the validity and truth of initiatives to contrast and compare poetry and literary prose with the other arts. Only by stripping conceptions of literature's nature of all of these previous beliefs in its differential immateriality will we allow it to reveal the artistic universality of its structure and constitutive processes.

3.3.2. *The Generic Deployment of Universal Artistic Structures*

The relationship I am examining between universality and poeticity, can be considered in terms of a cause and effect sequence. With regard to the two items composing the correlation, it can be expressed in any order. Still, the most common cause and effect relationship is usually that stated so that the feature of universality appears as a property or consequence of the literary utterance's poetic condition. This understanding is especially common today, when art's poetic universality is seen as a simple mechanism of reception and consensus; those works of art that are universally accepted across the ages and from the multiple perspectives of individual taste are consecrated as poetic, that is, achieve the greatest artistic value. The truth is that this way of posing the matter is both unoriginal and unproblematical. In fact, it coincides with the traditional understanding of "classical" works as eternal models.

It is necessary, however, to delve a little more deeply into the aesthetic and anthropological reasons for this historical, receptive social consensus. As I have already asserted when faced with this very issue earlier, the apparent historical *conventionality* of a social accord on the poetic value of literary works or on the system of artistic rules and principles on which it is founded does not necessarily mean said cultural system is arbitrary. For this reason, the universality of the anthropologico-imaginary symbol, which I have emphasized before as a fundamental principle underlying artistic texts' poetic value, guarantees the natural and causal nature of poetic value; that is, it guarantees that this value is not purely conventional and contingent. The essential anthropological unity of conscious and unconscious structures, mobilized by the imagination and communicated through the various processes producing the effectively and perfectly artistic text, is the basis for the universality which we locate as the origin and justification of the aesthetic sanction of poetic value.

It seems to me that my understanding of poetic universality in these terms — or, to put it another way, the anthropologico-imaginary universal basis of aesthetic judgments on poetic value — isolates the matter from its closest logical contaminations, like those implied in the extreme terms of the old debates on the theory of literary genres (P. Hernadi, 1972, pp. 152—156; R. Champigny, 1981, pp. 145—174), itself a central question and a traditional content of poetics and literary theories. On this issue, contemporary theory has arrived at a situation mixing abandonment with frustration (R. Wellek, 1970, pp. 236—238; F. Lázaro Carreter, 1979, p. 114; A. Fowler, 1982, p. 236); the interminable bibliography on the matter is dominated by merely repetitive proposals of solutions without much of a future. Hence, J. M. Schaeffer, for example, recently called attention to the "great confusion" reigning in this area of literary theory (J. M. Schaeffer, 1983, p. 3). Even authors who have produced the most rigorous modern syntheses, like Hernadi, or the clearest summaries, like Genette, have expressed reservations as to the possibility of any viable and interesting developments appearing in the theory of genres (P. Hernadi, 1972, p. 3; G. Genette, 1977).

As may be recalled, Croce's objection to the *generic* treatment of literary aesthetics referred to sublime poetic value's necessarily unrepeatable *singularity* and, hence, its unforeseeable nature (B. Croce, 1907; P. Hernadi, 1972, pp. 10—11). Still, the textual phenomena of literary expression's structurali-

3.3. Universality as a Property of Poetic Value

zation in genres, which the different kinds of literary utterances join and in which they are channeled, whether or not they achieve poetic value, is so obvious as to be undeniable (C. Guillén, 1985, p. 149). Hence, *singularity* and *generality* are the two new properties confronting one another, the dialectical parameters affecting the judgment of poetic value and through which it circulates (W. D. Stempel, 1979; C. F. P. Stutterheim, 1969).

Nevertheless, it seems apparent that the variety of possibilities for textual structural realization offered by the different categories of genre, does not in the very least affect the identification of the anthropologico-imaginary universals I have presented before at the very roots of poetic value. The rules governing the diversification of generic modes serve to determine a literary discourse's definitive textual physiognomy in its final form — that is, as a literary utterance — and are therefore of an optional nature and subsequent to the universal anthropologico-imaginary elements which initially establish the radically essential consistency of the poetic. The familiar expressive options — exegematic, dramatic or mixed — or those which make up the *dialectics of symbolic representation* — lyrical-subjective, epic-objective, and theatrical-mixed — are deployments made subsequent to the genre of spatio-temporal experiences which are channeled through the textual schemes of the artistic discourse in its greatly varied literary forms and manifestations (R. Champigny, 1978, pp. 94—111; J. P. Strelka, ed., 1978; V. M. de Aguiar e Silva, 1967 [1984, pp. 331—393]).

It is true, nevertheless, that the activity of the rules of genre in the construction of the text's material scheme is decisive for the artistic construction of the poetic effect (H. Dubrow, 1982). In this, the structural fit of an expression suitable to initial imaginary drives and their symbols reaches all levels of the utterance's linguistic constitution, including the macro-textual and micro-textual rules determining the differential physiognomy of different literary genres and their respective classes of texts. Taken together, they all contribute to the success and suitability of linguistic *expressiveness*, as I have presented it in this theory of the literary text. In terms of my own scheme on the construction of literary and poetic meaning in texts of verbal art, the expressive-rhetorical performative-conceptual rules which determine texts' *generic modes* should be generalized only as a specific subclass of the literary rules of expressiveness (C. Guillén, 1971, pp. 111—130; A. Fowler, 1982, p. 31). Under this category of the theoretical judgment of literary works I include the traditional objectives characterizing the specific and very well-defined theory of literary genres to be found in traditional poetics since antiquity (R. Champigny, 1978, pp. 94—111; M. L. Ryan, 1981 a) and, especially, under the Enlightenment's speculative model of literary aesthetics, insofar as it assumes its canonical form in Hegel's aesthetics (G. Genette, 1977).

Having affirmed the principle of universality as the constitutive guarantee of poetic value, I am here trying to look ahead and clear up, as far as possible, the problems of contiguity and terminological parallelism that may arise in the theory's reformulation, which will include forms of literary meaning. However, this should not be interpreted as an effort to resolve, in the narrow focus and reduced space of this section, the role of a theory of genre in the general structure of the theory of the literary text.

It has frequently been said that the theory of literary genres represents a dead end for historical discussion (F. Lázaro Carreter, 1979, p. 114; B. E. Rollin, 1981, pp. 127–128; J. M. Schaeffer, 1983, p. 3). Of course, at the very least it seems somewhat audacious to think, after the innumerable historical debates that have tried to fix the terms and content of the matter in its most precise details, that there still remains a definitive, *unique*, and *best* solution, entirely new and unknown (T. Todorov, 1976, p. 145). We should not forget that the issue has already occupied the attention of the shrewdest thinkers and specialists (C. F. P. Stutterheim, 1969; K. W. Hempfer, 1973; H. Dubrow, 1982).

The two basic perspectives or essential approaches to the problem are already quite clear: *natural genres* or *historical genres* (A. Fowler, 1971; T. Todorov, 1976; C. Brooke-Rose, 1976; J. M. Schaeffer, 1983; A. Rosmarin, 1985, p. 49). What I am interested in noting and emphasizing here is the immediately evident parallelism between these two basic positions in the theory of genres and those approaches which make up the basic options on the nature of aesthetic meaning, as I have attempted to present them in this book. It goes without saying that my resolute search for a structure of literary and poetic meaning in the successive levels that range from the rhetorico-verbal to the anthropologico-imaginary and universal necessarily favors a *natural* understanding of the system of genres at their inception, compatible with their subsequent historical articulation. The theory naturally requires the location of its universal features for conceiving and representing reality, for the same reasons and along the same path that raised the issue of the poeticity of artistic messages (C. Guillén, 1985, p. 141). At the same time, historico-literary — or, rather, historico-poetic — considerations favor the contemplation of obvious differential features. Let it be clearly understood that the currently predominant role which I concede the investigation of the "natural" conditions of the structure of the genres corresponds to the theoretical emphasis at this moment in the book; but I do not ignore the interest of the complementary historical, pragmatic considerations. In this respect, I do not believe it is reasonable for me to participate in the partisan attitude which leads to the preliminary exclusion of possibilities which has characterized, among others, Alastair Fowler's approach (1982).

In the same way that one cannot negate the historical evidence of the role of perceptive and conventional accords in the constitution of other structures of the literary work which aim to materialize verbal texts' artistic uniqueness, the conjunctural, relatively "unnatural" and asystematic conditions which have given place to the evolution of the generic system of literary expressive, representative and communicative modes are also visible, and even are registered at a more explicitly conscious historical level (W. Ruttkovski, 1968; M. L. Ryan, 1981 a).

I will add another example, one which I have studied in great detail, to the many which have been advanced by the partisans of conventionality and of the exclusively historical nature of the system of genres. The thematic uniqueness of the lamenting and despairing Platonism which sustains courtly amorous poetry and its extension in the specific personal stamp of Petrarch's "dolcestilnovista" model, shaped a dissymmetric structure of a very precise and widely divulged kind. The immediate reasons for this are not to be found in any kind of *natural dialectic* with respect to the logical or traditional formulations of amorous content. The historical influence on literary forms of an entire set of doctrinal treatises — the *trattati d'amore* — represents an immediate and undeniable stimulus, as might also be the case with the peculiar structuralization of the social regime of the troubadours' clientele in the courts of Provence and "dolcestilnovista" Italy (A. García-Berrio, 1985 a, pp. 117—128). This second stimulus, related to the sociology of literary production, logically contributes an important argument to the historical physiognomy of generic evolution. Still, it is far more difficult to verify its influence than that of concrete literary mediations, like those of the *trattati* in our example (C. Guillén, 1985, pp. 165, 197—198).

Clearly, I am not attempting here to accumulate historico-literary facts to prove the historical nature of the evolution of artistic forms, quite opposed, in the unforeseeable dissymmetries of their highly individual final manifestations, to the economic systematicity of "natural" or "simple" forms. As I see it, the problem appears more or less complicated according to the level of observation one initially selects, which in turn depends on how far one wishes to take the results, as is only logical (G. Genette, 1977). The existence of explicit and conjunctural factors — cultural, economic, political —, or simply causal factors among the motives for historical genres' constitutive features is quite obvious (M. Steiman, 1981).

Nevertheless, the degree of tension or modification introduced by the dialectic of historical factors has not been satisfactorily considered, particularly with respect to the structural-systematic constants which regulate the fundamental modes of expressive formulations and the creation of representations of the world. The consideration of the structures of literary genre from the perspective of the minimal formal requirements of maximal structural economy for their constitution reveals the secondary nature — which is to say, the non-essential character — of the historical dialectic among genres (T. Todorov, 1976).

As we approach the structural level corresponding to individualizing features in our examination of particular works, it is only logical that the historical causes of singularity be revealed with greater immediacy and clarity (M. Fubini, 1956). As can be seen, the issue of the theoretical problems posed by literary genres does not modify a point we have made with regard to all of the major questions debated in literary theory — especially literariness and poeticity. Everything depends on the level of reference. Delving more deeply into the essential nature of the principles which establish the historically dialectical and tripartite basic generic divisions is a process of purification which reveals with undeniable clarity the natural reasons for the fundamental system of literary genres organized as textual classes (C. Brooks-Rose, 1976).

The attempt to discover a set of "natural" constants which set forth and explain an underlying initial model that has remained substantially unaltered throughout the historical evolution of literary modes goes hand in hand with the kinds of questions and problems about literary phenomena which are intrinsic to the methodological stance of literary theory. This kind of objective explains and justifies the interest of Goethe and Hegel, and, subsequently, a large number of thinkers focusing on literature as a system, in the taxonomy of the "natural classes" of literary discourse as a less immediately obvious — and hence more attractive and profound — way of explaining the generic format of literary works, compared to the historical-literary approach. Only taxonomies of the explicit are achieved when these types are superficially identified with the most obvious historical divisions. These taxonomies are perfectly legitimate from the perspective of the historian, given the level of explanatory immediacy which interests him, but not from the point of view of the theoretician of literature.

The best evidence for the situation I have just alluded to is the danger of inorganic dispersion and incompleteness which the known historical taxonomies have not managed to escape from, to the great annoyance of their readers. Recall that Goethe's proposal of three "Naturformen" — epic, lyric and dramatic — results from the inorganic nature of his summary of the historical "Dichtarten" — allegory, ballad, cantata, didactic poem, drama, elegy, epigram, epistle, epic, fable, heroic poem, idyll, novel, ode, parody, romance, satire and story, an enumeration of unfounded and suspiciously open historical completeness (C. Guillén, 1985, p. 163). Nor is this lack of organicity remedied in the enumerations of forms and inventories based on historico-typological criteria, put forward and adopted in the discussions most partial to the pragmatic historical approach to the theory of genres like that of Alastair Fowler, who himself admits the reasons behind his particular disposition of the materials are "informal", that is, unjustified (A. Fowler, 1982, pp. 60–74).

Though, in effect, their existence is not purely hypothetical and "theoretical", the difficulty of immediately intuiting the natural genres compared to the more self-evident nature of the historical classes has led to the appearance that the latter are more undeniably valid than the former, an appearance which is, at the very least, misleading. In fact, as long as there is no convincing definition of the criteria which vouch for the "necessity" — that is, the reality, essentiality and "closed" character — of a particular historical classification, one cannot speak of having contributed an objectively useful and realistic taxonomy to the theory of genres. And this kind of historical investigation has not been realized to date. Furthermore, it does not seem likely, in my judgment, for it to ever be accomplished so long as such efforts reflect a strong "antitheoretical" bias, which has been extended to the theory of genre and has been so rightfully decried by Adena Rosmarin (1985, pp. 5—6). The efforts which have most nearly fulfilled these preconditions, in spite of the objections normally leveled against them, are the historical organizations of literature which proceed on the basis of "mixed", historical and theoretical criteria. Among these, the most complete and, for this very reason, the least capricious, is that undertaken by Northrop Frye (1957).

I will make no attempt to discuss the usefulness or reasonableness of attending to the historico-pragmatic verifications of the traditional conception of three natural genres (C. Guillén, 1971, 1985; P. Hernadi, 1972; H. Dubrow, 1982), the natural forms for cognitively and expressively channeling the literary reference of reality's messages. I am above all concerned with not contributing to the state of confusion which was sown recently in the theory of genre. This resulted from an argument seeking to pass off the incorrect perceptions of historico-literary "reality" — due to their being diffuse, ahierarchical, and incomplete — as the most realistic and useful, motivated by the correlative prejudice against the "unrealistic", supposedly entelechical and "theoretical" nature of natural forms. The latter, after all, count on the not insignificant endorsement of having been proposed with substantial uniformity throughout the Renaissance and classical rhetorico-expressive tradition and beyond, in German Idealism's philosophico-aesthetic analyses of literature. This being the case, it would seem that the only objection to the otherwise well-constructed and convincing system of expressive and representative natural genres worth consideration is that it is unable to exhaustively explain all of the performative-historical "forms" and variables of literary expression. A limitation which only applies to those cases of classicist inertia which attempted to propose the system of natural genres as a terminal precept, governing the end products of literary expression, and not as a natural constitutive foundation, a starting point from which the "differences" of historical works are produced by processes of combination and variation.

Once more, it seems we are in the presence of another case in which it is necessary to break with the customary polemical method which has become the accepted view — or bias — of how scientific progression is achieved in the theory of literature. I believe that if the desire and will to locate unexpressed similarities were put into practice before the temptation to exaggerate the degree of proclaimed and apparent differences, it would be possible to find, among the most distant positions, the existence of areas of consensus never before recognized. With this we would achieve a basic balance as profoundly tranquilizing for many as it would be challenging and unassimilable to others. Assuming on the one hand the legitimate need to more deeply examine and develop the historical taxonomies of "forms" and "classes", understood in terms of the variations within the framework of the "family resemblance" Wittgenstein spoke of (A. Fowler, 1982, pp. 40—41), it is also clearly evident that the natural genres are a logical and necessary foundation from which to establish and measure historical classes as "differential" developments (A. Rosmarin, 1985, p. 46).

At the same time, it seems clear that the dialectically closed classical system of natural genres, understood as expressive-representative differences basic to the literary message, is at present far more adequately thought out and formulated, in spite of the healthy need to revise it according to each age's criteria, than the reasonably stable and exhaustive inventory seeking to fill the current needs of a literary history of genres or, more concretely, a poetic history of literary forms. What is perhaps most disturbing to certain determined polemical souls is precisely their eagerness as nonconformists when faced with the clear, definitive and stable situation — stable perhaps since Plato or Hegel — of a reasonably satisfactory theory of natural genres. Which is not by any means meant to imply that the investigation of this starting point, this foundation, is definitively complete and closed, since the "natural" and classical taxonomy of the genres is only a solid beginning, capable for this very reason of yielding excellent results when applied "differentially", to examine the innovations and modifications of historical classes and forms. A device capable, as a result, of defining the dimensions and nature, be it dialectical-natural or conjunctural-pragmatic, of the physiognomy of differential forms.

Only in this manner, from the hierarchical constancy of some principles as "natural" foundations and starting points, can we begin to resolve the difficulties that the theory of literary genres and forms has faced as a fundamental sector of a modernized historical poetics. Currently, the true problem for generic theory does not lie, in my opinion, in the presumed and hypothetical weakness or fancifulness of the traditional system of "natural" genres, which I conceive in terms of a generally reasonable and exhaustive system of the expressive and representative bases for explaining generic "differences". The weakness lies more in the vagueness or absence of morphological criteria capable of proposing a satisfactory or at least economical *level* from which work can begin on defining and setting the boundaries among the generic forms and the non-generic, singular variants of literary production.

For this reason, in order to calm the hypercritical urges of certain critics, I would propose as a model the reasonably pessimistic logic of Lázaro Carreter (1979, p. 112), for whom the historical perspective's lack of a clear discriminative "level", such as we called for earlier, focused only on its own internal observations, translates into the practical inoperativeness of a pragmatic theory of the genres, the ineffective critical sieve of which has always permitted the escape of an alarming plethora of exceptions, collateral forms, dissymmetries of axiology and point of view, and, in the final analysis, purely individual products. Compared to the real dangers this new approach presents, the point we started from is objectively more satisfactory. Hence, what I invoke here as the initial differential principle for a historical poetics of literary forms is the classical taxonomy known as that of "natural genres", whether it ultimately is referred to by its traditional name or by some other form. This taxonomy, which I do not call on vindictively or presume to adopt as an absolutely rigid end product, has acted as an effective balancing pole in the most productive modern efforts to walk the tightrope of literary theory, in the theory of literary genres (C. Guillén, 1971, 1985; T. Todorov, 1976, 1978; G. Genette, 1977, 1979; A. Rosmarin, 1985).

It is above all necessary to move away from the historical distrust towards the natural tripartite articulation of the dualist dialectic (E. Bovet, 1911; P. Hernadi, 1972, p. 13). Still, all of the historical paths carry us to this triad (K. Vietor, 1931, pp. 490–506). A quick review of the secondary and primary sources points to their agreement on this point. It is well illustrated in the different syntheses dealing with the history of these classifications (E. Bovet, 1911; L. Garasa, 1969; J. P. Strelka, ed., 1978; A. Fowler, 1971; K. W. Hempfer, 1973; G. Genette, 1977; P. Hernadi, 1972; J. Huerta Calvo, 1984, pp. 83–139; C. Segre, 1985, etc., to which our own discussions of the matter may be added: A. García-Berrio and M. T. Hernández, 1988, pp. 117–134; A. García-Berrio, 1988, pp. 24–27, 120–129) and also in the very accessible and rich references in the corresponding entries of the monumental histories of Renaissance and modern criticism by Bernard Weinberg and René Wellek, respectively.

In spite of the various points of view they have adopted, the majority of the classifications agree, in the final analysis, on a dialectically tripartite division (C. Guillén, 1971, pp. 390–419; 1985, p. 163). This is the case, both if we follow Hernadi's very complex system of orientation, classifying forms as expressive, pragmatic, structural and mimetic, or if we adopt the more restricted and, because of its greater clarity, effective system of considering the aspects *expressive of the uttering* or those *referential with regard to the utterance*. Recall that it was Plato who distinguished three basic expressive modes in his *Republic*: diegetic, mimetic and mixed (A. Fowler, 1982, pp. 235–236). Each of these corresponds to literary modes as follows: the first, to the poet's direct narration of real past, present or future experiences, realized by means of just one voice; the second, to the imitation of reality through characters' voices; and the third, to the system which blends the first two procedures (Plato, *The Republic*, 1981 edition, 391 d–394 d). This initial tripartite division based on a discourse's expressive mode was perpetuated until the Renaissance in the rhetorical division of the modes of expression: exegematic, dramatic and mixed (K. Weissenberger, 1978, pp. 229–253; A. García-Berrio, 1988, pp. 93–96).

The consolidation of this system was also encouraged by the important process of convergence with other very similar dialectical taxonomies, like that of the *classes of style*: high, middle and low. This particular system corresponded in part with the division of *man's modes of imitation* — better, identical and worse — in Aristotle's *Poetics*, originating with the axiologico-stylistic typologies of Hermogenes, Isocrates, and Theophrastus in Greek rhetoric and reaching its definitive form in Cicero and the *Rhetorica ad Herennium* (A. García-Berrio and M. T. Hernández, 1988, p. 123).

The diffusion of knowledge in the Middle Ages certainly affected, at certain moments and with regard to certain aspects, this process of convergence (H. R. Jauss, 1970; P. Zumthor, 1972, pp. 158—164), justifying the definitive merit of the subsequent Renaissance approaches and Minturno's final success. Nevertheless, the popularization during the intervening centuries of the widely-disseminated "Virgilian wheel" represents a privileged moment in the process of "natural" convergence towards a system of "simple literary forms", exceeding the immediate role of the deductions based on the classes of style and expository modes. By formulating an integrated model of styles, adapted to the nature of the characters — shepherd, farmer, soldier — and the specific themes of Virgil's three works — *Bucolics*, *Georgics* and the *Aeneid* —, the "rota Vergilii" manifested the converging general conviction by which literary discourse is constructed on the basis of enforced taxonomic courses, linked to a triple dialectic, natural and not merely conventionalized in its origins (A. García-Berrio, 1977—1980, I, pp. 99—104; A. Fowler, 1982, p. 291).

In the process of identifying the classes of expression with literary genres as general textual paradigms, the assimilation of the dramatic mode to theatrical literature and of the mixed mode to the epic genre never posed any difficulties, although the process of identifying the exegematic expressive mode with the unitary genre of lyrical poetry was far more laborious (C. Gallavotti, 1928, pp. 354—364; H. Färber, 1936). The assimilation of this final element was late, not definitively completed until 1564, with Sebastiano Minturno's work, *L'arte poetica*. The ambiguousness which Irene Behrens expressed on this point (1940, p. 192), vacillating between attributing the merit categorically to Minturno and favoring Francisco de Cascales' *Tablas poéticas* of 1614, helped to produce the uncommitted pronouncements of subsequent authorities on the matter, as was the case with Claudio Guillén (1971, pp. 390—396) and Gérard Genette (1979, pp. 33—34).

The direct comparison of the texts in question reveals without any doubt which of the two authors was responsible for this development. In 1973, I established Minturno's absolute originality as well as Cascales' *plagiarism* of entire fragments of the Italian's text, including those dealing both with this question and with other less important issues (A. García-Berrio, 1973, pp. 136—170; 1975; 1988, pp. 24—27 and 120—121; A. Fowler, 1982, pp. 236 and 319, notes). Minturno's discovery had been preceded in Renaissance poetics by a number of near misses, especially as far as concerns the unitary conception of lyrical poetry as a genre corresponding to the exegematic form.

Badio Ascensio, Trissino, Robortello and Tasso had all come very close to the solution of integrating the literary genres with the three modes of expression (A. García-Berrio, 1988, pp. 408—415).

Still, it is clear that the parameter of classifying the generic modes according to the dialectical deployment of modes of expression, in spite of the advantage of being immediately and objectively verifiable, which is what served to impose its historical precedence over other criteria, presents the inconvenience of being scarcely illustrative of the profound nature of the literary and the poetic, which is what is of primary interest to modern theoretico-literary speculation. This explains why, as we shall soon see, from Hegel, Schlegel and Vischer onwards, the notion of the genres as being modes for the representation of consciousness, is the conception which has imposed itself on contemporary criticism.

Nevertheless, in the rigorous synthesis which P. Hernadi has elaborated in our own century, there is no shortage of authors who have had recourse, in the opinion of the Hungarian theoretician, with which I do not always agree, to the criteria of the expressive modes which we have been discussing, within what Hernadi denominates "structural" perspectives (1972, pp. 54—83).

Petersen's attempt to bring Goethe's old tripartite scheme up to date stands out as among the purest and least debatable proposals (G. Genette, 1977). Petersen considers the lyric as "a soliloquial representation of a condition", "epos" as "the soliloquial report of a condition", and drama as the "representation of an action in dialogue". Also included among the classifications characteristic of this taxonomical mode is Wolfgang Kayser's well-known proposal, closely influenced in my opinion by Karl Bühler's tripartite scheme of the functions of language. In this scheme, the lyrical manifestation occupies the symptomatic center with the representative angle corresponding to epic communication and the angle of the appellation to the agent belonging to what Kayser characterizes as the "dramatic challenge".

Similarly, we should mention the use T. S. Eliot popularized of the three *voices* as features defining genre: the first voice corresponds to the "expiated soliloquy" of the lyrical; the second, the objectivized manifestation of the personal voice itself, to narration; and the third voice, entirely "alienated", corresponds to drama's expressive form. Hernadi charts other echoes of the old problem of expressive modes, in less evident and convincing terms to my mind, in the literary thought of Percy Lubbock, Roman Ingarden, Franz Stanzel, Norman Friedman and Wayne C. Booth (P. Hernadi, 1972, pp. 62—74). All of which demonstrates that these "structural forms" of the expressive taxonomy continue to be considered valid, particularly when taken together, in recent speculation on the nature and classes of genre, albeit if not usually considered as being at the core of the discussion.

The triple division of genres as it thus developed in the West is only rationally consolidated when the efforts to justify its components culminate; that is, the efforts to justify them not as rigorous categories corresponding to classical expressive and stylistic forms, but rather as natural symbolic modes in the necessary representation of the phenomena of consciousness. As is known, the key formulation of this consolidation belongs to Hegel's poetics (G. W. F. Hegel, 1970, Vol. III, Ch. III). In his poetics, Hegel establishes the lyric as the dialectical component of the *symptomatic-subjective* vision, the epic in its antithetical role within the *objective* perspective on the consciousness of otherness, and the dramatic as a dialectical *synthesis* of both positions (A. García-Berrio and M. T. Hernández, 1988, pp. 50–51). In my judgment, the most interesting contributions to the theory of genres in our century are those that follow the model of establishing the generic textual taxonomies as modes of representation of the dialectical deployment between intimacy and otherness.

Commenting on this feature, Hernadi has sanctioned the penetrating universality of the Hegelian influence in the following terms: "This dialectical tripartition of literature, foreshadowed by Novalis, Schelling and the Schlegel brothers, was to become embalmed and canonized in Friedrich Theodor Vischer's bulky *Ästhetik*. Small wonder that most German critics in the mimetic tradition have rather accepted or somewhat modified than ignored or altogether rejected the time-honored association of genres with an objective, a subjective and a 'synthetic' mode of mimesis" (P. Hernadi, 1972, p. 84). As a result, Hernadi offers a rigorous summary of the thinking on the purification of the categories of subjectivity and objectivity as concepts for the generic classification of literature, spanning from T. A. Meyer and Kate Friedmann with their profound reflections on epic objectivity to Ernst Hirt and his investigation of "dualism" as a natural constitutive category of reality, culminating with Theodor Adorno's well-known reflections concerning the dialectical correlation between literature's subjective and objective components.

Through it all, the combination of criteria set forth in our century by authors like Pierre Kohler or Paul van Thiegem (1938, pp. 95–101) seems to be on the mark, conceiving as they do the variety of genres as performative schemes with the capacity to orient and structure the literary construction of works from the exigencies implied in the contents of represented reality (P. Hernadi, 1972, pp. 21–24). A basic conception not entirely foreign to Emil Staiger's famous approach to the genres (1946). Staiger preferred opening the formal modes of stylistic classes corresponding to the different genres, emphasizing the structural "tonalities" of the form in correspondence with the demands exerted by the contents. He thus obtained diffuse — although not inexact — formulas like that of the subjective-objective "identification" of the lyric, the "distance" *(Abstand)* of the epic, and theater's "conflict" and "problem".

The speculative tradition, which underlies the Hegelian starting point in the dialectical deployment of literary genres, not only permits us to demonstrate the non-conventional roots of the trilogy of natural genres in terms of

3.3. Universality as a Property of Poetic Value

simple attitudes — causal equivalents to Jolles' "simple forms" (1930) —, but also helps facilitate the consideration of the artistically poetic at the natural level, exempt from conventionalizable aesthetic relativism. The expressive and communicative origin of literature is none other than the artistic experience of otherness. That is, art and literature multiply and complete, from their own point of view and with their specific, sentimental-imaginary instruments, the process of exploring and questioning reality which consciousness carries out, beginning with self-awareness, as the first mysterious and intimate articulation of the real constituted in the world (K. Hamburger, 1957). The human tendency towards the discovery and communication of otherness is common, therefore, to thought and art; they differ only in the capacities put into play in each case and, hence, in their results: artistic *images* and intellectual *concepts*.

Lodged in the natural situation underlying artistic experience, the dialectical deployment of the subjective quest in terms of an experience of our discovered or uncovered identity, and of otherness as the awareness of the other as different from the self, different from the *I* (H. Bovet, 1951, pp. 139—140), presupposes the natural division which differentiates between the lyric's symptomatic-expressive *diegesis* and representative-communicative *mimesis*, in terms of the double universe in which the forms of consciousness are manifested. The lyric and drama represent the pure discursive expression of this opposition; while the epos and its modern mode of novelesque narration constitute the synthesis and compromise of lyrical-diegetic reflection with mimetic exterior observation, as in the mix and synthesis of the modes of expression corresponding to the two genres of direct voices, that of the author and those of the characters, the agents, respectively, of the uttering and the utterance.

The interaction between the two modes of dialectical deployment, relative to the form of perception and subjective-objective representation of the world as a dialectic of identity-otherness which corresponds to literary discourse's modes of expression, determines as a result two sufficiently well-founded typologies. Both converge in the ideal ternary scheme as a dialectically reinforced natural category. The pragmatic proposal that has been mobilized, basing itself on the work of E. Staiger (1946), W. V. Ruttkovski (1968) and P. Hernadi (1972) does not seem to be as naturally integratable, because at bottom the appellative-communicative dimension, although without a doubt very important, does not achieve the fundamental unity which the expressive-symptomatic possesses in the classical process of utterance. The results to date of the integration of this third, pragmatic parameter — with fairly vague antecedents in the work of T. A. Meyer, W. Dohrn, and P. Kohler — have occasionally generated a hardly justifiable schematic complexity, as in Hernadi (1972, pp. 152—171). In other cases, it postulates generic categories which are difficult to reconcile with the three traditional classes, like E. Staiger's "artistic" type (1946), a genre defined by the strong pragmatic-actantional presence which potentializes its influence on the reader. For Staiger, this fourth category, the artistic, would determine the differential generic physiognomy of texts in which said form is manifested, and in which, basically, the appellative function of language predominates.

Nor has the recent importance of the receiver's role in literary theory provided the basis for valuable insertions of this third parameter in the theory of genres, at least to date. For J. M. Schaeffer, the awareness of rules of genre forms a part of the "horizon of expectations" which frames and permits the reader to approach a work, and is supposedly constructed, among other principles, according to the network of precepts and norms constituting the natural and historical ideal of genre (J. M. Schaeffer, 1983; A. Fowler, 1982). Genre is thus a decisive part of the "frame" of reception, according to W. D. Stempel (1979) and M. L. Ryan (1979), while for Wolfgang Raible the known nature of a work, as the element integrating corresponding texts to a particular genre, powerfully reduces receivers' freedom to interpret and de-codify it (W. Raible, 1980).

In conclusion, the universality of the anthropologico-imaginary foundations determining the category and sentiment of poeticity as an artistic value does not enter into conflict with the compartmentalization of generic criteria. In the first place, because, as I have said, the rules of genre are principles for the textual formation of the utterance subsequent to and nearer the manifested surface of the text than the anthropological causes of imaginary representation, themselves preceding generic compartmentalization and responsible for creating the matrix of poetic values in art. And finally, because, as we have just seen, the differential generic specificities correspond, in turn, to the universal dialectical deployment of natural ways of considering and textually formulating expressive tension, moving between identity and otherness as forms of consciousness.

3.3.3. The "Natural" Limitation of Historical Literary Genres

The question of the *naturalness* of the principles of generic organization in the basic situation characterizing poetic knowledge and feeling, is a fundamental area of interest affecting the perspective of the theoretician of literature and of his or her particular speculative discourses. The natural and necessary nature of the generic division is manifested especially in the quantitatively *limited* or *closed condition* of the resulting classes. In this sense, the traditional fixing of the number of generic divisions at three would not turn out to be the continued maintenance of a whim or a numerical superstition conventionalized by tradition, but rather the *natural* result of the dialectical deployment originating in a dual polarity, both archetypal and "natural" structures in the deployment of the human forms of representing reality.

On the other hand, the literary historian pursues an understanding of the formulation of the texts he examines with the notion of their being realities differentiated one from another and ultimately becoming unique products. The two visions, that of the historian and that of the theoretician, are complementary, when not antagonistic. The historian is not interested in delving into the final natural causes in the genesis of artistic products, but rather in describing, verifying and understanding the circumstantial differences among the same, which is what ends up yielding him a differentiated ordering of entities along the timeline of historical succession (A. Fowler, 1982). In this manner, the traditional epic and the modern novel, to cite the most characteristic and familiar examples, are of more interest to the historical mind as differentiated realities — the progressive loss of versified expression, transformation of the "high mimetic" epic heroism into the bourgeois normalcy of novelesque characters, etc. — than in all that both forms have in common with regard to their manner of conceiving and expressing the mimesis of objective reality. These are shared features which permit us to consider both as historical modalities of the same literary genre, that of mixed mimetic-fictional narration (other examples of this kind of historical modification are to be found in A. Fowler, 1982, and C. Guillén, 1985).

As a result of this double manifestation of the scientific-literary mind, which has been responsible for the familiar but problematic distinction between *historical* and *theoretical* literary genres in contemporary genre theory (T. Todorov, 1976; G. Genette, 1977; J. M. Pozuelo Yvancos, 1988, pp. 69–80), the natural genres are maintained at their most restricted and traditional number of three. The attempts to vary this scheme are few and far between: four polarities in certain formulations, either resulting from the pragmatic effort (W. V. Ruttkovski, 1968; P. Hernadi, 1972, pp. 156–171), or from the inclusion of a fourth genre, a "didactic" one in the case of Herbert Seidler or Ruttkovski himself, "essayistic" in that of Claudio Guillén (1971, p. 114). Of course, such a fourth genre is difficult to reconcile from the perspective of dialectic parallelism. Staiger also attempted this approach with the addition of a fourth "artistic tonality" (1946). On the other hand, there have been proposals reducing the dialectical triad to two groups, chosing not to pollute the radical contrast of subjective-identity and objective-otherness with subsequent differentiations, like K. Hamburger's scheme opposing the lyrical to the narrative (K. Hamburger, 1957; P. Hernadi, 1972, pp. 46–53).

Those given to classifying historical genres have not fixed the number of their minimal or basic entities. This purifying, "essentializing" operation is repugnant to the historicist mind. Its interest lies in identifying differences, without locating or hierarchicalizing their genetic origin in a particular strata, surface or deep, of textual structure. Those who defend the existence of so-called historical genres have until now limited themselves to locating individual variants, almost always superficial and adjectival, and to proposing them as numbing objections against those who insist on the existence of deep typological constants proclaiming the underlying community of origins over the divergent plurality of end products (B. E. Rollin, 1981).

The defense of the so-called historical genres takes the obviousness of its intended aim as its starting point (A. Rosmarin, 1985, p. 47), but this obviousness, given what I have just been saying, does not uproot or deprive the opposing, naturalist position of its attractiveness. Beyond the evidence that secondary generic differences exist and evolve (A. Fowler, 1971, pp. 199—216; 1982), the reasoned disarticulation of the classical criteria underlying and organizing the dialectical theory of the genres as logical developments of natural principles and origins has rarely been produced. I believe the "hydrostatic model" Fowler ironically alludes to as a preface to his defense of historical empiricism can itself be positively and reasonably illustrative: "There are those who have been tempted to conceive a system of genres based practically on a hydrostatic model, as though the total substance remained constant, subject to redistributions" (A. Fowler, 1979).

I see nothing wrong with adopting and assimilating this "total substance", which Fowler refers to ironically as the logical principle of cohesion, determining by its natural base the possibilities for dialectical differentiation among the genres, without this transforming the cohesive control into a system of rigidly demarcated rules (A. Fowler, 1982). In any case, these rules cannot limit or determine the terminal possibilities of individual historical development, since these end products consist of secondary transformations and complementary modifications, governed by historical chance. Genre rules act upon the antecedent mass of that "total substance," inherent to the nature of the literary and poetic event, which, as such, also regulates the essential deployment of its basic forms of manifestation. In this sense, the theoretician of literature will not be likely to share Fowler's prejudices, since the simplicity he attacked should not be confused with the non-problematical simplicity of the tangible. All the more so when one of the most undeniable properties of the traditional scheme of natural genres is the clear "simplicity" of the logic which sustains it, a logical simplicity which has given rise to the majority of the attacks on the supposed *a priori* arbitrariness of the natural system of genres (C. Guillén, 1971, p. 392).

There is no doubt that upon delving deeply into the radical space of poeticity's natural causes, the theoretician of literature must renounce the ease of moving in that world of tangible evidence so favored by historical positivism. But if the theoretician fears and distrusts the only partially immediate and verifiable nature of his hypotheses and surrenders to his anxiety, his particular activity will be severely threatened. It is also worthwhile asking those who, like the demanding Fowler, exaggerate the rigor of their reservations, whether or not the historical process of the fundamental convergence of criteria for the theory of genres, which, as we have already seen, spans the period of time from Plato to the great German Idealists, does not represent a "firm" enough historical base for the theory, one Fowler himself either unjustly silences or ignores. In the case of his analysis, contributors to the theory of genre as noted as Hegel and F. Schlegel do not merit a single mention. Moreover, the vague discussion of Goethe appears to come directly from Hernadi's summary (A. Fowler, 1982, p. 241).

Speculative work on the theory of natural genres neither excludes nor detracts from the legitimate historiographical activity of discovering, verifying and explaining the production of historical varieties. Far to the contrary, it is in this direction, I believe, that the theory of genre and even the general theory of literature itself can expect its advances to be channeled. To the extent that, once one abandons the simple programatic proclamation of principles, absolute exclusions between the historical and theoretical perspectives are usually not to be found. A characteristic example is B. E. Rollin's widely disseminated study, "Nature, Convention and Genre Theory" (1981), an organizational effort that manifests its reservations towards the uncertain "theory of genres" and does not attempt to hide, like Fowler, its predisposition towards centering itself on what is tangible in the historical task of "classification". Still, Rollin's criticism of "Aristotelian realism", which, according to him, only engenders a "naturalist" attitude that does not contribute any procedure for judging and resolving disagreements, takes note of the fact that its radicalization would degenerate into the opposite conventionalist extreme, making any form of mediation impossible.

This kind of fear and mistrust is always a matter of the time and culture in which these thinkers moved, a situation that is incompatible with the traditional and actual needs of literary theory which, insofar as it is a speculative option, must without fail assume the hypothetical risks from which it has historically extracted — and currently continues to extract — its most productive deductions (A. Rosmarin, 1985, pp. 5—6).

Even in the most radical critical formulations on the "theoretical" or "historical" theory of genres, like that Jean-Marie Schaeffer formulated proceeding from the suspicious pragmatism of the aesthetics of reception, there always exists an opening for compromise which permits us not to discard as useless the formula for the tripartite natural typology. In his study, "From the Text to the Genre: Notes on a Generic Problem", he begins by leveling very drastic accusations against Hegel's "social ontology", Croce's "nominalism", and the "dualist Romantic ontology" manifested in F. Schlegel's work (J. M. Schaeffer, 1983). But he ends up invoking, in agreement with Hempfer's stance as he understands it (1973, p. 2), the vague principle of Piaget's "constructivism". Such a device is obviously intended to be used to find a mediated course of action that saves us from the risk presented by the impossible "empirical" verification of naturalist hypotheses. In addition, it is an attempt to control the dispersion of all theoretical criteria by the extreme monism of historical empiricism, threatening not only the theory of genres but literary theory itself (K. W. Hempfer, 1973, p. 271).

As a theoretical model or an initial general program this invocation of constructivism can, in effect, be reasonable. One only has to notice the authorities — W. V. O. Quine and W. Stegmüller — that Schaeffer cites in support of his own postulates to infer the philosophical and methodological reach his ideas have. In any case, what has been missing until now is the effective construction of a theory of genres which identifies and relates the extent of historical tensions in order to test the true elasticity of natural forms. This pragmatic ideal of realist mediation, outlined as a step forward by Todorov and embraced by Genette, has guided my own efforts in this theory of the literary text but has not been tackled by authors like Schaeffer and Rollin, even in its most schematic form.

B. E. Rollin's starting point, based on biological taxonomies, explicitly recognizes the need to break with the immobilizing atmosphere of mistrust into which historicist empiricism has immersed the theory of genres (B. E. Rollin, 1981). But beyond the postulation of principles like those Rollin proposed, a mediative theory has rarely been satisfactorily undertaken to date.

Two of the more widely disseminated and authoritative treatments of the question, those authored by T. Todorov and G. Genette, respectively, have coincided in recognizing the need for mediation. In 1976, Todorov presented a strong case defending the reality of natural genres, their existence serving to control, as systems of general rules, the degree of dispersion and violation of historical variables. Among his clever affirmations along these lines, he writes: "That the work should disobey its genre does not make it non-existent; we are tempted to say: to the contrary ... because the transgression, in order to exist, needs a law, precisely that law which will be transgressed" (T. Todorov, 1976; A. Rosmarin, 1985, p. 47). This historical codification of the genres is consolidated based on the natural features of discursive properties: "A literary genre or not, it is nothing more than that codification of discursive properties." It is worth keeping in mind that, at the time he made these claims, Todorov found himself in the midst of the structural-universalist fervor which crystallized in his *Grammaire du Décaméron*. The program for investigating the natural-discursive properties constituting genre announced in this first work has since been discontinued, providing one of the more well-founded reasons for Christine Brooke-Rose's criticisms of Todorov (1976).

In spite of the defects and limitations of his bibliographical treatment of historical sources, it can well be argued that Gérard Genette's contributions represent the clearest and most thoughtful actualization of a program for the future of generic theory, which will involve the painstaking investigation of the development of the historical genres as events of conjunctural actualization — dissymmetric, discontinuous, lacunal, etc. — of the discursive classes of natural genres. Genette's effective synthesis makes a direct quote useful and economical: "... I do not in any way pretend to deny literary genres every kind of *natural* and transhistorical foundation: on the contrary, I consider as ambiguous evidence of this natural foundation the existence of an existential stance, of an *anthropological scheme* (Durand), of a *mental disposition* (Jolles), of an *imaginative scheme* (Mauron), or, as we might currently say, of a properly epic, lyrical and dramatic *sentiment* ... I only deny that a generic product can be defined solely in terms which exclude the historic ... but no instance is entirely determined by history" (G. Genette, 1977, and 1979, p. 420). Genette's appraisal of the situation is a model of balanced common sense which, in spite of its obviousness, has not customarily imposed itself on recent theoretical extremisms.

There are many reasons for the recent preference for the accessible but dispersive criteria of historical origin. Some are as ancient as those based on the example of Aristotle's *Poetics*, with its indiscriminate reference en bloc, at the beginning of the work, to generic modes (1447a 13—16), jumbling together the great entities — epic and tragedy — with minor species of imitation, like flute and lyre music and the art of mimes and dancers (A. García-Berrio, 1988, pp. 408—409). Aristotle's historico-empirical position at this point of his presentation represents an option, a non-polemical starting point which has attracted numerous authors down to our own times (F. Lázaro Carreter, 1979).

A second source of adherence to the historical principle originates in modern literature and art (A. Fowler, 1982, pp. 26, 32—55; A. Rosmarin, 1985, p. 7), with their tendency to eliminate conventional barriers and distinctions. As Todorov recalls, following Maurice Blanchot's profound diagnosis, each work of modern literature, in its "process of undoing" or deracination, effects the negation of systematic principles. In this regard, the principles of literary genre appear among the most classic, conventional and preceptive and, hence, as immediate targets for negation (T. Todorov, 1976). Of course, as Claudio Guillén has shrewdly pointed out, the modern consequences of this process, especially the most evidently intentional and pragmatic, have not always turned out to be very interesting (C. Guillén, 1985, pp. 177—179).

The third set of factors contributing to the vogue of historicism, not unrelated to the previously cited stimulus, is internal to the physiognomy of literary theory in recent times. I am referring to the widely held and radical mistrust felt towards traditional idealistic poetics' seemingly *a priori* and supposedly "natural" and universal categories. The expressive and conceptual principles traditionally invoked in the theory of literary genres are a favorite target of this bias (A. Fowler, 1982). Concretely, the attempt to discredit the concept of "natural" genres can be traced back, as is the case with so many of the matters I have been examining in this book, to the break with the idealism of Romantic aesthetics initiated by structuralist poetics, yielding generally opposing paradigms. The paradigms of structuralist poetics, in turn, gradually disintegrated through the exhaustion of said poetics, as represented by the various poststructuralist trends.

Nevertheless, from the perspective I have adopted in this theory of the literary text, I have no doubt as to the legitimacy and necessity of comparing and integrating the natural scheme of universal features, founded on the basic structure of literature's poetic function, with the variety of its historical realizations, without giving in to *a priori* reasoning. In essence, I am advocating a critical-literary program which joins theoretical intuition with historical verification as the most essential task facing contemporary literary theory.

As I have already mentioned, up to the present there have been very few projects even partially tailored to this task, although the need and viability of such endeavors has been unanimously recognized by the keenest observers, like Genette and Todorov. Once the coupled method for studying generic categories is fixed — involving, on the one hand, the "empirical observation" which conducts us through the evidence regarding historical genres and, on the other, the "abstract analysis" of the natural or theoretical genres — we can proceed to empirically examine the "recurring discursive properties" for elaborating and, at a second, more speculative stage of the system, "codifying these properties of discussion". At the end of said process, we will have closed, according to Todorov, the hermeneutical circle by which we can recognize the essential and secondary properties of genre in the real structures of historical texts. In this way, we identify the first, most radical and universal properties with those elements determining the general structure of natural genres, which does not imply the renunciation of Todorov's interpretative ideal (T. Todorov, 1976).

We can conclude, therefore, that the exclusion of any of the two series of data — historical or natural and theoretical —, which have recently been approached with reciprocally restrictive criteria in mind, is entirely arbitrary. On the one hand, it is absolutely necessary to historically confirm the maintenance and modification of the constitutive elements attributed to the great natural genres. Their evolution and the physiognomy of the modifications this development introduces offer a model for fixing exactly what is modified and what remains unchanged in the course of history (A. Rosmarin, 1985, pp. 44−47). But it is also clear that the purely empirical and unilateral observation of the modified features — and not of those which remain unchanged, which might tentatively be the generic universals — deprives the artistic work of one of the essential elements we turn to in order to affirm its transcendental value, while it does nothing to improve our historical diagnostic capacity, as Lázaro Carreter indicates: "A more closely-knit network of genres is not going to greatly facilitate the endeavor to understand the concrete work, which will always find a hole in the scheme through which it can escape" (1976, p. 115).

As with any other phenomena of language, every concrete actualization of the rules of the paradigm — in this case the paradigm of the genres — produces unique and relatively impure realizations of the perfect rules of the system. Hempfer emphasizes the fact that the model relating language to speech or the utterance can be extended to explain many events involving

3.3. Universality as a Property of Poetic Value

the correlation genre/text (K. W. Hempfer, 1973, pp. 222—223; W. D. Stempel, 1979). And, to continue with possible similarities within linguistic theory (E. Stankiewicz, 1984), numerous mechanisms illustrate the generic-specific gradation; for example, those comparing phonological entities with phonetic realizations, etc. Hence, we are dealing with an interdependence in which neither element can be ignored, as Christine Brook-Rose argues intelligently when censuring the widespread anti-idealist bias manifesting itself in the recent positivist stance of poststructuralism against any evidence supporting a claim for the existence of theoretical genres (C. Brooke-Rose, 1976).

Although I do not share her interest in the automatism of future diagnoses of literary phenomena, which can be inferred from the structure of theoretical genres, and myself prefer to continue considering them "natural" as opposed to "theoretical", there is no doubt that Brooke-Rose's proposals are stimulating. This is the case, not only in relation to historiographical analyses of the past, but also in regard to their immediate deductive consequences for the natural principles of permanence in terms of generic universals.

In the sphere of proposals for a program of generic investigation, which a future version of this theory of the literary text will undertake to discuss at greater length in studying forms of meaning, almost all of the efforts which have been made to naturalize the dialectical tripartite organization of genres and to lodge it in the analogy to anthropologically-rooted taxonomical constructions appear to me to be positive and promising. Although I am aware of the reticence to accept this naturalization and the widespread efforts in the opposite direction in recent years (A. Fowler, 1982), I am encouraged by the overwhelming multiplication of typological constructions, very deeply rooted in man's essential vision and experience of the world and corresponding to the triple taxonomical scheme of literary genres.

Of course, many such efforts fall short of being entirely convincing. Consider, for example, E. Bovet's well-known scheme establishing correspondences between the lyric and youth, the epic and mature adulthood and drama and old age. Initiatives of this type may at least involve some kind of metaphorical approximation to the nature of genres, but Bovet's does not stand up as a model of historical successiveness which attempts to establish the correspondences between discourse and correlative stages of life (P. Hernadi, 1972, pp. 9—14). Other attempts to relate the generic scheme to a tripartite model based on man's *vision of the world*, like those of T. Spoerri, R. Petsch and L. Beriger, also turn out to raise objections (P. Hernadi, 1972, pp. 15—17). Among them, M. Heidegger's familiar scheme stands out in terms of the anthropological medullarity of the *tertium comparationis*. Also traceable in the theoretico-literary writings of J. Kleiner, Heidegger's argument links lyrical expression with the sense of the past, the epic with that of the present and the dramatic with that of the future (P. Hernadi, 1972, pp. 89—91). Finally, there is Kenneth Burke's contribution, based on the dialectic among *yes*, *no* and *perhaps*.

Closer to our own times, more convincing and, in my opinion, more illustrative, are those other forms of tripartite parallelism which claim to reveal the predominance of certain psychological forms to explain the genetic peculiarities of each of the genres. These theories range from the now antiquated argument R. Hartl proposed, defining the lyric as emotional, the epic as an expression of imaginative activity and the dramatic as mobile, to E. Staiger's (1946) more recent and more well-known hypothesis, indicating sensual, intuitive and conceptual elements as predominating in lyric, epic and drama, respectively. These various stimuli are collected in Hernadi's persuasive synthesis, with its well-known tripartite division of literature into *ecumenical works*, characterized by the "intentional totality of their vision", *synesthetic works*, characterized by the "experienced identity of action and vision", and *concentrical works* (P. Hernadi, 1972, p. 182).

If I echo these proposals for parallelism, it is not because I consider them entirely suitable for precisely defining the genres, but, as I have already said, because almost all of them base the anthropological foundations of the ternary dialectic on the fundamental categories and forms of man's representation of the world. In this sense, not even the application of the three regimes of symbolic imagination developed by Durand, whose ideas I have used so extensively in my own discussion of the imaginary definition of the poetic, seems adequate for defining a taxonomy of the genres, at least in the form Durand proposed to accomodate them (G. Durand, 1971). The assimilation of the epic to the diurnal and the nocturnal to the lyric is not convincing, while the location of the novelesque at the moment of transition between the other two regimes is even less so.

It is true, however, that in those instances in which the typologies of simple forms cannot be accomodated to any natural scheme of organization, we are prone to be invaded by an inevitable sense of these schemes' lack of rigor or justification, at least as far as the number and nature of their proposed elemental generic forms. In the case of André Jolles' famous classification which, moreover, at the time constituted a very worthwhile effort to deepen the examination of literature in terms of anthropological universals, the author followed as his constitutive principle the path that ranges from language to literature and observed in the course of comparison, the repetition of one phenomena which becomes enriched as it passes to a higher level, and the fact that the force constituting and defining forms entirely dominates the system, elevating itself to an ever higher level. In his analysis, Jolles reveals the strictly natural level pertaining to some simple forms which are only secondarily and historically literary but whose natural cause is located in the linguistic nature of primary expressive gestures: forms which are produced in language and which proceed by language's own labor, so to speak, without the intervention of a poet (A. Jolles, 1930, pp. 17–22).

Jolles' argument on the universal elementariness of his generic forms is not any less convincing when he displaces his consideration of causal foundations from the "verbal gesture" to the mental disposition or "anthropological gesture". On the other hand, the historical development of each of these "language gestures" involves the transformation of the simple forms as initial seeds through their association with variables which adhere to them over time, sometimes yielding an aggregative state in which it is difficult to recognize the initial gesture. Nevertheless, the original gesture still maintains its nuclear nature, making it possible to identify the various literary forms with the radical poetic myth which supports them (A. Jolles, 1930, pp. 62–66).

In spite of all of the elements of depth and universal interest undoubtedly present in Jolles' attractive construction, the absence of an explicit articulation, be it dialectical or of any other logical kind, capable of explaining the causes producing the numerical restriction and reciprocal need for the elemental forms, detracts from the persuasiveness of his efforts, exemplary in so many other respects, to uncover the universal constitution of classes of literary texts (A. Fowler, 1982, p. 151).

The "natural", conceptual and expressive nature of the triad of theoretical genres justifies itself by its very clear rationality, in the terms in which it was explained by the German Enlightenment, from Hegel to F. Schlegel, without forgetting Goethe's influential contribution (G. Genette, 1977). The various successive demonstrations of the same point to be found in the bibliography of our own century, especially all those which establish parallelisms with other fundamental dialectical triads on the basis of man's view of the world and anthropological constitution, have contributed less to the doctrinal enrichment of a system already well-described in its natural coordinates (C. Guillén, 1971; W. D. Stempel, 1972; R. Champigny, 1978; M. Steiman, 1981). The only potentially fruitful task left pending, as I have been arguing here, is an unbiased critical examination of the historical variables; one which does not lose sight of their relationship to the well-consolidated dialectical scheme of three basic, expressive and representative generic modes.

These criteria are certainly met in the four famous essays Northrop Frye collects in his book *Anatomy of Criticism*. This fact undoubtedly helps explain the ambivalent judgments cast on this great theoretico-historical literary synthesis. In general, critics acknowledge Frye's superior effort of historical assimilation, while showing themselves more critical of his categories and theoretical decisions (C. Brooke-Rose, 1976). Personally, faced with Frye's monumental literary culture, I feel closer to those who openly praise the breadth of his "universalizing ambition" (P. Hernadi, 1978 a) than to those who relativize or ignore the importance of his efforts to achieve a very attractive synthesis of history and theory (G. Genette, 1977; A. Fowler, 1982, pp. 241–243).

In contrast to the monumental dimensions of his historico-critical synthesis, the arguments Frye raises for the "naturalization" of the historical literary materials do not in principle rest on any more credible bases than many similar metaphorical proposals. This is my opinion of the attempt to identify the four fundamental *mythoi* in his system with a set of categories rooted in the anthropologico-imaginary as much as in the annual rhythm of the seasons. Recall the four basic forms or stages in the deployment of the *mythoi*: comedy is identified with spring (N. Frye, 1957 [1968, pp. 163—182]), the "romance" with summer (pp. 186—205), tragedy with fall (pp. 206—223) and, finally, satire with winter (pp. 223—239). Overall, an assimilation with many attractive elements, but which generally appears quite forced in many cases, due in large part to the difficulty of accomodating the historical materials to the categories, never intersubjectively identifiable, of the four metaphorical references (R. Scholes, 1976, p. 119; P. Hernadi, 1972, pp. 106—107).

Frye's attempts at anthropological structuralization seem far more assimilable when he explores the most essential and spatial forms of categories in his generic organization of textual classes. This is what, in my judgment, the positive and negative tendency towards an ascending and descending generic "deployment" represents, permitting his four arguments to be incorporated therein: comedy and "romance" corresponding to the series of positive and ascending forms, irony and satire to the series of negative and descending forms. At its foundation, one can also sense the influence of the Aristotelian classification relating to the means of imitation of literary characters: better than, worse than and equal to those in reality (Aristotle, *Poetics*, 1448a 15—16; A. García-Berrio, 1988, pp. 58—59).

Recall how Frye directs his *mythoi* along the lines of the Aristotelian moral *pattern*. Frye conceives *myth* as the sublime and idealized form of the hero's imaginary representation, superior to common men and his circumstantial environment. The protagonist of the romance is also superior to men and his environment, but as a matter of degree rather than absolutely; that is, we recognize his moral superiority within an otherwise basic natural equality with normal men, an equality mythic heroes are always beyond.

The hero at the lowest degree of superiority within the ascendant and positive deployment of literary modes of invention, which Frye denominates *high mimetic*, is "superior in degree to other men, but not to his natural environment". The protagonist most favored by epic and tragedy in the majority of their historical expressions, he "has authority, passions and powers of expression far greater than ours, but what he does is subject both to social criticism and to the order of nature" (N. Frye, 1957 [1968, pp. 33—34]). When the literary character does not demonstrate his superiority to other beings or to his environment, the spatial development of the mimetic identification is fixed at its referential point of origin at absolute zero. This applies to the characters of the *low mimetic* mode, that is, the characters of realist fiction. Finally, the descending, inferior or negative stage of this process of the spatial deployment of literary modes of representation is occupied by forms of *irony* and *satire*. In this mode, characters are "inferior in power or intelligence to ourselves, so that we have the sense of looking down on a scene of bondage, frustration, or absurdity" (N. Frye, 1957 [1968, p. 34]).

My admiration for Frye's stimulating effort at historico-theoretical assimilation and systematization stops short of encompassing his attempts to impose the organization of his speculative categories as a diachronic outline of historical successiveness (A. Rosmarin, 1985, p. 32). This is true with regard to many of the historical facts he mobilizes. For example, immediately following the preceding systematization of modes, when Frye forcibly attempts the construction of the evolutive parallelism of said modes in literature's historical stages (N. Frye, 1957 [1968, pp. 34—35]). All the same, to be fair, I think it is essential, when faced with constructs as complex and ambitious as Frye's scheme, not to allow our general judgments of the same to stray excessively towards petty objections. We should keep in mind that, in the scientific explanation of culture, assimilative synthetic efforts are as important as is the critical readjustment of the deficiencies of such systems, a process of readjustment which is only natural to the creation of such "frames of reference". But without the breadth of vision of great syntheses, the source of inevitable elasticity and capaciousness, scientific reflection on culture would disperse into insignificant and atomized particularizations. Not to mention the specific feature of this kind of effort represented by the depth and wealth of literary culture brought into play, factors hard to equal in Frye's case.

Frye's powerful talent for synthetic penetration is not easily frustrated, even when it develops its arguments on the basis of very problematically established categories. It is well-known that, within the same theory of modes from which the *mythic* varieties just examined are deduced, Frye also discusses another group of modes denominated *thematic*. In this, Frye is developing the contrast between *mythos* and *dianoia* (μύθος and διάνοια), tragedy's "qualitative parts", easily extended to the structure of any narrative work. The definition of *dianoia* — a term not at all clear in the exegesis of Aristotle's *Poetics* (A. García-Berrio, 1988, p. 212) — is fairly simplistic: "The best translation of *dianoia* is, perhaps, *theme*, and literature with this ideal or conceptual interest may be called thematic" (N. Frye, 1957 [1968, p. 52]).

The Aristotelian use of the term *dianoia*, not very clearly defined in the fragment of the *Poetics* where the qualitative parts of tragedy are enumerated and described (1456a 36—37), refers literally to the *meaning* of the text's utterance — something entirely different from *theme* —, corresponding to the artistic signifier of the work, which Aristotle denominates *lexis*. In narrative works, the "theme", in the strictest sense, is determined by the synthesis of the action, *mythos*, and of the meaning, *dianoia*. Thus, it does not correspond, as Frye would have it, exclusively to the sector of conceptual content, independent from the characters' actions (A. García-Berrio, 1988b, pp. 211—222).

Still, basing himself on a categorical basis so superficially intuited, Frye deduces one of his most illustrative taxonomies. Thus, he opposed two great units. The first consists of the literary "mimetic cathartic" utterance, based on the psychological mechanism of "distancing", depending on the *mythos* and the modes of realistic invention. In the second, he locates the utterance "processed in *stasis*", founded on the general sense of "abysmalization" and depending on the lyrical predominance of *dianoia* (N. Frye, 1957 [1968, pp. 52—57]).

What bestows this dual comparison of fundamental literary modes — also proposed by K. Hamburger around the same time as Frye — with greater depth and, thereby, justifies it, is, once again, the essential nature of the imaginary-anthropological foundation on which the great Canadian critic attempted to lodge technicisms and formulas belonging to the Aristotelian tradition. For Frye, "the *mythos* is the *dianoia* in movement; the *dianoia* is the *mythos* in *stasis*", a formula in which an absolute representation of the spatio-temporal play of imaginary and existential coordinates of human experience is primary. Or, as Hernadi explains it in his exegesis of Frye's thought regarding these points in *Anatomy of Criticism*, *dianoia* keeps the work united in a pattern of meaning, thus being a representation of the spatio-simultaneous block, compared to which *mythos* is opposed as the development in the flow of time of meaning as a form of succession (P. Hernadi, 1972, pp. 140—141).

In short, Frye's generic taxonomies reveal their profound and necessary reasonings upon testifying to their solidarity with a radical anthropologico-imaginary understanding of literary meaning, or what Claudio Guillén calls the "most complex and paradigmatic mental spaces" (1985, p. 150). Recall how in his "Polemical Introduction" to *The Anatomy of Criticism* Frye alerts his readers to the "unconscious" nature of the majority of the facts which form the baggage of experience of the theoretician of literature (N. Frye, 1957 [1968, p. 11]). And, further ahead, he insists on the "impersonal nature of imaginary works"; that is, their universal nature in the sense which we have been speaking of: "The work of imagination presents us with a vision, not of the poet's personal greatness, but of something impersonal and far greater: the vision of a decisive act of spiritual freedom, the vision of the recreation of man" (1957 [1968, p. 94]). All of this because the universality of literary utterances is not only the result of their capacity for symbolization based on integral forms of present reality, but is achieved and realized from the conscious and unconscious psychological depths which the artist commits to his work as forms of *desire*.

3.3.4. The Universal Structure of the Artistic Text: From Diversity to Singularity

The scheme of the literary text's constitutive and descriptive levels which I have set forth in this book is reproduced in the characterization of plastic works. It is no mere coincidence that the humanist theory of the visual arts, beginning especially with Alberti's famous systematization, bases itself on the scheme of rhetorical parts — *inventio*, *dispositio* and *elocutio* — for tracing the principle moments of a theory of painting: *rudimenta*, corresponding to *inventio*, and *pictura*, related to *elocutio*. Moreover, the subsequent division of *pictura* into *circumscriptio*, *compositio* and *lumina* corresponds even more precisely to the tripartite division of rhetorical parts (A. Chastel, 1959; A. García-Berrio and M. T. Hernández, 1988a, pp. 24—25). This fact naturally testifies to the superior tradition and development the disciplines of rhetoric and poetics possessed when the time came to produce an initial theory of painting; but it also corroborates the reasonableness of establishing such parallels.

In the plastic text, as in the verbal text, what is of first importance is the set of *pre-meaningful* features: brushstrokes, glaze, gestures of pattern and design preceding any constructed meaning. That is to say, Martinet's famous division concerning the *double articulation* of language is fulfilled in a very similar way in the constituents of the structure of both kinds of texts. As happens in the case of the specifically artistic *intensionalization* of the pre-meaningful elements of the second linguistic articulation, which acquire an autonomous meaningful value according to the effects of poetic endodeixis (R. Jakobson, 1960) proper to secondary systems of symbolization (J. Lotman, 1970, Ch. I), so, too, in the case of painting, the aesthetic effect of these pre-meaningful forms is important for establishing the poetic value of plastic works. In the same sense, the aformalism of modern painting plays above all on the endodeictic capacity of said entities of secondary articulation (A. García-Berrio and M. T. Hernández, 1988a, pp. 44—45, 177—178).

The transformation of the meaningful neutrality of plastic materials by means of poetic intensionalization is already classically understood in the use of different materials: fresco, tempera, oil, acrylic, wax, wood panel, copper, canvas, etc. A characteristic example might be the role as pre-meaningful components played by the different layers of paint superimposed in glazing. Many of the greatest revolutions in painting stem from the modification of such techniques and materials. But it is modern art which has discovered and made use of the revolutionary potential of all of these effects, with the widespread use of such techniques as "collage" and "grattage" and the reworking of the textures of the base, or of paper and layers of paint, in order to formulate new aesthetic proposals based on the materials' own capacities for suggestion. For example, the so-called material abstraction practiced by Dubuffet, Burri and Tapies, relies heavily on the autonomous, endodeictic meaningful effects of materials traditionally considered inert in the creation of painting's meaningful effects (A. García-Berrio and M. T. Hernández, 1988a, pp. 89—92).

Ascending semiotic levels according to their complexity and degree of responsibility for meaning, we can perceive the extension of the parallelism between painting and poetry, even at the highest strata. Both the verbal and plastic texts in their respective systems of symbolization and communication participate in the differentiation between syntax and semantics, making it possible, at each level, to distinguish between macrostructural and microstructural problems.

For example, the development of iconography and iconology since Aby Warburg and Erwin Panofsky exploits the parallelism in the relationship between morphological entities and the unitary textual set. In effect, the symbolic construction of the meaningful references in classical art counted on the morphological value sustaining certain isolated forms, as differential constituents of the global meaning. Thus, certain attributes enable the identification of Saint Peter — keys, for example —, independent and apart from the rest of the different morphological elements added in concrete individual variants.

With the liberation of meaning in modern art, plastic morphology has seen its potential realized in revolutionary formulas for variation. In this manner, the fertile proliferation of its formal morphematic constituents underlies the protean wealth of Picasso's art in his various stages. A genre like that of the cubist still life, in the work of Léger, Braque, Gris or Picasso himself, consecrates the morphological aesthetic capacity of the work's individual components — bottles, mandolins, pieces of paper, pages from newspapers, etc. — which, thanks to the cubist geometry, maintain a powerful degree of their substantive manifestation, in addition to contributing to and participating in the general, global constructive effect of the overall representation. In this same order of things, the contemporary Spanish painter Luis Gordillo constructs the surprising plasticity of his work through the unstable flow of inventive originality and renovation the morphologico-formal constituents of his compositions possess (A. García-Berrio and M. T. Hernández, 1988 a, pp. 45—46, 179—180).

But in classical as in modern painting, the fundamental path of artistic perfection lies in the *syntactical construction* of the painting as a textual whole. In the painting, as in the text of verbal art, the careful selection of syntactical solidarities and contrasts among individual morphemes is decisive in contributing to the general aesthetic effect. Recall, for example, the composition of Velázquez's *La túnica de José (Joseph's Bloody Coat Brought to Jacob)*. The painting's overall aesthetic effect is in part the result of the judicious selection of details: not only the positions and expressions of the various characters, but also the little dog in the foreground and the staff allowed to fall in desperation emphasize their dispositive, plastic and narrative dependence on the expositive center of interest governing the composition — the bloodied tunic. The luminous effects of the painting behave similarly: from the marvelous anatomical detail of the brother's back, bathed in light, which is located in the foreground on the lefthand side of the painting to the blurred and shaded figure of the troubled father at the other extreme of the composition.

The consideration of the dispositive structure of a painting as a textual whole, in the terms with which we have just approached *La túnica de José*, refers to the work's dispositive or syntactical macrostructure. But the demarcation of the compositional or microsyntactic work — to appeal to the rhetorical opposition between *compositio* and *dispositio* — is also possible. Consider, for example, the compositional effect played by the position of the hands or the orientation of the facial expression of each of the figures in the gallery of living characters in *El Entierro del Conde de Orgaz (The Burial of the Count of Orgaz)*. Analogously, recall the concrete details of the Count's armor, or the little scenes embroidered on the chasubles and copes of the saints represented as priests, etc.

As we have been indicating with respect to the other levels, the linguistic parallelism between the syntax of verbal and plastic texts is not altered when considered in light of the variations introduced by modern art, even in its most outstandingly abstract realizations. All to the contrary, upon relinquishing the semantic support of the iconographico-descriptive, the abstract artist concentrates on the contrasted and compensatory construction of his text as a harmonic combination of form of pure plasticity. Sometimes he concentrates on the yield achieved from the graphic results of his gestures, distributed proportionally over the entire extension of the painting, as in Pollock's action paintings. At other times, he takes exquisite care in distributing the brushstrokes and varied surfaces with color in order to obtain a general luminous effect in the work, as in the poetics of radical abstraction of the Spaniard, Luis Feito (A. García-Berrio and M. T. Hernández, 1988a, pp. 84—89).

Certainly, the widespread geometrical trend based on Mondrian's new plasticism consists of the absolute radicalization of the compositional syntax in the scheme of the entire work. Numerous other developments are based on the same notion, including the principles behind Vassarely's geometrical abstraction, modular art or even abstract informalism. All of these plastic models try to experience the perceptive economy of regular systems of combined forms, with their distributive syntactic rules for determining the variety of results based on certain minimal morphological constants.

The parallelism between the painting as a plastic structure of constituents and the literary text represents the culminating expression of this system for legitimizing similarities between painting and literature. We have already seen how the perceptive syntax *functionally* regulates the micro- and macrocomponential options for textual construction. If we consider the specific problem of the *lexical level*, there are important resemblances between literature and plastic discourse. Classical literature defends its peculiarities, as is known, in terms of the limitation of a particular lexicon, which deliberately restricts the entire field of standard vocabulary to the conventions of *decorum* corresponding to the different expressive genres, themes, characters, situations, meters, or modes of discourse in prose, etc. In painting, the strict conventions of classical iconography similarly create a framework of symbolic restrictions, very much equivalent to those of lexical decorum. Only in this way, in the terms of an auto-restrictive lexicon, the respective dictionaries of classical literature and painting reveal the common tone as *de-automatizing devices* in which they find their conventional pragmatic characterization as artistic languages.

Also in this case, the abolition of the iconographic limitations of classicism by modern painters coincides with the analogous process of the destitution of the rules of selective decorum in the classical lexicon practiced by recent literature. Recall how modern art since Majakovsky and Marinetti has revolutionized the poetic lexicon, rescuing forms from technology and daily civil life, previously looked on with disdain by artistic criteria. The process is the same in modern painting, which begins to thematically vindicate vulgar images in Van Gogh's old shoes or in Duchamp's "ready-made" pieces, and culminates with present forms of "minimalist" and "poor" painting, as extremisms in the representative assimilation of references and referents never before accepted in the *onomasiological* creative process. The painter selects a particular color or concrete suggestion of form in a certain place of his text "as a function" of the presence of other brushstrokes and other corresponding forms, in complementary similarity or contrast, present in other spaces of the same work. Similarly, the spectators in the complementary process of perceptively receiving and attributing meanings realize their particular "reading" of the painting exercising the associations and rejections which are created by the characteristically sensitive optical rhythms, which bear no small portion of the responsibility in the process of effecting sensual optical pleasure. These act sensorially or imaginarily in a way very similar to the manner in which temporal and auditory rhythms are channeled in poetry (A. García-Berrio and M. T. Hernández, 1988a, pp. 13–14).

Considered from a different perspective, the constitution of a painting registers forms of *isotopy* entirely analogous to those manifested by literature's verbal texts (F. Rastier, 1972, pp. 80–105). The structures of functional correspondence and contrast which I just referred to are enormously complex and varied in compositions of such great symbolic density as Picasso's almost monochrome *Guernica*, even more so when the chromatic isotopic networks complicate the composition in paintings like the Venetian pieces of El Greco or Tintoretto. In this way, each concrete element of the text, each individual morphemic form or each iconographico-lexemic entity is perceived within a powerful dynamizing acceleration, which is highly analogous to that which characterizes the increment of the functional play of morphological and lexical units in verbal artistic texts (A. García-Berrio, 1973, pp. 145–150).

What already stands out clearly at this point in the comparison which we are developing between the two artistic systems of literature and painting is the common systematic nature characterizing them. In the chapter dealing with literariness I indicated that this feature was a property common not only to the standard system of language, but also to the peculiar set of "exceptions" which determine the verbal expressiveness of literature. Now, analogously, we see the same systematicity in the principles and operations which regulate the textual constitution of the aesthetic message in works of visual art.

As regards the system of linguistic anomalies regulating the workings of literary expressiveness we distinguished, as will be recalled, between *exception* and *violation*, indicating the lack of grammaticality and sense as the limit establishing the distinction between one and the other, and particularly the pertinence or exclusion of the expression deviating from the literary system. Now, in the same manner, the set of strictly material and compositional rules of painting as a text testify to the same systematicity of plastic expressiveness, and to the limits of verisimilitude and harmony, the violation of which destroys the painting's aesthetic prospects (A. García-Berrio and M. T. Hernández, 1985—1986, p. 52).

Once again, the modifications of traditional plastic "grammar" introduced by the various revolutions which, taken together, may be denominated modern art, corroborate the unmodifiable reach of these universals, affecting the system of all the arts equally. The semantic alterations of modern art, like the license taken with the logical associationism of images introduced by dadaism or surrealism, or those which decompose the perceptive structure of the object in the multiplication of the elements of cubist reference, or even the destitution of every form of iconicity in the symbolic process of informalism and, in general, of the various abstract poetics, all share in common the fact that they fix their own limits based on the plastic principles corresponding to *agrammaticality*. The functionalist rules of chromatic and formal proportionality which I was referring to previously as constitutive of the construction of the classical work of art, are fulfilled even more strictly with regard to the poetics of modern aformalism. In antitraditional painting the limits to the boldness and audacity of plastic exception are regulated by the kind of aesthetico-perceptive violation which would delegitimize the work as antisystematic and antiaesthetic (A. García-Berrio and M. T. Hernández, 1988a, pp. 54—64).

From the semantic point of view, we discover in the first place the common fictional nature of the supposed plastic and literary realisms. The mechanisms of realist referential illusion are materially different, but they yield results very similar as far as their common nature as forms of *illusion* are concerned. Beginning with Mikhail Bakhtin's work, we have acquired the basis for observing that the novel's realistic "painting", the most descriptive mode of the various forms of literary reference, is better understood as the representation of "voices" and ways of talking than as true descriptions. Analogously, examined in terms of their conventions, flat plastic forms producing the realistic illusion of three-dimensionality incorporate the same process of detailed saturation as that utilized in literature, based on a set of *semantic minimums* by which the pragmatic effect of reality is produced.

As with literature, the accumulation of details in realist painting is quite limited and restricted, according to strict laws of perceptive and communicative economy. Detailed naturalism in painting and literature eventually becomes counterproductive and unviable. Hence, the process of accumulating details deriving from the thesis of the naturalist novel, or the intense focus on minimal spaces of reference in certain texts belonging to the "nouveau roman", is equivalent in its lack of efficiency and effectiveness to the most extreme forms of plastic "hyperrealism". This effort attempts to make the characteristic visual illusion created in painting vanish, to the extent that it exceeds the limits of saturation dictated by the "law of semantic maxima" (T. Albaladejo Mayordomo, 1986).

In the area of semantics, the revolution of modern art affords us with the illustration of the same situation as prevailed at the other levels we have considered, demonstrating the parallel workings of the constitutive exigencies governing the two great artistic systems, plastic and literary, even in regard to their respective evolutionary needs. Aformalism and the various manifestations of abstraction, upon relinquishing the immediate representation of the painting's meaning, a source of much of the criticism the traditional detractors of these tendencies level against them, attempt to make gains through their semantic breadth. Traditional naturalist painting was forced by the verisimilar iconography of classical semantics to powerfully restrict the natural, absolute capacities of formal gestures and patches of color. The "opening" to the freedom of meaning informalism and abstraction represent also implied a massive increase in painting's symbolic possibilities. As a result of this opening, painting communicates its meaning by way of fantastic and sentimental contents both inconcrete and inaccessible in the reductive referentiality of traditional realism's semantic iconography (A. García-Berrio and M. T. Hernández, 1985–1986, p. 50).

In this sense, aformalist and abstract painting represent a certain *polysemic liberation of meaning* very much more natural and complete than that pretended for "open" literary works. Compared to similar trends in the visual arts, the contemporary trend towards "open" literature, and especially the critical doctrines which encourage it, are characterized by a far more inaccessible entelechy, as I have already indicated in my examination of the corresponding concepts in the thought of Barthes, and, to some extent, in the more extreme cases of the aesthetics of reception. In the case of literature, it is difficult, perhaps impossible, to avoid the automatic contamination posed by the standard meaning of the terms it utilizes in constructing its discourses. Messages are necessarily imposed in literature. This does not occur to the same extent in the case of modern painting, which finds it easier to abandon automatic contaminations of meaning, through its legitimate capacity for playing only with the aesthetic power of pure plastic forms, freed from the monosemicalizing control of iconography's conventions of meaning. Modern painting represents the culmination of the kind of trend towards polysemical radicalization the literatures and poetries of modernity proclaim as their own, generally with less perfect, more limited results.

Finally, considering the pragmatic point of view, the essential similarities between the communicative mechanisms of the plastic arts and literature are clear. The fictional and conventional nature of reference is identical. Words in the expression of lyrical intimacy, and even more so in the narrative or

3.3. Universality as a Property of Poetic Value

descriptive symbolization of the beings and objects of reality, are very incomplete and highly inadequate mediations. The difficulty of verbal art resides above all in this essential feature, restricted in successful cases to the verbal talents of a very restricted group of speakers possessing a truly exceptional and superior linguistic competence.

In spite of appearances to the contrary, the symbolization of the visual arts is no more proportional and direct. In the phenomenology of painting, conventions similar to those necessary for the constitution of verbal discourse circulate between artist and spectator. The cultural history of the perception of the visual arts as traced by Gombrich (1959) reveals how the symbolic effect creating the realistic illusion is nurtured by these kinds of conventions and accords, without which every visual discourse, from those of Egypt to those of the societies of our own contemporary culture, can be considered as a complete stylization. Hence, procedures like chiaroscuro and perspective would not easily be persuasive to an eye not educated in our conventional plastic system, which is based, lest we forget, on a stylization converting the flat surface supporting the painting into a three-dimensional space.

From the point of view of the pragmatic realistic illusion, critics have been pointing out since Aristotle that every artistic mimesis is based on the intellectual principle of *re-cognition* (M. Bakhtin, 1975, p. 52; A. García-Berrio and M. T. Hernández, 1988a, pp. 127–130) as opposed to *cognition* (knowledge); that is, in contrast to the acquisition of an absolutely unknown novelty, proper to logico-scientific experience. The sentimental and imaginary results of this intellectual process are those which customarily appear as what is characteristic in artistic experience. The philosophy of artistic mimesis from Aristotle to Bakhtin or Francastel has not substantially distinguished the differences among the various artistic genres which create it. In effect, what is important in a definite way in a comparison of literary mimesis and plastic mimesis are the analogies in the pragmatico-communicative convention of the communicative mode of recognition.

The pragmatic process of artistic re-cognition does not so much refer to the pleasure of discovering the referents of reality, which are sometimes trivial, as in the famous still lifes of Rembrandt and Velázquez, or Braque and Gris, and other times refer to persons, scenes or things which are well-known and familiar to us. Rather, the kind of intense satisfaction produced by this mode of cognitive experience derives from the very nature of the artificial objects, paintings or sculptures which artistic references introduce in this process. What especially interests us in the communicative scheme creating the effect of recognition are the technical difficulties we see the painter or author overcome in the materialization of the reference; or rather, the deforming stylizations of said referential materialization which emphasize and make visible the subjective facts of the represented entity. This is what produces the pleasure in the artistic manifestation of the personality traits emphasized in portraits, be it Velázquez's Innocent X or Dicken's Scrooge, or in the sentimental accent created through the stylized selection of details, in objects or scenery which might be entirely familiar to us, as in the still lifes of Zurbarán or Sánchez Cotán, or the idyllic setting of Constable's *Wivenhoe Park* (E. H. Gombrich, 1959).

The focalization of perceptive pleasure in the artistic referential structure, which is natural to the psychological, intellectual and affective process of art, translates what Shklovsky brilliantly formulated as the "artifice" or "procedure" *(priem)*, the determining factor among the peculiarities of artistic communication.

As we have seen, the similarities are very great between the respective structures of the components particularized as artistic in the artistic processes of "speech acts" and "visual acts". From the point of view of their pragmatic singularities, the aesthetic phenomena corresponding to the different arts — here I have analyzed only those belonging to the plastic and literary arts — reinforce the similarities. That is, the artistic modification which stylizes and adapts the aesthetic effect to the peculiar nature of pragmatico-communicative structures, natural to visual perception and verbal symbolization, intensifies the common rendering of uniquely similar features of each of the standard pragmatico-communicative systems.

But this property does not exclusively belong to the artistic pragmatic perspective, as I have emphasized with regard to each of the semiotic levels I have analyzed. At every step of the way, I have indicated the important community of natural and artistic roots underlying the resemblances under discussion. And above all, I have been able to show that these common foundations grow and are condensed in forms of identity when the process of stylization belonging to the artistic procedure intervenes with regard to the respective understanding and operations of standard, verbal and iconico-visual symbolization. As a result, one can with absolute propriety speak of an aesthetic universality of the artistic text, both in terms of the constitutive physiognomy of its structure and in that of the *poietic* and *aisthetic* (creative and perceptive) processes converting the text into *experience*.

The artistic text's unique structure, which has been examined here in some detail as regards the similarity of texts of verbal, plastic and visual art, justifies the claim of the universality of textual principles underlying the nature and value of the artistic. Compared to the temptation, very widespread today, to attribute all of this to cultural conventionalisms, the deep analysis of the structure of these different textual classes of various arts reveals that all of them are articulated on the basis of surprisingly homogeneous and common structural and pragmatic *universals*. The firm generality which we saw at all of these levels and in all of these mechanisms of the structural constitution of works corresponding to the different arts, constitutes the best proof of the determination of symbolic forms capable of producing the process of artistic illusion as a general, global phenomena, unifying the most superficial and immediate differences visible among diverse phenomena. *Universality* is

3.3. Universality as a Property of Poetic Value

thus the property of artistic texts which justifies the *necessity* of art as an entity, irreducible in its nature and axiology to the negative bias of the conventional.

3.3.5. The Imaginary Foundations of the Universality of Artistic Systems: Painting and Poetry

In the preceding section's analysis of the material and immanent structure common to texts of different arts I did not mention their underlying anthropologico-imaginary foundations. At the most, I have alluded to the sensorial conditions of visual perception and the psychologico-cognitive components of memory which are involved in the general configuration of the texts of different modes of general communication. Nevertheless, up to this point I have not attended to the most definitive arguments for establishing the principle of the *universality* of aesthetic factors. These ultimate foundations are lodged, from my point of view, in the peculiarities of the imagination's behavior, which are decisive factors, as we saw in the previous chapter, in the constitution of artistic *experience*.

As brilliant as the material and immediate elements put into play in the material confection of plastic texts may be, and as great as their capacities for mimetic representation, artistic works would not achieve the aesthetic transcendence which they have been conceded individually and collectively in the social and personal scheme of culture were it for these factors alone. Reducing the art of painting purely to its directly and immanently visible *expressiveness*, would be to reduce it to the status of a trivial simulacrum, of puerile intranscendence. This explains the inevitably disquieting feelings that sometimes affect the lovers of painting when they are able to sense, in momentary successful efforts to distance themselves, the materially fungible nature of great works. This feeling corresponds to the opposite case of the incomprehension of the uncultured observer, surprised by experts' enthusiasm or the high economic value society concedes to what for him are nothing more than painted cloths and papers. A vulgar incomprehension, motivated no doubt by the fungibility of the plastic objects and their material bases, which is to be found frequently in modern art, even as regards its most undeniably valuable pieces, like Bacon's tryptichs or the monumental *Les Demoiselles d'Avignon*.

As has been demonstrated with regard to literature, the sublime nature of a visual work of art is bestowed on the *text's material scheme* by virtue of its nature as the efficient foundation of imaginary activity. The material nature, in itself intranscendent, of a painting's brushstrokes and patches of color, or of the words of communicative usage in the poem, finds itself heightened and transfigured when it is able to express transcendentally subconscious impulses and symbolic sets due to its successful expressive structure. Through such impulses and symbols of the artistic imagination, as I have discussed in the preceding chapter with regard to poetry, man expresses and communicates his representation of the world in terms of an awareness of identity and otherness, which is ultimately based on anthropological references to essential coordinates of time and space.

Recall how beyond the dense immediacy of the symbolic universe, the complex atlas of symbols and myths is absorbed in the final analysis by the singularity of the temporal coordinates of essential anthropological orientation. Represented under diurnal symbols and myths, posturality is a relational structure measuring the consciousness and symbols of time. A second coordinate responds to the digestive sense of night, as an unformed space of that which is alien to the temporal dimension and our consciousness of it. And, finally, copulative symbols represent a temporal compromise achieved in erotic activity; an eros which dislodges the consciousness of diurnal pleasure from the temporal dimension to which it belongs, elevating it in the ecstatic plenitude of its momentary and definitive triumph over the temporal limits of existence.

At the same time, as I indicated before, the temporal symbols of imaginary semantics are forms of visible or otherwise sensibly accessible coatings cloaking the most profound structural patterns of the imagination. Thus, the myths of ascent and fall of Phaethon and Icarus embrace the two senses — a *positive* sense of flight and a negative one of inhumation — of the vertical axis of anthropological spatial orientation, in which all of the celestial myths are distributed — Elijah, Jesus, etc. — along with the infernal myths of descent — Orpheus, etc.

All that has been said in the preceding chapters concerning the literary structures which give shape to the set of possibilities for the actualization of the imaginary scheme of spatio-temporal anthropological orientation, we can repeat here as applicable to the case of the visual arts, in very similar if not identical terms (A. García-Berrio and M. T. Hernández, 1988a, pp. 204—209). In the first place, there are plastic universes conceived as diurnal forms of postural exploration. The various classical genres of painting — landscape, still life, portrait, etc. — fall into this category as forms of representing reality. From this characteristic classicist restriction of plastic mimesis, modern art heightens and focuses on pragmatic tendencies towards the expression of the intimately subjective and the subconscious and nocturnal, as in surrealism or certain poetics of aformalism and of so-called magical realism. These movements almost always explore the intimate landscapes of the subjective, excluded from the postural experience of classical painting.

The uprooted characters of Dalí and De Chirico move in this subjective space. And, if we focus on the best plastic creation in the rich panorama of contemporary Spanish art, we discover the interior and subconscious quest of such varied artists as Gordillo, Feito and Lucio Muñoz. While the spatial foundations underlying Farreras' work and Chillida's or José Luis Sánchez's sculpture correspond to an absolute nocturnal space, without postural references to grasp onto, Brinkmann's creations embrace the visceral setting of the digestive nightmare, while an exterior and realistic oneiricism is articulated in the uchronic forms of Ignacio Berriobeña, or in José Hernández's lavish scenes of sepulchral corruption (A. García-Berrio and M. T. Hernández, 1988 a, pp. 150—175).

Still, if one looks closely enough, all of these nocturnal and even digestive tendencies — the programatic constituents for a very broad and representative sector of modern art — are easily traceable in the nocturnal plastic poetics of individual artists and even entire periods of classicism. Hence, the work of some contemporary nocturnal painters like José Hernández immediately recalls the sepulchral themes of certain artists and schools of Spanish Baroque painting, the culminating expression of which is the work of Valdés Leal. Analogously, a discussion of the digestive spatiality characterizing the most hypochondriacal moments of Brinkmann's painting inevitably suggests Bosch's universe of symbolic abstraction, which Salvador Dalí's oneiric settings are not entirely alien to either.

In the visual arts, Romanticism and Mannerism are among the historical moments and tendencies characteristically open to the nocturnal scheme. It is not even worth insisting very much on the explicitly nocturnal themes and the art of ruins and interiors so characteristic of the former movement, a very familiar and well described fashion of the age so prevalent it leaves its traces in Stendhal's Roman walks, Byron's Mediterranean fantasies and in the directly nocturnal and sepulchral art of Novalis, Young, Foscolo and Cadalso. As concerns Mannerism, considered as a labyrinthian form of imagining the world according to Hocke's terms (G. R. Hocke, 1959), rather than as a moment or period of international art as European art criticism has described it, there is no doubt that its most outstanding characteristics can be linked to the desire to express the subconscious and its specifically nocturnal referential thematism.

We can find no better example combining the characteristics of the Mannerist historical moment with the expression of an individual temperamentally digestive singularity than the case of El Greco. His nocturnal will is manifested not only in the explicit scenery which envelops his characters or even the view of Toledo in almost abstract backgrounds of tenebrous vibrations, or in the contrasted tones of his chromatic range of Venetian blacks and purples, but above all in the postural instability of his creations, burning with anxiously transcendent curiosity. El Greco's characters are provisional and barely substantial inhabitants of the diurnal universe of plenary forms of posturality. Recall, for example, the Toledan gentlemen and ecclesiastical figures in his portraits, those making up the memorable gallery of figures in his *Entierro del Conde de Orgaz (The Burial of the Count of Orgaz)*, the figures in his historical and sacred scenes like *El martirio de San Mauricio* or *El expolio*, the Virgins and saints in ecstasy and the alienated protagonists of his portraits of the Apostles.

El Greco's characteristic ascendancy, manifested in the stylized verticality of his characters, in the central orientation of facial expressions, and in the always ascendant sense of his celestial visions, serves as the spatial mode for the expression of his diurnal uprootedness. Compare this to the plenary forms of Zurbarán's postural consciousness, present even when he constructs scenes of transcendent eschatology. In fact, the inhabitants of his paradises sit heavily on a stage of solid clouds. With El Greco, on the other hand, even his most earthbound figures demonstrate an untiring and vehement curiosity, inquiringly searching eternal space. Hence, his *Caballero de la mano en el pecho* probes the depths of an infinite horizon delineated beyond the contemplator's back, while almost all of those convoked to *The Burial of the Count of Orgaz* disperse their attention to the winds of an all-enveloping ethereal spatiality, foreign to a gaze attempting to find any solid resting point.

The symbolic coordinates of El Greco's faith, like the imaginary forms of the mystic's certainty, conjure up the security of a radiant paradise in a celestial plenitude able to cast out the nocturnal torment following death. This explains why El Greco's night only envelops those of his figures illuminated and enlightened by a strong faith able to resist any vacillations regarding the radiant certainty of the theological universe, a heavenly sky abbreviated in geometrical patterns in *La visión de Felipe II*. In fact, El Greco's strongly orthodox beliefs project diurnal forms on the hypothetical space of transcendence. But the torments and nocturnal anxieties of the void facing the individual beyond death fill the space of his paintings with shadows, barely broken by brilliant hints of deep red (A. García-Berrio and M. T. Hernández, 1988a, pp. 220–230).

The contrasts between Zurbarán and El Greco, like those we could draw between painters of every period — Leonardo and Raphael, the surrealist De Chirico and Gris the cubist, etc. — highlight the eternal contrast in painting between the need to give symbolic form to the plenary pleasure of postural luminosity in the face of the inaccessible density of the nocturnal and digestive premonition. Two systems of reference to the concrete and the inconcrete which are immediately evident in mimetic and iconographic representation, of fears and messages. But said explicit manifestations of referential mimesis are not the only instruments for communicating these basic schemes. Consider again, for example, the contrast between an El Greco enveloping his most earthly figures and scenes in mysterious nocturnal clouds of color, and a Zurbarán who manages to animate his paradisiacal scenes with earthly, weighted human figures, or who sets his beautiful saints, all dressed up in their Sunday best, walking the streets of Seville and Madrid.

The symbolization of the opposing nocturnal and diurnal imaginary regimes can rely on a much broader range of resources in classical and modern painting. As concerns El Greco and Zurbarán, we have referred to fundamental features like drawing and coloring, the very obviousness of which leads me not to discuss them at greater length. However, it is worthwhile noting those elements constitutive of the very spatiality of the canvas as a textual universe. It is obvious that the symbolic expression of the postural is reinforced by means of the structural dispositions underlining certain iconographic forms or objects in paintings. This is visible in the role played by the traditional recipes for the centric or non-centric disposition — classical and Mannerist, respectively — of the central thematic content of the narration or plastic description, assisting the perceptive focalization of values. This perception and judgment of the painting's elements is assisted by other classical dispositive structures — triangle, diagonal, etc. —, like the contrasted dialectic between backgrounds and theme, all of which are geared towards producing a greater or lesser testimonial emphasis for the objects of postural representation or digestive diffusion.

In this respect, it is also true that the chaotic symbolization of the nocturnal makes use of the formal device of densely multiplying, concentrating and crowding the painting's iconographic or formal constituents. I have outlined this in terms of the amassing of contrasts in El Greco, but it is also clearly visible in the scenes of destruction which Picasso later, symptomatically, entitled *Guernica*. For the same reason, the visceral and nocturnal basis of the stages of sharpest civil conscience in Antonio Saura's work is visible in his chaotic crowding of expressive gestures — in eyes, mouths and arms twisted every which way. Through these gestures, Saura distorts the clarity of the canonical structures of posturalism classically associated with the portrait to the point of sheer confusion, as with the lines — head, neck, bust — in the many variations of Phillip II and Dora Maar in *Imaginary Portraits* or in the figures in his numerous *Crucifixions*.

But the most direct expression of the digestive confusion of the nocturnal is achieved in those paintings involving the plenary occupation of space, either through the chaotic accumulation of iconographic nocturnal symbols, as in Valdés Leal's sepulchral scenes, or through the simple accumulation of neutral forms, as in the infinite variations in the composition of Saura's *Multitudes*. Using this same procedure, Luis Gordillo, in series as characteristic as that entitled *Mosaico*, manages to evoke the confused complexity of the subconscious, symbolized by the multitudinous density of highly plural forms of the most diverse morphology (A. García-Berrio and M. T. Hernández, 1988a, pp. 198—199).

In the spatial poetics of his texts, Velázquez communicates the narrative normalcy of a world without anxieties through a clear horizontal and seriated disposition of the iconographic constituents of his scenes, without emphasizing any superpositions. This is the case from the earliest *costumbrista* pieces and still lifes of his Seville period, like *El almuerzo (The Breakfast)* and *El aguador de Sevilla (The Water Carrier)*, to the maturity of his two great pieces from the Italian period: *La túnica de José (Joseph's Bloody Coat Brought to Jacob)* and *La fragua de Vulcano (The Forge of Vulcan)*. A formula he adopts without exception for his most complex scenes, like *La corte de Baco (Bacchus' Court)*,

La rendición de Breda (The Surrender of Breda), *Las hilanderas (The Tapestry Weavers)*, and even the clever spatial structure of *Las meninas*.

Velázquez's art at this level of textual space lends itself entirely to an earthly posturalism. Together with the previously mentioned spatial dimensions of the scenes, this can be observed directly in the presence and expression of the best domestic portraits of the Conde Duque de Olivares. In contrast to the spatial sublimity of the expressions and glances of El Greco's characters, Velázquez's sacred figures concentrate their glance in lower earthly regions, as in his humble Immaculate Mary's or the Christ figure of his *Cristo en la cruz (Christ on the Cross)*, contravening the customary iconographic canons for the representation of these figures, even going so far, in the crucifixion scene, as to ignore the stipulations of his teacher and father-in-law, Pacheco, concerning Christ's heaven-ward gaze. Even in scenes where the thematic requirements of ascendant eschatology normally would impose themselves, such as in the *Coronación de la Virgen (The Coronation of the Virgin)* or the *Imposición de la casulla a San Ildefonso (The Virgin Delivering the Chasuble to St. Idelfons)*, Velázquez hardly ever makes any postural concession to the figures' sublime ecstasy by incorporating plastic forms of ascent entirely removed from the diurnal and earthly.

But the postural naturalness of the textual disposition of Velázquean mimesis does not imply that his objects and characters are easily and immediately grasped or accessible to the viewer. On the contrary, Velázquez is one of the most mysterious and withdrawn painters in the history of art. His poetics of postural manifestations, which revels in a naturalistic obsession for detail in his Court portraits of Isabel and Margarita, Don Fernando or the multiple representations of Phillip IV, to the point of disrespect and contempt in some cases, also marvelously expresses the distance of royalty in all of these extremely solemn figures, preserved from the immediate accessibility of the tangible. Moreover, Velázquez symbolizes intemporal depth, compatible with the realistic representation of the diurnal, in the flight of his figures towards the spatial depth of his canvases. His creations are of course exceptional and perhaps unique in the history of painting, precisely because he has managed to spatially superimpose the most immediate forms of diurnal luminosity with the nocturnal and digestive forms of man's phantasmagorical temporal destiny (A. García-Berrio and M. T. Hernández, 1988a, pp. 231−234).

Velázquez's sublime creativity is above all the fruit of his analytical eye, which diffused the temporal dream of diurnal forms in the enveloping ardor of their reality as essences alien to time. In the case of Picasso's creative vigor, the message is far less subtle, more direct, blunt and forceful. The universal painter from Málaga possessed a poetic talent for meaningful and interesting creation based on the unleashing of uncontainable eros as a polemical form of saving the immediate and diurnal, rescued by the power of the copulative from the always threatening abyss of nonexistence. Picasso, like perhaps Rubens, represents one of the clearest manifestations of the poetic sublimation of immediate artistic texts charged with the imaginary transcendentality of the essential copulative and amorous impulses of the third regime.

Picasso himself proclaimed this repeatedly in the area of his own experiential consciousness, affirming that he only painted for the love of his successive lovers. He thus, in the most natural way, confessed the exact roots of his most powerful creative impulse. A general consideration of his work, through its various formal moments, corroborates this. Nevertheless, reading the explicit message Picasso left in some of his fundamental works is sufficient proof of this, such as that piece which for many reasons is considered of capital importance in the evolution of his poetics: *Les Demoiselles d'Avignon*.

This work represents a complete and explicit synthesis of the three imaginary regimes which I have been considering in terms of their role in the visual arts. In the foreground, we see Picasso's symbolic sailor, traveler and discoverer of the postural order, reinforced by the representation of food and fruit, which establish his deep rootedness in vital experience. In the familiar genesis of the painting, the vague figure in the background, about to enter the brothel scene, according to Picasso's own symbolic intention, is the student; that is, the reflexive representation of the unconscious structure of the immediately real. In case there is any doubt as to the symbolico-nocturnal role of this second figure, Picasso represented him in the known drafts and first versions of the painting holding a skull. Finally, occupying the canvas' entire spatial center, the magnificent female nudes, provoking an elementary erotic impulse by means of the elemental cubist schematism of their forms and the expressionist primitivism of their features, reminiscent of feminine African masks; this erotic impulse acts as a life-giving form interposed between the consistency of the plenary and diurnal and the permanently threatening presence of the eventuality of dispersion in nocturnal death (A. García-Berrio and M. T. Hernández, 1988a, pp. 234–236).

In conclusion, through the examination of all of these obvious materials and traces in the plastic poetics of some of art's most brilliant creators, the fundamental role of symbols and spatial imaginary structures in the poetic constitution of the artistic work is made clear. The expressiveness of the textual material scheme in painting, as in that of texts of verbal art, is only the necessary *basis* for justifiably locating the *space* of imaginary productivity in which the transcendental nature of the poetic consists. The synthetic summary of all of these temporal symbols and patterns of spatial orientation testifies to the definitive anthropological radicalness of the categories of time and space as principles of sensible orientation in the coordinates created by the eternal dialectic between *identity* and *otherness* as expressions of consciousness. Finally, the same essential radicalness of the imaginary foundations of artistic poeticity, common to literature and the plastic arts, proclaims the principle of *universality* as the ultimate raison d'être of the poetic, its nature and axiology.

Bibliography

Works are cited in the body of the text according to their first original-language editions, which is therefore how they are initially cited in this bibliography. Where pages are cited according to a different edition, be it an English translation or a later foreign-language edition, the year of this citation appears bracketed in the text (together with the appropriate page numbers) and is indicated at the end of the entry in this bibliography. In the few cases where it has not been possible to consult the English translation of a particular work, we have retained the citation to the original edition, indicating the chapter and/or paragraph in which the reader may locate the cited passage (with the exception of those cases where we are aware of significant revisions to the English edition, as with Eco, 1990).

Abrams, M. H.
1953 *The Mirror and the Lamp: Romantic Theory and the Critical Tradition*, New York, Oxford University Press.
1979 "How to Do Things with Texts", in *Partisan Review*, XLVI, pp. 566–588.
Adam, J. M.
1976 *Linguistique et discours littéraire*, Paris, Larousse.
Adorno, T. W.
1958 *Noten zur Literatur*, Berlin, Suhrkamp.
1986 *Aesthetic Theory*, New York, Routledge and K. Paul, 1986.
Aguiar e Silva, V. M. de
1967 *Teoria da Literatura*, Coimbra, Almedina, 1984 (6th edition).
1977 *Competencia lingüística y competencia literaria (Sobre la posibilidad de una Poética generativa)*, Madrid, Gredos, 1980.
Albaladejo Mayordomo, T.
1979 "Aplicación analítica de la teoría de la estructura del texto y de la estructura del mundo a un texto de J. Guillén", in Petöfi, J. S. and García-Berrio, A., pp. 267–307.
1981 "Aspectos del análisis formal de textos", in *Revista Española de Lingüística*, II, I, pp. 117–160.
1982 "Struttura comunicativa testuale e proposizioni performativo-modali", in *Lingua e Stile*, XVII, I, pp. 113–159.
1983 "Componente pragmático, componente de representación y modelo lingüístico-textual", in *Lingua e Stile*, XVIII, I, pp. 3–43.
1984 "La crítica lingüística", in Aullón de Haro, P. (ed.), pp. 141–207.
1986 *Teoría de los mundos posibles y macroestructura narrativa*, Alicante, Universidad de Alicante.
1986 a "La organización de mundos en el texto narrativo. Análisis de un cuento de *El Conde Lucanor*", in *Revista de Literatura*, XLVIII, 95, pp. 5–18.
1986 b "Sobre lingüística y texto literario", in *Actas del III Congreso Nacional de Lingüística Aplicada*, Valencia, Universidad de Valencia, pp. 33–46.
1989 *Retórica*, Madrid, Sintesis.
1991 *Semántica de la narración: la ficción realista*, Madrid, Taurus.
Aldridge, J. W. (ed.)
1952 *Critics and Essays in Modern Fiction*, New York, Ronald Press.

Alighieri, Dante
    De vulgari eloquentia, by A. Marigo and P. Ricci (eds.), Florence, Le Monnier, 1957 (reprinted, 1968).
Allén, S. (ed.)
    1989   *Possible Worlds in Humanities, Arts and Sciences*, Berlin, De Gruyter.
Alonso, A.
    1954   *Poesía y estilo de Pablo Neruda*, Barcelona, Edhasa, 1979.
    1955   *Materia y forma en poesía*, Madrid, Gredos, 1977 (3rd edition).
    1961   *Estudios lingüísticos: Temas españoles*, Madrid, Gredos.
    1961   "Estilística y gramática del artículo en español", in *Estudios lingüísticos: Temas españoles*, pp. 125—160.
Alonso, D.
    1952   *Poesía española. Ensayo de métodos y límites estilísticos*, Madrid, Gredos, 1976 (5th edition).
Ambrogio, I.
    1968   *Formalismo e avanguardia in Russia*, Rome, Editori Riuniti.
Amossy, R.
    1984   "Stereotypes and Representation in Fiction", in *Poetics Today*, 5, 4, pp. 689—700.
Arac, J. (ed.)
    1983   *The Yale Critics: Deconstruction in America*, Minneapolis, University of Minnesota Press.
Aristotle
    Poética, trilingual edition by V. García Yebra, Madrid, Gredos, 1974.
Arnheim, R.
    1954   *Art and Visual Perception*, Berkeley, University of California Press.
    1982   *The Power of the Center*, Berkeley, University of California Press.
Arrivé, M.
    1972   *Les langages de Jarry. Essai de Sémiotique littéraire*, Paris, Klincksieck.
    1973   "Pour une théorie des textes polyisotopiques", *Langages*, 31, pp. 53—63.
Aschenbrenner, K.
    1974   *The Concepts of Criticism*, Dordrecht, Reidel.
Atkins, J. W. A.
    1934   *Literary Criticism in Antiquity*, Gloucester, Mass., P. Smith, 1961 edition.
Auerbach, E.
    1946   *Mimesis: Dargestellte Wirklichkeit in der abendländischen Literatur*, Berne, A. Francke (*Mimesis: The Representation of Reality in Western Literature*, Garden City, Doubleday, 1957).
Aullón de Haro, P. (ed.)
    1984   *Introducción a la crítica literaria actual*, Madrid, Playor.
Austin, J. L.
    1962   *How To Do Things With Words*, Cambridge, Mass., Harvard University Press.

Bachelard, G.
    1957   *La Poétique de l'espace*, Paris, P. U. F., 1970 (6th edition) (*Poetics of Space*, New York, Orion Press, 1964).
Badouin, C.
    1952   *Le triomphe du héros. Étude psychoanalytique sur le mythe du héros et les grandes épopées*, Paris, Plon.
    1972   *La Psychanalyse de Victor Hugo*, Paris, A. Colin.
Bailey, R. W., et al. (eds.)
    1978   *The Sign. Semiotics Around the World*, Ann Arbor, University of Michigan Press.
Bakhtin, M.
    1929   *La Poétique de Dostoievski*, Paris, Seuil, 1970 (*Problems of Dostoyevsky's Poetics*, Minneapolis, University of Minnesota Press, 1970).

1929 a   *Marxism and the Philosophy of Language*, Cambridge, Harvard University Press, 1980.
1955   *Rabelais and His World*, Cambridge, M. I. T. Press, 1968.
1978   *Esthétique et théorie du roman*, Paris, Gallimard.
Bal, M.
1977   *Narratologie*, Paris, Klincksieck.
Baldensperger, F.
1946   *La critique et l'histoire littéraires en France au XIX et au debout du XX siècles*, Paris, Montaigne.
Baldwin, C. S.
1924   *Ancient Rhetoric and Poetics*, Gloucester, Mass., P. Smith, 1959.
1928   *Medieval Rhetoric and Poetics*, London, MacMillan.
1939   *Renaissance Literary Theory and Practice*, Gloucester, Mass., P. Smith, 1959.
Bally, C.
1921   *Traité de stylistique française*, Paris, Klincksieck, 1952 (3rd edition).
Banfi, A.
1987   *Filosofía del arte*, Barcelona, Península.
Baquero Goyanes, M.
1956   *Prosistas españoles contemporáneos*, Madrid, Rialp.
1963   *Perspectivismo y contraste*, Madrid, Gredos.
1970   *Estructuras de la novela actual*, Barcelona, Planeta, 1989 (4th edition).
1972   *Temas, formas y tonos literarios*, Madrid, Prensa Española.
1976   *Introduction* to his edition of M. de Cervantes Saavedra, *Novelas Ejemplares*, Madrid, Editora Nacional.
Barilli, R.
1979   *Retorica*, Milan, Isedi.
Barnstone, W. (ed. and trans.)
1968   *The Poems of St. John of the Cross*, Bloomington, Indiana University Press.
Barthes, R.
1953   *Le degré zéro de l'écriture*, Paris, Seuil (*Writing Degree Zero*, London, Cape, 1970).
1957   *Mythologies*, Paris, Seuil (*Mythologies*, New York, Hill and Wang, 1972).
1963   *Sur Racine*, Paris, Seuil (*On Racine*, New York, Performing Arts Journal, 1983).
1964   *Essais Critiques*, Paris, Seuil (*Critical Essays*, Evanston, Northwestern University Press, 1972).
1966   *Critique et vérité*, Paris, Seuil (*Criticism and Truth*, London, Athlone Press, 1987).
1967   *Système de la mode*, Paris, Seuil (*The Fashion System*, London, Cape, 1983).
1969   *Michelet par lui-même*, Paris, Seuil.
1970   "L'Ancienne Rhétorique. Aide-memoire", in *Communications*, 16, pp. 172–223.
1970 a   *S/Z*, Paris, Seuil (*S/Z*, New York, Hill and Wang, 1975).
1971   "The Struggle with the Angel", in R. Barthes, 1977 b.
1973   *Le plaisir du texte*, Paris, Seuil (*The Pleasure of the Text*, New York, Hill and Wang, 1975).
1975   *R. Barthes par R. Barthes*, Paris, Seuil.
1977   *Fragments d'un discours amoureux*, Paris, Seuil (*A Lover's Discourse: Fragments*, New York, Hill and Wang, 1978).
1977 a   *Poétique du récit*, Paris, Seuil.
1977 b   *Image, Music, Text*, London, Fontana Press, 1987 (5th edition).
 et al. 1966 *L'analyse structurale du récit*, Communications, 8, Paris, Seuil.
Bate, W. J.
1946   *From Classicism to Romanticism*, Cambridge, Mass., Harvard University Press.
Battistini, A. and Raimondi, E.
1984   *Retoriche e Poetiche dominanti*, in Asor Rosa, A. (ed.), *Letteratura italiana*, Turin, Einaudi, vol. III (T. I., *Teoria e poesia*).

Bau, G., Ubersfeld, A. and Piers, B.
    1979   *L'espace théâtrale*, Paris, C. N. R. S.
Baudelaire, C.
    1935   *The Flowers of Evil*, ed. by Marthiel and Jackson Mathews, Norfolk, New Directions Books.
    1985   *66 Translations from Charles Baudelaire's Les Fleurs du Mal*, ed. and trans. by James McGowan, Illinois, Spoon River Poetry Press.
Baumgarten, A.
    1735   *Reflections on Poetry*, Berkeley, University of California Press, 1954.
Becker, C.
    1963   *Das Spätwerk des Horaz*, Göttingen, Vandenhoeck und Rupprecht.
Behrens, I.
    1940   *Die Lehre von der Einteilung der Dichtkunst*, Halle, Supplement to *Zeitschrift für Romanische Philologie*, XCII.
Benjamin, W.
    1969   *Illuminations*, New York, Schocken Books.
Ben-Porat, Z.
    1986   "Represented Reality and Literary Models", in *Poetics Today*, 7, I, pp. 29—58.
Berger, B.
    1964   *Der Essay*, Berne, Francke.
Berlin, I.
    1976   *Vico and Herder. Two Studies in the History of Ideas*, New York and London, Viking Press.
Bertinetto, P. M.
    1973   *Ritmo e modelli ritmici*, Turin, Rosemberg e Sellier.
Bierwisch, M.
    1970   "Poetics and Linguistics", in Freeman, D. C. (ed.), 1970, pp. 69—115.
Black, E.
    1965   *Rhetorical Criticism. A Study in Method*, Madison, University of Wisconsin Press, 1978.
Black, M.
    1962   *Models and Metaphors*, Ithaca, Cornell University Press.
Blanchot, M.
    1943   *Faux pas*, Paris, Gallimard, 1975.
    1949   *La part du feu*, Paris, Gallimard, 1972.
    1949 a   *Lautréamont et Sade*, Paris, Ed. de Minuit, 1963.
    1955   *L'espace littéraire*, Paris, Gallimard (*The Space of Literature*, Lincoln, University of Nebraska Press, 1982).
    1959   *Le livre à venir*, Paris, Gallimard.
    1969   *L'entretien infini*, Paris, Gallimard, 1971.
    1973   *Le pas au-delà*, Paris, Gallimard.
Bloom, H.
    1961   *The Visionary Company*, Ithaca, Cornell University Press, 1971 (3rd printing, 1987).
    1973   *The Anxiety of Influence: A Theory of Poetry*, New York and London, Oxford University Press.
    1975   *A Map of Misreading*, New York, Oxford University Press, 1980.
    1975 a   *Kabbalah and Criticism*, New York, Seabury.
    1982   *Agon: Towards a Theory of Revisionism*, Oxford, Oxford University Press, 1983.
    1982   *The Breaking of the Vessels*, Chicago, University of Chicago Press.
    1989   *Ruin the Sacred Truths: Poetry and Belief from the Bible to the Present*, Cambridge, Harvard University Press.
    et al. 1979 *Deconstruction and Criticism*, New York, Seabury.

Bloomfield, L.
1933 *Language*, New York, Holt.
Bobes Naves, M. del C.
1973 *La semiótica como teoría lingüística*, Madrid, Gredos.
1975 *Gramática de "Cántico"*, Madrid, Cupsa.
1985 *Teoría general de la novela. Semiología de "La Regenta"*, Madrid, Gredos.
1987 *Semiología de la obra dramática*, Madrid, Taurus.
Boccaccio, G.
De genealogia deorum, by V. Romano (ed.), Bari, Laterza, 1951.
Bodkin, M.
1934 *Archetypal Patterns in Poetry. Psychological Studies in Imagination*, London and New York, Oxford University Press, 1974.
Bolgar, R. R.
1971 *Classical Influences on European Culture*, Cambridge University Press.
Bonaparte, M.
1933 *Poe, étude psychanalitique*, Paris, Denoël-Steele (*The Life and Works of Edgar Allen Poe*, London, Hogarth Press, 1949).
Bonheim, H.
1977 "Für eine Modernisierung der Rhetorik", in Plett, H. F. (ed.), pp. 109—124.
Bonomi, A.
1975 *Le vie del riferimento*, Milan, Bompiani.
1979 *Universi di discorso*, Milan, Feltrinelli.
Booth, W. C.
1961 *The Rhetoric of Fiction*, Chicago, University of Chicago Press.
1965 "The Revival of Rhetoric", in *Publications of the Modern Language Association of America*, 80, pp. 8—12.
Borinski, K.
1914 *Die Antike in Poetik und Kunsttheorie*, Darmstadt, Wissenschaftliche Buchgesellschaft, 1965.
Bornscheuer, L.
1977 "Zehn Thesen zur Ambivalenz der Rhetorik und zum Spannungsgefüge des Topos-Begriffs", in Plett, H. F. (ed.), pp. 23—44.
Bourneuf, R. and Ouellet, R.
1972 *L'Univers du Roman*, Paris, P. U. F.
Bousoño, C.
1952 *Teoría de la expresión poética*, Madrid, Gredos, 2 volumes, 1976 (6th edition).
Bové, P. A.
1983 "Variations on Authority: Some Deconstructive Transformations of the New Criticism", in Arac, J. (ed.).
Bovet, E.
1911 *Lyrisme, épopée, drame: une loi de l'évolution générale*, Paris, Colin.
1951 *Roman et poésie. Essai sur l'esthétique des genres*, Paris, Nizet.
Bowra, C. M.
1961 *The Romantic Imagination*, London, Oxford University Press.
Bray, R.
1957 *La formation de la doctrine classique en France*, Paris, Nizet.
Brecht, B.
1983 edition *Brecht on Theater*, New York, Hill and Wang.
Bremond, C.
1966 "La logique des possibles narratifs", in *Communications*, 8, pp. 60—67.
1973 *Logique du récit*, Paris, Seuil.
Breuer, D.
1974 *Einführung in die pragmatische Texttheorie*, Munich, Fink.

1977 "Die Bedeutung der Rhetorik für die Textinterpretation", in Plett, H. F. (ed.), pp. 23–44.
Brik, O.
1965 "Rhythme et syntaxe", in Todorov, T. (ed.), pp. 143–153.
Brink, C. O.
1963–1982 *Horace on Poetry*, Cambridge, Cambridge University Press.
Brooke-Rose, C.
1976 "Historic Genres-Theoretical Genres. Reflections on Todorov's Concept of the Fantastic", in *New Literary History*, VIII, 1, pp. 145–158.
Bruck, J.
1982 "From Aristotelean Mimesis to 'Bourgeois' Realism", in *Poetics*, 11, 3, pp. 189–202.
Brunel, P.
1971 *Le mythe d'Electre*, Paris, A. Colin.
1974 *Le mythe de la métamorphose*, Paris, A. Colin.
Brunetière, F.
1980 edition *L'évolution de la critique*, Paris, Hachette.
1890 *L'évolution des genres dans l'histoire de la littérature*, Paris, Hachette.
Bryant, D. C.
1967 *Rhetorical Dimensions in Criticism*, Baton Rouge.
Buch, H. C.
1972 *Ut pictura poesis. Die Beschreibungsliteratur und ihre Kritiker*, Munich, Fink.
Buch, A., Heitman, K. and Mettman, W.
1972 *Dichtungslehren der Romania aus der Zeit des Renaissance und Barock*, Frankfurt, Athenäum.
Burger, P.
1974 *Theorie der Avantgarde*, Frankfurt, Suhrkamp.
Burgos, J.
1982 *Pour une Poétique de l'imaginaire*, Paris, Seuil.
Burke, K.
1969 *A Grammar of Motives*, Berkeley, University of California Press.
1969 a *A Rhetoric of Motives*, Berkeley, University of California Press.
Butcher, S. H.
1955 *Aristotle's Theory of Poetry and Fine Art*, New York, Dover.

Caillois, R.
1974 *Approches de l'imaginaire*, Paris, Gallimard.
Calabrese, O.
1985 *Il linguaggio dell'arte*, Milan, Bompiani.
Cambon, G.
1980 *Ugo Foscolo, Poet of Exile*, Princeton, Princeton University Press.
Caplan, H.
1934–1936 *Medievales artes praedicandi*, Ithaca, Cornell University Press.
Carnero, G.
1983 *La cara oscura del Siglo de las Luces*, Madrid, Fundación Juan March/Cátedra.
Cassirer, E.
1932 *Philosophie der Aufklärung*, New Haven, Yale University Press.
Cellier, L.
1971 *L'épopée humanistique et les grandes mythes romantiques*, Paris, Sedes.
Cervantes Saavedra, M. de
1976 edition *Novelas Ejemplares*, ed. by M. Baquero Goyanes, Madrid, Editora Nacional
1989 edition *El Ingenioso Hidalgo Don Quijote de la Mancha*, ed. by J. J. Allen, Madrid, Cátedra, (*The Adventures of Don Quixote*, translated by J. M. Cohen, New York, Penguin, 1950 edition).

Chabrol, C. (ed.)
1973 *Sémiotique narrative et textuelle*, Paris, Larousse.
Chambers, R.
1984 *Story and Situation. Narrative Seduction and the Power of Fiction*, Minneapolis, Manchester University Press, University of Minnesota.
Champigny, R.
1978 "Semantic Modes and Literary Genres", in Strelka, J. P. (ed.), pp. 94–111.
1981 "For and Against Genre Labels", in *Poetics*, 10, 2/3, pp. 145–174.
Chapman, R.
1973 *Linguistics and Literature*, London, E. Arnold.
Charland, T. M.
1936 *Artes praedicandi: contribution à l'histoire de la Rhétorique au Moyen Âge*, Paris, Vrin.
Charles, M.
1977 *Rhétorique de la lecture*, Paris, Seuil.
Chassegnet-Smirgel, J.
1971 *Pour une psychanalyse de l'art et de la creativité*, Paris, Payot.
Chastel, A.
1959 *Art et Humanisme à Florence au temps de Laurent le Magnifique*, Paris, P. U. F.
Chateaubriand, R. de
1974 edition *René*, Paris, Larousse.
Chatman, S.
1965 *A Theory of Meter*, The Hague, Mouton.
1971 "La struttura della comunicazione letteraria", in *Strumenti Critici*, 23, pp. 1–40.
Chiarini, P.
1983 *Brecht, Lukács, e il realismo*, Bari, Laterza.
Chico Rico, F.
1988 *Pragmática y construcción literaria. Discurso retórico y discurso narrativo*, Alicante, Universidad de Alicante.
Clancier, A.
1973 *Psychanalyse et critique littéraire*, Toulouse, Privat.
Cohen, J.
1966 *Structure du langage poétique*, Paris, Flammarion.
Cohen, T. and Guyer, P. (eds.)
1982 *Essays in Kant's Aesthetics*, Chicago, University of Chicago Press.
Collin, F.
1971 *Maurice Blanchot et la question de l'écriture*, Paris, Gallimard.
Coquet, J. C.
1972 *Sémiotique littéraire*, Paris, Marne.
Corti, M.
1976 *Principi della comunicazione letteraria*, Milan, Bompiani.
1978 "Modelli e antimodelli nella cultura medievale", in *Strumenti Critici*, XII, 35, pp. 3–30.
Coste, D.
1980 "Trois conceptions du lecteur et leur contribution à une théorie du texte littéraire", in *Poétique*, 43, pp. 354–371.
Cremante, R. and Pazzaglia, M. (eds.)
1972 *La Metrica*, Bologna, Il Mulino.
Croce, B.
1907 *Aesthetics as Science of Expression and General Linguistics*, New York, Noonday, 1953.
Crosman, I.
1983 "Reference and the Reader", in *Poetics Today*, 4, 1, pp. 89–97.

Culler, J.
1975 *Structuralistic Poetics: Structuralism, Linguistics and the Study of Literature*, Ithaca, Cornell University Press.
1982 *On Deconstruction*, New York, Cornell University Press.
Curtius, E. R.
1948 *European Literature and the Latin Middle Ages*, Princeton, Princeton University Press, 1973.

Dähl, O.
1973 *Topic and Comment. Contextual Boundness and Focus*, Hamburg, Buske.
Dällenbach, L. (ed.)
1979 "Théorie de la Reception en Allemagne", in *Poétique*, 39.
Decaunes, L.
1976 *Clefs pour la lecture*, Paris, Seghers.
Delas, J. and Filliolet, J.
1973 *Linguistique et Poétique*, Paris, Larousse.
Derrida, J.
1967 *L'écriture et la différence*, Paris, Seuil (*Writing and Difference*, Chicago, University of Chicago Press, 1978).
1967 a *De la Grammatologie*, Paris, Gallimard (*Of Grammatology*, Baltimore, Johns Hopkins University Press, 1976 [6th printing, 1984]).
1972 *La dissémination*, Paris, Seuil (*Dissemination*, Chicago, University of Chicago Press, 1981).
Dijk, T. A. van
1972 *Some Aspects of Text Grammars*, The Hague, Mouton.
1972 a *Beiträge zur generativen Poetik*, Munich, Bayerischer Schulbuch Verlag.
1976 *Per una poetica generativa*, Bologna, Il Mulino.
(ed.) 1976 a *Pragmatics of Language and Literature*, Amsterdam, North Holland.
1976 b "Pragmatics and Poetics", in Dijk, T. A. van (ed.), pp. 23—57.
1977 *Studies in the Pragmatics of Discourse*, The Hague, Mouton.
1977 a *Text and Context. Explorations in the Pragmatics and Semantics of Discourse*, London, Longman.
1979 "Advice on Theoretical Poetics", in *Poetics*, 8, pp. 569—608.
(ed.) 1985 *Discourse and Literature. New Approaches to the Analysis of Literary Genre*, Amsterdam, J. Benjamins.
1983 *Strategies of Discourse Comprehension*, New York, Academic Press.
Dijk, T. A. van and Kintsch, W.
1977 "Cognitive Psychology and Discourse", in Dressler, W. U. (ed.), pp. 61—80.
Dimter, M.
1985 "On Text Classification", in Dijk, T. A. van (ed.), pp. 215—230.
Dockhorn, K.
1968 *Macht und Wirkung der Rhetorik*, Bad Homburg.
Dodds, E. R.
1957 *The Greeks and the Irrational*, Boston, Beacon.
Doležel, L.
1966 "Vers la stylistique structurale", in *P. T. L.*, I, pp. 257—266.
1976 "Narrative Worlds", in Matejka, L. (ed.), *Sound, Sign and Meaning*, Ann Arbor, University of Michigan Press, pp. 524—533.
1976 a "Narrative Modalities", in *Journal of Literary Semantics*, 5, I, pp. 5—14.
1976 b "Narrative Semantics", in *P. T. L.*, I, pp. 129—151.
1979 "Extensional and Intensional Narrative Worlds", in *Poetics*, 8, 1—2, pp. 193—211.
1979 a "In Defence of Structural Poetics", in *Poetics*, 8, pp. 521—530.
1980 "Truth and Authenticity in Narrative", in *Poetics*, 1, 3, pp. 7—25.

1983	"Intensional Function, Invisible Worlds, and F. Kafka", in *Style*, 17, 2, pp. 120—141.
1983a	"Proper Names, Definite Descriptions and the Intensional Structure of Kafka's 'The Trial'", in *Poetics*, 12, 6, pp. 511—526.
1986	"Semiotics of Literary Communication", in *Strumenti Critici*, 1, 1, pp. 5—48.
1989	"Possible Worlds and Literary Fictions", in S. Allen (ed.), pp. 221—242.

Domínguez Caparrós, J.
1981   "Literatura y actos de Lenguaje", in *Anuario de Letras*, 19, pp. 89—132.

Doubrovsky, S.
1966   *Pourquoi la Nouvelle-Critique?*, Paris, Mercure de France.

Dressler, W. U. (ed.)
1978   *Current Trends in Textlinguistics*, Berlin and New York, De Gruyter.

Dubois, C. G.
1984   "Problems of 'Representation' in the Sixteenth Century", in *Poetics Today*, 5, 3, pp. 461—478.

Dubrow, H.
1982   *Genre*, London, Methuen.

Ducrot, O.
1972   *Dire et ne pas dire*, Paris, Hartmann.

Ducrot, O. and Todorov, T.
1974   *Encyclopedic Dictionary of the Science of Language*, Baltimore, Johns Hopkins University Press.

Durand, G.
1960   *Les structures anthropologiques de l'imaginaire. Introduction a l'archetypologie générale*, Paris, Bordas (9th edition, 1969).
1971   *Le decor mytique de la "Chartreuse de Parme"*, Paris, Corti.
1979   *Figures mytiques et visages de l'oeuvre*, Paris, Berg.

Eco, U.
1962   *Opera aperta*, Milan, Bompiani.
1964   *Apocalittici e integrati*, Milan, Bompiani.
1968   *La struttura assente*, Milan, Bompiani.
1968a   *La definizione dell'arte*, Milan, Mursia.
1971   *Le forme del contenuto*, Milan, Bompiani.
1977   *A Theory of Semiotics*, Bloomington, University of Indiana Press.
1978   "Possible Worlds and Text Pragmatics: 'Un dramme bien parisien'", in *Versus*, 19—20, pp. 5—72 (later included in *Lector in fabula*, 1979).
1979   *Lector in fabula. La cooperazione interpretativa nei testi narrativi*, Milan, Bompiani (partial translation in *The Role of the Reader*, London, Hutchinson, 1981).
1990   *I limiti dell'interpretazione*, Milan, Bompiani (*The Limits of Interpretation*, Bloomington, Indiana University Press, partially revised edition).

Eggert, H., Berg, H. and Rutschky, M.
1975   "Zur notwendigen Revision des Rezeptionsbegriffs", in Müller-Seidler, W. (ed.), pp. 423—432.

Eikhenbaum, B.
1922   *Il giovane Tolstoj*, Bari, De Donato, 1968.
1969   "Die Illusion des 'skaz'", in Striedter, J. (ed.), 1969, pp. 161 ff.

Eisenweig, U.
1976   *L'espace imaginaire d'un récit: "Sylvie" de G. de Nerval*, Neuchâtel, La Baconnière.

Eliade, M.
1962   *Mephistopheles et l'Androgyne*, Paris, Gallimard (*Mephistopheles and the Androgyne*, New York, Sheed and Ward, 1965).
1963   *Aspects du mythe*, Paris, Gallimard.

Ellis, J.
1974 *The Theory of Literary Criticism: A Logical Analysis*, Berkeley, University of California Press.
Else, C. F.
1957 *Aristotle's Poetics*, Cambridge, Harvard University Press.
Empson, W.
1930 *Seven Types of Ambiguity*, London, Chatto and Windus, 1977 (3rd revised edition).
Enkvist, N. E.
1973 *Linguistic Stylistics*, The Hague, Mouton.
1978 "Stylistics and Text Linguistics", in Dressler, W. U. (ed.), pp. 174–190.
Enkvist, N. E., Spencer, J. and Gregory, M.
1971 *An Approach to the Study of Style*, London, Oxford University Press.
Erlich, V.
1955 *Russian Formalism: History, Doctrine*, Gravenhage, Mouton.

Facciani, R. and Eco, U. (eds.)
1969 *I sistemi di segni e lo strutturalismo sovietico*, Milan, Bompiani.
Falk, E. H.
1981 *The Poetics of Roman Ingarden*, Chapel Hill, The University of North Carolina Press.
Fanto, J. A.
1978 *Speech Act Theory and Its Applications to the Study of Literature*, in Bailey, R. W., et al. (eds.), pp. 208–304.
Faral, E.
1928 *Les Arts Poétiques du XIIe et du XIIIe siècles*, Paris, Champion, 1971.
Felman, S. (ed.)
1982 *Literature and Psychoanalysis*, Baltimore, Johns Hopkins University Press.
Felpering, H.
1985 *Beyond Deconstruction: The Uses and Abuses of Literary Theory*, Oxford, Clarendon Press.
Ferraris, M.
1984 *La svolta testuale. Il decostruzionismo in Derrida, Lyotard, gli "Yale Critics"*, Pavia, Cluep.
Fetterley, J.
1978 *The Resisting Reader*, Bloomington, Indiana University Press.
Fish, S. E.
1970 "Literature in the Reader: Affective Stylistics", in *New Literary History*, II, pp. 123 ff.
1973 "How Ordinary is Ordinary Language", in *New Literary History*, 5, pp. 41–54.
1976 "How to Do Things With Austin and Searle: Speech Act Theory and Literary Criticism", in *Modern Language Notes*, 91, pp. 983–1025.
1980 *Is There a Text in This Class?*, Cambridge, Harvard University Press.
1986 "Anti Professionalism", in *New Literary History*, XVII, pp. 89–108.
Fischer, E.
1970 *À la recherche de la réalité. Contribution à une esthétique marxiste moderne*, Paris, Les Lettres Nouvelles.
Flahault, E.
1978 *La parole intermédiaire*, Paris, Seuil.
Foerster, H. von
1985 "Das Konstruierenden einer Wirklichkeit", in Watzlawick, R. (ed.), pp. 39–60.
Fokkema, D. W.
1976 "Continuity and Change in Russian Formalism, Czech Structuralism and Soviet Semiotics", in *P. T. L.*, I, I, pp. 317–388.

Fokkema, D. W. and Ibsch, I.
1986   *Theories of Literature in the Twentieth Century*, New York, St. Martins Press.
Fonagy, I.
1961   "Communication in Poetry", in *Word*, 17, pp. 194—218.
1965   "Le langage poétique", in Benveniste, E., *et al.*
Fontanier, P.
1968 edition *Les figures du discours*, Paris, Flammarion.
Forastieri-Braschi, E.
1978   "La base hermenéutica del conocimiento literario", in *Dispositio*, 3, 7—8, pp. 103—125.
Forastieri-Braschi, E. *et al.* (eds.)
1980   *On Text and Context. Methodological Approaches to the Context of Literature*, Puerto Rico, Universidad de Río Piedras.
Forster, E. M.
1927   *Aspects of the Novel*, New York, Harcourt.
Foucault, M.
1966   *Les mots et les choses*, Paris, Gallimard.
Fowler, A.
1971   "The Life and Death of Literary Forms", in *New Literary History*, 2, I, pp. 199—216.
1979   "Genre and the Literary Canon", in *New Literary History*, I, 1, pp. 97—119.
1982   *Kinds of Literature. An Introduction to the Theory of Genres and Modes*, Cambridge, Harvard University Press.
Fowler, R. (ed.)
1966   *Essays on Style and Language*, London, Routledge and Kegan Paul.
1970   "Prose Rhythm and Meter", in Freeman, D. C. (ed.), pp. 347—365.
1986   *Linguistic Criticism*, Oxford, Oxford University Press.
Frank, J.
1952   "Spatial Form in the Modern Novel", in Aldridge, J. W. (ed.), pp. 43—66.
1963   *The Widening Gyre*, New Brunswick, New Jersey, Rutgers University Press.
Freeman, D. C. (ed.)
1970   *Linguistics and Literary Style*, New York, Rinehart and Winston.
Frenzel, E.
1969   *Stoff-, Motiv- und Symbolforschung*, Stuttgart, Metzler.
Freud, S.
1976 edition *The Complete Psychological Works*, New York, Norton, 24 volumes.
Fricke, H.
1982   "Semantics or Pragmatics of Fictionality? A Modest Proposal", in *Poetics*, 11, 4—6, pp. 439—452.
Frye, N.
1957   *Anatomy of Criticism*, New York, Atheneum (6th printing, Princeton, Princeton University Press, 1968).
1963   "The Developing Imagination", in *Learning in Language and Literature*, Cambridge, Mass., Harvard University Press.
1963 a "The Archetypes of Literature", in *Fables of Identity*, New York.
Fubini, M.
1956   *Critica e poesia*, Bari, Laterza.
Fumaroli, M.
1980   *L'Âge de l'Eloquence*, Geneva, Droz.
Furst, L. R.
1979   *Romanticism in Perspective*, London, MacMillan.

Gadamer, H. G.
1960   *Truth and Method*, New York, Seabury, 1975.

1967   "Rhetorik, Hermeneutik und Ideologiekritik", in *Kleine Schriften*, Tübingen, I, pp. 113—130.

Gaillard, F.
1984   "The Great Illusion of Realism, or the Real as Representation", in *Poetics Today*, 5, 4, pp. 753—766.

Gallacher, C.
1982   "Re-Covering the Social in Recent Literary Theory", in *Diacritics*, XII, 4, pp. 40—48.

Garasa, D. L.
1969   *Los géneros literarios*, Buenos Aires, Columba.

García-Berrio, A.
1966   "La figura de don Juan en el postromanticismo español", in *Anales de la Universidad de Murcia*, XXIV, 3, pp. 279—321.
1967   "El mito de don Juan sometido a revisión", in *Anales de la Universidad de Murcia*, XXV, 1/2, pp. 71 ff.
1968   *España e Italia ante el conceptismo*, Madrid, C. S. I. C.
1970   "Bosquejo para una teoría de la frase compuesta en español", in *Anales de la Universidad de Murcia*, XXVII, 3/4, pp. 209—230.
1973   *Significado actual del formalismo ruso*, Barcelona, Planeta.
1975   *Introducción a la Poética clasicista: Cascales*, Barcelona, Planeta.
1976   "Ideas lingüísticas en las paráfrasis renacentistas de Horacio", in *Homenaje al Profesor Muñoz Cortés*, Murcia, Universidad de Murcia, pp. 181—201.
1977   "Crítica formal y función crítica", in *Lexis*, I, 2, pp. 187—209.
1977 a   "Historia de un abuso interpretativo: 'Ut pictura poesis'", in *Estudios ofrecidos a E. Alarcos Llorach*, Oviedo, Universidad de Oviedo, pp. 291—307.
1977—1980   *Formación de la teoría literaria moderna*, 2 volumes, Madrid, Cupsa; Murcia, Universidad de Murcia.
1978   "Tipología textual de los sonetos españoles sobre el 'carpe-diem'", in *Dispositio*, III, 9, pp. 243—293.
1978 a   "Lingüística del texto y texto lírico. La tradición textual como contexto", in *Revista Española de Lingüística*, 8, I, pp. 19—75.
1979   "Lingüística, literaridad/poeticidad (Gramática, Pragmática, Texto)", in *1616. Anuario de la Sociedad Española de Literatura General y Comparada*, II, pp. 125—168.
1979 a   "Text and Sentence", in Petöfi, J. S. (ed.), I, pp. 24—42.
1979 b   "Poética e ideología del discurso clásico", in *Revista de Literatura*, 41, 81, pp. 5—40.
1979 c   "A Text-Typology of the Classical Sonnets", in *Poetics*, 8, pp. 435—458.
1979 d   "Construcción textual en los sonetos de Lope de Vega. Tipología del macrocomponente sintáctico", in *Revista de Filología Española*, 60, pp. 23—147.
1980   "Una tipologia testuale di sonetti amorosi nella tradizione classica spagnola", in *Lingua e Stile*, 15, 3, pp. 451—478.
1980 a   "Text Linguistics and the Lyric Text", in Forastieri, E., *et al.* (eds.), pp. 95—138.
1980 b   "Estructura y función del personaje en la lírica amorosa del Siglo de Oro", in *Lexis*, IV, 1, pp. 71—77.
1980 c   "Quevedo y la conciencia léxica del 'concepto'", in *Cuadernos Hispanoamericanos*, 361—362, pp. 1—16.
1981   "Poetica e ideologia del discorso classico", in *Intersezioni*, 3, pp. 501—527.
1981 a   "La poética lingüística y el análisis literario de textos", in *Tránsito*, h—i, pp. 11—16.
1981 b   "Macrocomponente textual y sistematismo tipológico: el soneto amoroso español de los siglos XVI y XVII y las reglas de género", in *Zeitschrift für Romanische Philologie*, 97, 1—2, pp. 146—171.
1982   "Definición macroestructural de lírica amorosa de Quevedo (Un estudio de 'forma interior' en los sonetos)", in *Homenaje a Quevedo. Actas de la II Academia Literaria Renacentista*, Salamanca, Universidad de Salamanca, pp. 261—293.

1983	"Il ruolo della retorica nell'analisi/interpretazione dei testi letterari", in *Versus*, 35—36, pp. 99—154.
1983 a	"Problemas de la determinación del tópico textual. El soneto en el Siglo de Oro", in *Anales de Literatura Española*, Universidad de Alicante, I, pp. 135—205.
1983 b	"Las letrillas de Góngora. Estructura pragmática y liricidad del género", in *Edad de Oro*, II, pp. 89—97.
1983 c	"Nuevas perspectivas para el estudio de la lírica en los Siglos de Oro", in Rico, F. (ed.), *Historia crítica de la literatura española*, III, Barcelona, Crítica, pp. 736—741.
1984	"Retórica como ciencia de la expresividad (Presupuestos para una Retórica general)", in *Estudios de Lingüística. Universidad de Alicante*, 2, pp. 7—59.
1984 a	"Más allá de los 'ismos': sobre la imprescindible globalidad crítica", in Aullón de Haro, P. (ed.), pp. 349—387.
1984 b	"Testo, classe testuale, genere", in *Diacronia, Sincronia e Cultura. Saggi linguistici in onore di L. Heilmann*, Brescia, La Scuola, pp. 267—280.
1984 c	"Topical Tradition and Textual Complexity", in *Poetics Today*, 4, pp. 707—721.
1985	*La construcción imaginaria en "Cántico" de Jorge Guillén*, Limoges, Trames.
1985 a	"Sociocrítica y formalismo a la luz de las tipologías textuales", in *Homenaje a J. A. Maravall*, Madrid, C. S. I. C., II, pp. 117—128.
1985 b	"Poesía galante, poesía amorosa y poesía erótica; sistemas literarios de legitimación", in Redondo, A. (ed.), pp. 241—249.
1987	"¿Qué es lo que la poesía es?" in *Lingüística española actual*, IX, 2, Homenaje al Profesor Julio Fernández-Sevilla, pp. 177—188.
1988	*Introducción a la Poética clasicista. Comentario a las "Tablas Poéticas" de Cascales*, Madrid, Taurus (2nd revised edition).
1989	*Teoría de la literatura: la construcción del significado poético*, Madrid, Cátedra.
1989 a	"La ambigüedad como máscara de la memoria: Anselm Kiefer", *Revista de Occidente*, 100, pp. 123—191.
1989 b	"La lecture lyrique", in *Versus*, 52/53, pp. 71—80.
1990	"Ingenio clásico e imaginacíon moderna: una acotación postestructuralista al estudio del intertexto en el Siglo de Oro", in *Castilla. Estudios de Literatura*, 15, pp. 105—119.
1990a	"Don Giovanni, mito spagnolo e universale", in Camerini, S. (ed.), *Don Giovanni*, Bologna, Nuova Alfa, pp. 25—38.
1991	"Gustavo Torner, en la consistencia expresiva del arte moderno" in *Torner*, Madrid, Museo Nacional Reina Sofía, pp. 25—44.

García-Berrio, A. and Hernández, M. T.
1987	"The Semiotics of Discourse and of the Plastic Text: On the Textual Scheme and Imaginary Construction", in *Dispositio*, X, 27, pp. 127—160.
1988	*La poética: tradición y modernidad*, Madrid, Síntesis.
1988 a	*Ut poesis pictura. Poética del arte visual*, Madrid, Tecnos.

Garin, E.
1952	*L'Umanesimo italiano. Filosofia e vita civile nel Rinascimento*, Bari, Laterza, 1973.
1965	*Scienza e vita civile nel Rinascimento italiano*, Bari, Laterza, 1972.

Garrido Gallardo, M. A.
1978	"Todavía sobre las funciones externas del lenguaje", *Revista Española de Lingüística*, 8, 2, pp. 461—480.

Garvin, P. L.
1964	*A Prague School Reader on Aesthetics, Literary Structure and Style*, Washington, Georgetown University Press.
1970	*Cognition: A Multiple View*, New York, Spartan Books.

Gary-Prieur, N.
1971	"La notion de connotation(s)", *Littérature*, 4, pp. 104—106.

Garza-Cuarón, B.
1978 *La connotación: problemas del significado*, Mexico, Colegio de México.
Gendarme de Bevotte, G.
1929 *La légende de don Juan*, Paris, Hachette.
Genette, G.
1966 *Figures*, Paris, Seuil.
1968 "Preface", to Fontanier, P.
1969 *Figures II*, Paris, Seuil.
1969 a "Vraisemblance et motivation", in Genette, G., 1969, pp. 71–99.
1972 *Figures III*, Paris, Seuil (*Figures of Literary Discourse*, New York, Columbia University Press, 1981).
1977 "Genres, types, modes", in *Poétique*, 32, pp. 389–421.
1979 *Introduction a l'architexte*, Paris, Seuil.
1980 *Narrative Discourse*, Oxford, Blackwell.
Getto, G.
1951 *Letteratura e critica nel tempo*, Milan, Marzorati.
Gianformaggio, L.
1981 "La nuova retorica di Perelman", in Mosconi, G. *et al.*, 1981, pp. 110–188.
Girolamo, C. Di
1978 *Critica della letterarietà*, Milan, Il Saggiatore.
1982 *Teoría crítica de la Literatura*, Barcelona, Crítica.
Glasserfeld, E. von
1985 "Einführung in den radikalen Konstruktivismus", in Watzlawick, P. (ed.), pp. 16–38.
Goldmann, L.
1955 *Le dieu caché*, Paris, Gallimard (*Hidden God*, New York, Routledge, 1976).
1964 *Pour une sociologie du roman*, Paris, Gallimard (*Towards a Sociology of the Novel*, London, Tavistock Publications, 1975).
Gombrich, E. H.
1959 *Art and Illusion*, Oxford, Phaidon Press.
1966 *Norm and Form: Studies in the Art of the Renaissance*, London, Phaidon.
1986 "Sind eben alles Menschen gewesen? Zum Kulturrelativismus in den Geisteswissenschaften", in A. Schöne (ed.), *Akten des VII Internationalen Germanisten-Kongresses*, Tübingen, N. Niemeyer, pp. 17–28.
Gómez de Liaño, I.
1982 *El idioma de la imaginación*, Madrid, Taurus.
Gómez Moriana, A. and Gürttler, K. R. (eds.)
1980 *Le vraisemblable et la fiction*, Montréal, Université de Montréal.
Goriély, B.
1967 *Le avanguardie letterarie in Europa*, Milan, Feltrinelli.
Göttner, H.
1973 *Logik der Interpretation*, Munich, Fink.
Grabes, H. (ed.)
1977 *Text, Leser, Bedeutung. Untersuchungen zur Interaktion von Text und Leser*, Grosse Linden, Hoffmann.
Gray, B.
1975 *The Phenomenon of Literature*, The Hague, Mouton.
1977 *The Grammatical Foundations of Rhetoric*, The Hague, Mouton.
Greimas, A. J.
1966 *Sémantique structurale*, Paris, Larousse (*Structural Semantics*, Lincoln, University of Nebraska Press, 1984).
1970 *Du sens*, Paris, Seuil (*On Meaning*, London, Pinter, 1987).
(ed.) 1972 *Essais de sémiotique poétique*, Paris, Larousse.
1972 "Pour une théorie du discours poétique", in Greimas, A. J. (ed.), pp. 6–24.
1973 "Les actants, les acteurs et les figures", in Chabrol, C. (ed.).
1976 *Maupassant. La sémiotique du texte: exercises pratiques*, Paris, Seuil.

Grimm, G. (ed.)
1975 *Literatur und Leser. Theorien und Methode zur Rezeption literarischer Werke*, Stuttgart, Reclam.
1977 *Rezeptionsgeschichte*, Munich, Fink.
Groeben, N.
1977 *Rezeptionsforschung als empirische Literaturwissenschaft*, Kronberg, Athenäum.
Group μ
1970 *Rhétorique générale*, Paris, Larousse.
1977 *Rhétorique de la poésie*, Brussels, Complexe.
Grube, G. M. A.
1968 *The Greek and Roman Critics*, London, Methuen.
Gueunier, N.
1969 "La pertinence de la notion d'ecart en stylistique", *Langue Française*, 3, pp. 34–35.
Guillén, C.
1971 *Literature as System*, Princeton, Princeton University Press.
1986 *Entre lo uno y lo diverso*, Barcelona, Crítica.
Guiraud, P.
1955 *La Stylistique*, Paris, P. U. F., 1975 (8th edition).
Guiraud, P. and Kuentz, P.
1970 *La Stylistique. Lectures*, Paris, Klincksieck.
Gülich, E. and Quasthoff, U. M. (eds.)
1986 "Narrative Analysis. An Interdisciplinary Dialogue", in *Poetics*, 15, 1–2.
Gülich, E. and Raible, W. (eds.)
1972 *Textsorten*, Frankfurt, Athenäum.
Gülich, E. and Raible, W.
1977 *Linguistische Textmodelle. Grundlagen und Möglichkeiten*, Munich, Fink.
Gullón, R.
1980 *Espacio y novela*, Barcelona, Bosch.
Gumbrecht, H. U.
1975 "Konsequenzen der Rezeptionsästhetik oder Literaturwissenschaft als Kommunikationssoziologie", in *Poetica*, 7, pp. 388–413.
Gusdorf, G.
1952 *Mythe et métaphysique*, Paris, Flammarion, 1963.
1976 *Naissance de la conscience romantique au Siècle des Lumières*, Paris, Payot.

Habermas, J.
1971 *Hermeneutik und Ideologiekritik*, Frankfurt.
Hamburger, K.
1957 *Die Logik der Dichtung*, Stuttgart, E. Klett (*The Logic of Literature*, Bloomington, Indiana University Press, 1973).
Hancher, M.
1977 "Beyond a Speech-Act Theory of Literary Discourse", *Modern Language Notes*, 92, pp. 1081–1098.
Harshaw, B.
1984 "Fictionality and Fields of Reference. Remarks on a Theoretical Framework", in *Poetics Today*, 5, 2, pp. 227–251.
Hartman, G. H.
1970 *Beyond Formalism*, New Haven, Yale University Press, 1978 (4th edition).
1975 *The Fate of Reading and Other Essays*, Chicago, University of Chicago Press.
1979 *Deconstruction and Criticism*, New York, The Seabury Press.
1980 *Criticism and Wilderness*, New Haven, Yale University Press.
1985 *Easy Pieces*, New York, Columbia University Press.

Hartmann, P.
1978 "Textlinguistik als linguistische Aufgabe", in Dressler, W. U. (ed.), pp. 93—105.
Harweg, R.
1973 "Textgrammar and Literary Text", in *Poetics*, 9, pp. 86—87.
Hathaway, B.
1962 *The Age of Criticism. The Late Renaissance in Italy*, Cornell University Press (reprinted, 1972, Westport, Greenwood Press).
Haubrichs, W.
1975 "Zur Relevanz von Rezeption und Rezeptionshemmung in einem kybernetischen Modell der Literaturgeschichte", in Müller-Seidler, W. (ed.), pp. 97—122.
Haugon Olsen, S.
1978 *The Structure of Literary Understanding*, London, Cambridge University Press.
Hauptmeier, H. and Schmidt, S. J.
1985 *Einführung in die empirische Literaturwissenschaft*, Braunschweig, Vieweg.
Havránek, B.
1964 "The Functional Differentiation of the Standard Language", in Garvin, P. L. (ed.), pp. 3—16.
Hayes, C. M.
1966 "Transformational-generative Approach to Style", *Language and Style*, I, pp. 39—48.
Hegel, G. W. F.
1970 edition *Vorlesungen über die Ästhetik*, in *Werke*, Frankfurt, Suhrkamp, V. 13—15.
Heidegger, M.
1971 *Erläuterungen zu Hölderlins Dichtung*, Frankfurt, Klostermann.
Heilmann, L.
1978 "Retorica, Neoretorica, Linguistica", in Ritter-Santini, L. and Raimondi, E. (eds.), pp. 9—24.
Heintz, J.
1979 "Reference and Inference in Fiction", in *Poetics*, 8, 1—2, pp. 85—99.
Hempfer, K. W.
1973 *Gattungstheorie*, Munich, Fink.
Hendricks, W. O.
1973 *Essays on Semiolinguistics and Verbal Art*, The Hague, Mouton.
Henn, T. R.
1934 *Longinus and English Criticism*, Cambridge, Cambridge University Press.
Henry, A.
1971 *Métonymie et métaphore*, Paris, Klincksieck.
Hernadi, P.
1972 *Beyond Genre: New Directions in Literary Classification*, Ithaca, Cornell University Press.
1976 "Literary Theory: A Compass for Critics", in *Critical Inquiry*, III, pp. 369—386.
1978 "Order Without Borders: Recent Genre Theories in the English-speaking Countries", in Strelka, J. P. (ed.), pp. 192—208.
Hernández, M. T.
1986 "La teoría literaria del conceptismo en Baltasar Gracián", in *Estudios de Lingüística. Universidad de Alicante*, 3, pp. 7—46.
Hernández Guerrero, J. A.
1987 *La expresividad literaria*, Cádiz, Universidad.
Herrick, M. T.
1946 *The Fusion of Horatian and Aristotelian Literary Criticism*, Urbana, University of Illinois Press.
Hester, M.
1967 *The Meaning of Poetic Metaphor*, The Hague, Mouton.

Heuermann, H., Hühn, P. and Rötger, B. (eds.)
1975   *Literarische Rezeption: Beiträge zur Theorie des Text-Leser-Verhältnisses und seiner empirischen Erforschung*, Paderborn, Schöningh.
Hidalgo Serna, E.
1983   *Das ingeniöse Denken bei Baltasar Gracián*, Munich, Fink.
Hill, A. A.
1976   *Constituent and Pattern in Poetry*, Austin, University of Texas Press.
Hintikka, J.
1989   "Exploring Possible Worlds", in S. Allén (ed.), pp. 52—73.
Hintzenberg, D. and Schmidt, S. J. (eds.)
1980   *Zum Literaturbegriff in der Bundesrepublik Deutschland*, Braunschweig, Vieweg.
Hirsch, E. D.
1967   *Validity in Interpretation*, New Haven, Yale University Press.
Hocke, G. R.
1959   *Die Welt als Labyrinth*, Hamburg, Rowohlt.
Hohendahl, P. U.
1974   "Zur Lage der Rezeptionsforschung", in *Zeitschrift für Literaturwissenschaft und Linguistik* 4, 15, pp. 7—11 (New Haven, Yale University Press, 1979, 9th edition).
1974a   *Sozialgeschichte und Wirkungsästhetik*, Frankfurt, Athenäum.
Hölderlin, F.
1966 edition   *Poems and Fragments*, trans. by Michael Hamburger, London, Routledge and K. Paul.
Herrstein-Smith, B.
1980   *On the Margins of Discourse: The Relation of Literature to Language*, Chicago, University of Chicago Press.
Holub, R. C.
1984   *Reception Theory: A Critical Introduction*, New York, Methuen.
Howell, R.
1979   "Fictional Objects: How They Are and How They Aren't", in *Poetics*, 8, 1—2, pp. 129—177.
Howell, W. S.
1961   *Logic and Rhetoric in England 1500—1700*, New York, Russell and Russell.
Hrushovski, B.
1972   "I ritmi liberi moderni", in Cremante, R. and Pazzaglia, M. (eds.), pp. 169—176.
Huerta Calvo, J.
1984   "La crítica de los géneros literarios", in Aullón de Haro, P. (ed.), pp. 83—139.

Ihwe, J.
1972   *Linguistik in der Literaturwissenschaft*, Munich, Schulbuch Verlag.
Ingarden, R.
1931   *Das literarische Kunstwerk*, Tübingen, Niemeyer (*The Literary Work of Art*, Evanston, Northwestern University Press, 1973).
Ingen, F. van (ed.)
1974   "Die Revolte des Lesers oder Rezeption versus Interpretation", in Labroise, R. (ed.), pp. 83—148.
Iser, W. (ed.)
1969   *Immanente Ästhetik, ästhetische Reflexion*, Munich, Fink (Poetik und Hermeneutik).
1971   "Indeterminacy and the Reader's Response in Prose Fiction", in Miller, J. H. (ed.), pp. 1—45.
1972   *Der Implizite Leser*, Munich, Fink (*The Implied Reader*, Baltimore, Johns Hopkins University Press, 1974).
1972a   "The Reading Process: A Phenomenological Approach", in *New Literary History*, 3, pp. 279—294.
1975   "Die Appellstruktur der Texte", in Warning, R. (ed.), pp. 228—252.

1975 a   "The Reality of Fiction: A Functionalist Approach to Literature", in *New Literary History*, VIII, 1, pp. 7—38.
1976   *Der Akt des Lesens*, Munich, Fink (*The Act of Reading*, Baltimore, John Hopkins University Press, 1978).
1979   "The Current Situation of Literary Theory: Key Concepts and the Imaginary", in *New Literary History*, 11, pp. 1—20.

Jaeger, W.
1934   *Paideia: die Formung des griechischen Menschen*, Berlin, De Gruyter (*Paideia: The Ideals of Greek Culture*, Oxford University Press, 1944).

Jakobson, R.
1960   "Linguistics and Poetics", in Sebeok, T. (ed.), pp. 350—377.
1971   *Selected Writings*, The Hague, Mouton, 6 volumes (esp. Volumes 3 and 5).
1973   *Questions de Poétique*, Paris, Gallimard.

Jakobson, R. and Lévi-Strauss, C.
1962   "'Les Chats' de Baudelaire", in *L'homme*, II, 1, pp. 401—419.

Jameson, F.
1971   *Marxism and Form*, Princeton, Princeton University Press.
1972   *The Prison-House of Language: A Critical Account of Structuralism and Russian Formalism*, Princeton, Princeton University Press, 1974.
1981   *The Political Unconscious: Narrative as a Socially Symbolic Act*, Ithaca, Cornell University Press.

Jauss, H. R.
1967   *Literaturgeschichte als Provokation der Literaturwissenschaft*, Konstanz, Konstanzer Universitätsreden (in *Towards an Aesthetics of Reception*, 1982, pp. 3—45).
1973   "Die Parzialität der rezeptionsästhetischen Methode", in Warning, R. (ed.), 1975, pp. 343—352.
1973 a   "Levels of Identification of Hero and Audience", in *New Literary History*, 5, pp. 283—317.
1975   "Negativität und Identifikation. Versuch zur Theorie der ästhetischen Erfahrung", in Weinrich, H. (ed.), pp. 263—339.
1977   *Ästhetische Erfahrung und literarische Hermeneutik*, Munich, Fink (*Aesthetic Experience and Literary Hermeneutics*, Minneapolis, University of Minnesota Press).
1982   *Toward an Aesthetic of Reception*, Minneapolis, University of Minnesota Press.

Jefferson, A. and Robey, D. (eds.)
1986   *Modern Literary Theory: Comparative Introduction*, London, Botsford.

Jehn, P. (ed.)
1972   *Toposforschung*, Frankfurt, Athenäum.

Jessi, F.
1968   *Letteratura e Mito*, Turin, Einaudi.

Jiménez, J.
1986   *Imágenes del hombre. Fundamentos de Estética*, Madrid, Taurus.

Johansen, S.
1949   "La notion de signe dans la glossématique et dans l'esthétique", in *Travaux du Cercle Linguistique de Copenhague*, V, pp. 288—303.

Jolles, A.
1930   *Einfache Formen*, Tübingen, Max Niemeyer.

Jones, L. K.
1977   *Theme in English Expository Discourse*, Lake Bluff, Illinois, Jupiter Press.

Juan de la Cruz, S.
1964   *The Collected Works of Saint John of the Cross*, trans. by Kieran Kavanaugh and Otilio Rodríguez, New York, Doubleday and Co., 1964.

Kamerbeer, J.
1977   "Le concept du Lecteur ideal", *Neophilologus*, 41, pp. 2-7.
Kant, M.
1985 edition *Critique of judgment*, New York, MacMillan.
Kennedy, G. A.
1963   *The Art of Persuasion in Greece*, Princeton, Princeton University Press.
1980   *Classical Rhetoric in its Christian and Secular Tradition*, Chapel Hill, University of North Carolina Press.
Kennedy, W. J.
1978   *Rhetorical Norms in the Renaissance*, New Haven, Yale University Press.
Kerbrat-Orecchioni, C.
1977   *La connotation*, Lyon, Presses Universitaires de Lyon.
Kibédi-Varga, A.
1970   *Rhétorique et Littérature*, Paris, Didier.
1981   *Théorie de la Littérature*, Paris, Picard.
Klinkenberg, J. M.
1973   "Le concept d'isotopie en sémantique et en sémiotique littéraire", in *Le français moderne*, 41, pp. 285—290.
1977   "Rhétorique et Specificité Poétique", in Plett, H. F. (ed.), pp. 77—92.
Kloepfer, R.
1975   *Poetik und Linguistik*, Munich, Fink.
Kopperschmidt, J.
1976   *Allgemeine Rhetorik*, Stuttgart, Kohlhammer (2nd edition).
1977   "Von der Kritik der Rhetorik zur kritischen Rhetorik", in Plett, H. F. (ed.), pp. 213—229.
Kripke, S. A.
1959   "A Completeness Theorem in Modal Logic", in *The Journal of Symbolic Logic*, 24, 1, pp. 1—14.
Kristeller, P. O.
1956   *Studies in Renaissance Thought and Letters*, Rome, Edizioni di Storia e Letteratura.
Kristeva, J.
1969   *Semeyotiké. Recherche pour une Sémanalyse*, Paris, Seuil.
1970   *Le texte du roman*, The Hague, Mouton.
1974   *La révolution du langage poétique*, Paris, Éditions du Seuil (*Revolution in Poetic Language*, New York, Columbia University Press, 1984).
Kroll, W.
1977   "Bibliographie deutscher Arbeiten zur Rezeption und Wirkungsästhetik ... Auswahl: 1966—1977", in *Wortkunst*, pp. 212—275.
Krysinski, W.
1977   "The Narrator as a Sayer of the Author", in *Strumenti Critici*, XL, 32—33, pp. 44—89.
Kubczak, H.
1977   *Die Metapher*, Heidelberg, C. Winter.
Kuentz, P.
1971   "Rhétorique générale ou Rhétorique théorique?", in *Littérature*, 4, pp. 108—115.
Kuiper, K. and Small, V.
1986   "Constraints of Fiction", in *Poetics Today*, 7, 3, pp. 495—526.
Kuroda, S.-Y.
1976   "Reflections on the Foundations of Narrative Theory", in Dijk, T. A. van (ed.), pp. 107—140.

Labroise, R. (ed.)
1974   *Rezeption — Interpretation. Beiträge zur Methodendiskussion*, Amsterdam, Rodopi (Amsterdamer Beiträge zur neueren Germanistik, 3).

Lachmann, R.
1977 "Rhetorik und kultureller Kontext", in Plett, H. F. (ed.), pp. 167—186.
Lämmert, E.
1985 *Bauformen des Erzählens*, Stuttgart, Metzlersche.
Landwehr, J.
1975 *Text und Fiktion*, Munich, Fink.
Lanhan, R. A.
1976 *The Motives of Eloquence. Literary Rhetoric in the Renaissance*, New Haven, Yale University Press.
Lausberg, H.
1960 *Handbuch der literarischen Rhetorik*, Munich, Max Hueber.
Lázaro Carreter, F.
1956 "Quevedo entre el amor y la muerte", in *Papeles de Son Armadans*, I, 11, pp. 145 ff.
1966 *Estilo barroco y personalidad creadora*, Salamanca, Anaya.
1975 "¿Es poética la función poética?", in *Nueva Revista de Filología Hispánica*, XXIV, 1, pp. 1—12.
1976 *¿Qué es la literatura?*, Santander, Publicaciones de la Universidad Internacional Menéndez Pelayo.
1976 a "The Literal Message", in *Critical Inquiry*, 3, pp. 315—322 (Spanish version in *Estudios de lingüística*, Barcelona, Crítica, 1980, pp. 173—192).
1976 b *Estudios de Poética*, Madrid, Taurus, 1979 (2nd edition).
1976 c "El realismo como concepto crítico-literario", in *Estudios de Poética*, pp. 121—142.
1976 d "Sobre el género literario", in *Estudios de Poética*, pp. 113—120.
1980 "Leo Spitzer o el honor de la Filología", in Spitzer, L., pp. 7—27.
1981 "Imitación compuesta y diseño retórico en la 'Oda a Juan de Grial'", in *Actas de la I Academia Literaria Renacentista*, Salamanca, Universidad de Salamanca, pp. 193—224.
Le Guern, M.
1973 *Sémantique de la métaphore et de la métonymie*, Paris, Larousse.
Lee, R. W.
1964 *"Ut pictura poesis". Humanistic Theory of Painting*, New York, Merton and Co.
Leech, G. N.
1966 "Linguistics and Figures of Rhetoric", in Fowler, R. (ed.), pp. 135—156.
1970 "This Bread I Break — Language in Interpretation", in Freeman, D. C. (ed.).
Leech, G. N. and Short, M. N.
1981 *Style in Fiction*, London, Longman.
Lefebve, M. J.
1971 *Structure du discours de la poésie et du récit*, Neuchâtel, Ed. de la Baconnière.
Leitch, V. B.
1983 *Deconstructivism: An Advanced Introduction*, London, Hutchinson.
Lejeune, P.
1975 *Le pacte autobiographique*, Paris, Seuil.
Lentricchia, F.
1980 *After New Criticism*, Chicago, University of Chicago Press.
Leoni, A. and Pigliasco, M. R. (eds.)
1979 *Retorica e scienze del linguaggio*, Rome, Bulzoni.
Leopardi, G.
1966 edition *Selected Prose and Poetry*, ed. and trans. by I. Origo and J. Heath-Stubbs, Oxford, Oxford University Press.
Lessing, G. E.
1967 edition *Laokoon oder über die Grenzen der Malerei und Poesie*, in *Schriften*, vol. III, pp. 7—173, Frankfurt, Insel.

Lévi-Strauss, C.
1958   *Anthropologie Structurale*, Paris, Plon (*Structural Anthropology*, New York, Basic Books, 1963).
Levin, H.
1968   "Thematics and Criticism", in Demetz, P. *et al.* (eds.), in *The Disciplines of Criticism ... in Honor of R. Wellek*, New Haven, Yale University Press, pp. 125–145.
Levin, S. R.
1962   *Linguistic Structures in Poetry*, The Hague, Mouton.
1965   "Internal and External Deviation in Poetry", *Word*, 21, pp. 225–237.
1971   "The Conventions of Poetry", in Chatman, S. (ed.).
1976   "Concerning What Kind of Speech Act a Poem Is", in Dijk, T. A. van (ed.), pp. 141–160.
Levinas, E.
1975   *Sur Maurice Blanchot*, Montpellier, Fata Morgana.
Li, C. N. (ed.)
1975   *Subject and Topic*, New York, Academic Press.
Litman, C. A.
1971   *Le sublime en France (1600–1714)*, Paris, Nizet.
Lotman, Y. M.
1970   *The Structure of the Artistic Text*, Ann Arbor, University of Michigan Press, 1977.
1976   "The Content and Structure of the Concept of 'Literature'", in *P. T. L.*, 1, 2, pp. 339–356.
Lotman, Y. M. and Uspenskij, B. A. (eds.)
1973   *Ricerche semiotiche. Nuove Tendenze delle scienze umane nell'URSS*, Milan, Einaudi.
Lotman, Y. M., Ivanov, V. V., Pjatigoskij, A. M., Toporov, V. N. and Uspenskij, B. A.
1979   "Tesi per un'analisi semiotica de la cultura", in Prevignano, C. (ed.), 1979, pp. 194–220.
Lukács, G.
1920   *Die Theorie des Romans*, Berlin, P. Cassirer (*The Theory of the Novel*, Cambridge, M. I. T. Press, 1971).
1947   *Goethe und seine Zeit*, Bern, Francke (*Goethe and His Age*, London, Merlin Press, 1968).
1954   *Prolegomena zu einer marxistischen Ästhetik* (*Prolegómenos a una estética marxista*, Barcelona, Grijalbo, 1969).
1955   *Der historische Roman*, Berlin, Aufbau Verlag (*The Historical Novel*, Boston, Beacon Press, 1962).
1958   *Wider den mißverstandenen Realismus*, Hamburg, Claasen.
1963   *Ästhetik*, Berlin-Spandau, H. Luchterhand, 1966–1967, four volumes.
Lüking, B.
1977   "Rhetorik und Literaturtheorie. Überlegungen zu einer interpretativen Poetik", in Plett, H. F. (ed.), pp. 45–61.

Macrí, O.
1962   "La storiografia sul Barocco letterario spagnolo", in *Manierismo, Barocco e Rococo: Conceti e termini*, Rome, Academia Naz. dei Lincei, pp. 149–198.
Macherey, P.
1974   *Pour une théorie de la production littéraire*, Paris, Maspero.
Maffesoli, M. (ed.)
1980   *La galaxie de l'imaginaire*, Paris, Berg.
Man, P. de
1971   *Blindness and Insight: Essays in the Rhetoric of Contemporary Criticism*, Minneapolis, University of Minnesota Press, 1986 (2nd rev. edition, 1983, 4th printing).

1979 *Allegories of Reading: Figural Language in Rousseau, Nietzsche, Rilke and Proust*, New Haven, Yale University Press.
et al. 1984 *The Rhetoric of Romanticism*, New York, Columbia University Press.
1986 *The Resistance to Theory*, Minneapolis, University of Minnesota Press.
1989 *Critical Writings*, ed. by L. Waters, Minneapolis, University of Minnesota Press.
Mandel, K. R.
1970 "Probleme der Wirkungsgeschichte", in *Jahrbuch für Internationale Germanistik*, 2, 1, pp. 71—84.
Mandelkow, K. R.
1975 "Rezeptionsästhetik und marxistische Literaturtheorie", in Müller-Seidler, W. (ed.), pp. 379—388.
Mannoni, O.
1969 *Clefs pour l'imaginaire ou l'autre scéne*, Paris, Seuil.
Mansuy, M.
1970 *Études sur l'imagination et la vie*, Paris, Corti.
Maravall, J. A.
1975 *La cultura del Barroco*, Barcelona, Ariel.
Marchese, A.
1978 *Dizionario di Retorica e di Stilistica*, Milan, Mondadori.
Margghescou, M.
1974 *Le concept de littérarieté*, The Hague, Mouton.
María, R. de
1978 "The Ideal Reader: A Critical Fiction", in *Publications of the Modern Language Association of America*, 93, pp. 463—473.
Marichal, J.
1971 *La voluntad de estilo*, Madrid, Revista de Occidente.
Marín, L.
1978 *Estudios semiológicos (La lectura de la imagen)*, Madrid, Comunicación.
Marshall, D. G.
1983 "History, Theory and Influence: Yale Critics as Readers of Maurice Blanchot", in Arac, J. (ed.), pp. 135—156.
Martin, J.
1974 *Antike Rhetorik. Technik und Methode*, Munich, Fink.
Martinet, A.
1965 *Elements de Linguistique Générale*, Paris, A. Colin, 1960 (*Elements of General Linguistics*, London, Faber and Faber, 1964).
Martínez Bonati, F.
1960 *La estructura de la obra literaria*, Barcelona, Seix Barral, 1972 (2nd revised edition).
1978 "El acto de escribir ficciones", in *Dispositio*, III, 7—8, pp. 137—144.
1981 "Representación y ficción", in *Revista Canadiense de Estudios Hispánicos*, VI, I, pp. 67—89.
Martínez García, J. A.
1975 *Propiedades del lenguaje poético*, Oviedo, Universidad de Oviedo.
Marx, K. and Engels, F.
1978 edition *On Literature and Art*, Chicago, Progress Publs.
Matoré, G.
1976 *L'Espace Humain*, Paris, Nizet.
Maturana, H. R.
1985 *Erkennen: Die Organisation und Verkörperung von Wirklichkeit*, Braunschweig, Vieweg.
Maurer, K.
1977 "Formen des Lesens", in *Poetica*, 9, pp. 472—498.

Mauron, C.
1962 *Les métaphores obsédantes au mythe personnel*, Paris, Corti.
Mayoral, J. A. (ed.)
1985 *Pragmática de la comunicación literaria*, Madrid, Arco.
1987 *Estética de la recepción*, Madrid, Arco.
Mazzacurati, G.
1961 *La crisi della retorica umanistica nel Cinquecento*, Naples, Libreria Scientifica.
Mazzeo, J. A.
1933 "Metaphysical Poetry and the Poetic of Correspondence", in *Journal of the History of Ideas*, 2, pp. 221—246.
Megaldo, P. V.
1978 *Linguistica e retorica di Dante*, Pisa, Nistri Lischi.
Mendonça Telhes, G.
1979 *A retórica do silêncio*, São Paulo, Cultrix.
Menéndez Pelayo, M.
1883—1891 *Historia de la ideas estéticas en España*, Madrid, C. S. I. C., 1949.
Metz, C.
1973 *Language and Cinema*, The Hague, Mouton.
Michel, A.
1982 *Le parole et la beauté. Rhétorique et Esthétique dans la tradition occidentale*, Paris, Les Belles Lettres.
Miller, J. H.
1963 *The Disappearance of God*, Cambridge, Harvard University Press.
1970 *Thomas Hardy: Distance and Desire*, Cambridge, Harvard University Press.
(ed.) 1971 *Aspects of Narrative*, New York, Columbia University Press.
Miner, E.
1976 "That Literature Is a Kind of Knowledge", in *Critical Inquiry*, 2, 3.
1976 a "The Objective Fallacy and the Real Existence of Literature", in *P. T. L.*, I, I.
Mitchell, W. J. T. (ed.)
1981 *On Narrative*, Chicago, University of Chicago Press.
Molino, J.
1971 "La connotation", in *La Linguistique*, 7, 1.
Moreno Cabrera, J. C.
1985 "La teoría de los objetos no existentes de T. Parsons y el análisis de la ficción narrativa", in *Teoría Semiótica. Lenguajes y textos hispánicos. Actas del Congreso Internacional sobre Semiótica e Hispanismo*, Madrid, 20—25 de junio de 1983, C. S. I. C.
Morpurgo-Tagliabue, G.
1960 *La esthétique contemporaine. Une enquête*, Milan, Marzorati.
Morris, C.
1946 *Signs, Language, and Behavior*, New York, Prentice Hall.
Mosconi, G., et al.
1981 *Discorso e retorica*, Turin, Loescher.
Mounin, G.
1969 *La communication poétique*, Paris, Gallimard.
Muir, E.
1928 *The Structure of the Novel*, London, Hogart Press, 1967 (10th edition).
Mukařovský, J.
1964 "Standard Language and Poetic Language", in Garvin, P. L. (ed.).
Müller-Seidler, W. (ed.)
1975 *Historizität in Sprach- und Literaturwissenschaft*, Munich, Fink.
Muñoz Cortés, M.
1986 *Estudios de Estilística textual*, Murcia, Universidad de Murcia.

Murray, H. A.
1943 *Thematic Apperception Test Manual*, Cambridge, Harvard University Press.
Murphy, J. J.
1974 *Rhetoric in the Middle Ages*, Berkeley, University of California Press.
1983 *A Synoptic History of Classical Rhetoric*, Davis, Hermagoras Press.
(ed.) 1983 *Renaissance Eloquence*, Berkeley, University of California Press.
1985 *Three Medieval Rhetorical Arts*, Berkeley, University of California Press.

Nadeau, M.
1945—1948 *Histoire du Surréalisme*, Paris, Seuil, 2 volumes (*The History of Surrealism*, London, Cape, 1968).
Naess, A.
1975 *Kommunikation und Argumentation*, Kronberg, Skriptor.
Naumann, M.
1971 "Autor, Adressat, Leser", *Weimarer Beiträge*, 17, pp. 163—169.
(ed.) 1973 *Gesellschaft, Literatur, Lesen, Literaturrezeption in theoretischer Sicht*, West Berlin, Aufbau Verlag.
Navarro Tomás, T.
1966 *Métrica española*, New York, Las Américas.
Nemoianu, V.
1984 "Societal Models as Substitute Reality in Literature", in *Poetics Today*, 5, 2, pp. 275—297.
Norden, E.
1898 *Die antike Kunstprosa vom IV Jahrhundert vor Christ in der Zeit der Renaissance*, Stuttgart, Teubner, 1974 (7th edition).
Norris, C. H.
1982 *Deconstruction: Theory and Practice*, London and New York, Methuen.
1983 *The Deconstructive Turn*, London and New York, Methuen.
Novalis
1960 *Hymns to the Night and Other Selected Writings*, trans. by C. Passage, New York, Bobbs-Merrill.

Ohmann, R.
1971 "Speech Acts and the Definition of Literature", in *Philosophy and Rhetoric*, 4, pp. 1—19.
1972 "Speech, Literature and the Space Between", in *New Literary History*, 4, 1, pp. 47—63.
Ong, W. J.
1975 "The Writer's Audience Is Always a Fiction", in *Publications of the Modern Language Association of America*, 90, pp. 9—21.
Ortega y Gasset, J.
1966 *Obras Completas*, Madrid, Revista de Occidente.
Owen, G. (ed.)
1968 *Aristotle on Dialectic. The Topics*, Oxford, Clarendon Press.

Pagnini, M.
1970 "La critica letteraria come integrazione dei livelli dell'opera", in *Studi offerti a M. Fubini*, Padua, Liviana, I, pp. 87—102.
1980 *Pragmatica della letteratura*, Palermo, Cellerio.
Pajano, R.
1972 *La nozione di Poetica*, Bologna, Pàtron.

Panofsky, E.
1974 edition *Idea. A Concept in Art Theory*, New York, Marc Row.
Paraíso de Leal, I.
1976   *Teoría del ritmo de la prosa*, Barcelona, Planeta.
Pareyson, L.
1954   *Estetica. Teoria della formatività*, Turin, Edizioni di Filosofia (new print., Milan, Bompiani, 1987).
Partee, B. H.
1989   "Possible Worlds in Model-Theoretic Semantics", in S. Allén (ed.), pp. 93–123.
Pasoli, E.
1964   *Le epistole letterarie di Orazio*, Bologna, Pàtron.
Pavel, T. G.
1975   "Possible Worlds in Literary Semantics", in *Journal of Aesthetics and Art Criticism*, 34, 2, pp. 165–176.
1979   "Fiction and the Causal Theory of Names", in *Poetics*, 8, 1–2, pp. 179–191.
1980   "Les mondes possibles et la logique du vraisemblable", in Gómez-Moriana, A. and Gürttler, K. R. (eds.), 1980, pp. 182–194.
1983   "The Borders of Fiction", in *Poetics Today*, 4, 1, pp. 83–88.
Pelletier, A. M.
1977   *Fonctions poétiques*, Paris, Klincksieck.
Perelman, C. and Olbrechts-Tyteca, L.
1958   *Traité de l'argumentation*, Paris.
Petöfi, J. S.
1973a   "Towards an Empirically Motivated Grammatical Theory of Verbal Texts", in Petöfi, J. S. and Rieser, H. (eds.), pp. 207–275.
1975   "Beyond the Sentence, Between Linguistics and Logic", in *Style in Text*, Stockholm, Skriptor.
1975a   *Vers une théorie partielle du texte*, Papiere zur Textlinguistik, Hamburg, Buske.
1977   *Text and Discourse Constitution*, Berlin, De Gruyter.
(ed.) 1979 *Text vs. Sentence. Basic Questions of Text Linguistics*, Hamburg, Buske, two volumes.
1979a   "La representación del léxico como red semántica", in Petöfi, J. S. and García-Berrio, A., pp. 216–242.
Petöfi, J. S. and Franck, D.
1973   *Präsuppositionen in Philosophie und Linguistik*, Frankfurt, Athenäum.
Petöfi, J. S. and Güriía-Berrio, A.
1979   *Lingüística del texto y crítica literaria*, Madrid, Comunicación.
Petöfi, J. S. and Rieser, H. (eds.)
1973   *Studies in Text Grammar*, Dordrecht, Reidel.
Piaget, J.
1950   *Introduction a l'épistémologie génétique*, Paris, P. U. F.
1954   *La construction du réal chez l'enfant*, Neuchâtel, Delchamp et Nistlé (3rd corrected edition) (*The Construction of Reality in the Child*, New York, Basic Books, 1954).
Picard, M.
1948   *Die Welt des Schweigens*, Zürich, Rentsch.
Pir, F.
1967   *De l'imagination poétique dans l'oeuvre de Gaston Bachelard*, Paris, Corti.
Plato
1979 edition *The Republic*, Arlington Heights, H. Davidson.
Plett, H. F.
1971   *Rhetorische Textanalyse*, Hamburg, Buske.
(ed.) 1977 *Rhetorik. Kritische Positionen zum Stand der Forschung*, Munich, Fink.
1977   "Die Rhetorik der Figuren. Zur Systematiker Pragmatik und Ästhetik der Elocutio", in Plett, H. F. (ed.), pp. 125–166.

Poggioli, R.
 1962 *Teoria dell'arte d'avanguardia*, Bologna, Il Mulino.
Popovich, A.
 1979 "Testo e metatesto (Tipologia dei supporti intertestuali come oggetto delle ricerche della scienza della letteratura", in Prevignano, C. (ed.), pp. 521—545.
Posner, R.
 1976 "Poetic Communication vs. 'Literary Language': The Linguistic Fallacy in Poetics", in *P. T. L.*, I, 1, pp. 1—10.
Poulet, G.
 1950 *Études sur le temps humain*, Paris, Gallimard.
 1961 *Le métamorphose du cercle*, Paris, Gallimard.
 1963 *L'espace proustien*, Paris, Gallimard.
 1970 "Phenomenology of Reading", in *New Literary Criticism*, I, pp. 53—68.
Pozuelo Yvancos, J. M.
 1983 *La lengua literaria*, Málaga, Agora.
 1986 "Retórica y narrativa: 'la narratio'", in *Epos*, II, pp. 231—252.
 1988 *Teoría del Lenguaje literario*, Madrid, Cátedra.
 1988a *Del Formalismo a la Neorretórica*, Madrid, Taurus.
Pratt, M. L.
 1977 *Toward a Speech Act Theory of Literary Discourse*, Bloomington, Indiana University Press.
 1986 "Ideology and Speech-Act Theory", in *Poetics Today*, 7, 1, pp. 59—72.
Praz, M.
 1975 *Studies in Seventeenth-century Imagery*, Rome, Edizioni di Storia e Letteratura.
Prevignano, C. (ed.)
 1979 *La semiotica nei Paesi slavi*, Milan, Feltrinelli.
Prince, G.
 1973 *A Grammar of Stories*, The Hague and Paris, Mouton.
 1973a "Introduction à l'étude du narrataire", in *Poétique*, 14, pp. 178—196.
 1982 *Narratology. The Form and Functioning of Narrative*, Berlin, Mouton.
Prior, A. N.
 1962 "Possible Worlds", in *Philosophical Quarterly*, 12, 46, pp. 36—43.
Propp, V.
 1928 *Morphology of the Folktale*, Austin, University of Texas Press, 1968.

Quevedo, F. de
 1980 edition *Songs of Death and Love and in Between*, trans. and ed. by D. M. Gitlitz, Lawrence, Kansas-Coronado Press.
Quine, W. V. O.
 1960 *Word and Object*, Cambridge, Technology Press of M. I. T.

Rabinowitz, P.
 1977 "Truth in Fiction: A Reexamination of Audiences", in *Critical Inquiry*, 4, pp. 121—141.
Raible, W.
 1980 "Was sind Gattungen? Eine Antwort aus semiotischer und textlinguistischer Sicht", in *Poetica*, 12, pp. 320—349.
Raimondi, E.
 1961 *Letteratura barocca*, Florence, Olschki.
 1974 *Il romanzo senza idilio*, Turin, Einaudi.
 1983 "Retorica e linguaggio letterario", in *Intersezioni*, III, pp. 484—503.
 1985 *Le pietre del sogno*, Bologna, Il Mulino.

Ransom, J. C.
1941   *The New Criticism*, Norfolk, New Directions.
Rasmussen, D.
1974   *Poetry and Truth*, The Hague, Mouton.
Rastier, F.
1972   "Systématique des isotopies", in Greimas, A. J. (ed.), pp. 80—105.
1973   *Essais de sémiotique discursive*, Paris, Marne.
Raymond, M.
1947   *De Baudelaire au Surréalisme*, Paris, Corti.
Redondo, A.
1980   "El personaje de don Quijote; tradiciones folklórico-literarias. Contexto histórico y elaboración cervantina", in *Nueva Revista de Filología Hispánica*, XXIX, pp. 36—59.
(ed.) 1985 *Amours légitimes et amours illégitimes en Espagne (XVIe—XVIIe siècles)*, Paris, Publications de la Sorbonne.
Reeves, C. E.
1986   "The Languages of Convention. Literature and Consensus", in *Poetics Today*, 7, 1, pp. 3—28.
Reisz de Rivarola, S.
1979   "Ficcionalidad, referencia, tipos de ficción literaria", in *Lexis*, 3, 2, pp. 99—170.
Rewar, W.
1976   "Tartu Semiotics", in *P. T. L.*, I, 1, pp. 153—196.
Rey-Debove, J. (ed.)
1973   *Recherches sur les signifiants*, The Hague, Mouton.
Reyes, A.
1941   *La crítica en la edad ateniense*, Mexico, Colegio de México.
Revzin, I. I.
1979   "Alcune nozioni semiotiche e i principi generali dell'analisi dei sistemi segnici", in Prevignano, C. (ed.), pp. 316—321.
Richards, I. A.
1929   *Practical criticism*, London, Routledge and Keagan Paul.
1936   *The Philosophy of Rhetoric*, New York, Oxford University Press, 1965.
Ricoeur, P.
1969   *Le conflit des interprétations*, Paris, Seuil.
1975   *Le métaphore vive*, Paris, Seuil.
1983—1986   *Temps et récit*, Paris, Seuil, 3 volumes (*Time and Narrative*, Chicago, University of Chicago Press, 1984).
Rieser, H. (ed.)
1982   *Semantics of Fiction*, special issue of *Poetics*, 11, 4—6.
Riffaterre, M.
1971   *Essais de Stylistique Structurale*, Paris, Flammarion.
1978   *Semiotics of Poetry*, Bloomington, Indiana University Press.
1979   *La production du texte*, Paris, Seuil (*Text Production*, New York, Columbia University Press, 1983).
Ritter Santini, L. and Raimondi, E. (eds.)
1978   *Retorica e Critica letteraria*, Bologna, Il Mulino.
Rockinger, L.
1863—1864   *Briefsteller und Formelbuch des elften bis vierzehnten Jahrhunderts (1863—1864)*, New York, Franklin (reprint, 1961).
Rodríguez Adrados, F.
1974   "Las unidades literarias como lenguaje artístico", in *Revista Española de Lingüística*, 4, 1, pp. 133—134.

Rollin, B. E.
   1981   "Nature, Convention and Genre Theory", in *Poetics*, 10, pp. 127–143.
Romberg, B.
   1962   *Studies in the Narrative Technique of the First-Person Novel*, Stockholm, Almqvist and Wiksell.
Romero de Solís, D.
   1981   *Poiesis. Sobre las relaciones entre filosofía y poesía desde el alma trágica*, Madrid, Taurus.
Ronen, R.
   1986   "Space in Fiction", in *Poetics Today*, 7, 3, pp. 421–438.
Rorty, R.
   1982   "Idealism and Textualism", in *Consequences of Pragmatism*, Minneapolis, University of Minnesota Press.
Rosmarin, A.
   1985   *The Power of Genre*, Minneapolis, University of Minnesota Press.
Rostagni, A.
   1930   *Arte Poetica di Orazio (Introduzione e Commento)*, Turin, Chiantore.
Rothe, A.
   1987   "Le rôle de lecteur dans la critique allemande contemporaine", in *Littérature*, 3, 2, pp. 96–104.
Rousse, J.
   1972   "La prima persona nel romanzo. Abbozzo di una tipologia", in *Strumenti Critici*, VI, 19, pp. 259–274.
Rousset, J.
   1945   *La littérature de l'âge baroque en France. Circe et le paon*, Paris, Corti.
Ruttkovski, W. V.
   1968   *Die literarischen Gattungen*, Bern.
Ruwet, N.
   1972   *Langage, musique, poésie*, Paris, Seuil.
Ryan, M. L.
   1979   "Towards a competence theory of Genre", in *Poetics*, 8, 3, pp. 307–377.
   1980   "Fiction, Non-Factuals and the Principle of Minimal Departure", in *Poetics*, 9, 4, pp. 403–422.
   1981   "The Pragmatics of Personal and Impersonal Fiction", in *Poetics*, 10, 6, pp. 517–539.
   1981 a   "On the Why, What and How of Generic Taxonomy", in *Poetics*, 10, 2/3, pp. 109–206.

Sacks, S. (ed.)
   1980   *On Metaphor*, Chicago, University of Chicago Press.
Sager, P.
   1974   *Neue Formen des Realismus*, Köln, Du Mont Schauberg.
Saintsbury, G. E. B.
   1902–1904 *A History of Criticism and Literary Taste in Europe*, Geneva, Slatkine, 1971, three volumes.
Saitta, G.
   1949–1951 *Il pensiero italiano nell'Umanesimo e nel Rinascimento*, Bologna, Zuffi.
Samarini, A. N.
   1979   "Particolarità dello sviluppo di alcuni sistemi segnici", in Prevignano, C. (ed.), pp. 309–315.
Sartre, J. P.
   1950   *L'imagination*, Paris, Seuil.
Saussure, F. de
   1916   *Course in General Linguistics*, London, Duckworth, 1983.

Scrivano, R.
1959   *Il manierismo nella letteratura del Cinquecento*, Padua, Liviana.
Schaeffer, J. M.
1983   "Du genre au texte. Notes sur la problematique générique", in *Poétique*, 53, pp. 3–18.
Scheglov, J. K. and Zholkovskij, A. K.
1979   "I concetti di 'tema' e di 'mondo' poetico", in Prevignano, C. (ed.), pp. 302–345.
Schlegel, F.
1956 edition *Schriften und Fragmente*, Stuttgart, Kröner.
Schlosser-Magnino, J.
1924   *Die Kunstliteratur*, Wien, Anton Schroll and Co.
Schmidt, S. J.
1970   *Text, Bedeutung, Ästhetik*, Munich, Bayerischer Schulbuch Verlag.
1972   *Ästhetizitat. Philosophische Beiträge zu einer Theorie des Ästhetischen*, Munich, Bayerischer Schulbuch Verlag.
1973   *Texttheorie*, Munich, Fink.
1974   *Elemente einer Textpoetik*, Munich, Bayerischer Schulbuch Verlag.
1976   "Towards a Pragmatic Interpretation of 'Fictionality'", in Dijk, T. A. van (ed.), pp. 161–178.
1979   *Grundriß der empirischen Literaturwissenschaft*, Braunschweig, Vieweg.
1979 a   "Empirische Literaturwissenschaft als Perspektive", in *Poetics*, 8, pp. 557–568.
(ed.) 1979 b *Empirie in Literatur und Kunstwissenschaft*, Munich, Fink.
1980   "Fictionality in Literary and Non-Literary Discourse", in *Poetics*, 9, 5–6, pp. 525–546.
1981   "Empirical Studies in Literature: Introductory Remarks", in *Poetics*, 10, pp. 317–336.
1983   *La comunicazione letteraria*, Milan, Il Saggiatore.
1983 a   "L'interpretation: veau d'or ou necessité", in *Versus*, 35–36, pp. 77–98.
1984   "The Fiction Is That Reality Exists. A Constructivist Model of Reality, Fiction and Literature", in *Poetics Today*, 5, 2, pp. 253–274.
Schmidt, S. J. and Henkel, G.
1972   "Die Trivialliteratur im Kanon der Literaturwissenschaft", in *Sprachen im technischen Zeitalter*, 44, pp. 258–269.
Scholes, R.
1976   *Structuralism in Literature*, New Haven, Yale University Press.
Scholes, R. and Kellog, R.
1966   *The Nature of Narrative*, Oxford, Oxford University Press.
Schor, N.
1984   "Details and Realism: 'Le Curé de Tours'", in *Poetics*, 5, 4, pp. 701–709.
Schramm, W. (ed.)
1970   *Grundfragen der Kommunikationswissenschaft*, Munich.
Schunk, P.
1971   "Zur Wirkungsgeschichte des Misantrope", in *Germanisch-Romanische Monatsschrift*, 52, pp. 1–15.
Searle, J. H.
1969   *Speech Acts: An Essay in the Philosophy of Language*, London, Cambridge University Press.
1977   "Reiterating the Difference. A Reply to Derrida", in *Gliph*, 1.
Sebeok, T. A. (ed.)
1960   *Style in Language*, New York–London, The Technology Press of M. I. T. and J. Wiley.
Segers, R. T.
1975   "Readers, Text and Author: Some Implications of Rezeptionsästhetik", in *Yearbook of Comparative Literature*, 24, pp. 15–24.

Segre, C.
1969 *I segni e la critica*, Turin, Einaudi.
1974 *Le strutture e il tempo*, Turin, Einaudi (*Structures and Time*, Chicago, University of Chicago Press, 1979).
1979 "Generi", in *Enciclopedia*, Turin, Einaudi, pp. 581–584.
1985 *Avviamento all'analisi del testo letterario*, Turin, Einaudi (*Introduction to the Analysis of the Literary Text*, Bloomington, Indiana University Press, 1988).
Selden, R.
1985 *A Reader's Guide to Contemporary Literary Theory*, Brighton, The Harvester Press.
Sgall, P., Hajicova, E. and Benesova, E.
1973 *Topic, Forms and Generative Semantics*, Kronberg, Skriptor.
Shapiro, K.
1976 *Asymmetry. An Inquiry into the Linguistic Structure of Poetry*, Amsterdam, North Holland.
Shapiro, K. and Beum, R.
1972 "Metro, ritmo, espressività", in Cremante, R. and Pazzaglia, M. (eds.), pp. 109–116.
Shibles, K. W. A.
1971 *Metaphor. An Annotated Bibliography and History*, Whitewater, Language Press.
Shklovsky, V.
1925 *Una teoria della prosa*, Bari, De Donato, 1970.
Shukman, A.
1977 *Literature and Semiotics. A Study of the Writings of J. M. Lotman*, Amsterdam, North Holland.
1978 "Soviet Semiotics and Literary Criticism", in *New Literary History*, IX, 2, pp. 189–197.
Sirri, R.
1974 *Che cosa è la letteratura*, Naples, De Simone.
Sloan, T. O. and Waddington, R. B. (eds.)
1974 *The Rhetoric of Renaissance Poetry*, Berkeley, University of California Press.
Sobejano, G.
1970 *El epíteto en la lírica española*, Madrid, Gredos.
Spillner, B.
1974 *Linguistik und Literaturwissenschaft*, Stuttgart, Kohlhammer.
1977 "Das Interesse der Linguistik an der Rhetorik", in Plett, H. F. (ed.), pp. 93–108.
Spingarn, J. E.
1908 *A History of Literary Criticism in the Italian Renaissance*, New York, Columbia University Press, 1963.
Spitzer, L.
1948 *Linguistics and Literary History*, Princeton, Princeton University Press.
Staiger, E.
1946 *Grundbegriffe der Poetik*, Zürich, Atlantis.
Stalnaker, R. C.
1976 "Possible Worlds", in *Noûs*, 10, pp. 67–75.
Stankiewicz, E.
1984 "Linguistics, Poetics and the Literary Genres", in *New Directions in Linguistics and Semiotics*, Amsterdam, J. Benjamins.
Stanzel, F. K.
1955 *Die typischen Erzählungssituationen im Roman*, Vienna, Bronmuller.
Stégen, G.
1960 *Essai sur la composition de cinq epîtres d'Horace*, Namur, Wemael-Charlier.
Steinmetz, M.
1981 *Réception et interpretation*, in Kibédi Varga, A. (ed.), pp. 193–209.

Steiman, M.
1981 "Superordinate genre conventions", in *Poetics*, 10, 2–3, pp. 243–261.
Stempel, W. D.
1972 "Gibt es Textsorten?", in Gülich, E. and Raible, W. (eds.).
1979 "Aspects génériques de la réception", in *Poétique*, 39, pp. 353–362.
Stender-Petersen, A.
1949 "Esquisse d'une théorie structurale de la littérature", in *Travaux du Cercle Linguistique de Copenhague*, V, pp. 277–287.
Stern, J. P.
1973 *On Realism*, London, Routledge and Keagan Paul.
Stierle, K.
1979 *Texte als Handlung: Perspektiven einer systematischen Literaturwissenschaft*, Munich, Fink.
1975 a "Was heißt Rezeption bei fiktionalen Texten?", in *Poetics*, 7, pp. 345–387.
1977 "Identité du discours et transgression lyrique", in *Poétique*, 32, pp. 422–441.
Strelka, J. P.
1978 *Theories of Literary Genre*, Pennsylvania–London, Pennsylvania State University Press.
Striedter, J.
1969 *Texte der russischen Formalisten*, Munich, Fink.
1989 *Literary Structure, Evolution and Value*, Cambridge, Harvard University Press.
Stutterheim, C. F. P.
1969 "Prolegomena to a Theory of Literary Genres", in *Zagawnienia Rodzajow Literackich*, 6.2, 11, p. 524.
Suleiman, S. R. and Crossman, I.
1980 "The Reader in Text", in *Essays on Audience and Interpretation*, Princeton, Princeton University Press.
Suvin, D.
1979 *Metamorphoses of Science Fiction*, New Haven, Yale University Press.
Sypher, W.
1956 *Four Stages of Renaissance Style*, Garden City, Doubleday and Co.

Tadié, J. Y.
1987 *La critique littéraire au XXe siècle*, Paris, Belford.
Tatarkiewicz, W.
1970 *History of Aesthetics*, The Hague, Mouton, three volumes.
Tateo, F.
1960 *Retorica e poetica fra Medioevo e Rinascimento*, Bari, Adriatica.
Terracini, B.
1966 *Analisi stilistica. Teoria, storia, problemi*, Milan, Feltrinelli.
1976 "Analisi del concetto di lingua letteraria", in *I Segni, la storia*, Naples, Guida, pp. 175–204.
Terracini, L.
1988 *I codici del silenzio*, Turin, Ed. dell'Orso.
Thompson, E. M.
1971 *Russian Formalism and Anglo-American New Criticism*, The Hague, Mouton.
Tieghem, P. van
1938 "La question des genres littéraires", in *Helicon*, 1, pp. 95–101.
1946 *Les grandes doctrines littéraires en France*, Paris, P. U. F., 1974.
Timpanaro, S.
1965 *Classicismo e illuminismo nell'Ottocento italiano*, Pisa, Nistri Lischi.

Todorov, T. (ed.)
1965 *Théorie de la littérature*, Paris, Seuil.
1966 "Las categorías del relato literario", in VV. AA. 1974, pp. 159–192.
1967 *Littérature et signification*, Paris, Larousse.
1968 *Poétique, Qu'es-ce que l'estructuralisme*, Paris, Seuil.
1969 *Grammaire du Decameron*, The Hague, Mouton.
1970 *Introduction a la littérature fantastique*, Paris, Seuil.
1976 "The Origin of Genres", in *New Literary History*, VIII, 1, pp. 159–170.
1978 *Les genres du discours*, Paris, Seuil.
Tomashevsky, B.
1928 *Teoría de la Literatura*, Madrid, Akal, 1981.
1928a "La nouvelle école d'histoire littéraire en Russie", in *Revue d'études slaves*, V, pp. 226–240.
1965 "Thématique", in Todorov, T. (ed.), pp. 263–307.
Tompkins, J. P. (ed.)
1980 *Reader-Response Criticism. From Formalism to Post-structuralism*, Baltimore, Johns Hopkins University Press.
Torre, G. de
1966 *Problemática de la literatura*, Buenos Aires, Losada.
Trabant, J.
1970 *Zur Semiologie des Literarischen Kunst-Werks*, Munich, W. Fink.
Tynjanov, J.
1924 *Il problema del linguaggio poetico*, Milan, Mondadori, 1968 (*The Problem of Verse Language*, Ann Arbor, Ardis Publs., 1981).
1929 *Avanguardia e tradizione*, Bari, Dedalo, 1968.

Ueding, G.
1976 *Einführung in die Rhetorik*, Stuttgart, Metzler.
Uehling, T. F.
1971 *The Notion of Form in Kant's Critique of Aesthetic Judgement*, The Hague, Mouton.
Uitti, K.
1969 *Linguistics and Literary Theory*, Englewood Cliffs, New Jersey, Prentice-Hall.
Uspensky, B.
1973 *A Poetics of Composition*, Bloomington, Indiana University Press.

Vajda, G. M.
1981 "Points de vue pour la théorie esthétique de la Recéption", in *Neohelion*, 8, 2, pp. 291–297.
Valéry, Paul
1977 edition *Paul Valéry: An Anthology*, ed. by James R. Lawler, Princeton, Princeton University Press.
Valesio, P.
1967 *Struttura dell'alliterazione*, Bologna, Zanichelli.
1980 *Novantiqua. Rhetorics as a Contemporary Theory*, Bloomington, Indiana University Press.
1986 *Ascoltare il silenzio*, Bologna, Il Mulino.
Veltrusky, J.
1977 *Drama as Literature*, Lisse, Ridder Press.
Verene, P.
1981 *Vico's Science of Imagination*, New York and London, Cornell University Press.
Vickers, B.
1988 *In Defence of Rhetoric*, Oxford, Clarendon Press.

Vierne, S.
1980 "La littérature dans le labyrinte", in Maffesoli, M. (ed.), pp. 202—210.
Viëtor, K.
1931 "L'histoire des genres littéraires", in *Poétique*, 32, 1977, pp. 490—506.
Villegas, J.
1973 *La estructura mítica del héroe*, Barcelona, Planeta.
1976 *Estructuras míticas y arquetipos en el 'Canto General' de Neruda*, Barcelona, Planeta.
Vinogradov, V.
1969 "Das Problem des 'skaz' in der Stilistik", in Striedter, J. (ed.), pp. 203 ff.
Volli, U.
1978 "Mondi possibili, logica, semiotica", in *Versus*, 16—20, pp. 123—148.
VV. AA.
1970 *Lo verosímil*, Comunicaciones, 11, Buenos Aires, Tiempo Contemporáneo.

Walton, K. L.
1978 "How Remote are Fictional Worlds from the Real World", in *Journal of Aesthetics and Art Criticism*, 37, pp. 11—23.
Walzel, O.
1952 *German Romanticism*, New York, MacMillan.
Warneker, B. J.
1972 "Abriß einer Analyse literarischer Produktion", in *Das Argument*, 72, pp. 27—232.
Warning, R.
1977 "Hermeneutik, Semiotik und Rezeptionsästhetik", in *Romanistische Zeitschrift Literaturgeschichte*, I, pp. 126—131.
(ed.) 1975 *Rezeptionsästhetik. Theorie und Praxis*, Munich, Fink.
Watzlawick, P. (ed.)
1985 *Die erfundene Wirklichkeit. Wie wissen wir, was wir zu wissen glauben? Beiträge zum Konstruktivismus*, Munich, Piper.
Weber, H. D.
1978 *Rezeptionsgeschichte oder Wirkungsästhetik*, Stuttgart, Klett-Cotta.
Weber, J. P.
1960 *Génèse de l'oeuvre poétique*, Paris, Gallimard.
1963 *Domaines thématiques*, Paris, Gallimard.
Weimann, R.
1970 "Gegenwart und Vergangenheit in der Literaturgeschichte", in *Weimarer Beiträge*, 5, pp. 31—57.
1973 "'Rezeptionsästhetik' und die Krise der Literaturgeschichte", in *Weimarer Beiträge*, 8, pp. 5—33.
Weinberg, B.
1961 *A History of Literary Criticism in the Italian Renaissance*, Chicago, University of Chicago Press, two volumes.
1970—1973 *Trattati di Poetica e Retorica del '500*, Bari, Laterza, four volumes.
Weinrich, H.
1967 "Für eine Literaturgeschichte des Lesens", in *Mercur*, 234, pp. 1026 ff.
1971 *Tempus*, Stuttgart, Kohlhammer.
1971 a *Literatur für Leser*, Stuttgart, Kohlhammer.
(ed.) 1975 *Positionen und Negativität*, Munich, Fink.
Weise, G.
1961 *L'ideale eroico del Rinascimento e le sue premesse umanistiche*, Naples, Ed. Scientifiche.
1969 *Il Rinascimento e la sua eredità*, Naples, Signori.
1978 *Il manierismo. Bilancio critico del problema stilistico e culturale*, Florence, Olschki.
Weissenberger, K.
1978 "A Morphological Genre Theory", in Strelka, J. P. (ed.), pp. 229—253.

Wellek, R.
1946 "The Concept of Baroque in Literary Scholarship", in *Journal of Aesthetics and Art Criticism*, V, pp. 79—109.
1955 *A History of Modern Criticism: 1750—1950*, New Haven, Yale University Press.
1963 *Concepts of Criticism*, New Haven, Yale University Press.
1970 *Discriminations: Further Concepts of Criticism*, New Haven, Yale University Press.
Wellek, R. and Warren, A.
1956 edition *Theory of literature*, New York, Harcourt.
Wienold, G.
1974 "Textverarbeitung. Überlegungen zur Kategorienbildung in einer strukturellen Literaturgeschichte", in Höhendahl, P. U. (ed.), pp. 97—134.
1978 "Textlinguistic Approaches to Written Works of Art", in Dressler, W. U., pp. 133—154.
Williams, G.
1968 *Tradition and Originality in Roman Poetry*, Oxford, Oxford University Press.
Williams, R.
1980 *Marxism and Literature*, Oxford, Oxford University Press.
Wilson, E.
1931 *Axel's Castle: A Study in the Imaginative Literature of 1870—1930*, New York, Charles Scribner's Sons.
Wolff, I.
1971 "Der intendierte Leser", in *Poetics*, 3, pp. 141 ff.
Wood, T. E. B.
1972 *The Word 'Sublime' and Its Context*, The Hague, Mouton.
Woods, J. and Pavel, T. G. (eds.)
1979 "Formal Semantics and Literary Theory", in *Poetics*, 8, 1—2, 1979.
Woolf, W.
1928 *The Common Reader*, New York, Harcourt.
1932 *The Second Common Reader*, New York, Harcourt.
Wright, A.
1987 *Fictional Discourse and Fictional Space*, London, MacMillan.

Yllera, A.
1974 *Estilística, poética y semiótica literaria*, Madrid, Alianza, 1979 (2nd edition).

Zeraffa, M.
1966 "Le temps et ses formes dans le roman contemporain", in *Revue d'esthétique*, 1, pp. 43—65.
Zgorzelski, A.
1984 "On Differentiating Fantastic Fiction: Some Supragenological Distinctions in Literature", in *Poetics Today*, 5, 2, pp. 299—307.
Zimmermann, B.
1974 "Der Leser als Produzent: Zur Problematik der rezeptionsästhetischen Methoden", in *Zeitschrift für Literaturwissenschaft und Linguistik*, 4, 15, pp. 12—26.
Žirmunsky, V.
1966 *Introduction to Metrics*, The Hague, Mouton.
Zumthor, P.
1972 *Essai de Poétique Mediévale*, Paris, Seuil.
1975 *Langue, texte, énigme*, Paris, Seuil.

Index of Contents

Actio   119, 125
Aesthetic effect   89
Aesthetic function   87
Aesthetic value   41, 97, 148, 268, 285, 324, 329, 423
Aesthetics of reception   147—150, 170—179, 186, 262, 263, 271
Aisthesis   175, 493
Agrammaticality   485
Ambiguity (as poetic property)   294—300, 306, 307
Anagnorisis   441
Antidistributive structures   280
Anthropological orientation   358—360, 363, 393, 402, 450, 490
Anxiety (of influence)   84, 290, 292, 294
Appellative structures   177
Appreciation (theory of)   139—141
Arbitrariness
— of the textual construction   145, 146, 153
— theoretical   271
— of the system of genres   470
Archetypal image   379
Archetypal lexeme   317
Archetypal psychology   312
Archwriting   212, 234
Argumentation (theory of)   139—141
Argumentative parameter   282

Basic dominant   335

Carnavalesque space   441
Catharsis   7, 10, 175, 176
Chronotope   109, 440
Classes of style   464
Classical sonnet (structures of)   273, 274, 276—279, 280—284
Cognition   487
Compositional structures   290
Connotative periphery   103, 178, 340
Consistency of poetry   221, 222, 224, 228, 241, 245, 246
— of artistic texts   447, 457
— Construction (macrotextual)   275, 280
— syntactical   482

Context   65, 272, 273, 276, 327
— conventional context   265, 264, 274
— internal context   263, 265
— contextual frame   327
— contextually motivated causes   67
Conventionality of literature   41, 145, 156, 266, 267, 270, 283—289, 465
— negatively conventional   271
— positively conventional   271
Convergence (ideology of)   291
Cotext   65
— co-textually motivated causes   67
Crisis
— of superproduction of formalist schools   4, 34, 319
— of structuralist poetics   33, 36
— of poststructuralism   152—170, 317
Critical writing   162—164, 298
Crystallization   269, 270, 348
Cultural imagination   347—351, 354
Cultural series   264
Cultural stereotypes   351
Cultural topics   269

Deautomatization   20, 29, 47, 66, 227, 339
— de-automatizing devices   483
Deconstructionism   3, 206, 210, 218—225, 230, 237, 240, 262
Decorum   11, 67, 68, 76, 184, 483
Delectare   125, 135
Denotative mode   87
Dianoia   378, 479, 480
Dialectics of symbolic representation   457
— natural-   459
Diegesis   467
Différance   130, 211—214, 232, 234—237, 306
Différence (in the deconstruction)   211—214, 230, 250, 251, 255, 338
Digestive regime   19, 336, 399, 400
— dominant in painting   491—495
Discourse (in narratology)   32, 78
Displacement   235
Dispositio   10, 11, 21, 72, 73, 76, 77, 114, 116, 119—121, 124, 125, 140, 141, 381, 480, 483

Disproportion (principle of)   433, 434
Dissemination (semantic)   218, 219, 222, 231, 237
Diurnal experience   19, 355, 356, 370—372, 374—376, 384, 385, 388, 394, 395, 408
Docere   125, 135
Double articulation   481

Elocutio   11, 72, 76, 77, 114, 119, 121, 124—126, 140, 480, 481
Embellished discourse   13
Ethical exchange   133
Ethical factor   132
Ethical incarnation   132
Ethical value   131
Ethos   132, 378
Expansion (as poetic tendency)   359, 360
— unlimited -   394
Expressiveness
— fantastic nature of   18, 19, 342
— in classical poetics   97—100, 421, 423
— in classical literature   104—112, 314
— macrostructure of   123 and foll.
— of the de-automatizing mechanism   11, 13
— persuasive -   131, 135, 437
— plastic-   485
— poetic effects of   90, 288
— rhetorical -   136, 267, 340, 437, 438
— stylemes of   115
— verbal and fantastic constituents of   94—97, 343, 345, 352, 357, 360, 368, 376, 401—403, 405, 452, 457, 484, 489
Evocative myth   353

Fabula (or plot)   75, 121, 197, 276, 336, 443
Fantasy (aspects and definitions of)   17 and foll., 90, 95, 102, 106, 180, 184, 185, 295, 318, 336, 340—345, 347, 354, 368, 373, 375, 392, 396, 398, 440, 443, 446
Fantastic fictionality   91, 341
Fantastic literature   325
Fantastic operations   18, 316, 317
Fantastic sensations   384
— types of
— elevation and constitution   388
— fall and dissolution, expansion, collision, retraction, centering, etc.   389, 394, 396, 401
Fantastic structure   92
Fiction   90, 94, 95, 313, 318—326, 331—342, 355

Fictional pragmatics   341
Fictional saturation   313, 337, 338
Fictional semantics   340
Fictional syntax   341
Fictional world   322
Fictionality   90. 91, 94, 95, 130, 197, 317, 319, 321, 323—325, 329, 330, 337, 339, 341, 342, 254, 402, 438
Figure   388
Fissure   213
Form
— architectonic   35, 169, 290
— conventional   337
— essential   336
— historical   297
— imaginary   316, 358
— linguistic   296
— literary   312
— of fantasy   342, 343, 446
— symbolic   355, 357, 488
— simple   464
— performativo-historical   461
Formativity   190—192
Function of relation   356

Gaps (in the text)   173, 175, 179—182, 184, 185
Generality (of poetic value)   446, 457, 488
Generalization (or archetypal universalization)   334
Generic treatment of literature   456
Genre of contents   277
Genres (lyric, narrative and dramatic)   273, 325, 326, 436, 437, 439, 445
— expressive options of   457
— natural and historical   458—468, 469 and foll.
— natural limitation of   468—480
— of painting   490
— theory of   456—458 and foll., 470—472
— tripartite division of   463—466
Gesture
— onomatopoeic   356
— verbal   477
— anthropological   477

Historic thought   114
Horizon of expectations   150, 171, 173, 176, 179, 468

Identity (structures of)   158, 418, 447, 451, 467, 468
— subjective   469, 495
Illocutionary properties   321

Imaginary activity 312 and foll., 489
Imaginary mode 413
Imaginary myth 388
Imaginary process 313, 356, 389
Imaginary rhythms 358, 366, 388
— diurnal and nocturnal 405, 414
Imaginary semantics 360
Imaginary space 264, 318, 371, 385, 386, 389 and foll., 418 and foll.
Imaginary syntax 17, 316, 358, 380, 381, 387, 437
Imaginary uniqueness 363
Imitatio (as poetic procedure) 291, 292
Implicit crossings 196
Individual myths 388
Individually poetic (the) 271
Individualization 335
Influence (literary) 290, 292, 294
Inscriptions (of poetic experience) 236
Intensionalization 124, 125, 317, 357, 358, 436, 481
Intentio auctoris 202, 205
Intentio lectoris 194, 195, 203, 205
Intentio operis 201, 202
Interpretation 194—200, 203, 208
Interpretative communities 168—170
Interpretative strategies 168, 175
Intertextuality 102, 269, 276, 292, 294, 388, 423
Inventio 11, 72, 76, 77, 119, 124—127, 140, 141, 480, 481
Ironic indeterminacy 300 and foll.
Isodistribution (metrico-syntactical) 280
Isotopy 66, 121, 197, 207, 484

Law of semantic maxima 151, 337 and foll., 486
— universal laws 387
— hidden laws 387
Lexis 479
Literal language 160
Literal message 147
Literariness
— aspects of 21, 25, 26, 39—44, 84—93, 151, 266, 272, 284, 285, 317, 401, 452, 484
— and the pragmatic perspective 55—63
— semantic structures of 49—55
Literary hermeneutics 186—190, 260, 317
Literary myth 327, 328, 355
Literary options 41 and foll.
Literary psychoanalysis 311 and foll.
Literary space 245—247, 268, 275, 277, 417

Literary writing 158—163, 240, 241, 243, 245, 249, 262
Locutionary properties 321
Logic
— of difference 212
— of interpretation 186
— of possible narratives 33
Logocentrism 211, 212, 214, 233, 234, 236
Logos 378

Macrostructural construction 274, 280, 282—285, 298, 382
— rules of 457
Macrostructural space 381
Material scheme 264
Meaning
— as heuristic type 186, 187
— literal 199, 200
— meaningful boundary 187—189
— nucleus of 178
— of the text's utterance 479
— polysemic liberation of 486
— pre-meaningful features 481
— trajectory of 197
Mention 317, 364, 367
Metalinguistic reflection 348
Metapoetry 348, 350
Metrical rule 276
Microtextual components 274, 280, 283—285, 298, 382, 457
Mimesis 6, 10, 14, 146, 184, 272, 288, 297, 311, 319, 324, 329—341, 365, 378, 419, 422, 449, 543, 466, 467, 487, 490, 494
Misreading 191, 203, 267, 286, 290, 293, 294
Modes of imitation 464
— of expression 465, 467
— of mimesis 466
— generic 92, 93, 457, 463, 473
Monosemicalization 386
Motivation 446
Movere 125, 135, 148
Mystical literature 428—434
Mytheme 279
Mythic archetypes 335, 352, 354
Mythocriticism 343, 355, 359, 375, 379, 380, 408, 450
Mythologeme 379, 395
Mythos (in the theory of genres) 478—480

Narratio 325
Narrative syntax 437

Naturalness (of artistic text)   288, 408, 417, 468, 494
Necessity (of art)   489
Neutral (the)   253—261
Nocturnal regime   19, 355, 370, 371, 374—376, 385, 399
— scheme   400
— spatiality   402, 406, 490—493
Nomic (nature of imagination)   102, 354
Nomical products   341, 354
Novel (generic definition)   436 and foll
— Novel's spatiality   439 and foll.

Obsessive metaphors   380
Opacity of artistic text   296
Openness   190, 191, 194, 297
Ordo naturalis   439
Originality   80—82, 84, 266, 273, 292, 293, 420
Other (as imaginary representation)   16, 17, 249, 254—257, 261, 343, 360
Otherness   6, 246, 254, 255, 261, 356, 376, 418, 420, 451, 466—469, 495

Parts of discourse   125—128
Performative efficacy   132
Perlocutionary properties   321
Personal myth   357, 358, 380, 381, 388
Pluriaxiality (of poetic texts)   70
Plurisignification   35, 52
Poetic competence   58, 267
Poetic function   87, 193
Poetic reality   322
Poeticity   19, 25, 26, 39—44, 85—93, 151, 152, 233, 248, 265, 272, 285, 313, 325, 326, 343, 346, 358, 376—378, 388—390, 393, 398, 402, 413, 415, 419, 423, 436, 438, 442, 455, 495
— of fictional discourse   329, 330
Poetics
— as classical science   6—13, 453—455
— general   27, 35, 36
— historical   423
— in the romantic literary theory   13—20
— linguistic and semiological   7, 8, 20—33, 44—49
— of expressiveness   89, 438
— of reception and reading   39
— of symbol   312
— of the imagination   158, 311, 312, 314, 315, 379, 381 and foll, 422
Poiesis   10, 175, 286, 320, 325, 330, 336, 337, 342
Poietic vector   146

Polyphonic novel   109, 334, 440
Polyphony   135, 295, 440
Polysemy   52, 69, 70, 109, 193, 217, 218, 222, 268, 294, 295, 298, 299, 386, 415
Possible worlds   90, 336, 342
Possible worlds theory   326
Postural dominant   19, 355, 356, 358, 370—373, 375, 384—386, 395, 407, 492—494
Practice of exception   59—63, 227
Pragmatic elements of fiction   323, 324
— perspectives   39, 40, 147, 323
— relativism   26, 27, 152, 157, 199
Predifferential space   211, 212, 231, 232, 236

Quantitative involution   444
Qualitative parts of tragedy   10

Reader
— implied   135, 147, 149, 166, 170, 173, 177, 179, 188, 190, 311
— in the story   296
— response   192, 199, 210, 290
Realist fiction   322, 333, 334, 336
Receiver   4, 176, 323, 369, 468
Re-cognition   15, 196, 288, 289, 319, 331, 333—336, 339, 355, 378, 411, 414, 487
Regimes of imagination   355, 357, 359, 370—374
— system of   383, 384, 386, 414, 476
— in painting   491—495
Retractatio   82—85, 265—267, 286, 288, 290, 292, 347
Rhetoric
— and its relations with the poetics   11—13, 22
— and linguistic analysis   76, 77
— as science of verbal expressiveness   95—97, 112—123, 438
— general   95, 116—123
— integration of rhetoric and linguistic poetics   123 and foll.
— of silence   416, 417

Scheme (of textual complex)   315, 316, 318, 347, 355, 358, 364, 366—368, 385—388, 394, 399, 405, 408, 412, 413, 417, 437
Semantic
— contents   274
Semantico-extensional code   323, 330
Semantics of imagination   355, 375, 379, 414
— of the poetic text   275

Semiosis (unlimited)   190, 191, 194, 204, 207, 208
Semiotic scheme   275
Sentimental experience   356, 416
Silence (and meaning)   242—244
Singularity of poetic value   456, 457
Singularization (as literary mechanism)   335
Spatial myth   390, 395, 403, 404, 407, 417, 418 and foll.
Story   32, 78
Style (and levels of expressiveness)   103, 104
Styleme   21, 40, 115, 283
Stylistics
— expressive   135
— European   29, 122
— macro and microstructural   268
Stylization   317, 318, 334, 338, 357, 374, 487, 488
Sublime   15, 98, 254, 288, 317, 336, 377, 378, 409, 414, 416, 423, 435, 446, 450, 451, 478
Suggestive utterances   297
Suggestion (aesthetic and imaginary)   364—369, 390, 422
— acoustical   416
— spatial   395
Suplementarity   213
Symbol
— anthropological   91, 355—357, 370, 386, 456, and foll.
— conventional   336, 394, 395
— copulative   490
— ethical   91
— imaginary   92, 185, 355, 369, 370, 375 and foll.
— temporal   359, 376, 385, 386
Symbolic reading   315
Symbolic semantics   380
Symbolic structure   313
Symbolico-spatial relations   229
Syntactical imaginary-structures   274, 381, 382, 414
Syntax   275
— of imaginary space   495
System of options   76
System of transferences   316

Temporal structure   418
Text
— and literary studies   63 and foll.
— linguistics and grammar of   71—78
— text's general structure   22
Textual constitution   274

Textual dispositio   73—75
Textual dynamization   66
Textual macro and microcomponents   275
Textual typology (of classical lyrical poetry)   78—95
Textual scheme   26, 282, 283, 316, 366, 367, 368, 370, 393, 416, 422, 457, 489
Thematic   275, 279, 285, 380, 479
Thematic class   277, 279
Thematic genre   277, 279
Thematic level   275
Thematic restriction   279
Topic   197, 231, 233, 270, 276, 380
— topics of Renaissance aesthetics   270, 277—279
Topical convergences   235, 237, 251, 266, 269, 282
Topical system   270
Topicality   80, 81, 90, 328
Trace (deconstructive concept)   130, 211, 212, 214, 215, 223, 227, 230, 314, 339
Tradition   79, 173, 265, 266, 275, 276, 285—287, 292
Traditional context   173, 263, 264, 291
Transrationality   20, 28, 121, 227, 313
Typological organization   277
Typological processing of texts   275
Typological scheme   79, 282

Universal
— truth   438
— value   403
Universalization (process of)   378
Universals
— aesthetic structure of   287, 420
— anthropologico-aesthetic   5, 40, 271, 290, 342, 347, 354, 358, 376—378, 445, 448, 450, 453
— architectonic   342, 435
— structural and pragmatic -   488
Universalist model   19, 20, 31, 447
Universality   377, 420
— imaginary   446—448, 453, 455, 456, 468, 488, 489, 495

Value (the poetic as)   415, 420, 453
— universal foundation of   455, 456
Variation (principle of)   443, 444
Verbal material   21, 119, 314, 318, 369
Verisimilar fiction   323—325, 330—332, 337, 338, 340
Verisimilitude   7, 90, 184, 197, 324, 332, 333, 360, 445

Vision
— symptomatic-subjective 466
— objective 466
— of the world 475
Voice 133, 135, 318, 334
— in the theory of genres 465, 485
Voyage structure 443

Withdrawal (impulse of) 384

Writing (poetics of) 232—237, 250—259, 298
Work
— concentrical 476
— ecumenical 476
— synesthetic 476
— open 190, 191, 198, 297, 486
World models 321—326, 330, 332, 333, 335, 337

Index of Names

Abrams, M. H.   15, 164, 314, 391, 423
Adam, J. M.   28
Adorno, T. W.   138, 261
Aguiar e Silva, V. M. de   28, 41, 50, 58, 87, 226, 267, 456
Albaladejo Mayordomo, T.   12, 21, 24, 44, 72−75, 81, 85, 90, 94, 124, 127, 137, 138, 149, 151, 197, 313, 317, 320, 322, 323, 326, 332, 333, 336, 337, 357, 486
Alberti, L. B.   347, 480
Alberti, R.   350
Aleixandre, V.   350, 357, 422
Alfieri, V.   356
Alonso, A.   15, 16, 29, 39, 112, 122
Alonso, D.   15, 16, 29, 30, 122
Álvarez, J. M.   347, 348, 422
Álvarez Quintero, S. and J.   328
Aristotle   6−8, 10, 14, 20, 43, 46, 132, 147, 184, 249, 288, 301, 319, 321, 325, 330, 331, 335, 398, 413, 414, 437, 449, 455, 464, 473, 478, 479, 487
Arnheim, R.   355, 414, 419
Arnold, M.   392
Arrivé, M.   28, 30, 66, 70
Artaud, A.   233
Atkins, J. W. H.   9
Auerbach, E.   334, 335
Augustine, Saint   415, 416
Avalle, D'A. S.   32
Azúa, F. de   207

Bacon, F.   489
Bachelard, G.   17, 229, 312, 313, 343, 368, 370, 375, 377, 380, 384, 387, 389, 391, 392, 394, 395, 399, 450
Badio Ascensio, D.   447
Badouin, Ch.   311, 370
Bakhtin, M.   32, 33, 35, 36, 55, 91, 109, 119, 132, 133−136, 169, 288, 290, 331, 334, 342, 440, 485, 487
Bal, M.   20, 439
Baldwin, Ch. S.   8, 11, 12, 120
Balzac, H. de   133, 318, 334
Bally, Ch.   21, 50

Baquero Goyanes, M.   32, 108, 110, 318, 319, 334, 436, 439, 440
Barilli, R.   137
Baroja, P.   333
Barthes, R.   4, 7, 22, 25, 34, 35, 52, 71, 74, 117, 128, 138, 145, 149, 158−164, 166, 186, 188, 190, 193, 205, 216, 217, 250, 251, 259, 268, 295, 298, 382, 486
Bate, W.   14
Battistini, A.   12, 14, 16
Baudelaire, Ch.   30, 87, 91, 314, 392, 395−401
Baumgarten, A.   326
Becker, C.   9
Beckett, S.   436
Bécquer, G. A.   126
Behrens, I.   464
Bembo, P.   347
Ben-Porat, Z.   335
Benavente, J.   328
Benjamin, W.   221, 239, 240, 261
Berg, H.   171
Berlin, I.   16
Berriobeña, I.   491
Bertinetto, P. M.   44
Betcherev, W.   355
Bettetini, G.   33
Bierwisch, M.   56, 58
Black, E.   115−117, 119, 134, 138
Black, M.   140
Blanchot, M.   7, 16, 92, 101, 211, 213, 216, 219, 220, 221, 225, 231−233, 236, 240−262, 371, 375, 417, 455, 473
Bloom, H.   82, 84, 227, 228, 266, 286, 290−294, 299, 347, 390
Bloomfield, L.   100
Bobes Naves, M. C.   328, 361, 436, 439
Boccaccio, G.   8, 89, 300
Bodkin, M.   34, 370, 438
Boileau, N.   12, 15
Bolgar, R. R.   7
Bonaparte, M.   311, 370, 380
Bonomi, A.   321, 326
Booth, W. C.   22, 115, 323, 465
Borges, J. L.   134

Borinski, K. 13
Bornscheuer, L. 140
Botticelli, S. 347
Bousoño, C. 153, 348, 355, 358
Bovet, E. 463, 467, 475
Bowra, C. M. 15
Braque, G. 482, 487
Bray, R. 12
Bremond, C. 22, 31–33, 121, 383
Breton, A. 249
Breuer, D. 120, 126, 138
Brik, O. 45, 48
Brink, C. O. 9, 345
Brinkmann, E. 491
Brooke-Rose, Ch. 458, 460, 472, 475, 477
Bröndal, V. 201, 235
Brunel, P. 370
Brunetière, F. 43
Bruyne, E. de 17, 446
Bryant, D. C. 122
Buch, H. C. 454
Bühler, K. 465
Burgos, J. 70, 71, 313, 315, 316, 357, 381, 388, 390, 409
Burke, K. 475
Burri, A. 481
Butcher, S. H. 6
Butor, M. 177, 436
Byron (Lord) 134, 327, 491

Cadalso, J. 491
Caillois, R. 167
Calabrese, O. 454
Cano Ballesta, J. 134
Caplan, H. 8, 72, 120
Carnero, G. 13, 347–350, 422
Cascales, F. 464
Castellet, J. M. 347
Castelvetro, L. 270
Castilla del Pino, C. 184
Castro, A. 300
Cellier, L. 375
Cernuda, L. 422
Cervantes, M. de 9, 21, 88, 89, 100, 103, 105, 109–112, 132, 182, 183, 207, 225, 261, 295, 299, 300–307, 327, 358, 360, 415, 423, 436, 440–446
Cicero, M. T. 12, 98, 125, 184, 421, 464
Clancier, A. 184, 311
Clarín (Alas, L.) 340, 469
Cohen, J. 40
Cohen, T. 14
Coleridge, S. T. 16, 17, 98, 185, 228, 229, 287, 354

Collin, F. 262
Coquet, J. C. 21, 383
Corti, M. 26, 39, 55, 152, 205
Coste, D. 27, 35, 51
Cremante, R. 46
Croce, B. 54, 85, 87, 151, 207, 227, 240, 456, 471
Crosman, I. 165, 183, 322, 323
Culler, J. 8, 21, 23, 33, 34, 35, 44, 163, 193, 210, 218, 230
Cummings, E. E. 100
Curtius, E. R. 269

Chabrol, C. 73, 74
Chambers, R. 438
Champigny, R. 456, 457, 477
Chapman, R. 40
Char, R. 244, 254
Chardin, T. de 420, 421
Charles, M. 58, 134
Chassegnet-Smirgel, J. 184
Chastel, A. 454, 481
Chatman, S. 24, 45, 153, 205
Chekhov, A. 183
Chiabrera, G. 347
Chiarini, P. 335
Chico Rico, F. 113, 138
Chirico, G. de 490, 492
Chillida, E. 490

Dähl, O. 275
Dalí, S. 370, 490, 491
Dällenbach, L. 487
Dante (Alighieri) 12, 156, 174, 183, 225, 276, 291, 299, 300, 326, 346, 347, 358, 423, 446
Delas, D. 41
Demetrius 12
Democritus 454
Derrida, J. 16, 17, 34, 46, 129, 130, 156, 195, 205, 206, 210–240, 242, 248, 250, 251, 262, 286, 339, 455
Dickens, Ch. 318, 487
Dijk, T. A. van 3, 26, 34, 39, 56, 57, 65, 72, 77, 78, 116, 145, 152, 153, 156, 186, 197, 205, 317, 321, 380
Dilthey, W. 12
Dockhorn, K. 124
Dodds, E. R. 7
Dohrn, W. 467
Doležel, L. 3, 22, 32, 48, 56, 102, 156, 164, 197, 204, 207, 321, 326, 342
Domínguez Caparrós, J. 44, 58
Dostoyevsky, F. 132, 133, 318

Doubrovsky, S.   229
Dragomirescu, E.   488
Dressler, W. U.   21, 71, 273
Du Marsais, C. Ch.   114
Dubois, J.   115
Dubrow, H.   457, 458, 461
Dubuffet, J.   481
Ducrot, O.   195
Duchamp, M.   484
Durand, G.   17, 19, 33, 91, 92, 101, 184, 185, 229, 312, 315, 316, 327, 343, 355, 363, 368–371, 373, 376, 379, 381, 383–387, 414, 437, 438, 440, 450, 472, 476

Eco, U.   4, 34, 49, 58, 75, 137, 147, 149, 150, 182, 186, 190–210, 217, 222, 223, 324, 326
Eggert, H.   171
Eikhenbaum, B.   31
Eisenzweig, V.   440
Eliade, M.   369, 370, 376, 409, 438
Eliot, T. S.   4, 186, 207, 422, 465
Else, C. F.   6
Ellis, J. M.   26, 39, 42, 155
Emerson, R. W.   294
Empson, W.   294–298
Enkvist, N. E.   21, 41, 71, 72, 74
Erlich, V.   20, 22
Espronceda, J.   134
Euripides   103

Fabbri, P.   51, 223
Falk, E. H.   44
Fanto, J. A.   152
Faral, E.   8, 12, 121
Färber, H.   464
Feito, L.   483, 490
Felman, S.   184
Ferraris, M.   3, 51, 165
Fetterley, J.   52
Fillmore, Ch.   33
Filliolet, J.   41
Fischer, E.   335
Fish, S.   26, 35, 39, 153, 165–169, 221
Flahault, E.   87
Flaubert, G.   334
Foerster, H. von   455
Fokkema, D. W.   34, 87
Fonagy, I.   47, 153
Fontanier, P.   114, 115, 272
Forastieri-Braschi, E.   56, 186, 265
Forster, E. M.   39

Foscolo, U.   376, 491
Fowler, A.   456–458, 460, 462–464, 468, 469–471, 473, 475, 477
Fowler, R.   21, 24
Franck, D.   181
Franck, J.   391, 436, 440
Freeman, D. C.   21
Frege, G.   187
Freud, S.   198, 225, 294, 311, 370, 387
Fricke, H.   323
Friedman, N.   465
Friedmann, K.   466
Frost, R.   89
Frye, N.   20, 91, 286, 367, 370, 374, 377, 378, 390, 423, 435, 477–480
Fubini, M.   459
Fumaroli, M.   13, 118
Furst, L.   16

Gadamer, H. G.   34, 114, 156, 171, 186, 205
Gaillard, F.   322
Galdós, B. Pérez   111, 134, 318, 328, 333
Gallavotti, C.   464
Garasa, L.   463
Garcilaso de la Vega   101, 269, 282, 347, 422
García Lorca, F.   87, 350, 357, 422
Garin, E.   8, 13
Garrido Gallardo, M. A.   87
Garvin, P. L.   155
Gary-Prieur, M. N.   28
Garza Cuarón, B.   50, 94, 156
Genette, G.   22, 117, 177, 205, 324, 383, 456, 457, 459, 463–465, 469, 472–474, 477
Getto, G.   18
Gianformaggio, L.   114
Gil de Biedma, J.   345, 346, 349, 422
Gimferrer, P.   347, 422
Guiraud, P.   21
Girolamo, C. di   39, 41, 42, 55, 165
Glassersfeld, E. von   155
Godzich, W.   266
Goethe, J. W.   16, 100, 291, 300, 327, 346, 447, 448, 460, 465, 477
Gogh, V. van   484
Gogol, N.   27
Goldmann, L.   36, 169
Gombrich, E. H.   170, 203, 223, 224, 334, 335, 339, 419, 447–450, 487, 488
Gómez de la Serna, R.   108
Gómez de Liaño, I.   438
Gómez Moriana, A.   324

Góngora, L. de   269, 273, 274, 300, 347
Gordillo, L.   490, 493
Goriély, B.   13
Göther, H.   186
Grabes, H.   183
Gracián, B.   99, 100, 104, 108, 267, 421
Gray, B.   66, 73, 319, 333
Greco, El   297, 300, 484, 491, 492–494
Gregory, M.   21
Greimas, A. J.   30, 33, 49, 50, 65, 66, 73, 74, 77, 78, 121, 383
Grimm, G.   137, 175, 183, 186
Gris, J.   482, 487, 492
Groeben, N.   171
Group μ   53, 61, 113, 114, 116–121
Grube, G. M. A.   9, 12
Guillén, C.   456, 461–464, 469, 470, 473, 477
Guillén, J.   47, 61, 62, 92, 189, 350, 356, 357, 360–367, 389, 391, 395, 418, 422, 424, 434
Gülich, E.   22, 33, 74
Gullón, R.   418, 436, 438
Gumbrecht, H. U.   173, 174, 176
Gürttler, K. R.   324
Gusdorf, G.   13, 95, 375, 438
Guyer, P.   14

Habermas, J.   114
Hall, V.   81
Hamburger, K.   319, 322, 324, 467, 469, 480
Hancher, M.   152
Harshaw, B. (vid. Hrushovski, B.)   333
Hartl, R.   476
Hartman, G. H.   200, 227, 228
Hartmann, P.   73, 162, 204
Harweg, R.   42
Hathaway, B.   8
Hatzfeld, H.   15
Haubrichs, W.   171
Haugom-Olsen, S.   186
Hauptmeier, H.   155
Hegel, G. W. F.   12, 19, 20, 36, 243, 249, 435, 447, 457, 460, 462, 466, 470, 471, 477
Heidegger, M.   16, 156, 215, 390, 409, 411, 418, 475
Heilmann, L.   96, 131
Heintz, J.   321
Hempfer, W.   458, 463, 471, 474, 475
Hendricks, W. O.   32, 58, 72
Henkel, G.   176
Henry, A.   53, 116

Herder, J. G.   98, 228, 240
Hermogenes   12, 464
Hernadi, P.   456, 461, 463, 465–467, 469, 475–478, 480
Herrera, F. de   269
Herrick, M. T.   10, 75
Herrstein-Smith, B.   59
Hester, M.   116
Heuermann, H.   183
Hidalgo Serna, E.   99
Hill, A. A.   39, 48
Hillis Miller, J.   201, 390, 391, 392
Hintikka, J.   207, 294
Hintzenberg, D.   154
Hirsch, E. D.   150, 186–190
Hirt, E.   456, 457
Hjelmslev, L.   28, 50, 81
Hocke, G.   491
Hohendahl, D. U.   173, 263
Hölderlin, F.   243, 244, 261, 350, 353, 370, 375, 392, 403–412, 418
Holub, R. C.   27, 34, 39, 51, 165, 170
Homer   291, 359, 423
Horace, Q.   9, 11, 95, 98, 147, 295, 300, 345, 421, 453
Howell, W. S.   321
Hrushovski, B.   494
Huerta Calvo, J.   463
Huizinga, J.   435
Husserl, E.   187, 225, 237, 418

Ibsch, E.   34
Ihwe, J.   21, 44
Ingarden, R.   44, 181, 465
Iser, W.   4, 40, 47, 49, 71, 135, 138, 148, 149, 150, 171–179, 180 ff., 203, 205, 222, 311, 331

Jaeger, W.   7
Jakobson, R.   7, 8, 21, 25, 29, 30, 87, 88, 287, 288, 298, 315, 316, 481
Jameson, F.   33–35, 264, 423
Jauss, H. R.   4, 35, 40, 135, 138, 148–150, 170, 171–179, 203, 205, 311, 327, 464
Jefferson, A.   24, 34, 137
Jessi, F.   417
Jiménez, J. R.   102, 225, 245, 314, 412, 418, 422, 424–427, 434
Johansen, S.   496
John of the Cross, Saint   91, 371, 372, 424–427, 434
Jolles, A.   20, 467, 472, 476, 477
Jones, L. K.   275

Index of Names 541

Jouve, P. 377
Joyce, J. 191, 200, 208, 299, 436
Jung, C. G. 311, 312, 343, 370, 375, 387, 413, 437, 450

Kafka, F. 244, 245, 257, 311
Kamerbeer, J. 183
Kant, I. 14, 23, 36
Kayser, W. 440, 465
Keats, J. 294, 353, 354
Kellog, R. 322
Kennedy, G. A. 11, 12, 114
Kerbrat-Orecchioni, K. 28, 50, 156
Klee, P. 261
Kleiner, J. 475
Klinkenberg, J. M. 30, 70, 122, 137
Kloepfer, R. 21, 44
Kohler, P. 466, 467
Kopperschmidt, J. 72, 96, 113, 114, 123, 130, 138
Kripke, S. A. 326
Kristeller, P. O. 8
Kristeva, J. 22, 25, 43, 49, 77, 78, 85, 102, 205, 312
Kroll, W. 171
Krysinsky, W. 51, 58
Kubczak, H. 116
Kuiper, K. 323
Kuentz, P. 113
Kummer, W. 152
Kuroda, S. Y. 57, 317, 321, 329

Lachmann, R. 115, 116, 128
Landwehr, J. 322
Lanham, R. 498
Lausberg, H. 11, 111–114, 125, 140, 181
Lautréamont, Count of 133, 260
Lázaro Carreter, F. 18, 29, 43, 58, 64, 82, 87, 90, 147, 153, 274, 456, 458, 462, 474
Le Guern, M. 53, 116
Lecourt, D. 268
Lee, R. W. 453, 454
Leech, G. N. 62, 85, 116, 334
Lefebve, M. 85
Léger, F. 482
Leitch, V. B. 219
Lejeune, P. 312
Lenin, V. I. 27
Lentricchia, F. 23, 35
León, Fray Luis de 95, 421
Leoni, F. A. 11
Leopardi, G. 200, 228, 353, 393, 394
Lessing, G. E. 453, 454

Lévi-Strauss, C. 213, 235, 315, 316, 439
Leucipus 454
Levin, S. R. 29, 30, 40, 43, 56, 57, 85, 87, 152, 153, 321
Levinas, E. 16, 211, 212, 220, 249, 254–257
Li, Ch. N. 275
Litman, T. A. 15
Longhi, R. 261
Lope de Vega 269, 273, 280, 281, 300, 301, 454
Lotman, Y. 21, 56, 58, 60, 87, 179, 205, 280, 298, 481
Lubbock, P. 465
Luisini, F. 270
Lüking, B. 116, 120, 123
Lukács, G. 238, 261, 288, 335
Lledó, E. 7

Machado, A. 350, 357, 422
Macherey, P. 181
Macrí, O. 18
Majakovsky, V. 421
Mallarmé, S. 91, 102, 222, 241, 242, 244, 260, 299
Malvezzi, V. 421
Man, P. de 85, 86, 159, 212, 215, 216, 221, 225, 227–229, 237–240, 299, 390–392
Mandelkow, K. R. 172
Mann, T. 261
Mannoni, O. 184, 353
Manrique, J. 88
Mansuy, M. 184
Manzoni, A. 86, 264
Marañón, G. 328
Maravall, J. A. 18
Marchese, A. 40
Martial, M. V. 267
Margghescou, M. 41, 53
María, R. de 183
Marin, L. 454
Marinetti, A. 484
Marino, G. 273
Marshall, D. F. 220
Martin, J. 112
Martin, W. 3
Martinet, A. 481
Martínez Bonati, F. 52, 319, 321, 322, 323
Matoré, G. 390, 418–421, 435–437, 440
Maturana, H. R. 155
Maurer, K. 138, 171, 172, 177, 178
Mauron, Ch. 161, 184, 241, 311, 313, 316, 317, 368, 369, 380, 381, 388, 424

Mayoral, J. A.   137, 152
Mazzacurati, G.   12, 13
Mazzeo, J. A.   104
Megaldo, P. V.   12
Mendonça-Telhes, G.   96, 416
Meyer, T. A.   466, 467
Michaux, H.   388
Michel, A.   13, 33
Miner, E.   39, 42
Minturno, S.   464
Molière, J. B. P.   36, 327
Moler, A.   418
Molina, T. de   327
Molino, J.   28, 50, 160, 226
Mondrian, P.   483
Moreno Cabrera, J. C.   321
Morpurgo-Tagliabue, G.   15
Mosconi, G.   138
Mouloud, A.   387
Mounin, G.   327
Mozart, W. A.   327
Muir, E.   31
Mukařovský, J.   24, 40, 54, 62, 85, 172, 205
Muratori, A.   12
Murphy, J. J.   12, 16, 114, 120
Murray, H. A.   138

Nadeau, M.   13
Naess, A.   275
Nanni, L.   194, 205
Naumann, M.   176
Navarro Tomás, T.   46
Nemoianu, V.   335
Nietzsche, F.   240, 294
Norden, E.   13
Norris, Ch.   34, 213
Novalis, F.   189, 372–374, 401, 402, 466, 491

Ohmann, R.   57, 153
Olbrechts-Tyteca, L.   114, 138
Ong, W.   183
Ortega y Gasset, J.   163, 174, 261
Ovid, P.   9

Pagnini, M.   44, 58, 63
Painter, G. D.   311
Pajano, R.   8
Panofsky, E.   339
Paraíso de Leal, I.   45
Pareyson, L.   191
Partee, B. H.   207
Pasoli, E.   9

Pavel, T. G.   197, 321, 326, 331
Pazzaglia, M.   46
Peirce, Ch. S.   190, 194, 204, 208–210
Pellegrini, M.   99
Pelletier, A. M.   87
Perelman, Ch.   114, 138, 140, 437
Pérez de Ayala, R.   328
Petersen, J.   465
Petöfi, J. S.   21, 22, 70, 71, 73, 74, 75, 77, 115, 121, 126, 147, 181, 190, 270, 275, 322, 323
Petrarch, F.   273, 274, 293, 374
Philostratus   453
Piaget, J.   383, 471
Picard, R.   375
Picasso, P.   482, 484, 493–495
Piera, C.   343, 344
Pigliasco, M. R.   11, 13
Pindar   9
Pir, F.   184
Plato   8, 134, 301, 462, 463, 470
Plett, H. F.   96, 116, 118, 119
Plutarch   447, 453
Poe, E. A.   195, 311
Poggioli, R.   13
Pope, A.   449
Popovich, A.   102
Popper, K.   224
Posner, R.   56, 152
Poulet, G.   183, 221, 239, 390, 391, 436
Pound, E.   57, 235, 422
Pozuelo Yvancos, J. M.   8, 21, 42, 44, 73, 100, 113, 172, 469
Pratt, M. L.   39, 55, 137, 152, 321
Prince, G.   22, 33, 176, 444
Prior, A. N.   326
Propp, V.   21, 27, 30, 31, 280
Proust, M.   311, 391
Pseudo-Longinus   12, 15, 98, 240, 415

Quasthoff, U. M.   33
Quevedo, F. de   104–108, 269, 273, 301
Quine, W. V. O.   471
Quintilian, M. F.   12, 184

Rabelais, F.   301
Raphael   347, 492
Raible, W.   22, 74, 468
Raimondi, E.   11–14, 18, 99, 356, 393
Ransom, J. C.   72
Rasmussen, D.   326
Rastier, F.   30, 65, 66, 121, 383, 484
Raymond, M.   13, 91, 92

Reeves, Ch.   151, 321
Reisz de Rivarola, S.   321
Rembrandt   487
Revzin, I.   280
Reyes, A.   9
Rewar, W.   28, 87
Ricoeur, P.   116, 186, 188, 324, 331–333
Richards, I. A.   115, 156, 166, 186, 238
Rieser, H.   74
Riffaterre, M.   21, 24, 43, 54, 64, 166, 176, 205, 238, 239
Rilke, R. M.   247
Ritter Santini, L.   11
Robortello, F.   10, 465
Robey, D.   24, 34, 137
Rockinger, L.   120
Rodríguez Adrados, F.   41
Rollin, B. E.   458, 469, 471, 472
Romberg, B.   58
Romero de Solís, D.   6, 59, 415
Ronen, R.   336
Rorty, R.   200
Rosmarin, A.   458, 461–463, 470, 471, 473, 474, 479
Rothe, A.   171, 173
Rousse, J.   51
Rousseau, J. J.   225, 235, 236
Rousset, J.   231
Rubens, P. P.   495
Rutschky, M.   171
Ruttkovsky, W.   459, 467, 469
Ruwet, N.   41
Ryan, M. L.   323, 459, 468

Sade (Marquis of)   133
Sager, P.   330
Saitta, G.   8
Salinas, P.   422
Samarini, A. N.   280
Sánchez, J. L.   422
Sánchez Cotán, J.   488
Sartre, J. P.   184, 225, 229, 324, 394, 420
Saura, A.   493
Saussure, F. de   225
Scheglov, J. K.   275
Scott, W.   353
Scrivano, R.   8
Schaeffer, J. M.   456, 468, 470
Schelling, F. W.   466
Schiller, F.   16
Schlegel, A. W.   16, 17, 36, 228, 466
Schlegel, F.   18, 98, 228, 466, 470
Schmidt, S. J.   26, 34, 39, 44, 57, 86, 87, 137, 145, 152, 154–157, 176, 186, 205, 317, 321, 322, 329

Scholes, R.   24, 44, 322
Schunk, P.   174
Searle, J. R.   138, 153, 321
Sebeok, T.   21
Segers, R. T.   183
Segre, C.   21, 44, 58, 63, 65, 66, 86, 142, 268, 326, 439, 463
Selden, R.   24, 35
Sgall, P.   275
Shakespeare, W.   255, 261, 291, 292, 295, 299, 300, 345, 358, 446
Shapiro, K.   88
Shibles, K. N. A.   53
Shklovsky, V.   21, 24, 25, 27, 29, 488
Short, M. N.   334, 335
Shukman, A.   28, 87
Siles, J.   348
Simonides   453
Sloan, T. O.   12
Sobejano, G.   30
Sophocles   198
Spencer, J.   21
Spengler, O.   419, 435
Spillner, B.   120, 126, 131
Spingarn, J. E.   8, 121
Spitzer, L.   15, 72
Staiger, E.   467, 476
Stalnaker, R. C.   326
Stankiewicz, E.   475
Stanzel, F. K.   58, 205
Stegen, G.   9
Stegmüller, W.   471
Steihmetz, M.   27, 34, 51
Steiman, M.   459
Stein, G.   252
Stempel, W. D.   27, 170, 457, 468, 475
Stendhal   133, 264, 491
Stern, J. P.   333, 335
Sterne, L.   172
Stierle, K.   102, 171–174, 178, 181, 263
Strelka, J.   463
Striedter, J.   20, 49, 72
Stutterheim, C. F. P.   457, 458
Suleiman, S.   164, 183
Suvin, D.   325
Sypher, W.   18

Tacitus, C.   421
Tadié, J. Y.   124
Tapies, A.   481
Tasso, T.   274, 465
Theophrastus   464
Theresa of Avila, Saint   424, 428, 430–434

Terracini, B.   21, 72, 102, 375, 416
Tesauro, E.   99, 100, 104, 267
Thibaudeau, J.   163
Thieghem, P. van   466
Thomson, E. M.   23
Timpanaro, S.   14
Tintoretto   484
Todorov, T.   8, 22, 29, 32, 48, 77, 78, 116, 145, 205, 325, 458, 459, 473, 474
Tolstoy, L.   27, 133, 318
Tomashevsky, B.   21, 27, 75, 183
Torre, G. de   314
Trabant, J.   28
Trissino, G. G.   465
Tynjanov, J.   20, 313

Ueding, G.   117, 119
Uehling, G.   14
Unamuno, M. de   89, 174, 225, 328, 412

Vajda, G. M.   170
Valéry, P.   92, 189, 412, 413
Valesio, P.   19, 45, 46, 96, 131, 357, 416, 417
Valle Inclán, R. M. del   329
Vassarely, V.   483
Velázquez, D. de   102, 300, 482, 483, 487, 493, 494
Veltruský, J.   15
Verene, P.   87
Vickers, B.   117
Vico, G.   87, 240, 435
Vierne, S.   313
Viëtor, K.   465
Villegas, J.   314, 438
Vinogradov, V.   31
Virgil, P.   300, 347, 421–423, 464
Vischer, T.   466

Vitruvius   347
Volli, U.   326

Waddington, R. B.   12
Walton, K. L.   323, 324
Walzel, O.   14
Warning, R.   137
Warren, A.   16, 17, 463
Weber, H. D.   170
Weber, J. P.   103, 184
Weimann, R.   263
Weinberg, B.   8, 10, 120, 463
Weinrich, H.   58, 137, 175, 439
Weise, G.   7
Weissenberg, K.   463
Wellek, R.   16–18, 333, 463
Wienold, G.   71, 171
Wilson, E.   91
Wittgenstein, L.   223, 462
Woods, J.   321
Woolf, V.   172, 180
Woolf, W.   183
Wordsworth, W.   291, 392
Wölfflin, H.   435
Wrigth, A.   333

Young, E.   189, 491

Zeratta, M.   439
Zgorzelski, A.   325, 330
Zimmermann, B.   176
Žirmunsky, V.   44–46
Zola, E.   180
Zholkowsky, A. K.   56, 275
Zorrilla, J.   328
Zumthor, P.   464
Zurbarán, J.   300, 488, 492

Walter de Gruyter
Berlin · New York

RESEARCH IN TEXT THEORY
UNTERSUCHUNGEN ZUR TEXTTHEORIE

Literary Discourse
Aspects of Cognitive and Social Psychological Approaches
Edited by László Halász
Large-octavo. VI, 242 pages, 12 tables, 6 figures.
1987. Bound DM 112,- ISBN 3 11 010685 X (Volume 11)

Connexity and Coherence
Analysis of Text and Discourse
Edited by W. Heydrich, F. Neubauer, J.S. Petöfi, E. Sözer
Large-octavo. XII, 404 pages. 28 illustrations, 5 tables.
1989. Bound DM 198,- ISBN 3 11 011102 0 (Volume 12)

Comprehension of Literary Discourse
Results and Problems of Interdisciplinary Approaches
Edited by D. Meutsch and R. Viehoff
Large-octavo. VI, 259 pages, 25 figures, 8 tables. 1989.
Bound DM 128,- ISBN 3 11 011111 X (Volume 13)

Prices are subject to change

Walter de Gruyter
Berlin · New York

RESEARCH IN TEXT THEORY
UNTERSUCHUNGEN ZUR TEXTTHEORIE

Possible Worlds in Humanities, Arts and Sciences
Proceedings of Nobel Symposium 65

Edited by Sture Allén
Large-octavo. X, 453 pages, 25 illustrations, 10 tables.
1989. Bound DM 188,- ISBN 3 11 011220 5 (Volume 14)

Intertextuality

Edited by Heinrich F. Plett
1991. Large-octavo. VIII, 268 pages. Cloth DM 142,-
ISBN 3 11 011637 5 (Volume 15)

Subject-oriented Texts
Languages for Special Purposes and Text Theory

Edited by Hartmut Schröder
Large-octavo. VIII, 322 pages. 1991. Cloth DM 164,-
ISBN 3 11 012568 4 (Volume 16)

Prices are subject to change